From Ancient Cham to Modern Dialects

Oceanic Linguistics Special Publication No. 28

From Ancient Cham to Modern Dialects:
Two Thousand Years of
Language Contact and Change

With an appendix of Chamic
reconstructions and loanwords

Graham Thurgood

University of Hawai'i Press

Honolulu

Library of Congress Cataloging-in-Publications Data
Thurgood, Graham.
From ancient Cham to modern dialects : two thousand years of
language contact and change / Graham Thurgood.
p.   cm. — (Oceanic linguistics special publication ; no. 28)
Includes bibliographical references (p.   ) and indexes.
ISBN 0–8248–2131–9 (pbk. : alk. paper)
1. Cham language—Dialects. 2. Cham language—History.
3. Language in contact—Southeast Asia. I. Title. II. Series.
PL4491.94.T47   1999
499'.22—dc21   98–54334
                                              CIP

Camera-ready copy prepared by the author.

Printed by Cushing-Malloy, Inc.

Contents

Appendix I: Language Names (and transliteration tables)   261

Appendix II: The Chamic Lexicon 277

Preface

The title of this book *From Ancient Cham to Modern Dialects: Two Thousand Years of Language Contact and Change*, even more than showing my admiration for J. Marvin Brown's work on Thai, reflects my belief that the term 'Cham' was used at an earlier time as a general term for all the Chamic-speaking peoples of Vietnam. It is reflected in the name of the kingdom, Champa, it the etymological source of the name Tsat used by the Utsat people of Hainan to describe their language, and it occurs quite early in the Chinese dynastic records in their references to Champa.

Leaving the title aside, two quite different views of research exist, each with its own place, one more conservative, the other more exploratory. One view is typified by the comment of the English poet Pope to lesser poets advising them to keep their piece nine years. In this view, the endpoint is reached when everything is completely clear and thoroughly documented. As will become evident to readers, this monograph has been written in a quite different tradition: it is an exploratory study that first reconstructs proto-Chamic and then, based on that reconstruction, focuses on 2000 years of language contact and change. Central themes in this exploration include the adaptation of Chamic to the Southeast Asian linguistic area, the canonical restructuring of the basic shape of the word, major changes to the consonant and vowel inventories, the development of register, tone, and restructured register, and, of course, the role played by bilingualism in all these developments.

However, from the outset it must be acknowledged that these analyses offered here are, even more than usual, tentative, preliminary, and undoubtedly in need of correction and amplification. In part, this reflects the fact that Chamic studies are, in some senses, still in their infancy; in part, the numerous gaps in my background; and, in part, it reflects things that I have simply missed or misanalyzed, and it would be surprising if all my errors should prove minor. In a number of ways, the conclusions presented here differ from conclusions reached in my own earlier work, and where they differ, these conclusions supersede the earlier ones. In Chamic studies, only the outlines seem to be clear; far more remains to be discovered than has been found thus far.

The preoccupation throughout with borrowed forms directly reflects the preoccupation with language contact and the relative chronology of language contact. Thus, their presence in the tables and text is relevant, *not only to the reconstructions involved,* but also to the relative chronologies of the borrowings themselves. If the loans participated in a change, they predate the change; if they did not participate, then they were borrowed after the change.

The original plan for this work did not include Acehnese. It was only as the first draft was nearing completion that a comparison with Acehnese made it absolutely obvious that Acehnese was simply a Chamic language whose speakers had migrated to Sumatra, not a separate branch collateral with the mainland languages. At that point the whole manuscript was reworked to incorporate Acehnese, not with the intent of being definitive, but hoping to confirm beyond all *reasonable* objections that Acehnese was Chamic. A myriad of details has been left for another time when more is known.

In addition to the main texts, this work is accompanied by three appendices: one is a set of transliteration tables, another is an appendix of reconstructed and borrowed forms, and the last is an appendix of forms arranged alphabetically by English gloss. The transliteration of a multitude of differing orthographies was necessary for clarity of exposition. Almost without exception, this was done mechanically, aside from an error that may have crept in here and there.

The other appendix lists both the proto-Chamic reconstructions and the borrowings found throughout the manuscript, along with the forms that these assessments are based on. Not all the languages are included, but there are enough so that the reconstructions can usually be done on the basis of the forms given.

Within this appendix, both reconstructed forms and borrowings are listed. Undoubtedly there is some error in the identification of borrowings, but none that invalidate any of the conclusions. A number of marginally attested forms are included in this appendix, along with the supporting data, with the hope that other researchers will help clarify their etymologies. Where Chamic forms are suspected of having as of yet unidentified Mon-Khmer counterparts, it is hoped that various scholars will help fill in these gaps.

Finally, it is expected that the forms reconstructed in this work for Proto-Chamic will be revised in the direction of the forms found reconstructed for Proto-Malayo-Chamic, as better and more thorough use is made of the Written Chamic inscriptional data.

Graham Thurgood
California State University, Chico

Acknowledgments

Despite the single author, this work is a collaborative effort, only made possible through the generous help of countless others. Much of my work on Chamic would not have been possible without the help of Bob Blust, who provided me with encouragement, insights, and copies of crucial papers. In particular, the Malayo-Polynesian side of this work heavily reflects his help. He gave freely of his time, energy, and considerable expertise, making it possible not only to look at the Chamic historical changes from the bottom-up—from the modern Chamic looking back to Proto-Chamic, but also to look at them from the top down—from the perspective of reconstructed Proto-Malayo-Polynesian. These twin perspectives produced a much more sophisticated and insightful reconstruction and analysis than would have been otherwise possible.

The Acehnese portion of this work owes much to Mark Durie, who constantly supplemented my meager knowledge of Acehnese, patiently pointing out over email what worked and what did not. He not only supplied most of the Acehnese forms—including a wealth of forms in an extremely valuable thesaurus (Daud Bukhari and Mark Durie, n.d.) and a hypercard program containing Chamic-Acehnese comparative material (Durie, 1990b), but he also looked them over after the first draft of the manuscript was written, and supplied many that were still missing. In a similar way, he critiqued and improved many of the analyses, not just of Acehnese but also those of Chamic. In many instances, he played the devil's advocate, forcing me to rethink, clarify, reformulate, and, with some frequency, change positions taken in earlier drafts.

Whatever merits the analyses may have also owe a great deal to David Solnit, who significantly improved a number of the analyses in both major and minor ways. The phonetic analysis of Tsat owes its essence to work done on it by Ian Maddieson, who supplied a significant number of the forms. Gérard Diffloth, Theraphan Luangthongkum, Arthur Abramson, and, most recently, David Thomas labored hard providing insights and straightening out my use of terminology with regard to the terms register, voice quality, register complex, and so on and clarified my discussion of the Chamic interaction with the MK. In addition, he sent me invaluable materials on Mon-Khmer reconstruction as well as a copy of Phraya Prachakij-karacak's (1995) *Some Languages of Siam,* containing a Jarai

xi

and a Rade wordlist from the last century. At a much later point, Peter Ladefoged suggested the explanation for the connection between breathiness and vowel raising and creakiness or tenseness and vowel lowering included here. Ouyang Jueya kindly sent me additional forms, several of which turned out to be crucial for the analysis of Tsat historical developments. Neil Baumgartner let me use the Cham font he developed. A large number of other people made substantive suggestions that are directly reflected in the ideas presented here: Eric Oey, Patricia Donegan, David Stampe, Jean Tempeste, Zane Clark, Ibrahim b. Ismail, Ni Dabai, Joel Nevis, Jerry Edmondson, George Grace, Paul Benedict, Jim Collins, Alan Stevens, David Thomas, Osh Larish, Keng-Fong Pang, Karen Mistry, and Elzbieta Thurgood. There is no reason to believe, however, that those thanked will even recognize what I have done with their suggestions, let alone agree with them.

In addition to Mark Durie, who read the original "first" draft, a number of other people kindly offered to read an earlier draft and provide me feedback: David Thomas, Paul Benedict, John Wolff, Malcolm Ross, Martha Ratliff, Jim Matisoff, and Jerry Edmondson, and Sander Adelaar. Paul Benedict send me some useful notes about wider Austronesian connections as well as about the etymology of the *u*- prefix found in Tsat. The feedback has been invaluable and has, in some cases, substantially improved the description.

The Chamic lexicon contained in Appendix 2 has been painstakingly gone through by a number of scholars, all of whom know more about Austronesian than I do. The usefulness and accuracy of the appendix owes its merits to their help. Specifically, Bob Blust, Mark Durie, K. Alexander Adelaar, David Thomas, and Paul Benedict have all contributed time and energy to the appendix. In particular, Bob Blust, Mark Durie, and K. Alexander Adelaar commented on the forms, one-by-one where necessary. For this labor, I cannot thank them enough.

In addition, various people have knowingly or unknowingly helped me with my understanding of the history and the historical documents pertaining to Champa and the surrounding area. I wish to thank the following people for their suggestions and help: Bob Hsu, Barbara Andaya, Hilary Chappell, Pang Keng-Fong, Ngo Thanh Nhan, Arun Sinha, John Wolff, Mike Feener (by way of John Wolff), John Marston, Mackie Blanton, Chris Court, Mark Durie, Sander Adelaar, and the late Gwyn Williams.

In a more general way, I wish to acknowledge my intellectual debts to my early teachers: my friend and mentor Jim Matisoff, who introduced me to Southeast Asia, Mary Haas, who taught me much of what I know about the comparative method, and Paul Benedict, who never lost track of the big picture.

Even more than usual, I fully expect some of the analyses presented here to be modified on the basis of better and more detailed studies of the languages cited, as well as on the basis of instrumental studies on these same languages. I shall be astonished if all my errors should prove minor and grateful to readers for their corrections. It goes without saying that, where these analyses differ, they supersede my prior work on Chamic. This work is based upon research supported by the National Science Foundation under Grant No. SBR-9512101.

List of Abbreviations and Conventions

AC	Aymonier and Cabaton (1906)
Aceh.	Acehnese
Bahnar (AC)	refers to the Bahnar forms cited in Aymonier and Cabaton (1906)
breathy register	a term used to designate the register complex that includes a breathy-voiced component
C	refers to a form in Aymonier and Cabaton (1906) from Cabaton
CEMP	Central-Eastern-Malayo-Polynesian
Coastal Chamic	Haroi, Western Cham, and Phan Rang Cham
early-PC	a stage not fully recoverable by reconstruction but hinted at by the transcriptions used in early inscriptional Chamic
Headley	Headley 1976; the numbers following 'Headley' identify specific words discussed in this work
Highlands Chamic	Rade, Jarai, Chru, N. Roglai, and Tsat
Nb.	Nonthaburi Malay
NR	Northern Roglai
PAn	Proto-Austronesian
PC	Proto-Chamic; the earliest stage reliably recoverable by reconstruction
Phan Rang Cham	In this work, the Phan Rang Cham forms come largely from Moussay's dictionary, with the consequence that they are heavily influenced by Written Cham—and thus at times, more archaic than the modern spoken forms. Cited modern spoken forms are specifically labeled as spoken forms.
PL	Pierre-Bernard Lafont

PMK	Proto-Mon-Khmer
PMP	Proto-Malayo-Polynesian; in a table, it refers to an Austronesian reconstruction that at least predates Chamic; some of these forms do not reconstruct all the way back to PMP
PNB	Proto-North-Bahnaric (Smith 1972)
PR Cham	Phan Rang Cham
PSB	Proto-South-Bahnaric
register complex	a complex of features that may include length, pitch, and voice quality (phonation type)
register	the same as register complex
Roglai	Roglai always refers to Northern Roglai unless specifically otherwise noted
tense register	a term used to designate the register complex that includes a tense-voiced component
WMP	Western Malayo-Polynesian; specifically, the PMP languages not in CEMP
*	reconstructed
x	borrowed and not reconstructable to PC
x*	borrowed earlier than PC so reconstructable to PC
x/*	borrowed but not clear if it reconstructs to PC
∅-	indicates that the sound completely disappeared
---	indicates that no relevant examples have been found
(m)	metathesis
(n)	vowel reflex the result of nasalization
-X	Apparent irregularities in the correspondences are indicated by a hyphen followed a consonant indicating precisely what is irregular:
-v	= irregular vowel,
-c	= irregular consonant,
-f	= irregular final,
-vR	= irregular vowel register,
-t	= irregular tone,
-n	= irregular nasalization, and so on. As the historical phonology is better understood, at least some

	of these apparent irregularities should disappear, while others will doubtless remain puzzles.
subscribed dot	The dot subscribed under various voiceless stops indicates that the following vowel is breathy, or behaves as if it were in the so-called breathy voice. This orthographic convention makes the historical developments far, far more transparent, because it matches the transliteration found in Moussay (1971), and because it allows for a straightforward, largely phonetically transparent transliteration of Western Cham.
Wr. Cham	Written Cham from Aymonier and Cabaton (1906)

From Ancient Cham to Modern Dialects

1

Introduction

Beyond the no longer fully-understood deteriorating temples and an abundance of beautiful statuary, little now remains of the Champa civilization that once flourished along the coastal plains of central and southern Vietnam (Ciochon and James 1992:52-55). Almost a hundred temples along the coastline from Quang-Tri in the north to Phan Rang in the south give silent testimony to a mostly-forgotten, once-formidable civilization of traders and artisans. Fragments of knowledge of the past can still be retrieved, even from the crumpling remains of Tra-kiêu in the north, the first political capital of the Champa civilization. Today, however, much of what is standing is no longer easily recognized, having been absorbed into the walls of modern buildings. In a valley seventeen miles to the west of Tra-kiêu is a much richer cluster of still upright buildings in Mi-son, once a center of Hindu worship where today twenty of the roughly seventy temples built between the seventh and twelfth centuries AD still stand. Further south, present-day Binh-dinh is the site of Vijaya, the new capital built after Indrapura fell in 982. Here there is another group of temples built, not in a valley like Mi-son, but on high places, possibly reflecting the more perilous times in which they were built. And, still further south, near the modern cities of Nha Trang and Phan Rang, are the important complex of temples called Po Nagar, the spiritual center in the south. These ruins are the physical remains of the Champa civilization, which reached its zenith in the sixth or seventh century but has long since returned to obscurity. Traces of its history remain in these fading temples and sites, their legacy in an archaeological record now inaccessible, as Ciochon and James wrote, except to trained archaeologists and historians.

However, alongside the physical legacy embodied in these silent temples from the distant past stands an enormously rich, still-living legacy, the modern descendants of the Chamic language that was once the lingua franca of Champa. This rich linguistic record lives on in the Tsat spoken on Hainan, the Rade, Jarai, Haroi, Chru, and Roglai spoken in the southern Vietnam highlands, the Cham spoken along the Vietnamese coast and the various Cham communities of Cambodia, and in the Acehnese of north Sumatra—in all the Chamic languages.

The Chamic languages have an incredibly rich story to tell, one that may ultimately prove more valuable to historians of language than the archaeological records will prove to archaeologists. Captured in the Chamic linguistic record is a luxurious complex of language changes, following a myriad of internal paths, and responding to a diverse array of influences from other languages, that is remarkable for both its richness and its clarity. The Chamic linguistic record has much to tell us about the history of the Chamic languages and about the nature of historical change and the role of contact in that change.

The use of 'Cham' in title of the book *From Ancient Cham to Modern Dialects: Two Thousand Years of Language Contact and Change* reflects an interplay between its earlier usage and its modern usage. As back as a thousand years ago and probably earlier, Cham was used as a general term for all the Chamic-speaking peoples of Vietnam. It is reflected, not just in the name of the kingdom, Champa (Cham + pa), but also in the Chinese dynastic records. For example, the *History of the Song Dynasty* (960-1279) records that, in 986, some Cham arrived in Hainan from Zhancheng (Zheng 1986:37). Zhancheng (etymologically, Zhan 'Cham' + cheng 'city') refers to Champa, with Zhan having subsequently undergone various sound changes within the history of Chinese. The form Zhan in the dynastic source matches the phonetics of the language name Tsat (etymologically from Cham *cam) used by the Utsat people of Hainan (U 'people' + Tsat 'Cham', that is 'Cham people') perfectly. Other Chamic language names also appear to have at one time included Cham as part of the name. The Phan Rang Cham traditions refer to four different peoples with Cham as a component of their name (Goschnick 1977:106): the Cham Raglai (the Roglai; from *ra* 'people' + *glai* 'forest'),[1] the Cham Jarai (the Jarai), the Cham Kur (Cham + kŭr 'Khmer', the Western Cham of Cambodia and Southern Vietnam), and the Cham Ro (from Cham + rɔ 'remnant'). Goschnick very tentatively associates the term Cham Ro with the Haroi, but the match is far better with the Chru (from Cham + rɔ); it is clear from its syllable structure that Chru is the reduction of two morphemes and Cham Ro is a perfect etymological fit. As for the Haroi, it is quite likely that their name comes from the MK name Hrê, particularly in light of some of the other variants of Haroi including Hroi and so on. However, an alternate designation of the Haroi is the Bahnar Cham. That leaves only the Rade for which I have not yet found a variant that includes Cham. To return to the main point, Cham was once used widely to refer to the various groups of Chamic-speaking people.

---

1.   It is likely that the designation 'forest people' was applied at different times to more than one group of Chamic speakers. It cannot be automatically assumed that all dialects designated Roglai are dialects of the same language.

From Ancient Cham to modern dialects: Two Thousand Years of Language Contact and Change is a preliminary reading of that linguistic record. It reconstructs an early stage of Chamic as the foundation for tracing the developments of Chamic from its Austronesian forebears through early Chamic down to its modern descendants, sketching the internal developments, noting the nature of external contact, and examining the role played by each in the nature and direction of change. In the Chamic languages is hidden a rich storehouse of knowledge, not just about the Chams and the history of the region, but also about the interaction of language change and language contact: about external contact and internal change, about the origins of register complexes from systems without such complexes, about the origins of tones from nontonal languages, and about the convergence of languages in a new linguistic area.

Not to be ignored is the potential Chamic contribution to the unraveling of various puzzles about linguistic and non-linguistic history. Cham is the earliest attested Austronesian language. Coedès (1939, cited in Marrison 1975:53) dates the inscription found at Tra-kiêu near the old Cham capital of Indrapura (Amaravati) from the middle of the fourth century, noting that this inscription is "le plus ancien texte, actuelle connu, écrit dans un dialecte malayo-polynésien", that is, "...the oldest text, presently known, written in a Malayo-Polynesian dialect".

The Cham inscription is older by three centuries than the "Old Malay" inscriptions of Srivijaya in southeastern Sumatra. The text itself, associated with a well near Indrapura, the old northern capital, is short but linguistically revealing, as Marrison notes.

> Siddham! Ni yang nāga punya putauv. Ya urāng sepüy di ko, kurun ko jemā labuh nari svarggah. Ya urāng paribhū di ko, kurun saribu thun davam di naraka, dengan tijuh kulo ko.

> fortune! this YANG serpent possess king. YA person respect DI him, for him jewels fall from heaven. YA person insult DI him, for one-thousand year remain DI hell, with seven family he.

> Fortune! This is the divine serpent of the king. Whoever respects him, for him jewels fall from heaven. Whoever insults him, he will remain for a thousand years in hell, with seven generations of his family. (Marrison 1975:53)

Marrison (1975:53) observes that the language of the text is not that far from modern Cham or Malay in its grammar and its vocabulary. The similarities to modern Malay and modern Cham grammar are evident in the *yang* and *ya* relative markers, both found in Cham, in the *dengan* 'with' and *di* 'locative', in the syntax of the equative sentence *Ni yang nāga punya putauv* 'This the one possessed by the king', in the use of *punya* as a genitive, and so on Hindu influence is evident in the Sanskrit terms *"siddham* — a frequently used invocation of fortune; *nāga* — serpent or dragon; *svarggah* — heaven, *paribhu* — to insult, *naraka*— hell, and *kulo* — family". Most of the remaining vocabulary is transparently Chamic. And, from the earliest times, as the oldest Malayo-Polynesian text shows by the presence of Hindu terminology and its Indic script, contact has played a significant role in Chamic.

Although the major focus of this study is on the history of language contact and change, the bulk of its work revolves around historical reconstruction of proto-Chamic (PC) and to the problems inherent in trying to reconstruct it, since a historical reconstruction is necessary for recognizing, unraveling, and interpreting historical language contact. Without a reconstruction, it is often not possible to differentiate between similarities that are genetically-inherited and those that are contact-induced. However, driven by concern with understanding the prior history of Chamic language contact, the attempt has been made throughout this work to identify and to determine, where possible, when individual loans were incorporated into Chamic. There has been a consistent concern with differentiating loans that predate the formation of PC and loans that postdate the breakup of PC. These loans are an important source of information, not just about the sources and the chronology of contact, but also sometimes about its nature and intensity. Even more important, these loans are a crucial source of information about the historical contact between the peoples involved.

CHAMIC CONVERGENCE WITH SOUTHEAST ASIA

Without doubt the Chamic languages have only begun to reveal what they can about the history of the peoples of this area but certainly even this modest study reveals some important historical relationships. Nonetheless, as valuable as the non-linguistic considerations may be, the greatest value of the Chamic data may lie in the insights that Chamic gives us into the effects of language contact on language change. As Eric Oey wrote (n.d.:1), the "closer study of the Chamic languages within their historical context offers an unparalleled opportunity to better understand the nature of mainland Southeast Asian areal influences that the Chamic languages have undergone together with many of their non-PMP [Proto-Malayo-Polynesian] neighbors." More recently, Solnit (1993:109) wrote expressing a similar view of the Chamic developments: "Clearly Chamic provides multiple examples of the spread of Southeast Asian areal features including monosyllabicity, tonality, and glottalized consonants, none of which are otherwise characteristic of Austronesian. Its linguistic neighbors, from which the features are spread, are all Mon-Khmer: Bahnaric, Katuic, Viet-Muong, Khmer." Indeed, because so much evidence is available concerning insular PMP languages, the Chamic languages of the mainland provide us with crucial information about linguistic contact and adaptation to a new linguistic area.

About 2000 years ago, when the Austronesian-speaking traders, artisans, and seafarers that were to become Chamic arrived on the mainland of Southeast Asia, the language they spoke was disyllabic, nontonal, and nonregistral. Just as importantly they had not had contact with the languages of the mainland for some four thousand years—recurrent, constantly self-renewing myths about Austronesian speakers having reached the islands through the Malay peninsula notwithstanding.

The linguistic record attests to the relatively "recent" arrival of Chamic speakers in Vietnam: proto-Chamic, the immediate predecessor of all the modern Chamic languages is a single unitary language, still quite close to its daughter languages, with an obviously short time depth. If there is a single, linguistically-obvious, uncontroversial conclusion that can be drawn from the reconstruction of proto-Chamic, it is that, despite the incessant uninformed statements to the contrary, the linguistic evidence alone establishes unequivocally that the Chamic speakers of Vietnam represent an incursion of Austronesian speakers from the islands, not the remnants of Austronesian speakers left on the mainland from the initial expansion of Austronesian speakers out into the Pacific some six or eight thousand years ago. That the Chamic speakers are recent arrivals on the mainland is established beyond question by the linguistically-unitary, quite tight-knit, rather easily-reconstructed nature of PC. Chamic has absolutely none of the diversity nor any of the time-depth associated with an older primary branch of a language family and all of the characteristics of a recently-arrived, dialectally-unified immigrant group.

In the last 2000 years, the Chamic languages of Vietnam have undergone radical restructuring in the canonical shape of their words, major changes in their consonantal and vocalic phonological inventories, and, in some cases, even in the basic structure of their phonological systems.

THE GENERAL TENDENCIES: A BROAD OVERVIEW

The return to the mainland by a pre-Chamic Austronesian language that was almost certainly disyllabic and atonal has provided us with an unusually clear picture of the interaction between internal developments and external contact. Despite the essentially identical starting point provided by PC, the histories of the individual languages differed, although only moderately, in the subsequent paths

of internal change and differed often radically in the nature of the resulting phonological system. The crucial cause of these differences in the internal path followed and in the ultimate phonological system attained was the differences in the
contact situation, specifically, the differences in the phonological models encountered through contact. This exposure to new phonological systems—through
external contact—determined to a significant degree which of the myriad of
available paths of change a given Chamic language actually took. External contacts supplied the new models for phonological restructuring and thus gave directionality to the changes by selectively making some phonological features, but
not others, salient.

Among the general tendencies arising from contact with the languages
of the Southeast Asian mainland, beginning with the registral Mon-Khmer (MK)
languages and continuing with the tonal Vietnam and Hainanese (Min), are the
following:

- increasing monophthongization, that is,
  the movement from disyllabic > iambic > monosyllabic
- adjustments in vowel and consonant inventories, that is,
  the addition of glottalized consonants
  the proliferation of vowel contrasts
  the merger and ultimate loss of finals
  the loss of voicing distinctions among the obstruents
- radical changes in the phonological systems, that is,
  the development of register complexes and then tone systems

All of these represent areal tendencies in Southeast Asia and, in the Chamic data,
all of them represent directions of linguistic "drift" adapted under the influence
of contact with languages already containing the features in question.

PREVIOUS WORK ON CHAMIC RECONSTRUCTION

In order to distinguish between contact-induced and historically-inherited similarities, it is minimally necessary to have knowledge of language history. In this
case, some of what is needed can be found in older texts, but given the relative
paucity of extensive early texts this also means that it is imperative to have a historical reconstruction of PC. In the case of Chamic, we are dealing not with a single contact situation but with a series of contact situations stretching over a long
period of time. And, given the limitations of the written records, it would not be
possible to discuss the contact in any meaningful way without a historical reconstruction: on a non-trivial but simple level, it would neither be possible to accu-

rately identify the loans—let alone begin to stratify them accurately as to when and where they were borrowed, nor would it be possible to subgroup the dialects and thus determine what changes correlate with changes in the contact patterns. Thus, a reconstruction of Chamic is crucial to the unraveling the layers of historical contact.

Although a number of earlier scholars recognized the Austronesian affiliations of Chamic, or at least Cham, the earliest actual lexical reconstructions of Chamic were those of Lee (1966) in his doctoral dissertation. A little earlier, some of the sound correspondences between proto-Malayo-Polynesian and Cham had already been set out by Doris Blood (1962) in her concise and still useful "Reflexes of Proto-Malayo-Polynesian in Cham" Dyen (1971), often referring to Blood (and to Thomas (1963)) also discussed the correspondences between proto-Malayo-Polynesian and Chamic. Within Chamic itself, using data supplied by Pastor Pham Xuan Tin, Dorothy Thomas (1963) laid out some of the internal correspondences in her insightful "Proto-Malayo-Polynesian reflexes in Rade, Jarai, and Chru". Lee's 1966 work followed. Then, Burnham (1976) incorporated Haroi data into the reconstructions, while modifying and improving a number of Lee's reconstructions in his work "The place of Haroi in the Chamic languages" (sometimes citing personal communication with Lee).

In a general sense, Lee's 1966 dissertation, as modified by Burnham 1976, still remains the basic framework for the PC historical reconstructions. Lee's dissertation contains 700 plus lexical reconstructions accompanied by preliminary inventories of the PC consonant and vowel systems. Aside from the occasional modification or addition of several forms here or there by Lee, Burnham, or others (cf. Durie 1990a), these reconstructions have remained essentially unaltered until now, simply because so little has been done in the meantime on Chamic reconstruction.

Increases in the database since Lee 1966

Since Lee 1966, our knowledge of the mainland Chamic languages has increased significantly, and much of this has been incorporated into these reconstructions. Lee basically used four mainland languages: N. Roglai, Rade, Jarai, and Phan Rang Cham. The data base for this work not only includes additional sources for Lee's four languages but has been expanded to include another four mainland languages: Haroi (Burnham 1976), Chru, Western Cham, and Written Chamic as well as Tsat, spoken on Hainan, and Acehnese, spoken in northern Sumatra. The addition of Haroi, Chru, and Western Cham resulted in minor adjustments here and there, but little more. Further, although the additional use of Written Chamic forms was sometimes valuable for its occasional preservation of an older form, aside from certain insights into the older vowel system, it has led to only minor advances in the reconstructions.

Far more significant was the inclusion of Acehnese, a language whose affinity with Cham was seen by Niemann as early as 1891. Subsequent scholars examining the issue of its affiliation such as Cowan, Shorto, Durie and others have also reached similar conclusions. The argument for this position will be made later in this work. The significance of Acehnese for reconstruction comes from its early departure from the mainland, which sometimes enabled it to retain archaic features that bear significantly upon PC reconstruction but which have disappeared from the dialect continuum left behind on the mainland.

Increases in Austronesian comparative material

A second area where our knowledge has increased is in the availability of reliable, accessible proto-Austronesian (PAn) and PMP reconstructions. Far more is readily available to the comparativist now than was available in the late 1960s and the early 1970s, leading to modifications of our PC reconstructions and increasing our ability to differentiate between native PC material and MK borrowings, an area that is difficult but in which important progress has been made.

This work has benefited greatly from having access to the extensive PMP reconstructions of Blust and to the proto-Malayic reconstructions of Adelaar. Access to clear, internally consistent reconstructions of PMP and proto-Malayic has made it possible to examine how prospective PC reconstructions fit in with the higher order reconstructions of Austronesian (AN), specifically with PMP (based on Blust's dictionary files (1990-1995) and personal communication with Blust) and proto-Malayic (based on Adelaar (1988, 1992) and personal communication).

In particular, the presence of a large body of reliable PMP reconstructions allows the Chamic reconstructions to be done on both a bottom-up and a top-down basis. Here, the term bottom-up refers to the more common procedure in comparative work and requires no explication. The term top-down, however, is less common and does require comment. This term was apparently introduced into Austronesian comparative literature by Blust (1972:1), who was discussing what he termed "reconstruction from the top down". Certainly, this top-down reconstruction is what Anttila (1972:346) explicitly refers to by the term "inverted reconstructions", which in reference to Chamic would simply mean that the interpretations of the sound correspondences within Chamic are not based solely on the data within Chamic itself but are also based on our knowledge of higher-level PMP reconstructions. This use of an outside witness is of particular value when there is no obvious directionality to a sound change, that is, in those cases when a sound change could have gone either way, the ability to use PMP reconstructions as a check often makes the direction of the change clear, thus making it obvious which of the alternatives within Chamic represents the older stage.

The availability of these MK and Austronesian sources, when used along with our understanding of the PC correspondence patterns, often makes it possible to not just identify loans but frequently to determine whether the loan pre-dates or post-dates the breakup of PC. Beyond the expanded database—even the invaluable inclusion of Acehnese, the major impetus behind the adjustments in the reconstruction of PC comes from the greatly improved ability to identify loanwords.

However, there is one potentially invaluable source that remains only partially tapped—the earlier records of inscriptional Chamic. The more that we know about the earlier inscriptions, the further back that we will be able to push the PC reconstructions. The value of these older inscriptions is greatly increased by the fact that early Chamic itself was a dialect continuum—a string of related and interacting dialects along the coast of Vietnam. As a consequence, there is every reason to believe that there were Post-PC changes that affected all the members of the dialect continuum, with the result that the evidence of an earlier stage was lost everywhere. Thus, when we reconstruct PC, in reality, what we are reconstructing is not the earliest stage of Chamic but a somewhat later stage. What evidence we have of the earlier stages is, in part, provided by Acehnese, which dropped out of the dialect chain, when it left the mainland, thus saving evidence of earlier stages, and, in part, by the inscriptional evidence, which should fill in some of the gaps.

Borrowings: their identification and interpretation

In order to analyze PC, it is essential to identify borrowings. The reason is that the Chamic languages have been in intimate contact with MK languages for about two thousand years and during that time have borrowed extensively from them. Without identifying the various layers of borrowings, it is neither possible to reconstruct the history of the Chamic contact with MK nor to reconstruct Chamic itself. Fortunately, it is usually possible, not just to identify borrowed items, but also to determine their relative chronology.

The problem of detecting borrowings is complicated by the existence of mutual borrowing between Chamic speakers and the MK groups with which they had contact. Thus, as David Blood points out (p.c.), there are numerous Cham loans in Chrau, as the Chrau were dominated by the Chams, so the existence of a form in Chrau does not authenticate it as originally MK. He adds that Mnong evidence is also suspect, as the central and eastern Mnongs have been under heavy Rade dominance and Bahnar evidence is also suspect because of heavy mutual cultural interaction with the Jarai. Hrê evidence is similarly suspect because of heavy interaction with the Haroi, as is at least some Katu evidence, as the Katu have clearly borrowed extensively from Haroi (Gérard Diffloth, p.c.).

Although it is likely that individual MK languages are largely free from Chamic borrowings (David Thomas suggests Koho, Stieng, Rengao, Jeh, and West Bahnaric), this work has tended to identify loans, not on the basis of any single factor, but on an evaluation of the overall evidence: the degree of regularity of the Chamic sound correspondences, the existence or non-existence of a good Austronesian etymology, the existence or non-existence of the form in the available reconstructions of various MK subgroups, and so on. In particular, among the MK sources, the existence of a form in Bahnar is much weaker evidence of its being MK in origin, than for example, its existence in Thomas' (Prachacakij-karacak 1995) West Bahnaric reconstructions, H. Blood's (1967, 1968, 1974) proto-Mnong reconstructions (which, in many cases, are often actually proto-South-Bahnaric as he draws heavily on Koho, Stieng, and Chrau (David Thomas, p.c.)), Efimov's (1987) proto-South-Bahnaric reconstructions (from the Gage translation of Efimov's wordlist), and Smith's (1972) proto-North Bahnaric. The existence of a form in several MK subgroups, of course, is still stronger evidence.

The most valuable single work for the identification of MK borrowings is Headley (1976), who focused on the potential MK borrowings in Lee's Chamic reconstructions. He estimated that 10% of Lee's reconstructions were MK borrowings, a number that now appears to be on the low side. Headley listed those forms he thought might be borrowings, either from MK or, in a small number of cases, from elsewhere; in most cases, based on his familiarity with MK, Headley identified particular Chamic items as potentially borrowed from MK. In all but a few cases, subsequent research has borne out his suspicions. Looking at his identification from a Chamic perspective, some of Headley's putative borrowings display irregular correspondences within Chamic, some have sounds not found in inherited AN forms, and some exist both in MK and Chamic but have no history elsewhere in AN. Further, some have been reconstructed in one or more branches of MK (see sources listed in the paragraph above). In fact, further investigation has fully confirmed most of the identifications. In addition to those, other forms also reconstructed for PC by Lee (1966) and by Burnham (1976) have also turned out to be MK borrowings.

The identification of the extensive layer of MK (and, occasionally, other) borrowings in Chamic has had several consequences. First, and in a sense most important, is the realization of how extensive and how intimate the MK contact was. The second consequence is that the identification of these as borrowings has led to a reassessment of the consonant and vowel inventories reconstructed by Lee (and, by Burnham).

The bases for the identification of certain words as loans needs to be discussed, particularly as the strength of the supporting evidence may vary considerably from case to case. It would be, of course, possible to simply assume that all words are native words unless there is overwhelming, irrefutable evidence that they are borrowings, including a precise identification of the source. In the Chamic context, this theoretical stance would make it quite impossible to effectively distinguish between inherited AN forms and borrowed MK forms, leading to the reconstruction of a PC that contained a large number of post-Chamic MK loans. Thus, a less dogmatic, more pragmatic approach to loan identification has been taken: if the sum of the evidence, taken as a whole, suggests that the word is more likely a borrowing than an inherited form, then it is treated as such; if the bulk of the evidence suggests that it is native, then it is treated as native.

In actual fact, few of the words are problematic. Certain words are unquestionably loans. For example, if a form which occurs in Chamic is also found reconstructed in one or more of the MK subgroups thus far reconstructed for Vietnam, that is, if it occurs in one or more of Smith's proto-North-Bahnaric, Blood's proto-Mnong, Efimov's proto-South-Bahnaric, or Peiros' proto-Katuic— a preliminary reconstruction of PKatuic, then from a Chamic viewpoint it is loan, with the regularity of the intra-Chamic correspondence patterns determining whether it reconstructs to the PC stage or whether it was borrowed after the breakup of PC. Further support is often provided by the failure of such forms to occur in AN languages outside of Chamic, although occasionally such a form may have a cognate in Malay.

Even without an identified MK donor language it may still be possible to reliably designate a form as a loan. For instance, there are a number of words which lack AN etymologies and which do not show up in any of the MK reconstructions available but which contain "loan phonemes", that is, sounds which only occur in borrowed words. Aside from the handful of AN words that have developed implosives under very specific conditions, forms with implosives can usually be designated as loans. Similarly, as is established later in this work, certain PC words contain vowels which only occur in MK borrowings; these too are marked as borrowings.

In other cases, it is not the presence of an unexpected sound that identifies the word as a loan but instead the existence of marked irregularities in the correspondence patterns; for instance, if the initial and the vowel are irregular in several languages and the word does not appear to exist in AN outside of Chamic, it is a likely loan. Similarly, if the correspondences are quite irregular within mainland Chamic, the word does not seem to exist in AN outside of Chamic, and the form apparently does not occur in Acehnese, it is likely a post- PC loan that post-dates not just the breakup of Chamic but also the movement of the Acehnese to Sumatra. The case would, of course, become even more convincing with the discovery of a likely MK source for the loan, but even without such a source, the bulk of the available evidence suggests such forms are loans, not inherited forms.

Certain words are unquestionably native AN. Certain forms reconstruct back to PMP or even back to PAn. The PAn and PMP forms cited in this work (unless otherwise noted) come exclusively from Blust's published work (or, personal communication); it is obvious even on the basis of my own limited personal "expertise" that many of the various PMP forms found floating around in the literature are unreliable. Not surprisingly, the PMP forms with PC reflexes have PC correspondences that show the forms are inherited, not borrowed.

Other forms for which we have limited documentation seem to be inherited, at least at the PC level. Some forms occur outside Chamic, for instance, in Malay, and pattern quite regularly within Chamic, but do not seem to reconstruct to PMP. These are treated as inherited, at least from the Chamic perspective, a decision without any significant consequences for the analyses in this work, as the words pattern regularly and there is no evidence of borrowing. Within this context, the Malay borrowings into Acehnese sometimes present a particular problem, as not only was there a long period of mutual interaction between the Acehnese and the Malay, but also some of the borrowings may not be readily distinguishable from inherited material.

In practice, of course, a specific word might be difficult to evaluate. Usually the problem revolves around the lack of information about its wider distribution, particularly its wider distribution in the MK languages. For AN, Blust's files and his comparative dictionary (in progress) are extensive enough to provide a reasonably accurate estimate about a particular word's distribution in AN as a whole; however, for MK if a form does not occur in either Smith (1972), in Blood (1967, 1968, 1974), in Efimov (1987), in Thomas (Prachacakij-karacak 1995) or in Peiros (1996), it is difficult to tell if the gap is fortuitous or meaningful. That is, there is no obvious way for me to determine if the word is likely to be a native MK etymon or not. A particular area of indeterminacy involves words found in Bahnar and one or more Chamic languages but not in any of the MK reconstructions; since Bahnar has borrowed numerous Chamic words, without more evidence it is unclear what the direction of the borrowing was.

Nonetheless, despite the existence of countless potential areas of difficulty in the identification of loans, the actual task is usually not problematic with the overall level of reliability quite high. Discussions of the status of particular words are scattered throughout this work, as are discussions of the evidence for the designations.

Finally, it is important to distinguish between pre-PC borrowings and post-PC borrowings. Thus, if the intra-Chamic correspondence patterns are regular, the loan predates the breakup of PC. In such cases, the word is marked by the accompanying asterisk as reconstructing to PC, while at the same time also marked with ˣ to indicate that, although it reconstructs to PC, it is nonetheless an early pre-Chamic borrowing from MK, e.g., ˣ*ɓaŋ 'hole; door' was borrowed from MK before the PC stage. On the other hand, if the intra-Chamic correspondences are irregular, the form was borrowed after the breakup of PC. In these cases, the form is simply labelled with ˣ indicating it is a borrowing, one that postdates the formation of PC, e.g. ˣsrăp 'crossbow' is a post-PC borrowing from MK.

THE DEGREE OF ADJUSTMENT

The improved identification of loans—particularly the late MK loans, the expanded data base—particularly due to the inclusion of Acehnese, occasional adjustments in the earlier analyses, and the increased availability of reconstructions of PMP and proto-Malayic—providing a clearer picture of the language that PC evolved out of, all have resulted in the accumulative modification of countless details: roughly 60% of the specific lexical reconstructions differ in minor or major ways from the reconstructions found in Lee (1966). This accretion of small changes combined with the identification of the bulk of the post-PC MK loans has resulted in revisions in the PC vowel and consonant inventories (with the specific details found scattered throughout this work). Nonetheless, despite the large number of smaller changes, Lee's pioneering work still remains the framework for these reconstructions.

2

The Geographical
and Historical Setting

The history of Chamic linguistic contact needs to be placed in a broader historical and geographical context.

THE GEOGRAPHICAL SETTING

The geographical setting has played its part in the history of the Chamic-speaking people. Vietnam is readily divided into the highlands formed by the Annamite Cordillera and an often quite narrow strip of land that runs along the coastline, with the north-south coastline itself being cut up into segments by the various rivers that flow eastward into the South China Sea. Thus, these rivers, which provided good harbors, carved the geographical configuration around which various riverine political entities developed. The rivers contained the harbors, with the surrounding coastal strips integrated as rice growing areas, and the highland areas were more loosely integrated into the coastal political entities as sources of highlands forest products, often as important for trade as for consumption. In the early years, there were frequent power struggles between the political units that developed in the various river basins, first between Funan and Champa and later, after the decline of Funan, between the various riverine entities within Champa itself, with frequent shifts in power as one or the other river-mouth harbors rose to ascendancy (cf. K. R. Hall, 1985). Later, the Vietnamese would move south along the coast, settling in the areas most suited to wet rice irrigation; this movement naturally forced the Chams away from the coastal strip up into the highlands.

Austronesian settlements existed in coastal areas because of the harbors, with the first major harbor being at Oc-eo, the port city of Funan (see "Chamic history" on page 17). As is typical of Austronesian settlement elsewhere, other later settlements were scattered along the narrow belt of land along the coast, typically close to river mouths. As part of the trading network, trading posts were also established in various places, including the southeast part of Hainan island, where some of the northern Cham would flee in 986, with a second migration following in 1486, and in parts of Cambodia. During most of its history and certainly during its ascendancy, Champa remained coastal. And, despite the fact that the MK speakers are now largely found in the highland areas, it was in and around these coastal communities that the initial, intense contact between Austronesian speakers and MK speakers occurred. However, first after the loss of the northern capital in 982 and then again after 1471 when the Vietnamese moved down along the narrow coastal plain, Chamic speakers retreated into the highlands, while still remaining in contact with MK speakers.

CHAMIC PREHISTORY

As Keyes (1995:182) observes, Southeast Asian prehistory has often been divided into periods named after sites found in northern Vietnam: the Hoa-binh, the Bac-son, and the Dong-son cultures. However, the Chamic speakers are only marginally associated with the Dong-son cultural complex, and instead are associated with a fourth complex, the Sa Huynh culture of southern Vietnam.

In Bellwood's summary of the Sa Huynh culture (1985:275-279ff; the sites Bellwood mentions have been indicated in Figure 1), he writes that the sites stretch from Hue and Da Nang in the north, to the type site Sa Huynh near the central Vietnam coastline, and then southwards to the Mekong Delta. Bellwood (1985:278) reports that the carbon dates from Phu Hoa and Hang Gon suggest an overall date range for the Sa Huynh culture between 600 BC and 0, but he goes on to say that the assemblages continue well into the middle of the first millennium, making the first part contemporary with the Funan civilization and the later with the early Champa civilization.

Bellwood (1985:276) associates the Sa Huynh culture with the Chamic settlers from the islands. The Sa Huynh burial jars have close parallels in the Early Metal phase jars in the Philippines, northern Borneo, and the Celebes Sea region of northern Indonesia. The dates at Niah and Tabon for jar burial go back as early as the end of the second millennium BC, suggesting that the practice in northern Borneo predates the practice in Sa Huynh. Bellwood dismisses suggestions that the stone burial jars of the Sa Huynh should instead be associated with similar practices in northern Laos. Other parallels are found in the "almost identi-

cal knobbed pennanular stone earrings (the so-called 'lingling-o'), and of a special kind of earring or pendant with two animals heads (presumably deer), in a
number of sites in Vietnam, Palawan and Sarawak".

Figure 1: The Sa Huynh culture

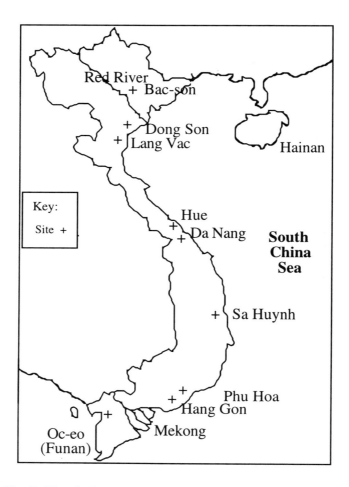

The Sa Huynh sites reflect the Austronesian-speaking group that settled
on the coast of Vietnam from an earlier homeland in perhaps Malaya or, more
likely, Borneo, sometime before 600 BC, although even earlier dates are now
being reported by Vietnamese archaeologists. It was some of these Austronesian-
speaking people who, after extended contact with the MK people then living
along the coast, would become the speakers of Chamic.

Here the archaeological records are supplemented by the linguistic record, salvaged through historical reconstruction, which indicates that this period included intense, intimate, assimilative linguistic and non-linguistic contact between the pre-Chamic Austronesian-speaking people and MK-speaking peoples, as evidenced from the massive incorporation of loan words (including pronouns, kinship terms, basic vocabulary, and so on), the restructuring of the basic word structure, the incorporation of new consonants, new vowels, vowel length contrasts, and so on.

CHAMIC HISTORY

The first Austronesian incursions onto the mainland must have immediately brought them into contact with MK speakers. Hall (1955; 1981) and Blust (1992a) argue that the first contact was probably not along the Vietnamese coast facing the South China Sea, but rather at Funan, facing the Gulf of Thailand, around 500 BC, or perhaps even earlier—at the site at Oc-eo, the port city of Funan. By the middle of the sixth century, Funan had been conquered by the Khmers, but both Hall (1955:23; 1981:25) and Blust (1992a:50) suggest that earlier Funan was Austronesian speaking. In the first edition of his 1955 history of Southeast Asia, Hall asserted that the Funanese were Malays (1955:23, cited in Blust (1992a:50)), a position that he repeated some twenty-five years later, when he wrote writes that the "Funanese were of Malay race, and still in the tribal state at the dawn of history" (1981:25). Blust, citing Hall (1955) with approval, points out that (1992a:50):

> The fall of Funan probably has a special significance for understanding the history of AN [AN] languages on the Southeast Asian mainland. If Funan was AN-speaking, in the early centuries of the Christian era a single dialect chain would have extended almost unbroken from the southern tip of the Malay Peninsula to Champa. The expansion of the Khmers into the region of the Mekong delta would then have divided an earlier language continuum into two separate and smaller dialect chains,...

The question of whether or not Funan was originally Austronesian-speaking aside, it is likely that the long period of contact between Austronesian and MK speakers began at Funan. If so, this would further suggest that the initial language contact was not with the more northerly Bahnaric but rather more southerly Mon-Khmer groups; and, even if Hall and Blust are not correct, the first intense contact also began at Funan. In any case, one would certainly still speculate that there was a string of trading posts down along the coast, stretching as far south as the eastern coast of modern Malaysia which were dominated by Austronesian-speaking traders.

Without records of the actual language spoken, the evidence for Funan being Austronesian speaking remains circumstantial. Nonetheless, the available Chinese descriptions record at least an Austronesian presence in Funan and along the coast to the south. K. R. Hall (1985:38) notes that, in 240, K'ang T'ai, a Wu envoy to Funan, reported to the emperor that Funan's authority reached from the lower Mekong Delta to the upper Malay Peninsula, a stretch coterminous with what was almost assuredly a string of Austronesian speaking trading colonies. In the Southern Ch'i history, the Funan of Jayavarman, the great king who died in 514, is described (D. G. E. Hall 1981:33) as a community of seafaring people, "carrying on both trade and piracy, and constantly preying on their neighbours", a picture that would just as accurately describe the neighboring Chams. To extend Durie's characterization of the Acehnese to the people of Funan, they were "a people of the coastal margins, engaged in fishing the sea, in wet rice cultivation of their preferred homelands, in maritime trade (and sometimes piracy)..." (1996:114). That is, the descriptions are of a very Malay-like people.

The archaeological record also suggests what Hall interprets as an Austronesian connection. K. R. Hall (1985:40) describes the archaeological remains at Oc-eo as showing that "the coast was occupied in the early first century AD by Malay fishing and hunting groups". This interpretation is based on the conclusion that Funan and the Chamic Sa Huynh culture both show the influence of Borneo people, although it is not clear that the influence is from the same region of Borneo. K. R. Hall (1985:40) writes that archaeological evidence from Borneo from the presumed site of Yeh-po'-t'i, an ancient trade port believed to have been on the west coast of Borneo, which notably included "carved sacrificial posts known as yūpas" and which "substantiate a Borneo cultural link to Funan". Elsewhere Bellwood (1985:276) has suggested that aspects of the Chamic Sa Huynh culture show links with northern Borneo culture.

More than one explanation, however, exists to account for the archaeological evidence. If, as speculated by Hall and Blust, the Cham were simply an extension of the an earlier Austronesian-speaking Funanese kingdom, these connections receive a simple explanation. First, however, it is not clear that the Borneo influences on Funan and on the Sa Huynh cultures were the same, leaving the possibility we talking about more than one group of people. And, second, the establishment of a Borneo connection does not automatically make it with Austronesian-speaking people. It seems evident to Adelaar and to myself that many of the now Austronesian languages on Borneo show a MK substratum, one that I would associate with a language shift from MK to Austronesian.

The historical records provide several types of evidence that indicate that the people of Funan were the same people found in neighboring Champa, but this leaves open the possibility that the people themselves were MK speaking. For instance, there is a fifth-century Chinese report of a Funan prince who fled to Lin-yi, that is, Champa, and eventually became king of the Chams (K. R. Hall, 1985:71). However, it is easy to read too much into this since the later history of Champa is dominated by intense contact and extensive cooperation between MK and Austronesian speakers. For instance, to paraphrase K. R. Hall (1985:178), the Chinese envoys who visited Funan in the 240s reported that around 220 the Chams and the Funanese were making joint naval raids and land attacks against the Red River Delta region. Thus, these frequent reports of joint Funanese and Cham raiding ventures only argue for mutual cooperation.

It is important to point out both that there was also frequent tension not just between Funan and Champa but also between the various coastal centers within Champa itself. As K. R. Hall (1985:178) writes, "... the Cham realm's early history was characterized by shifting alliances among regional centers that were concentrated at the river mouths of the Cham coast..." Changing power relationships were at the root of this factionalism. Funan's power base was mostly solid when trade routes were either overland or at least followed the coastline closely. As better sailing techniques and improved knowledge allowed more direct routes to be taken to China, the geographical position of Funan ceased to be an advantage and instead became a deterrent, with the bulk of the international trade shifting to Champa along the eastern coast of Vietnam. As these shifts worked themselves out, some tension between Funan and Champa was inevitable. By the end of the sixth century, however, the changes in trading routes left Funan a commercial backwater, as virtually all international trade shifted to the ports along the Vietnamese coast. In part as a reaction to these changes, the Funanese rulers withdrew inland, refocusing their economy on developing rice-lands in the upper Mekong Delta (K. R. Hall, 1985:75), and by the end of the sixth century Funan had ceased to be even partially Austronesian-speaking, becoming instead part of the Khmer world.

As for Champa itself, the first date of import for its future historical path is probably 111 AD, before the first historical reference to the Chamic people themselves. In that year, northern Vietnam became a province of the Han empire, an event that would lead to the Sinicization of north Vietnam. In particular, the "Vietnamese peasantry began to use Chinese methods of irrigation and agricultural terracing" (Keyes 1995:182). In later centuries, these methods of irrigation and terracing would be brought to the south, with consequences for the MK and Chamic peoples then living on the coastal plains.

The initial historical appearance of the Chams themselves—a term referring at that time to all the Chamic speaking people—was in a role that they would
play repeatedly over the centuries. In the year 137 AD, Coedès suggests
(1968:43), "a band of about a thousand barbarians from beyond the frontier of
Jih-nan" attempted to invade Hsiang-lin. Coedès continues, "their name Ch'ü-
lien, although written with different characters, can scarcely be dissociated from
that of the founder of Lin-yi."

However, the first recognition of Champa itself, writes Coedès
(1968:17), was by the Chinese, who began to speak of the kingdom of Champa
along the coast of Vietnam around 190 to 193 AD. Coedès wrote (1968:42) that
The History of Chin includes, around the year 280, a report in which the Chinese
governor of Tongking complains about the raids of the kingdom of Lin-yi
(Champa). The governor, T'ao Huang, says of the kingdom that it "touches Funan
in the south. Their tribes are numerous; their friendly bands render mutual aid
taking advantage of the ruggedness of their region, they do not submit [to
China]."

By about the sixth century the Champa civilization reached its zenith,
but continued to flourish until the Vietnamese "push to the South" began in the
tenth century. Meanwhile a writing system based on Indic models evolved, in
which the earliest Cham linguistic record is the inscription found at Tra-kiêu, dating from the middle of the fourth century (The inscription is cited in full on
page 3). Various temples were built in the north, particularly around the spiritual
capital of Mi-son, another cluster to the south at the site of Vijaya, and still further south are the important complex of temples called Po Nagar near the modern
cities of Nha Trang and Phan Rang. This whole period involved continued contact with MK speakers.

The Chamic dialect chain extended north at least as far as Quang-Tri,
where they undoubtedly encountered Katuic speakers. The linguistic evidence
suggests that it was the Chamic speakers who left their linguistic imprint on the
Katuic languages in the form of borrowings and perhaps even some morphology,
if as Reid (1994) argues the morphology found in some dialects of Katu is Austronesian, particularly Katu proper. Under pressure from the north, these Chamic
speakers left, probably to become the modern Acehnese of northern Sumatra.

The beginning of the rapid decline started when the Vietnamese sacked
the capital at Indrapura in 982. From this point on, the remaining history of
Champa is dominated by what the Vietnamese historians term the "push to the
South", the Vietnamese movement down along the coastal plains of Vietnam.
Within twenty years after the sacking of Indrapura, the Chams had effectively
abandoned their northern provinces and the capital was moved further south to
Vijaya.

Figure 2: Champa from inception to absorption (important sites)

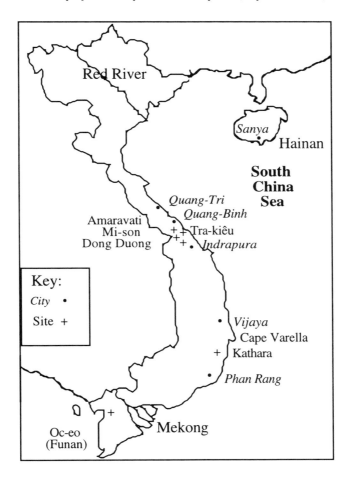

With the fall of Indrapura, the Chams inhabiting the northern provinces resettled elsewhere. With the departure of the Acehnese, the northern Cham consisted of two groups of still identifiable modern descendants: the Tsat speakers of Hainan ("The history of Tsat contact" on page 224), who are quite probably the refugees from Champa mentioned in the Chinese report of 986, and the Northern Roglai, who fled to the south with the fall of the capital, eventually coming to live in the Vietnamese highlands. History also records a third group of refugees from northern Champa, the group recorded by Guangzhou (Canton City) as 310 refugees from Zhancheng. Although cited by Zheng (1986:37) in connection with providing confirmation of the dating the arrival of the Tsat in Hainan, the group itself seems to have fled to Guangzhou, not Hainan. Since the Chams more than likely had trading connections in Guangzhou (Canton) at the time, Guangzhou makes sense as a destination for the emigrants.

The linguistic evidence shows that the Northern Roglai and the Utsat were once speakers of the same northern Cham dialect. Zheng (1986:37) notes that the *History of the Song Dynasty* (960-1279) makes it clear that some of the northern Cham went to Hainan. Specifically, in 986, Pu-Luo-E and a hundred of his clan arrived, having not just fled Zhancheng (Champa) but having been harassed by the people of Jiaozhi, the name given by the Northern Sung dynasty to northern parts of Vietnam. This report, including the Pu used in the name of the leader, affirms the arrival of the Cham from Champa, the group we now identify as the Utsat. Having arrived in Hainan, these Cham entered into the Hainanese linguistic area, an area characterized by the richly tonal Be and Li of the Tai-Kadai family and the Southern Min Hainanese dialect of Chinese.

The effective end of Champa as a regionally-dominant political entity came with the fall of the southern capital at Vijaya in 1471. Much of the remainder of Champa was incorporated into Vietnam and, although remnants of Champa existed for quite some time, it was now reduced to small territories situated south of Cape Varella, where even today many Cham still live.

Just as happened after the fall of the northern capital, the fall of Vijaya also led to a diaspora of Chamic speakers, some to the highlands, some to Hainan, Guangzhou (Canton), Malaka, Aceh, Java, Thailand, and Cambodia (the Western Cham). With reference to Hainan, again citing from Zheng (1986:37), in 1486 the *True Records of the Emperor Xian Zong of the Ming Dynasty* (1368-1644) record over 1000 new refugees in Hainan from Zhancheng (Champa). With reference to Guangzhou (Canton City), in 988 AD the Guangzhou records report 310 refugees from Zhancheng. The *Sejarah Melayu* records that after the fall of Vijaya, the two sons of King Pau Kubah fled, with Syah Indera Berman going to Malaka, and Syah Pau Ling going to Aceh where he started the line of Aceh kings (Abdul Rahman al-Ahmadi 1994 [1987]:104). Other sources and texts record the arrival of Cham in Java. In Thailand, a 1662 missionary account notes the existence of a Cham colony at Ayudhya (Lafont 1994b:73) these appear to the same group now found in Bangkok, where they still exist as an identifiable ethnic community. At various times, Cham also fled to Cambodia. For instance, after the fall of Vijaya in 1471, the *Khmer Annals* record that many Cham took refuge in Cambodia; later, in 1692, the *Khmer Royal Chronicles* record another large migration (Mak Phoen 1994:76-77).

As Figure 3 shows, this last major ancient diaspora along with several still later, more modern migrations correlates with the modern distribution of the Chamic languages. Some of the Chamic speakers retreated into the highlands of

Vietnam, others fled to Hainan to become speakers of Tsat, some went to Cambodia (apparently some as war captives, others willingly) where they speak what are Western Cham dialects, and still others ultimately went to northern Sumatra, eventually to become speakers of Acehnese.

Figure 3: The modern distribution of Chamic

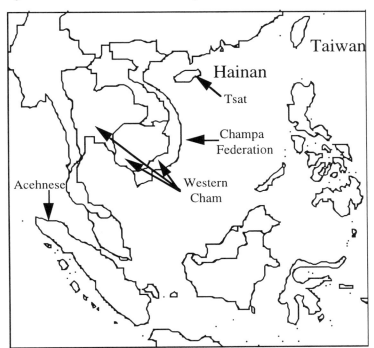

Once they were separated from the Chamic community, as Durie notes (p.c.), the Acehnese re-entered the Austronesian world, greatly expanding their contacts with Malay while their language's typological convergence with MK languages was largely arrested. However, it remains unclear when and by what route the Acehnese made their way to north Sumatra. As for dating their arrival in Sumatra, Durie (1996:115), for example, assumes that Acehnese may have been there for a period of more than a thousand years, based on the striking dialect diversity. Any real precision with respect to an arrival date is not possible without more information than we now have.

The Acehnese and Kelantan

With respect to the path the Acehnese took on their travels, there is evidence that there was an important, Chamic presence in Kelantan, on the east coast of the

Malaysian peninsula but this influence looks to have been quite late. As Abdul Rahman al-Ahmadi (1994 [1987]: 105-106) notes, local Kelantanese traditions have the King of Kelantan coming from Kembayat, an area some authors believe to be Champa, although others maintain it is Cambodia. Less controversial evidence of a Chamic presence is found in the numerous place names related to Champa: Pengkalan Cepa, Kampong Cepa, and Gong Cepa, to cite but a few. The Cepa of these names is obviously Champa, with the expected sound changes. These place names and other influences were the result of an Acehnese presence in Kelantan, not just a Chamic presence. Gérard Diffloth has suggested that Acehnese contains loanwords restricted to Aslian; however, even if data showing Aslian loanwords from groups on the Malay peninsula can be assembled, the finding would only provide substantiation for the contention that the Acehnese had a presence in Kelantan.

Table 1: The Malayic dialects of Nonthaburi, Pattani, and Kelantan (I)

PMP	Malay	Nb.	Pattani	Kelantan	PC	
*-i	-i	-i	-i	-i	*-ɛy	
*laki	lakilaki	laki	---	llaki	*lakɛy	'male; person'
*waʀi	hari	---	---	aɣi	*hurɛy	'day; sun'
*gigi	gigi	gigi	gigi	gigi	*gigɛy	'tooth'
*beli	bĕli	---	---	bəli	*pə-blɛy	'sell'
*-u	-u	-u	-u	-u	*-ɔw	
*taqu	tahu	tahu	tahu	tahu	*thɔw	'know; can; able'
*kutu	kutu	gutu -i?	kutu	---	*kutɔw	'louse, head'
*kuku	kuku	kuku	kuku	---	*kukɔw	'claw; fingernail'
*kahiw	kayu	kayu	kayu	kayu	*kayɔw	'tree; wood'
*batu	batu	batu	batu	batu	*batɔw	'stone'
*baqeʀu	baharu	baɣu	baɣu	baɣu	*bahrɔw	'new; just now'
*aku	aku	ku	---	---	*kɔw	'I (familiar)'
*qabu	abu	ʔabu	abu	---	*habɔw	'ashes'

Two things argue for this Acehnese presence in Kelantanese being fairly recent. First, the records of Acehnese presence in the area themselves suggest a fairly recent presence. Second, Kelantanese itself shows little other Acehnese influence. Despite the obvious Chamic influences in the place names, the modern dialects of the northeast coast of Malaysia and southern Thailand, Nonthaburi

Malay (a group relocated from Pattani to central Thailand), Pattani Malay and Kelantanese Malay subgroup, not with PC, but with Malayic. As Tables 1 and 2 show, with reference to four obvious vocalic innovations differentiating the Malayic and the Chamic branches of Malayo-Chamic, Nonthaburi (data from Tadmor 1995), Pattani (data from Tadmor 1995), and Kelantan (data from Abdul Hamid Mahmood, 1994) consistently pattern with Malay, the representative of Malayic, not with PC.

Specifically, as Table 1 shows, in final position Chamic has innovated, diphthongizing the two high PMP vowels *-i and *-u, giving *-ɛy and *-ɔw, respectively; not one of these three dialects shares this Chamic innovation.

Table 2: The Malayic dialects of Nonthaburi, Pattani, and Kelantan (II)

PMP	Malay	Nb	Pattani	Kelantan	PC	
*-ay	-i	-i	-i	-i	*-ay	
*ma-atay	mati	mati	mati	mati	*matay	'die'
*qatay	hati	ati	hati	ati	*hatay	'liver'
(*qaqay)	kaki	kaki	kaki	kaki	*kakay	'leg; foot'
*-uy	-i	-i	-i	-i	*-uy	
*hapuy	api	ʔapi	api	api	*ʔapuy	'fire'
*babuy	babi	---	---	---	*babuy	'wild pig'

As is obvious both from the PMP forms in Table 2 and from Adelaar's 1992 reconstruction of Malayic, Malayic has innovatively monophthongized the two PMP final diphthongs *-ay and *-uy, merging both as *-i; the three dialects share this Malayic innovation. Thus, although there have been some Acehnese influence in Kelantan, it is obvious not just from this evidence but from all the linguistic evidence that Kelantanese is not Acehnese, nor Chamic, but a Malayic dialect.

Two other general observations can also be made about the forms of Table 2, neither of which invalidates their subgrouping implications. First, it is not the case that PMP *-ay forms all have -i reflexes in Malay (and in western Indonesia as well as in a small set of languages historically heavily influenced by Malay); some forms keep -ay reflexes in Malay (Blust, p.c.). Dyen, for example, reconstructed *-ey (in addition to *-ay) for precisely those forms that have Malay -i reflexes. However, whatever the ultimate solution to the problem posed by the -i/-ay split in reflexes for higher level reconstruction, the fact remains that the Kelantanese reflexes pattern with Malayic, not with PC. To the degree that the Malayic -i reflexes are unexpected, the argument that Kelantanese subgroups with Malayic, not Chamic, is only strengthened.

Note that the limited amount of data presented here makes the solution to the problem seem obvious: simply reconstruct both *-ey and *-ay. However, the apparent obviousness disappears once it is realized that this particular split in reflexes is limited basically to PMalayic and, as noted already, to a number of languages in western Indonesian known to have been strongly influenced by Malay. Thus, I fully sympathize with Blust's reluctance to posit an additional vowel phoneme solely on the basis of one segment of one subgroup of Austronesian. Bear in mind, however, that Dyen's reconstruction of both *-ey and *-ay is based on different subgrouping assumptions and these assumptions, coupled with his methodology, requires reconstructing another proto-phoneme.

Second, the PMP form *qaqay should be the nonexistent *hahi in Malayic and the nonexistent *hahay in PC, but it is *kaki in Malayic and *kakay in PC. And, how both Chamic and Malay developed the same aberrant reflex remains an unsolved problem. Again, however, whatever the ultimate source of this irregularity, the fact the Chamic and Malayic share this oddity supports rather than refutes the arguments for the unity of Chamic and Malayic as a superordinate subgroup (both subgroups share reflexes of this unexpected lexical innovation) and for the patterning of the Kelantanese languages with Malayic (as the *-ay component of the form becomes -i, rather than remaining -ay).

The Cham remaining on the mainland

The MK and Chamic speakers who stayed on the mainland continued to undergo significant, long-term changes in their patterns of language contact, changes directly related to the Vietnamese-dominated inhabitation of the coastal plain, an area suitable for wet-rice irrigation. The Vietnamese movement into these areas was abrupt in times of war and gradual in times of peace, but incessant. In response to this incursion, some segments of the Chamic and MK groups inhabiting the coastal plains adapted, assimilated, and in some cases even shifted to Vietnamese, although not without changing the incoming Vietnamese culture in the process, while other segments of the Chamic and MK peoples reacted by retreating into the hills, pushed not so much by the march of an army but more by the almost imperceptible conversion of the coastal plains, by the Vietnamese farmers, slowly but steadily, one field at a time.

Steadily over time, the once coastal-dwelling speakers of Cham languages have either adapted and assimilated or continued to move further into the highlands. The previous extensive interaction networks between Chamic speakers were often weakened and sometimes even broken, with new patterns of affiliation evolving, but now in some cases not with fellow Chamic speakers, but with

MK speakers. The Haroi, who have effectively become a Chamic-speaking branch of the otherwise Bahnaric-speaking Hrê are an excellent example of this sort of cultural realignment. Eventually, as a consequence of the breaking of old alliances and the substitution of new linguistic and cultural realignments, the differentiation among many of the Chamic languages became more marked, becoming the Rade, the Jarai, the Chru, the Haroi, and the modern Cham.

Typically the Chamic and MK speakers that remained in the coastal plain eventually assimilated into the Vietnamese culture, a process found throughout Southeast Asia. As Keyes (1995:19) wrote:

> Despite a growing distinction between the hill and lowland peoples, sharp boundaries did not develop between the two. Rather, throughout most of Southeast Asia, hill peoples were incorporated into social systems dominated by the lowland peoples.

And, although some of the MK and Chamic speakers retreated into the hills, much of the disappearance of the Chamic MK speakers along the coastal plain must be attributed not to their being killed or even displaced but to their absorption into the emerging lowland civilization. Again, Keyes (1995:183-184) writes:

> Once the various territories had been conquered, Vietnamese migrants would move into and settle these areas. Here, they often intermarried with Chams and Khmer, and, even when they did not, they were exposed to the different social and cultural patterns of these Indianized peoples. These contacts tended to result in some compromising of the dominant Chinese-derived tradition, at least among the peasantry. Many of the cultural differences between northern and southern Vietnamese can be traced to such compromises.

In many cases, such assimilation led to the total absorption of peoples into the dominant Vietnamese culture, but even in cases where the group has maintained a distinct linguistic identity, there have not only been enormous cultural changes but the languages have been slowly restructured in the direction of Vietnamese, as exemplified by the dramatic evolution of tones in Phan Rang Cham.

THE CHAMIC AND MK LANGUAGES IN VIETNAM

The modern distribution of Chamic and MK languages is shown in Figure 4. The Chamic languages are found in central and southern Vietnam interspersed with MK languages.

Figure 4: The modern distribution of Chamic and Mon-Khmer

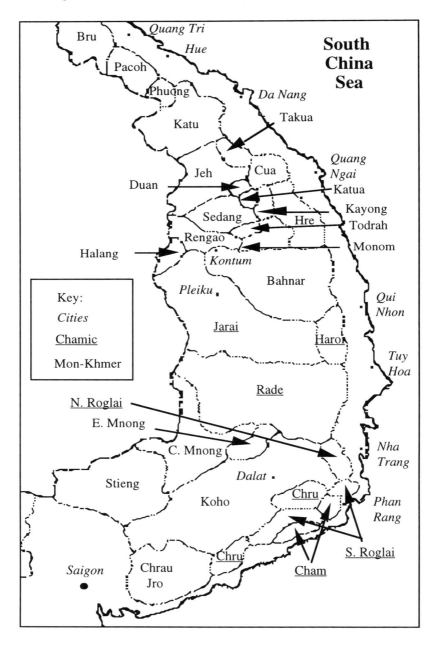

Most of the Chamic languages are now highlands languages spoken by hill tribesmen living away from the coastal plains. For those in the southern Vietnamese highlands, the major linguistic contact has been with MK highlands languages, and this mutual contact has resulted in what Solnit termed "the southern Vietnamese highlands subregion", a linguistic area defined by certain common linguistic characteristics ("Reflexes of PC glottalized obstruents" on page 91).

What is equally evident from Figure 4 (from Gregerson and Thomas (1980:xi)) is that there are no longer any Chamic speakers living in the north, but as already mentioned, the Acehnese were at one point the most northerly Chamic speakers, and upon the departure of the Acehnese, the descendants of then most northerly Chamic speakers live on in the modern Tsat speakers of Hainan and the modern Northern Roglai speakers found in the south (page 224).

Finally, of course, there is the modern diaspora of Chamic and other speakers from Vietnam, as a result of the conflicts of the Vietnam war, and from Cambodia, as a result of the Khmer Rouge genocidal killings. These modern refugees are found scattered throughout the world, in Malaysia, Hong Kong, France, Australia, and so on — even occasionally showing up in places as distant as the central valley of California and the large and growing Chamic (Dega) community in central North Carolina (David Thomas, p.c.).

3

Classification of the Chamic Languages

The classification of the Chamic languages as Austronesian and the determination of their relationship to the rest of Austronesian has clear implications for our understanding of the prehistory and the history of this part of Southeast Asia. John Crawfurd, one of the earliest scholars to examine Cham recognized its Austronesian character, describing Cham as the "Malay of Champa" as early as 1822. However, by the turn of the century the classification of Cham, and, thus, Chamic, had become controversial, a controversy that resulted from a failure to distinguish between genetic and typological criteria for classification.

The scholars following Crawfurd were inclined either to be confused by the MK-like typology of Chamic or to view it as an "intermediate link" between the MK languages of the mainland and the Austronesian languages of the islands. Thus, in 1889, Étienne Aymonier, who believed, along with many of his contemporaries, that the Malayo-Polynesians migrated to the islands from this part of the Southeast Asian mainland, wrote that Cham formed a kind of intermediary link between Khmer and Malay (Aymonier 1889:5-6 (translation mine)):

> ...that like the Khmer language as well as the majority of the tribes in the forests of southern Indo-China, the Cham language represents a mainland group related to the Polynesian family of languages found in all the islands of Pacific and of the Indian Ocean; knowledge of it will help balance the study of these languages; one can suggest that Cham serves as an intermediate link between Khmer and Malay, for example.

The MK-like typological features in Chamic coupled with the presence of some borrowed material also accounts for Schmidt's (1906) description of the Chamic languages as "Austroasiatische Mischsprache" and for Thomas Sebeok's misguided 1942 claim that these languages are Austroasiatic. Despite this earlier confusion, the Chamic languages are indisputably Austronesian from a modern perspective,[1] and what is of interest is determining how and under what influences these languages came to acquire the often typologically MK-like forms and systems which they possess today.

THE PLACE OF CHAMIC WITHIN AUSTRONESIAN

The existence of the Austronesian family was certainly recognized early by Hadrianus Relandus in 1708. In 1852 its geographical extent was sketched nicely by Crawfurd, who described what he called the "Malayan" languages in the following terms (1852:cxxxiii):

> A certain connexion, of more or less extent, is well ascertained to exist between most of the languages which prevail from Madagascar to Easter Island in the Pacific, and from Formosa, on the coast of China, to New Zealand. It exists, then, over two hundred degrees of longitude and seventy of latitude, or over a fifth part of the surface of this earth.

Crawfurd continues with his geographical survey of languages, adding to his Malayan

> ... the innumerable islands of the Indian Archipelago, from Sumatra to New Guinea — of the great group of the Philippines — of the islands of the North and South Pacific — and of Madagascar.

In 1852, the Austronesian language family was the most geographically dispersed language family in the world.

Placing Chamic more precisely within the Austronesian family requires a family tree, along with its subgroups, but none of the subgrouping assumptions about PAn are totally without their distractors. Nonetheless, while there are differences in details, except for Dyen (1965; 1995), who has his own family tree, and two of Dyen's students (Wolff 1991, 1995; Tsuchida 1982), who regard For-

---

1. The modern perspective probably begins with Pittman (1959), who clearly recognized the Austronesian nature of Jarai, one of the Chamic languages.

mosan languages as branching off from Philippine languages, modern scholars agree in placing the Austronesian homeland in Formosa and, in one sense or another, in their recognition that the Austronesian languages of Formosa represent a higher branch on the family tree than the remaining Malayo-Polynesian languages (cf. the discussion in Tryon (1995)). In Blust's view (1977 and elsewhere), for example, there are four primary subgroups of AN, three of them Formosan (Atayalic, Tsouic, and Paiwanic) and one non-Formosan (MP), the configuration presented in Figure 5. Others argue that the Formosan languages consist of a single branch; still others argue about the subgrouping of the Formosan languages (cf. Starosta 1995). Again, however, most scholars place the homeland on Formosa.

　　　Non-linguistic arguments also exist for a Formosan homeland for the insular Austronesian languages. Bellwood (1978, 1985, 1991) has argued for such a homeland on archaeological grounds. The dating of the archaeological record suggests that Neolithic sites on the east coast of Formosa are part of the Yüan-shan culture, which Bellwood associates with later Philippine and Indonesian settlement. Bellwood places the Yüan-shan culture complex on Formosa (4300 BC) earlier by some 800 years or so than the earliest dates in the Philippines (c. 3500 BC or later) and far earlier than the dates for Indonesia (c. 2500 BC) and Melanesia (1870 BC) (dates from Blust 1995:592).

　　　However, it is misleading to regard Austronesian languages themselves as having originated in Formosa. The Formosan languages represent a starting pointing for the migration into the Pacific, but there is also linguistic evidence for an earlier Austronesian presence on the mainland. While no early Austronesian language has left modern descendents, the earlier Austronesian presence has left Austronesian loans in the non-Austronesian languages of the mainland. For example, in at least two branches of Tai-Kadai, there are early, readily identifiable Austronesian borrowings (Thurgood, 1994). The unique correspondence patterns of borrowed Austronesian disyllabic roots are particularly conspicuous in among the overwhelmingly monosyllabic forms of proto-Tai and proto-Kam-Sui. For example, PAn *βolan corresponds to proto-Tai *ʔbl/rien[1], and proto-Kam-Sui *ñ'a:n[2] 'moon'; PAn *danum corresponds to the proto-Tai *nl/rəm[4], and proto-Kam-Sui *ñ'am[3] -t-i-f '(fresh)water'; and Proto-Western-Malayo-Polynesian (PWMP) *bujak corresponds to proto-Tai *ʔbl/rɔ:k[7] 'flower'.[2] These are but

---

2.　Thai scholars often attribute many of these words to Thai contact with Malay in southern Thailand, but for at least these forms the reconstructions date back to proto-Tai and the forms are found even in the Tai dialects spoken in southwestern China, the area of the Tai homeland. The dating of proto-Tai and the distribution of the forms makes it clear that these forms were borrowed long before the earliest contact with Malay in southern Thailand.

a few of many early Austronesian words borrowed early into proto-Tai and proto-Kam-Sui (see Thurgood 1994 for details and more examples).

These forms are significant because the Tai-Kadai reconstructions and the subgrouping evidence show that these words represent, not recent borrowings into the Tai and Kam-Sui languages, but ancient borrowings into proto-Tai and proto-Kam-Sui from early Austronesian sources which make it possible to provide the approximate time and place of the borrowings. Both the Tai and the Kam-Sui borrowings reconstruct to proto-Tai and proto-Kam-Sui and thus predate the breakup of these proto-languages. An examination of the geographical distribution of the Tai languages makes it clear that the area where the proto-Tai began to break up must be somewhere in the Guizhou area (if not even further to the north) and since the area where the proto-Kam-Sui began to break up must be in the Guizhou and Guangxi area, it follows that the early Austronesian contact, which predates the breakup of proto-Tai and proto-Kam-Sui, must also have occurred — at the very least — as far north as Guizhou. The proto-Tai and the proto-Kam-Sui homelands place these early Austronesian speakers somewhere south of the Yangtze some 8,000 years ago or so (see Thurgood 1994 for a fuller discussion). What this does is to establish the existence of early Austronesian speakers presumably along the south bank of the upper reaches of the Yangtze— early Austronesian speakers whose descendants later left the mainland to become Austronesian speakers. Given that the Austronesian arrival in Indonesia and Melanesia was considerably later in prehistory than estimated dates for Formosa and the northern Philippines, it also makes a departure point somewhere across from Formosa and the Philippines the most reasonable place to begin the journey out into the Pacific.

In any case, despite differences of opinion about some of the higher-level subgrouping details, the place of Malayo-Chamic within this configuration does not itself seem controversial, nor do any of the disagreements about the higher-level subgroupings seem to have any consequences for the conclusions reached about Chamic. It at least seems evident that Chamic subgroups neither with one the Formosan branches nor with the Central-Eastern Malayo-Polynesian subgroup, leaving Malayo-Chamic uncontroversially a part of the languages usually termed Western Malayo-Polynesian. However, as Blust has pointed out (p.c.), it is important to realize that PWMP is not a well-defined subgroup defined by the existence of its own set of independent innovations; instead, PWMP is basically those Malayo-Polynesian languages *not* included in Central-Eastern-Malayo-Polynesian, that is, PWMP is a cover term for those PMP languages that fall outside of Central-Malayo-Polynesian. Thus, the split of PMP is not binary; indeed, it is quite probable that CEMP is a subgroup within a MP dialect continuum, with Malayo-Chamic simply being a subgroup within the continuum.

Following a convention found in Ross (1995b:263), language subgroupings established on the bases of shared innovations are distinguished orthographically from collections of languages placed together for other reasons. In Figure 5, subgroupings established on the bases of shared innovations are in boldface, while language groupings that do not have an exclusively shared ancestor (Ross 1995b:263) are in italics. Thus the italicized label "Formosan languages" indicates a collection of languages descended (along with PMP) from PAn. However, the claim is not being made that there was a single, unified "Proto-Formosan" from which the Formosan languages descended. Moving down the tree, Malayo-Polynesian is itself defined by a set of shared innovations. In turn, it consists of Central-Eastern-Malayo-Polynesian, an innovation-defined subgroup; its complement is Western Malayo-Polynesian, those Malayo-Polynesian languages not part of the innovation-defined Central-Eastern-Malayo-Polynesian.

It is worth bearing in mind that the historical subgrouping of languages, when properly done, as these subgroupings are, is done not on the basis of the geographical distribution of the languages, but on the basis of shared historical innovations (Blust 1995b, Ross 1992). The Austronesian family tree above is based on such shared historical innovations; the fact that the family tree has such striking correlations with geography is because, to a large degree, the current linguistic distribution still reflects the older migration patterns fairly accurately.

MALAYO-CHAMIC AND BROADER AFFILIATIONS

Within Western Malayo-Polynesian, the Chamic languages are part of what Blust (1992a) terms the Malayo-Chamic subgroup, a subgroup that pairs the Chamic languages including Acehnese (cf. "Acehnese, a Chamic language" on page 47) with Adelaar's (1988, 1992) Malayic languages, a cluster of languages which includes Malay. The existence of a special relationship between both the mainland Chamic languages and Acehnese and, on a higher level, between the Chamic and the Malayic languages has long been argued for in the literature. The reconstructions found in this work serve to confirm what earlier scholars have long maintained.

Marrison (1975), Blust (1981), Adelaar (1985), and James Collins (1991) have all argued for a special connection between the Chamic and the Malayic languages. Collins (1992:110), however, adds a word of caution, writing that without full reconstructions of PC, Proto-Malayic, and Proto-Acehnese, "comparisons are superficial". Now, with this reconstruction of PC, with Adelaar's proto-Malayic, and Durie's partial reconstruction of proto-Acehnese, it is far more evident that the uniquely Malay elements in Acehnese are borrowed, while the uniquely Chamic elements are inherited.

Figure 5: Proto-Austronesian family tree
(modified from Blust 1977; Ross 1995b)

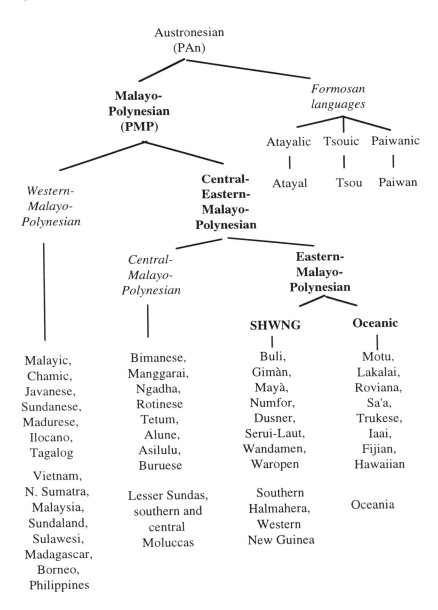

Figure 6: The Malayo-Chamic languages

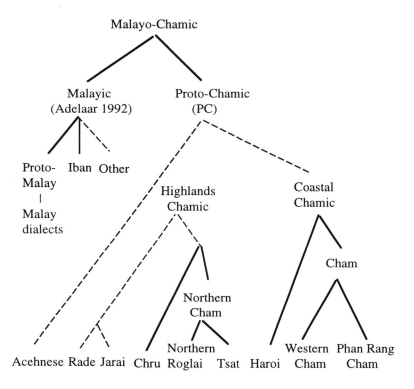

Another language that Blust suggests might fall in a wider subgroup that includes Malayo-Chamic is Sundanese (1992a:44). However, Moken definitely falls outside of this group, as most likely do Rejang and Maloh.[3]

The innovated numerals

One piece of evidence for Malayo-Chamic and, potentially, for its broader affiliations are a series of innovated numerals. Although, as Nothofer has quite correctly pointed out, the numerals alone are not sufficient for subgrouping, certainly the innovated numerals for seven, eight, and nine, which are unquestionably not reconstructable back to PMP, do provide highly suggestive sub-

---

3. Collins (personal communication cited in Blust 1992a:74, fn. 6) appears to be alone in his opinion that the most immediate relatives of Acehnese are Malayic, not Chamic.

grouping evidence (cf. discussions in Dyen (1965), Blust (1981), and Nothofer (1975), as emended in Nothofer (1985)).

Table 3: Innovated numerals in Malayo-Chamic

PMP	PC	Malay	Iban	
*esa; *isa	*sa	satu	satu	'one'
*duha	*dua	dua	dua	'two'
*telu	*klɔw	(**tiga**)	(**tiga**)	'three'
*epat	*paːt	ĕmpat	empat	'four'
*lima	*lima	lima	---	'five'
*enem	*nam	ĕnam	---	'six'
*pitu	*tujuh	tujuh	tujoh	'seven'
*walu	*dua-lapan	dĕlapan	delapan	'eight'
	> *lapan	lapan	lapan	
	< 'nine'	---	selapan	
*siwa	*sa-lapan	---	---	'nine'
	*samilan	sĕmbilan	---	
	< 'eight'	---	---	
*puluq	*pluh	puluh	---	'ten'
*Ratus	*ratus -f	ratus	---	'hundred'
*ribu	*ribɔw	ribu	ribu	'thousand'

Note that the Malayic languages, represented in Table 3 by Malay and Iban, share the innovation of *tiga 'three', reflecting a genetic closeness not shared with the Chamic languages.

Table 3 compares the numerals of PMP with the numerals of PC, Malay, and Iban, making the innovations apparent. The most widely distributed innovation is in the number 'seven', which is not only distributed throughout Malayo-Chamic but also is found in languages beyond this group, and thus may correlate with a broader subgroup. Although not as widely distributed as the innovations for 'seven', the innovations for 'eight' and 'nine' occur not just throughout Malayo-Chamic but also within a number of other languages, including Maloh and Rejang. However, as Blust (1992a:44) cautions, emending Blust 1981, the appearance of these innovated numerals in Rejang and Maloh may be due to borrowing.

Table 4: The Chamic numerals

	PC	Aceh.	Rade	Jarai	NR	Tsat	Haroi	PR Cham
'one'	*sa	sa	sa	sa; hə-	sa	sa^{33}	sa; ha; hɔ	tha
'two'	*dua	duwa	dua	dua	dua	thua^{11}	thua	ţwa
'three'	*klɔw	lhɛə	tlău	kləu	tləu	kiu^{33}	tlău	klŏw
'four'	*paːt	pɯət	pă?	pă?	paː?	pa?^{24}	pa?	pa?
'five'	*lima	limʌŋ	ema	rəma	lumă	ma^{33}	ləmĭa	lamɨ
'six'	*nam	nam	năm	năm	năm	naːn?^{33}	năm	năm
'seven'	*tujuh	tujoh	kjuh	təjuh	tijuh	su^{55}	cəsŭh	tacŭh
'eight'	*dua-lapan		---	cəpan	---	paːn?^{42}	---	ţalipăn
>	*lapan	lapan	---	rəpan	---	lapat	ləpăn	---
'eight'	< 'nine'	---	sapăn	səpan	---	---	---	---
'eight'	*dua-ambil-an	---	---	---	---	---	---	tàmpăn
'nine'	*sa-lapan	---	---	---	salapat	---	---	thalipăn
'nine'	*samilan	---	---	---	---	---	---	samilan
'nine'	< 'eight'	---	duapăn	dua	dua	thua^{11}	thua-	---
		---	---	rəpan;	cəpan	paːn?^{42}	ləpăn	
'ten'	*pluh	ploh	pluh	pluh	spluh	piu^{55}	apoh	plŭh

Notes: For 'nine', the second N. Roglai form and the Tsat form are from < *dua *dua-lapan, that is, another *dua added to the original *dua-lapan. In 'eight' and 'nine', the Jarai morpheme *-pan* has unexpected length. The PR Cham for 'nine' is from Aymonier and Cabaton (1906).

The innovated forms for 'seven', 'eight', and 'nine' in Table 3 make it abundantly clear that PC subgroups with the Malayic languages.

Table 4 shows the distribution of these innovated numerals within the Chamic languages. Notice the regularity of the Acehnese reflexes ("Acehnese, a Chamic language" on page 47, discusses the membership of Acehnese within PC). In Table 4, there is an interesting indeterminacy in the reconstruction of some of the forms listed in the table as descended from PC *lapan. Forms with a reflex of *lapan could be the truncation of *dua-lapan or be from *sa-lapan; in most cases, it is not possible to tell. As a consequence, as many as four of the Chamic languages might have a word for 'eight' that was descended from 'nine'.

This widespread confusion of the forms for 'eight' and 'nine' both within Chamic (Table 4) and outside of Chamic (Minangkabau, Kerinci), the double-prefixed forms for 'eight' in Northern Roglai and Tsat and for 'nine' in

Phan Rang Cham, and the complete inversion of 'eight' and 'nine' in Rade and Jarai, all indicate that the semantics of the original roots was anything but transparent. It certainly appears as if the Rade and Jarai speakers ignored the subtractive meaning of the root and instead, not totally unreasonably, ordered the numeral beginning with *sa- 'one' (*sa-lapan) before the numeral beginning with *dua 'two' (*dua-lapan).

The existence of reflexes of PMP *telu 'three' in Acehnese and the rest of Chamic, rather than the later Malay and Iban innovation *tiga* 'three', indicates that Malay and Iban are closer to each other than either of them is to PC as well as being another piece of evidence that Acehnese patterns more closely with the Chamic than the Malayic languages (page 47). Within Chamic, the fact that Rade and Jarai have both reversed the reflexes of 'eight' and 'nine' (one suspects that they were no longer primarily traders and merchants) suggests that Rade and Jarai have been in particularly close contact, a conclusion that is supported by all sorts of other evidence.

The intriguing semantics behind the Malayo-Chamic innovations of 'seven', 'eight', and 'nine' are discussed by Blust (1981:467, fn. 5). He writes that the forms for *tujuh 'seven' are usually thought to be from the word for 'index finger', which Blust notes is "the second finger of the second hand in finger-counting". The form *tujuh itself does not date back as far as PMP, but precisely where and when it was innovated is not yet clear. The other innovations for 'eight' and 'nine' involve what Blust terms "subtractives". These forms he relates to the roots *alap and *ambil 'fetch, take', with *dua-lap-an being 'two taken away (from ten)' and both *sa-alap-an and *sa-ambil-an being 'one taken away (from ten)', with an the etymology based on 'one less' also occurring in many Borneo languages and in South Sulawesi languages (Adelaar, p.c.). In the PR Cham form *tàmpăn* 'eight' (from Blood 1962:11), the -p- is unexpected, but the presence of the medial -m- suggests that it comes from *dua-ambil-an 'two taken away (from ten)', which would make it semantically parallel to *dua-lap-an above. The Acehnese form *sikurɯəŋ* 'nine' from *sa-kura:ŋ, although involving the root *kura:ŋ 'less', appears to have originated independently but from almost identical semantics.

THE MALAYO-CHAMIC SUBGROUP

The Malayo-Chamic subgroup is justified by a set of shared innovations. In addition to the innovated numerals, which may not be confined just to the Malayo-Chamic languages, there are several innovations largely but apparently not exclusively restricted to the Malayo-Chamic subgroup. Blust (1992a:34-44, emending

Blust 1981) discusses the following: (1) the shift of PMP *q > *h, although the scope of PMP *q > h is somewhat wider than just Malayo-Chamic, including as it does Balinese, Javanese, Sundanese, and the Batak languages, (2) the merger of PMP *R and *r but with the merged reflex remaining at the same time distinct from other proto-phonemes, and (3) the loss of PMP *w in initial position. The merger of *R and *r also happened in Batak and Balinese, and so did the loss of *w (although some Batak languages have a residue of it). The lexically-specific innovation Blust cites is the introduction of an initial *h in PMP *waRi (*waRi > *ari > *hari), an innovation that follows the loss of PMP *w in initial position.

Two observations need to be made about these shared innovations. First, the PC reconstructions reflect all of these changes; thus, there is no question that PC falls within the parameters of the subgroup. Second, while there is some question about precisely where to draw the lines at the periphery of the Malayo-Chamic subgroup, the linguistic distribution of the innovations mentioned here define a core.[4]

WITHIN THE CHAMIC LANGUAGES: A SKETCH

Pawley and Ross (1995:39-74) have noted with reference to other Austronesian languages that there are two distinct patterns of shared innovations, each pointing to a different historical origin. In one pattern, which reflects genetic inheritance (1995:50), "all member languages of a subgroup exclusively share a common set of innovations", from which it can be inferred that "the subgroup has been formed because a community speaking a single language has become separated geographically and/or socially into two or more communities after separation,

---

4. The history of Chamic studies shows some promising early work but then scholars appear to have turned to Thai and Khmer studies, leaving Chamic studies largely dormant until a mild resurgence of interest in the last several decades. The earliest wordlist is that in Crawfurd (1822, discussed by Crawfurd himself 1852). The history of much of the early research is set out by Lafont (1987b; 1994b), who notes that much of the early work on Chamic was linguistic. In addition to Crawfurd's list, there was a two-page list published in 1868 by A. Bastian, who two years later published a paper on the language and the origins of the Cham people. Several years later in 1875, Lafont continues, A. Morice published the first Cham glossary, containing some 800 words, as part of a work on the Cham and Stieng (a MK language) languages. Then, in 1880 K.F. Holle published a replica of the Cham alphabet, following up this publication with a commentary on it in 1882.

[and] changes have occurred in the speech of each of the new communities until what was one language has become two or more."

In the pattern reflecting areal diffusion of changes along a dialect continuum (1995:50), "innovations form an overlapping pattern, such that, for example, languages A, B, and C reflect one bunch of innovations, languages C, D, and E another bunch, languages D, E, F, and G yet another, and languages G and H still a different bunch of innovations", from which can be inferred that "the languages of the subgroup once formed a network of related dialects. During this phase, innovations occurred at various places in the network, spreading from their dialect of origin into neighbouring dialects, but without affecting the whole network. Over time the dialects have diverged until they have become mutually unintelligible for practical purposes, but they continue to reflect the innovation pattern of the former" dialect chain.

In the case of the Chamic languages both genetic inheritance and areal diffusion have produced their patterns of shared innovations, but fortunately in most although not all cases it is possible to distinguish one from the other and thus to infer information about which dialects developed from an earlier common source and also to infer much about the earlier patterns of contact and bilingualism.

The initial period of contact with MK speakers, undoubtedly very early in the establishment of Champa. It involved intense contact including considerable bilingualism and led to the dramatic restructuring found in PC. After that initial contact-induced restructuring, the language of Champa seems to have continued for some time as a largely differentiated dialect chain in coastal communities along the coast of Vietnam. There is no evidence in the linguistic record of any marked dialect differentiation until the historical events associated with the Vietnamese push to the south forced radically new patterns of language contact as the result of the partial destruction of the old language contact patterns.

Perhaps for as long as the first millennium, the Chamic languages constituted a dialect chain that certainly extended along the coast of Vietnam (Blust 1981:32; cf. also Blagden 1929 (summarized in Dyen 1971a:202)) and may even have extended as far south as the east coast of the Malaysian peninsula, although it is more likely that the Chamic-like features found along the east coast of Malaysia date from a much later Acehnese influence. The breakup of the dialect chain along the coast of Vietnam into clearly distinct languages occurred after the rich interactional network between the coastal communities was disrupted by the Vietnamese push to the south, a push that caused many Chamic speakers to move back into the highlands. This retreat into the highlands resulted in a new set of language networks for almost all Chamic speakers, with some like the Haroi eventually coming to be part of a MK social network, while others like the Phan

Rang Cham eventually came to be part of the lowlands society dominated by the Vietnamese.

Figure 7: The PC dialect chain and its modern reflexes

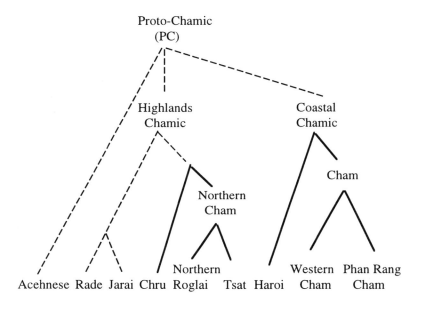

The basic relationships among the Chamic languages are shown in Figure 7, which shows groupings due to common genetic inheritance and linguistic convergence due to bilingualism. Often the data reflects both types of influence: in many cases, languages reflect genetically-inherited similarities as well as similarities due to areal contact. The interplay between these two factors, recognized from the beginning of the comparative method and reflected in the well-known distinction between the "family tree" model and the "wave" theory, is found throughout the Chamic data.

The genetic and the areal relationships between the various modern languages are illustrated in Figure 7. Although future research may show that Acehnese is particularly close to one or another of the mainland Chamic languages, the evidence thus far suggests that the Acehnese left Champa before any strongly marked distinction developed among the Chamic languages. It appears that at the time of their departure, the Acehnese were the most northerly of the Chamic groups, covering an area now populated by, among others, the modern Katuic speakers. Only subsequent to the Acehnese departure did the remaining languages split into two major areal configurations: the Highlands Chamic languages and the Coastal Chamic languages. Thus, in Figure 7 Acehnese is shown as separated from the other languages. It was undoubtedly only after 1000 AD or so that a distinction of any significance existed between these two areas, with the sharp separation of the Chamic speakers into Highlands Chamic and Coastal Chamic developing largely after the Vietnamese began moving south. In Figure 7, these two linguistic areas are indicated by dotted lines. In the case of Jarai and Rade, where the evidence for mutual influence is clear but the evidence for genetic subgrouping is not, only the influence of contact is indicated (by dotted lines).

Within these areal configurations are subgrouping relationships (shown by solid lines): specifically, the Coastal Chamic languages look to have once been a single dialect before splitting up into Haroi, Western Cham, and Phan Rang Cham. Similarly, within the Highlands Chamic area at least the Chru, Northern Roglai, and Tsat were a single dialect before splitting up. However, the Rade and the Jarai were probably never a genetic subgroup but instead were simply the middle members of the original dialect chain, which were eventually forced up into the highlands. Naturally, all these languages also participated in various patterns of areally-induced changes.

The subgrouping relationships merit a special comment. Tsat and Northern Roglai represent a Northern Cham dialect that split into two under the impetus provided by the Vietnamese capture of the northern capital at Indrapura. The division of Cham into Western and Phan Rang Cham represents another dialect division, this time following the Vietnamese capture of the southern capital. Their early relationship with Haroi is also apparently a subgrouping one, but the evidence for this is not as clear because the relationships are obscured by the fact that Haroi would later go on to participate in two additional areal configurations: the Haroi first interacted with the Highlands Chamic group before becoming socially and linguistically realigned with the MK-speaking Hrê.

The relationship of Tsat and Northern Roglai

Despite the radical differences in the phonology, the morphology, and the syntax of the modern languages, the subgrouping relationship between Tsat of Hainan island and Northern Roglai of the Vietnamese highlands is obvious from the comparative evidence. These two languages share two quite distinctive, quite unusual innovations, either one of which would by itself suggest a subgrouping relationship: Tsat and Northern Roglai share the innovation of preploded final nasals and the shared loss of PC *-s in PC *-a:s. As late as around 1000 AD, these two languages probably constituted a single Northern Cham dialect.

Northern Roglai and Chru seem to have a special relationship. First, there are various shared similarities among the nasalized vowels. Second, there is the simple note in Grimes (1988:615), which states without further comment that Southern Roglai is closely related to Chru and Northern Roglai.

Note that Tsat is subgrouped specifically with Northern Roglai, not simply with Roglai. Cac Gia Roglai (Cobbey 1977) and Cat Gia Roglai[5] (Lee 1998) both share reflexes of earlier preploded final nasals, with the denasalization having occurred under the same conditions. Several other dialects of Roglai share reflexes of earlier preploded final nasals as evidenced by the occasional final -p, -t, or -k from a former nasal final, but Gia Lê Roglai is almost entirely lacking in evidence of preploded finals.[6] However, a brief examination of Cobbey's 1977 fiche containing wordlists made it clear that neither his Cac Gia Roglai nor Gia Lê Roglai share the sound change PC *-a:s > N. Roglai/Tsat -a and Lee's Cat Gia Roglai lacks the crucial forms. Thus, the Tsat subgrouping is specifically with N. Roglai to the exclusion of the other Roglai dialects for which I have seen data.

The subsequent developments in Tsat are quite unrelated to any of the developments among the remaining mainland Chamic languages. Instead, despite the obvious parallels with developments elsewhere in Chamic, the Tsat developments reflect contact with the tonal, monosyllabic languages of Hainan: the movement from iambic to monosyllabic, the reduction of the *-l- and *-r- in onset clusters to /-i-/, the drastic reduction of final consonant contrasts, and the appearance of tones are all the product of contact pressures that developed after the Tsat arrival on Hainan.

The relationship of Haroi with Western and Phan Rang Cham

The other subgrouping relationship is between the Coastal Chamic languages. There is really no question about the relationship between Western and Phan Rang Cham, as they were the same language until the fall of the southern capital in 1471.

A more interesting question involves the nature of the Haroi relationships. Haroi no longer resembles its closest genetic relations as it has changed radically under the influence of Hrê. Specifically, modern Haroi has become a restructured register system under the influence of Hrê. It has also come under the influence of contact from the Highlands languages Rade and Jarai, but the evidence indicates that, prior to this social and linguistic realignment with Hrê,

---

5. It is unclear to me whether we are talking about two languages or one here.
6. The one exception seems to be the reflex of *duŋ 'nose' əduŋʔ, with its glottalized final nasal.

Haroi's genetic affiliations were with Western Cham dialects. Although Haroi and Western Cham are now no longer in contact, two interesting changes probably induced by contact are shared with it. One is the lowering of centering diph-thongs and triphthongs as part of a set of changes that also affected both Kvoeu-Hor and Timothy Friberg's Cham and Headley's Kompong Thom Cham (see page 133 and page 135). The second change is that Haroi and Headley's Kompong Thom Cham (but not Kvoeu-Hor and Timothy Friberg's Western Cham (1978)) shared the change of the PC *-əŋ > *-iŋ (§8.3.2).

A third innovation, however, most likely reflects an early common inher-itance from Haroi's origin as a Cham dialect. This change is the early develop-ment of breathy-voiced register complex, often termed "second register". Although aspects of second register development differ from language to lan-guage, the basic core of second register development looks like it occurred early in Cham, before Cham broke up into Haroi and Cham, with Cham subsequently breaking up into Phan Rang and Western Cham. Thus, the evidence seems to sup-port what Lee (1966:2-3) noted in passing, "Hroy [Haroi] or Bahnar Cham may be a dialect of Cham proper."

In a later 1974 paper about advanced-tongue-root and register in Haroi, Lee again considered the possibility that both Haroi and Cham developed register together. However, his assumptions about Chamic subgrouping presented formi-dable obstacles to such an analysis. Lee had apparently forgotten or abandoned an earlier subgrouping suggestion made in his thesis where he suggested that Haroi and Cham subgrouped together. Almost in indirect reference to his earlier suggestion, Lee wrote (1977b:97), "The difficulty in trying to make it a shared innovation stemming from an era when they were still one language is that Northern Roglai, which is *evidently* much closer to Cham than either Cham or Northern Roglai is to Haroi, shows no evidence that I have been able to observe of a register system" [italics mine]. However, this comment fails to distinguish similarity due to inheritance from that due to contact.

In short, Haroi has undergone at least three distinguishable layers of areal influence beyond the MK influence common to all PC languages: the early influence of Coastal Cham (or perhaps, just Western Cham), the later influence of Highlands Chamic, and the restructuring influence of Hrê. It is not surprising that Burnham (1976) ended up placing Haroi squarely between Highlands and Coastal Chamic, as the Haroi have related to and been influenced linguistically at different times by both groups.

The relationship of Rade and Jarai

The similarities between Rade and Jarai appear primarily contact-induced: among other similarities they share the change of PC *-a:s > -aih, PC *-us > -uih and *rVl- > hl- as well as a number of other minor similarities, including the interesting switching of 'eight' and 'nine', noted already in "Malayo-Chamic and broader affiliations" on page 34. However, it is also evident from the large number of differences in the two that much of the similarity between them, aside from shared retentions may be contact induced.

Rade appears to constitute the end point in a Chamic dialect chain that was only broken up after the Vietnamese occupation of the south. More specifically, Rade, but not Jarai, retains the PC *-εy < PMP *-i that became *-əi̯ throughout the rest of the mainland Chamic languages. Presumably, a dialect chain still existed after Acehnese speakers left the mainland, and this change appears to have spread through all but Rade, which with the departure of the Acehnese became the most geographically isolated of the languages in the chain, and, one assumes, was likewise the most isolated when the change spread through the other remaining mainland languages. Rade has reduced its inventory of presyllable onsets much more radically than Jarai or any of the other Chamic languages. Other distinctions also suggest that some the similarities between these two languages are either independent developments or the result of contact.

A second change that appears to have swept through the dialect chain that existed until roughly 1000 AD is the loss of the nasal component of medial clusters consisting of stops preceded by homorganic nasals. Clearly such medial clusters still appeared in Chamic languages after the breakup of PC as these are still found in modern Acehnese, but these have long since totally disappeared from all the mainland Chamic languages.[7] For instance, in Crawfurd's 1822 wordlist the only forms with such medial clusters are forms identifiable as recent loans. The native clusters had long since lost their nasal component.

The Highlands versus Coastal Chamic distinction

The next major development is the split of the mainland Chamic languages into a Highlands Chamic region and a Coastal Chamic region. The distinction between the Highlands Chamic area and the Coastal Chamic area could only have come into existence as a distinct linguistic area after the fall of the northern capital of Champa in 982, which drove Chamic speakers back from their coastal communities and into the highlands. And, in a sense, the changes characteristic of the Coastal Chamic region probably emerged only much later after the fall of the southern capital in 1471, a date that marks the beginning of the emergence of new

---

7. In light of this, it is quite surprising that there is an apparent lack of evidence in early Cham written records for the nasal component of these clusters. This lack, however, may merely reflect my own lack of expertise about inscriptional Cham.

patterns of Cham contact with Vietnamese, a language with a distinctly different phonological structure.

The Highlands Chamic languages have certain similarities that led Solnit (1993:110) to characterize it as the Southern Vietnam highlands sub-area. In general terms, the Highlands languages have not undergone as radical a restructuring process as the Coastal Chamic languages, in keeping with the similarities between the structures of the Chamic and the MK languages of the highlands. Most of the forms are iambic in structure and have remained that way for some time, unlike the Coastal languages and Tsat, which under contact with more monosyllabic languages, have themselves become more monosyllabic.

More specifically the Highlands Chamic languages have kept the PC contrast between *b and *ɓ. As a common retention, of course, this does not provide evidence of any sort of subgrouping relationship, but it does provide an interesting example of the influence of patterns of bilingualism on what does and does not change (cf. discussion in "Solnit's Southern Vietnam Highlands sub-area" on page 91).

The Coastal Chamic languages are marked by changes in a number of salient features. Among these changes is the development of a breathy-voiced register complex from the voiced obstruents, a development that happened in somewhat parallel but somewhat distinct ways in Phan Rang Cham, Western Cham, and Haroi, suggesting that the partial influence of patterns of areal contact rather than just common inheritance is needed to account for the developments. A second and obviously related change is the subsequent loss of the voicing of the voiced obstruents and the co-occurring loss of the distinction between voiced obstruents and glottalized obstruents throughout these languages, which is clearly an areal feature, not a shared innovation, as it happened independently in the different coastal languages. Not coincidentally, these changes are in the direction of the structure of Vietnamese, the dominant language in the Coastal Chamic area.

ACEHNESE, A CHAMIC LANGUAGE

It is quite correctly simply assumed in the literature that the mainland Chamic languages form a subgroup. The questions that exist revolve around the relationship of Acehnese with the mainland Chamic languages. That there is a special relationship between Acehnese and the Chamic languages was recognized as early as 1891 by Niemann, who subgrouped Acehnese and Cham together, noting similarities in their verb morphology, in their treatment of inherited vowels, and in various instances of apparent lexical agreement. Along these lines, Cowan (1981:523) writes:

> The Achehnese language belongs to the West-Austronesian languages but, although situated in Sumatra, it has its nearest relatives in the Chamic languages of the South-East Asian continent. This relationship is evident on all levels: phonology (e.g. final stress, large-scale monosyllabism, consonant clusters, diphthongization of certain final vowels deriving originally from long vowels), morphology (e.g. lack of suffixes, use of the substantival infix *-n-*), and lexicon.

Quite early, Niemann suggested a migration of Chams to Aceh—which, in fact, is what happened.

Over the years various other scholars have agreed with Niemann and Cowan at least to the extent of recognizing not only that a special subgrouping relationship exists between Acehnese and the mainland Chamic languages but also that there are similarities between Acehnese and mainland Chamic that need to be accounted for. Among these scholars are Blagden[8] (1929), Cowan (1933, 1948, 1974, 1981, 1983, 1988), Shorto (1975, 1977), I. V. Collins (1975), Blust (1981), and Durie (1990a). The literature leaves no question that there are striking parallels between Acehnese and Chamic.

Thus, the claim that Acehnese has a special subgrouping relationship with Chamic is not original to this work, and the more specific claim that Acehnese is simply a Chamic language has also already been made in the literature. In fact, the belief that a special subgrouping relationship exists between Acehnese and the mainland Chamic languages seems to be shared by all but one of the scholars who have done extensive, detailed comparisons of the languages involved.

---

8. Blagden's view, however, was quite distinct from the views of other scholars cited here. He followed Kern's 1889 hypothesis in which Austronesian speakers originated on the mainland and the Cham represent the remaining remnants of this original group of Austronesian speakers on the mainland. Thus, although he viewed the Acehnese as related to the Chamic speakers, he also viewed the Cham including the Acehnese as having originated on the mainland (specifically somewhere between Kra and Penang). Thus, Blagden's scenario is quite at odds with the migrations supported by the reconstructions in this work, which instead suggest the Chams originated through a migration to coastal Vietnam from Southwest Borneo and then only subsequent to that did the Acehnese migrate from there to northern Sumatra (conceivably with stops along the way).

Only J. Collins (1991), who has noted the parallels between Acehnese and Malay, seems to dissent. While recognizing the existence of parallels between Acehnese and mainland Chamic, Collins argued for the possibility that Acehnese and Malay subgrouped more closely than either with mainland Chamic and that the Acehnese and mainland Chamic parallels were due to parallel but independent developments combined with the mutual but independent influence of MK contact on both Acehnese and mainland Chamic. Collins has argued that detailed reconstructions are needed to settle the question. It is easy to see his point, as *without such reconstructions,* it would not be possible to determine where the parallels reflect contact and where they reflect genetic inheritance. However, now the reconstructions and the accompanying correspondence patterns exist: not only do they make it clear that Acehnese is a Chamic language but establish that the very real special connection with Malay, aside from features also found in Chamic, reflects the long history of contact between Acehnese and Malay.

The precise nature of the special subgrouping relationship between Acehnese and the mainland Chamic languages was impossible to determine without reconstructions. The specific question that required more reconstruction to resolve was whether Acehnese and mainland Chamic were sister languages or whether Acehnese was simply another of the Chamic languages. Here, the reconstructions provide substantiation for the claim that Acehnese is simply another Chamic language. Thus, Niemann (1891) was correct when he suggested that Acehnese is a Chamic language whose speakers migrated to northern Sumatra, a position also taken by Cowan (n.d.:1), who specifically states that, before the migration of the Acehnese speakers to Sumatra, Acehnese was not distinct from Chamic.

The evidence presented in various works of Cowan, in Shorto, and Durie is certainly substantial enough to establish the special relationship of Acehnese and Chamic. However, for those with doubts, the integration of the Acehnese data into the reconstruction of Chamic, along with the numerous subgrouping arguments, should provide a conclusive demonstration of the nature of the relationship. These reconstructions fully substantiate the claim that Acehnese is not just subgrouped with Chamic but that it is a Chamic language.

None of this, however, is to claim that modern Acehnese looks like the modern mainland languages—it does not. In fact, Acehnese often looks more like PC than any of the modern mainland Chamic dialects do. This often striking similarity to PC is not at all surprising, however. The Acehnese speakers left for Sumatra while all the mainland Chamic languages still looked a lot like PC, preserving many of its PC-like features, while the remaining mainland Chamic languages were subsequently subjected to even more intense language contact over a long period of time—at the very least for another six or seven hundred years.

Meanwhile the Acehnese speakers, having left much of the MK contact behind, have in many cases retained elements lost on the mainland. For example,

Acehnese still preserves the four-way distinction in first syllable vowels inherited from PMP.[9] Elsewhere in Chamic, this distinction has been reduced either partially or drastically, although its earlier existence is hinted at in the data. On the other hand, like the rest of Chamic, Acehnese has a rich array of second syllable vowels, including those borrowed into pre-PC from MK sources. Thus, modern Acehnese is witness to a stage after the incorporation of MK vowels into PC but before the four-way distinction had been reduced to a limited three-way distinction. And, Acehnese's potential for providing a window into the paths of morphological and syntactic change is still largely unexplored.

The patterns of innovated numerals in "Malayo-Chamic and broader affiliations" on page 34 provided some evidence that Chamic was part of a broader, not yet fully defined group, termed Malayo-Chamic that included both the mainland Chamic languages and Acehnese, but at best this only establishes that both the Chamic languages and Acehnese were all part of a larger subgroup. It does not provide evidence that Acehnese should be subgrouped together with mainland Chamic, nor does it provide evidence that Acehnese is a Chamic language.

However, it is now possible to provide evidence that establishes the integrity of PC, including Acehnese, as a distinct subgroup of PMP. The evidence consists of a cluster of shared innovations—shared innovations found among the consonants, among the vowels, in the shared borrowings of pre-PC material borrowed from MK sources, and so on. Some of the shared innovations are innovations not found anywhere else in Austronesian; for others, individual parallels are found elsewhere but certainly not in the particular configuration found here.

Shared innovations among the consonants

(1) Both Acehnese and mainland Chamic presyllables have precisely the same consonantal onset inventories, including the identical change of the PMP first syllable *n- to /l-/ (Table 11; "Presyllable onsets: retention and reduction" on page 75ff).

(2) As H. K. J. Cowan (1948), among others, noticed much earlier, the restructuring of PMP disyllabic forms produced the same clusters in Acehnese as can be reconstructed for PC (see the discussion of primary clusters in "Primary clusters" on page 93).

---

9. In place of MK contact, however, there has been intense contact with Malay, as J. Collins makes clear. One consequence of this Malay contact is that in a number of ways Acehnese now looks somewhat more Malay-like than PC or the Chamic languages remaining on the mainland, particularly in the lexicon.

In addition to the reduction in the primary clusters, there is also the shared presence of onset clusters with medial *-h- as the second element of the cluster (see "The loss of the vowel before medial -h-" on page 63 and "Voiced and voiceless 'aspirated' consonants" on page 84).

Not only do the mainland Chamic languages and Acehnese reduce the same PMP disyllables to monosyllables with cluster onsets, both languages also maintain disyllabicity in the same forms (see the discussion of secondary reduction "Secondary clusters" on page 94).

(3) Both Acehnese and mainland PC merge *kl- and *tl- to *kl- and *gl- and *dl- to *gl-, although Acehnese then goes a step further merging both to *kl- > lh- in Durie's Acehnese.

(4) Finally, in both Acehnese and mainland PC, there are a handful of native PMP words which developed glottalized obstruents (see "The origins of glottalized obstruents" on page 86). The monosyllabic forms with glottalized obstruents on the mainland now have glottal stop reflexes in Acehnese; the disyllabic forms have voiced obstruent reflexes in Acehnese. This shared innovation of glottalized obstruents, otherwise unattested in Austronesian, constitutes by itself strong subgrouping evidence.

Shared innovations among the vowels

(1) The diphthongization of the high vowels interacts with the loss of final *-r ("The splits in the PMP high vowels *i and *u" on page 114). In syllable-final position, PAn *-u (possibly early PC *-u) diphthongizes, becoming PC *-ɔw. However, with PAn *-ur forms, which have PC *-u reflex, the Chamic reflexes do not reflect any diphthongization, making it clear that the forms with final *-ur had not yet lost the final *-r when the PMP *-u in open syllables went to PC final *-ɔw. Instead, the PMP *-ur lost the final -r only after this change, and thus did not diphthongize. Acehnese shares not only the diphthongization of the *-u but also shares the constraint that the loss of final /-r/ must be sequenced after the diphthongization of open final *-u, resulting in undiphthongized final open /-u/ in the Chamic languages.

The subgrouping value of the diphthongization, which occurs independently elsewhere in Austronesian, is increased greatly by the presence of this shared sequencing constraint. It is worth noting that, while the typological parallelism is interesting, it is the occurrence of these changes in precisely the same words that makes it of interest for subgrouping.

(2) As Durie (1990a) noticed, Acehnese and PC share regular reflexes of vowels borrowed from MK into PC. More specifically, the PC vowels borrowed from MK, *ɛ, *ɔ, *ə, *ia, *ua, and *iaw, all turn up in the same borrowed words

in Acehnese and with regular reflexes (see the discussion of borrowed main syllable vowels "The borrowed PC main syllable vowels" on page 126). In addition,
for most of these vowels, the vowel itself is not completely restricted to borrowed
words, but instead it also turns up in one or two native PMP words as well and, in
these cases, the Acehnese word also has the innovated vowel in precisely the
same native Austronesian words.

Note that only a shared common inheritance from PC can account for
this sort of configuration. Aside from the question of how and where Acehnese
would have access to the borrowed MK vocabulary involved, it is unlikely in the
extreme that two languages would independently borrow essentially the same
words, while also innovating new vowels in a handful of Austronesian inherited
roots, resulting in the same adjustments to the vowel configurations in both Acehnese and the mainland languages and leaving both the mainland languages and
Acehnese in virtually perfect correspondence patterns with each other.

The distribution and patterning of the borrowed MK vowels by itself
constitutes strong evidence that Acehnese is a Chamic language that migrated
from the mainland to northern Sumatra, evidence only made stronger by the
handful of parallel innovations found in the inherited Austronesian vocabulary.

(3) As discussed in considerable detail in "The borrowed PC main syllable vowels" on page 126, Cowan (1948, 1974), Shorto (1975), and this work all
correlate vowel length in mainland Chamic vowels with the subsequent development of diphthongization in modern Acehnese. Cowan (1948, 1974) wrote extensively on the topic, as did Shorto (1975); both noticed that the vowel length
contrast between long and short /a/ in closed syllables correlated with vocalic distinctions in Acehnese, including in PMP roots. Shorto concludes that the correspondences he found are proof of a subgrouping relationship between Acehnese
and the rest of Chamic. Collins (1991:116), in contrast to Cowan, Shorto, and the
position taken in this work, argues that the diphthongization in Acehnese and the
vowel length in PC are historically distinct phenomena.

Both Cowan and Shorto are correct. The correlation in closed syllables
between PC length and modern Acehnese diphthongization is well-attested in the
literature; the existence of PC reconstructions only strengthens the case, establishing that the PC length contrast between *-a- and *-a:-, which was inherited
into Acehnese as a length distinction, subsequently developed into diphthongization. Note, as Cowan (n.d.:4) argued with reference to this development, that the
Acehnese diphthongization of certain long vowels in closed syllables is of a
much younger date than the diphthongization of PMP final *-i and *-u in open
syllables, a fact "confirmed by the fact that it was still active in North Sumatra at
the time of Islamization; witness its occurring in Arabic loanwords with long /a/
in final closed syllables."

The reconstructed PC length distinctions correspond almost exceptionlessly with the modern Acehnese closed syllable diphthongs and also with the skewed distributional patterns, making it quite impossible to attribute the correspondences to parallel but independent developments. Specifically, PC length in / a/ is distinguished, not before all finals, but only before final *-ʔ, *-ŋ, *-k, *-l, *-r, *-n, and *-t. Where the Acehnese data is available, with a handful of irregular forms, the same distributional constraints apply to the diphthongization of /a/ in Acehnese (see the examples and discussion in §6.5). There is little likelihood of independent developments in both Acehnese and the rest of Chamic.

PC also displays length distinctions for two other vowels, in *-ɔ:- vs. *-ɔ- and in *-u:- vs. *-u-, but again only in very limited contexts. Whether the length distinctions with these two vowels will also have Acehnese correlates remains to be seen.

Shared innovations in the lexicon

(1) Both Acehnese and the rest of PC share a great deal of vocabulary borrowed from MK sources (Proto-North-Bahnaric (PNB), Proto-Mnong, Proto-South Bahnaric, Proto-Katuic), as many people have pointed out.

Table 5 shows a handful of MK borrowings that reconstruct to PC and have regular reflexes in Acehnese; others are found throughout this work and in Appendix II. While individual words may well have been borrowed independently into both Acehnese and the mainland Chamic languages, it is highly unlikely that all or even most of the shared MK borrowings can be accounted for in this way.

The word 'cotton' reconstructs to PWMP, but not to PMP. The word itself also appears to be a late loan into WMP, but the variant in Acehnese and mainland Chamic comes from MK.

Table 5: MK borrowings found in Acehnese and mainland Chamic

PNB	PMnong	PC	Acehnese	
---	*kroŋ	ˣˣ*krɔ:ŋ	kruən	'river'
---	*tăp	ˣˣ*kləp	tob, top	'stab; poke'
*čĕm	*sĭm	ˣˣ*cim	cicém	'bird'
*ha	*ha	ˣˣ*ha	hah -f	'open (mouth to say sthg.)'
*ĭč	---	ˣˣ*ʔɛh	èʔ -f	'excrement; defecate'
*joh	---	ˣˣ*cɔh	coh	'peck (of bird)'
*kaŋ	*kaŋ	ˣˣ*ka:ŋ	kɯən	'chin; jaw'
*păr	*păr	ˣˣ*pər	phʌ -i	'to fly'
*kapayh	---	ˣˣ*kapa:s	gapɯəh	'cotton'

(2) A second set of MK borrowings provides even more insight into the relationship between Acehnese and the mainland languages—the MK borrowings that do not reconstruct to PC but which nonetheless show up in Acehnese! [Note that the forms listed in the post-PC column in Table 6 are explicitly marked with the ˣ as *not* reconstructing to PC].

Some of these words show up elsewhere in Austronesian, although usually in a slightly different form. However, the Acehnese variants look to be forms that were borrowed into various Chamic dialects after the breakup of PC. The presence of these forms in Acehnese shows that Acehnese speakers left Champa not only after the breakup of PC but also after these words were borrowed from MK sources.

Table 6: Post-PC MK borrowings in Acehnese and mainland Chamic

PNB	PMnong	post-PC	Acehnese	
---	*groh	ˣgrɔh	kloh	'to bark'
---	*čəkăw	ˣcagəu	cagəə	'Malaysian bear'
---	---	ˣdhual/r -f	dhoi	'dust; fog, mist'
---	*bərtoh	ˣpatuh	bɯrɯtoh -i	'to explode'
*mon	*kəmon	ˣkəmuan	kɯmuən	'nephew; sister's son'
---	*thəl	ˣɗɛl	dɯə	'shallow'
*baɗŭk	---	ˣpruac (?)	pruet	'stomach; intestine'
*oŋ	---	ˣhɔːŋ -f	h'uəŋ	'wasp'
*tačhŭm	*cŭm	ˣcum	com	'kiss; smell'
---	*brak	ˣʔəmraːk	mɯraʔ	'peacock'

(3) In addition to the borrowings, there are also various bits and pieces of the pronoun system that look to be related as well as some shared borrowed MK kinship terms (cf. ˣkəmuan 'nephew, sister's son' and ˣ*ʔuːŋ 'husband; male'). However, among the singular pronouns, the only particularly noteworthy innovation shared with Acehnese is the use of the innovated first person polite form PC *hulun from 'slave', but this innovation is not restricted just to Chamic.

More interesting are the plural pronouns, which at the PC level have PC *gəp 'group; other', which shows up as a part of various plural pronouns. The form is borrowed from MK and, of relevance here, found in Acehnese.

The evidence from Acehnese epic poetry

Cowan observed in Acehnese epic poetry what he described as "the similarity between the national Achehnese verse form *sanja'* and a related Cham verse used in the song of the *kadhar* (a musician-officiant) at the ceremony of the sacrifice of

the buffalo" (in 1933, cited from Cowan 1982:156). Cowan observed the existence of a structure that consisted of lines of eight disyllabic metrical feet, alternately describable as four pairs of such feet, with specific patterns of internal
rhyming.

However, in addition to what Cowan noticed, there are other indications
of the origins of the *sanja'* poetic tradition. Preserved in the rhyme schemes is
evidence of early vowel changes, changes so early that they predate the origin of
Acehnese itself. As G. W. J. Drewes wrote (1979:4), Acehnese epic poetry is
written in what the Acehnese called *sanja'* (from the Arabic *saj*), several features
of which are of particular interest. First, for the purposes of rhyming, long and
short syllables are not distinguished, the significance of which will be made clear
in a moment. Second, two syllables make up a foot, with the accent on the second
syllable. As Drewes notes the foot is iambic or, from the viewpoint of historical
comparison, not unlike the structure of Chamic. And, in this poetry, the most
common rhyme scheme consists of the last vowel of the sixth foot rhyming with
the last syllable of the fourth foot. Thus, in the following example from Drewes
(1979:4), the two italicized words rhyme:

> gah ban / gadjah / sië ban/ *piti* //
> phét di / *gaki* // sa ngon / rusa,

> 'fame as an elephant, a body as a ricebird;
> his sense of honour is in his legs, just as with the deer'

However, if one examines, for example, *Hikajat Potjut Muhamat*, an epic poem
from roughly the end of the 17th century, it becomes clear that, while most of
what counts as a rhyme actually does rhyme, not all of the so-called rhymes are
still phonetically transparent. As Drewes notes, in this epic the following vowels
count as rhyming (using Drewes' orthography):

counted as rhyming with	*a*		are *eu* [ɯ] and	*eue*	[ɯə],
counted as rhyming with	*i*		are *è* [ɛ] and	*é*	[e],
counted as rhyming with	*u* [ɔə]	are *o* [ɔ] and	*eu*	[ɛə].

In the *Hikajat Potjut Muhamat* these rhymes are bizarre phonetically, but if the
vowels in the *Hikajat Potjut Muhamat* are replaced with their corresponding
forms from PC, the rhyme scheme, which ignores length differences, is perfect:

counted as rhyming with	*a*	are *-aː- (nasalized) and *-aː-,
counted as rhyming with	*i*	are *i (nasalized) and *-i -,
counted as rhyming with	*u* [ɔə]	are *-u- and *-ɔə < *-ɛə < *-ɛw < *-u.

That is, all the forms that count as rhyming with /a/ were /a/ earlier in history, all the forms that count as rhyming with /i/ were /i/ earlier, and all the forms that count as rhyming with /u/ were /u/ earlier. The comparative evidence suggests that the first two rhymes were phonetic rhymes in an earlier stage of Acehnese. However, the third set of rhyming forms is astounding: the last time these rhymes actually rhymed phonetically has to be at the very least contemporary with an early stage in the history of Chamic! That is, by the most conservative estimate at least 800 years earlier!

Acehnese as a Chamic language

Even though the linguistic evidence presented so far is more than adequate to establish the relationship beyond question, the countless other details given throughout the remainder of this work give full substantiation to the long-held belief that Acehnese is a Chamic language. Certain of the shared innovations are so specific and so striking in their uniqueness that even on their own they would constitute evidence that Acehnese is a Chamic language.

Following Durie's suggestion (p.c.), since in subgrouping terms Acehnese is simply another Chamic language, this work will simply use the designation "Chamic" to refer to the Chamic family, rather than Durie's earlier suggestion Aceh-Chamic (1990a), Cowan's Chamo-Achehic (1988), or Shorto's Achino-Chamic (1975).

The contribution of Acehnese to PC reconstruction

The finding that Acehnese is a Chamic languages makes it invaluable as a source of information on the reconstruction of PC and on language contact and change—one that has only been modestly tapped in this work. Before the Acehnese speakers split off, it seems reasonable to assume that Chamic speakers constituted a relatively homogenous dialect chain along the Vietnamese coast—a relative homogeneity which was maintained in part by the fact that the dialects were most likely subject to essentially the same type of pressures from MK language contact and by the tendency for changes originating in one part of the dialect chain to spread throughout the whole (cf. "Diphthongization of PC *-ay in Rade" on page 125), for a post-PC change found everywhere on the mainland, except Rade). Even after the breakup of PC, convergence among the mainland languages was promoted both by the similarities in the MK contact patterns and by the tendency for innovations to spread throughout a dialect chain—tendencies which among the mainland Chamic languages have continued until modern times.

When the Acehnese speakers left the mainland, they left behind the leveling effects of the spread of changes through the dialect chain—a chain that existed at least well into the 18th century and the linguistic pressures arising out of the continuing MK contact on the mainland. As a consequence, for possibly as much as a thousand years, Acehnese has been outside the influence of many of the linguistic pressures that have influenced the mainland Chamic languages. And also as a consequence, Acehnese preserves a living record of an intermediate stage in the history Chamic, one that has been largely lost through subsequently leveling in the languages remaining on the mainland, albeit a stage that must be used with some caution, but which nonetheless is potentially invaluable.[10]

The methodological problem, of course, lies in figuring how to interpret differences between Acehnese and the mainland Chamic languages. If a linguistic feature occurs only in Acehnese, does it represent an independent innovation in Acehnese or a retention preserved only in Acehnese and lost on the mainland? Sometimes it is clear; for example, it is clear from comparisons with non-Chamic Austronesian languages that the medial homorganic nasal plus stop clusters in Acehnese are a retention.

In other cases, the answer is not as readily apparent. An area of potential difficulty is interpreting the apparently large number of lexical innovations, particularly MK borrowings, shared by the mainland languages but not Acehnese and reconstructed by Lee (1966). Subsequent work has shown many of these to be post-PC borrowings, whose occurrence only in the mainland simply indicates that the borrowings took place after the Acehnese speakers had left the mainland. Their status as borrowings is sometimes evident from the presence of otherwise unexpected clusters or from irregular correspondence patterns ("Post-PC clusters in mainland Chamic languages" on page 96). However, in other cases, a post-PC borrowing from MK may not leave recognizable traces. Thus, even some of the MK forms reconstructed in this work at the PC level may in reality be post-PC borrowings, not yet formally detectable as such.

---

10. In this regard, Acehnese is certainly not without parallels. Within Austronesian, Malagasy presents another example of a language being removed from a linguistic area before the areal tendencies have an opportunity to fully affect it. Malagasy, as Blust (p.c.) points out, has a Philippine-type morphosyntax, unlike any other language in its immediate subgroup (Barito), or any language of southern or western Borneo. The detailed agreements of grammatical morphemes show clearly that this is due to retention. Malagasy left southern Borneo before the widespread breakdown of this type of system spread through much of western Indonesia.

The areas of indeterminacy about when and from where forms are borrowed has been significantly reduced, but there is still a small subset of forms whose history is unclear. Certainly one problem is that the MK borrowings are from several MK sources: some are from Bahnaric, some are from Katuic, and, possibly, some are from the MK languages spoken in Funan.

Comparisons of the MK borrowings in the modern mainland Chamic languages with the MK borrowings in Acehnese adds several new wrinkles to the problem: first, it is at least possible, as Durie (p.c.) has suggested, that the Acehnese picked up some MK words from the Aslian MK languages spoken in the Kelantan area, a possibility suggested earlier by G. Diffloth (p.c.). It is well-established that there was a Chamic influence in Kelantan and there is no reason to assume that this influence did not include Chamic speakers. Second, as the well-known Mon-Khmer specialist Gérard Diffloth has said on a number of occasions, the northeast coast of northern Sumatra has a number of MK place names, certainly leaving open the possibility that some of the MK borrowings in Acehnese were borrowed even after the arrival of the Acehnese in Sumatra.

Thus, interpretation of the MK component in Acehnese is complicated. In some cases, our understanding is improved. For example, much of the MK material that Lee reconstructs for PC does not occur in Acehnese. The reworking of Lee's PC reconstructions in light of additional evidence has made it clear that many of these MK forms absent from Acehnese do not actually reconstruct back to PC; rather many of these forms are post-PC MK borrowings which presumably entered various mainland languages after the Acehnese departed from the mainland. In other cases, if as Diffloth notes (p.c.), there is MK material in Acehnese which does not appear in the mainland languages, it must be accounted for, but if Acehnese speakers were the most northerly of the Chamic speakers, they may have picked up some of this vocabulary from Katuic speakers, also in the north, before leaving for Sumatra. In any case, although there are obvious potential sources for these forms, the answers to these questions have not yet been found.

A DIGRESSION ON MOKEN, A NON-CHAMIC LANGUAGE

Here might be the most appropriate place for a note on Moken, just to point out that Moken is not Chamic and to give some of the obvious evidence. Moken, at least the sixty or so Moken words recorded by Martha Blanche Lewis (1960) and cited in Blust's dictionary, are enough to demonstrate that Moken is not a Chamic language. It does not share the PAn *q > *h change found in the whole of Malayo-Chamic, a lack which sets it, not just outside of Chamic, but outside Malayo-Chamic as well; instead, it has the change PAn *q > Moken /k/, a rather unusual reflex of PAn *q. Like Chamic, it does diphthongize both the high vowels in word-final position, but in this its similarity to Chamic is only typological. The Chamic and Moken reflexes of the word-final high vowels are split in entirely different ways in the two languages. Instead of PC *-εy (< PAn *-i) and *-ɔw (< PAn *-u), Moken has *-uy, -oi* and *-ui, -oi,* respectively, at least suggesting that the PAn *-i and *-u have been merged in Moken. In any case, the Moken developments make it clear that Moken does not share in the Chamic diphthongization of word-final high vowels nor in the PAn *q > PC /h/ change. In fact, thus far, although there are some typologically similarities, there is no evidence that Moken shares any of the more marked inherited innovations characteristic of the Chamic languages.

4

Altering the Basic Word:
From Disyllabic to Monosyllabic

On the basis of the material in Blood (1962), Greenberg (1970:139) wrote, concerning Phan Rang Cham:

> This language, like the closely related Jarai, Rade, and Chru mentioned earlier, tended toward loss or reduction of the vowel of the first syllable, thus producing extensive monosyllabism.

Although not in precisely these terms, early writers commented on the movement from canonically disyllabic forms to canonically iambic forms, that is, to forms with an unstressed presyllable and a stressed main syllable. For instance, Thomas (1963:61) notes that for Jarai and Chru, PMP disyllabic forms with medial *r, *R, *q, or *h usually lose the first vowel, while in most other instances the first syllable vowel is reduced to shwa. Greenberg (1970:137), characterizing the process in more global terms, writes, "These languages have generally reduced the typical Austronesian canonical CVCVC to the monosyllabic norm by reduction or loss of the first vowel". That is, the PMP canonical CVCVC has became sesquisyllabic with an iambic stress pattern or else simply monosyllabic.

This adjustment of the canonical morpheme structure has its correlates in both the reduction in the membership and the restrictions in the distribution of the consonant and vowel inventories. Various new consonants (and vowels) were introduced from MK in borrowed words. The most salient of these borrowed consonants were the series of voiced glottalized obstruents, since there were no glottalized consonants in the PMP predecessor, but there have also been a myriad of less conspicuous changes, one of the most widespread being the introduction of new clusters through the borrowing of words containing them. As for the vowels, there has been proliferation through outright borrowing from MK sources as well as through internal developments under MK influence.

THE IAMBIC SYLLABLE: EARLY MON-KHMER INFLUENCE

Throughout the history of Chamic, there is a clearly-marked, continual movement from disyllabic to iambic and from iambic to monosyllabic, but the initial impetus for these changes was the PC shift to a preference for final stress under MK influence. Once the canonical preference was set for stress on the final syllable, the preconditions had been set up for the restructuring of the Chamic lexicon.

In general, MK morphemes are either monosyllabic or what Matisoff (1973) picturesquely termed sesquisyllabic, i.e., a syllable and a half, with a stress pattern characterized by Donegan (1993:5) as iambic, that is, "words in which a light (open) syllable precedes a heavy (closed or long-voweled) second syllable", that is, words with an unstressed presyllable and a stressed main syllable. Both Matisoff (1973) and Donegan (1993) note in passing that words in proto-Austroasiatic (of which MK is one of the two major branches) were either iambic or monosyllabic. Of direct interest here is the fact that this characterization fits the MK languages of Vietnam perfectly; for example, Chrau (Thomas 1971) is iambic, Mnong and Rolom are monosyllabic, Vietnamese is monosyllabic, and so on. As Lee (1974:645) mentions, "Ultimate stress in languages with phonological words of more than one syllable is regular throughout much of Southeast Asia." And then he adds, "The Chamic languages without exception have only ultimate stress."

The restructuring of Chamic lexicon and phonology both provide eloquent testimony to the intensity and the intimacy of the Austronesian contact with MK. Lexically, of the roughly 700 forms Lee (1966) reconstructed for PC, Headley (1976) identified roughly 10% of them as MK in origin—and, 10% is a conservative figure. Included among the MK incorporated early enough to be incorporated into PC are basic vocabulary including pronouns, and a number of kinship terms. The fact that these reconstruct to PC shows that the early contact was intense and intimate, suggesting both considerable bilingualism and intermarriage.

While the nature of the earlier system is not absolutely clear, the first Austronesian speakers to come into contact with the MK speakers along the coast most likely had a system, not with exclusively penultimate stress, but a system like that in modern Malay with penultimate stress in the vast majority of disyllabic words but ultimate stress in a small group of words with a reduced shwa as the initial syllable, as Lee (1974:646) suggests. In this interpretation, contact with MK led to a shift of preference from penultimate to ultimate stress, rather than introducing an entirely new stress pattern.

The shift in preference, however, set in motion a chain of events that has manifested itself in different ways in different languages and, of course, under different contact conditions with the consequences already present in the consonant and vowel inventories of PC: The PC presyllable inventories are reduced versions of the earlier PMP first syllable inventories, while the PC main syllable inventories are larger than the inventories found in the earlier PMP second syllables.

The internal paths of this historical developmental continuum from disyllabicity to monosyllabicity are transparent. The adoption of canonical final stress by PC was enough to set up the internal preconditions for movement in the direction of monosyllabicity. All that remained was for the changes to be triggered by subsequent intense, extended contact with a monosyllabic language. In PC, the pretonic syllable still had four possible distinct vowels, but since then all the mainland Chamic languages have shown a steady erosion of the pretonic syllable, beginning with the reduction of vowel distinctions. With the exception of Acehnese, the descendant languages have reduced the vowel distinctions at least somewhat, although in a language such as Roglai, the presyllable still shows a three-way distinction in certain environments. In some of the other languages, the pretonic syllable still exists but in still others the presyllable has undergone a complete loss of vowel distinctions; for example, in Chru and Rade (for the Rade, see Table 9, page 66), only one vowel is found in the pretonic syllable—a shwa.

The movement toward monosyllabicity

In individual modern languages, the PC disyllabic, iambic forms have preceded even further in the direction of monosyllabicity, with the number of consonantal and vocalic contrasts in the presyllable being even more reduced. After the break-up of PC, some languages, such as Roglai, Rade, and Jarai, apparently in contact with languages typologically very much like PC and thus under minimal external pressure to modify the basic word shape, have remained largely unchanged. However, other Chamic languages, under the influence of different patterns of contact, have in varying degrees gone even more towards monosyllabicity.

One path that leads to a dramatic movement from disyllabic to monosyllabic within a generation or two is illustrated by Phan Rang Cham, where the presyllables were first omitted in informal, colloquial speech and now seem to have been dropped entirely by some speakers. Doris Blood (1962:11) writes,

Cham words may have two or rarely three syllables, but there is a strong tendency toward monosyllabicity. The final syllable of disyllabic words, here referred to as the main syllable, carries the primary stress. The consonants and vowels of the initial syllable... may vary considerably or may be dropped entirely. Often in normal speech a word that is sometimes heard as a two-syllable words is fused into one, as in perèw > prèw <u>new,</u> and in kelĕk > klĕk <u>to tickle</u>. The following variations have been observed: perèw ~ prèw ~ phirèw ~ phrèw ~ firèw ~ frèw.

Scholars tend to maintain full forms of words in their speech. As a general rule the speech of non-scholars is characterized by the loss of preliminary syllable, reduction in vocalism or assimilation of that syllable with the main syllable.

In these examples, the reduced forms have come about by rather natural reductions and then loss of the presyllable vowels, but the complete loss of the presyllable can come about quite dramatically.

Although not as marked as in PR Cham, this tendency to drop syllables in more colloquial speech is also found throughout Chamic, even in Acehnese, long removed from the MK sphere of influence. Durie (p.c.) comments that it occurs in personal names and in certain highly frequent terms. Thus instead of *anɯk manok*, a villager might say *nɯk manok* 'chicken' and instead of *miyup rumoh* 'under the house', they might say *yup moh*.

Although usually not as dramatically captured in mid-change, throughout Chamic the reduction of disyllables, sometimes all the way to monosyllables, has occurred and almost all of it has in part been motivated by the tendency of the presyllable vowel to reduce to shwa and then drop, as shown in colloquial Phan Rang Cham variation, collapsing the disyllabic forms into monosyllabic forms. The bulk of such reductions follow one of three patterns of reduction.

THE LOSS OF THE VOWEL BEFORE MEDIAL -h-

The first of the three patterns which led to monosyllables may have been completed by the PC stage. When the initial of the main syllable was *h, as in Table 7, the initial of the pretonic syllable and the initial of the main syllables coalesced into an initial cluster, a pattern noticed by Blood (1962) and commented on by Greenberg (1970:139). One consequence of their origin from the coalescence of disyllables is that such clusters only occur in modern monosyllabic forms.

Table 7 illustrates these developments nicely. In Malay, a closely-related but non-Chamic language, the forms are still disyllabic with the medial -h- as the onset of the second syllable. However, in PC, as reflected both in Acehnese and in the various mainland Chamic languages, these forms have been reduced to mono-syllables beginning with various clusters in which the second consonant is -h-.

*Table 7: From disyllabic syllables with medial *h to monosyllables*

PMP	Malay	PC	Aceh.	Chru	NR	Tsat	
*paqit	pahit	*phit	phet	phi:ʔ	phi:ʔ	phiʔ^{24}	'bitter; bile'
*paqa	paha	*pha	pha	pha	pha	pha^{33}	'thigh'
---	pohon	*phun	phon	phun	phut	phun^{33}	'trunk; stem'
*paqat	pahat	*pha:t	phɯət	pha:ʔ	---	pha:ʔ^{24}	'chisel; to plane'
*daqan	dahan	*dha:n	dhɯən	tha:n	tha:t	---	'branch; bough'
*taqu	tahu	*thɔw	thɛə	thəu	thəu	tiauʔ^{42}-i	'know; able'
*taqun	tahun	*thun	thon	thun	thut	thun^{33}	'year'

In some instances, as Gérard Diffloth (p.c.) has pointed out, these conso-nant plus -h- combinations are actual clusters, not aspirated stops. Fuller (1977:78) noted that in Chru such forms behave phonologically as clusters, not as unitary phonemes, citing as evidence alternations such as *phà* 'to plane' and *p-ən-hà* 'a plane', in which an infixed nominalizing -ən- occurs. Certainly, where there is an established etymology, such clusters inevitably come from the reduc-tion of disyllables. This too is a point of convergence with MK languages, many of which have parallels, for example, Khmer *khaat* 'lose' and *k-om-haat* 'loss'.

DISYLLABLES WITH LIQUIDS > MONOSYLLABLES AND CLUSTERS

Table 8 shows a second pattern in which disyllables, but with an originally medial *-l- or *-r-, coalesced into monosyllables with initial clusters. Notice that the original disyllabic forms are still retained as disyllables outside Chamic in PMP and Malay and within Chamic in PC as well as in the modern Chamic lan-guages Acehnese and Northern Roglai (not shown in Table 8), but the disyllables have been reduced to clusters in Chru and Tsat. Within Chru and Tsat following the loss of the shwa in the presyllable, the initials of the pretonic syllable and the main syllable coalesced, producing monosyllables. In Tsat, the process of mor-pheme structure simplification has gone one step further with the *-l- or the *-r- of initial cluster becoming an -i- glide.[1]

---

1. The patterns of these secondarily-derived clusters are discussed in more detail in Chapter 5.

Table 8: From disyllabic syllables with medial liquids to monosyllables

PMP	Malay	PC	Aceh.	Chru	Tsat	
*daʀaq	darah	*darah	darah	drah	sia[55]	'blood'
*daʀa	dara	*dara	dara	dra	---	'girl'
*bulu	bulu	*buləw	bulɛə	bləu	phiə[11]	'body hair'
---	pulau	*pulaw	pulɔ	pəlaːu -1	---	'island'
*bulan	bulan	*bulaːn	buluɯən	blaːn	-phian[11]	'moon'
*baqeʀu	baharu	*bahrɔw	baro -f	bərhəu	phiə[11]	'new'
*palaj	---	*palaːt -1	paluɯət	plaːʔ	pieʔ[24] -v	'palm; sole'
---	---	*pula	pula	pəla	pia[33]	'to plant'
*gulung	gulung	*guluŋ	guloŋ	pərləŋ-v	---	'to roll'
*qabaʀa	---	*bara	---	bra	phiə[11]	'shoulder'
---	karam	*karam	---	kram	---	'sink; sunk'
---	kura	*kura	---	kra	---	'turtle'
---	---	*palɛy	---	pləi -v	piai[33]	'village'

Quite parallel to these secondary clusters, which have developed within the history of Chamic, are a set of earlier primary clusters, that is, clusters which had already become clusters by the PC stage and which had developed in a similar way from the loss of the vowel preceding a medial *-l- or *-r- in an earlier disyllabic form.

LOSS OF THE UNSTRESSED INITIAL SYLLABLE

In most cases, however, the loss of the shwa of the presyllable resulting in the juxtaposition of the presyllable initial and the main syllable initial would have resulted in a highly-marked cluster. Thus, it is not surprising that when the main syllable began with any other consonant than *h- or a liquid, the whole pretonic syllable was lost (see Table 9).

Table 9 shows the unidirectional movement from disyllabic to iambic to monosyllabic. As this table shows, throughout Chamic there has been a unidirectional movement along the path to monosyllabicity. Outside of Chamic, PMP has fully disyllabic forms as does Malay. Within Chamic, the disyllables are rapidly becoming monosyllables through the reduction and loss of the presyllables: the four-way vowel distinction of the PC presyllable still exists in Acehnese, but it has been reduced to a limited three-way distinction in Northern Roglai, while in Rade the presyllable has been reduced even more, with the four-way vowel contrast reduced to just a shwa and several of the initial consonants having been dropped. In Tsat, the process has gone even further, with almost all the remaining disyllables reduced to monosyllables through the total loss of the presyllable.

Table 9: From disyllables to monosyllables

PMP	Malay	PC	Aceh.	Rade	Tsat	
*mamaq	mamah	*mamah	mamʌh	məmah	ma^{55}	'chew'
*qumah	huma	*huma	umʌŋ	həma	ma^{33}	'dry field'
*lima	lima	*lima	limʌŋ	ema	ma^{33}	'five'
*taŋan	tangan	*taŋaːn	---	kəŋan	ŋaːn^{33}	'hand; arm'
*lapaʀ	lapar	*lapa	---	epa	pa^{33}	'hungry'
---	padi	*paday	pade	mədie	thaːiʔ^{42}	'rice (paddy)'
*panaq	panah	*panah	panah	mənah	na^{55}	'shoot (bow)'
*baseq	basah	*basah	basah	məsah	sa^{55}	'wet; damp'
*m-uda	muda	*muda	muda	məda	tha^{11}	'young; tender'

Thus, although achieved through the interaction of various internal pressures and paths, the Chamic tendency toward monosyllabicity was originally set into motion by language contact and, where the movement toward monosyllabicity has continued, it is due to continued language contact with languages that have even more restricted preferred morpheme structures. That is, the process was set into motion by MK contact, resulting in iambic forms; the subsequent reduction to monosyllables seems to be due in large part to subsequent Phan Rang Cham contact with the monosyllabic Vietnamese and Utsat contact with the monosyllabic languages of Hainan.

5

Chamic Consonants

The shift to a preference for final stress has its consequences for the developments among the consonants: not only do final consonants have their own unique path of development, but so do the presyllable and the main syllable initial consonants. For the presyllable initials, the tendency is for the contrasts to be steadily reduced, beginning with the transition from PMP to PC. For the main syllable initials, the opposite was initially true; the initial contact with MK languages expanded the inventory, as did the reduction of disyllables to monosyllables, which introduced new clusters. However, this introduction of new contrasts is best viewed as an incidental byproduct of the reduction of disyllables to monosyllables; as with all consonants, the central tendency among the main-syllable initials was also towards the reduction of contrasts.

Making sense out of these tendencies and, in particular, the language-to-language variation in what gets reduced and by how much, requires looking beyond just the language internal motivations to the differences in patterns of bilingualism. It becomes clear that direct correlations exist between the internal developments and the external bilingualism.

PRESYLLABLE CONSONANTS: THE DETAILS

There is only a very limited number of consonants that can begin the presyllable (Table 10). Specifically, there are six voiceless obstruents: three stops, an affricate, and two fricatives. There are four voiced obstruents: three voiced stops and a voiced affricate. Finally, there are three sonorants: one nasal (*m-), and two liquids (*l- and *r-), with the further likelihood of an additional, marginal *ñ-, which seems to occur only in two words: *ñamuk 'mosquito' and *ñawa 'breath; life'.

Table 10: The presyllable consonants

*p-	*t-	*c-	*k-	
	*s-			*h-
*b-	*d-	*j-	*g-	
*m-	*l-	*ñ- (rare)		
	*r-			

All of these presyllabic consonants existed as such in the PMP language spoken by the PMP speakers who originally came to Vietnam, although of course various MK forms with similar structures have been added to the total number of forms. Within Chamic itself, the full array of these forms is found unaltered within the older written records of Cham, although many of these presyllable consonants have since undergone the changes reflected in the modern Phan Rang Cham and Western Cham dialects. Similarly, even in modern Acehnese, all of the presyllable consonants except for *h- are still found as such.[1]

Changes in the presyllable consonants have occurred in all the Chamic languages, with the distribution of the changes suggesting that contact patterns were a major determinant of the paths of change. Acehnese, which retains all the presyllable consonants except *h-, left the mainland before the bulk of the changes began. The languages remaining on the mainland, except for Rade, underwent changes that were at least in part influenced by contact, as many of the similarities in the developments cut across subgrouping lines but match contact patterns. The lone exception is Rade, which, as the geography suggests, patterns as if it were on the edge of the dialect chain existing among the Chamic dialects remaining on the mainland. Certainly, the developments among the Rade presyllable initial consonants are unique to Rade.

The rather salient lack of presyllables beginning with *n-, despite the existence of *n- in the presyllables of PMP, seems to correlate directly with a similar scarcity of such forms in, say, Malay, where, although a handful of apparently disyllabic native words with *n-* seems to exist, the overwhelming majority of disyllabic forms beginning with *n-* are either obviously borrowed or just as obviously a secondary result of the effects of verbal prefixes. In this context, Lee (1974:652) writes that, although only Manley (1972:25) seems to specifically note the absence, "apart from reduplicative patterns and some cases of syllabic nasals homorganic with the first consonant of the following syllable, normally *m* is the only nasal that can occur as the onset syllable in many languages of Vietnam."

---

1. Initial *h- in presyllables does not occur in Durie's reconstructions of Proto-Acehnese.

Then, Lee suggests the thus-far-unexceptional correspondence of PMP
*n- to PC *l-, citing five of the examples in Table 11.

Table 11: PMP *n- > PC *l-

PMP	Malay	PC	Aceh.	NR	W. Cham	
*niyuʀ	nyor	*laʔur	bɔh u	laʔu	laʔu	'coconut palm'
*h-in-ipi	mimpi	*lumpɛy	lumpɔə	lupəi	lapay	'to dream'
*nanaq	nanah	*lanah	---	lanãh	---	'pus'
*nipis	nipis	*lipih	lipeh	lupih	lapih	'thin (material)'
*niwaŋ	---	*lawaːŋ	---	luwaːk	lawaŋ	'thin'
---	nasi	*lasɛy	---	---	lasǎy	'cooked rice'

In the case of 'dream', the PC forms and the Acehnese form in particular look to
be the product of the string PMP *h-in-ipi > *nipi > *lipi > *l-um-pi > *lumpɛy,
with two layers of distinct verbal morphology stuck into the ultimate Acehnese
form. This particular change is restricted to the Chamic component of Malayo-
Chamic, including Acehnese.

The Indic borrowing into mainland Chamic, ˣnagar 'country, city; area'
and the Acehnese borrowing naŋgroe represent distinct variants borrowed independently. The Acehnese initial is not the expected /l-/ and its vowel suggests an
earlier *-i, both of which suggest that the Acehnese form is borrowed from
Malay.

The voiceless obstruents

The reflexes of the voiceless obstruents are, by and large, straightforward. In
Rade, the *p- has merged with the *b- and the *m-, all becoming m-; Rade has
also merged *t-, *k-, and *c- as k-, a merger also found in the minor syllables of
a number of MK languages. In fact, Chong (MK) allows only k- as the first consonant of a minor syllable. In Haroi, the PC presyllable *t- has merged with *c-
as c-. Elsewhere, as Table 12 shows, the various series are kept distinct.

Certain other Chru reflexes not listed in Table 12 are of particular interest and merit more discussion than they will be given here. In addition to the
listed *p-, *t-, and *k- reflexes, there are also forms with what appear to be the
reflexes pər-, tər-, and kər-, respectively. However, these forms are most likely
related to the reduction of earlier trisyllabic (or, polysyllablic) forms, rather than
being phonologically conditioned. Some of the trisyllabic forms apparently were
the residue of either borrowed or native morphology. For example, in some
instances, the pər- may be related to the Haroi pala- 'RECIPROCAL' (Goschnick
1977:115). Thus, in Chru the form for 'divide; share' is pərpha, while in Phan
Rang Cham there are three forms, one of which is parapha. In addition, there is
the form 'rabbit', which is tərpaːi in Chru, but *tarapay in PC. Finally, there are

many such forms which apparently do not occur elsewhere in PC, and thus may be borrowings.

Table 12: The voiceless obstruents

PC	Aceh.	Rade	Jarai	Chru	NR	Tsat	Haroi	W. Cham	PR Cham
*p-	p-	m-	p-	p-	p-	ø-	p-	p-	p-
*k-	k-; g-	k-	k-	k-	k-	ø-	k-	k-	k-
*t-	t-	k-	t-	t-	t-	ø-	c-	t-	t-
*c-	c-; j-	k-	c-	c-; ˣs-	c-	ø-	c-	c-	c-
*ʔ-				(unmarked)					

In most cases, it is not possible to tell from the material available whether or not forms written with a word-initial vowel actually have glottal onsets. However, at least so far, it really does not seem to have any consequences for the analysis. In Western Cham the pretonic syllable is lost more often than not. With the *ʔa-* pretonic syllable, for instance, it is lost in every case except *atau* 'ghost; corpse'.

Acehnese reflexes of presyllable initial *k- and *c-

The Acehnese reflexes of PC presyllable *k- and presyllable *c- are voiced if and only if the main syllable initial is also a voiceless stop (see Table 13, page 70), but not if the main syllable initial is a sonorant (Mark Durie, p.c., informs me that this process is productive in modern Acehnese).

Were it not a borrowing, the word *guda* 'horse' would be an exception to this pattern; that is, *guda* 'horse' has a presyllable voiced stop preceding a main syllable voiced stop. However, there is good evidence it is borrowed: Aside from not patterning as might be expected diachronically, it is not widespread in Austronesian and it is suspiciously close to the Gujarati *ghoḍa* 'horse' (Karen Mistry, p.c.), and it is well-known that Gujarati traders were early visitors to this region.

*Table 13: PC *k- > Acehnese g-; *c- > Acehnese j-*

Malay	PC	Acehnese	
---	*campa	jɯmpa	'Champa'
kita	*k-ita	gɯ-ta-ñɔə	'we (incl.)'
kaki	*kakay	gaki -v, gateh -f	'foot; leg'
kapas	ˣ*kapaːs	gapɯəh	'cotton'
kuku	*kukɔw	gukɛə	'claw; fingernail'
kĕntut	*kəntut	toh gɯntət	'fart; flatus ventrus'
kutu	*kutɔw	gutɛə	'louse, head'
kuda	ˣ---	guda	'horse'

PC *s- and *h-

In Table 14 and 15, the reflexes of presyllabic *s- and *h- are examined. In Acehnese the *s- has been retained in presyllables, while the *h- has been lost. In Chru and N. Roglai, the two series are retained largely unchanged. In Chru, there is a minor but interesting split in the reflexes of *s-. If the main syllable began with a voiceless stop, the vowel of the presyllable was completely dropped, leaving the Chru monosyllabic with an initial sp-, st-, or sk- cluster as its onset; otherwise, the complete presyllable remains unaltered. This association of consonant manner with a split in consonantal reflexes reflects voice quality differences (Cf. Thurgood, 1980).

*Table 14: Reflexes of PC presyllabic *s-*

PC	Aceh.	Rade	Jarai	Chru	NR	Haroi	W. Cham	PR Cham
*s-	s-	h-;	h-	sə-;	s-	h-;	h-	h-
		ø-		s-		ø-		
/___p, t, k	ø-	h-	s-	s-	ø-	h-	h-	h-
/___vd. obst.	h-	h-	h-	sə-	s-	ø-	h-	h-
elsewhere	h-	h-	sə-	s-	h-	h-	h-	h-

In the remaining five languages, the reflexes of *s- and *h- have merged completely. In Jarai, Western Cham, and Phan Rang Cham, both *s- and *h- have merged, becoming *h-*, although this development is made somewhat less transparent by the frequent total loss of the whole presyllable in Western Cham and Phan Rang Cham.

*Table 15: Reflexes of PC presyllabic *h-*

PC	Aceh.	Rade	Jarai	Chru	NR	Haroi	W. Cham	PR Cham
*h-	ø-	h-;	h-	h-	h-	h-;	h-	h-
			ø-				ø-	
/___p, t, k	ø-	h-	h-	h-	ø-	h-	h-	h-
/___vd. obst.	h-	h-	h-	h-	ø-	h-	h-	h-
elsewhere	h-	h-	h-	h-	h-	h-	h-	h-

Finally, in Rade and Haroi, the merged reflexes are further split, although in each case it is on the basis of slightly different conditioning factors. In both Rade and Haroi, if the main syllable began with a voiceless stop, the *h-* initial was simply lost (some transcriptions show a glottal onset being added secondarily to what would otherwise be a vowel-initial word). In Haroi, the process went a step further with *h*- also being lost before main syllables with a voiced obstruent initial. Cf. also "Secondary clusters" on page 94. Again, the association of manner differences with splits in consonantal reflexes reflects voice quality differences (Cf. Thurgood, 1980).

The voiced stops and breathiness

The correspondence patterns for voiced stops shows an association of with breathiness that probably dates back to PC. All the modern Chamic languages except Acehnese and Rade have split reflexes of presyllable *b-, *d-, and *g-, with the splits conditioned by the manner of the initial consonant of the main syllable. The reflexes of PC *j- have not undergone such splits.

Table 16: Examples of reflexes of the PC presyllable voiced obstruents

PC	Jarai	Chru	NR	W. Cham	PR Cham	
*batɔw	pətəu	pətəu	patəu	patau	patŏw; patŏw	'stone'
*bituʔ	pətuʔ	pətuʔ -f	pituʔ	patŭʔ	pitŭʔ; patŭʔ	'star'
*basah	pəsah	pəsah	pasah	pasah	pathăh	'wet; damp'
ˣ*batɔ	pəto	pətɔ	pato	patɔ	patɔ	'teach'
*batuk	pətŭk	pətuʔ	pituʔ	patŭʔ	patŭʔ	'cough'
*dikit	---	təki:ʔ	tiki:ʔ	takiʔ	takiʔ	'few; little'
*dəpa	təpa	təpa	tupa	tapa	tapa	'armspan'
*gatal	kətal	kətal	katan	katăl	katăl	'itchy'
*gətak	kətăk	kətaʔ	kataʔ	katăʔ	katăʔ	'sap; resin'
*babah	---	---	---	papah	papah	'mouth'
*babuy	bəbui	pəbui	babui	papui	papuy	'wild pig'
*dada	təda	təda	dada	tata	tata	'chest'
*bulɔw	bləu	bləu	biləu	plau	palŏw	'body hair'
*buŋa	bəŋa	bəŋa	buŋă	paŋur -f	piŋu	'flower'
*bula:n	blan	bla:n	bila:t	plan	pilan	'moon'
*darah	drah	drah	darah	tarah	tarăh	'blood'
*dara	dra	dra	dara	tra	tara	'girl'
*dalam	dlăm	dərlam	dalap	talăm	talăm	'inside'
*gunam	gənăm	gənam	---	---	kanăm	'cloud'

All the evidence indicates that Acehnese left the mainland before the loss of the presyllable initials took place. Rade, apparently on the edge of the Chamic dialect chain left behind, underwent its own series of developments largely if not totally independent of the other mainland dialects. All the remaining Chamic languages have undergone splits correlated with the manner of the initial of the main syllable.[2] As for Haroi, although subsequent changes have resulted in the total devoicing of all PC presyllable voiced stops, traces of earlier split patterns are reflected in the vowel reflexes of the presyllables.

Table 16 shows examples of the split in the reflexes of PC presyllable voiced stops, which depend upon the nature of the main syllable initial. In Jarai, Chru, N. Roglai, W. Cham, and PR Cham, if the main syllable began with a voiceless stop, the voiceless stop reflex is rarely but occasionally accompanied by breathy voice on the vowel. If the main syllable began with a voiced obstruent, the reflexes may be either voiced or voiceless in Jarai, are voiceless in Chru, are voiced in N. Roglai, are voiceless in W. Cham but with variable residual breathy voice on the vowel, and are voiceless in PR Cham but without any residual breathy voice. Finally, if the main syllable consonant is a sonorant, the reflex is voiced in Jarai, Chru, and N. Roglai, and voiceless but with accompanying residual breathy voice on the vowel in W. and PR Cham.

The same patterns (although based on all the data, not just the examples in Table 16) are presented schematically in Table 17.

Table 17: The reflexes of the PC presyllable voiced obstruents

PC	Aceh.	Rade	Jarai	Chru	NR	Haroi	W. Cham	PR Cham
*b-	b-	m-	p-;	p-;	p-;	p-	p-/;	p-/;
			b-	b-	b-		p̣-	p̣-
/__vl. stops		m-	p-	p-	p-	p-	p-	p-/; p̣-
/__vd. stops		m-	b-	p-	b-	p-	p-/; p̣-	p-
/__sonorants		m-	b-	b-	b-	p-	p̣-	p̣-
*d-	d-	ø-	t-;	t-;	t-;	c-	t-/;	t-;
			d-	d-	d-		ṭ-	ṭ-
/__vl. stops		ø-	t-	t-	t-	c-	t-	t-
/__vd. stops		ø-	t-	t-	d-	c-	ṭ-/; t-	t-
/__sonorants		ø-	d-	d-	d-	c-	ṭ-	ṭ-
*g-	g-	k-	k-;	k-;	k-;	k-	k-;	k-;
			g-	g-	g-		ḳ-	ḳ-
/__vl. stops		k-	k-	k-	k-	k-	k-	k-
/__sonorants		k-	g-	g-	g-	k-	ḳ-	ḳ-
*j-	j-	ø-	j-	j-	j-	c-	ç-	ç-

---

2.   Tsat has essentially lost all its presyllables, leaving too little trace of earlier stages of the process of loss to determine whether Tsat also split the reflexes of the PC voiced stops.

The patterns themselves are as described for the examples in Table 16, although in general terms, the cross-linguistic patterning of the changes illustrates a persistent drift towards voiceless obstruents. The pattern of the drift is evident in the table: in terms of the manner of the main syllable consonant, the loss of voicing (and breathiness) is most favored before voiceless obstruents, less favored before voiced obstruents, and least favored before voiced sonorants.

The sonorants

The nasals

The reflexes of the PC nasals *m- and *ñ-, shown in Table 18, require two comments. First, in Rade, the *p- and the *b- have also merged with the *m- giving m-.

*Table 18: The reflexes of the PC presyllable nasal *m- (and, possibly, *ñ-)*

PC	Aceh.	Rade	Jarai	Chru	NR	Haroi	PR Cham	
*m-	m-	m-	m-	m-	m-	m-	m-	
*mata	mata	---	məta	məta	mata	məta	mɨta	'eye'
*manu?	manɔ?	mənŭ?	mənŭ?	mənŭ?	manŭ?	mənŭ?	mɨnŭ?	'chicken'
*muda	muda	məda	məda	məda	mida	məthɨa	mɨṭa	'young'
*ñamuk	jamɔ?	---	---	jəmŭ?	jamŏ?	---	çamɔ̆?	'mosquito'
*ñawa	---	ewa	jəwa	jəwa	lawa	cəwɨa	yawa	'breath'

Second, the near nonexistence of PC *ñ- indicates the phoneme was marginal at the PC level, and the reflexes show its dissolution in various ways throughout Chamic. In large part the reflexes of initial *ñ- have blended with those of *j-, although there is also merger with the reflexes of *y-. The change of PC first syllable *ñ- to /l/ in N. Roglai is at least reminiscent of the change of PMP first syllable *n- to /l/ in PC. It is worth, however, noting that 'breath, breath, life, soul' is still manifested as /ñawà/ 'soul' in Headley's Western Cham, suggesting that this Western Cham initial still reflects the PMP initial quite faithfully.

The liquids

In terms of Chamic reflexes, the *r- and the *l- are a little more interesting than the PC *m-. The distinction between the presyllable *r- and the *l- has been totally lost in Rade, Haroi, and Jarai, with the Rade reflexes further merging with *d- and *j-, and then ultimately disappearing completely.

Table 19: Reflexes of PC presyllable liquids

PC	Aceh.	Rade	Jarai	Chru	NR	Haroi	PR Cham	
*r-	r-	ø-	r-	r-	r-	l-	r-	
*rata:k	rɯtɯə?	etak	rɤtǎ?	rəta:?	rata:?	ləta? -l	rata?	'bean; pea'
*ribɔw	ribɛə	ebǎu	rɤ̆bəu	rəbəu	rubəu	ləphɨau	ripɔ̆w	'thousand'
*rusa	rusa	---	rɤ̆sa	rəsa	rusa	ləsa	ratha	'Sambhur deer'
*l-	l-	ø-	r-	l-	l-	l-	l-	
*lima	limʌŋ	ema	rəma	ləma	lumǎ	ləmɨa	limɨ	'five'
*lakɛy	lakɔə	ekɛi	rɤ̆kəi	ləkəi	lakəi	ləkŏi	likɛ̆y	'male; person'
*laŋit	laŋɛt	eŋĭt	---	ləŋi:?	laŋi:?	ləŋi?	laŋi?	'sky'
*luka	luka	eka	---	ləka	---	ləka	lika-	'wound, scar'

Presyllable onsets: retention and reduction

Within the history of Chamic, the persistent movement towards monosyllabicity includes the gradual reduction of the presyllable: first, the consonant and vowel inventories are progressively reduced and then eventually the entire presyllable is lost. Acehnese retains 12 of the 13 distinctions (marginally 14), undoubtedly in part because it left the mainland early, thus avoiding the subsequent bilingual contact which would lead the other languages toward the reduction of the initial contrasts.

Rade displays the most drastic reductions in the presyllable consonantal onsets. In Rade, the original 13 consonants have been reduced to just three. The apical voiced consonants *r-, *l-, *j-, and *d- have been lost, the bilabials *m-, *b-, and *p- have merged, becoming *m-,* the *t-, *c-, *k-, and *g- have merged, becoming *k-,* and, the two voiceless fricatives have merged, becoming *h-* (with the *h-* subsequently disappearing in some contexts (see "The voiceless obstruents" on page 69; Table 14)).

Haroi has reduced the original 13 distinctions to just six, paralleling Rade in the reductions it makes. The *l- and *r- have coalesced, becoming *l-;* the *t- and *c- coalesced, becoming *c-;* the *s- and *h- have coalesced, becoming *h-* (with the *h-* subsequently disappearing in some contexts (see Table 14, page 71)).

And, as happens partially or completely throughout Chamic, the voicing distinction is lost with the voiced obstruents. The obvious parallels between Rade and Haroi apparently reflect the influence of a period of mutual contact.

Jarai, like both Rade and Haroi, coalesces *r- and *l- as well as *s- and *h-, leaving Jarai with 11 presyllable onsets.

Table 20: Retention and reduction in presyllable consonants

PC	Aceh.	Rade	Jarai	Chru	NR	Haroi	W. Cham	PR Cham
*r-	r-	ø-	r-	r-	r-	l-	r-	r-
*l-	l-	ø-	r-	l-	l-	l-	l-	l-
*j-	j-	ø-	j-	j-	j-	c-	ç-	ç-
*d-	d-	ø-	t-; d-	t-; d-	t-; d-	c-	t-/; ṭ-	t-; ṭ-
*t-	t-	k-	t-	t-	t-	c-	t-	t-
*c-	c-	k-	c-	c-	c-	c-	c-	c-
*k-	k-	k-	k-	k-	k-	k-	k-	k-
*g-	g-	k-	k-; g-	k-; g-	k-; g-	k-	k-; ḳ-	k-; ḳ-
*m-	m-	m-	m-	m-	m-	m-	m-	m-
*p-	p-	m-	p-	p-	p-	p-	p-	p-
*b-	b-	m-	p-; ɓ-	p-; ɓ-	p-; ɓ-	p-	p-; ᵱ-	p-; ᵱ-
*s-	s-	h-; ø-	h-	sə-; s-	s-	h-; ø-	h-	h-
*h-	ø-	h-	h-	h-	h-	h-; ø-	h-	h-

Totals:

| 13 | 12 | 3 | 11 | 13 | 13 | 6 | 12 | 12 |

In all the languages except Rade and Haroi, at least some of the voiced stops have devoiced coalescing with the reflexes of the voiceless stops in the process. Also, in both dialects of Cham, *s- and *h- have merged as *h*.

Notice that the table does not include Tsat, which does not have presyllables, let alone presyllable onsets. Tsat has dropped all presyllable consonants except those that have coalesced with the initial of the main syllable to become part of the onset of a monosyllable.

Sporadic "dissimilation"

As is quite obvious (cf. text above and Table 20), throughout Chamic particularly within the mainland Chamic languages after the breakup there has been a tendency toward the reduction of the contrasts in the initials of the presyllables. This reduction has been accomplished, not so much through the dropping of initials, although this happens occasionally, but instead largely through the merger of various presyllable initials (cf. the situation in Rade in which some initials have disappeared while others have undergone widespread merger).

Mark Durie (p.c.) pointed out another set of presyllables in which there has been sporadic "dissimilation" of the presyllable initial (see Table 21). These dissimilations involve instances where both the presyllable and the main syllable begin with the same initial: both begin with /k-/, both begin with /c-/, or, more problematically, both begin with /s-/. When the change occurs, the presyllable initial usually becomes /t-/, but sometimes it becomes /c-/ and sometimes /k-/. In each case, the change has occurred sporadically, sometimes happening, sometimes not. As with the changes discussed earlier, the result of these changes in the reduction of number of patterns found involving the presyllable initials.

It is instructive to discuss the developments of the presyllable initials in the examples of Table 21 one-by-one, beginning with the forms with initial *k-. In those cases where there is a Malay form, the initial of that form faithfully reflects the older Austronesian form. For the form 'claw; fingernail', most of the languages reflect the original PC *k-: The Acehnese form *gukɛə* is quite regular including the voiced initial (see "Acehnese reflexes of presyllable initial *k- and *c-" on page 70), and most of the remaining forms have also retained a velar reflex. However, two forms do reflect a change: the Jarai (PL) form *təkəu* has a /t-/ reflex, and both the Jarai (Lee) form *cəkəu* and the Phan Rang Cham (Lee) *cəkăw* have initials reflecting neither a *k- nor *t-.

*Table 21: Sporadic change from *k- to /t-/ in initials of the presyllable*

Malay	PC	Aceh.	Jarai	NR	PR Cham	Wr. Cham	
kuku	*kukɔw	gukɛə	---	kukəu	kakŏw	kukau	'claw;
	> /t-/	---	təkəu	---	cəkăw	---	'fingernail'
kaki	*kakay	gaki -v	---	---	---	kakai	'foot'
	> /t-/	---	təkai	takai	takay	takai	
---	*kakaːs	---	rə̆kăh -i	kaka	kakăh	kakah	'fish scales'
	> /t-/	---	---	---	təkah	---	
gigi	*gigɛy	gigɔə	---	---	---	---	'tooth'
	> /t-/	---	tə̆gəi	digəi	takĕy	tagĕi	

For 'foot', only the Acehnese *gaki* -v (unless, as the vowel suggests, this is a borrowing from Malay), and one of the two Written Cham forms recorded by Aymonier and Cabaton *kakai* reflects the original *k-. The remaining forms reflect an initial /t-/. The pair of Written Chamic (AC) forms make it clear that both variants have existed within the history of Cham, and suggest that the *k- developed into

/t-/ during that time. For 'fish scale', the form in Jarai (PL) should be compared with Khmer *sraka* (listed in Aymonier and Cabaton). Of the remaining forms all seem to have retained reflexes of the original *k- except for one of the two Phan Rang Cham variants. The variant recorded by Lee *təkah* reflects /t-/, not the *k-, but the presence of both variants within Phan Rang Cham suggests that the *k- variant existed within the history of Cham. Finally, with the voiced velar of 'tooth', only the Acehnese form has retained evidence of the older velar; else-where the reflexes have become alveolar stops.

Several observations can be made about these changes. First, the changes postdate the breakup of PC: Acehnese, Jarai, Northern Roglai, Western Cham, and Phan Rang Cham all retain evidence of the earlier *k-. Second, the changes are sporadic in nature: the *k- only changes sometimes, and when it does change it sometimes becomes /c-/ and sometimes /t-/. The reflex sometimes appears to reflect an earlier *k-, sometimes a *t, and sometimes a *c. Third, two words changed almost everywhere while two others only changed sporadically, a pattern consistent with the existence of a tight-knit dialect chain in which changes in one dialect often spread to contiguous dialects. Fourth, the apparent failure of Acehnese to participate in this change (or, in the change of *c- to /t-/ discussed below (with the marginal exception of the word 'lizard')) suggests that Acehnese had already the mainland when the bulk of these changes took place.

Consider the forms in Table 22 with initial *c-. With 'grandchild', the older *c- is still faithfully retained only in two Chamic sources, Acehnese and the Written Cham (AC) *čačauv* (along with the variant with the initial /t-/). Similarly, with 'chop; strike', only the Written Cham (AC) *čačauh* retains the older initial. Fortunately, the Aymonier and Cabaton dictionary contains numerous older forms. With 'great grandchild', again only the Written Cham (AC) retains the older initial (along with a form reflecting the more recent /t-/). Finally, the MK borrowing 'lizard' is interesting primarily because it is a late borrowing but none-theless it has sporadically undergone the change from *c- to /t-/ in Acehnese (see the doublet in Acehnese) suggesting that, although the change from *c- to /t-/ must have occurred long enough after the breakup of PC for Acehnese to have escaped most of its influence, it is still reflected in this late borrowing.

As with the *k- to /c-/ and /t-/ changes, several observations can be made about this data. First, the change postdate the breakup of PC, as the Acehnese and Written Cham doublets make clear, and, if 'lizard' is ignored, it is only the Writ-ten Cham doublets that do so. Second, the apparent failure of Acehnese to partic-ipate in this change, with the exception of the word 'lizard', suggests that Acehnese left before much of this occurred. Finally, the doublets in Written Cham indicate that the change occurred after the breakup of PC and spread throughout the dialect chain.

Table 22: Sporadic change from *c- to /t-/ in initials of the presyllable

Malay	PC	Aceh.	Jarai	NR	PR Cham	Wr. Cham	
cucu	ˣ*cucɔ	cucɔ	---	---	---	čačauv;	'grandchild'
	> /t-/	---	təco	tico	tacɔ	tičauv	
---	ˣ*cacɔh	---	---	---	---	čačauḥ;	'chop, strike'
	> /t-/	---	tə̆cɔh	ticoh	tacŏh	tičauḥ	
cicit	ˣ*cicĕt	cʌt	---	---	---	čačaiʔ;	'great
	> /t-/	---	təcĕʔ	ticĕʔ	tacĕʔ	tičaiʔ	grandchild'
cicak	ˣ*cicaʔ	cicaʔ;	că̆ŋ că̆ʔ	---	---	čačaʔ	'lizard;
	> /t-/	ticaʔ	kă̆ŋ kă̆ʔ	tacă̆ʔ	kacă̆ʔ	---	gecko'

Finally, there is a third set of forms which behave in a parallel way but which are only apparent when one looks outside of the Chamic languages, that is, there is a pair of words in which /t-/ reflects what extra-Chamic evidence makes clear was an earlier /s-/ (see Table 23). Within Chamic itself, however, there is no attestation that I am aware of for an earlier *s-; and, unless an Acehnese or a Written Cham form turns up unexpectedly, I do not expect to find any.

Table 23: Sporadic change from *s- to /t-/ in initials of the presyllable

Malay	PC	Jarai	NR	W. Cham	PR Cham	Wr. Cham	
susu	**susɔw	---	---	---	---	'breast'	
	> *tasɔw	tə̆səu	tisəu	tasau	tathŏw	tasŏu	
sisir	ˣˣsisi(r)	---	kasi -i	---	---	---	'a comb'
	> ˣtasi	tə̆si	---	tasi	tathi	tasi; tasiʔ -f	

Nonetheless, on the basis of the parallels with the forms in Tables 16 and 17 combined with the external evidence offered by the Malay forms, it is likely that these forms were **susɔw and ˣˣsisi 'comb; hand of bananas' in post-PC and have simply dissimilated giving the forms found in the tables.

In any case, the "dissimilations" discussed above, despite their sporadic nature, despite the fact that they postdate the breakup of PC, and despite their sometimes idiosyncratic patterning have in common that they are part of the change toward the reduction of presyllables—a change that has its impetus supplied not by the internal dynamics of these languages but by the structures of the languages that the Chamic languages are in contact with.

The extra-Chamic correspondences

As the patterns in Table 24 and the examples in Table 25 show, in Malay, a language clearly subgrouped outside of Chamic, the first syllable consonants correspond precisely with the onsets reconstructed for Chamic.

Table 24: Reflexes of PC presyllable liquids

Malay	PC	Aceh.	Rade	Jarai	Chru, NR	Haroi	W. & PR Cham
l-	*l-	l-	ø-	r-	l-	l-	l-
r-	*r-	r-	ø-	r-	r-	l-	r-
j-	*j-	j-	ø-	j-	j-	c-	j-
d-	*d-	d-	ø-	d-	t-; d-	c-	t-/; ṭ-

The PC presyllable liquids are retained unaltered in Acehnese. The identical patterns of reflexes in Chru and Roglai as well as those in Western and Phan Rang Cham reflect the subgrouping.

Table 25: Reflexes of PC presyllable liquids (examples)

Malay	PC	Aceh.	Rade	Jarai	Haroi	PR Cham	
lima	*lima	limʌŋ	ema	rəma	ləmɨa	limɨ	'five'
lapar	*lapa	---	epa	rəpa	ləpa	lapa	'hungry'
rusa	*rusa	rusa	---	rəsa	ləsa	ritha	' Sambhur deer'
dara	*dara	dara	era	dra	cərɨa	ṭara	'girl'
darah	*darah	darah	erah	drah	cərɨah	ṭarăh	'blood'
danau	*danaw	danɔ	enau	dənau	cənɨau	ṭanaw	'lake'
jarum	*jarum	jarom	erŭm	jrŭm-v	cərŭm	çarŭm	'needle'
jalan	*jala:n	-lɯən	elan	jəlan	cəlɨan	çalan	'road; path'

The Malay forms, the PC forms, the Acehnese, and the Phan Rang Cham forms all agree in their reflexes.

MAIN SYLLABLE ONSET CONSONANTS

Once the borrowings have been culled out, the correspondences among the remaining main syllable onsets are straightforward. If these reflexes are compared with the reflexes of the presyllable onsets, it becomes apparent that certain consonants have different reflexes, depending upon whether they were presyllable or main syllable onsets.

The voiceless obstruents

The voiceless obstruents have been retained largely unaltered. Only the *s- in Phan Rang Cham has changed, and, even in this case, it is obvious both from Western Cham and from the older inscriptional citations that it was an *s-* at an earlier point in Cham.

Table 26: Reflexes of the voiceless obstruents

PC	Aceh.	Rade	Jarai	Chru	NR	Tsat	Haroi	W. Cham	PR Cham
*p-	p-	p-	p-	p-	p-	p-	p-	p-	p-
*t-	t-	t-	t-	t-	t-	t-	t-	t-	t-
*k-	k-	k-	k-	k-	k-	k-	k-	k-	k-
*c-	c-	č-	c-	c-	c-	ts-	c-	c-	c-
*ʔ-	ø-	ø-;	ʔ-	ø-;	ø-;	ʔ-	ø-;	ø-;	ˌø-
		-ʔ-		-ʔ-	-ʔ-		-ʔ-	-ʔ-	
*s-	s-	s-	s-	s-	s-	s-	s-	s-	th-
*h-	h-	h-	h-	h-	h-	h-	h-	h-	h-

Notice that, while the main syllable PC *s- onset is retained as such in all modern languages except Phan Rang Cham, the presyllable PC *s- became *h-* except in Chru and N. Roglai. It is worth noting that Written Cham has two distinct representations for /s-/, with the one Moussay transliterates as /th-/ being the older form, and the one transliterated as /s-/ being more recent. Thus, in some sense, the forms with /s-/ are suspicious; that is, these may eventually turn out to be borrowed but this remains to be seen.

The apparent two-way alternation in the reflexes of the PC glottal stop is more a question of orthographic conventions than of reality. In several languages, a clear reflex of the PC glottal stop occurs intervocalically in word-medial position, where the retained glottal stop is written as either a glottal stop or a hyphen. In word-initial position before a vowel, nothing occurs in the orthographies but from the various phonetic descriptions it seems evident that such forms actually begin with a glottal onset—it simply is not indicated in the orthographies.

To digress for a moment, Adelaar (1988:62) writes that, for his proto-Malayic, the proto-phoneme *c is not well-attested, citing certain words, including a form with the PC counterpart ˣcum 'kiss; smell'[3] and another with the PC counterpart ˣˣpicah 'broken; break':

> the number of etyma with *c is restricted, and many of the Malayic lexemes containing c are borrowed. But there is still a number of them which hitherto could not be explained away as borrowings, and the

---

3.   As Blust pointed out (p.c.), if PC 'kiss; smell' is a MK borrowing, its distribution in western Indonesia is interesting. Iban doesn't seem to have it, but as Blust (p.c.) suggested this would be because Iban is part of the Malayo-Chamic population that never left the southwest Borneo homeland. He further notes that Malay, Minangkabau and Banjarese all have it, as do some other languages which may have borrowed it from Malay (Sundanese, Madurese; Ngaju Dayak presumably got it from Banjarese).

elimination of PM *c will ultimately depend on the reduction of their number, which includes e.g. PM *cari, *cu(ŋ)kup, *curi, *cium. It appears that reflexes of *cium and *curi must have been borrowed from Northern Indian languages, where we find Bengali *cum(a)* 'a kiss', *curi, cori* 'theft', and *cor* 'thief', and Hindi *chúma* 'a kiss', *chori* 'a theft', and *chor* 'thief'. Since other Northern Indian languages usually have similar or related terms for 'kiss' and 'theft' or 'thief', and the regular PMP etyma for these notions are *ajek and *taŋkaw respectively, *cium and *curi must be erroneous reconstructions built on Northern Indian loanwords. Other instances of PM *c, such as *kuciŋ 'cat', *pəcah 'scattered', and *kəcil 'small' may be the result of secondary phonological developments within Malayic itself (cf. Zorc 1983:12-3). It is very likely that these phonological developments on the one hand, and borrowing from Chinese, Northern Indian, Dravidian, and Southeast-Asian languages on the other, will ultimately eliminate the evidence for PM *c. And the elimination of PM *c has far-reaching consequences for PAn/PMP *c.

Of the two PC counterparts he mentions specifically, the first is a borrowing, but the second reconstructs at least within Chamic. However, as Adelaar observes for Malayic, the vast majority of the words within Malayo-Chamic with *c- are borrowed. Only one of the forms with a presyllable *c- looks to be PMP, the word *caba:ŋ 'branch', but in PC it is ˣˣcaɓaŋ, with an unexpected glottalized /b/. Of the 30 or so PC forms whose main syllable begins with *c, although many reconstruct to the PC level, other than ˣˣpicah, none appear to have strong PMP reconstructions!

The voiced obstruents

As is clear from the reflex patterns in Table 27, before it became differentiated into a Highlands and Coastal Chamic, PC had four voiced obstruents.

Table 27: Reflexes of PC voiced obstruents

	Highlands Chamic (Plateau Chamic)					**Hainan**	**Coastal Chamic** (Lowlands Chamic)	
PC	Aceh.	Rade	Jarai	Chru	NR	Tsat	Haroi	W. & PR Cham
*b-	b-	b-	b-	b-	b-	ph-	ph-	p-
*d-	d-	d-	d-	d-	d-	th-	th-	ṭ-
*g-	g-	g-	g-	g-	g-	kh-	kh-	ḳ-
*j-	j-	j-	j-	j-	j-	s-	s-	ç-

We know that the Cham initials were voiced in the inscription found at Tra-kiêu (Coedès (1939; cited in Marrison (1975))); for example, *di* 'at', *dengan* 'with', and *tujoh* 'seven'. There is no reason not to trust that the words written with voiced stops in the script were voiced stops, at least originally.

The real questions revolve around when the various devoicings took place. Much of this must be surmised as all we know directly is that, on the basis of Cabaton (1901), the voiced stops had become voiceless by 1901. The devoicing in Tsat and the Coastal Chamic are instructive for two reasons: first, the two occurred independently of each other and, second, the reflexes correlate with different linguistic sub-areas. In the southern Vietnamese highlands, Rade, Jarai, Chru, and N. Roglai have preserved the original PC voicing; in the Hainan linguistic sub-area Tsat has devoiced, and in the linguistic sub-area along the coastline, the Haroi and Cham have undergone devoicing.

In Tsat, closely-related to N. Roglai, the devoicing probably occurred only after the arrival in Hainan in 986, having fled Champa following the Vietnamese sacking of the northern capital at Indrapura in 982. The change was undoubtedly influenced by the language contact situation in Hainan, as much of the phonological system of Tsat has been restructured under the influence of the languages of Hainan. Notice that, in any case, the Tsat is most closely related to Northern Roglai, a language which still has voiced obstruents; thus, the devoicing in Tsat happened after — long after — the separation of Cham and Roglai.

It is likely that the devoicing in Coastal Chamic, that is, in Haroi and in Cham, postdates the emergence of the distinction between Coastal Chamic and Highlands Chamic. There is also every reason to suspect that Haroi and Cham were by then quite separate and that the parallel developments in each were the result of a similar response to similar situations — that is, the type of convergence typical of a linguistic area.

What must be resisted, however, is the temptation to attribute the changes in Coastal Chamic to Vietnamese influence. The reason that this temptation must be resisted is that the same changes are found in Western Cham, a group that apparently split off from Cham immediately after the Vietnamese conquest of the southern capital at Vijaya. Thus, if this historical scenario is accurate, it is quite unlikely that the innovated changes in Coastal Chamic are primarily due to Vietnamese influence. It is possible, however, that the various changes common to Coastal Chamic might be the modern reflexes of changes that occurred before Cham differentiated into Haroi, Western Cham, and Phan Rang Cham.

Even more important to the history of these languages is the fact that the voiced obstruents are associated with breathiness throughout Chamic. For example, in the two Cham dialects, the reflexes are voiceless unaspirated stops followed by a breathy voiced vowel. Also, for Chru, Fuller (1977:85) writes that the voiced initial stops are often accompanied by a breathy quality on the vowel. In Haroi, various vowel splitting patterns make it clear that the voiced obstruents are to be associated with breathy voice. And, in the earlier discussion of the reflexes of the presyllable voiced stops, the patterns of splitting in the reflexes suggest that breathy phonation is associated with the voiced stops. In short, this and other evidence makes it clear that throughout Chamic voiced stops are associated with breathiness.

The sonorants

The PC sonorants are retained as such throughout Chamic. As noted elsewhere, the sonorants behave as a natural class for the sake of certain register complex and tonal developments.

Table 28: Reflexes of PC sonorants

PC	Aceh.	Rade	Jarai	Chru	NR	Tsat	Haroi	W. Cham	PR Cham
*m-	m-	m-	m-	m-	m-	m-	m-	m-	m-
*n-	n-	n-	n-	n-	n-	n-	n-	n-	n-
*ŋ-	ŋ-	ŋ-	ŋ-	ŋ-	ŋ-	ŋ-	ŋ-	ŋ-	ŋ-
*ñ-	ñ-	ñ-	ñ-	ñ-	ñ-	ñ-	ñ-	ñ-	ñ-
*l-	l-	l-	l-	l-	l-	l-	l-	l-	l-
*r-	r-	r-	r-	r-	r-	z-	r-	r-	r-
*y-	y-	y-	y-	y-	y-	z-	y-	y-	y-
*w-	w-	w-	w-	w-	w-	v-	w-	w-	w-

Also, as might be expected, in various languages the reflexes of *y- and *w-, alternate in a fully-predictable way between -y- and -i- and between -w- and -u-, respectively, depending on whether or not the reflex has been analyzed as vocalic or consonantal in the grammar in question (cf. Lee 1974:662, fn. 5).

It is important to note that, while an initial *w- is reconstructable in some words for PC *w-, none of the words with an initial PC *w- reconstruct to the PMP level. The secondary nature of such forms is fully consistent with Blust's (1992a:34-44) claim that word-initial *w- was lost in proto-Malayo-Chamic.

Voiced and voiceless 'aspirated' consonants

These voiced and voiceless 'aspirated' initials come from two sources. The inherited initials result from the coalescence of the initial of the presyllable with the *h- of the main syllable (see Table 29, below, for examples). In addition, there are a number of examples that are MK borrowings, for example, PC *pha 'different' and PNB *pha 'different' and PC ˣ*khan 'blanket; cloth' and PNB *khǎn 'blanket'.

In Chamic, although there is some question about whether these are units or clusters, they often behave as clusters, not just phonologically but also phonetically. They frequently sound like clusters and they partake in morphological alternations in which they are split as if they were clusters (see "The loss of the vowel before medial -h-" on page 63). Of course, such an analysis rests crucially on the assumption that alternating forms are synchronically related to one another, an assumption that is clearly true diachronically but may be questionable synchronically. With reference to Jarai, Blust (1980b:133) records the alternation [phíʔ] ~ [pəhíʔ] 'bitter' < PC *phiʔ (his own transcription), an alternation that suggests that the initial is phonetically a cluster. With reference to Acehnese, as Durie (1985:19) makes clear, both the voiceless aspirated and the voiced aspirated (his murmured) stops can be treated as phonemic sequences of C + h. Durie (p.c.) argues that there are both phonetic (1985:19) and phonological grounds for treating Acehnese C + h sequences as demonstrably phonological clusters. Acehnese (Durie 1985:19) nicely illustrates the evidence found in morphological alternations; cf. /phet/ 'bitter', which, when it takes the infix /-ɯn-/, becomes /pɯnɯhet/ 'bitterness'. And, in Acehnese, this process of infixation is widespread enough to make it clear not only that the infixation itself is productive but also that these onsets are not just historically but also synchronically clusters.

The diachronic source of such C + h clusters in all those instances where there is a clear etymology and the forms have not been borrowed is from the reduction of disyllables.

Table 29: Reflexes of voiceless and voiced 'aspirated' consonants

PC	Aceh.	Rade	Jarai	Chru	NR	Tsat	Haroi	W. Cham	PR Cham
*ph-	ph-	ph-	ph-	ph-	ph-	ph-	ph-	ph-	ph-
*th-	th-	th-	th-	th-	th-	th-	th-	th-	th-
*kh-	kh-	kh-	kh-	kh-	---	kh-	kh-	kh-	kh-
ˣch-	---	čh-/; s-	s-	s-	ch-/; c-	---	c-/; s-	ch-	s-/; ch-/; thy-
*bh-	---	bh-	bh-/; ph-	ph-	ph-	---	---	ph-/; pah-	ph-
*dh-	dh-	dh-	th-	th-	th-	th-	th-	ṭh-	ṭh-
*gh-	kh- ?	gh-	kh-	kh-	kh-	kh-	kh-	ḳh-	ḳh-

The voiceless 'aspirates' are retained as such throughout Chamic, but the voiced series has been largely lost. Thus, the voiced aspirates are only retained as such in the orthography of Cham and in Rade, with the *bh- variably retained as /bh-/ in Jarai and the *dh- apparently retained as /dh-/ in Acehnese. Nonetheless, evidence for a former voiced series is found in both Western and Phan Rang Cham, where the reflexes of these obstruents are in the breathy-voice quality often found on the vowels after the former voiced obstruents; as Lee notes (1974:648-649), this is a clear indication that these initials were once voiced obstruents. In discussing these aspirates, Lee also notes that there are also some voiced affricates in Roglai, but he assumes these are probably Rade borrowings.

It needs to be pointed out that ˣch- does not reconstruct to the PC level, nor apparently do the forms containing it occur in Acehnese. Notice the considerable, unconditioned variation in its reflexes.

The process of reducing the PMP forms to aspirates in PC was not totally completed by the PC stage; as Lee (1974:649) again notes, PMP *tuqah 'old' is PC *tuha which drops the vowel in Rade *kha*, sometimes in Jarai *təha* vs. *tha*, but not in Roglai *tuha* and Cham *taha*. Undoubtedly, some variation in such forms has existed in Chamic for a considerable period of time.

As pointed out earlier, the development of PC and post-Chamic clusters consisting of stop plus -h- is an obvious adaptation to the MK languages with which the PC speakers had come into contact.

Glottalized voiced obstruents

The immediate problem in talking about glottalized voiced obstruents is determining just what they are. Greenberg (1970:134), paraphrasing Ladefoged, mentions at least three phonetically distinct possibilities, all referred to as implosives: "segments in which the larynx is actually lowered producing an ingressive air stream upon the release of the oral stop, segments with laryngealized voicing, and segments which are preglottalized." In the literature on the Chamic languages, these segments are frequently termed "preglottalized". Certainly some manifestations, such as the glottalized obstruents of Jarai, are definitely phonetically preglottalized (Bob Blust, p.c.); other manifestations may very well not be. Nonetheless, since the variants never actually contrast with one another synchronically and all pattern together in Chamic, the variants can be treated as diachronically non-distinctive.

The origins of glottalized obstruents

The overwhelming majority of PC glottalized obstruents are pre-Chamic borrowings from MK sources; a large number of the remaining forms with glottalized obstruents represent borrowings post-dating the breakup of PC. As an example, Solnit (1993:109) cites the MK loan PC ˣɗiŋ -f 'tube; pipe (for smoking)'. However, the earliest layer of glottalized obstruents was not borrowed but rather developed in a small set of PMP forms.

Over the last forty years, linguists have largely focused their attention on this small subset of inherited forms with glottalized obstruents. The first author to comment on the crucial correspondences was Dorothy Thomas, who wrote about the glottalized /ɓ/ in the Rade, Jarai, and Chru forms for 'hair' (cf. Rade ɓŭk 'hair'). Comparing the Chamic forms to Dyen's (1953) PMP *buhuk 'hair', she commented (1963:63), "The preglottalized b of *buhuk reflexes probably represents a metathesis of the *b and *h."

A little later, Greenberg (1970:137), in his oft-cited paper "Some generalizations concerning glottalic consonants, especially implosives", noting that for Chamic, Dyen's *h > pre-Chamic *ʔ (and, as will be relevant for other examples, Dyen's *q > pre-Chamic *h), recognized that the PMP *buhuk had been replaced by the pre-PC level by *buʔuk. He then stated that when the first consonant in a CVCV(C) structure is a voiced stop and the second is the laryngeal ʔ; the result is a glottalized voiced obstruent, or, in his terms, a voiced injective.

To the word 'head hair', Greenberg added 'stench' and Lee (1974:649; 653-654) added 'climb', both of which work in a parallel way. Later writers, e.g. Blust (1980b) and Solnit (1993), have also cited the forms and the analysis approvingly. For the forms, see Table 30.

Table 30: PC glottalized obstruents in PMP words

PMP	Malay	Pre-PC	PC	Aceh.	Rade	PR Cham	
*buhuk	---	*buʔuk	*ɓuk -1	ʔoʔ	ɓŭk	ɓuʔ	'head hair'
*nahik	naik	*daʔik	*ɗiʔ	ʔeʔ	ɗĭʔ	ɗiʔ	'climb; ascend'
*bahu	bau	*baʔu	*ɓɔw	---	ɓău	ɓɔ̆w	'stench'
			*bɔw	bɛə	---	---	'stench'
*daqan	dahan	*dahan	*dhaːn	dhɯən	adhan	ʈhan	'branch'
*daqis	dahi	*adahi	*ʔadhɛ̆y	dhɔə	adhɛi	ʈhɛ̆y	'forehead'

Ignoring for a minute the last two forms on Table 30, several additional comments might be made about the data and its analysis. First, the form for 'climb; ascend' looks good, despite the PMP initial; if the PMP form is accurate, the *d- is simply a backformation from what was misanalyzed as a nasal prefixed *dahik. However, the form does occur in Bahnar (AC) dɘ̆k; it conceivably could turn out to simply be a lookalike borrowed from Bahnar. Second, although both Thomas

(1963) and Lee (1974) mention metathesis, it is more likely that the change involved deletion of the first syllable vowel, particularly if we include 'climb; ascend' in the set. Once the two segments are juxtaposed, metathesis hardly seems necessary.

Finally, it is necessary to note that Acehnese seems to have a glottal stop reflex for glottalized obstruents heading monosyllabic forms, but voiced obstruent reflexes for forms in disyllables or as part of an onset cluster. Further, in the case of the Acehnese forms, it is likely that coalescence rather than first syllable dropping was involved. As Durie (p.c.) points out, although Acehnese does drop syllables independently of other Chamic languages on some occasions, this is rare—mostly the dropping in Acehnese is consistent with the dropping in the mainland languages. Thus, it would be surprising for Acehnese to have consistently dropped syllables just in this particular CV? environment when other Chamic languages did not.

In addition, the word 'stench' requires some discussion, as its analysis is complicated by the existence of a variant with a voiced rather than a glottalized initial. The most wide spread Chamic reflexes of 'stench' point to a form with a glottal initial, but the Acehnese example points instead to a *b-; aside from the patterning, the existence of a *b- variant finds support in Aymonier and Cabaton's dictionary, which lists two variants, one with an initial voiced stop and one with a glottalized initial. Doris Blood (1962) also recorded a Phan Rang Cham variant that reflects an initial voiced stop.

Now turning to the interaction between the first three forms, which contain the PMP *-h- and the two additional forms on Table 30, which contain PMP *-q-, it becomes clear that the changes were chronologically ordered:

(1) PMP *-h-> PMalayo-Chamic*-h-> Pre-PC*-?- /V__V
(2) PMP *-q-> PMalayo-Chamic*-?-> Pre-PC*-h-.

That is, the change of PMP *-h- to pre-PC *-?- occurred before the change of PMP *-q- to pre-PC *-h-. It is only after these ordered changes, that the loss of the first syllable vowel led to the development of the Chamic glottalized initials.

Note that this change is shared throughout PC: these forms have the expected glottal stops as their reflexes in Acehnese and the expected glottalized obstruents as their reflexes in mainland Chamic.

Other sources have also been suggested for the origins of other Chamic glottalized obstruents, but as of yet the data has yet to provide any clear substantiation for any of these suggestions. For instance, Greenberg (1970), following Thomas (1963:60), proposed that some Chamic glottalized obstruents might have developed from the loss of the first vowel in disyllabic forms with a glottal presyllable onset and a voiced stop main syllable onset. The suggestion itself seems plausible but the data cited in support of the notion is most likely spurious. Greenberg (1970:137) writes, "...from PMP ʔijuŋ 'nose' Thomas (1963) gives Jarai, Chru ʔduŋ, Rade ʔduŋ or ʔaduŋ." However, contra Greenberg, neither the Jarai nor the Chru forms actually occur in Thomas; instead, both Chru and Jarai have ʔadŭŋ instead. And, while the Rade forms ʔduŋ and ʔaduŋ do occur in Thomas, the crucial Rade form ʔduŋ, likewise seems spurious as a form for 'nose'. It does not occur with a glottalized consonant in Lee 1966, Tharp and Y-Bham 1980, Y-Chang 1979, or Egerod 1978 — all of which are sources for Rade. It is, of course, possible that the form in Thomas is not an error, but it would take more than this one form to substantiate the hypothesis. Another similar spurious pair of forms also appears to exist in Thomas (1963:66), which lists the forms ʔdok, ʔdoʔ 'stand' from PC *dɔːk 'sit', but which again do not occur in the Rade sources consulted. Contrary to what has been indicated, the Chamic forms for both PC *iduŋ 'nose' and *dɔːk 'sit; stay' show completely regular reflexes of the original voiced stops, with no evidence of the secondarily-derived implosion.

Nonetheless, as various authors have noted, still other forms with unexpected glottalized obstruents do occur in the Chamic data (see Table 31). Lee (1974:654) cites two forms with reservations, one for 'open the eyes' and another for 'pain; ache'. The first, has a strong PMP etymology and patterns regularly in Chamic *ɓlaːʔ, despite the potentially irregular vowel in Acehnese. However, the glottalized initial is unexpected and not possible to account for. As for ˣ*padiʔ 'pain; ache', it is regular within most of Chamic, but it is not directly related to the Acehnese or to the extra-Chamic Malay forms. Thus, Lee's reservations about these forms seem well-founded.

Table 31: Unexpectedly glottalized obstruents

PMP	Malay	PC	Acehnese	Rade	PR Cham	
*bulat	---	*ɓlaːt	ɓlɯt -vʔ	---	ɓlaʔ	'open eyes wide'
---	---	ˣ*padiʔ	---	---	padiʔ	'pain; ache'
*cabaŋ	cabang	ˣ*caɓaːŋ	cabɯəŋ	kəɓaŋ	caɓaŋ	'branch; tree fork'
*lindiq	---	ˣ*ɗih	---	ɗih	ɗĭh	'sleep; lie down'
---	---	ˣ*ɓaŋ	---	ɓăŋ	ɓăŋ	'hole; door'

However, other anomalous forms remain in need of explanations. For instance, the glottalized medial consonant in ˣ*caɓaːŋ 'branch of a tree' cannot be explained, if the PMP etymology of the form is reliable. Further, the medial /b/ of the Malay form should be a /w/, but it isn't. Within Chamic at least, the form looks as if always had a glottalized medial consonant: the Acehnese /b/ is the normal reflex of a glottalized consonant in a disyllable.

In another form, suggested by Solnit, ˣ*ɗih 'sleep; lie down', if it is related to cited provenience PMP *lindiq, the glottalized obstruent needs an explanation. Elsewhere Blust (1980b:143) notes two words as possibly PMP in origin but with preglottalized initials. The first, meaning 'sticky, as glutinous rice', looks to have been independently borrowed more than once into Chamic and reflects something like ˣ(ma)klit, ˣɓlit 'sticky, as glutinous rice'; note the similarity to the well-attested PMP root reflected in Malay *pulut*. The other root is *ɗɔh 'distant; far', which is regular in Chamic, which has apparent PMP correspondences (cf. Malay *jauh*), and which has an inexplicably glottalized initial.

More intriguing is the suggestion by Blust (1980b) that some of the Jarai glottalized initials may derive from earlier clusters of homorganic nasal plus stop, but thus far the crucial forms needed to confirm or disconfirm the suggestion are missing.

Finally, there are glottalized consonants, including various nasals, scattered seemingly randomly throughout various Jarai dialects (mentioned by Haudricourt 1950) that require more careful examination. To take a single example, the PC form ˣ*ɓaŋ 'hole; door' unexpectedly turns up in Jarai with a preglottalized nasal, despite the rest of the reflexes of PC *ɓ- showing up as preglottalized stops, at least in that dialect in this particular case, the presence of Bahnar *maŋ* and proto-North-Bahnaric *qmăŋ 'door' suggest that the Jarai form is a late borrowing from either Bahnar or one of the Bahnaric languages in the area. The Jarai data in Lafont's (1968) dictionary include a rich array of oddities in which homorganic nasals appear sporadically in lieu of anticipated stops, sometimes preglottalized and sometimes not. Whether this can be explained in the same way remains to be seen. In any event, the alternation of glottalized voiced stops and homorganic nasals is found throughout at least the Tai-Kadai family (cf. the Tai subgroup (Li 1977), the Kam-Sui subgroup (Thurgood 1988a), and the Hlai (Li) subgroup (Thurgood 1991).

Understanding what is happening in Jarai will doubtless require more data. However, an examination of the Jarai dialect forms in Lafont's dictionary suggests that in at least one of the Jarai dialects the voiced stops may have become glottalized, as in certain Vietnamese dialects, and that some dialect borrowing has occurred.

Finally, it is likely that some of the forms with glottalized consonants but nonetheless reconstructed in this work to PC are actually post-PC loans that are formally undetectable. Despite their regular correspondence patterns in the languages in which they occur, their limitation to the highlands Chamic languages strongly suggests they were borrowed after the breakup of PC, but that they nonetheless fit the correspondence patterns. See Appendix II for such cases.

Reflexes of PC glottalized obstruents

In PC, the correspondences and their reflexes are straightforward (see Table 32). The PC correspondences consist of two layers: an older layer limited to three or four native PMP words with glottalized obstruents inherited from PC and a large number of MK borrowings incorporated along with their glottalized obstruents.

Table 32: Reflexes of PC glottalized obstruent

								W. & PR
PC	Aceh.	Rade	Jarai	Chru	NR	Tsat	Haroi	Cham
*ɓ-	ʔ-; b-	ɓ-	ɓ-	ɓ-	ɓ-	ɓ-	ɓ-	ɓ
*ɗ-	ʔ-; d-	ɗ-	ɗ-	ɗ-	ɗ-	ɗ-	ɗ-	ɗ-
×*ʔj-	---; j-	ʔj-	ʔj-	i-	ʔj-	ʔi-	ʔj-	ʔj-

As Table 32 shows, PC has three glottalized obstruents, which have been retained as such in the modern languages, except for the reflexes of *ʔj- in Tsat and Chru. In Acehnese, the reflexes of glottalized obstruents in disyllables or in onset clusters seem to be the corresponding homorganic stops, but otherwise they seem to be a simple glottal stop (see "The origins of glottalized obstruents" on page 86 for discussion of specific examples; this entire section owes much of its merit to email discussions with Mark Durie).

Solnit's Southern Vietnam Highlands sub-area

In the area of Southern Vietnam in which PC and the contemporaneous MK languages were spoken, there was a contrast between glottalized voiced obstruents[4] and plain voiced obstruents. At some point probably postdating the Vietnamese conquest of the south, southern Vietnam was split into two smaller sub-areas. One, described by Solnit (1993:110) as the Southern Vietnam Highlands sub-area, is the home of the Highlands Chamic languages (Rade, Jarai, Chru, and N. Roglai) and Bahnaric languages this area is characterized by contrastively glottalized voiced obstruents.

The other area, now far more influenced by Vietnamese, consists of the Coastal Chamic languages (Haroi and Cham) and is characterized by the loss of this contrast. It is that the Coastal Chamic languages share the range of innovations that they do in part because at one time these were all the same dialect and

---

4. As Blust notes (p.c.), preglottalized stops are also an areal feature in central Taiwan and implosives are found in a number of languages of northern Sarawak, and in a region extending from Bimanese (eastern Sumbawa) through much of Flores in the Lesser Sunda Islands, and into southeastern Sulawesi.

that changes occurred before the original language differentiated into Haroi, Western Cham, and Phan Rang Cham and in part because of similar influences.

The Tsat-speakers had most likely moved to Hainan before the distinction between the Highlands and the Coastal Chamic came into being, and thus they participated in neither linguistic area, but instead were influenced by the Hainan sprachbund. Sometimes change in Tsat parallel changes in Coastal Chamic, but in each case these are developments characteristic of Hainan languages. In addition, at least with some of the changes, the similarity is only typological as the details differ significantly.

Table 33: The PC contrast between voiced and glottalized obstruents

PC	Rade	Jarai	Chru	NR	Tsat	Haroi	W. Cham	PR Cham
*ɓ-	b-	b-	b-	b-	ph-	ph-	p-	p-
*d-	d-	d-	d-	d-	th-	th-	t̪-	t̪-
*j-	j-	j-	j-	j-	s-	s-	ç-	ç-
*ɓ-	ɓ-	ɓ-	ɓ-	ɓ-	ɓ-	ɓ-	ɓ-	ɓ
*ɗ-	ɗ-	ɗ-	ɗ-	ɗ-	ɗ-	ɗ-	ɗ-	ɗ-
×*ʔj-	ʔj-	ʔj-	i-	ʔj-	ʔi-	ʔj-	ʔj-	ʔj-

Among the Coastal Chamic languages—Haroi, Western Cham, and Phan Rang Cham, the voiced obstruents have devoiced, removing the contrast between the glottalized and the plain series. As Lee points out (1974:653) for Cham, now that the PC voiced obstruents have devoiced, the old glottalized series tends to vary freely between voiced and glottalized variants.

This phonetic variation should not be surprising as voiced stops (plosives) and voiced glottalized obstruents (implosives) are not all that unlike one another. Ladefoged (1971:26-27) writes:

> The difference between implosives and plosives is one of degree rather than kind. In the formation of voiced plosives in many languages (e.g., English) there is often a small downward movement of the vibrating vocal cords. This allows a greater amount of air to pass up through the glottis before the pressure of the air in the mouth has increased so much that there is insufficient difference in pressure from below to above the vocal cords to cause them to vibrate. An implosive is simply a sound in which this downward movement is comparatively large and rapid.

Beyond the phonetic plausibility, there is another factor that contributes to the variation. As Lee (1974:653) notes, there is similar variation in Vietnamese dialects, where the voiced alveolars and bilabial segments are voiced in some dialects but glottalized in others. As Henderson (1965:422-425) has written, such variation is characteristic of Southeast Asia.

CONSONANT CLUSTERS

The clusters distributed throughout the modern Chamic languages can be grouped into three historical strata: primary clusters inherited at the PC level, secondary clusters derived from PC disyllabic forms, and MK borrowings.

Primary clusters

All of the clusters reconstructed at the PC level have either *l- or *r- as the second member of the cluster. Either these clusters were already clusters in the language that PC descended from, or these clusters developed early in pre-Chamic—it is not possible to tell from internal evidence.

Table 34: Reflexes of PC primary clusters

PC	Aceh.	Rade	Jarai	Chru	NR	Tsat	Haroi	W. Cham	PR Cham
*pl-	pl-	pl-	pl-	pl-	pl-	pi-	pl-	pl-	pl-
*bl-	bl-	bl-	bl-	bl-	bl-	phi-	pl-	pl-	pl-
*kl-	lh-	tl-	kl-	tl-	kl-	ki-	tl-	kl-	kl-
*gl-	lh-	dl-	gl-/; dl-	gl-	dl-	khi-	tl-	ḳl-	ḳl-
*pr-	pr-	pr-	pr-	pr-	pr-	pi-	pr-	pr-	pr-
*tr-	tr-	tr-	tr-	tr-	tr-	ts(i)-	tr-	tr-	tr-
*kr-	kr-	kr-	kr-	kr-	kr-	ki-	kr-	kr-	kr-
*br-	br-	br-	br-	br-	br-	phi-	pr-	pr-	pr-
*dr-	dr-	dr-	dr-	dr-	dr-	si-	tr-	ṭr-	ṭr-

Note that in Tsat, the medial *l- or *r- has been vocalized, becoming -*i*-. The forms for *kl- and *gl- also merit comment. Lee (1966) reconstructs both *tl- and *kl- as well as both *dl- and *gl-, but aside from one word in Rade—the word for Roglai, the distinction between /gl-/ and /dl-/ seems to be restricted to Jarai. In Jarai, the variation that exists looks cross-dialectal rather than genuinely contrastive, including variation within dialects (cf. *dlɛh, glɛh* 'tired').

Acehnese makes it particularly obvious that C + h sequences derive from the coalescence of what were at an earlier point distinct segments. For example, both *kl- and *gl- have merged to a single /lh-/ reflex, which Durie still treats as a synchronic cluster (1985:20). As he notes with regard to not just /lh-/ but to all Acehnese clusters including an /h/ (1985:19) "The /h/ is psychologically real to native speakers, who intuitively use *h* to transcribe these consonants, and it simplifies the description of the phonotactics."

Even more indicative of the diachronic origins are examples in which the C + h are morphologically separable. Durie notes that infixes often split up C + h clusters, as with /phet/ 'bitter' which, when it takes the infix /-ɯn-/, becomes /p-ɯn-het/ 'bitterness' (cf. "Voiced and voiceless 'aspirated' consonants" on page 84). As both Durie and Cowan note, the morphological alternations often preserve both components of the earlier cluster intact. Durie (p.c.), for example, notes that the combination of consonants that led to the initial /lh-/ in *lhʌ* 'thresh grain' is preserved in the form *c-ɯm-ɯlʌ,* which has the otherwise lost *c-*. Much the same point was made by Cowan (1981:539):

> ...it should be noted that, historically speaking, the initial cluster *lh* derives from *sl, *tl [*kl-, in this work], or *cl, clusters that are not admitted in present-day Achehnese, but apparently were in an earlier period of the language. In derivations with the infix, however, the original consonants tend to reappear; e.g., *lhɔ* 'stamp, tread upon something forcibly': *c-ɯm-ɯlɔ; lhab* 'paint, dye': *s-ɯm-ɯlab; lhan* 'swallow' ....

Cowan suggests that the *sl-, *kl-, and *cl- clusters were in "an earlier period of the language". The crucial question, of course, is precisely how much earlier---a question to which I have no answer.

These PC primary clusters are inherited from PMP disyllables in which the initial of the initial syllable coalesced with the *r- or *l- initial of the main syllable to form a main syllable cluster onset (see Table 35, for examples).

Table 35: Sources of PC primary clusters

PMP	PC	Aceh.	NR	PR Cham	
*beli	*blɛy	blɔə	blai	plɛ̆y	'buy'
*belaq	*blah	plah -i	blah	plah	'chop; split'
*tuʀun	*trun	trən	trut	trŭn	'descend'
*beʀay	*brɛy	bri -f	brai	prɛ̆y	'give'
*beʀas	*braːs	brɯəh	bra	prah -1	'rice (husked)'
*puluq	*pluh	siploh	sa pluh	plŭh	'ten'

In Table 35, the PMP and the Malay counterparts of the PC primary clusters are disyllabic.

Secondary clusters

Although no reduction occurred at either the PC stage, as the PC reconstruction indicates, various secondarily-derived clusters are scattered throughout Chamic which resulted from the collapse of an original disyllabic form when the onset of the main syllable was *r- or *l- and the vowel of the presyllable was completely lost. See also the discussion in "Disyllables with liquids > monosyllables and clusters" on page 64.

Table 36: Clusters from the reduction of PC disyllabic forms

PC	Aceh.	Rade	Jarai	Chru	NR	Tsat	Haroi	W. Cham	PR Cham
*kar-	kar-	kr-	kr-	kr-	kar-	---	kr-	kar-	kar-
*par-	par-	pr-	pr-	pr-	par-	---	---	par-	par-
*bar-	bar-	mr-	br-	br-	bar-	phi-	pr-;	pr-;	par-
							pər-	par-	
*sar-	sar-	hr-	hr-	sr-	sar-	---	hər-	hr-	har-
*har-	ar-	hr-	hr-	hər-	har-	ø-	hər-	hr-	har-
*mar-	mar-	---?	mr-	mər-	mar-	ø-	mər-	mar-	mɨr-
*jar-	jar-	ø-	jr-	jr-	jar-	s-	cər-	çr-	çar-
*dar-	dar-	ø-	dr-	dr-	dar-	---	cər-	ʈar-;	ʈar-
								ʈr-	
*sal-	---	hl-	hl-	səl-	sal-	---	həl-	hl-	hal-
*hal-	al-	hl-	hl-	həl-	hal-	---	həl-	hl-	hal-
*ral-	---	hl-	hl-	rəl-	ral-	---	həl-	ral-	ral-
*mal-	mal-	ml-	ml-	məl-	mal-	---	məl-	mal-	mɨl-
*tal-	tal-	kl-	təl-	təl-	tal-	ø-	cəl-	tal-	tal-
*jal-	jal-	ø-	jəl-	jəl-	jal-	ø-	cəl-	çal-	çal-
*dal-	dal-	ø-	dl-	dəl-	dal-	ø-	cəl-	ʈal-	ʈal-
*kal-	kal-	kl-	kl-	kəl-	kal-	ki-	kəl-	kl-	kal-
*gal-	gal-	kl-	gl-	gəl-	gal	khi-	kəl-	ḳl-	ḳal-
*bal-	bal-	ml-	bl-	bl-	bal-	phi-	pəl-	pl-	ṗil-
*pal-	pal-	pl-	pl-	pl-;	pal-	pi-	pəl-	pl-	pal-
				pəl-					

This widespread reduction largely represents what was historically independent but parallel developments. In the Rade-Jarai cluster of languages, Rade has clusters in all cases, while Jarai has clusters in all but two cases. In the Chru-Roglai-Tsat cluster of languages, N. Roglai has not reduced any of the forms to clusters, Chru has reduced some to clusters but not others, while Tsat has only remnants of clusters and then only in those forms where the presyllable was not completely lost. Finally, in the Haroi-Cham subgroup, Haroi and Phan Rang Cham have essentially retained the disyllabic forms, while Western Cham has reduced some to clusters.

The secondarily-derived Chamic clusters are still disyllabic not only in Malay, an extra-Chamic language, and in PC, but also in, for example, modern Northern Roglai and modern Phan Rang Cham, as the examples in Table 37 show.

Table 37: PC disyllabic forms in Malay and Acehnese

Malay	PC	Aceh.	NR	PR Cham	
bulu	*bulɔw	bulɛə	biləu	pilɔ̆w; palɔ̆w	'body hair'
dalam	*dalam	dalam	dalap	ṭalăm	'inside; in'
ulat	*hulat	ulat	hula?	hală?	'worm'
jalan	*jalaːn	-luən	jalaːt	çalan	'road; path'
kulit	*kulit	kulet	kuliː?	kali?	'skin'
malam	*malam	malam	malap	mĭlăm	'night; evening'
tali	*talɛy	talɔə	taləi	talĕy	'rope; string'
barah	*barah	barah	barah	---	'swell; swollen'
darah	*darah	darah	darah	ṭarăh	'blood'
hari	*hurɛy	urɔə	hurəi	harĕy	'day; sun'
jarum	*jarum	jarom	jurup	çarŭm	'needle'
kĕram	*karəm	karɔm	karəp	karăm	'to hatch'
mérah	*mahirah	mirah	mariah	mĭryăh	'red'
pérak	ˣpirak -lf	pira?	paria? (m)	pirak	'silver; money'
surat	*surat	surat	sura?	hară?	'write; letter, book'

The Southeast Asian tendency towards reduction of disyllables to mono-syllables is nicely illustrated in the cross-linguistic treatment of disyllables in Chamic.

Post-PC clusters in mainland Chamic languages

Lee reconstructed four clusters to the PC level that subsequent research has shown to have entered various mainland Chamic languages after the breakup of PC: ˣcr-; ˣjr-, ˣsr-, and ˣgr-.

Table 38: Post-PC clusters in mainland Chamic languages

post-PC	Aceh.	Rade	Jarai	Chru	NR	Tsat	Haroi	W. Cham	PR Cham
ˣcr-	---	cr-; tr-	cr-	cr-	cr-	---	cər-	cr-	cr-
ˣjr-	---	dr-	jr-	jr-	jr-	si-	cər-	çr-; cr-	çr-
ˣsr-	sr- ?	hr-	hr-	sr-	sr-	---	sr-	sr-	thr-
ˣgr-	gr- ?	gr-	gr-	gr-	gr-	khi-	kr-	ḳr-	ḳr-

These clusters do not reconstruct to the PC level. The first indication of their status as post-PC borrowings is their attestation pattern. Even in the patterns in Table 38, representative forms are, if not lacking, at least marginally represented in both Acehnese and Tsat. The extensive gaps, however, are far more readily apparent in Table 39, when unlike the typical Chamic cognate, items are frequently unattested in the majority of the languages examined. Bear in mind these sets are the strongest sets available; items excluded are weaker in one way or another than those in Table 39.

Table 39: Post-PC clusters in mainland Chamic languages (examples)

post-PC	Aceh.	Rade	NR	Tsat	Haroi	W. Cham	PR Cham	
ˣcr-	---	cr-; tr-	cr-	---	cər-	cr-	cr-	
ˣcrɛh	---	trɛh	---	---	---	---	crĕh	'to mark'
ˣcrih	---	---	crĭh -n	---	---	---	crĭh	'strange'
ˣcrɔh	---	crɔk -f	croh	---	cərŏh	crɔh	crŏh	'a stream'
ˣjr-	---	dr-	jr-	si-	cər-	çr-	çr-	
ˣjrɔ	---	---	jro	---	---	---	---	'large jar'
ˣjrăw	---	drau	jrău	siau[11]	cəriău	çru	çru	'medicine'
ˣjrɔ	---	ero	jro	---	cərɔ -VR	crɔ -i	---	'rainbow'
ˣsr-	sr-	hr-	sr-	---	sr-	sr-	thr-	
ˣsrăp	---	---	srã?	---	srău?	---	thru?	'crossbow'
ˣsrɛ̆	---	---	srĕ	---	---	srɛ	---	'debt, owe'
ˣsrŏh	srɔh	---	---	---	---	---	---	'polish rice'
ˣsrŏ?	---	hrŏ?	---	---	---	---	---	'subside'
ˣsrɔːk	---	hrok	sroː?	---	---	---	---	'fishtrap'
ˣgr-	---	gr-	gr-	khi-	kr-	ḳr-	ḳr-	
ˣgrit	---	---	---	---	kri?	---	---	'dirty'
ˣgriaŋ	---	griăŋ -v	giaŋ -f	---	---	ḳrĕŋ -v	ḳrĕŋ	'fang; tusk'
ˣgruă?	---	---	---	---	---	ḳru?	---	'lie prone'
ˣgrəm	---	grăm	grəm	khiːn[11]	kriam	ḳrəm	ḳrŭm	'thunder'
-vf			-f			-v	-v	
ˣgrək	---	---	grə?	---	kri?	ḳrə?	ḳră?	'vulture'
ˣgrɔh	*grŏh	grɔh	groh	khiə[55]	krŭh -v	/krŏh/	ḳrŏh	'to bark'

Typical of the sets for these clusters are the form 'dirty', which is attested in Jarai and Haroi as well as by a highly irregular form in Western Cham, and the form 'lie prone', which, although attested also has a variant completely lacking the medial -r-, an alternation which is otherwise quite unexpected. Each of the forms has something that makes it suspect. One of the forms with an Acehnese counterpart is *grɔh 'to bark' (Durie's proto-Acehnese reconstruction) but 'to bark' does not reconstruct to the PC level; the two forms in Durie's Acehnese are *dloh* and *kloh* -i; aside from having two variants, the second form has an irregular initial.

Stronger evidence of the non-PC nature of these forms, however, is found in three other areas. First, all the more widely attested sets show irregularities; with the less attested patterns, there are often not enough forms to establish a regular reflex, let alone an irregular one. Second, the vowel of many of the forms is either the /ə/ or the /ɔ/, both vowels only marginally attested in forms inherited from PMP, with the overwhelming attestation in MK borrowings. Third, and quite telling, none of the forms with these clusters is attested in PMP.

The under-representation in Acehnese and Tsat along with the strongest representation in the highlands languages combines to suggest that many of these forms were borrowed after the Acehnese had left the mainland on the journey that would eventually take them to Sumatra and after the Tsat had broken from the Roglai and gone to Hainan, fleeing the Vietnamese push to the south.

The most probable sources of these forms are the MK languages, but if so, the equivalent words in the MK languages have not yet been identified. Thus, for example, with ˣsr- clusters, it is evident that both PMnong and PNB have an *sr- cluster, but to confidently identify MK as the source requires finding the same words.

Still other borrowed clusters exist. In PC, all of the forms beginning with the clusters ˣɓl-, ˣnr-, ˣʔjr- and ˣmr- are borrowings, see Table 40.

Table 40: Other clusters borrowed after the breakup of PC

post-PC	Aceh.	Rade	Jarai	Chru	NR	Tsat	Haroi	W. Cham	PR Cham
ˣɓl-	ɓl-	l-	ɓl-; ɓl-	ɓl-; l-	ɓl-; l-	---	ɓl-	ɓl-	ɓl-
ˣnr-	---	n-	n-; r-	n-	nr-	n-	n-; r-	n-	n-; r-
ˣʔjr-	---	ɗr-	ʔjr-	ir-	ʔj-; ʔjr-	---	ʔjr-	ʔj-	ʔjr-
ˣmr-	mɯr-	mr-	mr-	mr-	mr-	z-	mr-	mr-	mr-
						< *r-			

An examination of the actual forms shows that they are irregular in various ways. In addition, the clusters themselves often indicate these are borrowed, not only from the viewpoint that they are otherwise not permitted PC clusters but also because two of them include imploded consonants.

Table 41: Post-PC borrowed clusters

post-PC	Aceh.	Rade	Chru	NR	PR Cham	
ˣʔjraw	---	ɗrau	iraːu -1	ʔjrau	---	'bamboo sp.'
ˣʔjruah	jlɯh; glɯh	---	iruah	ʔjuah	ʔjrwăh	'barking deer'
ˣɓluar -f	---	luar -v	lər -i	lə -i	---	'to lie'
ˣɓlaŋ	blaŋ	---	ɓlaːŋ	ɓlaːk	ɓlaŋ	'plains; yard'
ˣʔəmraːk	mɯraʔ -v	amrak	amră:ʔ	amra:ʔ	amraʔ	'peacock'
ˣʔamrɛc	---	amreč -v	amrɛʔ -f	amreʔ	amrɛ̆ʔ -f	'pepper; hot'
ˣmray	---	mrai	məraːi	murai	mray	'thread'
ˣʔanrɔːŋ	---	enoŋ -v	anɔːŋ	anroːk	anɔŋ	'carry on pole'
ˣnrən -if	---	---	prən -i	---	---	'numb'
ˣʔanrɔŋ -f	---	---	---	anroʔ -f	arɔ̆ʔ	'toad'

Not surprisingly, not one of these forms has an established PMP etymology. It is also evident from examination not just of the forms in Table 41 but the rest of the data that these forms are concentrated among the Highlands Chamic languages, that is, the languages with the most intense recent contact with MK languages.

WORD-FINAL CONSONANTS

The reflexes of the PC word-final consonants are straightforward. Most of the original finals are preserved in Rade, in Jarai, in Acehnese, and in the older inscriptional Cham. In some words, all the mainland languages have lost the final -t and -p, all, leaving within Chamic only the Acehnese evidence. Everywhere on the mainland, there has been a strong tendency for all the stop finals to reduce to a glottal stop.

Final voiceless stops and affricates

The voiceless final stops and affricates are rapidly losing their contrastiveness throughout Chamic. As Table 42 indicates, the Jarai final glottal stops tend to have two reflexes: one reflecting the proto-final itself, the other a final glottal stop. For instance, there are two reflexes of *-k in Jarai: the dominant reflex is -*k*, and a sizable number of glottal stops. Durie (p.c.) notes that in the Acehnese traditional orthography the final -c is still preserved.

Table 42: Reflexes of PC final voiceless stops and affricates

PC	Aceh.	Rade	Jarai	Chru	NR	Tsat	Haroi	W. Cham	PR Cham
*-p	-p	-p	-p	-ʔ	-ʔ	-ʔ	-ʔ	-ʔ	-ʔ
*-t	-t	-t; -ʔ	-t; -ʔ	-ʔ	-ʔ	-ʔ	-ʔ	-ʔ	-ʔ
*-k	-ʔ	-k	-k; -ʔ	-ʔ	-ʔ	-ʔ	-ʔ	-ʔ	-ʔ
*-ʔ	-ʔ	-ʔ	-ʔ	-ʔ	-ʔ	-ʔ	-ʔ	-ʔ	-ʔ
*-c	-t	-ʔ; -č	-iʔ; -c / u___	-iʔ	-ʔ	-iʔ	-iʔ	-ʔ	-yʔ

Throughout Chamic, as Lee (1974:659-661) has written, there has been a progressive reduction in the number of word-final consonants. Although PMP had at least some voiced word-final obstruents, no word-final voiced consonants are reconstructed as such for PC. This is not surprising as no languages in contact with the mainland Chamic languages have final voiced stops. Similarly, PC *-s and *-h, although reconstructed for PC, have subsequently merged to final -h throughout Chamic, except where the *-s is simply lost. As for the liquids, the final *-r is being lost throughout Chamic, while in Roglai final *-l has become -n, merging with those examples of Roglai -n that have not denasalized.

The final *-h and *-s

Throughout Chamic, both final *-s and *-h have merged almost completely in the modern languages, but in two cases they can still be separated by the differences in the accompanying vowel reflexes. Thus, after two vowels *-u- and *-a:-, the difference between final *-s and *-h is reconstructable. In addition, sometimes the final -s is still preserved in the Acehnese orthography, as Durie notes (p.c.).

After PC short and long *-a-, it is possible to sort out the difference between final the final *-h and *-s, a gap reflecting an earlier merger within PMP. Before final *-h the PMP distinction between PAn *-ə- < e > and *a merged (Bob Blust, p.c.). Since the major source of the length distinction in PC between long and short -a- is the earlier distinction between PMP *-ə- > PC short *-a- and PMP *a > both PC short *-a- and long *-a:-, before final *-h PC did not develop a distinction between PC *-a- and *-a:-.

However, a limited PC length distinction does appear to have developed before the final *-s. In inherited PC words the PAn *a > PC *-a:-, while it appears that the PAn *-ə- > PC *-a-, although this is speculative without more attestation.

The correspondence of PAn *-a- > both PC *-a- and *-a:- is well-attested, but the number of PAn *-ə- to PC *-a- forms is quite marginal with the attestation possibly limited to two examples: *ma-alas 'lazy' and *dras 'fast'. For the first, Blust (1992a) reconstructs *males (the -e- is a schwa) for 'lazy' in his proto-Malayic; for the second, he reconstructs PMP deʀes, both with a schwa before the final *-s.

In Table 43, the length contrast before PC final *-s is widely supported: there are differences between *-as and *-a:s in all the languages in the table. In contrast, the distinction between PC *-as and *-ah depends upon the two Acehnese examples, which conceivably could be the result of widely-attested later Malay influence on Acehnese.

However, even if the distinction between PC *-as and *-ah fails to hold up, the PC sets reconstructed as *-a:s still need to be reconstructed with length: the diphthongization in Acehnese clearly reflects an earlier long vowel, and the length is still retained as such in Chru. Thus, as Durie (p.c.) wrote me, the loss of the final *-s in Tsat reflects a two-stage process: first, the final *-s and *-h merged to *-h, and then the final *-h was lost after long *-a:-.

*Table 43: PC short *-ah and *-as versus long *-a:s*

PC	Aceh.	Rade	Jarai	Chru	NR	Tsat	
*-ah	-ah	-ah	-ah	-ah	-ah	-a^{55}	
*blah	plah -i	blah	blah	blah	blah	phia^{55}	'chop; split'
*lagah	---	egah	rəgah	ləgah	lagah	khe^{55}-v	'tired'
*panah	panah	mənah	pənah	pənah	panãh	na^{55}	'shoot (bow)'
*basah	basah	məsah	pəsah	pəsah	pasah	sa^{55}	'wet; damp'
*-as	-aih	-ah	-ah	-ah	-ah	-a^{55}	
*ma-alas	malaih	alah	ʔalah	alah	alah	---	'lazy'
*dras	draih	---	drah	drah	drah	sia^{55}	'fast'

Versus:

*-a:s	-ɯəh	-aih	-aih	-a:h	-a	-a$^{33/11}$	
*bra:s	brɯəh	braih	braih	bra:h	bra	phia^{11}	'husked rice'
ˣ*kapa:s	gapɯəh	kəpaih	kəpaih	kəpa:h	kapa	pa^{33}	'cotton'
*kaka:s	---	kaih	---	kərka:h	kaka	ka^{33}	'fish scales'
*ʔata:s	atɯəh	taih	ʔataih	ata:h	ata	ta^{33}	'far; above'

There is one more set of forms that need to be mentioned in connection with the discussion of *-as and *-a:s—the forms for 'gold'. Forms for 'gold' resembling the Malay ĕmas are found throughout Southeast Asia. Within PC, reconstruction suggests a borrowed form such as ˣama(:)s, with variable vowel length. The Acehnese mɯih, Chru mĭːh, and Tsat ma^{33} suggest a long vowel, while Western and Phan Rang Cham suggest a short vowel.

In a similar way, the preservation of the *-uh versus *-us distinction is illustrated by the examples in Table 44. Although there is a complete merger in the Bireueng dialect of Acehnese (although not in all dialects), Northern Roglai, and Tsat, the vowel reflexes retain traces of the former distinction between *-uh and *-us in Rade, Jarai, and Chru. The final *-s again produces a final -i- glide in Rade and Jarai and vowel length in Chru, but is merged in N. Roglai and Tsat, becoming *-h (the Tsat 55 tone is a reflex of an earlier *-h).

*Table 44: PC *-uh versus *-us*

PC	Aceh.	Rade	Jarai	Chru	NR	Tsat	
*-uh	-oh	-uh	-uh	-uh	-uh	$-u^{55}$	
^{x}*ʔjuh	---	ʔjuh	ʔjuh	iuh	ʔjuh	$ʔiu^{55}$	'firewood'
*tujuh	tujoh	kjuh	təjuh	təjuh	tijuh	su^{55}	'seven'
*pluh	---	pluh	pluh	spluh	pluh	piu^{55}	'ten'
*labuh	---	ebuh	rəbuh	ləbuh	labuh	phu^{55}	'fall down; drop anchor'
*-us	-oh	-uih	-uih	-uːh	-uh	$-u^{55}$	
*tabus	---	---	---	---	---	phu^{55}	'ransom; save'
*ñus	---	añih	ñuih	ñiːh	ñũh	$ñau^{55}$ -v	'blow nose'
*tikus	tikoh	kəkuih	təkuih	təkuːh	tukuh	ku^{55}	'rat'
*marus	---	ruih lak	---	---	maruh	---	'itch'

The Acehnese treatment of final *-s is of particular interest. The written script preserves -s, as well as also other archaisms, such as final -l, and -c, as both Cowan and Durie have noted, strongly suggesting that the merger of these conso-nants with -h, -y, and -t, respectively, has taken place within the history of Ace-hnese. As Durie notes (p.c.), although final *-s has merged with *-h, the distinction is still preserved in some dialects (e.g. the dialect preserved in the great Djajadiningrat dictionary) where before front vowels the *-s has simply merged with /h/, but after /a/ in particular, the reflex shows up as /-ih/.

The final sonorants

The PC final sonorants are retained essentially unchanged, with the exception of the loss of final *-l and *-r in Acehnese and the N. Roglai alternations.

Table 45: Reflexes of PC final sonorants

PC	Aceh.	Rade	Jarai	Chru	NR	Tsat	Haroi	W. Cham	PR Cham
*-m	-m	-m	-m	-m	-m; -p	-n	-m	-m	-m
*-n	-n	-n	-n	-n	-n; -t	-n	-n	-n	-n
*-ŋ	-ŋ	-ŋ	-ŋ	-ŋ	-ŋ; -k	-ŋ	-ŋ	-ŋ	-ŋ
*-l	-ø	-l	-l	-n	-l	-n	-l	-l	-l
*-r	-ø	-ø; -r	-ø; -l	-ø; -n	-ø; -r	-ø	-ø; -r	-ø; -r	-ø; -r

The splits in the N. Roglai final nasals are regular and are discussed in some detail in the chapter on nasals and nasalization). Durie (p.c.) notes that in Acehnese traditional orthography the final -l, and -r are both preserved, e.g. *wil 'circle' is *wil* in the traditional writing. In some cases in spoken Acehnese, it is lost after front vowels and diphthongs but in other instances it shows up as the glide -y; in other dialects a reflex is preserved even after the diphthongs.

6

Chamic Vowels

The Austronesian speakers who arrived on the coast of the Southeast Asian mainland spoke a basically disyllabic language with a relatively modest vowel inventory. There were four basic vowels: *-a, *-i, *-u, *-e ([-ə]) as well as three final diphthongs: *-ay, *-uy, and *-aw; the four vowels occurred in both syllables of the disyllabic forms, while the diphthongs were restricted to the final syllable.

Under the influence of intense contact with MK languages, this pre-Chamic PMP language adopted the main syllable stress of the neighboring MK languages, a change that is reflected in the contrasts between the vowel inventories of the pre- and the main syllable. Unlike the PMP disyllables where there was a balanced four-way vowel contrast in both the syllables, in PC the vowel inventories were anything but symmetrical: in the unstressed PC pretonic syllable, the four-way PMP vowel distinction has been retained in the presyllable, but in the stressed main syllable the four-way distinction has been expanded to roughly 18 or so distinct vowels, not counting length contrasts.

Some of these new main-syllable vowels developed out of splits of inherited PMP vowels, but the bulk of the forms with new vowels are found in pre-Chamic borrowings from MK. Thus, the main vowels of PC include two readily-discernible historical layers: those vowels inherited from PMP, which form the core of the basic vowel system, and those vowels which primarily reflect MK influence and overwhelmingly occur in pre-Chamic MK borrowings.

While often distinguishable, the two layers are not always completely distinct: sometimes the phonology of the MK borrowings matched the phonology of the PMP lexicon, making the borrowed form indistinguishable on purely phonological grounds from inherited PMP forms; undoubtedly, sometimes the phonology of the MK borrowings was restructured by the pre-Chamic speakers to match the phonology of the PMP lexicon, again making the forms blend phonologically with the inherited PMP forms. In other instances, new phonological contrasts entered pre-PC with the MK borrowings.

Among forms carrying new phonological contrasts, the majority of the words are identifiable as MK loans into pre-Chamic, while the bulk of the remaining forms are potentially of MK origin as they lack etymologies, PMP or otherwise. However, although the preponderance of forms containing new vowels are MK borrowings, usually sprinkled in among the MK forms are also one or two words with straightforward, well-attested PMP etymologies. Two stages appear to have occurred with such words: First, the MK contact led to the development and phonemicization of a vowel distinction already present in the phonetics of the PMP forms. Second, the development of the new sound in an PMP form would have significantly lessened the need to restructure the incoming MK loanwords containing the new vowel. Thus, when MK loanwords with new loan phonemes were encountered, the new phonemes were borrowed along with the loanword.

THE LITERATURE

While earlier writers stopped at noting and commenting on the resemblances between Cham and other languages—sometimes showing great insight, the scientific study of comparative Chamic vowels can only be said to have begun with the first attempts to establish sound correspondences. Sound correspondences between PMP and PC were first given by Pittman (1959), followed by Blood (1962), and Thomas (1963), and later by Dyen (1971a). In addition, the sound correspondences within the modern Chamic languages were discussed by Lee (1966), primarily, but also Burnham (1976), and others. With these works, the comparative study of Chamic began.

Now, in light of the work of Headley (1976) and of several writers who have tentatively reconstructed subgroups of MK languages of Vietnam it is usually possible to sort out the MK borrowings from the native PC material, and, as a consequence, it is now also possible to revise these earlier analyses. For the identification of MK words, in addition to Headley, there are reconstructions available of two branches of Mon-Khmer found in Vietnam. Within the Bahnaric branch, reconstruction work on three subgroups have been carried out: South Bahnaric: Efimov 1987; H. Blood (on the Proto-Mnong subset of South Bahnaric) 1967, 1968, 1974; North Bahnaric: Smith 1972; and West Bahnaric: Thomas (in Prachacakij-karacak 1995). Two reconstructions of the Katuic branch have been

done: Peiros 1996 and Thomas 1967. These works make possible the identification of a large number of MK loans while particular phonological features often
make it possible to classify them as either pre-Chamic or post-PC loans.

Further, the expansion of the data has led to numerous revisions of individual lexical reconstructions and minor modifications in the overall vowel
inventory, although Lee's basic outline is still quite workable today. In addition,
of course, more recent studies of various Chamic languages has also led to
increased understanding of PC vowels and their correspondences (Edmondson
and Gregerson 1991; Friberg and Kvoeu-Hor 1977; Thurgood 1998).

As for PC vowel correspondences, only Lee (1966) actually set out the
main vowel correspondences, but he based his analysis on a corpus with numerous unidentified MK words. As a result, over 10% of his reconstructed forms are
actually MK borrowings, many of them borrowed after the breakup of PC. Once
these are identified some of Lee's marginally-attested vowel correspondences
either disappear or merge with other better-attested correspondences. Another
adjustment to Lee's scheme involves the reanalysis of his treatment of nasalized
vowels. Lee reconstructed a number of nasalized vowels in PC to account for the
failure of certain Roglai word-final nasals to denasalize. However, once the post-
PC MK borrowings are removed from the data base, it becomes clear that the
majority of the Roglai changes are internal to Roglai, leaving only a handful of
nasalized vowels in PC. Finally, as the result of the identification of loans and
modifications in the analysis of countless individual words, Lee's *ɔ and *o have
both been reconstructed as just a single *ɔ, in part by assigning some *ɔ reflexes
to *ə, but occasionally by assigning some elsewhere. This accumulation of minor
revisions has resulted in a modification of the general scheme in Lee 1966.

As is true throughout this work, in the discussion to follow four major
time divisions are distinguished: (i) the PMP period predating contact with MK
languages the pre-Chamic period, (ii) the period in which early contact occurred
but which predates what we reconstruct as PC, (iii) the stretch of time during
which what we reconstruct as PC was spoken, and (iv) the period following the
breakup of PC, including the modern period.

THE PC PRESYLLABLE VOWELS

The fully disyllabic forms of PMP were radically restructured in pre-Chamic. In
fact, by PC the reflexes of these once truly disyllabic forms had come to consist
of an unstressed atonic presyllable followed by an enriched, stressed tonic syllable. Under the influence of contact with neighboring MK languages, pre-Chamic
developed word-final stress, leading to the proliferation of contrasts in the
stressed final syllable and eventually to the reduction of contrasts in the
unstressed syllable.

This reduction of the first syllable of the PMP disyllable to an atonic presyllable in most of the modern languages is reflected both in the fact that the presyllable has become exclusively CV in structure and in the widespread reduction in vowel contrasts. Both the first syllable of the PMP ancestral disyllable and the first syllable of PC had a four-way contrast, but this four-way distinction is only preserved in Acehnese—the remaining Chamic languages have essentially lost most of the vowel contrasts, at most preserving a three-way distinction in specific contexts.

And, while Acehnese still preserves a four-way contrast, many of the other individual daughter languages have proceeded further along a path toward monosyllabicity, with the directionality and the end point of these changes often provided not so much by internal forces within the phonologies of the daughter languages but by the phonological structures of the languages these languages were in contact with.

PC still maintains the four-way distinction, as is evident in the comparison of the Acehnese data with, for example, PMP or Malay, but, within mainland Chamic, a three-way, rather than four-way, contrast can only be partially reconstructed and then only in certain contexts. Some evidence is found in Northern Roglai and some appears to exist in early inscriptional Cham, with additional bits and pieces of evidence found scattered elsewhere. The evidence provided by the existing forms in the various daughter languages must, however, be used with some caution as there have been several internal realignments of the presyllable vowels both in Roglai and in Cham, often giving the illusion that vowel contrasts have been preserved but with the vowels in question actually being the product of secondary developments. Thus, as comparisons among PMP, Acehnese, and mainland Chamic make clear, in the mainland Chamic languages, the presyllable vowels have undergone secondary shifts and reductions that sometimes totally obscure the nature of the original vowel.

The Written Cham data has undoubtedly preserved more information than is contained in this work, as Written Cham records contain the earliest Austronesian recorded, but this would require considerable philological work and careful diachronic analysis. Perhaps some of this has been done already and I am simply unaware of it. In any case, it is unclear how much would be learned from such philological work since Acehnese also preserves the PMP four-way vowel distinction, so such work would very likely do little more than simply confirm what is already known.

Preservation of the original PC four-way distinction

In the modern mainland Chamic languages, the four-way contrast is still largely preserved as a three-way distinction after initial glottal stops, and remnants of the system are preserved in Roglai and Cham, but in these languages subsequent secondary vowel shifts have obscured what little remains of the original vowels. Occasional glimpses of the original vowels have been preserved as the result of sporadic metathesis in which the first syllable vowel shifts to the main syllable.

Preservation after initial glottal stops

In mainland Chamic, there is a three-way distinction between *i, *u, and *a (with the merger of PMP *ə and *a) still largely preserved in both Roglai and Cham after an initial glottal stop.

Table 46: The preservation of PC first syllable vowels after glottal initials

Malay	PC	Aceh.	Chru	NR	PR Cham	
ikan	*ʔikaːn	---	akaːn	ikaːt	ikan	'fish'
hidung	*ʔiduŋ	idoŋ	aduŋ	idŭk	iʈŭŋ	'nose'
ikat	*ʔikat	ikat	akaʔ	ikaʔ	ikăʔ	'to tie'
urat	*ʔurat	urat	araʔ	uraʔ	urăʔ	'vein, tendon'
ular	*ʔular	ulɯə	ala	ula	ula	'snake'
akar	*ʔughaːr	ukhɯə	akha	ukha	uӄha	'root'
orang	*ʔuraːŋ -1	urɯəŋ	araːŋ	uraːk	uraŋ	'person; someone'
anak	*ʔanaːk	anɯ	anaːʔ	ană:ʔ	aniʔ	'child'
atas	*ʔataːs	atɯəh	ataːh	ata	atăh	'far; above; long'
asah	*ʔasah	asah	asah	asah	ʈhăh	'sharpen'
asap	*ʔasap	asap	asaʔ	asaʔ	athăʔ	'smoke (of a fire)'
api	*ʔapuy	apui	apui	apui	apuy	'fire'
angin	*ʔaŋin	aŋɛn	aŋin	aŋin	aŋĭn	'the wind'
hantu	*ʔantɔw	ɯntɛə	atəu	atəu	atŏw	'ghost; corpse'

The Malay in Table 46 reflects the original PMP first syllable vowels fairly well, although the first vowel of *orang* comes from an earlier /u/. It is also worth noting that, while the Roglai data appears to reflect both the PMP and the PC distinctions rather faithfully, several of the Cham reflexes also have another reflex, one reflecting the older vowel and the other reflecting the vowel's subsequent reduction to /a/.

Preservation in other phonetic environments

The PMP four-way distinction between *u, *i, *a, and *ə has been preserved in Malay and in Acehnese (three of these are reflected in Table 47), but is reduced to a three-way distinction in mainland Chamic with the merger of *a and *ə to *a, probably phonetically a shwa in the onset syllable. This preservation is somewhat sporadic, with much of the crucial evidence coming from much, much earlier Written Cham records and inscriptions.

Table 47: The preservation of PC first syllable vowels in other environments

Malay	PC	Aceh.	NR	PR Cham	Wr. Cham	
dikit	*dikit	dit -mv	tikiːʔ	takiʔ	dikik	'few; little'
timun	*timun	timɔn	tumŭn	tamŭn	tamun	'melon'
---	*gigɛy	gigɔə	digəi	takĕy	tagĕi	'tooth'
tulang	*tulaːŋ	tulɯəŋ	tulaːk	talaŋ	tulaŋ; talaŋ	'bone'
kuku	*kukɔw	gukɛə	kukəu	kakŏw	kukau; kakŏu	'claw'
rusa	*rusa	rusa	rusa	ritha; ratha	rusā; rasā	' Sambhur deer'
huma	*huma	umʌŋ	humã	hamu -v	humā; hamū	'field'
bunga	*buŋa	buŋɔŋ	buŋã	piŋu	buŋə; baŋɨ	'flower'
kutu	*kutɔw	gutɛə	kutəu	katŏw	katŏu	'head louse'

Notice that a three-way distinction is partially retained in Roglai, and almost totally lost elsewhere in mainland Chamic. Despite the occasional illusion of having kept an original PMP vowel in the first syllable, modern Phan Rang Cham has virtually lost these distinctions. In fact, the vowels in all, not just some, of the Phan Rang Cham forms are the result of reduction—in most instances, they have an /a/ reflex. In other cases, they are the result of a secondary development—in these cases, they have an /i/ reflex. Modern Phan Rang Cham does have its own distinctions among these vowels, but these distinctions are the result of various secondary developments.

In contrast, the Written Cham forms, particularly the forms recorded in the dictionary of Aymonier and Cabaton (1906) seem to preserve a great number of older vowel distinctions. However, this material must be used with great caution. The entries reflect various time periods and sources blended together. As a consequence, the Aymonier and Cabaton Written Cham material has a great deal of variation, some of which can be made sense of and some of which is simply quite puzzling.

Sporadic preservation of /u/ through metathesis

Aside from what has been preserved in Roglai and Cham, there are also a handful of cases in which an original first vowel /u/ was preserved through sporadic metathesis (m).

*Table 48: Sporadic metathesis of first syllable *u*

PC	Aceh.	Rade	Jarai	Chru	NR	
*hurɛy	urɔə	hrue (m)	hrəi	hərəi	hurəi	'day; sun'
*huma	umʌŋ	həma	həma	həma	humã	'field'
*hubɛy	ubi -f	habɛi	habəi	habəi	habuəi (m)	'taro; yam'
*durɛy	durɔə	erue(m)	drəi; trəi	druəi (m)	daruəi (m)	'thorn'
*ʔurat	urat	aruăt (m)	ʔaraʔ -v	araʔ	uraʔ	'vein'
*hulat	ulat	hluăt (m)	hluăt (m)	hэlaʔ	hulaʔ	'worm'

Note that in Table 48, there is sporadic metathesis of first syllable *u, resulting in a /u/ showing up in the second syllable, often along with the expected vowel reflex. Although they are not included in the table, in a number of cases, the languages in question also have a non-metathesized variant. The directionality of these changes is particularly clear when the forms are compared with the non-metathesized Acehnese forms.

Various shifts in the three-way distinction

In addition to the massive reduction of the four-way distinction in first syllable vowels throughout much of Chamic, at times in Roglai and at times in Cham there have been secondary vowel shifts further hindering the identification of the original PC vowel.

Independent secondary shifts in Roglai and Cham

Two separate shifts are illustrated in Table 49. In Roglai, one well-attested shift is the change of an earlier vowel to /u/ after *r-, *l-, *m-, *t- and before a bilabial. Often Roglai has variant forms, one with the secondary /u/ and one without; occasionally, one variant shows up in the data recorded by Awoi-hathe *et al.* while another shows up in the material collected by Lee. An additional complicating factor is the apparent sporadic vowel harmony in Roglai, in which the presyllable vowel assimilates to the /u/ in the main syllable, as in 'needle', 'that', and so on (see Appendix II).

The other secondary development illustrated by much of the same data in Table 49 is the change in Phan Rang Cham of a presyllable vowel to /i/ after either *r- or *l-. As with any vowel in the presyllable, there is variation between /i/ and the reduced /ə/. This Cham development, however, is only a part of a more general change in Cham (see "Secondary shifts in Cham" on page 112 just below). Cabaton (1901) noted that the first vowel in *ribut* 'storm' was, apparently, at that time, a barred-i.

Table 49: The Roglai shift to /u/ and the Cham shift to /i/

Malay	PC	Aceh.	NR	PR Cham	Wr. Cham	
lapar	*lapa	---	lapa	lipa; lapa	lipā; lapa	'hungry'
lĕmbu	ˣ*ləmɔ	lɯmɔ	lamo -n	limɔ; lamɔ	lamau	'cow; ox'
---	*lamaːn	---	lumãn	limɨn	limɨn; lamɨn	'elephant'
labuh	*labuh	---	labuh	lipuh; lapuh	libuh; labuh	'fall down'
lĕmak	ˣ*ləmaʔ	lɯmaʔ	lumãʔ	limɨ̆ʔ; lamɨ̆ʔ	liməʔ; laməːʔ	'fat, oil'
lĕbih	*ləbɛh	lɯbɛh	lubeh	lipɛh; lapĕh	lubaih; labaih	'more'
	-v					
lipan	*limpaːn	limpɯən	lupaːt	lipan; lapan	lipan; lapan	'centipede'
mimpi	*lumpɛy	lumpɔə	lupəi	lipĕy; lapĕy	lipĕi; lapĕi	'to dream'
luka	*luka	luka	---	lika-likĕh	likā; lukā	'wound'
lubang	*lubaːŋ	---	lubaːk	lipaŋ; lapaŋ	liɓāng; lubaŋ; labaŋ	'hole; pit'
rĕbung	*rabuŋ	---	rubuk	ripuŋ; rapŭŋ	rabung	'bamboo shoot'
nipis	*lipih	lipeh	lupih	lipĭh; lapĭh	lapih	'thin'
lima	*lima	limʌŋ	lumã	limi; lamɨ	limi; limə̄	'five'
ribut	ˣ*ribuːʔ	---	rubuːʔ	ripuʔ; rapuʔ	rabuʔ	'storm'
ribu	*ribɔw	ribɛə	rubəu	ripŏw; rapŏw	ribuv; ribŏu	'thousand'
mamah	*mamah	mamʌh	mumãh	mɨmih	mɨmih	'chew'
babah	*mabah	---	mubah	papah	babah, pabah	'mouth'
---	*mamih	mamɛh	mumĩh	mɨmĭh	mɨmih, mamih	'sweet'
timun	*timun	timɔn	tumũn	tamŭn	tamun	'melon'
tumbuh	*tamuh	---	tumũh	tamŭh	timuh; tamuh	'to grow'
dĕpa	*dəpa	---	tupa	tapa	dapā	'armspan'

In another subset of forms, various presyllable vowels have become /i/ in Roglai before certain alveolars,[1] but without more examples even a general idea of what is conditioning this change is difficult to figure out.

---

1. As is well known, in a large number of AN languages /t/ is dental while /d/ and /n/ are alveolar.

Table 50: The Roglai shift to /i/ before an alveolar

Malay	PC	Aceh.	NR	PR Cham	Wr. Cham	
---	*batɛy	---	pitəi	patĕy	patĕi	'banana'
darah	*darah	darah	darah	ʈarằh	daraḥ	'blood'
dada	*dada	dada	dada	taʈa	dadā, tada	'chest'
dalam	*dalam	dalam	dalap	ʈalằm	dalaṃ	'inside; in'
batuk	*batuk	bato?	pitu?	patŭ?	batuk	'cough'
---	*gigɛy	gigɔə	digəi	takĕy	tagĕi	'tooth'
---	*bitu?	---	pitu?	pitŭ?; patŭ?	batuk; butuk	'star'
bini	*binay	---	binằi	pinay	binai	'virgin'
bulu	*bulɔw	bulɛə	biləu	pilɔ̆w; palɔ̆w	bulɔ̆u; baluw	'body hair'
bulan	*bula:n	bulɯən	bila:t	pilan	bulan; balan	'moon'
gatal	*gatal	gatai	katan	katằl	gatal; katal	'itchy'
---	*gətak	---	kata?	katằ?	gatak; kātak	'sap; resin'

The interaction of these various secondary developments makes the reconstruction of presyllable vowels extremely tenuous at least on the basis of non-Acehnese Chamic data alone. However, since these are well-preserved in Acehnese and elsewhere outside of mainland Chamic, it is of little consequence.

Secondary shifts in Cham

In Phan Rang Cham, there is a somewhat similar shift from various presyllable vowels to /i/, but with several more conditions than in the Northern Roglai examples: the initial must be a bilabial stop and the following main syllable onset not only must be an alveolar but it also must be either a sonorant or be a sonorant descended from a voiced obstruent (and, thus, the following vowel has breathy voice).

Table 51: Shifts in Cham to /i/ before alveolars

Malay	PC	Aceh.	Rade	W. Cham	PR Cham	
---	*bara	---	mra	pra	pirā	'shoulder'
---	*banut	---	mənŭt	---	pinu?	'banyan, balete'
bini	*binay	---	mənie	panai	pinay	'virgin; woman'
bulan	*bula:n	bulɯən	mlan	ea plan	pilan	'moon; month'
bulu	*bulɔw	bulɛə	mlằu	plau	pilɔ̆w	'body hair'
biji	ˣ*bijɛh	bijɛh	mjɛh	paçɛh	paçɛh	'seed'
babi	*babuy	bui	---	papui	papuy	'wild pig'
---	*babah	babah	---	papah	papah	'mouth'

This change, like many of the secondary shifts of presyllable vowels discussed in this section, seems to be relatively recent as only a small number of these second-arily-derived vowels are in Aymonier and Cabaton's 1906 dictionary, but they are rather common in Moussay's 1971 dictionary.

THE INHERITED PC MAIN SYLLABLE VOWELS

The PC vowel system developed out of an PMP system with four basic vowels and three diphthongs. The typical morpheme was disyllabic, with each of the four vowels occurring in either syllable, but with the diphthongs restricted to the final syllable.

Figure 8: PMP second syllable vowels > PC main syllable vowels

PMP second syllable vowels			PC main syllable vowels		
*i		*u	*-i-,		*-u-,
			*-ụ̣ > *-ɛy	*-ʊy̦ > *-ɔw	
	*-ə- < e >	>	*-ə-		
*a			*a (short) / *-a:-		
*-ay	*-uy		*-ay	*-uy	
*-aw			*-aw		

The transition from PMP to PC vowels was not particularly complex. Both PMP high vowels split, becoming diphthongs in final position (at least when lengthened by stress), but remaining unchanged in closed syllables. The PMP shwa, which never occurred word-finally in PMP, everywhere ceased to be a shwa; in all contexts, it became PC *a. The old PMP *a reflexes split before certain finals, with some reflexes of PMP *a becoming PC *-a- and others becoming PC *-a:-, thus introducing in those positions a PC length distinction. In PC, the old PMP shwa disappeared as such, although a new shwa appears in the PC inventory brought in by pre-PC borrowings from MK. As for the old PMP diphthongs, they entered PC unchanged.

The path from PMP to PC was illustrated in Figure 8. The next stage involves the breakup of PC into its various daughter languages, including Ace-hnese, a stage which is more complicated than the transition from PMP to PC and cannot be fully represented in Table 52 (cf. Figure 12 and accompanying text).

Although this table introducing the vowels is somewhat simplified, it is a good representation of the basic vowel reflex patterns, with several qualifications. First, in two languages, the vowels correspondences are too complicated to repre-sent clearly on the table. The vowels of Haroi, which have registrally-induced vowel splits, are discussed later (in "Haroi vowels and restructured register" on page 197). The vowels of Acehnese, which often have multiple reflexes due to vowel lowering induced by nasalization, are also treated later, as the correspondences (Table 52), although regular, are somewhat over-simplified.

Table 52: The basic main syllable vowel reflexes

PMP	PC	Aceh.	Rade	Jarai	Chru	NR	Tsat	W. Cham	PR Cham
*i	*-ɛy	-ɔə	-ɛi	-əi	-əi	-əi	-ai	-ay	-ɛ̆y
*i-	*-i-	-e-; -ɛ-	-i-	-i-	-i-	-i-	-i-	-i-	-i-
*u	*-ɔw	-ɛə	-ău	-əu	-əu	-əu	-au; -(i)ə	-au	-ɔ̆w
*u-	*-u-	-o-; -ɔ-	-u-	-u-	-u-	-u-	-u-	-u-	-u-
*ə-	*-a-	a	-a-	-a-	-a-	-a-	-a-	-a-	-a-
*a-	*a	a; ɯə	a	a	a	a	a	a	a
*-uy	*-uy	-ui	-ui	-ui	-ui	-ui	-ui	-ui	-uy
*-ay	*-ay	-e; ---	-ie	-ai	-ai	-ai	-aːiʔ[42]	-ai	-ay
*-aw	*-aw	-o; -ɔ	-au	-au	-au	-au	-au	-au	-aw

Second, the crucial issue of vowel length, of considerable importance to both the analysis of borrowing and to PC subgrouping questions, is given a long and detailed treatment later ("PC vowel length" on page 138). Third, various minor subpatterns are treated elsewhere as they come up, including the sporadic metathesis found scattered throughout Chamic, the Western and Phan Rang Cham reflexes of nasalized reflexes of PC *a found in Western and Phan Rang Cham, and the interesting reflexes of PC *-ay and *ɛy found in Rade.

The splits in the PMP high vowels *i and *u

Thomas (1963) laid out the basic patterns for the splitting of the PMP high vowels into two conditioned reflexes: For both high vowels, her tables make it clear that in open syllables (and before -h), the PMP *i and *u lengthen in open syllables and subsequently diphthongize, while in closed syllables (except before -h), they remain high monophthongs.

An examination of Thomas' distributions, suggests that except for the forms with final -h, the splits correlate with whether or not the forms occur word-finally. And, in fact, the final -h in these forms is spurious. Thomas's analysis of the patterns was obscured by a spurious final -h in Dempwolff's PMP reconstructions (Dempwolff's "spiritus asper"); once Dempwolff's spurious final -h is eliminated from Thomas' reconstructions, her description of the split is accurate.

Despite using Dyen (1953) in which Dyen corrects Dempwolff, Thomas was nonetheless misled by Dempwolff's spurious finals since, for the forms not found in Dyen, she reverted to Dempwolff's reconstructions.

The diphthongization patterns

Several diphthongization cases will be discussed in this chapter, but the first to occur historically and thus the most central is the chain by which the high, stressed *i and *u of PMP first lengthened under stress, becoming early-PC *-ị̈ and *-ụụ (the *-ụụ is apparently preserved as such in the older Written Cham records as < -uw >), going on to become < -ɛ̆y > and < -ɔ̆w > in later Written Cham (with the /-ɛi/ also preserved as such in Rade), next becoming /-əi/ and /-əu/ (preserved as such in Jarai, Chru, and Northern Roglai), and then ultimately ending up as /-ăị/ and /-ăụ/ in modern spoken Phan Rang Cham and Tsat.

The diphthongization was restricted to the high, stressed vowels, and, as Cowan (1974:189) emphasized, the stressed vowels became long before diphthongizing. The unstressed high vowels did not lengthen, and thus did not participate in the changes. Acehnese provides some clear examples of the distinct treatment of stressed and unstressed vowels. In particular, Acehnese has several reflexes of PMP *aku 'I': the vowel in the stressed independent morpheme *keə* is a diphthong, while the vowels in the two unstressed affixes, the prefix *ku-* and the suffix *-ku(h)*, have remained undiphthongized.

The initial part of this diphthongization chain reflects what Donegan (1985, and, p.c.) describes as the tendency for tense vowels to lengthen and then diphthongize as upgliding: the PMP *-i and *-u become early-PC *-ị̈ and *-ụụ, respectively. Subsequently, both onsets underwent lowering, leading to the PC vowels *-ɛy and *-ɔw, respectively. Next, the onsets of both vowels lose their color, that is, the *-ɛy loses its palatality, while the *-ɔw loses its labiality, producing *-əị and *-əụ, respectively.

Figure 9: Diphthongization chains for PC word-final high vowels

PMP	>	early-PC	>	PC	>	Jarai...	>	PR Cham, Tsat
*-i	>	*-ị̈	>	*-ɛy	>	*-əị	>	/-ăi/
*-u	>	*-ụụ	>	*-ɔw	>	*-əụ	>	/-ău/

Finally, the further lowering of *-əị and *-əụ in Tsat and in spoken Phan Rang Cham to -ăi and -ău was noted in Blood 1967 and later discussed in Donegan (1985:133). Note that, except for the PC form *-ị̈, each of the posited steps is attested either in one of in Written Cham or in one of the modern Chamic languages.

Most stages in the diphthongization chain posited in Figure 9 are attested in the variation in Aymonier and Cabaton's 1906 dictionary of Cham, a dictionary that is panchronic in the sense that the spellings of the words apparently come from texts spanning the whole history of Cham writing.

Figure 10: Diphthongization chain steps attested in Written Cham

PMP	>	Early	>	Later	>	...		>	Modern
*-i	>	*-ɨi̯	>	*-ɛy	>	-əi̯		>	/-ăi/
*-u	>	*-Uṷ	>	*-ɔw	>	-əṷ		>	/-ău/
*baru	>	baruw	>	barɔw	>	...		>	barau 'new'
*təbu	>	tābuw	>	tabɔw	>	...		>	tabauw 'sugarcane'

Although the entries in Aymonier and Cabaton are not dated, if the range of Written Cham variation is placed on the chain, three of the four stages posited for the transition from early-PC *-Uṷ to modern PR Cham /-ău/ are attested.

The diphthongization chain in Figure 9 and Figure 10 should be familiar to historical linguists because it is also well attested in the history of Germanic. As Donegan (1985:214) points out, the following diphthongization chain has occurred repeatedly in Germanic, citing Stampe (1972) for the history of English, Priebsch and Collinson (1966) for Standard German, and Sapir (1915) for Yiddish.

Figure 11: Germanic diphthongization chains

i̱	>	ɨi̯	>	ɛy	>	ʌi̯	>	ɑi̯
u̱	>	Uṷ	>	ɔw	>	ʌṷ	>	ɑṷ

Note that the Germanic process has stressed vowels becoming long and only after becoming long do they diphthongize. It is also worth noting that, if the shwa in PC were replaced by ʌ and the -ă- in Phan Rang Cham were replaced by ɑ, the PC chains and the Germanic chains in Figure 11 would be identical.

Along with the rest of Chamic, Acehnese inherited diphthongized variants of proto-Malayic word-final *-i and *-u, where the stressed PMP > proto-Malayic high vowels *-i and *-u underwent lengthening and then diphthongization. Within PC, the chain of Acehnese diphthongization was, of course, identical with the developments in mainland Chamic up to the point where the Acehnese migrated to northern Sumatra, which seems to be while the PC diphthongs were still preserved as *-ɛy and *-ɔw. As Durie notes (p.c.), the dialect data preserves a complete record of the various Acehnese stages in the development of PMP *-i > proto-Malayic *-i > PC *-ɛy to Acehnese *-ɛy > Acehnese -ɔi̯ to Acehnese (Bireuen) -ɔə̯, that is, the dialect data contains the -ɛy posited for PC as well as both the -ɔi̯, and the -ɔə̯ posited as stages in the development of the Bireuen forms. However, the dialect data has not preserved parallel forms for the stages in the development of *-u > -ɛə̯.

Figure 12: Acehnese diphthongization chains

						modern
PMP >	early-PC >	PC	> Acehnese >	Acehnese >	Acehnese
*-i	> *-i̯i̯	> *-ɛy	> -ɛy	> -ɔi̯	> -ɔə̯
*-u	> *-u̯u̯	> *-ɔw	> *-ɛu̯	> *-ɛy	> -ɛə̯

After that, the mainland Chamic languages and certain dialects of Acehnese took different paths of development. First, some Acehnese dialects dissimilated the syllabic onsets of both *-ɛy and *-ɔw, producing *-ɔi̯ and *-ɛu̯, respectively. This dissimilative fortition effectively reversed the earlier vowel quality distinctions in the onset of the diphthongs! Then, apparently reflecting the tendency for lax vowels to develop ingliding diphthongs (Donegan 1985), these Acehnese dialects reduced both diphthong upglides into shwa, turning pre-Acehnese *-ɔi̯ and *-ɛu̯ to Acehnese -ɔə and -ɛə, respectively.

Thus, despite the common starting point and the early shared paths of development, the PC and some of the Acehnese chains ultimately diverged sharply, resulting in reflexes that correspond perfectly diachronically but are quite distinct phonetically.

Reflexes of PMP *-i- and *-i

In the transition from PMP to PC, the reflexes of the PMP high vowel *i split: in closed syllables and in unstressed open syllables, it remained *-i-, while in open stressed syllables, it became early-PC *-i̯i̯ and then PC *-ɛy. It is important to note that, while most PMP forms do, not all the PMP open syllable *-i reflexes go to PC *-ɛy. For a small number of grammatical forms, the PMP open-syllable *i displays a Chamic pattern of reflexes that matches the reflex pattern for *-i-.

The last two of the three grammatical morphemes in Table 53 sometimes pattern with the *-ɛy forms and sometimes pattern with the *-i forms, suggesting that there was originally an unstressed and a stressed variant, with the unstressed variant going on to pattern with *-i and the stressed one with *-ɛy. Acehnese supplies several nice pairs of contrasting stressed versus unstressed reflexes, with one of these being the stressed Acehnese sɔə 'who' and the unstressed si 'title for people's names'.[2]

*Table 53: PC open syllables with *-i in unstressed syllables*

PC	Aceh.	Rade	Jarai	Chru	NR	Haroi	PR Cham	
*dĭ	di	ţi	---	tə-	---	---	ţi	'at'
*-nĭ	---	---	---	ni	tinĭ	ni	ni	'this'
*-nɛy	-nɔə	-nɛi	-nai	---	---	---	---	
*kamĭ	---	---	---	---	---	---	kami	'we (ex.)'
*kamɛy	kamɔə	həmɛi	gəmai	---	labu?-	kəmei;		
		-iv	-iv		kamîn ?	kəme -v		

It is important to note that the forms themselves are inherited, not borrowed. Malay, for example, has the preposition *di*, the demonstratives *ini* and *ni*, and the pronoun *kami* for the corresponding forms. Their unique reflex pattern comes from their occurrence in a unique phonological environment: these forms typically occur stressed in some contexts but unstressed in others.

Other sources

The majority of the remaining PC *-i finals are in early borrowings, although two of these forms are found elsewhere in Austronesian.

*Table 54: Two other early borrowings with PC open syllable *-i*

PC	Rade	Jarai	Chru	NR	Haroi	PR Cham	
ˣˣsisi(r)	kəsi	təsi	təsi	kasi	cəsei	tathi	'a comb'
*pagi	məgi	pəgi	pəgi	pagi	pəkhι	paķe	'tomorrow'
	-v					-v	

Headley suggests that 'comb' is a borrowing from MK, but, if so, its presence in Malay as *sisir* requires that it also have been borrowed into Malay. In

2.   The pattern reflects a restriction on stress distribution, not the difference between content words and grammatical morphemes. The apparent exceptions—the grammatical morphemes—are in practice usually encliticized into larger constructions and are thus a part of a larger phonological word.

any case, the actual PC reflex may simply reflect the final *-ir. As clearly occurred with PMP forms ending in final *-ur, the vowel was not in an open syllable when open syllable PMP *-i went to PC *ɛy. Rather, the *-ir lost the final -r only later, and thus did not diphthongize. However, with the form *pagi*, which shows up in Malay as *pagi*, the PC final *-i is both unexpected and unexplainable, unless it is a Malay borrowing.

All the remaining forms that pattern like PC final *-i are loans, in many cases loans that postdate the breakup of PC. Headley has identified a number of these as loans; many also evidence irregular correspondence patterns. For 'scissors', Headley (#1.54) suggests that it is a MK loan, while another author has suggested the less likely Tamil form *kĕlĕkati* 'areca-nut scissors'. For 'horn; antler', Headley (#1.34) identifies it is MK in origin, while it also looks like a PLB form.

Most, and probably all, of the forms below are loans. Headley (1976) has suggested that three of these forms are borrowed on the basis of the MK data. His contention receives support from Chamic: for all three forms, the correspondence patterns within Chamic are irregular, indicating that the borrowing postdates the breakup of PC. With 'horn' even the representation of the borrowed form as ˣtuki is quite problematic: first, it is quite possible it was borrowed more than once with different forms. And, second, there are at least three distinct variants in the data: Northern Roglai (Lee) *tukɨ* (with the barred-ɨ being the expected reflex of an earlier medial -r-), PNB *ake, and Proto-Mnong *ŋke. It is instructive that Acehnese only has a form for one of these, *unɔə* for 'honey bee'.

*Table 55: Borrowings with post-PC open syllable *-i*

post-PC	Rade	Jarai	Chru	NR	Haroi	W. Cham	PR Cham	
ˣkatri	kətrɛi	---	kətrəi -f	katri	kətrǒi -vf	katray	---	'scissors'
ˣtuki -v	ki -v	təki	təki	tuki	cəke -v	take -v	take	'horn; antler'
ˣlaʔi -f	ei	rəʔi	ləʔi	laʔi	ləʔi	laʔi	lii	'winnowing basket'
ˣtali	---	kli -i	---	---	cəlei	---	tali	'flat (of rocks)'
ˣhuni	hənue	həni	həni	hunî	həni	hani	hani	'honey bee'

Throughout Chamic, the reflex of PC *-i- was simply -i-, often marked in closed syllables as short or long by various authors but although length is apparently contrastive in individual languages, the length does not reconstruct to PC. Not only does the length not agree across languages but within the individual languages its occurrence can be predicted on the basis of the environments.

Table 56: Reflexes of PC *-i- < PMP *-i-

Acehnese	Rade	Jarai	Chru	NR	W. Cham	PR Cham
-eh; -ɛh	-ih	-ih	-ih	-ih	-ĭh	-ĭh; -ih
-em; ---	-ĭm	-ĭm; -im	-im	-ip	-ĭm	-ĭm
-eʔ; -ɛʔ	-ĭʔ	-ĭʔ	-iːʔ	-iːʔ	-iʔ	-iʔ
-et; -ɛt	-ĭt; -ĭʔ	-it; -iʔ	-iːʔ	-iːʔ	-iʔ	-iʔ
---	-ĭl	-ĭl	-il	-in	-ĭl	-ĭl
-en; -ɛn	-ĭn	-in; -ĭn	-in	-in; -it	-ĭn	-ĭn
---	-ĭŋ	-ĭŋ	-iːŋ	-iŋ	-əŋ	-ĭŋ
-ep; ---	-ĭp	-ip	-iuʔ	-iuʔ	-iuʔ	-ĭwʔ

The Acehnese forms reflect two processes: the lowering of all high vowels and the further lowering of all nasalized vowels ("Nasalization in Acehnese" on page 176). The variability of the Jarai reflexes seems to represent something about Jarai rather than something about the source, as the variation shows up in both available sources on Jarai.

The upglide developing from PC *-ip in Chru, Northern Roglai, Western Cham, and Phan Rang Cham represents the fortition of the second formant transition to the final -p, rather than assimilation to the "labiality" of the *-p, as the "labiality" of the *-p involves lip spreading while the "labiality" of the glide represents lip rounding (see Thurgood and Javkin (1975), for an acoustic explanation of this class of sound changes). A parallel change occurs with PC *-ap.

The PC reflexes of the PC *-ɛy show more variation. The Acehnese developments were discussed above. The PC *-ɛy is retained as such in Rade and Written Cham.

Table 57: Reflexes of PC *-ɛy (< PMP *-i)

PMP	PC	Aceh.	Rade	Jarai	Chru	NR	Tsat	W. Cham	PR Cham
*-i	*-ɛy	-ɔə	-ɛi; -ue (m)	-əi	-əi	-əi; -uəi (m)	-ai	-ay	-ɛ̆y

In Rade, Jarai, Chru, and Northern Roglai, the reflexes of PC *-ɛy become -əi. In Tsat, Haroi, and Phan Rang Cham /-ai/ developed, through the lowering of -əi.

Reflexes of PMP *-u- and *-u

In the transition from PMP to PC, the reflexes of the PMP high vowel *u split: in closed syllables and in unstressed open syllables, it remained *-u-, while in open stressed syllables,[3] it became early-PC *-uṵ and then PC *-ɔw. PC also developed restricted length distinctions in the reflexes of *-u, but only before final glottal stops and velar nasals. (See "PC *-u- length distinctions" on page 141, for further discussion).

The reflexes of PC *-u are typically -u throughout Chamic, except in Haroi (see "Haroi vowels and restructured register" on page 197) and Acehnese. In Acehnese, the reflexes of PC high vowels are regularly lower, with reflexes after a nasal lower still ("Nasalization in Acehnese" on page 176).

The Chamic reflexes of PC *-ɔw parallel the reflexes of PC *-ɛy. In written Phan Rang Cham the *-ɔw is represented as -ŏw (the Phan Rang Cham in Table 59); but in the modern spoken Phan Rang Cham, it first delabialized, becoming -əi, and then lowered, becoming -ăw, as it has in Rade, Tsat, Western Cham, and Haroi.

*Table 58: Reflexes of PC *-u- < PMP *-u-*

PC	Aceh.	Rade	Jarai	Chru	NR	Tsat	W. Cham	PR Cham
*-uh	-oh; ---	-uh	-uh	-uh	-uh	-u^{55}	-uh	-ŭh
*-us	-oh; ---	-uih	-uih	-uːh	-uh	-u^{55}	-uh	-ŭh
*-un	-on; -ɔn	-ŭn	-ŭn	-un	-ut; -un	-un	-ŭn	-ŭn
*-um	-om; -ɔm	-ŭm	-um; -ŭm	-um	-up	---	-um	-ŭm
*-uŋ	-oŋ; ---	-ŭŋ	-uŋ; -ŭŋ	-uŋ	-uk; -uŋ	-uŋ	-uŋ	-ŭŋ
*-uːŋ	---	-uŋ	-ɔŋ; -uŋ	-ɔːŋ; -oːŋ	-uːk	-uŋ	-oŋ	-oŋ
*-uʔ	-oʔ; -ɔʔ	-ŭʔ	-ŭʔ	-uʔ	-uʔ	---	-ŭʔ	-ŭʔ
*-uːʔ	---	-ŭʔ	-ŭʔ	-uːʔ	-uːʔ	---	-uʔ; -oʔ	-uːʔ; -oʔ

Although preserved in the orthography, in the modern spoken Coastal languages, the onset of PC *-ɔw has been unrounded to /-ăṵ/.

*Table 59: Reflexes of PC *-ɔw < PMP *-u*

PC	Aceh.	Rade	Jarai	Chru	NR	Tsat	Haroi	W. Cham	PR Cham
*-ɔw	-ɛə	-ău	-əu	-əu	-əu	-au; -(i)ə	-ău; -ɨau	-au	-ŏw

---

3. It is worth noting that in all vowels in word-final open syllables are phonetically long.

Other sources

It is important to note that some forms that initially appear to come from a PC
*-u actually reflect an early PMP open syllable *-ur. Although the final -r itself is
no longer directly reflected anywhere in Chamic, PMP forms ending in final *-ur
have non-diphthongized reflexes throughout Chamic.

(1) PMP   *-u >   PC   *-ɔw
(2) PMP   *-ur >   PC   *-u

The Chamic /u/ reflexes make it clear that the forms with *-ur were not yet in
open syllables when the PMP *-u in open syllables went to PC *-ɔw. Instead, the
PMP *-ur lost the final -r only after this change, and thus did not diphthongize.

*Table 60: Reflexes of PMP *-u vs. *-ur in Chamic*

PMP	Malay	PC	Aceh.	Rade	PR Cham	
*bulu	bulu	*bulɔw	bulɛə	mlău	palŏw	'body hair'
*aku	aku	*kɔw	kɛə	kău	kŏw	'I'
*kutu	kutu	*kutɔw	gutɛə	kətău	katŏw	'head louse'
*ikur	ékor	*ʔiku	iku	ku	iku	'tail'
*telur	tĕlur 'egg'	*klu	---	---	klu	'testicles (animal)'
*niyur ?	nyor	*laʔur	u	---	liu	'coconut palm'
*kajur ?	kujur	*kaju	---	kəju	---	'spear; lance'

Notice that the Malay forms have retained the final -r. In Acehnese, the forms
without final -r have a diphthong, while the form for 'tail', which had an earlier
PMP -r, has no such diphthongization. Similarly, in the rest of the Chamic languages, the forms with PMP -r did not diphthongize along with the forms in open
syllables. This striking parallelism in the changes and in their relative chronology
is just one of many pieces of evidence that demonstrates that Acehnese was a
Chamic dialect that left for Sumatra ("Acehnese, a Chamic language" on
page 47).

Reflexes of the PMP shwa

In all contexts, the original PMP shwa disappeared, merging with the reflexes of
PC short *a. Meanwhile, the PMP *a became PC long *-a:- before the finals * -ʔ,
-ŋ, -k, -l, -r, -n, -p, and, more marginally, before -t, producing in these words a
length contrast with the former PMP -ə- reflexes, which always remained short in

PC. The introduction of various pre-PC MK borrowings strengthened the PC length contrast between long and short *a (for a further discussion of the length contrast, see "PC *-a- length distinctions" on page 146).

Table 61: The reflexes of PMP shwa

PMP	PC	Aceh.	Rade	Chru	NR	Haroi	PR Cham	
*gatel	*gatal	gatai	kətăl	kətal	katan	kətăl	katăl	'itchy'
*tanek	*tana?	---	kənă?	təna?	tană?	cənă?	tanĭ?	'cook'
*iket	*?ikat	ikat	---	aka?	ika?	akă?	ikă?	'to tie'
*qajeng	*hadaŋ	araŋ -m	hədăŋ	hədaŋ	hadak	athĭaŋ	haţăŋ	'charcoal'
*qulej	*hulat	ulat	hluăt (m)	həla?	hula?	---	hală?	'worm'

In the examples in Table 61, as in all the examples found so far, PMP -ə- has become PC *-a- (The Chamic reflexes of PC *-a- are discussed on page 146ff.).

Reflexes of PMP *a

Within PC, a length contrast developed before final -?; -ŋ; -k; -l; -r; -n; and marginally before -t. (See page 138ff. for further discussion of the length distinction.) The Chamic reflexes of PC *a show a minimum of variation; the variation that does occur is usually conditioned by the syllable-final consonant.

The Haroi reflexes, obscured by the secondary development of registrally-induced vowel splitting, are discussed in "Haroi vowels and restructured register" on page 197. The Tsat correspondences are too marginally attested to be included in the table.

The table is organized by the manner and place of the final consonant. Among the final stops, the steady, incessant Chamic lenition of final *-p, *-t, *-k, and *-c to a glottal stop is somewhat irregular in its reflexes. The upglide developing from PC *-ap in Chru, Haroi, and Western Cham is acoustically rather than articulatorily based. (See the brief discussion of the development of *-ip in page 117.) The reflexes of PC final nasals are split in Roglai, with some forms retaining the nasals and others developing homorganic voiceless stops (see "Nasalization in Northern Roglai" on page 170). The short vowel reflex of PC *-a:ŋ only occurs occasionally in Phan Rang Cham. In Western Cham and Phan Rang Cham nasalization has sometimes produced a high vowel reflex. Finally, the Acehnese reflexes are often split, with the most frequent conditioning factor being whether or not the vowel is nasalized, typically by the preceding nasal consonant.

*Table 62: The reflexes of PC *a*

PC	Aceh.	Rade	Jarai	Chru	NR	W. Cham	PR Cham
*-a	-a; -ʌŋ	-a	-a	-a	-a	-a	-a
*-ah	-ah; -ɔh	-ah	-ah	-ah	-ah	-ah; -ih	-ah; -ih
*-aːs	-ɯəh	-aih	-aih	-aːh	-a	-ah	-ăh
*-as	-aih	-ah	-ah	-ah	-ah	-ah	-ah
*-ap	-ap	-ăp	-ăp	-aʔ	-aʔ	-auʔ	-ăʔ
*-aːp	-ɯəp	-ap	-ap	-aːuʔ	-aːʔ; -ăʔ	-auʔ	-awʔ
*-at	-at	-ăt; -aʔ	-ăt; -ăʔ	-aʔ	-aʔ	-ăʔ	-ăʔ
*-aːt	-ɯət; -ɯt	-at	-at; -aʔ	-aːʔ	-aːʔ	-aʔ	-aʔ
*-ak	-aʔ	-ăk; -ăʔ	-ăk; -ăʔ	-aʔ	-ak; -aʔ	-aʔ	-aʔ; -ak
*-aːk	-ɯək; -ɯk	-ak	-ak	-aːʔ	-aːʔ	-aʔ; -iʔ	-aʔ; -iʔ
*-aːʔ	-at; -aʔ	-ăʔ	-ăʔ	-aːʔ	-aːʔ	-aʔ	-aʔ
ˣ*-ac	-ɯət	-ač	-ăiʔ	-aːiʔ	-aːiʔ	-aiʔ	-ayʔ
*-am	-am	-am; -ăm	-am; -ăm	-am	-ap; -am	-ăm	-ăm
*-aŋ	-aŋ	-ăŋ	-ăŋ	-aŋ	-ak	-ăŋ	-ăŋ
*-an	-an	-ăn	-ăn	-an	-an; -at	-ăn; -in	-ăn
*-aːn	-ɯən	-an	-an	-aːn	-aːn; -aːt	-an; -in; -in	-an; -in; -in
*-aːŋ	-ɯəŋ; -ɯŋ	-aŋ	-aŋ	-aːŋ	-aːk	-aŋ; -iŋ	-aŋ; -ăŋ
*-aŋ	-aŋ	-ăʔ	-ăʔ	-aʔ	-aʔ	-ăʔ; -əʔ	-ăʔ; -iʔ
*-ar	-ɯə; -iə	-ar	-ar-; -ăr	-aːr	-a	-ar	-ăr; -ar
*-aːr	-ɯə	-a	-a	-a	-a	-a	-a
*-al	-ai	-ăl	-al	-al	-an	-ăl	-ăl
*-aːl	-ɯə	-al	-al	-aːl	-an	-al	-al

Reflexes of the PMP diphthongs

The reflexes of PMP *-ay, *-aw, and *-uy are PC *-ay, *-aw, and *-uy, respectively. It is worth noticing that the first two diphthongs are, in effect, the long counterparts to the word-final PC *-εy and *-ɔw, which developed word finally from PMP *-i and *-u.

The Chamic reflexes of PC *-ay, *-aw, and *-uy are straightforward and well-attested. Two things are particularly interesting about these correspondences. The split in the Acehnese reflexes of *-aw correlates with vowel nasalization; the lower vowel reflex is the nasalized one. In Rade, Chru, and Tsat, loans are sometimes distinguishable on the bases of their distinctive reflexes. Thus, the Rade reflex -ai indicates a loan; the actual reflex is the much more aberrant looking -*ie*. In Tsat, the regular reflex of PC *-ay is -aːiʔ[42], with the *-y final strengthened to a glottal stop; the lack of a final glottal stop marks a form as a loan. Finally, in Chru, otherwise unexpected vowel length seems to occur with loans, although more work needs to be done on this.

*Table 63: The reflexes of PC *-ay, *-aw, and *-uy*

PC	Aceh.	Rade	Jarai	Chru	NR	Tsat	W. Cham	PR Cham
*-ay	-e; ---	-ie; ˣ-ai	-ai	-ai	-ai	-aːiʔ[42]; ˣ-aːi	-ai	-ay
*-aw	-o; -ɔ	-au	-au	-au; ˣ-aːu	-au	-aːu; -au	-au	-aw
*-uy	-ui	-ui	-ui	-ui	-ui	-ui	-ui	-uy

Diphthongization of PC *-ay in Rade

In Rade, the regular reflex of PC *-ay is -ie, a change that only occurred in final, accented open syllables, as PC *-ay was restricted to such syllables.

PC	Rade	Jarai	NR	W. Cham	PR Cham
*-ay	-i̯e	-ai	-ai	-ai	-ay

Commenting on the correspondence, Lee (1974:655) terms this change from PC *-ay to Rade -i̯e (Lee's -ye) metathesis, a characterization which is not unreasonable as a description of the diachronic correspondence with PC. However, the actual mechanism of change was undoubtedly not metathesis.

Instead, a more likely chain involves a series of steps well-attested in the literature: the change of PC *-ay to *-eę̆, dissimilative raising of the onset, and a shift in syllabicity.

PC	>	assimilation	>	onset raising	>	syllabicity shift
*-ay	>	*-eę̆	>	-ię̆	>	-i̯ę̆

The first step involving assimilation is a variant of the change of *-ay to -e, that is, essentially a monophthongization, but accompanied by the natural conse- quences of retaining length. The onset raising of the next step is illustrated by Donegan (1985:142-143) with examples from Finnish (*ee > ie in initial stressed syllables), from the transition of Vulgar Latin to Old French (ẹ > ie, in accented open syllables), and from the Finca Valparaiso dialect of Pokomchi, a Quichean language, (e: > ie, but apparently with no mention of stress or accent). Donegan's examples parallel the Rade change. The final step, of course, involves a shift in syllabicity, with the onset becoming a glide and the second part becoming the syllable nucleus. Note that this last step changes a more closed syllable into a more open syllable.

THE BORROWED PC MAIN SYLLABLE VOWELS

In addition to the vowel categories inherited from PMP, PC included a number of vowels that were borrowed into pre-Chamic from MK sources. Of course, many MK borrowings fit nicely with the consonant and vowel categories inherited from PMP. On the one hand, these are difficult to identify on internal grounds; on the other hand, these had only a limited effect on the PC segmental inventory.

Table 64: PC main syllable vowels, inherited and borrowed

*-ia	*-i-, *-i			*-u	*ua
[ˣ-iåw]				*-u-, *-u:-	ˣˣ-uay
[ˣ-iaw]					*uəy
		*-εy, *-ɔw,			
*ε		*ə		*-ɔ	
				*-ŏ-, *-ɔ:-	
		*-a			
	*-a-, *-a:-				
		*-ay		*-uy	
		*-aw			

Other MK borrowings, however, had a significant effect on the vowel categories of PC, an effect made salient by the fact that some vowel types are exemplified overwhelmingly, but *not* exclusively, by MK borrowings. In effect, these new vowel types have been borrowed from MK. However, the mechanism for developing the new category always seems to involve more than simply bor- rowing words containing the vowel. Typically, but not invariably in this data, the borrowing of a new vowel category also seems to be accompanied and, indeed, facilitated by the innovative development of the new category out of native material. The number of native tokens of the new type may be small — perhaps only one or two — but there are usually some.

In the table, the vowel categories associated with MK borrowings are in boldface to distinguish them from inherited vowel categories. As for the vowels themselves, the *-i in open syllables, despite being in boldface, originates from two sources, one involving borrowed MK forms, the other involving forms inherited from PMP (page 117). And, finally, most of the vowel length distinctions involve the interaction of influence of MK borrowings and inherited PMP material.

PC *ε

The examination of words containing PC *ε produces some fascinating asymmetries. Despite the fact that there are only a small number of PC forms that reconstruct with *ε and that their etymologies are far from worked out, what we do know provides a clear outline of the history. The distribution of reflexes in the modern languages is uncontroversial. In Acehnese (Durie 1990a), before certain finals the *ε is retained as such, and before others is backed to *ʌ. And, on the mainland, the Chamic languages Rade and Jarai, as is not unexpected given their close mutual interaction, have the same conditioned set of reflexes: the -ε- occurs in closed syllables, the -e in open. The remaining languages each have but a single reflex.

*Table 65: The reflexes of PC *ε*

PC	Aceh.	Rade	Jarai	Chru	NR	Tsat	W. Cham	PR Cham
*ε	ε; ʌ	-ε-; -e	-ε-; -e	ε	e	e	ε	ɛ

The full set of reconstructed forms is worth listing. The first word in the list is the Acehnese form lɯbɛh, PC *ləbɛh 'more, surplus', related to Malay lĕbih 'more' and a native PMP root. This word, however, is the only clearly PMP word in the entire list. However, as Durie notes, the Acehnese /-ε-/ vowel is irregular.

*Table 66: The reflexes of PC *ləbɛh*

PNB	PMnong	Malay	PC	Aceh.	Rade	PR Cham	
---	---	lĕbih	*ləbɛh	lɯbɛh -v	ebɛh	lipɛh	'more; surplus'

The next group of words all reconstruct fairly regularly to PC, but they have neither a Malay or other PMP counterpart, nor a MK counterpart in PNB or PMnong.

*Table 67: Reflexes containing PC *ε*

PC	Aceh.	Rade	PR Cham	
ˣ*hagɛt -f	---	---	haķɛ̆t -f	'why? what?'
ˣ*lɛʔ	---	lɛʔ	lɛ̆ʔ	'fall into'
ˣ*nɛh	---	---	---	'to elbow'
ˣ*palɛʔ	---	kəplɛ̆ʔ	---	'to drop'
ˣ*pɛt	pʌt	pɛ̆ʔ	pɛ̆ʔ	'pick, pluck'
ˣ*raɗɛ	---	eɗe	raɗɛ	'Rhade'
ˣ*tɛʔ	---	tĭʔ -v	---	'torn, worn'
ˣ*klɛʔ	---	tlɛ̆ʔ	klɛ̆ʔ	'steal'
ˣ*tulɛh	---	---	talɛ̆h	'untie'
ˣ*tamɛh	tamɛh	kəmɛh	---	'pillar; post'
ˣ*ɓɛʔ	---	---	ɓɛ̆ʔ	'clf. long, thin objects'
ˣ*gɛ	---	---	ķɛ	'boat'

With the next group of words, two pieces of evidence suggest that, except for the last two which are post-PC borrowings, these forms are also early MK incorporations but reconstructable to at least to PC. Note that the imperative not only reconstructs to PC but also occurs in Acehnese. Each has a plausible MK etymology, that is, each word looks like a MK word reconstructed for either proto-North-Bahnaric (PNB), proto-Mnong, or PKatuic; none of them seems to have a Malay (or other PMP) counterpart.

*Table 68: PC *ε forms with MK etymologies*

PNB	PMnong	PC	Aceh.	Rade	PR Cham	
*beq	---	ˣ*ɓɛʔ	ɓɛʔ	---	pɛ̆ʔ	' IMPERATIVE'
---	*rəndeh	ˣ*radɛh	---	edɛh	raţeh -v	'vehicle'
---	---	ˣ*glɛh	---	---	ķlɛh	'tired'
---	---	ˣ*hurɛt	---	hruɛ̆ʔ	---	'rope; vine'
---	ˣsreh	ˣ*rɛh	---	---	---	'cut'
*ajeq	---	ˣ*jɛʔ	---	jɛ̆ʔ	çɛʔ	'near(ly); about to'
*aseh	*ʔaseh	ˣ*ʔasɛh	---	asɛh	athɛ̆h	'horse'
*ĭč	---	ˣ*ʔɛh	---	ɛh	ɛ̆h	'excrement'
*pale	*gle	ˣ*ʔalɛ	---	ale	---	'medium bamboo'
*babe	*be	ˣbubɛ	---	be	papɛ	'goat; sheep'
*weh	---	ˣwɛh-vf	---	wɛh	wɛ̆h	'turn aside'

The next group of words all reconstruct fairly regularly to PC, but they have neither a Malay or other PMP counterpart, nor a MK counterpart in PNB or PMnong.

*Table 69: Reflexes containing PC *ε*

PC	Aceh.	Rade	PR Cham	
ˣ*hagɛt -f	---	---	hakɛ̆t -f	'why? what?'
ˣ*lɛʔ	---	lɛʔ	lɛ̆ʔ	'fall into'
ˣ*nɛh	---	---	---	'to elbow'
ˣ*palɛʔ	---	kəplɛ̆ʔ	---	'to drop'
ˣ*pɛt	pʌt	pɛ̆ʔ	pɛ̆ʔ	'pick, pluck'
ˣ*radɛ	---	edɛ	radɛ	'Rhade'
ˣ*tɛʔ	---	tĭʔ -v	---	'torn, worn'
ˣ*klɛʔ	---	tlɛ̆ʔ	klɛ̆ʔ	'steal'
ˣ*tulɛh	---	---	talɛ̆h	'untie'
ˣ*tamɛh	tamɛh	kəmɛh	---	'pillar; post'
ˣ*ɓɛʔ	---	---	ɓɛ̆ʔ	'clf. long, thin objects'
ˣ*gɛ	---	---	kɛ	'boat'

The last set consists of the three words, aside from *ləbɛh, which actually occur both in Malay and Chamic. Neither the word for 'seed' nor the form for 'tickle' reconstruct to PC; in any case, the word for 'seed' is apparently a Sanskrit borrowing. More of interest, however, is the fact that both appear to reconstruct to the PC level, with the Acehnese forms corresponding nicely.

As a possible native PMP root, only the form for 'great grandchild' requires any careful examination. As for the initial c-, Adelaar (1988:62) writes with respect to his proto-Malayic that the proto-phoneme *c is not well-attested, making words containing it at least mildly suspect. In any case, if the PC and Malay forms are related and if both are not MK in origin, 'great grandchild' might constitute a second native PMP root in Chamic containing *ε, although I suspect that the form is ultimately MK.

*Table 70: PC *ε forms without MK etymologies*

Malay	PC	P-Aceh.	Aceh.	PR Cham	
cicit	ˣ*cicɛ̆t	*(cɛ)cɛt	cʌt	tacɛ̆ʔ	'great grandchild'
ɓiji	ˣ*bijɛh	*bijeh	bijɛh	paçɛh	'seed'
gɛ̆lak	ˣgilɛk -lv	*glɛʔ	gliʔ-gliʔ -iv	kalɛ̆k	'tickle'
'laugh'					

In any case, the MK origins of PC *ɛ are firmly established. Further, the handful of irregular PC roots with PC *ɛ ultimately from MK but with regular proto-Acehnese roots are what one expects if Acehnese is a Chamic dialect. (The proto-Acehnese reconstructions are from Durie 1990a).

PC shwa

The original PMP shwa merged with the PC reflexes of short *a, allowing a new PC shwa to develop out of material incorporated from MK sources. The Chamic reflexes of this new shwa are given in the table.

*Table 71: Reflexes of PC *ə*

PC	Aceh.	Rade	Jarai	Chru	NR	Tsat	W. Cham	PR Cham
*-əh	-ʌh	-ih	-əh; -ih	-əh	-əh	---	-əh	-ŏh; -əh
*-ət	-ʌt	-ɨʔ	-ɨʔ	-əʔ	-əʔ	-əʔ	-əʔ; -ɨʔ	-əʔ; -ɨʔ
*-ək	---	-ŏk	-ɨk; -iʔ	-əʔ	-əʔ	-əʔ	-əʔ	-ŏʔ
*-əp	-ɔp	-ŏʔ	-ŏʔ	-əuʔ	-əʔ	---	-auʔ	-ŏwʔ
*-əŋ	-ʌŋ	-ŏŋ	-ŏŋ	-əŋ	-ək	-aŋ	-əŋ; -ɨŋ	-aŋ; -ɨŋ
*-əm	-ɔm	-ăm	-ŏm	-əm	-əp	-an	-ŏm	-ăm
*-ən	-ʌn	-ăn	-ŏn	-ən	-ət	---	-ɛ̆n	-ăn
*-ər	-ʌ	-ər	-ər; -ŏr	-ər	-ə	-an	-ăr	-ăr

Even if the final *-p were not retained in Acehnese, it would be obvious from the vowel reflexes in the mainland languages that *-əp correspondences reflect a final *-p. Parallel changes happen with *-ap and *-ip; see "Reflexes of PMP *-i- and *-i" on page 117 for a brief discussion of the acoustics of the change. The -ɨ- reflexes in Western and Phan Rang Cham result from nasalization.

The sources of shwa

Thus far, only a handful of forms reconstructed with shwa have potential Austronesian etymologies. When there is a readily-determinable source, forms with shwa are overwhelmingly from MK, and even when the source is not fully identifiable, it is often obvious from either the phonotactics or from the presence of a non-PMP phoneme that the form was not PMP in origin.

The handful of PC forms containing shwa and potentially related to Malay (or PMP) forms are listed in Table 72. Of these only *bukən with its proto-Malayic *bukən reconstruction is totally convincing, although *lən also looks plausible. The form *lən has a potential PMP source in *talun 'fallow land; secondary forest'. In the case of the Malay word for 'hatch', the first syllable vowels in Malay and Acehnese do not match, possibly indicating that the word was independently borrowed into Malay and PC. The last word, although related to the Indonesian mythical bird the *garuda*, is a borrowing in Chamic.

*Table 72: Malay and PC words with PC *ə*

PNB	P-Malayic	Malay	PC	Aceh.	Rade	PR Cham	
---	*bukən	bukan	*bukən	bukʌn	məkăn	ḳŏw'-ḳən	'other; different'
---	---	---	*lən	lʌn	lăn	lăn	'earth; soil'
---	---	kĕram	*karəm	karɔm	krăm	karăm	'to hatch'
---	---	garuda	ˣgrək	---	---	ḳrə̆ʔ	'vulture; garuda'

All the words in the following table have probable etymological connections to MK. Some are reconstructed for the Mnong branch of MK and some are reconstructed for the North Bahnaric branch. None of them appear in Malay. The Proto-Mnong reconstructions are from H. Blood (1968). The Proto-North-Bahnaric reconstructions are from Smith (1972), occasionally with minor modifications.

*Table 73: MK words with PC *ə*

PNB	PMnong	PC	Aceh.	Rade	PR Cham	
---	*kăm	ˣ*ɓrəm	---	ɓrăm	ɓrăm	'arrow'
---	*klə̆m	ˣ*səm	sɔm ?	---	---	'to wrap'
---	*pə̆ŋ	ˣ*pəŋ	---	pə̆ŋ	pəŋ	'to nail; hammer'
---	*tə̆p	ˣ*kləp	---	tlŏʔ	---	'stab; poke'
---	*yəh	ˣ*yəh	---	---	mɨyăh	'PARTICLE'
---	*də̆k	ˣ*dəŋ	dʌŋ	dŏŋ	tăŋ	'stand; stop'
*čŏŋ	*sŏŋ	ˣ*ɓəŋ	---	ɓə̆ŋ	ɓăŋ	'to eat'
*gă̆ŋ	---	ˣ*gəŋ	---	---	ḳăŋ	'pole; post'
*hagăr	---	ˣ*sagər	---	həgər	haḳăr	'drum'
*joq	---	ˣ*ʔjəp	---	ʔjŏʔ	ʔjŏwʔ	'correct; right'
*pă̆y	---	ˣ*pə-pət	---	---	---	'to fan'

The root ˣ*bət 'to dam; to fence', which is the root used for the formation of ˣ*b-an-ət 'a dam; a fence', contains an instrumental prefix. The prefix itself, although apparently originally borrowed from MK, is not restricted just to a handful of fossilized forms. In Acehnese, for instance, this infix not restricted to specific forms but instead occurs productively in disyllables (cf. Chapter 9), a characteristic that says something about the intensity of the MK-Chamic language contact on the mainland that led to the borrowing.

Although not reconstructed for proto-North-Bahnaric (with one exception), the words in Table 74 appear in Bahnar (Aymonier and Cabaton (1906)). It is not obvious what significance, if any, to attach to the fact that Smith did not reconstruct these for proto-North-Bahnaric. On the one hand, a lot of the Bahnar lexicon is borrowed from Cham; on the other, these forms do not appear to have AN counterparts, suggesting that they were not originally AN.

Table 74: Other PC *ə forms with MK affiliations

PNB	Bahnar (AC)	PMnong	PC		Acehnese
---	bənot	---	ˣ*b-an-ət	---	'a dam, fence'
---	brəm; mrəm	*kăm	ˣ*ɓrəm	---	'arrow'
---	gər	---	ˣ*gər	gʌ	'handle (knife)'
---	gàŋ; gə̆ŋ	---	ˣ*gəŋ	---	'pole; post'
---	tâl; tol	---	ˣ*təl	---	'arrive; until'
*păr	apăr; păr	*păr	ˣ*pər	phʌ -i	'to fly'
---	gâp	---	ˣ*gəp	gɔp	'other; group'

The final set of forms have neither established MK nor Malay counterpart. Nonetheless, the first form looks unquestionably MK because of its glottalized stop. It is possible that careful search of MK sources would turn up counterparts for at least some of these.

Table 75: PC *ə words without PMP or MK etymologies

PNB	PMnong	PC	Aceh.	Rade	PR Cham	
---	---	ˣ*ɓəŋ	---	---	ɓă̆ŋ	'to burn'
---	---	ˣ*gəm	gɔm	gă̆m	kă̆m	'to cover'
---	---	ˣ*katər	---	kətər	---	'corn; grain'
---	---	ˣpayər -f	---	myər	payal -f	'to offer'
---	---	ˣ*ləp	---	---	lə̆wʔ	'fold'
---	---	ˣ*madəh	---	mədih	miṭəh	'awaken'
---	---	ˣ*məŋ	---	mə̆ŋ	mĭŋ	'from'
---	---	ˣ*rək	---	rə̆k	rə̆ʔ	'grass; weeds'
---	---	ˣ*sadər	---	hədər	haṭăr	'remember'
---	---	ˣ*wər	tuwʌ	wər	wă̆r	'forget'
---	---	ˣ*yər	---	---	yer	'lift, raise'

It is likely that these tables include at least some mistaken identifications and misassociations, but the overall configuration is unmistakable: the shwa has entered PC through MK material incorporated into pre-Chamic.

PC *ia, ˣ-iău, and ˣ-iaw

Three diphthongs were borrowed from MK sources: *ia was borrowed into pre-Chamic, becoming PC *ia, while ˣ-iăw and ˣ-iaw occur in post-PC borrowings. For the diphthong *ia:, only the word 'water' appears to be a PMP root.

*Table 76: Reflexes of PC *iar 'water'*

PC	Aceh.	Rade	Jarai	Chru	NR	Tsat	Haroi	W. Cham	PR Cham	
*ʔiar	iə	ɛa	ʔia	ia	ia	ʔia³³	ʔea	ea	ýa;	'water
-f									ier	(fresh)'

The Chamic reflexes of *ia are regular, with the slight variation conditioned by the finals. The two forms with nasalized vowels are marked with (n). In working with Chamic forms containing the sequence -ia-, the main difficulty is in distinguishing forms that were originally disyllabic, such as the disyllabicity reflected in Malay *tian* 'stomach', from forms with an -ia- borrowed from MK. This problem has not been completely solved here.

*Table 77: Reflexes of PC *ia*

PC	Aceh.	Rade	Jarai	Chru	NR	Tsat	Haroi	W. Cham	PR Cham
*-ia	---	-ia	-ia	-ia	-ia	-ia	-ea; ---	-ea	-ya
*-iar	-iə	-ea	-ia	-ia	-ia	-ia	-ea; ---	-ea	-ya
*-iaʔ	-iəʔ; -eʔ	-iăʔ	-iăʔ	-iaʔ	-iaʔ	-iaʔ	-eaʔ; -iaʔ -iiʔ (n)	-eaʔ;	-yăʔ
*-iat	-eʔ	-iăʔ	-iăʔ	-iaʔ	-iaʔ	-iaʔ	-ĕaʔ; -iaʔ -iiʔ (n)	-eaʔ; -iʔ (n)	-yăʔ;
*-iaŋ	-iəŋ	-ieŋ	-ɛŋ	-iaŋ	-iaŋ; -iak; (-yak)	-iaŋ	-eaŋ; ---	-iaŋ	-ieŋ

In both Haroi and Western Cham, the onsets of these centering diphthongs have been lowered in every case, except for *-iaŋ in Western Cham. This parallels but is more extensive than the lowering of the centering diphthongs beginning with /u/, which similarly occurs in Haroi and Western Cham (see page 135). In the case of Haroi, the second reflex shows the result of subsequent raising and backing of the onset to /ɨ/ under the influence of breathy voice (page 197).

In Table 78, the PC *ia and *-iya- have clear examples in Acehnese, with all of the examples except for 'dance' attested in Acehnese. The PC form for 'dance' may have a counterpart in Vietnamese *múa* 'dance'.

The word *tiya:n 'stomach' is PMP in origin, with a counterpart in Malay *tian*. It is interesting that, within Malay, *tian* is disyllabic. The last two forms, 'stomach' and 'wing', behave like disyllabic forms in some languages, in which case the second vowel is long, and sometimes like monosyllabic forms, in which case the vowels behave as if they were *-ia-. The final *-iap produces upglides, as does final *-p elsewhere.

*Table 78: The reflexes of PC *-iya-*

PC	Aceh.	Rade	Jarai	Chru	NR	Haroi	PR Cham	
*liyah	liəh	---	liah	ləyah	liah	leah	lyăh	'lick; taste'
*liya	haliya	eya	rɜ̆ya	lia	riya -i	ləyɨa	liya	'ginger'
*timiya	---	---	---	təmia	timiya -v	---	tamya; mya	'dance'
*tiya:n	tiyɯən	tian	kiăn	tia:n	matia:t	tean	tyan	'stomach'
*tiya:p	tiyɯəp	tiɜ̆ʔ -vf	---	tia:uʔ	tia:ʔ	teauʔ	tyawʔ	'chase'

Aside from the obviously onomatopoetic word 'cat', which is obviously onomatopoetic, the ˣ-iaw and ˣ-iăw only occur in forms postdating the breakup of PC.

Table 79: The forms with ˣ-iaw and ˣ-iăw

PC	Rade	Jarai	Chru	NR	Tsat	W. Cham	PR Cham	
*miaw	mieo	---	miau	miău	miau³³	maɲiau	mɨyaw	'cat'
ˣkriăw	---	krɛŭ	---	kiău -i	---	---	---	'castrate'
ˣdriaw	---	dreu	---	---	---	---	ʈriew	'exclaim'
ˣʔiăw	ɗiăŭ -iv	ǐaŭ	iău	iău	ta:iʔ⁴² -iv	iu	iw	'left (side)'
ˣliɲiaw	eɲau -v	rɜ̆ɲǐaŭ	---	---	---	laɲiu	liɲiw; laɲiw; ɲiw	'outside'

Not only are there irregular correspondences in one language or the other for all the forms, except for 'left (side)', but these forms are unattested in a number of languages.

PC *ua and ˣ*uay

Although no doubt exists that the majority of PC forms with *ua and ˣ*uay were incorporated into Chamic as the result of pre-Chamic contact with MK speakers, two of the *ua forms are undoubtedly PMP: the PC *buat 'to do' and *dua 'two' are identical in form and meaning to their Malay counterparts.

The rhymes marked with ˣ*- only occur in PC words ultimately from MK sources. That is, even at this preliminary stage of investigation, it seems evident that six of the twelve rhymes are exclusively MK in origin.

*Table 80: Reflexes of PC *ua and ˣ*uay*

PC	Aceh.	Rade	Jarai	Chru	NR	Tsat	Haroi	W. Cham	PR Cham
*-ua	-uwa	-ua	-ua	-ua	-ua	-ua	-oa; -ua	-oa	-wa
ˣ*-uah	---	-uah	-uah	-uah	-uah	-ua[55]	-oah; -ŭh	-oah	-wăh
*-uat	-uət	-ăt; -uot	-uă?; -ɔ̆t	-ua?	-uă?	-ua?	-oa?	-oa?	---
*-ua?	---	-uă?	-uă?	-ua?	-ua?	-ua?	-ŭ?	-oa?	-wă?
ˣ*-uam	---	-uom	-ɔm	-ɔːm	-ɔːp	-uan	-ɔm; -ŭm	-ɔm	-ɔm
ˣ*-uan	-uən	-uon	-ɔn	-uan; -uən	-uat; -uan	-uan	-ɔ̆n; -ŭn	-uan	-ŏn
ˣ*-ual	---	-ul	-ul	-ual; -uəl	-uan; -uən	---	-ul	-ual	-ŏl
ˣ*-uay	-uə	-ue	-uai	-uai	-uai	-uaːi	-oai; ---	-uai	-oy
ˣ*-uac	-uət	-uɛ̆?	-uăi?	-uai?	-ue?; -uai?	-oi?	-ŏai?; ---	-uai?	-ŏy?
ˣ*-uəy	---	-ui	-ui	-uəi	-uəi	-oi	-ui	-uai	-oy
ˣ*-uc	---	-uč	-ui?; -uc	-ui?	-ui?	---	-ŏi?; -ŭi?	-ui?	-ŭy?
ˣ*-uar	---	-uor; -ua	-ua	-ua	-uă	-ua	-oa; ---	-ur	-ur

There are two major tendencies which are evident in the reflexes of these diphthongs. There is a tendency to monophthongize, a tendency that seems to have existed in Chamic ever since it acquired diphthongs and triphthongs through contact with MK. Notice that the reduction of triphthongs to diphthongs and of diphthongs to monophthongs is scattered throughout these languages, and is particularly evident in Haroi, Phan Rang Cham, and Jarai.

The second tendency is to lower the onset of centering diphthongs. For the first five rhymes listed in Table 80, the onset is lowered in Haroi and Western Cham but without monophthongization. In a number of other languages, there is both lowering and monophthongization, although in several cases length is preserved. PR Cham, for instance, frequently reduces /ua/ to /o/.

Haroi goes further than any of the other languages in lowering the onsets of these diphthongs. In fact, Haroi appears to have lowered the onsets of all these diphthongs except for three: ˣ*uəy , *-uat, and ˣ*-ual. In the column for Haroi, the first reflex given shows the reflexes with the lowered onset. The second reflex given shows the effects of breathy voice, which in most cases raised the vowels to /ŭ/ but sometimes backed it to /u/, typically monophthongizing them at the same time (see "Haroi vowels and restructured register" on page 197, for further discussion).

PC *ɔ

With the exception of at most six words, when the reflexes of PC *-ɔ have etymologies, they have MK etymologies. Two obviously PMP forms are *dɔːk 'sit; stay' and *bɔh 'fruit; egg; clf. for small round objects', related to Malay *duduk* and *buah*, both of which have unquestionable PMP etymologies, with the Malay *duduk* representing a reduplicated form of the root.

*Table 81: PC *ɔ words with Malay (or AN) counterparts*

PNB	Bahnar	Malay	PC	Aceh.	Jarai	NR	PR Cham	
---	lɛmō;	lĕmbu	ˣ*lɔmɔ	lɯmɔ	rɔmɔ	lamo	limɔ;	'cow; ox'
	rɔmō					-n	lamɔ	
*troŋ	---	tĕrung	ˣ*trɔŋ	truəŋ	trŏŋ	trok	trŏŋ, crŏŋ	'eggplant'
---	---	buah	*bɔh	bɔh	bɔh	boh	pɔh	'fruit; egg; clf.'
---	---	duduk	*dɔːk	duəʔ	dŏːʔ	doːʔ	tɔʔ	'sit; live; stay'
---	---	empu	*pɔ	pɔ	po -v	po	po -v	'master; lord'
---	---	---	*lɔn	lʌn	lŏn	lət	lăn	'earth; soil'

The next two forms are the far more problematic ˣ*lɔmɔ 'cow' and ˣ*trɔŋ 'eggplant', which although found in MP (cf. Malay *lembu* and *tĕrung*), are not widespread in MP and do not reconstruct back to PMP. The evidence that these two are borrowings includes the dual reflexes for 'eggplant' found in Phan Rang Cham and the fact that both forms are found in MK: ˣ*trɔŋ 'eggplant' reconstructs as *troŋ in proto-North Bahnaric and 'cow; ox' is found in Bahnar.

In both cases, these forms may have been late borrowings into Malay. The last two words *pɔ 'master; lord' and 'earth, soil' look to be old AN roots, cf. Malay *empu* and PAn *Calun and PMP *talun 'fallow land, secondary forest'.

Table 82 illustrates reflexes of open syllable PC *-ɔ without AN counterparts. Among the open syllable examples, only 'cow; ox' and 'master; lord' seem to have PMP counterparts; in contrast, at least three of these reconstruct to proto-North-Bahnaric. The length distinction between the reflexes of PC *-ɔː- and *-ɔ- is discussed in the section on vowel length.

*Table 82: The reflexes of PC *ɔ*

PNB	PC	Aceh.	Rade	Jarai	Chru	NR	W. Cham	PR Cham	
---	ˣ*batɔ	---	məto	pɐ̆to	patɔ	pəto	patɔ	patɔ	'teach'
---	ˣ*blɔ	---	---	---	blɔ	---	---	---	'split'
---	ˣ*glɔ	---	dlo	dlɔ	glɔ̃ -n	dlo	ḳlɔ	ḳlɔ	'brain'
---	ˣjrɔ	---	---	---	jrɔ	jro	---	---	'large jar'
---	ˣjrɔ	---	ero -i	---	---	jro	crɔ -i	---	'rainbow'
---	ˣ*krɔ	---	kro	krɔ	---	kro	---	---	'dry'
---	ˣ*ləmɔ	lɯmɔ	emo	rəmo	ləmɔ	lamo -n	lamɔ	lamɔ; limɔ	'cow; ox'
---	ˣ*pɔ	pɔ	po	po	po -v	po	pɔ	po -v	'master'
---	ˣ*ralɔ	---	[hlɔ]	---	rəlɔ	ralo	ralɔ	ralɔ	'flesh; meat'
---	ˣ*rɔ	---	---	---	rɔ	ro	rɔ	---	'cage'
---	ˣ*tamɔ	---	---	---	tərmɔ	---	tamɔ	---	'intact'
---	ˣ*tuhɔ	---	kəho	---	---	tuho	---	---	'snare'
---	ˣkuhɔ	---	kəhɔ -iv	---	kəhɔ -iv	kuho -v	kahɔ	---	'Koho'
*čǎw	ˣ*cucɔ	cucɔ	čo	təcɔ	cɔ	tico	tacɔ	tacɔ	'grand -child'
*čano	ˣ*tanɔ	---	kəno	tɐ̆no	tənɔ	tano -n	tanɔ	tanɔ	'male'

Two of the forms in Table 82 have Malay counterparts in *lĕmbu* 'cow; ox' and *cucu* 'grandchild', but *lĕmbu* looks to have been independently borrowed into Malay and PC, as the medial correspondence of Malay -mb- to Acehnese -m- is unexpected.

The majority of the *ɔ vowels lack any sort of PMP etymology. And, although the MK etymologies have not yet been worked out, it appears that most of these forms entered PC through MK sources. Nonetheless there is a minority that appear to have come from PMP forms with *u.

PC VOWEL LENGTH

The PC vowel length distinctions are a major source of controversy, with the sole point of agreement being that a vowel length distinction existed in the mainland Chamic languages. Both Shorto (1975) and Cowan (1974; n.d.) claim that the long vowels in mainland Chamic correlate with diphthongization patterns in Acehnese—a position that Collins (1991:116) disputes, while asserting that the Acehnese diphthongization and the mainland Chamic vowel length distinctions are distinct phenomena occurring independently within each language, presumably also having developed independently within the various Chamic languages.

In contrast, Shorto (1975) and Cowan (1974; n.d.) not only correlate the vowel length distinction of mainland Chamic with Acehnese diphthongization but go much, much further, asserting the PC vowel length distinctions are not the results of developments at the PC level but instead are themselves inherited from PAn. Shorto argues, apparently on the basis of general beliefs about what can be borrowed, that the vowel length distinction found in Acehnese and mainland Chamic does not result from borrowing (1975:90):

> ...the creation of so fundamental a distinction as that of vowel length by borrowing seems intrinsically unlikely. On the other hand, contact with MK languages, in many of which (as in PMK) a vowel-length distinction operates, would favour the *retention* of an original distinction conceivably lost elsewhere.

That is, like Cowan, Shorto suggests that PAn had an original vowel length distinction which was retained in Chamic but lost elsewhere.

Shorto's reluctance to accept that a length distinction could have been borrowed would have more merit if the PC speakers were totally unfamiliar with vowel length. However, the population that spoke PC was not solely Austronesian speaking. The massive incorporation of MK vocabulary and the restructuring of the AN lexicon along MK lines strongly suggest that PC was spoken by population that included a large number of originally MK speakers who had shifted to PC along with an originally Austronesian speaking population that was itself bilingual. For such speakers, the vowel length distinctions would have been brought into PC as part of the borrowed MK lexicon that constitutes such a prominent part of the PC vocabulary.

As part of their proposed scenarios for the retention of an earlier PAn vowel length distinction in PC, both Cowan (n.d.:3) and Shorto (1975:100) present the thesis that PC was able to retain its distinctive length while it was for the most part lost in the rest of AN, because PC remained on the mainland in contact with MK languages with a length distinction, while the remainder of the AN languages left the mainland, breaking off contact with MK languages, and thus lost vowel length. One of the many problems with this position is that the bulk of modern scholarship views the Chamic speakers as having returned to mainland from the islands within the last two thousand years or so—a contention that is fully supported by the reconstructions of PC, which shows PC as a subgroup with a relatively shallow time depth.

Collins (1991:116) rejects both the contention that vowel length in PC is the retention of a PAn vowel length distinction and the claim that Acehnese diphthongization patterns correlate with PC vowel length. Collins is certainly correct in stating that PC vowel length was not inherited from PAn; in fact, much of this section on PC vowel length is devoted to showing how PC length distinctions evolved out of the interaction of PAn materials with MK contact and borrowings.

Undoubtedly based in large part on the materials available to him at the time, Collins' suspicion that the Acehnese diphthongs are not correlated with PC vowel length has not held up. Once the various late MK borrowings have been culled out, and the PC vowel length reconstructions established, it becomes clear that the correlation between PC vowel length and Acehnese diphthongization is fully documented, and, with many of the potential exceptions mentioned by Cowan and Shorto now accounted for. Further, as Cowan noted more than once (1948; 1974), for many of the forms in modern Acehnese, the transition from a stressed, long vowel to a modern Acehnese diphthong is attested, that is, documented within the history Acehnese (1974:188):

> Now it had been realized long ago, on the evidence of the related languages and the loanwords, as well as the archaic spellings in the Arabic script and local dialect forms, that in very many cases the Acehnese diphthongs derive from simple vowels in the final, i.e., stressed syllables. Thus it appeared that ɯə derived from a in closed syllables, exceptionally (in PAn *apa if this reconstruction is correct) also in an open syllable; ɔə and iə derived from i, and ɛə and uə from u, in the latter two cases according to whether the syllable is open or closed (originally closed).

Cowan (1974:189) continues, noting

> ...that the original simple vowels must have been lengthened before diphthongizing. This conclusion seems to be confirmed by the fact that, with certain morphemes, forms with the simple vowel still exist side by side with forms with diphthongs. In these cases the former are used

without and the latter with stress and the implication is that this stress first produced non-phonemic lengthening and then diphthongization.

Thus, unlike Collins, Cowan and Shorto view the transition from long vowels to diphthongs as straightforward with the correlation uncontroversial.

The PC vowel length distinctions are readily reconstructable, although the earliest system that can be reconstructed looks to have been oddly configured: In the reconstructed system, only PC *-u-, *-ɔ-, and *-a- show contrastive length, and then only before certain finals. As Lee (1966:117) noted, the "length contrast seems to be fairly certain for *a, *u, and *ɔ, but (as is true of the daughter languages) is limited to certain environments."

There is a subpattern to the way in which vowels show length before specific finals: the high vowel *-u- has a length contrast before glottal stops and velar nasals; the mid vowel *-ɔ- has a length contrast before glottal stops, velar nasals, and *-k; and the low vowel *-a- has a length contrast before glottal stops, velar nasals, and *-k as well as before four other finals (*-l, *-r, *-n, and, marginally, *-t).

Figure 13: Long versus short vowels and their environments

*-u- vs. *-uː-	*-ɔ- vs. *-ɔː-	*-a- vs. *-aː-
/____ʔ	/____ʔ	/____ʔ
/____ŋ	/____ŋ	/____ŋ
	/____k	/____k
		/____l
		/____r
		/____n
		/____t

Perhaps, as suggested by length distinctions in Rade, a distinction may once have existed between -aːm and -am as well. However, it will never be possible to reconstruct a full, balanced system of length contrasts as one most likely never existed — length contrasts were probably always asymmetrical.

This highly-skewed system of vowel-length contrasts directly reflects MK contact. This typologically-marked distribution matches the types of asymmetry found in the MK languages of Vietnam, in which the back vowels show more distinctions than in the front vowels (Gérard Diffloth, p.c.). The system itself is not just found in the mainland languages, but is also directly reflected in the diphthongization patterns of Acehnese (in Acehnese the inherited long vowels of PC subsequently diphthongized), providing yet another piece of evidence that Acehnese is simply another Chamic language.

It is reasonably clear just how the system of contrastive length came into being. In general terms, the vowel length contrasts in PC reflect the interaction of three major factors and one minor one: the major factors are intense contact with MK languages with vowel length contrasts, the incorporation of numerous MK loanwords containing such contrasts into pre-PC, and internal developments with the material inherited from AN.

With the long and short PC *-u- and *-ɔ- the incorporated material borrowed from MK seemed to play the central role in the phonemicization of the change, especially in the case of *-ɔ-, where all but a handful of the forms containing the sound, regardless of length, are MK in origin.

With the length distinctions associated with PC *-a-, however, the much of the distinction came about through the internal-developments in the inherited material as through as through contrasts with incorporated pre-PC MK loans. Statistically, the prime catalyst was the developments in the reflexes of PMP *-a- and *-ə- < -e- >, which established a distinction between PC *-a- and *-aː- in inherited words. The contrasts developed through this internal mechanism were augmented by the incorporation of countless MK -a- forms into Chamic, each entering with either a long or short vowel. For further discussion, see "PC *-a- length distinctions" on page 146.

The minor factor has to do with required syllable weight. Most PC content words are disyllabic or sesquisyllabic (syllable and a half). However, some PC content words are monosyllabic. In PC, all monosyllabic content words have long vowels. Sometimes the long vowel is etymologically expected; sometimes a short vowel would otherwise be expected and the long vowel simply reflects the requirement that, for those vowels with a PC length contrast, the vowel of a monosyllabic content word be long. Thus, *dɔːk 'sit', *yaːp 'count', and *paːt 'four' all have long vowels precisely because otherwise these forms would not meet the minimal requirements for a content word. PC is not unique in this respect; the requirement that monosyllabic content words be bimoraic is widespread in Austronesian (Blust, p.c.). For instance, in the Isbukun dialect of Bunan (data from Paul Li, class notes), a Formosan language of eastern Taiwan, in the pairs *paat* 'four' but *saspat* 'four (for counting people)' and *nuum* 'six'/ *ʔaʔabnum* 'six (for counting people)', the vowels in the monosyllabic roots are secondarily long in the monosyllabic roots, but short as expected elsewhere.

PC *-u- length distinctions

PC *u has a limited and asymmetrically-distributed vowel length distinction: *u is found both short (Table 83) and long (Table 84) in two environments: before final -ʔ and before final -ŋ. Etymologically, the short vowels descend both from PMP sources and from MK sources.

Among the reflexes of the PC *-u- short vowel, there are words with PMP etymologies (apparently, for example, 'flour', and 'nose') mixed in with words with established MK backgrounds (Table 83). No doubt exists that PC *-u- came from both sources.

*Table 83: Reflexes of PC *-u-*

PNB	Bahnar	Malay	PC	Rade	NR	
---	---	---	*ʔañuʔ	añŭʔ	añŭʔ	'beads'
---	---	---	*bituʔ	mətŭʔ	pituʔ	'star'
---	---	---	*katuŋ	kətŭŋ	katuk	'pull'
---	---	---	ˣ*ñuʔ	ñŭʔ	ñŭʔ	'dive; submerge'
---	---	---	*ʔaduʔ	adŭʔ	aduʔ	'room'
---	jəlu	---	*jaluʔ	elŭʔ	jaluʔ	'bowl'
---	---	manuk	*manuʔ	mənŭʔ	manŭʔ	'chicken; fowl'
---	bək ?	mabuk	*mabuʔ	---	babuʔ	'drunk'
---	---	gulung	*guluŋ	---	-guluk	'to roll'
---	---	hidung	*ʔiduŋ	adŭŋ	idŭk	'nose'
---	---	jantung 'heart'	*tuŋ	---	tuk	'stomach; abdomen'
---	---	lĕsung	*ləsuŋ -i	esŭŋ	risuk -i	'mortar'
---	---	rombong	*buŋ	bŭŋ	---	'large basket'
---	anuŋ	---	*ʔanuŋ	anŭŋ	---	'package'
---	duŋ	---	ˣ*ɗuŋ	ɗŭŋ	ɗuk	'wrap up; bundle'
---	təpuŋ	tĕpung	*tapuŋ	kəpŭŋ	tupuk	'flour'
*daqbăŋ	---	rĕbung	*rabuŋ	ebŭŋ	rubuk	'bamboo shoot'
*gadŭŋ	kəduŋ	kandung	ˣ*kaduŋ	---	---	'pocket; pouch'
			*-uʔ	-ŭʔ	-uʔ	
			*-uŋ	-ŭŋ	-uk; -uŋ	

More intriguing and indicative of the amount of work that still remains to be done are the words that appear in both MK and PMP, such as 'pocket; pouch' and 'flour'. For these the direction of the borrowing remains to be determined.

In contrast to short PC *-u-, the reflexes of the long PC *-uː- all seem to descend from MK sources (Table 84). The form *ribut* 'storm' is intriguing in that, in addition to occurring in Bahnar (MK), it also appears in Malay. In wider Austronesian, though, *ribut* is restricted geographically to western Indonesia and so is a likely loan.

*Table 84: Reflexes of PC *-uː-*

PNB	Bahnar	PC	Aceh.	Rade	PR Cham	
---	---	ˣ*ʔamuːŋ	---	amuŋ	---	'bunch; stalk'
---	---	ˣ*ʔamuːŋ	---	amuŋ	---	'snout; muzzle'
---	---	*bruːŋ	---	bruŋ	---	'streaked; striped'
---	---	ˣ*kaʔuːʔ	---	---	---	'worried; sad'
*ŏŋ	---	ˣ*ʔuːŋ	---	uŋ	---	'husband; male'
---	çəkuŋ	ˣcakuːŋ	---	kəkuŋ	cakoŋ	'carry (several)'
---	---	ˣ*puːŋ	jɯmpuŋ	---	apyăŋ	'straw (rice)'
---	---	ˣ*taguːʔ	---	kəgŭʔ	takoʔ	'get up; stand up'
---	---	ˣ*tuːʔ	---	tŭʔə	toʔ	'to receive'
---	---	ˣyuːʔ	---	---	---	'descend'
---	dôŋ	ˣɗuːŋ	---	ɗuŋ	---	'float'
---	gut	ˣ*guːʔ	---	gŭʔ	ķuʔ	'below; bottom'
---	həbut	*ribuːʔ	---	ebŭʔ	ripuʔ	'storm'
---	jŭ	ˣ*juːʔ	---	jŭʔ	çuʔ	'black'
---	pók	ˣ*puːʔ	---	pŭʔ	---	'carry in arms'
		*-uːʔ	---	-ŭʔ	-uːʔ	
		*-uːŋ	-uŋ	-uŋ	-uːk	

For PC *u, the vowel length distinction is the direct result of the incorporation of MK material. While the short vowels occur freely in both inherited PMP and incorporated MK words, the long vowels occur overwhelmingly only in words from MK sources.

PC *-ɔ- length distinctions

Both the distribution and the origins of PC *ɔ are of interest. Like all Chamic length contrasts, the distribution is anything but symmetrical. The PC *ɔ occurs long and short before final -ʔ, final -ŋ, and final -k.

*Table 85: Reflexes of PC *-ɔ-*

PNB	PC	Aceh.	Rade	NR	PR Cham	
*kasuq	ˣ*hɔʔ	---	kəhɔ̆ʔ	---	---	'sweat; bleed'
---	ˣ*ŋɔʔ	---	---	---	---	'upgrade; east'
---	ˣchɔʔ	---	---	chɔʔ	çhɔ̆ʔ	'scoop up; ladle'
---	ˣ*ʔakɔʔ	---	kɔ̆ʔ	akɔʔ	akɔ̆ʔ	'head'
*hăk	ˣ*ʔɔʔ	---	---	---	---	'vomit'
---	ˣʔanrɔŋ -f	---	---	anrɔʔ -f	arɔ̆ʔ	'toad'
---	ˣ*dhɔŋ	---	dhɔ̆ŋ	thok	ṭhɔ̆ŋ	'knife'
---	ˣ*prɔŋ	---	prɔ̆ŋ	prok	prɔ̆ŋ	'big'
---	ˣ*salɔŋ	---	hlɔ̆ŋ lar	---	klɔŋ -i	'forever'
---	ˣ*yɔŋ	---	yɔ̆ŋ	yok	---	'lift; take off'
*(ka)rɔ̆ŋ	ˣrɔŋ	ruəŋ	rɔ̆ŋ	-turok	rɔŋ -1	'back (anat.)'
*trɔ̆ŋ	ˣ*trɔŋ	truəŋ	trɔ̆ŋ	trok	trɔ̆ŋ	'eggplant'
---	ˣ*pɔk	---	pɔ̆k	poʔ	---	'to open'
---	ˣ*cɔk	---	---	---	cɔ̆ʔ	'to cry'
---	ˣ*tulɔk	---	---	---	---	'disk shaped'
*ŭk	ˣ*hɔk	---	hɔ̆k	---	hɔ̆ʔ	'pour out; spill'
---	ˣ*bɔk	---	---	boʔ	poʔ -v	'to swell'
	*-ɔʔ	---	-ɔ̆ʔ	-oʔ	-ɔ̆ʔ	
	*-ɔŋ	-uəŋ	-ɔ̆ŋ	-ok	-ɔ̆ŋ	
	*-ɔk	---	-ɔ̆k	-oʔ	-ɔ̆ʔ	

The vowel itself was almost but not entirely borrowed. Undoubtedly, it does occur in one native PMP form, the form *dɔːk 'sit', found throughout PMP and related to Malay *duduk*. Intriguingly, I suspect it is the word's monosyllabicity that accounts for the vowel length in this form. The forms ˣ*ləmɔ 'cow; ox; cattle' and ˣ*trɔŋ 'eggplant, although found in Malay as *lĕmbu* and *tĕrung*, are not widely attested in AN and are most likely early borrowings. If not, there are three PMP words with PC *ɔ; if these two are borrowings, there is but one native PMP form left.

The remaining words are apparently borrowings, some predating the formation of PC and some introduced later. Aside from the three words already mentioned, none of the words occurs widely attested in Austronesian. In contrast, four of the forms occur in Smith's (1972) proto-North-Bahnaric (see Table 85) and two more in Aymonier and Cabaton's (1906) dictionary of Cham (see Table

85). The -*nr*- cluster in 'toad', the glottalized stop in ˣcaɗɔŋ -f 'flat basket', and the initial *ch*- of 'scoop up; ladle' mark these as borrowed. Headley (1976) suggests that ˣ*yɔŋ 'to lift; take off' and ˣrɔŋ 'back (anat.)' are MK in origin, while Durie (1990a:106), citing Cowan (1983:177), labels ˣ*ŋɔʔ 'upgrade; above; east' a MK loan. That is, of 17 forms, at least 10 of them have MK affiliations; one may (or may not) have an Austronesian heritage.

*Table 86: Reflexes of PC *-ɔ:-*

PNB	Bahnar	PC	Aceh.	Rade	NR	PR Cham	
---	---	ˣ*sɔ:ʔ	sũəp -f	kəsŏʔ	-sɔ:ʔ	thɔʔ	'lungs; placenta'
---	---	ˣ*kɔ:ʔ	---	koʔ	ko:ʔ	kŏʔ -1	'white'
---	---	ˣ*mɔ:ʔ	---	moʔ	mõ:ʔ	---	'wife'
---	bòk; bŏ	ˣ*ɓɔ:ʔ	---	ɓŏʔ	ɓo:ʔ	ɓɔʔ	'face' cf. 'nose'
---	---	ˣ*ʔatɔ:ŋ	---	toŋ	ato:k	atɔŋ	'beat (gong)'
---	---	ˣ*khɔ:ŋ	khuəŋ	khoŋ	kho:k	khɔŋ	'dry (weather)'
---	kroŋ	ˣ*krɔ:ŋ	---	kroŋ	kro:k	krɔŋ	'river'
---	rõŋ	ˣ*rɔ:ŋ	---	roŋ	---	rɔŋ	'raise; nourish'
*boŋ	boŋ	ˣ*bɔ:ŋ	---	boŋ	bo:k	pɔŋ	'coffin; casket'
*čùŋ	---	ˣjɔ:ŋ	---	joŋ	jo:k	çɔŋ	'axe'
*kăn	---	ˣ*glɔ:ŋ	---	dloŋ	dlo:k	ḳlɔŋ	'tall; high; big'
*kôŋ	---	ˣ*kɔ:ŋ	---	koŋ	ko:k	kɔŋ	'bracelet'
*loŋ	---	ˣ*lɔ:ŋ	---	loŋ	---	---	'try, prove, test'
*oŋ	---	ˣhɔ:ŋ -f	---	hoŋ	hoŋ -f	---	'wasp'
*tùŋ	anoŋ	ˣʔanrɔ:ŋ	---	enoŋ -v	anro:k	anɔŋ	'carry (on pole)'
---	prõk	ˣ*prɔ:k	---	prok	---	prɔʔ	'squirrel'
---	lõk	ˣ*lɔ:k	pluəʔ	lok	lo:ʔ	lɔʔ	'to peel'
---	---	*dɔ:k	duəʔ	dok	do:ʔ	ṭɔʔ	'sit; live; stay'
		ˣ*-ɔ:ʔ	---	-ŏʔ; -oʔ	-o:ʔ	-ɔʔ; -ŏʔ	
		ˣ*-ɔ:ŋ	-uəŋ	-oŋ	-oŋ; -o:k	-ɔŋ	
		ˣ*-ɔ:k	-uəʔ	-ok	-o:ʔ	-ɔʔ	

With the long vowels, aside from the one obviously PMP form, the evidence for MK origins is impressive. All but six of these forms occur in PNB or in the Bahnar recorded by Aymonier and Cabaton. Headley (1976) labels six Chamic forms with long -ɔ:- as MK in origin: 'coffin; casket', 'axe', 'river', 'squirrel', 'wasp', and 'bracelet'. The remaining six, while not yet established as borrowings, certainly lack obvious PMP etymologies.

For PC *ɔ, both the vowel and its length distinction are the direct result of contact with MK, as both the vowel and its length distinction are present almost exclusively in material incorporated from MK.

PC *-a- length distinctions

Although for PC *-u- and PC *-ɔ- the PC vowel length distinction would at best be marginal without the forms with long vowels incorporated into Chamic from MK sources, the case is quite different with the length distinction associated with PC *-a-. While the influence of MK contact played a role, the length contrast in PC *-a- is fully and richly manifested in inherited Austronesian forms, largely due to the manifestation of PAn *e [ə] as PC *-ă-, while in many cases PAn *-a- is manifested as PC *-a:-.

The non-MK component of the PC *-a- versus *-a:- length contrast evolved from the PMP vowels *-ə- and PMP *-a-. And, with the possible exception of several thus far unexplained cases, these vowels have quite regular reflexes in PC. Cowan (1974) noted that for PMP *-ə- forms the PC reflexes are always short; however, for PMP *-a- both short and long PC reflexes are found. That is, while the PMP *-ə- unexceptionally merged with the PC short *-a- reflexes, the reflexes of PMP *a are split. Specifically, before final -ʔ, -ŋ, -k, -l, -r, -n, -p, and marginally before -t, PMP *a occurs long.[4]

These patterns are not, however, totally exceptionless. Before final -n, the PMP *a is -a:- in ten words, but not in the word 'name', where it has a short reflex. This exception is inexplicable unless 'name' occurred with considerable frequency in an unstressed syntactic slot, which, in turn, prevented length—a feature associated with stress—from developing. Before -t, PMP became long only marginally: specifically, it occurred long in words with a medial *-h- which dropped ('bad; wicked', 'chisel, plane, to chisel, plane'), in the number four *pa:t because it is a monosyllabic content word, and, for no apparent reason, in *pala:t -l 'palm; sole'. In the form 'palm; sole' the vowel pattern is irregular, with some languages having a short vowel reflex, and some a long vowel reflex. However, aside from this handful of cases, where PMP *a has long reflexes and where it has short reflexes is totally predictable from the final. [Note: The reconstructions

---

4.   Before *-h, PAn had already merged PAn *-e- and *-a- (Blust 1995b:622-623), with the ultimate consequence that the inherited Austronesian forms in PC did not develop a contrast between PC *-a and *-a:- before *-h. Nor did such a contrast develop in PC from borrowed MK material.

used in this work are Blust's for PMP (see References) and Adelaar's for Proto-Malayic.]

Among the reflexes of PC *-a- (Table 87) and of PC *-aː- (Table 88), words both of PMP and of MK origin can be found easily. Numerous forms have Malay counterparts, many of which are common PMP forms. Others have common MK origins.

In Table 88, seven examples are reconstructed for proto-North-Bahnaric; another ten are found in Aymonier and Cabaton's Bahnar. Still others such as ˣˣbaːl 'mɛnd; patch' are found in the MK subgroup PKatuic.

However, there are three Acehnese items that require discussion because in one variant or another they have a /-an/ final rather than the /-ɰən/ final expected from PC final *-aːn: 'fish', 'cup; bowl; dish', and 'road; path', and 'bowl'. According to Durie (p.c.), *ikan* is a Malay borrowing. As he notes, the usual Acehnese word for fish is ɰŋkot. The second word *cawan* 'cup; bowl; dish' is, according to Coope (1976) and Baxter (p.c.), a borrowing from Chinese. This analysis is consistent both with its failure to reconstruct within PMP and its irregular final. The last word needing discussion is the Acehnese -lɰən 'yard; space in front of the house', which Durie suggests is the regular reflex of PC *jalaːn 'road; path'. The difficulty involves the presence of another form in Acehnese *jalan* 'highway; main road' which at first glance looks like the appropriate cognate. On closer inspection, however, -lɰən looks to be the cognate form and *jalan* looks to be a later borrowing from Malay. As Durie points out, -lɰən corresponds quite regularly phonologically, while the final of *jalan* -v is irregular. Semantically, the *jalan* is interesting: *jalan*, as Durie notes, is used only marginally to refer to main roads and highways, while *ret/rot* is the normal word for road. This suggests that the semantic range of the original reflex of PC *jalaːn > -lɰən 'yard; space in front of the house' was narrowed under the influence of the word *ret/rot,* with the modern Acehnese *jalan* borrowed only later from Malay.

The fact that a length distinction between PC *-a- (Table 87) and PC *-aː- is found quite readily both in the inherited PMP forms and in the incorporated MK material suggests that the length distinction comes from two sources: one, it was developed internally from the inherited PMP material (as described above) and that it was also present in the material incorporated from MK languages.[5]

---

5. However, note that the contrast before PC *-r is found primarily in incorporated MK material, as most of the inherited PMP final -r's were lost.

*Table 87: Reflexes of PC *-a-*

PNB	Bahnar	Malay	PC	Aceh.	Rade	PR Cham	
---	ləmā	lĕmak	ˣ*ləmaʔ	lɯmaʔ	emăʔ	lamɨʔ	'fat, grease, oil'
---	tak	tĕtak	*taʔ	---	---	---	'chop; cut'
---	---	masak	*tasaʔ	---	kəsăʔ	tathăʔ	'ripe; cooked'
---	---	tanak	*tanaʔ	---	kənăʔ	tanɨʔ	'cook'
---	təgăk	---	*tagak -f	---	kəgăʔ	---	'cleaver'
---	---	---	*gətak	---	kətăk	katăʔ	'sap; resin'
---	araŋ	arang-	*hadaŋ	araŋ-m	hədăŋ	haʈăŋ	'charcoal'
*qmăŋ	maŋ	---	ˣ*ɓaŋ	---	ɓăŋ	ɓăŋ	'hole; door'
---	lăŋ	---	*glaŋ	---	dlăŋ	ḳlăŋ	'look at; watch'
---	păŋ	---	*paŋ	---	---	---	'to make a wall'
*hăŋ	---	---	ˣ*haŋ	---	hăŋ	hăŋ	'hot; spicy'
---	uāŋ	---	*waŋ	---	wăŋ-	wăŋ	'sickle'
---	anan	---	*ʔanan	nan	anăn	---	'name'
*khăn	khăn	kain	ˣ*khan	---	---	khăn	'cloth; blanket'
---	klăn	---	ˣ*klan	lhan	tlăn	klăn	'boa; python'
---	---	bantal	*bantal	bantai	---	patăr -f	'pillow'
---	---	gatal	*gatal	gatai	kətăl	katăl	'itchy'
---	---	sĕndal	ˣ*ɗal	---	---	ɗăl	'to wedge'
*baqar	---	---	ˣ*baʔar	---	məar	pɨʔar	'paper'
*-dăr	---	---	*dar	---	dar	---	'encircle'
*kăt	kât	ikat	*ʔikat	ikat	---	ikăʔ	'to tie'
---	---	surat	*surat	surat	hrăʔ	harăʔ	'write; letter'
---	təpăt	tĕpat	*təpat	tɯpat	kəpăʔ	tapăʔ	'straight; honest'
---	ara	urat	*ʔurat	urat	aruăt (m)	urăʔ	'vein, tendon'
---	---	kawat	*kawat	---	kəwăt	---	'wire'
---	---	sukat	*sukat	sukat	məkăʔ -i	---	'to measure'
---	---	pusat	*pusat	pusat	məsăt	pathăʔ	'navel; center'
---	---	ulat	*hulat	ulat	hluăt (m)	halăʔ	'worm'
---	---	---	*-aʔ	-at; -aʔ	-ăʔ;	-ăʔ; -ɨʔ
---	---	---	*-ak	-aʔ	-ăk, -ăʔ	-aʔ; -ak
---	---	---	*-aŋ	-aŋ	-ăŋ	-ăŋ
---	---	---	*-an	-an	-ăn; -an	-ăn
---	---	---	*-al	-ai	-ăl	-ăl
---	---	---	*-ar	---	---	---
---	---	---	*-at	-at	-ăt; -aʔ	-ăʔ

*Table 88: Reflexes of PC *-aː-*

Bahnar	Malay	PC	Aceh.	Rade	PR Cham	
---	ĕmpat	*paːt	pɯət	pǎʔ	paʔ	'four'
---	anak	*ʔanaːk	anɯʔ	anak	aniʔ	'child'
---	minyak	*miñaːk	miñɯʔ	---	miñiʔ	'oil'
uak	---	ˣ*ʔawaːk	awɯəʔ	awak	awaʔ	'spoon; ladle'
jāk	ajak	*jaːk	---	jak	çaʔ	'invite'
---	pinang	*pinaːŋ	pinɯŋ	mənaŋ	paniŋ	'betel(-nut)'
---	hudang	*hudaːŋ	udɯəŋ	hədaŋ	haṭǎŋ	'shrimp'
---	---	ˣ*kaːŋ	kɯəŋ	kaŋ	kaŋ	'chin; jaw'
iāŋ	yang	ˣ*yaːŋ	---	yaŋ	yaŋ	'spirit; god'
lāŋ	---	*laːŋ	---	laŋ	laŋ	'spread out'
---	orang	*ʔuraːŋ	urɯəŋ	arǎŋ -1	uraŋ	'person'
çaŋ	---	ˣ*caːŋ	---	---	coŋ	'wait'
---	tulang	*tulaːŋ	tulɯəŋ	klaŋ	talaŋ	'bone'
---	kĕrang	*kraːŋ	krɯəŋ	---	---	'clam'
---	lubang	*lubaːŋ	---	---	lipaŋ	'hole; pit'
---	---	ˣ*ɗaːŋ	---	ɗaŋ	ɗaŋ	'lie suppine'
---	lipan	*limpaːn	limpɯən	epan	lipan	'centipede'
---	hujan	*hujaːn	ujɯən	həjan	haçan	'rain'
---	bulan	*bulaːn	bulɯən	mlan	pilan	'moon'
---	dahan	*dhaːn	dhɯən	adhan	ṭhan	'branch'
---	tangan	*taŋaːn	---	kəŋan	taŋĭn	'hand; arm'
---	jalan	*jalaːn	-lɯən	elan	çalan	'road; path'
---	tampal	ˣ*baːl	---	---	pal	'mend'
---	pagar	*pagaːr	pagɯə	---	paḳa	'fence'
---	akar	*ʔughaːr	ukhɯə	agha	uḳha	'root'
---	tawar	*tabaːr	tabɯə	kəba	tapa	'tasteless'
---	jahat	*jəhaːt	jɯhɯət	jhat	çhaʔ	'bad; wicked'
---	pahat	*phaːt	phɯət	---	phaʔ	'to chisel'
---	---	*-aːʔ	-ɯəʔ; -ɯət	-ǎʔ	-aʔ	
---	---	*-aːk	-ɯək; -ɯk	-ak	-aʔ; -iʔ	
---	---	*-aːŋ	-ɯəŋ; -ɯŋ	-aŋ	-aŋ; -ǎŋ	
---	---	*-aːn	-ɯən	-an	-an; -in, -in	
---	---	*-aːl	-ɯə	-al	-al	
---	---	*-aːr	-ɯə	-a	-a	
---	---	*-aːt	-ɯət; -ɯt	-at	-aʔ	

Then, of course, there are a number of borrowings containing *-aː-, but these are transparently borrowings so these forms do not obscure the analysis of length in the Chamic languages.

*Table 89: Borrowings with *-aː-*

PMnong	Bahnar	Malay	PC	Acehnese	Rade	PR Cham	
*brak	amra	měrak	ˣʔəmraːk	mɯraʔ -v	amrak	amraʔ	'peacock'
*relat	---	---	ˣlaːt	---	lat	klɛt -ivf	'flat'
---	---	jaga	ˣjaːŋ	jaga -f	---	---	'to guard'

First, not one of the three forms in Table 89 reconstructs to the PC level. In addition, all three forms are attested in MK languages, although 'guard' is apparently ultimately Sanskrit (Coope 1986). The word 'peacock' has a medial /-mr-/ only found in MK borrowings. Headley (1976, #1.47) identifies it as a MK loan, it reconstructs as *brak in Proto-Mnong, *braːʔ in PSB (Efimov), and *riaʔ in PKatuic, and it has an irregular vowel reflex in Acehnese. In the case of 'flat' the forms were borrowed from MK. The word reconstructs as *relat in PMnong, which is the likely source of the forms scattered throughout the mainland Chamic languages. The lookalike form *rata* found in Malay and Acehnese is a quite unrelated borrowing from Javanese (see Appendix II). As for 'guard', Coope (1986) suggests that it comes from Sanskrit, which in light of the similarity between the Malay and Acehnese, on the one hand, and the PC, on the other, looks at least possible. What looks definite in any case is that the Acehnese and Malay cannot be directly related to the PC forms; the Acehnese looks like it came from Malay, with the question of the ultimate origin of the Malay being left open.

The Acehnese correlates of PC vowel length

The Acehnese data in the above tables is of particular interest. The claims in the literature by Cowan and by Shorto that the length distinction in PC correlates with certain Acehnese vowel distinctions are substantiated by a careful comparison of Acehnese vowels with these PC length distinctions. The distinction between long and short *a is clearly and unambiguously found in the tables above for the other two long vowels PC *-oː- and PC *-uː-, more Acehnese data will be needed to determine whether the distinction is preserved there too.

PAn stress and vowel length compared with PC vowel length

The data discussed in this section have shown that PC vowel length distinctions are not inherited from PAn but instead represent a secondary development, and, as a secondary development, appear to have nothing to say about whether or not stress (with resultant vowel length distinctions in various languages as a reflex) needs to be reconstructed for PAn. Certainly Zorc (1978, 1983) has shown that in certain Philippine languages the long/short vowel length distinction would correlate with the earlier existence of stress, and, as Ross (1992:47) writes, "Recent work suggests that Zorc's system is reconstructable for PAn, since there are relics of it in a few Formosan languages." Zorc and Ross are not alone in their suggestion that PAn had a stress distinction; Wolff (1991), Peiros (cited in Ross 1992), and Benedict (p.c.) also suggest reconstructing stress for PAn.

However, PC vowel length and the proposed PAn stress system (which correlates with vowel length in certain Philippine languages) have no correlation whatsoever with one another. First, as Ross (1992:47) notes, in the Philippine languages "the long/short distinction is limited to the vowel of the penultimate syllable", while the PC distinctions are limited to the ultimate syllable. Second, and more importantly, the PC vowel length distinctions between long and short *a correlate directly with the earlier distinction between PAn *e [ə] and *a reinforced by the borrowing of MK words with a length distinction, while the length distinctions between long and short *u and *o depend almost on length distinctions between originally inherited and originally borrowed material.

THE MAIN SYLLABLE VOWELS SUMMARIZED

It goes without saying that everywhere the details remain to be filled in and clarified. For instance, much more can be learned about the Acehnese correspondences from the incorporation of a more extensive number of forms. Similarly, a better understanding of borrowings will contribute to a better understanding of the systemic interactions between the PMP and the MK heritage.

Nonetheless, the outlines of the history of PC vowels seem clear. The PC vowel system consists of a core of elements inherited from PMP supplemented and enriched by MK borrowings. In addition, the subsequent reflexes of PC vowels in the various daughter languages is also straightforward, with the improvement upon the foundation laid by Lee 1966 and others made possible by an expanded understanding of which forms were borrowings and by a greatly expanded data base.

From these patterns we can learn something both about the nature of the earlier cultural contact and about the influence of language contact on vowel systems. The intensity of the early contact between MK speakers and the pre-PC speakers is attested to by the richness of the borrowed component of PC. The effects of language contact are attested to by the restructuring of the original PMP disyllables into the iambic morphemes of PC and by the incorporation of a number of new vowel distinctions into the linguistic system.

7

Nasals and Nasalization

Both nasal consonants and nasalized vowels are reconstructed for PC. For nasalized consonants, the reconstructions are straightforward and based on regular correspondence patterns. In fact, only two developments are worthy of comment: In Cham, word-final nasalization seems to trigger simplification of complex vowels. In Roglai and Tsat, there is widespread denasalization of word-final nasal consonants — a change that has two consequences: it makes late loans with word-final nasals conspicuous as they fail to undergo the change and it provides strong subgrouping evidence for the pairing of Tsat with Northern Roglai.

   For nasalized vowels, the bulk of the evidence comes from just three languages—the closely-related Chru and Northern Roglai, and, in certain cases, from Western and Phan Rang Cham. While there are sometimes questions about the data itself, sometimes about its interpretation, and sometimes about which forms are loans, there are, nonetheless, certain patterns which seem clear.

NASALIZATION IN PC

There are PC nasalized vowels not associated with adjacent nasal consonants. In these cases, the reconstruction of PC nasalized vowels is based on the nasalization recorded in Chru, Roglai, and Haroi forms, and, in those rare Phan Rang Cham forms with a reflex that would indicate prior nasalization (see "Nasalization in Cham" on page 155, for a discussion of the Cham reflexes).

   Table 90 includes words with reflexes of nasalized vowels. In Chru, all but one of the forms has an actual nasalized vowel; in Northern Roglai all of the forms have nasalized vowels; in Haroi about half the forms have nasalized vowels; and, in Phan Rang Cham, every word has evidence of prior nasalization,

either a vowel reflex characteristic of earlier nasalization or in the pattern of diphthong or triphthong simplification that indicates earlier nasalization.

Table 90: Reflexes of PC nasalized vowel

PC	Aceh.	Chru	NR	Haroi	PR Cham	
*maʔiăk	ʔiə?	məʔiaʔ	maʔiăʔ	məʔĕăʔ	miiʔ -v	'urinate'
*mahăw	---	məhău	mahău	məhău	mɨhu	'thirst'
*krăh	---	krăh	khrăh -i	krăh	krɨh	'middle'
*hă	---	hă	hă	hăi -v	hɨ	'you; thou'
x*bruăʔ	---	bruaʔ -n	bruăʔ	prʊ̈ʔ	prʊ̈ʔ	'work; do'
xʔiăw	---	iău	iău	eau	iw	'left (side)'
xsrăp	---	sră:uʔ -1	srăʔ	srău?	thru?	'crossbow'
xjrăw	---	jră:u	jrău	cəriău	çru	'medicine'
xsrʊ̈h	---	srʊ̈h	srʊ̈h	srouh -v	thrʊ̈h	'nest; swarm'
xkasuăr -f	---	kəsuă -f	kasuă -f	kəsoa	kathʊ̈r	'porcupine'
xjiă	---	jiă	jiă	sia -v	---	'taxes'

Notice that more than half of these have been identified as post-PC borrowings. Many of the nasalized vowels are found in borrowings, but not all. Certainly in this group, 'thirst; desire' appears to be related to an PMP form meaning
'want'.

NASALIZATION IN CHRU

The nasalization in Chru appears to be, etymologically-speaking, sporadic. When
it occurs, it occurs in the vicinity of initial nasals, *h-, and *ʔ- particularly when
these co-occur with final *-ʔ; however, the actual occurrence is, nonetheless, not
fully predictable on the basis of correspondence patterns.

In Table 91, there are Chru forms which have corresponding nasalized
vowels in Northern Roglai. With the exception of 'raw; green', the nasalized
vowel is preceded either by a nasal consonant or by a glottal stop, suggesting the
possibility of perseverative nasalization. In these cases, it is probably nothing
more than the variable marking perseverative vowel nasalization. The case of
'raw; green' is more surprising; however, it may be that the nasalization spreading from the earlier homorganic nasal is still found in Acehnese.

Table 91: Chru and Northern Roglai nasalization

PC	Aceh.	Chru	NR	Haroi	PR Cham	
*kuñit	kuñɛt	kəñĩ:ʔ	kuñĩ:ʔ	kəñei?	kañi?	'yellow; tumeric'
*banut	---	bənũ:ʔ	binũ?	---	pinu?	'banyan, balete'
*manuʔ	manɔ?	mənũ?	manũ?	mənŭ?	mĭnŭ?	'chicken; fowl'
*tamuh	---	təmũh	tumũh	cəmoh	tamŭh	'grow; sprout'
*tamut	---	mũ:?	mũ:?	---	---	'hammer'
*ñu	---	ñũ	ñũ	ñau -v	ñu	'he, she; they'
ˣ**k-am-lɔ?	klɔ	kəmlɔ̃	kumlo	kəmlɔ	kamlɔ	'dumb; mute'
ˣʔəmraːk	mɯraʔ -v	amrã:?	amra:?	amra?	amra?	'peacock'
ˣəm-aguăh	---	guăh	muguăh	---	---	'morning; dawn'
*məntah	mɯntah	mətăh	matăh	mətăh	mĭtăh	'raw; green'

A second interesting set of Chru correspondences is found in Table 92. These appear to exhibit what Matisoff (1985) has described as the tendency for vowels to nasalize spontaneously after glottal stops and /h/.

Table 92: Matisoff's vowel nasalization with glottal or /h/ initials

PC	Aceh.	Chru	NR	Haroi	PR Cham	
*tuʔut	tɯot	tə?ũ:?	tu?u:?	cə?u? -v	tau?	'knee'
ˣ**kaʔiaŋ	---	kə?ĩăŋ	ka?iak	kə?eaŋ	kaĭŋ	'loins; waist'
ˣ**ʔɛh	ɛʔ -f	ɛ̃h	eh	ɛh	ɛ̃h	'excrement'
ˣ**kaʔu:?	---	kə?ũ:?	---	kə?ou?	---	'worried; sad'
ˣ**haluaʔ	---	ləhũ?	hlua?	---	halwɔ̃? -i	'sharp'
ˣ**lahiã?	---	ləhĩa?	---	---	---	'to lose'

The third set of forms (Table 93), however, is not explicable in phonetic terms, that is, the nasalization on the vowel seems to have no obvious phonetic cause. What is immediately obvious, however, is the fact that, at the very least, four of the six forms are borrowed, not native.

Table 93: Unexpected vowel nasalization

PC	Aceh.	Chru	NR	Haroi	PR Cham	
ˣ**glɔ	---	glɔ̃ -n	dlo	---	klɔ	'brain; marrow'
*kakaːs	---	kərkã:h -n	kaka	kəkăh	kakăh	'fish scales'
*bhaːn	---	phã:n -n	pha:t	aphan	phan	'sneeze'
ˣ**ruay	---	ruăi -n	ruai	roai	roy	'fly; bug; insect'
ˣ**karah	---	krăh -n	karah	krăh	karăh	'ring'
ˣsraːp -f	---	srăp -n -f	---	srăp -fv	---	'tired of'

NASALIZATION IN HAROI

In Haroi, nasalized vowels are extremely rare. Tegenfeldt-Mundhenk and Goschnick (1977) note that there are 10 rarely occurring nasalized vowels and that there are only two examples of each. In addition, there is allophonic nasalization: "preceding final -p, -t, and -k, all vowels are nasalized" (1977:2).

Table 94: Haroi vowel nasalization in borrowed words

post-PC	Aceh.	Chru	NR	Haroi	PR Cham	
ˣsrăp	---	srã:uʔ -1	srãʔ	srãuʔ	thruʔ	'crossbow'
ˣtuăi	---	tuăi	thuăi -i	tõai	toy	'guest; stranger'
ˣjrăw	---	jrã:u	jrãu	cəriău	çru	'medicine'

The existence of nasalization in Haroi is interesting in that all the otherwise unaccountably nasalized words in Haroi are borrowed (cf. the similar situation in Chru, above).

NASALIZATION IN CHAM

One of the more striking effects of nasalization occurs in Cham, where nasalization appears to trigger vowel deletion. As Lee (1974:655) noticed, in Western and Phan Rang Cham PC *a vowels (and nasalized PC *ə vowels), either with inherited nasalized vowels or with vowels secondarily nasalized by a preceding nasal consonant, have special Cham reflexes. Sometimes PC *a becomes /ɨ/ (and, depending on additional conditioning factors, sometimes /i/ or /u/) and, in certain diphthongs, the original /a/ is dropped.

In the first set of examples, an inherited nasalized *a becomes /-ɨ-/. In the second set of examples, a preceding consonant secondarily nasalizes the vowel, leading to an /-ɨ-/ reflex. In the third set of examples, the reflex is /i/, rather than /ɨ/; the conditioning factor involved is unclear. In the fourth set of examples, three words ('flower', 'striped' (which may be the same root as 'flower'), and 'soul, spirit; shadow') have the reflex /-u-/. This reflex appears to be conditioned by a combination of their word-final position after a velar nasal and by the fact that the initial *b- makes the whole word breathy-voiced. In the next to last set of examples, it can be seen that some PC *-ə forms have also undergone the change. In the table in "Reflexes of PMP *-i- and *-i" on page 117, it can be seen that some PC *-ə became ă in Cham; perhaps the change from *-ə to ă occurred first, with the ă > -ɨ change following. The last set of examples constitutes a problem; despite the obviously nasalized vowel, the vowel reflex remains unaffected.

*Table 95: PC *a > -ɨ in PR Cham and Western Cham*

PC	W. Cham	PR Cham	
*krăh	krɨh; kɨh	krɨh	'middle; half'
ˣkrăm -1vn	krɨm -v	krɨm -v	'bamboo'
*mamah	mamɨh	mɨmɨh	'chew'
*tanah	tanɨh	tanɨh	'earth, soil'
*tama	tamɨ	tamɨ	'enter'
*ʔama	mɨ	amɨ	'father'
*huma	hamɨ	hamu -v	'field'
*lima	lamɨ	lamɨ; limɨ	'five'
*ʔina	nɨ	inɨ	'mother; major; big'
*panah	panɨh	panɨh	'shoot (bow); a bow'
*pina:ŋ	paniŋ	paniŋ	'betel (-nut)'
*ʔana:k	nɨʔ	anɨʔ	'child'
*lama:n	lamɨn	limɨn	'elephant'
*miña:k	mañɨʔ	miñɨʔ	'oil'
*laŋa -v	laŋɨ	liŋɨ; laŋɨ	'sesame'
*taŋa	---	tañɨ	'ask'
*taŋa:n	taŋən -v	tañɨn	'hand'
*tə(li)ŋa	---	taŋɨ	'ear'
*laŋit	laŋĩ:ʔ	liŋɨʔ	'sky'
*mañam -1	mañɨm	miñɨm	'weave; twill'
*buŋa	paŋur -f	piŋu	'flower'
*buŋa	---	piŋu	'striped'
*buŋat	paŋŭʔ	piŋŭʔ	'soul, spirit; shadow'
ˣ*b-an-ət	panəʔ	pinɨʔ	'a dam; a fence'
ˣ*məŋ	məŋ	mɨŋ	'from'
*gunam	---	ḳanăm	'cloud'
*nam	năm	năm	'six'
*ʔanan	nən	năn	'that (third p.)'

The direction of the nasalization is also of interest, being perseverative rather than anticipatory, a type of nasalization reminiscent of the nasalization in Malay and in other Austronesian languages of the region (cf. Court (1970)).

In addition, throughout the data, cases can be found in which the modern Cham reflex is an /a/, phonetically [ə], rather than /i/. These cases are examples of further reduction, in which a secondarily developed /i/ was subsequently reduced to a /ə/. An examination of the older Written Cham forms in Aymonier and Cabaton makes clear, many of the forms with an orthographic <a> in Modern Cham had an /i/ in the earlier records.

Finally, after *m- in the presyllable, the vowel reflex is almost exceptionlessly /ɨ/, rather than /i/, effectively neutralizing the earlier four-way vowel distinction. The patterns suggest that the various vowels were first reduced to shwa and then later became /-ɨ-/ under the influence of nasalization. Cabaton described this change in 1901.

Table 96: After Cham presyllable m-

PMP	Malay	PC	Aceh.	NR	PR Cham	
*mamaq	mamah	*mamah	mamʌh	mumãh	mɨmɨh	'chew'
*ma-atay	mati	*matay	mate	matai	mɨtay	'die'
*inum;	minum	*minum;	minom	---	mɨñŭm	'to drink'
*inem		*minam				
*mata	mata	*mata	mata	mata	mɨta	'eye'
*manuk	manuk	*manuʔ	manɔʔ	manŭʔ	mɨnŭʔ	'chicken; fowl'
*ma-qasin	masin	*masin	masen	masit (?)	mɨthɨn	'salted; salty'
*ma-esem	masam	*masam	masam	masap	mɨthăm	'sour; vinegar'
*m-uda	muda	*muda	muda	mida	mɨṭa	'young; unripe'

Note that the original presyllable vowel is still preserved in Acehnese, as is attested in both Malay and PMP.

Nasalization and vowel deletion in diphthongs

In addition to those environments in which a nasalized *a was reduced to a /ɨ/, there are also several cases, discussed by Lee, in which a nasalized *a was deleted. In Lee's terms, "In two other environments there are traces of earlier nasalization in Cham. One of these environments is where *ã is preceded by *i or *u as part of a complex peak" (1966:120).

Interpretation of the historical origins of these changes, however, is not as clear as it was in the case of a nasalized *ã being reduced to a /ɨ/. Lee pointed out the connection with nasalization, but other factors are also obviously involved. One factor is the non-Chamic-like syllable structure: all of these forms involve originally closed syllables were also originally heavy.

What is abundantly clear is that all five forms cited in Table 97 are post-Chamic borrowings. None of these forms shows up in Malay or PMP, but the first four are attested in either PSB (Efimov) or in PKatuic, and the one remaining form is also apparently a borrowing. One suspects that, in addition to simple nasalization, there may also have been some adjustment of borrowings to fit the more restricted syllable canon of Cham.

Table 97: Cham forms with lost nasalized vowels

P-Katuic	PSB	post-PC	NR	W. Cham	PR Cham	
---	*kʌːɲ	ˣkhiaŋ -fi	khiaŋ -f	khin -f	khĭŋ	'want; desire'
*əŋkʌɲ	---	ˣkasuăr -f	kasuã -f	kasur	kathŭr	'porcupine'
*kəmhuar	---	ˣmuăr -f	muã	mur	mu -f	'termite'
*br̩q	*bruə?	ˣˣbruă?	bruă?	prŭ?	prŭ?	'work; do'
---	---	ˣgruă?	---	k/rŭ?	---	'lie prone'

An examination of Table 97 makes it clear that the vowel deletion occurs in both Western and Phan Rang Cham.

Lee's second environment for deletion is where *ă preceded a following *u (Lee 1966:120). In this environment, Lee noted that the *ă was lost except when it followed a main syllable nasal, as in *naw 'go'. Rephrasing Lee's description, a nasalized vowel was lost when it preceded a *u, but not when it immediately followed a nasalized consonant.

Table 98: Loss of nasalized /a/ before /u/ in Cham

PC	Aceh.	Chru	NR	W. Cham	PR Cham	
*mahăw	---	məhãu	mahãu	mahu	mɨhu	'thirst; desire'
ˣjrăw	---	jrăːu	jrãu	çru	çru	'medicine'
ˣ?jraw	---	iraːu -1	?jrau	çrau < *jr-	---	'bamboo sp.'
*danaw	danɔ	dənau	danau -n	---	ṭanaw	'lake'
*bɔh maw	---	bəmau	bumãu	poh mau	pimaw	'mushroom'
*naw	---	nau	nãu	nau	naw	'go; walk'

In Table 98, the forms for 'medicine' and 'thirst; desire' reconstruct to PC and in both cases the vowels in question are nasalized. The form for 'bamboo species' is added for comparison; it provides an example of a word parallel to 'medicine' but without a nasalized vowel. The three remaining forms on the table confirm Lee's observation that, if the immediately preceding consonant was a nasal, the Cham deletion did not occur.

An examination of the relevant vowels in Chru and Northern Roglai shows that nasalization correlates with the Cham deletions, with the caveat that Cham deletion does not occur after an immediately preceding nasal consonant.

Lee (1966:120) notes that the deletions in the Cham forms in Table 99 could have been affected by either of the above conditioning environments, as the nasalized vowel both follows an *i and precedes a *u. Like the other deletions, these forms involve nasalized vowels in heavy syllables.

Table 99: Other deletions of nasalized vowels in Cham

PC	Aceh.	Chru	NR	W. Cham	PR Cham	
ˣʔĩãw	---	iãu	iãu	iu	iw	'left (side)'
ˣliɲiaw	---	---	---	laɲiu	liɲiw; laɲiw	'outside'
*miaw	miə	miau	miãu	maɲiau	mɨyaw -v	'cat'

Lee viewed the word 'cat', which he reconstructed with a PC nasalized vowel, as exceptional, as it failed to undergo vowel deletion in Cham. However, alternately, it is simply another form in which the vowel followed a nasal consonant, parallel to the four forms found Table 98.

Despite the apparent clarity of the examples in the last three tables, the analysis of Cham vowel deletion and nasalization is somewhat tentative. Most likely these partial patterns are not the product of internal developments within Chamic, but instead, the residue of MK developments that occurred before the forms were borrowed into Cham. After all, only one of the forms involving a deletion has a good PMP etymology—the form 'thirst; desire'. The form ˣkhiaŋ 'want; desire' is a late borrowing, as is made clear by the extreme irregularity in its correspondences. The form 'termite' is borrowed, and so are the forms for 'porcupine' and 'work; do'. The remaining forms could well be as of yet unidentified loans, possibly even late loans. In such cases, the apparent correspondence patterns would represent not what has happened in the history of Chamic, but instead may have come from different Chamic languages borrowing the various forms from different donor languages.

Other changes that at first appear to be connected are, on closer inspection, unrelated. The three forms below have only changed in Phan Rang Cham, but not in Western Cham, clearly indicating that the change is recent—post-dating the split of Western Cham and Phan Rang Cham.

Table 100: Vowel coalescence restricted to PR Cham

post-PC	Aceh.	Chru	NR	W. Cham	PR Cham	
ˣhanuã? -v	---	hənua?	ha nuã?	hanuɨ?	hanŭ?; nŭ?	'right (side)'
ˣtuãy	---	tuãi	thuãi -i	ʈuai	toy	'guest'
ˣkəmuan	kɯmuən	kəmuan	kamuãn	kamuan	kamon -v	'nephew'

Not only are these changes restricted to in Phan Rang Cham but also the language contains other parallels. These changes seem to reflect the trend toward diphthong simplification under the influence of Vietnamese playing itself out.

NASALIZATION IN TSAT

Tsat is an invaluable source of valuable information on Chamic nasalization. Unfortunately, the available Tsat material consists of preliminary sketches in a broad phonetic transcription. For the reflexes of PC finals, however, there is inconsistency in the recording of these finals, that is, variation beyond the expected variation found in a preliminary analysis. The rather wide-range of variation in the transcription of these finals cannot be blamed on Ouyang, Zheng, and Ni. All three are experienced and skilled field workers whose transcriptions of other languages has proved completely reliable in the past, so the variation reflects something about the nature of the Tsat data itself. Two possibilities, not mutually exclusive, suggest themselves: in part the variation may result from the fact that in certain sandhi environments the older place of articulation has been faithfully retained and in part it may result from its retention in careful speech. Nonetheless, all the critical elements for us to understand the basic developments involving the glottalization of final nasals in Tsat are present in the transcriptions of one or another of the linguists who have looked at Tsat— Ouyang, Zheng, and Ni, supplemented by the occasional word transcribed by Maddieson, who did some instrumental work on the tones working with Pang's tapes. Thus, despite considerable indeterminacy in the details, the overall pattern of development seems clear.

Two types of noticeable variation occur in the Tsat data: notational variation and actual variation. The notational variation is fully to be expected: the data is not only preliminary but comes from multiple sources and authors, from personal communication, from published papers, and from conference papers. The range of phonetic variation in the tonal transcription is clarified in Maddieson and Pang (1993), in which the various notational systems are standardized and it is established explicitly that Tsat has a five-way tone system, with three level tones, a rising tone, and a falling tone, an analysis implicit in Ouyang, Zheng, and Ni but certainly not transparent. The notational variation can be nicely illustrated by the single phonemic falling tone, which is marked at various times as 53, 42, 32, and 21 (following Ni and Maddieson, it is always marked in this work as 42). Part of this variation is subphonemic, as the falling tone is allophonically lower in the nasal finals than elsewhere, something consistently marked in Ouyang and Zheng. Similarly, a notational omission, rather than inconsistency, is worth noting: the glottal stop which appears to always accompany both the rising and the falling tone is not always marked in the Ouyang and

Zheng notation nor in the Ni notation, a reasonable enough omission given its predictability, but one that obscures the diachronic processes involved—thus glottal stops have been included in this transcription.

None of the notational variation, however, causes any problems. For all the Tsat forms cited in this work a standardized transcription of tones has been adapted and all final glottal stops are explicitly written; none of this involves substantive changes, but rather the standardization has been largely mechanical, aside from the handful of instances in which the various descriptions are actually different. Even in these cases, the decisions are trivial, as the correct choices in the cases of the few non-notational differences are glaringly obvious, and most likely reflect typographical errors rather than actual differences.

Reconstituting the nasalized finals

There is a second kind of "directional" variation, however, that is neither notational nor trivial, among the reflexes of PC final nasals. Fourteen of the forms in the data base differ in their transcription of vowel length, sixteen of the 53 nasal finals differ in their transcription of a nasal component, and six of the 53 nasal finals differ in their transcription of the place of articulation. Without question this fluctuation is in large part due to the fact that these distinctions are in the process of disappearing and are evidently quite hard to hear and in part due to contextually influenced variation, for example, in certain sandhi conditions the older place of articulation is preserved.

However, the variation obscures both the synchronic and the diachronic picture. Fortunately, in effect, it is possible, to use a term I first heard used by Marc Okrand, to "reconstitute" these Tsat finals by critically analyzing the data, that is, by a judicious comparison of the different transcriptions, supplemented by knowledge of the Tsat concurrence constraints, by taking into account Ouyang and Zheng's observations on the directionality of the variation, and by utilizing the insights provided by the occasional form that Maddieson transcribed. In this way, it is possible to determine with considerable accuracy what the modern Tsat finals must be.

Reconstituting the vowel length component

Vowel length is the easiest to reconstitute (Table 101). Fourteen of the forms in the data base and nine of the 53 nasal final forms differ in recorded vowel length. If Maddieson, Ouyang, Zheng, or Ni heard the vowel as long, it is long regardless of what the others recorded; this assumption leads to patterns of vowel length consistent with our diachronic and synchronic expectations.

Table 101: Reconstituting vowel length

PNB	PC	Tsat (reconstituted)	Tsat (O. & Z.)	Tsat (Ni)	
---	*nam	na:n$?^{33}$	na:t^{33}	nan$?^{33}$	'six'
---	*huda:ŋ	lə^{11} tha:ŋ^{11}	-tha:ŋ^{11}	lə^{11} thaŋ^{11}	'shrimp; lobster'
---	*sa:ŋ	sa:ŋ^{33}	sa:ŋ^{33}	saŋ^{33}	'house'
---	*hadaŋ	tha:ŋ$?^{42}$	tha:k^{42}	thaŋ^{42}	'charcoal'
---	*papa:n	pa:n^{11}	pa:n^{11}	pan^{11} -1	'board; plank'
*ka	*?ika:n	ka:n^{33}	ka:n^{33}	kan^{33}	'fish'
---	*padam	tha:n$?^{42}$	tha:t^{42}	than^{11} -t	'extinguish'

For 'extinguish' Ouyang and Zhang also have an intriguing phonetic form in square brackets [thatn^{42}] that foreshadows the discussion to come.

Reconstituting the nasalization component

The reconstitution of the nasalization component can be done almost mechanically (Table 102).

Table 102: Reconstituting the nasalization component

PC	Tsat (reconstituted)	Tsat (O. & Z.)	Tsat (Ni)	Tsat (Maddieson)	
x*haŋ	ha:ŋ$?^{42}$	ha:k^{42}	ha:$?^{42}$	[hæ$?^{42}$]	'hot; spicy'
*nam	na:n$?^{33}$	na:t^{33}	nan$?^{33}$	[næ$?^{33}$]	'six'
*lapan	pa:n$?^{42}$	pa:t^{42}	pa:n$?^{11}$-t	[pæ$?^{42}$]	'eight'
*?ariaŋ	liaŋ$?^{33}$ -i	liak^{33} -i	liaŋ$?^{33}$ -i	---	'crab'
x*prɔŋ	pioŋ$?^{33}$	pyok^{33}	pio$?^{33}$	---	'big'
x*trɔŋ	tsioŋ$?^{33}$	tsyok^{33}	tɕioŋ$?^{33}$	---	'eggplant'
*?ura:ŋ	za:ŋ$?^{33}$	za:k^{33}	za:n$?^{33}$	---	'person; someone'
x*dhɔŋ	thoŋ$?^{33}$ [thokŋ^{33}]	thok^{33}	tho$?^{33}$	---	'knife'
*khaŋ	kha:ŋ$?^{42}$	khak^{42}	kha$?^{42}$	---	'hard; stiff; strong'
*hadaŋ	tha:ŋ$?^{42}$	tha:k^{42}	thaŋ^{42}	---	'charcoal'
*klam	kian$?^{33}$	kiat^{33}	---	---	'afternoon; night'
*masam	sa:n$?^{42}$	sa:t^{42}	sa:n$?^{42}$	---	'sour; vinegar'
*hitam	ta:n$?^{42}$	ta:t^{42}	ta:n$?^{42}$	---	'black'
*dalam	la:n$?^{42}$	la:t^{42}	la:n$?^{42}$	---	'deep; inside'
*gulam	khiaŋ$?^{42}$ -ft	khiak^{42} -f	---	---	'carry on shoulder'
*padam	tha:n$?^{42}$	tha:t^{42}	than^{11} -t	---	'extinguish'

For the nasal finals, fully sixteen of the 53 forms differ in their recording of a nasalization component. Again, if Ouyang, Zheng, Ni, or Maddieson records nasalization, it is assumed to be present in the Tsat form. If we assume this, fully 48 of the 53 Tsat forms descended from PC final nasals turn out to have a nasalized reflex in modern Tsat.

As for the remaining five forms, these are also assumed to have (or, at least very recently had) a nasalized vowel. Not only are nasalized forms the expected reflexes of the PC final nasals, but non-nasalized final alveolar or velar consonants do not otherwise seem to occur in Tsat.

Further, while the nasals we are so carefully reconstituting still exist as nasals synchronically in specific sandhi contexts, they may only exist as vowel nasalization in citation forms, except possibly for careful speech.

Reconstituting the place of articulation

Finally, the place of articulation can be restored in a similar manner. Ouyang and Zheng note that, both with nasals and stops, older velars alternate with alveolars, an observation which is fully supported by the diachronic facts. In addition, it is clear that both older alveolars and velars sometimes alternate with glottal stops. Thus, if the "oldest" form found in Ouyang, Zheng, or Ni is taken as the basic place of articulation, all but two of the forms can be assigned a place of articulation that again fully accords with the diachronic facts.

The variation in the place of articulation for these reflexes is obvious in comparisons of Ouyang and Zheng with Ni, and has been specifically commented on by Ouyang and Zheng. The following patterns of variation are specifically noted by Ouyang and Zheng (1983:31); the directionality of the changes reflects in part the difference between what is retained in sandhi forms and what is found in citation forms, a directionality that mirrors the historical changes involved:

variation with velars becoming alveolars:

-k and -t   (with -k being the older form);
-ŋ and -n   (with -ŋ being the older form);

variation with nasals becoming homorganic stops:

-n and -t   (with -n being the older form);
-ŋ and -k   (with -ŋ being the older form);

variation with velar nasals disappearing leaving behind nasalized vowels:

-aŋ and -ã   (with -aŋ being the older form).

And, in addition, although not specifically noted by Ouyang and Zheng, on the basis of comparing Ouyang and Zheng with Ni, there is variation between -t or -k and glottal stop:

-t, -k and -ʔ   (with -t or -k being the older form).

Two of these patterns of variation are not just common in modern Tsat but also show up when Ouyang and Zheng's forms are compared with Ni's, that is, in two cases a velar varies with an alveolar—for which the original place of articulation is assumed to be velar, and in four cases, a velar varies with a glottal stop—for which the original place of articulation is again assumed to velar.

In short, despite variation in the marking of length, nasality, and place of articulation, it has been possible to determine with a fairly high degree of accuracy the basic phonemic shapes of the reflexes of the Tsat reflexes of PC final nasals.

Further, it is likely that the two places of articulation we are so carefully "reconstituting" are consistently present in modern Tsat in certain sandhi positions (as will become clearer later), but it is equally likely that in citation forms they have lost much of their distinctiveness, and may even have been largely reduced to nasalized vowels followed by a glottal stop, except perhaps in careful speech.

Table 103: Reconstituting the place of articulation

PC	Tsat (reconstituted)	Tsat (O. & Z.)	Tsat (Ni)	
*ʔuraːŋ	zaːŋʔ^{33}	zaːk^{33}	zaːnʔ^{33}	'person; someone'
*tulaːŋ	laːŋ^{33}	laːŋ^{33}	laːn^{33}	'bone'
$^{×}$*prɔŋ	pioŋʔ^{33}	pyok^{33}	pioʔ^{33}	'big'
$^{×}$*haŋ	haːŋʔ^{42}	haːk^{42}	haːʔ^{42}	'hot; spicy'
*khaŋ	khaːŋʔ^{42}	khak^{42}	khaʔ^{42}	'hard; stiff; strong'
$^{×}$*dhɔŋ	thoŋʔ^{33}	thok^{33}	thoʔ^{33} [thokŋ^{33}]	'knife'

Internal reconstruction of preploded nasals

This rather laborious reconstituting of the Tsat reflexes of the PC nasal finals was a necessary prelude to the internal reconstruction of Tsat sandhi forms, which are the final key to understanding the fate of PC nasal finals in Tsat. However, to begin we should examine the four attested sandhi forms to determine the patterning.

Table 104: The four attested sandhi forms

Sandhi form:		Reconstituted form:		PC
tatn^{42} (la:n^{11})	>	ta:n^{42}	'section'	---
tsiakŋ^{42} (lai^{33})	>	tsiaŋ^{42}	'where'	---
thokŋ^{33}-	>	thoŋʔ^{33}	'knife'	ˣˣdhɔŋ
thatn^{42}-	>	tha:nʔ^{42}	'extinguish'	*padam

Ouyang and Zheng (1983:31) list the first two forms of Table 104, noting that certain sandhi forms have nasal finals preceded by homorganic stops. The other two forms are also from Ouyang (p.c.). The first two forms are enough to make two things clear: First, ignoring the arrows on the table for a minute, the modern glottalized, nasalized finals have come from earlier final clusters consisting of a stop followed by a homorganic nasal. Second, now that the pattern is clear, it is possible to predict the sandhi forms from the reconstituted forms.

The sandhi forms cited by Ouyang and Zheng bring to mind Court's (1967:48) term preploded ṅasals, which he uses to describe the stop plus homorganic nasal combinations which occur in Měntu. To illustrate Měntu preploded nasals, he gives numerous Měntu examples, including the two forms cited in Table 105. To Table 105 have been added Malay, PC, Northern Roglai, and the four attested Tsat sandhi forms, along with the reconstituted forms.

Table 105: The preploded sandhi forms

Měntu	Malay	PC	NR	Tsat sandhi	>	Tsat reconstituted		
/burətn/	bulan	*bula:n	bila:t	---		-phian^{11}	'moon'	
/turakŋ/	tulang	*tula:ŋ	tula:k	---		-la:ŋ^{33}	'bone'	
---	---	ˣˣdhɔŋ	thok	thokŋ^{33}-	>	thoŋʔ^{33}	'knife'	
---	padam	*padam	padap	thatn^{42}-	>	tha:nʔ^{42}	'extinguish'	
---	---	---	---	tatn^{42}-	>	ta:nʔ^{42}	'section'	
---	---	---	---	tsiakŋ^{42}-	>	tsiaŋʔ^{42}	'at'	

In Měntu, a so-called Land Dayak language of Kalimantan, the preploded nasals have developed out of final nasals (cf. also the discussion in "Reflexes from PC word-final nasals" on page 171). In the Northern Roglai data listed here, PC final nasals presumably became preploded nasals before loosing the nasal component and becoming homorganic voiceless stops. And, in Tsat, as will be shown, the PC final nasals became preploded nasals (at least some of which are still preserved in the sandhi forms) and then in turn some of these developed final glottalization.

The patterns in Tables 105 and 106 allow us to internally reconstruct the Tsat sandhi forms on the basis of the reconstituted forms. The vowel length is inherited from PC.

In Table 106 are the internally-reconstructed sandhi forms. From these forms, not only the modern Tsat reflexes can be derived, but so can the Northern Roglai reflexes. Thus, there is no doubt that the modern Tsat and modern Northern Roglai forms descended from an earlier common source.

Table 106: The internally-reconstructed sandhi forms

PC	Tsat (sandhi)	>	Tsat (reconstituted)	
*nam	*natn	>	na:n$ʔ^{33}$	'six'
*ʔura:ŋ	*za:kŋ	>	za:ŋ$ʔ^{33}$	'person; someone'
*khaŋ	*khăkŋ	>	kha:ŋ$ʔ^{42}$	'hard; stiff; strong'
*hadaŋ	*thăkŋ	>	tha:ŋ$ʔ^{42}$	'charcoal'
ˣ*haŋ	*hăkŋ	>	ha:ŋ$ʔ^{42}$	'hot; spicy'
*masam	*satn	>	sa:n$ʔ^{42}$	'sour; vinegar'
*hitam	*tatn	>	ta:n$ʔ^{42}$	'black'
*dalam	*tatn	<	ta:n$ʔ^{42}$	'deep; inside'
*gulam	*khiakŋ -ft	>	khiaŋ$ʔ^{42}$ -ft	'carry on shoulder'
*padam	*thatn	>	tha:n$ʔ^{42}$	'extinguish'
*dua-lapan	*patn	>	pa:n$ʔ^{42}$	'eight'
*klam	*kiatn	>	kian$ʔ^{33}$	'afternoon; night'
*ʔariaŋ	*liakŋ -i	>	liaŋ$ʔ^{33}$ -i	'crab'
ˣ*trɔŋ	*tsiŏkŋ	>	tsioŋ$ʔ^{33}$	'eggplant'
ˣ*prɔŋ	*piŏkŋ	>	pioŋ$ʔ^{33}$	'big'
ˣ*dhɔŋ	*thŏkŋ	>	thoŋ$ʔ^{33}$	'knife'

Note that neither the Tsat preploded nasals nor the Northern Roglai preploded nasals discussed later should be confused with the post-nasalized final stops of Vietnamese, discussed by Ladefoged and Maddieson (1996:129). Not only has there been no contact between the Vietnamese and the Tsat speakers but the phenomena seem distinct; as Ladefoged and Maddieson write, in Vietnamese "word-final stops are usually released, but the release is by lowering the velum while the oral closure is maintained, so that a short voiceless nasal is produced".

The origin of these Vietnamese post-nasalized stops seems to have more in common with the origins of echo vowels found throughout much of Austronesian than with the Tsat, Roglai, and Land Dayak preploded nasals, which results from a change in the timing of velar lowering for what was originally a final nasal.

The distribution of modern glottalization

It is necessary to keep in mind that preploded final nasals are essentially final clusters consisting of a stop followed by a homorganic nasal. The glottal stop transcribed at various times by Ouyang, Zheng, Ni, and Maddieson developed when the stop component of these stop plus nasal combinations lost its place of articulation, becoming a glottal rather than an oral closure e.g., *-tn- > -ʔn- and *-kŋ- > -ʔŋ-. It was this process that produced what the various authors have written in their phonemic transcription as either -nʔ or -ŋʔ, depending on the place of articulation.

Given the assumption that the stop component of the preploded nasals was the source of glottalization, it is possible from the modern distribution of glottalization to reconstruct the earlier process. An examination of the modern distribution shows that glottalization occurs with a well-defined, specific subset of vowel plus final nasal combinations, that is, with two extremely interesting exceptions, just in the forms containing the PC short vowels *-a- and *-ɔ-, specifically, in the reflexes of the PC rhymes *-aŋ, *-am, *-ăn, *-iaŋ, *-ian, and *-ɔŋ, but nowhere else.

It is imperative not to miss the importance of the fact that glottalization was recorded in these forms. The only reconstructable source for the glottalization in forms ending in PC final nasals is the earlier preploded nasals of Tsat (and Roglai). Thus, just the occurrence of glottalization in the reflexes for PC *nam 'six', a form with a nasalized vowel (due to perseverative nasalization), and *ʔuraːŋ 'person', a form with a long vowel, argues for earlier preploded nasals in these forms.

Thus, the real puzzle is not why some Tsat forms have glottalization—it comes from Tsat forms descended from PC forms with nasal finals. The puzzle is why some Tsat forms descended from PC forms with nasal finals do not have glottalization. It is possible to be misled by a comparison with other languages containing preploded final nasals into thinking that the presence of nasal onsets prevents the development of preploded final nasals. However, at least in the case of Tsat, this is the wrong answer. The glottalization in the Tsat reflex of PC *nam 'six' makes that quite clear; the Tsat reflex of PC *nam 'six' obviously has a nasal onset and just as obviously has glottalization in its reflex. In fact, the presence of glottalization in the Tsat reflex of PC *nam 'six' suggests the right answer: all final nasals became preploded but it was only in certain highly favorably environments that this preplosion was retained long enough for the stop component to develop into glottal closure.

The solution to understanding the historical processes involved lies in realizing that all final nasals originally developed preplosion, which was then subsequently lost in most environments. Thus it is necessary to characterize the environments which favored the retention of preplosion. Certainly, preplosion is disfavored after nasal onsets, the retention of glottalization in 'six' notwithstanding. Beyond this, keep in mind that final preplosion is essentially a syllable-final cluster, so retention of the preploded nasals would have been least favored after long vowels and most favored after short vowels. After long vowels, simplification of the preploded cluster should be most likely; after short vowels, it should be least likely. And, in fact, this matches the modern distribution: except in the word 'person', after long vowels, there is no evidence of glottalization, while after the PC short vowels *-a- and *-ɔ-, glottalization always occurs. This distribution makes perfect sense if the preploded nasals had simplified to plain nasals everywhere except in the most favorable environment for retaining a final cluster, that is, except before the two short vowels *-a- and *-ɔ-.

Two additional pieces of evidence argue for the analysis in which all PC final nasals became preploded before being simplified to simple nasals in most environments in Tsat, one internal and one external. The internal evidence is the presence of glottalization on *ʔura:ŋ 'person' with its long vowel. While it is unclear just what special circumstances led to this particular word keeping its preploded nasal long enough to develop glottalization, it nonetheless did and it seems more likely that this is a specially-conditioned retention than a specially-conditioned development.

The second piece of evidence is even more compelling. The language most-closely related to Tsat, Northern Roglai has a startlingly similar set of developments. Even without considering the Tsat developments, it is necessary to conclude that Roglai also developed the highly-marked final preplosion in final nasals, and then subsequently simplified the preploded nasals, but with the nasal component, not the stop component being lost during the process. Instead of two separate but independent accounts of the development of final preploded nasals, it is much more plausible to assume that Tsat and Northern Roglai developed the preploded final nasals before they became separate languages, with each language then simplifying the preploded nasals in its own way.

It is in this context that the glottalization on the Tsat reflex of *nam 'six' becomes extremely interesting. In closely-related Roglai, only PC final nasals in forms like *nam with its nasal onset failed to ultimately have homorganic stop reflexes in modern Roglai. Thus, it is clear on the basis of internal evidence within Roglai that all the forms without syllable-initial nasals with their accompanying perseverative nasalization developed preploded final nasals on the path to the modern homorganic stop reflexes. What is left unclear from the Roglai material alone is whether the forms with syllable-initial nasals also developed preploded nasal finals and then subsequently lost them or whether the syllable-initial forms simply never developed preploded finals in the first place. The Tsat form *natn < na:n$?^{33}$, from PC *nam 'six', with its internally-reconstructed preploded nasal provides the answer; in the common ancestor of Northern Roglai and Tsat, in which the preploded nasals were originally innovated, all PC final nasals developed preplosion, with the subsequent simplification of these stop plus nasal clusters only occurring after Tsat and Northern Roglai had separated, as is evident from the often similar but clearly independent paths of cluster simplification taken in each language.

The modern distribution of glottalized, nasalized finals in Tsat came about as the result of a chronologically-ordered sequence of changes, which is represented in a somewhat simplified form in Figure 14:

Figure 14: Simplified derivation of glottalized nasal finals

	'hot; spicy'	'house'
PC	*haŋ	*sa:ŋ
P-Roglai-Tsat preploded final nasals	hăkŋ	sa:kŋ
coda simplification after long vowels	---	sa:ŋ
glottalization of prenasal stops	hă?ŋ	---
lengthening of /a/ before glottal stop	ha:?ŋ	---
tone assignment	ha:?ŋ^{42}	sa:ŋ^{33}
modern Tsat	/ha:?ŋ^{42}/	/sa:ŋ^{33}/

Figure 14, it should be emphasized, is only a rough schematic representation of the basic outlines. For discussion of the details and for a justification of the chronology, please see the preceding discussion.

The Tsat nasal reflexes with the 42 falling tone

Finally, the data base contains nine examples of former preploded nasals having developed a 42 falling tone. It is immediately obvious from examining the forms (Table 105) that the presence of a glottal stop is one prerequisite for the falling tone just as it is evident that the presence of a glottal stop by itself is not sufficient to predict the occurrence of the tone. The second prerequisite seems to be the presence of an inherited or a secondarily-derived long vowel in modern Tsat.

This pair of conditions accounts for the data in Table 106, with two exceptions: Tsat /khiaŋʔ⁴² -ft/ from *tsiakŋ -ft 'carry on the shoulder' and /zaːŋʔ/ from earlier *zaːkŋ 'person; someone'. The falling tone on 'carry on the shoulder' is unexpected, but so is the final; that is, the irregular tone is in a form that also has other correspondence problems.

The lack of a falling tone in PC *ʔuraːŋ > Tsat *zaːkŋ > zaːŋʔ, on the other hand, could be attributed to any one of a number of unique characteristics of this form: The PC vowel in this form was originally long; the PC vowels in the other forms were originally short. As a member of the classifier and of the pronoun systems, the word itself more than likely occurs in phonologically unstressed environments, unlike other otherwise similar forms in the data base. None of this, of course, tells us precisely why this particular form did not develop a falling tone; its unique characteristics do, however, make it clear that the word is not a counterexample to the proposed analysis.

NASALIZATION IN NORTHERN ROGLAI

The Roglai reflexes of PC final nasals are important for two things: Like Tsat, the Northern Roglai reflexes of PC final nasals have passed through a stage in which they were preploded final nasals (for a discussion of preploded nasals, see "Nasalization in Tsat" on page 160), providing compelling evidence that Tsat and Roglai were once the same dialect (namely, proto-Northern Roglai/Tsat). The Northern Roglai voiceless stop reflexes of PC final nasals in Table 107 have evolved from earlier preploded nasals shared by Proto-Northern-Roglai/Tsat, as indicated in the table.

Table 107: The presence of preploded nasals in Northern Roglai and Tsat

PC	>	P-NR/Tsat	NR	Tsat (sandhi)	
*nam	>	*năpm	nam	---	'six'
*bulaːn	>	*bulaːkŋ	ia bilaːt	---	'moon'
*tulaːŋ	>	*tulaːkŋ	tulaːk	---	'bone'
ˣ*dhɔŋ	>	*thŏkŋ	thok	thokŋ³³-	'knife'
*padam	>	*padăpm	padap	thatn⁴²-	'extinguish'
			---	tatn⁴²-	'section'
			---	tsiakŋ⁴²-	'at'

And, in addition to their importance for subgrouping, the unique treatment of word-final nasals in Northern Roglai is a rich source of information not only about the history of Roglai nasals but also about the history of PC nasals and about PC nasalized vowels. The modern Roglai reflexes often provide important evidence about which forms are inherited and which are borrowed. And, further, in the case of the borrowed forms, Roglai sometimes also provides information about the relative chronology of the borrowing.

Reflexes from PC word-final nasals

For PC word-final nasals, there are two basic Roglai reflex patterns. In the most dominant of these two patterns, the word-final nasal has as its Roglai reflex a homorganic stop.

Table 108: PC final nasals with Roglai stop reflexes

PC	Chru	NR	PR Cham	
ˣ*haːŋ	---	haːk	haŋ	'bank (river); shore'
*dalam	dəlam; dərlam	dalap	ʈalăm	'deep; inside'
ˣ*khɔːŋ	khɔːŋ	khoːk	khɔŋ	'dry (weather?)'
*khaŋ	khaŋ	khak	khăŋ	'hard; stiff; strong'
*saːŋ	saːŋ	saːk	thaŋ	'house'
*malam	məlam	malap	milăm	'night; evening'
ˣ_naːn	---	inaːt; rinaːt	---	'pineapple'
*hujaːn	həjaːn	hujaːt	haçan; çan	'rain'
*masin	məsin	masit (?)	mithĭn	'salted; salty'
*ʔiduŋ	aduŋ	idŭk	iʈŭŋ; ʈŭŋ	'nose'
*phun	phun 'stem'	phut	phŭn	'trunk; log; plant'
*pə-ghaːŋ	---	pakhaːk	paкhaŋ	'dry over fire'
*bhaːn	phắːn -n laːiʔ	phaːt	phan	'sneeze'
*lubaːŋ	ləbaːŋ	lubaːk	lipaŋ; lapaŋ	'hole; pit'
*halim	həlim	halip	halĭm	'rainy season'
ˣ*ɓaŋ	ɓaŋ 'door'	ɓak	ɓăŋ	'hole; door'
ˣ*haŋ	haŋ	hak	hăŋ	'hot; spicy'
ˣ*khan	khan	khat	khăn	'cloth; blanket'
ˣsuaːn -1	---	suaːt -1	swan	'soul'
ˣɗuan	---	ɗuat	ɗŏn	'bamboo hat'

As Table 108 shows, Chru and Phan Rang Cham both retain the PC final nasal, but in Roglai, the PC final nasal consonants have changed into homorganic oral stops. This homorganic stop is the unmarked reflex of word-final nasals in Roglai.

In Table 108, all the PC final nasals have denasalized becoming homorganic stops, the expected reflex. Of particular interest for relative chronology are the last two examples 'soul' and 'bamboo hat'. Neither form reconstructs to the PC level (as the ˣ without an accompanying * indicates), however, both forms have final stops, not nasals. Thus, these forms were borrowed into pre-Roglai after the breakup of PC but in time to take part in the denasalization of Roglai final nasals.

In the other basic pattern, the PC word-final nasal has been retained, a retention that correlates with the presence of a nasal consonant at the onset of the final syllable, that is, the PC word-final nasal has been retained as a nasal when the PC final syllable also began with a nasal. Notice that, in this data, there is a correlation between Roglai nasalization and vowel length.

As was true for Table 108, in Table 109 the forms inherited from PC include PC forms inherited from PMP (marked with *) and borrowings reconstructable back to PC (marked with ˣ*). Both sets of forms, of course, have undergone the change.

Historically, the Roglai forms have descended from forms that were once phonetically similar to the "preploded" nasals of Měntu Land Dayak described by Court (1967) (discussed also on page 164). Blust (1991:148), citing among others Court (1967), writes about preploded nasals:

> In certain Land Dayak languages of southwest Borneo (Scott 1964: Court 1967), final nasals are often combined with a preceding obstruent, voiced in some languages, voiceless in others: Mentu *ciupm* 'kiss' (Malay *cium*), Bukar-Sadong *kaidn* 'cloth' (Malay *kain*). Simple nasals occur in final position if the final syllable begins with a nasal consonant: Bukar-Sadong *teŋan* 'hand, arm'.

Continuing, he writes that similar distributions occur elsewhere:

> ...in Tunjung of southeast Borneo and in some dialects of Mentawai, spoken in the Barrier Islands west of Sumatra (Bernd Nothofer, personal communication). Northern Roglai, a Chamic language of Vietnam, reflects Proto-Austronesian final nasals as the homorganic voiceless stop. If the final syllable begins with a nasal, however, the final nasal is preserved — a clear indication of the former presence of preploded nasals in that language as well.

Table 109: PC final nasals with Roglai nasal reflexes

PC	Chru	NR	PR Cham	
*pina:ŋ	pəna:ŋ	pinăŋ	paniŋ	'betel (areca palm)'
ˣˣ*miaŋ	---	---	mieŋ	'cheek; jaw'
*gunam	gənam	---	ḳanăm	'cloud'
*lama:n	ləma:n	lumăn	limɨn	'elephant'
ˣcana:ŋ	cəna:ŋ	canăŋ	taniŋ -i	'furniture; bed'
*taŋa:n	təŋa:n	taŋăn	taŋɨn	'hand'
*timun	təmun	tumŭn	tamŭn	'melon; cucumber'
*ʔaŋan	aŋan	---	aŋăn; ŋăn	'name'
*ʔanuŋ	---	---	anŭŋ	'package'
*nam	nam	năm	năm	'six'
*mam -v	mɛm -v;	măm	mŭm -v;	'suck; suckle'
	măm		mum -v	
*ʔanan	nɨn	---	năn	'that (third p.)'
*binay	bənai	binăi	pinay	'virgin'
	'of animals'	'of animals'	'woman'	
*mañam -1	məña:m -1	mañăm	miñim	'weave; twill'
*ʔaŋin	aŋin	aŋɨn	aŋɨn; ŋɨn	'the wind'
ˣkəmuan	kəmuan	kamuăn	kamon	'nephew'
ˣrimɔ:ŋ	rəmɔ:ŋ	lumŏŋ -i	rimɔŋ;	'tiger'
			ramɔŋ	
ˣkrăm -1vn	kra:m -1	kram	krim -v	'bamboo'
ˣnrən -if;	drɨn -v	drɨn -vf	ṭrăn	'numb'
ˣdrə̃n -if		prən -i		
ˣcaŋuar -f	cənua -fŋ	caŋuă	---	'flat basket'
*miaw	miau	miău	miyaw -v	'cat'
*naw	nau	nău	naw	'go; walk'
*samaw	səmũ -f	---	---	'prompt; on time'
*danaw	dənau	danau -n	ṭanaw	'lake'
ˣhanuă?	hənua?	ha nuă?	hanŭ?	'right (side)'
*sana	səna 'fry'	sana -n	hana	'roast; parch'

One key to understanding the phonetics of these changes lies in recognizing that, as in many of the Austronesian languages of this area, in Northern Roglai the salient pattern of nasalization of vowels by adjacent nasal consonants is perseverative, not anticipatory. That is,

Roglai nasalization rule: v > ṽ / nasal _____ (C)#.

While not denying that there may also have been some anticipatory nasalization on the vowels preceding word-final nasal consonants, it was the perseverative assimilation that was crucial to blocking the denasalization of final nasals. Thus, the perseverative nasalization of the vowel from the syllable-initial nasal consonant of the forms in Table 109, alone or in combination with whatever anticipatory assimilation that may also have occurred, was salient enough to block the denasalization of the word-final nasals.

Forms with other reflex patterns

Most forms that fail to conform to one of the two basic reflex patterns are borrowings, although a subset of such aberrant forms may instead reflect PC nasalized vowels. Although the irregularities in their correspondence patterns make it obvious that most such forms are recent borrowings, a small number of these forms are regular in their correspondence patterns.

In addition to the secondarily nasalized vowels from perseverative assimilation from a preceding nasal consonant, there are also a handful of primary nasalized vowels with no obvious connection to an adjacent nasal consonant but which reconstruct with nasalized vowels at the PC stage.

Post-pre-Roglai borrowings

In Roglai, some the easiest post-PC borrowings to identify are those that have been borrowed so recently that they have not undergone the denasalization of final nasal consonants.

In Table 110, the final word-final nasals of the Roglai forms have not denasalized, despite the fact that there is no evidence of a preceding nasalized vowel to stop the denasalization from taking place. On the basis of this (and various other pieces of evidence) these forms have been identified as late borrowings post-dating the denasalization of Roglai final nasal consonants.

Table 110: Late borrowings into Northern Roglai

PC	Chru	NR	PR Cham	
ˣkhiːn	khin	khin -f	khĭn	'dare; brave'
ˣkhiaŋ -fi	khiaŋ -v	khiaŋ -f	khĭŋ	'want; desire'
ˣgriaŋ	griaŋ	giaŋ -f	ḳrĕŋ	'fang; tusk'
ˣdian	diən -v	diăn -f	ṭien	'candle'
ˣcum	ˣcum	cum -f	cŭm	'kiss; smell'
ˣphuŋ	---	phuŋ -f	---	'leper'
ˣ(li)huŋ	ləhɔŋ -v	lahoŋ -f	---	'papaya'
ˣɓaŋ	ɓaːŋ	ɓaŋ -f	---	'table'
ˣgrəm -vf	grəm	grəm -f	ḳrŭm -v	'thunder'
ˣhɔːŋ -f	hɔːŋ	hoŋ -f	---	'wasp'
ˣham -ln	haːm -l laːm	ham -f	---	'greed'

Secondary final nasals in Roglai

In addition to inherited final nasals, Roglai also has a set of final nasals derived secondarily from PC *-l. The original PC lateral final is still found in Cham and Chru.

*Table 111: PC final *-l > Roglai -n*

PC	Chru	NR	PR Cham	
ˣ*sapal	spal	sapan	hapăl	'arm'
*mal	mal	măn	măl	'beam'
*gatal	kətal	katan	katăl	'itchy'
*sanal	---	sanãn	---	'pillow'
*wil	wil 'circle'	win	wĭl	'round'
*kapaːl	kəpaːl	kapan	kapal	'thick'
ˣ*baːl	baːl	ban	pal	'mend; patch'
ˣ*b-an-aːl	---	banãn	---	'rag' cf. 'mend'
ˣkaɗual	kəduəl	kaɗuən	kaɗŏl	'heel'
ˣ*jaːl	jaːl	jan	çăl -l	'casting net'
ˣ*hual	hual	huan	hol	'cloud, fog'
ˣdhual/r -f	thul -v	thun -v	ṭhŭr -vf	'dust; fog'
ˣʔabual -v	buəl	abən -v	---	'blunt; dull'
ˣɗɛl	ɗɛl	ɗen	---	'shallow'
ˣsiʔjual -v	səʔuəl	siʔjuən	ʔjŏl; haʔjŏl	'light (weight)'

Although the change of final *-l (and *-r) to -n is an areal feature of Southeast Asia, within Chamic the change is apparently limited to Roglai. Note that this change even applies to post-PC loans. The relative lateness of the change within Roglai is apparent from relative chronology, that is, the shift postdates the shift of Roglai final nasals to homorganic stops.

NASALIZATION IN ACEHNESE

Nasalization in Acehnese, as elsewhere in Chamic, is perseverative. The most obvious manifestation of this nasalization is on the main syllable vowels of Acehnese, that is, the vowels in the second syllable, which it affects in several ways, as Table 112 shows.

Table 112: The effect of perseverative nasalization on Acehnese vowels

Malay	PC	Aceh.	NR	PR Cham	
kulit	*kulit	kulet	kuli:ʔ	kaliʔ	'skin'
nipis	*lipih	lipeh	lupih	lipĭh; lapĭh	'thin'
langit	*laŋit	laŋɛt	laŋi:ʔ	liŋiʔ; laŋiʔ	'sky'
---	*mamih	mamɛh	mumîh	mɨmĭh	'sweet'
angin	*ʔaŋin	aŋɛn	aŋin	aŋĭn; ŋĭn	'the wind'
kunyit	*kuñit	kuñɛt	kuñî:ʔ	kañiʔ	'yellow'
mabuk	*mabuʔ	maboʔ	babuʔ	---	'drunk'
manuk	*manuʔ	manɔʔ	manŭ̃	mɨnŭ̃ʔ	'chicken; fowl'
buta	*buta	buta	---	mita -i	'blind'
darah	*darah	darah	darah	ʈarăh	'blood'
tanya	*taŋa	tañʌŋ	tiñã	tañi	'ask'
huma	*huma	umʌŋ	humã	hamu -v	'field'
lima	*lima	limʌŋ	lumã	limɨ; lamɨ	'five'
bunga	*buŋa	buŋɔŋ	buŋã	piŋu	'flower'
---	*ʔina	inʌŋ	---	ini	'mother'
---	ˣ*ʔawa:k	awɯəʔ	---	awaʔ	'spoon; ladle'
---	*rəta:k	rɯtɯəʔ	rata:ʔ	riʈaʔ; rataʔ	'bean; pea'
dahan	*dha:n	dhɯən	tha:t	ʈhan	'branch; bough'
hudang	*huda:ŋ	udɯəŋ	huda:k	haʈăŋ; ʈaŋ	'shrimp'
anak	*ʔana:k	anɯʔ	anã:ʔ	aniʔ	'child'
minyak	*miña:k	miñɯʔ	mañã:ʔ	miñiʔ	'oil'
pinang	*pina:ŋ	pinɯŋ	pinãŋ	paniŋ	'betel (-nut)'

The PC second-syllable high vowels *-u- and *-i- are all lowered in Acehnese, but the non-nasalized variants become /o/ and /e/, while the nasalized variants become /ɔ/ and /ɛ/, respectively. The PC short *-a becomes /-a/, but the nasalized variant becomes /-ʌŋ/. The PC long *-a:- becomes /-ɯə-/, but the nasalized variant becomes the shorter /-ɯ-/.

8

The Origins of Registers and Tones

The Chamic languages present case studies of a clarity unparalleled in the literature illustrating the radical typological restructuring of phonological systems. The language that the seafaring Austronesian-speaking forerunners of the modern Chamic spoke when they arrived on the mainland was essentially disyllabic, nontonal, and non-registral. From this starting point have descended a startling array of phonological systems: the register system of Western Cham (Friberg and Kvoeu-Hor, 1977; Edmondson and Gregerson, 1993); the restructured register system of Haroi (Lee, 1974, 1977b; Burnham 1976; Thurgood, 1996); the quasi-registral, incipiently tonal system of Phan Rang Cham (Thurgood, 1993; Han, Edmondson, and Gregerson, 1992); and the fully-tonal system of Tsat (Haudricourt, 1984; Benedict, 1984; Ni 1990ab; Thurgood 1992b, 1993). All this variety has evolved from an essentially identical starting point, all of it has followed relatively transparent paths of internal restructuring, and in each case the unique endpoint has come about under the influence of contact with typologically different languages.

For each of these distinct developments, it is possible to reconstruct a clear outline of the entire internal path of development by which, from an essentially atonal and disyllabic pre-Chamic origin, the modern register system (in Western Cham), the modern restructured register system (in Haroi), the incipient tonal system (in Phan Rang Cham (Eastern Cham)), and the fully tonal system (in Tsat) developed. Due to the relatively shallow time-depth and the richness of the data, the Chamic languages provide outlines of the internal paths of development involved in all four cases that are rather clear and relatively complete.

178

For example, in the case of the Tsat data, we see a case in which we start from a completely atonal (and, largely disyllabic) stage and we end with a fully tonal (and, largely monosyllabic) stage. The completeness of the data is unlike much of the literature on tonogenesis, which typically involves just the later tone-splitting stage rather than true tonogenesis. And, further, in contrast to many of the instances of tonogenesis reported in the literature on tonogenesis, the end product is not a two-way tone contrast, but a rich five-way tone system.

There are, of course, several values to such case studies, among which is their value as models for less transparent, more controversial changes that, often because of the greater time-depth, require a high degree of extrapolation in the analysis.

WESTERN CHAM AND THE DEVELOPMENT OF REGISTER

Register itself constitutes a complex of features that tend to occur together: voice quality (phonation type), vowel length, pitch, and voice quality induced vowel gliding. Historically, as David Thomas has noted, individual languages may emphasize one or another of those features, suppressing the other features. Thus, as he notes, ancient Khmer emphasized the voice quality feature, while Vietnamese has progressively emphasized pitch. Modern Central Khmer has now subdued the voice quality feature and emphasized the vowel ongliding feature instead, while Modern Northern Khmer has emphasized the vowel height feature. And, Modern Vietnamese still has voice quality features in some of its tones.

The correlation of breathy voice with vowel raising and of creaky or tense voice with vowel lowering has long been noted in the literature on register complexes (noted at least as early as Henderson 1952). The explanation for this correlation is to be found in the mechanics of the production of breathy and tense voice: breathy voice characteristically involves a lowering of the larynx, a consequent enlongation of the vocal tract, and a resultant lower F1—hence vowel raising, while tense or creaky voice characteristically involves a raising of the larynx, a consequent shortening of the vocal tract, and a resultant higher F1—hence vowel lowering (Peter Ladefoged, p.c.).

There is a second correlation, not as widely reported, between voice quality and vowel centralization. Exactly the same laryngeal gestures that produce vowel height differences also affect the centralization of the vowels, except that it is the effect on the F2 that determines vowel centralization: the larynx is lowered in producing breathy voice, the vocal tract is lengthened, the lengthened vocal tract lengthens the wave lengths, lowering the formants and resulting in vowels with a lower F2. The result, of course, is that these vowels are more centralized. Conversely, the raising of the larynx in producing creaky voice, the consequent shortening of the vocal tract, and the resulting shortened wave lengths, produce higher formants. Vowels with a higher F2 are more peripheral.

As for Western Cham, its register system originated in two stages: first, a distinct breathy phonation developed after the voiced obstruents (second register) producing a phonation contrast with the vowel after the remaining consonants (first register); the two contrasting vowel quality differences—breathy versus modal voice—have resulted in two phonetically distinct sets of vowels, one associated with breathy voice and the other with the modal (or, clear) voice. Later, the register complex associated with breathy phonation was extended to the forms with sonorant initials, see Figure 15.

Figure 15: The development of Western Cham register

PC initial classes:		Distinct voice quality:		Vowel registers:
PC initials (except voiced obstruents + sonorants)	==>	modal voice	==>	breathy-voiced vowel set
PC voiced obstruents + sonorants	==>	breathy voice	==>	modal-voiced vowel set

The extension of the breathy register to include forms with initial sonorants (shown in Figure 15) is atypical and restricted to Western Cham. The developments in Haroi, Phan Rang Cham, and Tsat are more typical, with the sonorants patterning, not with the voiced obstruents, but with the other reflexes.

Again notice that these two distinct phonation types affected the vowel quality, resulting in two allophonically distinct sets of vowels (see Table 113). Finally, the voiced and voiceless obstruents lost their voicing contrast, merging into a single set of voiceless obstruents, phonemicizing the differences in voice quality and vowel quality, and producing the modern register system of Western Cham.

In modern Western Cham, the two vowel registers are distinct, although the two registers for the vowel /a/ are distinguished, not by vowel quality, but by other features. And, even now the two vowel sets are in part predictable from the modern initials. The original relationships are no longer transparent though, because of the mergers in the obstruents and because of the spreading, under specified conditions, of register from the pretonic first syllable to the stressed main syllable.

Table 113: Vowel registers in Western Cham

Modal register vowels:			Breathy register vowels:		
i	ə	ʉ	i	ɨ	u
e	ʌ	o	e^i	ə̦	o^u
æ	a	ɔ	e̦	a̦	o̦

[From Edmondson and Gregerson 1993:67]

The literature

The first synopsis of the diachronic origins of Western Cham register was Friberg and Kvoeu-Hor's (1977: 35-36, fn. 14) short footnote in their insightful paper on Western Cham register patterns. It has since been expanded and developed by Edmondson and Gregerson (1993), who supplement their analysis with instrumental data. The registers of Western Cham, like all registers, are clusters of co-occurring features: in modern Western Cham (Friberg and Kvoeu-Hor (1977) and Edmondson and Gregerson (1993:63-72)), first register vowels usually have tenser voice quality, lower voice quality, and higher pitch, while the second register vowels usually have laxer or breathy voice quality, high vowel quality, and lower pitch. And, as these authors observed, the first register vowels derive from the phonation type induced by proto-voiceless initials, while the second register vowels derive from the phonation type induced by proto-voiced initials. As Edmondson and Gregerson point out, the developments are reminiscent of Henderson's (1952) description of the feature complexes associated with Khmer register. See Table 114.

Table 114: Contrasts between modal and breathy register

	Modal voiced First Register	Breathy voiced Second Register
original initials	proto-voiceless	proto-voiced
voice quality	tense, clear	lax, breathy
vowel quality	lower (open)	higher (closed)
pitch distinctions	higher pitch	lower pitch

[Henderson, 1952; Edmondson and Gregerson, 1993:61-63]

Two things in Table 114 should be noted. First, although this is Henderson's (1952) description of the Khmer voice register distinctions, not of Western

Cham, the complexes also characterize the Western Cham distinctions (although Edmondson and Gregerson's instrumental description did not find systematic vowel quality differences between the registers). Second, the ordering of the features parallels the three historical stages: the original initials > voice quality distinctions > vowel quality & pitch distinctions.

The PC voiced consonants: the two layers

The first stage in the history of Western Cham register begins with the innovation of breathy voice after the voiced obstruents *b-, *d, *g-, and *j-. Later another layer was added when second register spread to the forms with sonorant initials. Thus, the sonorant initial forms were added to the nucleus of Western Cham second register forms from the voiced obstruents. Table 115 contains second register reflexes from originally voiced obstruents.

Table 115 shows the development of PC voiced obstruents into Western Cham second register. In Table 115 in both the monosyllables and the disyllables, it is the main syllable initial that developed into second register, regardless of the initial of the presyllable. Notice that all main syllable initial obstruents are marked with a subscribed dot, indicating a following second register vowel. This orthographic convention makes it easy to recognize second register by marking its presence the same way each time it appears, although it is of course the vowels, not the consonants, that show register distinctions. In actuality, the PC voiced obstruents have long since lost their voicing and merged with the voiceless series.

In Western Cham, it is possible for each syllable of a disyllabic word to be in a different register. In Table 115, 'seven' and 'rice (paddy)' have first register presyllable vowels because the presyllables originally began with a PC voiceless obstruent but second register main vowels, because the main vowel originally began with a PC voiced obstruent. In contrast, both syllables in the forms for 'mouth' and 'tooth' are in the second register because both syllables originally began with PC voiced obstruents. However, sometimes second register has been lost in the presyllable, cf. 'chest'.

As for the other languages in the table, they display similar patterns: In Tsat, both the 42 tone and the 11 tones show the effect of second register; only the 55 tone from *-h fails to do so. As for Phan Rang Cham, it is not a coincidence that all the second register Western Cham forms have either a corresponding low tone or a glottal-final low tone, as this tone developed from second register.

Table 115: PC voiced obstruents > Western Cham breathy register

PC	Tsat	Haroi	W. Cham	PR Cham	
*habɔw	phə¹¹	aphɨau	pau	hapɔ̆w	'ashes'
*babuy	phui¹¹	pəphŭi	papui	papuy	'wild pig'
*hubɛy	phai¹¹	aphui (m)	pay	hapɛ̆y	'taro; yam'
*ribɔw	phə¹¹	ləphɨau	rapau	ripɔ̆w	'thousand'
ˣ*kabaw	---	kəphɨau	kabau	kapaw	'water buffalo'
*dada	tha¹¹	cəthɨa	taṭa	taṭa	'chest'
*ʔiduŋ	thuŋ¹¹	athŭŋ	ṭuŋ	iṭŭŋ	'nose'
*hudaːŋ	thaːŋ¹¹	athiaŋ	niʔ ṭaŋ	haṭăŋ	'shrimp'
*dua	thua¹¹	thua	ṭoa	ṭwa	'two'
ˣ*glɛh	---	tlɪh	ḳlɛh	ḳlɛh	'tired'
*gigɛy	khai¹¹	cəkhɨi	ṭaḳay	taḳɛ̆y	'tooth'
*hujaːn	saːn¹¹	asɨan	çan	haçan	'rain'
*dɔːk	thoʔ⁴²	thuʔ	ṭɔʔ	ṭɔʔ	'sit; live; stay'
*ʔabih	phi⁵⁵	aphɨh	pih	apih	'all; finished'
*labuh	phu⁵⁵	ləphŭh	lapuh	lapuh	'fall down'
*babah	pha⁵⁵	pəphɨah	papah	papah	'mouth'
*tabus	phu⁵⁵	---	---	tapŭh	'ransom'
*tujuh	su⁵⁵	cəsŭh	taçuh	taçŭh	'seven'
*paday	thaːiʔ⁴²	pəthɨai	paṭai	paṭay	'rice (paddy)'

Western Cham also has second register after certain sonorant initials that are discussed in the section on phonation spreading ("Transparency and phonation spreading" on page 183).

Transparency and phonation spreading

For monosyllables, the situation is precisely as already described. However, for a subset of the disyllabic words, the modern distribution of register has been complicated by the spreading of the voice quality from the presyllable to the main syllable (The discussion here disagrees, although only in minor ways, from the Friberg and Kvoeu-Hor analysis of spreading found in Thurgood (1996)). Thus, it may be the PC initial of the presyllable, not the PC initial of the main syllable, that correlates with the modern register. Friberg and Kvoeu-Hor (1977:36), in the same footnote referred to earlier, have explicitly presented the patterns.

Breathy register after main syllable initial sonorants

Throughout Chamic there is a hierarchical pattern in the spread of the breathy voice associated with second register from the presyllable through the medial consonant to the main syllable: sonorants > voiceless fricatives > voiceless stops. Specifically, in Haroi, Phan Rang Cham, and Tsat, there is clear evidence that breathy voice has spread through the medial sonorants to the main syllable. In addition, there is every reason to assume that historically the same pattern of spreading occurred in Western Cham, thus accounting for the second register after the main-syllable initial sonorants in Table 116.

Table 116: Breathy voice spreading through a medial sonorant

PC	NR	W. Cham	PR Cham	
*barah	barah	parah	---	'swell; swollen'
*buŋa	buŋã	paŋur -f	piŋu	'flower'
*dalam	dalap	ṭalăm	ṭalăm	'deep; inside'
*darah	darah	ṭarah	ṭarăh	'blood'
*dilah	gilah < *g-	ṭalah	ṭalah	'tongue'
*durɛy	daruəi (m)	ṭaruai (m)	ṭaroy (m)	'thorn'
*jalaːn	jalaːt	çalan	çalan	'road; path'
*bɔh maw	bumãu	poh mau	pimaw	'mushroom'

In Table 116, the Western Cham disyllables are in second register, as indicated by the dot subscribed under the initial obstruents. The same patterns of spreading are found in the Phan Rang Cham forms.

Western Cham has second register reflexes after initial sonorants in two additional environments, environments where second register reflexes are not found elsewhere in Chamic: in monosyllables that begin with sonorants and in disyllables where both syllables begin with sonorants. See Table 117. The appearance of second register in these forms is unexpected. Perhaps it was extended to these forms due to some sort of acoustic similarity between nasalized and breathy-voiced vowels; perhaps it was extended to these vowels as these are the only other vowels following voiced consonants. In any case, the Friberg and Kvoeu-Hor (1977:36) analysis implicitly assumes that at some point all vowels following sonorants had developed second register, with it only to be lost later in some cases. It would be interesting to find out if all dialects of Western Cham have second register in these forms.

In Table 117, second register has not been marked in any special way, as it is fully predictable from the initials. The origin of second register with these forms will be speculated on after the discussion of register spreading on page 183, below.

There are two additional sets of disyllabic forms with sonorant main-syllable initials. In these, the vowels are in first register, rather than second register. In the Friberg and Kvoeu-Hor (1977:36) analysis (followed in Thurgood 1996), these are treated as the result of the spread of first register from the presyllable to the main syllable. Contra the Friberg and Kvoeu-Hor analysis, the first register vowels after the sonorants in Table 117 are assumed to be the expected reflex after a sonorant.

Table 117: Breathy-voiced is extended to the sonorants

PC	Tsat	Haroi	W. Cham	PR Cham	
x*1ɛʔ	leʔ^{24}	1ɛ̌ʔ	1ɛ̌ʔ	1ɛ̌ʔ	'fall into'
*ʔular	la^{33}	ali̇a	la	ula	'snake'
*mamah	ma^{55}	məmăh	mamɨh	mɨmɨh	'chew'
x*ləmɔ	mo^{33}	ləmɔ	lamɔ	lamɔ	'cow; ox; cattle'
*ʔama	ma^{11}	ama	mɨ	amɨ	'father'
*lima	ma^{33}	ləmi̇a	lamɨ	limɨ	'five'
*manuʔ	nuʔ^{24}	mənŭʔ	manŭʔ	mɨnŭʔ	'chicken; fowl'
*ʔana:k	naʔ^{24}	anaʔ	niʔ	aniʔ	'child'
*ʔini	ni^{33}	ni	ni	ni	'this'
*laŋit	ŋiʔ^{24}	ləŋiʔ	laŋiʔ	laŋiʔ	'sky'
x*wər	van^{33}	wɔl	wăr	wăr	'forget'

In the disyllabic forms in Table 118, the vowel after the main-syllable initial sonorant is in the first register, not in the second register. Thus, it is clear that it is initial of the first register, not the initial of the second register, that has determined the register of the second register. In short, the first register has spread from the first syllable to the second.

Table 118: Main syllable sonorants with first register reflexes

PC	Tsat	Haroi	W. Cham	PR Cham	
*pina:ŋ	na:ŋ^{33}	pənaŋ	panɨŋ	panɨŋ	'betel; betel-nut'
*tula:ŋ	la:ŋ^{33}	cəlaŋ	talaŋ	talaŋ	'bone'
*kumɛy	mai^{33}	kəmŏi	kamay	kamɛ̆y	'female, woman'
*pula	pia^{33}	pəla	pla	pala	'to plant'
*panah	na^{55}	pənăh	panɨh	panɨh	'shoot (bow); a bow'
*kulit	liʔ^{24} -i	kəleiʔ	kliʔ	kaliʔ	'skin'
*hurɛy	zai^{33}	hərɨi (m)	ea hray	harɛ̆y	'day; sun'
*huma	ma^{33}	həmɨa	hamɨ	hamu -v	'field'

Breathy voice spreading through other main syllable initials

As Friberg and Kvoeu-Hor observed, the breathy-voiced second register has also spread through the medial voiceless fricatives, producing second register vowels in the forms in Table 119. Note that in both 'new' and 'otter', the two words with medial /h/, the whole word is in second register, not just the second syllable.

*Table 119: Spreading of breathy voice through *s and *h*

PC	Tsat	Haroi	W. Cham	PR Cham	
*bəsɛy	sai¹¹	pəsŏi	pasay	piṭhɛ̆y	'iron'
ˣ*buhay	---	---	pahas -f	phay	'otter'
*bahrɔw	phiə¹¹	pr̆iau	pahau	pirɔ̆w	'new; just now'

All the Phan Rang Cham forms show evidence of the spread of second register in their low tone reflexes, as do both the Tsat forms in their 11 tones. In Haroi, however, only 'new' shows second register spreading.

The only Western Cham medials that block second register spreading are the medial voiceless stops. As Table 120 shows, second register failed to spread through the medial voiceless stops.

Table 120: Spread of breathy voice stopped by voiceless stops

PC	Tsat	Haroi	W. Cham	PR Cham	
*batɛy	u¹¹ tai¹¹	pətŏi	patay	patɛ̆y	'banana'
*batuk	tuʔ⁴²	pətoʔ	patŭʔ	patŭʔ	'cough'
*dikit	kiʔ⁴²	---	takiʔ	takiʔ	'few; little'
*batɔw	tau¹¹	pətău	patau	patɔ̆w	'stone'
ˣ*batɔ	to¹¹	pətɔ	patɔ	patɔ	'teach'

Perhaps, as Friberg and Kvoeu-Hor (1977:36) suggested, the voiced obstruents devoiced before spreading could occur, perhaps the medial voiceless stops are simply more resistant to spreading, or perhaps it is some combination of the two.

The history of Western Cham contact

Although there are gaps in our knowledge of Western Cham, it has apparently always been in contact with register languages. In the literature, the Western Chams are viewed as a recently split off dialect of Cham, with the Western Cham being a branch of Cham that migrated westward, particularly to Cambodia, after Champa collapsed in the sixteenth century (Headley, 1991), with this migration placing the split with Phan Rang Cham around 1471. Undoubtedly, many of the

Western Cham did migrate to Cambodia at that time, but it is also quite clear that a significant number of them remained in southern Vietnam and doubtless these continued to have contact with Phan Rang speakers. Be that as it may, judging from a comparison of Western and Phan Rang Cham, both Phan Rang and Western Cham had already developed a common register system by the time of the split, one probably shared by Haroi.

The gaps in our knowledge revolve around identifying the specific contact languages involved in the development of the original register system. Without more precise knowledge of the languages involved, it is impossible to do much more than speculate on the social mechanisms involved. However, from the nature and the number of MK loans incorporated into both Western and Phan Rang Cham, it is clear that at very least the contact involved long-term bilingualism and it also involved language shift from some MK languages to Cham, certainly at least in part from Bahnar.

It is not clear just how homogenous Western Cham is nor how similar the paths of development have been in different dialects. The two dialects used in this work, one described by Kvoeu-Hor and Friberg (1978) and one by Headley (1991), both differ, although only in minor details. When some of the other dialects of Western Cham are described, particularly those that have undergone different paths of contact since splitting off from Cham, it will be interesting to see how different these are.

Very speculatively, it may be that some of the Cham dialects in Cambodia date back, not to the fall of the southern capital in 1471, but even earlier to the fall of the northern capital roughly five hundred years earlier.

PHAN RANG CHAM, AN INCIPIENT TONE SYSTEM

For a long period after the breakup of PC, Cham was in contact with atonal, possibly registral MK languages and developed a register system, before breaking up into Phan Rang Cham, Western Cham, and Haroi. However, certainly since the fall of the southern capital Vijaya, in Binh-dinh, in 1471, a major influence on Phan Rang has been the fully tonal Vietnamese with many of the Phan Cham becoming bilingual in Vietnamese. In this setting, Phan Rang Cham has steadily become less registral and more tonal.

The literature

The available descriptions of Phan Rang Cham tones are excellent. The earliest description seems to be Doris Blood's in 1962, followed by David Blood's in 1967. These preliminary descriptions by the Bloods clearly distinguished a two-way tonal distinction for Phan Rang Cham. Later, on the basis of the material in Blood (1962), Greenberg (1970:139) wrote that Cham has followed a regional tendency, the development of lowered pitch after what were originally voiced obstruents, with the subsequent loss of voicing distinctions in the initial obstruents causing

> ...a hitherto atonal language to generate a tonal system of two levels, rather than to double the number of tones as in other languages of Southeast Asia.

Just four years later, Fr. Gérard Moussay analyzed Phan Rang Cham in his Chamic-French dictionary writing (1971:xiii-xiv) that there were four tones in the Cham language, and, although they are noted in the transcription by any sign, they are needed for speaking. He went on to describe them as: an even tone, occurring when the vowels are used alone or else when preceded by a normal consonant, a low tone when vowels are preceded by a long consonant (the examples indicate he meant the orthographically voiced obstruents), a departing ("rising") tone when the vowel is preceded by a normal consonant and followed by a glottal stop, and a falling tone when the vowel is preceded by a long consonant (again, what are orthographically voiced obstruents) and followed by glottal closure.

In 1992, Moussay's analysis was basically confirmed by the extremely useful instrumental study by Han, Edmondson, and Gregerson, who like Moussay analyzed Phan Rang Cham as having a three- or four-way distinction, depending upon whether or not Moussay's "departing" tone was phonemic.

The evolution of Phan Rang Cham tones

The path of Phan Rang Cham tonogenesis is quite transparent. The first stage probably dates back to before Phan Rang Cham, Western Cham, and Haroi split up into separate dialects: after voiced obstruents, breathy phonation (second register) developed while after the remaining obstruents there was the now contrasting unmarked, modal phonation (first register). Although it is not clear when the low-pitch that accompanied the breathy phonation developed into low tone, contrasting with the higher pitched modal phonation which developed into high tone, but from its inception that register system probably included redundant pitch distinctions.

Later, under the influence of bilingual contact with Vietnamese speakers, the pitch distinctions became more salient than the phonation differences and when the voicing distinction between obstruents was lost, the result was a two-way tonal distinction. With the loss of the voicing distinction in the initials, the originally breathy-voiced, low-pitched vowels became low-toned, while the remaining modal-voiced vowels automatically constituted a higher-pitched tone, essentially by default. The only remaining step was for the low tone and the high tone to each be split further on the basis of the presence or absence of a final glottal stop. With the final glottal stops, although it is obvious that Phan Rang Cham final glottal stops affect pitch, it is not clear if the pitch difference is still allophonically predictable synchronically or if it is already fully phonemic. However, diachronically, the source of the pitch is known, the direction of the change is clear, and even the inevitable outcome seems obvious. See Figure 16.

   For monosyllables, the developments are precisely as described, but for disyllabic forms the situation is more complicated. In some cases, the tone of the main syllable is not predictable from the initial of the main syllable, but instead must be predicted from the initial of the presyllable. Thus, if the PC presyllable originally began with a voiced obstruent and the main syllable initial was a sonorant or *-h-, it was the voiced obstruent of the presyllable that resulted in the low-toned reflex in modern Phan Rang. In such cases, the breathiness of the presyllable (originally, from its voiced obstruent), spread from the presyllable to the main syllable. When the main syllable began with other than a sonorant or *-h-, no such spreading from the presyllable to the main syllable took place, at least in Phan Rang Cham.

   Remnants of this earlier register system still exist in Phan Rang Cham. In their instrumental study, Han, Edmondson, and Gregerson point out (1992), for instance, that breathiness is regularly found in the monosyllables descended from PC voiced obstruents and it occurs, although only sporadically in the disyllabic forms.

Figure 16: Phan Rang Cham tonogenesis in monosyllables

Initials classes:	Resulting registers:	Resulting tone classes:
PC initials (except voiced obstruents) ⟶	modal voice + higher pitch	incipient high tone with glottal finals · high tone with non-glottal finals
PC voiced obstruents ⟶	breathy voice + lower pitch	low tone with glottal finals · low tone with non-glottal finals

Now, of course, as Doris Blood (1962:12) mentioned in passing and as was confirmed by the Han, Edmondson, and Gregerson studies, the Phan Rang forms are even more clearly distinguished by low or low-rising pitch.

PC voiced obstruents > breathy voice > low tone

It is important to realize that the path of development is from PC voiced obstruents to breathy phonation (second register) to low tone. If the middle step is left out, it leaves the impression that low tone developed directly from voiced obstruents—that synopsis would be not just misleading but quite false.

Table 121: PC voiced obstruent > breathy voice > low tones

PNB	PC	W. Cham	PR Cham	
---	*blɛy	p̪lay	p̪lĕy	'buy'
*pah	*blah	p̪lah	p̪lah	'chop; split'
---	*pə-blɛy	pap̪lay	pap̪lĕy	'sell'
---	*brɛy	p̪ray	p̪rĕy	'give'
---	*braːs	p̪rah	p̪rah -1	'rice (husked)'
*qyùŋ	ˣ*dəŋ	ţəŋ	ţăŋ	'stand; stop'
---	*dua	ţoa	ţwa	'two'
---	*dhaːn	ţhan	ţhan	'branch; bough'
---	ˣ*dhɔŋ	ţhŏŋ	ţhŏŋ	'knife'
---	*ʔadhĕy	ţhay	ţhĕy	'forehead'
---	ˣ*glɛh	ķlɛh	ķlɛh	'tired'
---	*glay	ķlai	răm-ķlay	'forest; wild, savage'
---	*gah	ķah	ķah	'side, direction; bank'
---	ˣ*gəm	ķŏm	ķăm	'to cover'
---	ˣ*gər	ķăr	ķăr	'handle (knife)'
---	ˣ*guy	ķui	ķuy	'carry on back'

The evidence for the earlier register stage with its contrast between modal and breathy register exists everywhere: in Phan Rang Cham clear traces of voice quality differences were found by Han, Edmondson, and Gregerson (1992) and in the closely-related Western Cham dialect, there is a register system that is very much like the earlier register system of Phan Rang. In addition, there is other evidence: notice that it is not voicing per se that led to low tone, but that the development of low tone was mediated through an intermediate stage of breathiness. Among other things, this apparently necessary intermediate stage accounts for the fact that it is only after the reflexes of the old PC voiced obstruents, which led to breathiness on the following vowel, that low tone developed. After the voiced sonorants, which are obviously voiced but which are far less likely to develop following breathiness on the vowel, low tone never developed.

Both the correlations with PC and the subsequent chain of developments are still evident from a comparison of PC, Western Cham, and the Phan Rang monosyllables. As Table 121 shows, if PC initial was a voiced obstruent, the Western Cham form has a breathy vowel, and the Phan Rang Cham monosyllable has low-tone with traces of residual breathiness.

Table 122: Other PC initials > modal register > high ton

PNB	PC	W. Cham	PR Cham	
---	*kra	kra	kra	'monkey'
---	ˣ*pɔ	pɔ 'title'	po	'master; lord'
---	ˣ*pəh	pəh	pə̆h	'to open'
*păr	ˣ*pər	păr	păr	'to fly'
---	*pluh	ha pluh	plŭh	'ten'
---	*tuh	tuh	tŭh	'to pour'
---	*tuŋ	tuŋ 'intestines'	tŭŋ	'stomach; abdomen'
---	*tuy	tui	tuy	'to follow'
---	ˣ*təl	tăl	tăl	'arrive; until'
---	*klaːs	klah 'to free'	klăh	'escape'
*trŏŋ	ˣ*trɔŋ	trŏŋ	trŏŋ	'eggplant'
---	*trɛy	tray	trɛ̆y	'full, satiated'
---	*klam	maklăm	klăm	'afternoon; night'
---	*klaw	klau	klaw	'laugh'
---	*klɔw	klau	klŏw	'three'
---	*trun	trŭn	trŭn	'descend'
---	*wah	w̥ah	wăh	'to fish'
*roy	ˣ*ruay	r̥uai	roy	'fly; bug; insect'
---	ˣ*wər	w̥ăr	wăr	'forget'
---	ˣ*məŋ	m̥əŋ	mĭŋ	'from'
---	*naw	n̥au	naw	'go; walk'
---	*wil	w̥ĭl 'circle'	wĭl	'round'
---	*nam	n̥ăm	năm	'six'
---	*ñu	ñ̥u	ñu	'he, she; they'

In Table 121, the Western Cham forms are all in the breathy register (marked by the dot under the initial obstruent). The Phan Rang Cham obstruents are marked in precisely the same way; in Phan Rang Cham the dot indicates not register but that the form has a low tone (although usually with residual accompanying breathiness).

Similarly, the origins of the contrasting Phan Rang tone are likewise evident from a comparison of the PC, Western Cham, and the Phan Rang monosyllables. As Table 122 shows, if PC initial was not a voiced obstruent, the Western Cham form has a first register vowel (except in the case of sonorants), and the Phan Rang Cham monosyllable has a high-tone without any traces of breathiness.

In Table 122, the Western Cham forms containing initial obstruents are in the unmarked modal register (indicated in the table by the lack of a dot under the Western Cham initial obstruent). However, there is a secondary development restricted to Western Cham (not found in either Phan Rang Cham or in closely-related Haroi), where all sonorant initial forms are also in the breathy register (marked in this table but not everywhere in this work by a dot under the initial sonorant). In Phan Rang Cham, all of the forms are in the unmarked high tone (indicated in the table by the lack of a dot under the initial consonant).

Registers split by final glottal stop

After the original register split, Phan Rang Cham developed a low tone from the second register and a default high tone from the first register. Then, these two tone classes were further split by the final glottal stop. The Phan Rang Cham low-tone with a final glottal stop became a low, glottal tone, indicated reasonably enough in Table 123 by the combination of the dot under the obstruent and the final glottal stop.

Table 123: Breathy register + final glottal stop

PNB	PC	W. Cham	PR Cham	
---	*ḅap	pau?	pḁ̆?	'fill; full'
---	*ḅru? -n -f	pṛŭ?	pṛŭ?	'rotten'
---	*ḍɔːk	ṭɔ?	ṭɔ?	'sit; live; stay'
---	ˣ*gɔ?	ḳɔ̆?	ḳɔ̆?	'kettle; glazed clay pot'
---	ˣgrək	ḳrə?	ḳrə̆?	'vulture; garuda'
---	*jahit	çhi?	çhi?	'sew'
---	ˣ*jɔh	jɔh 'snap'	çɔh	'broken; spoilt'
---	ˣ*juː?	çu?	çu?	'black'
*ajeq	ˣ*jɛ?	çɛ̆?	çɛ?	'near; about to'

Notice that the Western Cham forms are all in the breathy register (marked by the same dot under the obstruent that in Phan Rang Cham indicates low tone).

In a parallel way, the Phan Rang Cham high-tone with a final glottal stop became a high, glottal tone, which Moussay describes as rising, indicated reasonably enough in the Table 124 by the absence of a dot under the initial consonant and the presence of the final glottal stop.

An enlightening discussion of the tone splitting effect of final glottal stop on the Phan Rang tonal system is found in Han, Edmondson, and Gregerson (1992:41-42), in which they note that various excellent scholars have commented about the perceptible pitch difference between non-glottal final and glottal forms (which descend from the PC voiceless stops: *-p, *-t, *-k, *-ʔ). As Han, Edmondson, and Gregerson wrote, despite the fact that he considered the difference non-phonemic, Blood (1967:29) nonetheless wrote that such Cham forms had noticeably higher pitch before both the final glottal stop and before final -h. And, as discussed earlier, Moussay further splits the low-toned and high-toned into forms with and without final glottal stops. Similarly, Han, Edmondson, and Gregerson report that Hoang Thi Chau (1987) also posits a four tone system, with the glottal finals and the nonglottal finals distinguished.

Table 124: Modal register + final glottal stop

PC	W. Cham	PR Cham	
ˣ*puac	puaiʔ	poyʔ	'scold; talk'
*paːt	paʔ	paʔ	'four'
ˣ*pɛt	pɛ̆ʔ	pɛ̆ʔ	'pick, pluck'
ˣ*prɔːk	prɔʔ	prɔʔ	'squirrel'
ˣ*kɛʔ	kɛ̆ʔ	kɛ̆ʔ	'bite; snap at; peck'
ˣ*cət	cəʔ	cəʔ	'mountain range'
ˣ*kɔːʔ	kɔʔ	akɔ̆ʔ -1	'white'
ˣ*rək	rəʔ	harə̆ʔ	'grass; weeds'
ˣ*lɛʔ	lɛ̆ʔ	lɛ̆ʔ	'fall into'
*ŋaʔ	ŋă̆ʔ	aŋă̆ʔ	'make, do'
ˣ*lɔːk	lɔʔ	lɔʔ	'to peel'
*mat	məʔ	mɨʔ	'take; fetch, get'

Basing their analysis in part on instrumental findings, Han, Edmondson, and Gregerson (1992:41) differ from other investigators in distinguishing only three tones: the expected two low tones, one glottal-final and the other without a glottal final, but for the high tones they only posit a single tone, preferring to analyze Phan Rang Cham as having a single high tone but with allophonic pitch differences associated with the presence or absence of a glottal final.

From a historical perspective, the question of whether contemporary Phan Rang Cham has a four-tone system or a three-tone system is irrelevant. It is clear what the current system developed out of and even what direction it seems to be heading.

However, what is missing from these accounts is adequate information on the Phan Rang reflexes of PC forms that ended in *-h. Only Blood (1967) has commented on them specifically, and he treated them as patterning with the final glottal stops, that is, he reported such forms as having allophonic but noticeable extra high pitch. An instrumental examination of these forms would be quite interesting.

Transparency and phonation spreading

The situation in disyllabic forms is slightly more complicated. If the presyllable began with a PC voiced obstruent and the initial onset of the main syllable was either a sonorant or a medial voiceless fricative *s or *h, the breathy voice of the second register spread from the presyllable to the main syllable ultimately resulting in a low-toned main syllable.

As Table 125 shows, in disyllabic forms beginning with a PC voiced obstruent, the breathy voice of the register spread through medial sonorants resulting in the main syllable having second register in Western Cham, indicated by a dot under the obstruent, and in low tone in Phan Rang Cham, again indicated by a dot under the obstruent.

Table 125: Spreading through sonorants

PC	NR	W. Cham	PR Cham	
*ḅara	ḅara	pra	pirā	'shoulder'
*ḅarah	ḅarah	parah	---	'swell; swollen'
*ḅulɔw	ḅiləu	plau	pilɔ̌w	'body hair; feathers'
*ḅula:n	ia ḅila:t	ea plan	pilan	'moon; month'
*ḅuŋa	ḅuŋã	paŋur -f	piŋu	'flower'
*dalam	dalap	ṭalăm	ṭalăm	'deep; inside'
*danaw	danau -n	---	ṭanaw	'lake'
*darah	darah	ṭarah	ṭarăh	'blood'
*dilah	gilah < *g-	ṭalah	ṭalah	'tongue'
*durεy	daruəi (m)	ṭaruai (m)	ṭaroy (m)	'thorn'
*gunam	---	---	ḳanăm	'cloud'
*jala:n	jala:t	çalan	çalan	'road; path'
ˣ*ḅala	ḅala	pla	pila	'tusk; ivory'
*dara	dara	ṭra	ṭara	'girl (c. teenage)'

In addition to spreading through sonorants, the breathy voice of the second register also spread through medial *s and *h. All the Western Cham forms except 'iron' are in second register, just as all the Phan Rang Cham forms are in low tone.

*Table 126: Spreading through medial *s and *h*

Malay	PC	W. Cham	PR Cham	
jahit	*jahit	çhi?	çhi?	'sew'
jahat	*jǝhaːt	---	çha?	'bad; wicked'
dahi	*?adhĕy	ṭhay	ṭhĕy	'forehead'
akar	*?ughaːr	ḳha	uḳha	'root'
bĕsi	*bǝsɛy	pasay	piṭhĕy	'iron'

The form 'forehead' has been included in the table to show that voiced aspirated stops also show low tone. The Malay forms in the table show that one source of PC voiced aspirated initials is the reduction of earlier disyllabic forms.

However, the breathy voice of the second register did not spread through medial voiceless stops either in Western Cham or in Phan Rang Cham.

Table 127: Failure to spread through voiceless stops

PNB	Malay	PC	W. Cham	PR Cham	
---	batu	*batɔw	patau	patŏw, patŏw	'stone'
*prĭt	---	*batɛy	patay	patĕy	'banana'
---	batuk	*batuk	patŭ?	patŭ?	'cough'
---	dikit	*dikit	taki?	taki?	'few; little'
---	---	ˣ*batɔ	patɔ	patɔ	'teach'

None of the Western Cham forms in Table 127 show second register and none of the Phan Rang forms show low tone. Particularly interesting is the second Phan Rang form listed for 'stone'. The initial /p/ has a dot under it, indicating a second register vowel, but the /t/ beginning the main syllable does not. In effect, the first syllable of the form had second register, but the breathy voice did not spread to the second syllable, and thus the main syllable does not have a low tone reflex.

The patterns of spreading are in themselves interesting. Medial sonorants appear completely permeable to spreading, while medial obstruents are far more resistant, with only medial *s and *h allowing spreading.

The history of Phan Rang Cham contact

The Phan Rang data is interesting from the viewpoint of the mechanism of change involved. The Phan Rang Cham transition from a Western Cham style register system toward a Vietnamese style tone system represents more of an evolution than a revolution — the actual changes look to be little more than slight shifts in emphasis. To return to something Eugénie Henderson (1967:171) said thirty years ago:

> It is important to recognize that pitch is frequently only one of the phonetic components of "tone" as a phonological category. A phonological tone is in our area [South East Asia] very frequently a complex of other features besides pitch—such as intensity, duration, voice quality, final glottal constriction and so on.

The six tones of Vietnam are best described as complexes of features with pitch but one of these features (Thompson 1984-5:16). And, among these features, it is those which are salient in Vietnamese that are coming to the fore in the emergent Phan Rang Cham tone system. The Vietnamese system contains breathy versus non-breathy contrasts: the low-pitched huyền tone which is "often accompanied by breathy voice quality" contrasts with the clear register found with the mid or high-mid pitched ngang tone. And, among the forms with final stops, the nặng tone with its the low-dropping-pitch and which "ends in [a] stop or is cut off abruptly by [a] glottal stop" contrasts with the sắc tone with its high-rising pitch. That is, the Vietnamese tone system contains the very complexes of phonological oppositions that have formed the basis of the incipient tone system in Phan Rang.

The stages in Phan Rang Cham tonogenesis are still transparent. Distinct layers of external contact have precipitated each of the stages of internal change. Austronesian contact with MK led to the restructuring of evenly-stressed disyllables into iambic syllables with final stress. Later contact with MK register languages led to a register system, and intense contact the tone system of Vietnamese has produced an increasingly tonal Phan Rang. The entire history of successive Phan Rang Cham phonological restructurings has been the history of a language adjusting its internal paths of change to follow paths illuminated by language contact.

The social contact involved is bilingualism, with the Phan Rang Cham speakers being bilingual in Vietnamese, with no significant language shifting, except of course, away from Phan Rang Cham, when Phan Rang speakers shift to Vietnamese.

It seem appropriate to close this section with a quote from Lafont, who in the process of dismissing the very existence of tones in Cham, inadvertently adds an interesting twist:

> ...a few scholars have described Cham as a tone language but have never given evidence for this assertion, for there are no phonemic tones

in Cham as there are in Vietnamese. It seems that this error originated from l'Introduction (pp. xii-xiv) of the *Dictionnarie Cam-Vietnamien-Françis* (1971) in which the author talked about four tones while he referred to the intonation particular to the Phan Rang, Phan Rí region where the Cham people were educated in Vietnamese schools, intonation which is not to be found elsewhere, neither in the Chư-Đốc region nor among the Chams in Cambodia, except in interrogative sentences which are always characterized by a higher register. (1994b:12-13; note: the grammar of the translation has been emended)

The explicit and somewhat puzzling claim that Cham has no tones at all can simply be dismissed, although there is no question that the Cham tones are not as perceptually salient as the Vietnamese tones. More interesting, however, are the suggestion that not all dialects have tones and the almost inadvertent suggestion that Cham tonogenesis correlates directly with the degree of contact with Vietnamese.

HAROI VOWELS AND RESTRUCTURED REGISTER

Although comments on the Haroi vowels have been scattered throughout the chapter on vowels, their development is too complex to be explained in passing and too intimately involved with register and Hrê contact to be discussed in isolation. Thus, it is necessary to bring these prior observations together here and expand upon them as, from a Chamic viewpoint, the Haroi vowels have followed a unique, fascinating path of development.

The original PC vowel system underwent massive splitting and realignment before settling into the system of Modern Haroi. Prior to the realignments within Haroi, there were a series of other earlier realignments often shared with Western Cham ("Pre-Haroi vowel changes" on page 199), which were not recognized as such in Thurgood 1996. However, the major vehicle for this complete restructuring was voice quality-induced vowel splitting. Under the influence of tense voice (induced by the proto-voiceless obstruents) certain monophthongs were lowered. And, under the influence of breathy voice (induced by the proto-voiced obstruents), certain monophthongs were raised, other monophthongs developed on-glides, and still other diphthongs had their onsets raised.

The first indication of Haroi's uniqueness is the extraordinary number of vowels and, if one is doing historical work, the existence of two or more reflexes for each proto-vowel. In striking contrast to the typical nine- or ten-vowel systems of most Chamic languages, Haroi has a plethora of vowels: 11 simple vowels, each occurring both long and short (see Table 128; also cf. Tegenfeldt and Goschnick, 1977:1), and 17 diphthongs and triphthongs. Beyond these, Haroi also has some 10 rarely occurring nasalized vowels.

Table 128: Haroi simple vowels

		front	central	back
high:	closed	i	ɨ	u
	open	ι		ʊ
mid		e	ə	o
		ɛ		ɔ
low			a	

There are no vowel contrasts in the Haroi presyllable. As one consequence of the shift to final syllable stress into pre-Chamic, all of the common vowel distinctions in modern Haroi occur either in monosyllables or in the stressed main syllable of disyllables.

Table 129: Haroi diphthongs and triphthongs

	front		central		back	
high	ia	iau	ɨi	ɨai	ui	ua
			ɨa	ɨau		
mid	ea	eau			oi	oa
	ei				ou	oai
low			ai			
			au			

In addition, Haroi has a rich array of diphthongs and triphthongs (see Table 129), many the result of registrally-induced changes.

Although it is not clear what significance to attach to the fact, it is worth noting that Vietnamese also has an eleven-vowel system. Minimally, it would be important to examine the vowel inventories of various other languages of the region to see how common this particular configuration is in the area and in particular whether it occurs in Bahnar.

Haroi restructured register

Modern Haroi has what Huffman (1976) termed a restructured register system. In the case of Haroi, between PC and modern Haroi the following chain of events has occurred: (1) certain classes of initials led to distinctive phonation differences on the following vowels, that is, to voice quality distinctions; (2) the voice quality differences on the vowels produced vowel distinctions, that is, led to a register system with vowel registers—distinct vowel sets associated with different voice quality differences; and, (3) the voice quality distinctions that originally conditioned the vowel splits disappeared, leaving behind a large number of now unconditioned vowel distinctions; in Huffman's terms, it became a restructured register system with the proliferation of vowels associated with restructured register systems.

Pre-Haroi vowel changes

Prior to the alignments within Haroi, there were a series of other earlier realignments, often shared with Western Cham, which were not recognized as pre-Haroi in Thurgood 1966: the much earlier lowering of the onsets of certain diphthongs, a change which is largely shared with Western Cham; the merger of PC *-ɔw with the reflexes of *-ău, which is clear from the fact that the vowel of the rhyme behaves like a low vowel during the registrally-induced vowel splits; and, in a number of cases, PC shwa was raised or backed before specific finals, again a change that preceded the Haroi vowel shifts due to the influence of voice quality.

The early pre-Haroi reflexes of PC shwa

Among the changes that occurred before the registral realignment of the Haroi vowel system was the development of three distinct reflexes for PC shwa. In each case, the change was determined by the syllable-final consonant.

PC *-əŋ > *-ɨŋ

Before final *-ŋ, PC shwa became /-ɨ-/. The most obvious thing about Table 130 is that three of the four Haroi reflexes of PC *-əŋ contain a barred-ɨ. The shwa in the remaining form is the expected reflex of an earlier barred-ɨ which has been lowered due to the initial voiceless consonant (see "Registers and the vowel splitting patterns" on page 201, for discussion of this vowel lowering).

Beyond this, however, there is something else quite interesting about the chart: the reflexes in Headley's Western Cham match the Haroi reflexes perfectly, right down to the split conditioned by the voiceless obstruent initial. This suggests that this change predates from PC *-əŋ > *-ɨŋ predates Haroi, and that at least this dialect of Western Cham and Haroi were particularly close either genetically, through contact, or both. Note that this change is not shared, however, with the Kvoeu-Hor and Friberg Western Cham forms or with the Phan Rang Cham forms.

Table 130: The reflexes of PC *-əŋ

PNB	PC	Rade	Haroi	W. Cham (Headley)	W. Cham (Kvoeu-Hor)	PR Cham	
---	ˣ*ɓəŋ	ɓɜ̆ŋ	ɓɨŋ	bɨŋ	ɓəŋ	ɓă̆ŋ	'to eat'
---	ˣ*məŋ	mɜ̆ŋ	mɨŋ	---	məŋ	mɨŋ	'from'
*qyùŋ	ˣ*dəŋ	dɜ̆ŋ	thɨŋ	tɨŋ	ʈəŋ	ʈă̆ŋ	'stand; stop'
---	ˣ*pəŋ	pɜ̆ŋ	pɜ̆ŋ	pɜ̆ŋ	pəŋ	pəŋ	'to nail, hammer'

PC *-ət, *-ək, and *-əh remained -əʔ, *-ək, and *-əh

Before final *-t, final *-k, and final *-h, PC shwa was preserved as a shwa. Elsewhere it became something else.

Table 131: The reflexes of PC *-əʔ, *-ək, and *-əh

PNB	PC	Rade	Chru	Haroi	
---	ˣ*cət	čɨʔ -i	cəʔ	cɜ̆ʔ	'mountain range'
*pǎy	ˣ*pə-pət	---	---	pəpɜ̆ʔ	'to fan'
---	ˣ*rək	rɜ̆k	rəʔ	rɜ̆ʔ	'grass; weeds'
---	ˣgrək	---	---	kriʔ	'vulture; garuda'
---	ˣ*pəh	---	pəh	pɜ̆h	'to open'
---	ˣ*gləh	---	jərləh -i	tlɨh	'descend; collapse'
---	ˣ*madəh	mədih	mədəh	məthɨh	'awaken'

For these rhymes, the final shwa is preserved as such in Haroi, unless the syllable began in PC with a voiced obstruent. In that case, the shwa was raised to a barred-ɨ (see page 201, for discussion of this vowel raising).

All other examples of PC *-ə- > *-ɔ-

The remaining words with PC shwa backed to /-ɔ/, that is, the rhyme *-ən > *-ɔn, *-ər >, and *-əm > *-ɔm. In these cases, unless the initial of the main syllable or of the presyllable was originally a voiced obstruent, the vowel remained an open-ɔ. However, when the initial of the presyllable was a voiced obstruent, this open-ɔ was raised to /ŏ/ (see page 201, for discussion of this vowel raising).

Table 132: The reflexes of the other PC forms with *-ə-

PNB	PC	Rade	Chru	Haroi	
---	*lən	lăn	lən	lŏn	'earth'
---	*bukən	məkăn	pəkən	pəkŏn	'other; different'
---	ˣdrə̃n -if	---	drin -v	trŏn	'numb'
*păr	ˣˣpər	phiər -iv	pər	pɔl	'to fly'
---	ˣˣkatər	kətər	---	kətɔl	'corn; grain'
---	ˣˣwər	wər	wər	wɔl	'forget'
---	ˣˣyər	---	---	yɔl	'lift, raise'
---	ˣˣdər	dər	dər	thŏl	'bury'
---	ˣˣgər	grăn -ivf	gər	khŏl	'handle (knife)'
*hagẵr	ˣˣsagər	həgər	səgər	akhŏl	'drum'
---	ˣˣsadər	hədər	sədər	athŏl	'remember'
---	ˣˣʔəm	ăm	əm	ŏm	'to roast'
---	ˣˣpagəm	---	---	pəkhŏm	'dove'

It is obvious that the changes in the reflexes of the PC shwa forms took place before the registrally-induced vowel realignments (see page 201). Certainly, with the changes before the final velar nasal, this is obvious because the change is shared with Western Cham, but, even with the forms that backed to an open-ɔ, the modern Haroi distribution requires that the change preceded the vowel alignments discussed in "Registers and the vowel splitting patterns" on page 201.

Registers and the vowel splitting patterns

The two specific marked registers are associated with the remaining changes that produced the modern Haroi vowel splits: the first register, which consists of the allophonically-distinct conditioned set of vowels associated with the tense phonation type that evolved after the PC voiceless obstruents and the second register, which consists of the allophonically-distinct set of vowels associated with the breathy phonation that evolved after the PC voiced obstruents. When these vowel-quality-conditioning phonation differences were lost, allophonic vowel differences became phonemic, and Haroi became a restructured register language (see Figure 17).

Figure 17: Restructured register and Haroi vowel splitting

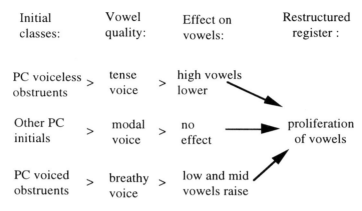

| Initial classes: | Vowel quality: | Effect on vowels: | Restructured register : |

For monosyllabic words, the various vowel types interacted with the manner of articulation of the PC syllable-initial consonant to produce the modern vowel splitting patterns. These vowel splitting patterns are summarized in Table 133.

Table 133: Consonant types, vowel classes, and vowel splitting

	voiceless obstruents > tense voice (= first register)	glottalized obstruents, voiced aspirates, & sonorants	voiced obstruents > breathy register (= second register)
high vowels; *-əŋ > *-iŋ	(onset) lowered; > -əŋ	unchanged	unchanged
centering diphthongs: *ua > *oa *ia > *ea	unchanged	unchanged	raised and backed: **-ia- > -ia-; **-ua- > -ua; -ʊ- /___m, -ʔ
mid *ɛ; *ə; *ɔ; *-ɛy > *-ŏi	unchanged	unchanged	raised: ɪ; ɨ; ʊ (u); -ɨi (+ fronted)
low vowels	unchanged	unchanged	developed -i- onset

After voiceless obstruents (tense voice)

The tense voice quality of first register vowels, from the PC voiceless obstruents, led to high vowel lowering. Otherwise, the voiceless obstruents did not affect vowel quality. Note that the high vowels include not just the high vowel inherited from PC high vowels, but also the secondarily-derived high barred-i that developed before final velar nasals in both Western Cham and Haroi (page 199).

Table 134: Tense voice and vowel lowering after voiceless obstruents

PNB	PC	Rade	Chru	Haroi	
---	ˣˣsisi(r)	kəsi	təsi	cəsei	'a comb'
*qb̆ič	ˣ*dhɔŋ	p̆ĭt	pi:ʔ	peiʔ	'sleep; close eyes'
---	*phit	phĭʔ	phi:ʔ	pheiʔ	'bitter; bile'
---	*jahit	jhĭt	si:ʔ	seiʔ	'sew'
---	*kulit	klĭt	kəli:ʔ	kəleiʔ	'skin'
---	*kuñit	kəñĭʔ	kəñi:ʔ	kəñeiʔ	'yellow; tumeric'
---	*tasiʔ	kəsĭʔ	təsiʔ	cəseiʔ	'sea; ocean'
---	*thu	thu	thu	thou	'dry'
---	*ʔiku	ku	aku	akou	'tail'
---	*lukut	ekŭt	ləku:ʔ	ləkouʔ 'avoid'	'absent'
---	*kəntut	---	kətu:ʔ	kətouʔ; tout	'fart'
---	ˣ*kaʔu:ʔ	---	kəʔŭ:ʔ	kəʔouʔ	'worried; sad'
---	ˣˣpəŋ	pŏ̆ŋ	pəŋ	pŏ̆ŋ	'to nail, pound'
---	ˣkhi:n	---	khin	khĕn	'dare'
---	ˣ*cuh	čuh	---	coh	'burn trns.'
---	*krih	krĭʔ -f	kri:h -1	kreh	'to whittle'
---	*phun	phŭn	phun	phon	'trunk; log; plant'
*trŭh	ˣ*truh	truh	truh	troh	'arrive'
---	*tuh	---	---	toh	'change'
---	*klum	---	klum	tlŏ̆m; kəlom	'to cover'
---	*trun	trŭn	trun	tron	'descend'
---	*pluh	pluh	spluh	aploh	'ten'
---	*thun	thŭn	thun	thon	'year'
---	*tuh	tuh	tuh	cətoh; toh	'to pour'
---	*tuy	tui hluɛ	tui	toi	'to follow'

As is evident from the examples in Table 134, both the /i/ and the /u/ develop into the diphthongs /ei/ and /ou/, respectively, word-finally or before a final glottal stop.

After glottalized obstruents and sonorants (modal voice)

No vowel quality changes occurred after either the glottalized obstruents nor after the sonorants. This is not surprising: both the glottalized obstruents and the sonorants were associated with modal voice, a clear phonation type that would not have been expected to affect vowel quality.

There is, however, a subset of reflexes after sonorants where the situation is complicated by an assimilative interaction involving a PC *i or *u in the presyllable or a *y as the onset of the main syllable that caused vowel raising, a phenomenon otherwise only associated with voiced obstruents (see Table 135). The existence of such irregular correspondences was noticed by Lee (1977b) and by Burnham (1976), who both commented on these unexpectedly high vowel reflexes.

Table 135: Height assimilation after high (semi-)vowels

PNB	PC	Rade	Chru	Haroi	
*yaŋ	ˣ*yaːŋ	yaŋ	yaːŋ	yɨaŋ	'spirit; god'
---	*yah	---	---	yɨah	'destroy; take apart'
---	*raya ?	---	---	ləyɨa	'big'
---	*yaːp	yap	yaːuʔ	yɨauʔ	'count'
---	*ɓuya	mya	bia	pəyɨa	'crocodile'
---	*ʔular	ala	ala	alɨa	'snake'
---	*huma	həma	həma	həmɨa	'field'
---	*lima	ema	ləma	ləmɨa	'five'
---	*ʔina	ana	---	anɨa	'mother; major; big'
---	*lamaːn	eman	ləmaːn	ləmɨan	'elephant'
---	*samaw	---	səmŭ -f	həmɨau	'prompt; on time'
*yun	ˣ*yuan -v	yuăn -v	ɣuən	yŭn	'Vietnamese'
*yor	*kayua	kəyua dah	kəyua	kəyua kə-	'because'
---	ˣ*hayuaʔ	---	yuaʔ	yŭʔ	'harvest (rice)'
---	*yua	---	---	yua	'use'

There are three groups of sonorant-initial forms in Table 135 which have unexpectedly high vowels. In each case, the presence of either *i, *u, or *y seems to correlate with the otherwise unexpected reflex. The first group contains low vowels, but with a barred-i onset; in each case, this onset follows *y. The second group also contains low vowels, but in this case it appears that it is the high vowel *i or *u in the immediately preceding syllable that conditioned the height. The last group contains an /-u-/ or /-ua/ which normally would have been lowered or had its onset lowered much earlier in the history of Haroi (page 135) but which is unexpectedly high in modern Haroi. This unexpected height correlates with the initial *y. These changes involve /a/ diphthongizing, with the onset of /iə/ increasing its palatality as it assimilates to the preceding element, while the second part of the diphthong decreases its sonority (Donegan 1985:145-46)

After voiced aspirates (modal voice)

Contrary to what is implied in a table in Thurgood (1996), once recent borrowings have been culled out, it becomes apparent that the so-called voiced aspirates behave just like the glottalized obstruents and the sonorants—they have no effect whatsoever on the vowel quality.

Table 136: Reflexes of the so-called voiced aspirates

PC	Rade	Chru	Haroi	
ˣ*dhɔŋ	dhɔ̆ŋ	thɔŋ	thɔ̆ŋ	'knife'
*ʔadhɛ̆y	adhɛi	thəi	thəi -v	'forehead'
*dhaːn	adhan	thaːn	than	'branch'
*jahit	jhĭt	siː?	sei?	'sew'
*jəhaːt	jhat	jəhaː?	săt	'bad; wicked'
*ʔughaːr	agha	akha	akha	'root'
*pə-ghaːŋ	bhaŋ -i	---	pəkhaŋ	'dry over fire'
*pə-gha?	---	kha?	khă?	'forbid'

The vowel in /ei/ in 'sew' is the expected diphthongization of /i/ before a glottal stop seen earlier.

After voiced obstruents (breathy voice)

As both Lee (1977b) and Burnham (1976) noticed, the breathy voice associated with the second register (from PC voiced obstruents) caused various mid vowels to raise and the low vowels to develop a barred-i onglide (see Table 137).

Table 137: Breathy voice quality and raising after voiced obstruents

PNB	PC	Rade	Chru	Haroi	
---	ˣ*glɛh	---	glɛh	tlɪh	'tired'
---	ˣ*jɔh	jɔh	jɔh	sŭh	'broken; spoilt'
---	ˣ*gɔʔ	gɔ̆ʔ	gɔʔ	khŭʔ	'kettle; clay pot'
---	*bɔh	bɔh	bɔh	phŭh	'fruit; egg; clf.'
---	*dɔːk	dok	dɔːʔ	thʊʔ	'sit; live; stay'
---	ˣ*gəm	gă̆m	gəm	khŭm	'to cover'
---	*braːs	braih	braːh	prɨah	'rice (husked)'
---	*ba	ba	ba	phɨa	'bring, take, carry'
---	*bap	---	---	phɨauʔ	'fill; full'
---	*gah	---	gah	khɨah	'side, direction; bank'
*pah	*blah	blah	blah	plɨah	'chop; split'
---	*glaŋ	dlă̆ŋ	---	tlɨaŋ	'look at; watch'
---	*jaːk	jak	---	sɨaʔ	'invite'
---	*glay	dlie lui	glai	tlɨai	'forest, jungle; wild'
---	ˣ*druam	druom	drɔːm	trŭm	'fell a tree'
---	*dua	dua	dua	thua	'two'

In addition, certain diphthongs monophthongize in specific environments. Additional examples of changes in PC shwa can be seen in page 199, above.

Transparency and phonation spreading

For disyllabic words, the situation is complicated by the fact that some classes of main-syllable initial consonants allow the phonation generated by the initial of the presyllable to spread to the vowel of the main syllable. In such cases it is initial of the presyllable, not the initial of the main syllable, that determines the register of the main vowel.

Except when the initial of the presyllable is *s or *h, the Haroi spreading patterns are remarkably straightforward. If the main syllable begins with a sonorant, it is the initial of the presyllable, not the initial of the main syllable, that determines the register of the main syllable vowel. In other words, except in the case of presyllable *s or *h, initial sonorants are transparent to register spreading. For example, as both Burnham (1976) and Lee (1977b:89) noticed, if the pretonic syllable begins with a voiced obstruent, the main syllable follows the vowel splitting patterns associated with breathy phonation (See Table 138).

Table 138: Breathy phonation spreading through sonorants

PC	Rade	Chru	Haroi	
ˣjawa	ewa	jəwa	cəwɨa	'breath, soul, air'
ˣ*bala	mla	bla	pəlɨa	'tusk; ivory'
*buŋa	məŋa	bəŋa	pəŋɨa	'flower'
*dara	era	dra	cərɨa	'girl (c. teenage)'
*bara	mra	bra	prɨa	'shoulder'
*darah	erah	drah	cərɨah	'blood'
*dras	---	drah	cərɨah	'fast'
*barah	---	brah	prɨah	'swell; swollen'
*dilah	elah	dəlah	cəlɨah	'tongue'
*gunam	kənam	gənam	kənɨam	'cloud'
*dalam	elam	dəlam	cəlɨam	'deep; inside'
*bulaːn	mlan	ea blaːn	pəlɨan	'moon; month'
*jalaːn	elan	jəlaːn	cəlɨan	'road; path'
*danaw	enau	dənau	cənɨau	'lake'
*bɔh maw	məmau	bəmau	pəmɨau	'mushroom'
*bulɔw	mlău	bləu	pəlɨau	'body hair'
*durɛy	erue (m)	druəi (m)	cərɨi (m)	'thorn'

In a parallel way, if the pretonic syllable begins with a voiceless obstruent (again, other than *s or *h) and the main syllable begins with a sonorant, the main syllable follows the vowel splitting patterns associated with voiceless obstruent phonation. The examples in Table 139 show forms in which the phonation induced by the initial voiceless obstruent of the pretonic syllable has spread to the main syllable. As a consequence, the reflexes of PC high vowels *-i and *-u after sonorants are the reflexes expected after voiceless stops, not the reflexes expected after monosyllables beginning with sonorants.

For the last two examples in Table 139, the final vowel can also be attributed to the otherwise well-attested process whereby a /i/ before a final glottal stop becomes /ei/.

In contrast to the sonorants that allow a great dealing of spreading, the syllable-initial obstruents allow none: indeed, it appears that main-syllable initial obstruents completely block spreading.

Table 139: Tense voice spreading through sonorants

PC	Rade	Chru	Haroi	
*tamuh	---	təmŭh	cəmoh	'grow; sprout'
*timun	kəmŭn	təmun	cəmon	'melon; cucumber'
*kalih	---	kərlih	kəleh	'miserly'
*kulit	klĭt	kəli:ʔ	kəleiʔ	'skin'
*kuñit	kəñĭʔ	kəñĭ:ʔ	kəñeiʔ	'yellow; tumeric'

It is important to note that the vowel splits cannot be attributed directly to the influence of PC initials; instead, the splits are due to the influence of an intervening phonation type. These two patterns of phonation spreading constitute strong evidence that it was the phonations correlated with the syllable-initial consonants, not the syllable-initial consonants themselves, that caused the vowel splitting. In phonetic terms, what must have spread from the pretonic syllable through the syllable-initial sonorant of the main syllable was a specific phonation type, not the manner of articulation or the voicing of the pretonic syllable-initial consonant.

Voice quality and the reflexes of PC presyllable *s- and *h-

In disyllabic forms when *s or *h is the initial of the presyllable, there is a voice quality-based split in the reflexes. It is more than likely that early in Haroi PC *s- and *h- merged as *h-. Then, before the before tense-voiced main syllables (< PC voiceless obstruents), the initial *h- was lost (the first set of examples in Table 140) but before breathy-voiced main syllables (< PC voiced obstruents the second set of examples in Table 140), this presyllabic *h- was retained.

However before the main-syllable initials associated with modal voice, that is, before glottalized obstruents or before sonorants (and, presumably, before voiced obstruents, if there were any), the *h- (< PC *s- and *h-) remained Haroi /h/.

Parallel developments in which the reflexes of initial consonants have differed depending upon voice quality, that is, phonation type, are attested in Thai, in the Yi languages (Lolo-Burmese), in Chinese, and elsewhere (cf. Thurgood, 1980, and numerous other sources).]

*Table 140: Register and the fate of PC presyllable *s- and *h-*

PNB	PC	Rade	NR	Haroi	
---	*hatay	tie	hətai	atăi -i	'liver'
---	*sapuh	---	---	apoh	'broom; sweep'
---	*satuk	tŭk	stuʔ 'boil'	atoʔ	'boil; cook'
---	*habɔw	həbău	həbəu	aphĭau	'ashes'
---	*hudip	hədĭp	hədiuʔ	athĭp	'live, alive'
---	*hudaːŋ	hədaŋ	hədaːŋ	athɨaŋ	'shrimp; lobster'
---	*hubɛy	həbɛi	həbəi	aphui (m)	'taro; tuber; yam'
---	*hujaːn	həjan	həjaːn	asɨan	'rain'
---	*sidəm	hədăm	adəm -i	athĭam	'ant'
---	*sijaw	---	---	asɨau	'hammock'
---	ˣ*haduah	duah	duah	athŏh	'look for; search'
---	ˣ*sadər	hədər	sədər	athŭl	'remember'
*hagăr	ˣ*sagər	həgər	səgər	akhŭl	'drum'
---	ˣsiʔjual -v	həʔjul	səʔuəl	həʔjul	'light (not heavy)'
---	*halɔw	hlău	hələu	həlău	'pestle'
---	*halim	hlĭm	həlim	həlĭm	'rainy season'
---	*hurɛy	hrue (m)	hərəi	hərii (m)	'day; sun'
*hare	*haway	həwie	həwai	həwăi	'rattan'
---	*haluh	hluh	həluh	həlŭh	'perforated; pierce'
---	*hulun	hlŭn	həlun	həlŭn	'slave; servant; I'
---	*sarip	---	---	hərip	'sip; slurp; suck in'
*hla	ˣ*sula	hla	səla	həla	'leaf'
---	*sarum	---	srum ?	hərŭm	'sheath-like'
---	*sana	---	səna 'fry'	həna	'roast; parch'
*čačhĕŋ	*saniŋ	hənĭŋ	sənəŋ	hənĭŋ	'think'
---	*samaw	---	səmŭ -f	həmĭau	'prompt; on time'

Haroi contact with Hrê

Certain things are known about Haroi from the linguistic evidence. The subgrouping evidence on page 40 argues that Haroi originated as a Cham dialect, along with Phan Rang and Western Cham. Similarly, the patterns of apparently non-inherited convergences with Rade suggest that Haroi was influenced by some contact with Rade. However, the strongest influence on the structure of modern Haroi was an extended period of intense contact with MK languages, especially with Hrê. In fact, the very name Haroi might be an adaptation of Hrê.

The evidence of Hrê contact is uncontroversial. The description in Schrock, et al. (1966:217) sums up the ethnographic situation nicely [although their description uses a single term to designate both the MK-speaking Hrê and the Chamic-speaking Haroi, both names will be used here]. The authors note that, although the Haroi and the Hrê speak two distinct languages, both linguistic groups are usually classified ethnographically as parts of a single tribe, with the Haroi speaking a Chamic language and being influenced by the Cham and the Rade and the Hrê speaking Hrê, a Northern Bahnaric language.

As an illustration of the linguistic differences, Schrock, et al. (1966:217) provide a brief table of linguistic forms (see Table 141, for an updated, slightly expanded, and slightly modified version of that table).

Table 141: The MK Hrê and the Chamic Haroi

	Eastern	Hrê		Haroi		PR		
PNB	Bahnar	(MK)		(Chamic)	Rade	Cham	PC	
---	sa	sa	l	ɓĭŋ	ɓɤ̆ŋ	ɓăŋ	ˣ*ɓəŋ	'to eat'
---	ec	ec	l	məɲ̆am	mənăm	miɲŭm	*minăm	'to drink'
---	hnan	hnamo	l	saŋ	saŋ	thaŋ	*sa:ŋ	'house'
*qbok	bok	bok	l	kə ɔi	ae	---	---	'grandfather'

What Schrock et al. intended the forms in Table 141 to show is the respective linguistic affiliations of Hrê and Haroi. And, from a modern viewpoint, it is uncontroversial that Hrê is MK, while Haroi is Chamic.

Here, however, it is not the genetic affiliations but the interlanguage contact that is of interest. It is evident from the Schrock et al. description that the Haroi are not only referred to as Bahnar Cham but are also from an ethnographic viewpoint (1966:217), "considered a subgroup of the eastern division of the Bahnar tribe". Certainly, the ethnography documents intense and extended contact, contact which obviously included bilingualism.

Although they incorrectly guessed that the contact language was Bahnar, rather than Hrê, Tegenfeldt and Goschnick (1977:1-2) correctly suggested a causal connection between MK contact and Haroi restructured register. That the language in question was Hrê, not Bahnar, is now clear as are the changes. Hrê has undergone vowel realignments quite parallel to those undergone in Haroi. The evidence can be culled, with some minor readjustments of the reconstructions, from Smith's (1972) reconstruction of Proto-North-Bahnaric (PNB), which includes Hrê.

However, before Haroi can be directly compared with Hrê (as seen in Smith's 1972 reconstructions), certain of Smith's reconstructions require modification. Typologically, there is usually a rather straight correlation between the voice quality differences of register complexes and vowel height movement: tense-register vowels tend to lower, while breathy-register vowels tend to rise; nonetheless, in Smith's reconstructions there is no regular relationship between the voice quality differences and vowel lowering and raising. In Smith's PNB reconstructions, under tense voice, certain reconstructed PNB vowels are sometimes raised and sometimes lowered; similarly, under the breathy voice, certain other PNB vowels are similarly sometimes raised and sometimes lowered.

With minor modifications in the vowel reconstructions, it is possible to reconstruct a system in which, when they changed height, the PNB vowels lowered under tense voice and raised under breathy voice. The solution to this was in the vowels themselves. In many cases, unless one took the effects of voice quality into consideration, the actual vowel reconstruction was somewhat arbitrary: that is, in many cases, it appears that Smith had no principled basis for deciding whether certain vowels should be reconstructed as, for example, mid in PNB and then raised in certain languages or whether they should be reconstructed as high in PNB and then lowered in certain languages. Working with the added constraint that tense voice causes vowels to lower and breathy voice causes vowels to rise, Smith's reconstructions can be adjusted rather easily, making the correspondences between voice quality and vowel movement both internally consistent and typologically expected.

Although more work needs to be done modifying Smith's reconstructions before it can be determined whether such changes are unexceptional or whether they are sometimes conditioned, the minor modifications already made have major additional benefits: it is now obvious that Hrê, the language most intimately in contact with Haroi, has undergone voice quality-related vowel height changes that closely parallel those found in Haroi. As Table 142 shows, at least some of the Hrê high vowels lowered under tense voice, the quality equivalent to the Haroi tense voice under which Haroi high vowels lowered.

And, as Table 143 shows, the Hrê mid and low vowels have raised under breathy voice, the voice quality equivalent to the Haroi breathy voice under which Haroi mid and low vowels raised.

In short, the Haroi and the Hrê changes are not just parallel, but the Haroi changes took place while in intense contact with Hrê.

Table 142: Hrê high vowels lowered under tense voice

PNB	Hrê	
(Smith, modified)		
*tum	tôm	'all'
*bič	bęč	'fat (v)'
*c(h)uy	čôy	'plant rice'
*pih	pêh	'pound rice'
*asih	asêh	'horse'
*rih	rêh	'play (instrument)'
*taqnih	taneh	'earth, soil'
*(q)bul	bo	'lizard; gecko; salamander'
*kačĭyh	kačêh	'sneeze'

It is tempting, by the way, to attribute the vowel raising in at least the PNB *-ày vowels in Table 143 to the final off-glide. However, a comparison of the Hrê reflexes of PNB *-ay under breathy voice with the reflexes of PNB *-ay under modal (that is, clear) voice makes it clear that breathy voice played a role in the vowel raising.

Table 143: Hrê mid and low vowels raised under breathy voice

PNB	Hrê	
(Smith, modified)		
*čèm	čìm	'bird'
*klèč	klǐč	'deaf'
*phèw	phềw	'happy'
*adrày	adrǐ	'pestle'
*hày	hǐ	'day; sun'
*plày	plǐ	'fruit; egg; clf. for round objects'

Note that when PNB *-ay has tense voice, the Hrê reflexes remain *-ay, but when the PNB *-ay was under breathy voice, the high vowel reflex occurs.[1]

---

1. Although these particular patterns appear quite clear, much reworking of Smith (1972) is needed to fully make sense of the interaction of vowel changes and phonation types.

Table 144: PNB *-ay reflexes under tense versus breathy voice

PNB (Smith, modified)	Hrê	
*bray	bray	'thread'
*katayh	katayh	'hip'
*may	may	'sister in-law; elder sister'
*baŋay	maŋay	'people'
*adrày	adrĩ	'pestle'
*hày	hĩ	'day; sun'
*plày	plĩ	'fruit; egg; clf. for round objects'
*qbǎyh	bĩh	'snake'

The conjectures about the earlier sociolinguistic situation are somewhat speculative, but it was likely a combination of some shift accompanied by long-term bilingualism. At the earliest stages, Haroi would still have been a dialect of the then prestigious Cham language, and thus some speakers of Hrê may have shifted to Haroi. Since then, however, Cham has suffered a considerable loss of prestige, and at some point the roles became reversed with the Haroi assimilating to the Hrê.

In any case, two things are well-attested: Ethnographically, the Haroi have been heavily influenced by Bahnar, in particular by the Hrê. Under these influences, Haroi has undergone a set of changes typologically parallel to the changes in Hrê. Specifically, during this period of social and linguistic contact, the Haroi vowel system has been realigned, coming to resemble the Hrê vowel system.

Conclusions

The Haroi case nicely illustrates the respective roles played by external language contact and by internal paths of change: the external contact has provided both the impetus and the directionality for the changes, while the language internal structures have provided constraints on the potential paths for the changes.

As a corollary to the primary role played by contact in this and other Haroi changes, the major Haroi changes have not come about gradually. Rather, the opposite is true: since the major changes in Haroi came about with the onset of intense contact, the major changes are characterized by short periods of rapid, assimilative restructuring, beginning with the onset of intensive contact and followed by periods of relative stasis and more minor changes—continuing until the next significant period of contact. The non-contact induced changes are far more minimal.

Similar restructurings, powered by contact situations and presumably abrupt rather than gradual, are found throughout Southeast Asia (for example, Thurgood 1992a, 1996). In fact, it would be reasonable to conclude that, in the Southeast Asian linguistic area, it is contact that has provided the impetus for most of the major changes with language-internal factors only influencing the paths by which such changes take place.

Finally, the most interesting part of this particular change may be that it seems to have been a change in part shared both by Haroi and Hrê. Given both the timing of the changes and their striking similarities, it looks like the best way to view the changes is as being one that was shared by the Haroi and the Hrê speakers. For monolingual Hrê speakers the changes occurred in their Hrê, but for those Haroi speakers bilingual in Hrê, the changes occurred not only in their Hrê but were also extended to their Haroi. Thus, in this sense, the change was shared between the two languages.

TSAT AND ITS FULLY-DEVELOPED TONAL SYSTEM

Tsat is a Chamic language spoken in the Muslim villages of Yanglan and Huixin near Sanya on Hainan island. Although there was undoubtedly a trading community established earlier, the first major migration to this area was apparently shortly after the fall of the northern capital at Indrapura to the Vietnamese in 982. Subsequent to that, there may also have been other immigrations.

The language itself is Tsat /tsaːnʔ⁴²/ (transcribed from a Keng-Fong Pang tape), a form that corresponds with absolutely complete regularity to the Cham name for themselves /căm/. The initial, the final, the vowel length, the glottalization, and even the tone are precisely what is expected (see Table 104 and the accompanying text for a discussion of the tonal developments). Although the language is Tsat, the people are called Utsat, an ethnonym consisting of the root /tsaːnʔ⁴²/ 'Cham', just discussed, with what is apparently the prefix /u-/ also seen in other ethnonyms in the language, an etymology suggested by Mark Durie (p.c.).

Evolution of the Tsat tones

Over fifty years ago, Paul Benedict (1941) recognized that Tsat is Chamic, but the Tsat tones were only reported more recently (Ouyang and Zheng, 1983; Ni, 1988ab, 1990ab). The comparative work has either accompanied the synchronic work or quickly followed it (cf. Benedict, 1984; Haudricourt, 1984; Zheng 1986; Ni, 1988ab, 1990ab).

The tone system itself is similar in its complexity to the tone systems of its Chinese neighbors and more complex than that of Phan Rang Cham, and the diachronic study of its tonal developments have been a major or minor focus of papers by various authors (Maddieson and Pang 1993; Benedict 1984; Haudricourt 1984; Ouyang and Zheng 1983; Zheng 1986; Ni 1988ab, 1990ab; Thurgood 1992b, 1993).

Tsat is of particular linguistic interest because in it, each stage in the transition from disyllabic and atonal to monosyllabic and fully-tonal is remarkably well-documented. Perhaps it is the clearest such case in the linguistics literature. Part of the clarity comes from the relatively short time-depth; the rest of the clarity is simply our luck in having most of the intermediate stages attested in related languages.

Figure 18: Tsat tonogenesis in monosyllables

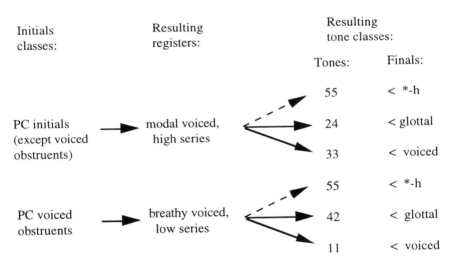

Tones are marked with Chao [Zhao] (1930) tone numbers. The numbers indicate relative pitch height, with 5 being high, 3 in the middle, and 1 low. The first number indicates where the tone begins the second where the tone ends. Thus, for example, 55 is a high, level tone.

Although a little more complicated, like the evolution of Phan Rang Cham tones, the evolution of tones in Tsat is relatively straightforward. The modern Tsat tones are predictable from the voicing differences in the earlier initials and finals. The 55 tone evolves from a final *-h; the relative chronology of this change with respect to the other changes is unclear, something indicated by the dotted line in Figure 18. Otherwise, the earliest stage involved a splitting of the lexicon into two groups — words with high-pitched, probably clear-voiced phonation and words with a low-pitched, breathy-voiced phonation (Figure 18).

Next, both of these groups were split further by the final consonant. All words with a final glottal stop developed a contour tone — a mid-rising 24s (-s indicates a stopped tone) tone from the high-pitched series and a mid-falling 42s tone from the breathy-voiced low-pitched series. All words with a nasal or a vowel final developed a level tone — a mid-level 33 tone from the high-pitched series and a low-level 11 tone from the breathy-voiced low-pitched series. Several other subsets developed in special ways, but these developments are also transparent.

From final *-h & *-s: (> tone 55)

Alone among the Chamic languages, Tsat has developed a unique tone from the reflexes of PC final *-h (< PMP *-q) and final *-s: the 55 high-level tone. Statistically, most such forms derive from final *-h, but a significant number of 55 tones also come from PC final *-s (for examples, see Table 145).

Table 145: Origin of the 55 high-level tone

Malay	PC	Chru	NR	Tsat	
nipis	*lipih	ləpih	lupih	pi^{55}	'thin (material)'
habis	*ʔabih	abih	abih	phi^{55} phi^{55}	'all; finished, done'
tikus	*tikus	təku:h	tukuh	(na^{11}) ku^{55}	'rat'
mamah	*mamah	---	mumãh	ma^{55}	'chew'
---	×*(si)ʔjɔh	səʔiɔh	siʔjoh	ʔiu^{55}	'drip; a drop'
tanah	*tanah	tənah	tanãh	na^{55}	'earth, soil'
deras	*dras	drah	drah	sia^{55}	'fast; short time'
buah	*bɔh	bɔh	boh	pho^{55}	'fruit; egg; clf.'
nanah	*lanah	---	lanãh	lə^{11} na^{55}	'pus'
tujuh	*tujuh	təjuh	tijuh	su^{55}	'seven'
mérah	*mahirah	məriah	mariah	za^{55}	'red'
sĕ-puluh	*pluh	spluh	sa pluh	piu^{55}	'ten'

For PC forms ending in either *-h or *-s (except the *-a:s rhyme), the Tsat reflex is invariably the 55 tone regardless of whether the syllable-initial consonant is a voiced obstruent, a voiceless obstruent, a sonorant, or whatever.

The shared Roglai and Tsat loss of PC *-s in reflexes of PC *-a:s

However, there is one fascinating and instructive exception to the generalization that PC final *-h and *-s led to tone 55 in Tsat: the PC *-a:s rhyme. As is particularly clear from the N. Roglai column in Table 146, the final *-s was simply lost after the four words ending in PC *-a:s.

Table 146: The shared Roglai and Tsat loss of PC *-s in reflexes of PC *-a:s

Malay	PC	Chru	NR	Tsat	
-as	*-a:s	-a:h	-a	-a$^{33/11}$	
atas	*?ata:s	ata:h	ata	ta^{33}	'far; above; long'
kapas	ˣ*kapa:s	kəpa:h	kapa	pa^{33}	'cotton'
---	*kaka:s	kərka:h	kaka	ka^{33}	'fish scales'
beras	*bra:s	bra:h	bra	phia^{11}	'rice (husked)'
-ah	*-ah	-ah	-ah	-a^{55}	
darah	*darah	drah	darah	sia^{55}	'blood'
panah	*panah	pənah	panãh	na^{55}	'shoot (bow); a bow'
pĕcah	ˣ*picah	pəcah	---	tsa^{55}	'broken; break'
bĕlah	*blah	blah	blah	phia^{55}	'chop; split'
basah	*basah	pəsah	pasah	sa^{55}	'wet; damp'

As a consequence in Tsat, these forms have tone 11 or tone 33 reflexes, not the 55 tone expected from words ending in a final *-s. Note first that this is a very restricted, very specific loss: only the *-s is lost and then, as Durie suggested (p.c.), only after long /a:/. In other environments. the *-s was not lost; that is, in other environments, the PC *-s remains /-s/: in Northern Roglai, it remains /-s/ and it shows up in Tsat as the 55 tone. Nor does the otherwise quite parallel PC *-ah loose its final *-h; in Northern Roglai, *-h is retained as such everywhere, and in Tsat the final *-h is reflected everywhere as the 55 tone (see the second set of examples in Table 146).

Given the highly specific environment for this change, the fact that it is shared by Northern Roglai and Tsat is strong evidence for subgrouping the two together. When combined with the fact that Northern Roglai and Tsat also both share the innovation of final preploded nasals, no doubt exists that these two languages should be subgrouped together.

From final stops

All PC final strops (*-p, *-t, *-k, *-c, *-ʔ) have as their Tsat reflex a final glottal stop. The transcriptions of both Ouyang and Zheng and of Ni give the misleading impression that even these final glottal stops have disappeared in some forms, but the instrumental studies in Maddieson and Pang (1993) make it clear the final glottal stops are still present.

These forms ending in final glottal stops have split into two tones, a distinction correlated with the manner of the initial consonant: monosyllables beginning with an originally voiced obstruent have a 42 falling tone; the remaining monosyllables have a contrasting 24 rising tone. The importance of initial voicing in the evolution of the 42 tones was suggested by Benedict (1984); this precise configuration of features as the origin of the 42 tone was pointed out to me by Eric Oey (p.c., 1992).

Table 147: Origin of the 42 falling tone

Malay	PC	Chru	NR	Tsat	
---	ˣtəbiat	təɓiaʔ	tubiaʔ	phiaʔ^{42}	'go out; appear'
hidup	*hudip	hədiuʔ	hadiuʔ	thiuʔ^{42}	'live, alive'
---	ˣ*jɛʔ	jɛʔ	jeʔ 'near'	seʔ^{42}	'near; about to'
duduk	*dɔːk	dɔːʔ	doːʔ	thoʔ^{42}	'sit; live; stay'
---	ˣ*juaʔ	jəwaʔ	juaʔ	suaʔ^{42}	'step on; tread'
---	ˣ*ŋɔʔ	ŋɔʔ	---	ŋoʔ^{42}	'upgrade; east'
buat 'do'	*buat	---	buãʔ	phuaʔ^{42}	'do; work'

The remaining monosyllables ending in a glottal stop but not beginning with an originally voiced obstruent have a rising 24 tone.

Just as with the 42 falling tone, the final glottal stop is also retained with the 24 rising tone. What is not yet obvious from these forms but what will become obvious when voice quality spreading is discussed is that it was the breathiness associated with the voiced obstruents, not the voicing per se, that led to the low tone reflexes ("Transparency and phonation spreading" on page 183).

Table 148 shows several pieces of evidence for the final stops, not the least of which is the extra-Chamic language Malay, which retains a number of the finals as such. In this respect, however, the Malay orthography is somewhat deceptive as the orthographic final <k> actually represents a glottal stop in most cases. Note that Acehnese (not included on the table) sometimes retains the final stops as such.

Table 148: Origin of the 24 rising tone

Malay	PC	Chru	NR	Tsat	
pahit	*phit	phi:?	phi:?	phi?^{24}	'bitter; bile'
---	*satuk	stu?	satu?	tu?^{24}	'boil; cook'
anak	*?ana:k	ana:?	anã:?	na?^{24}	'child'
pahat	*pha:t	pha:?	---	pha:?^{24}	'chisel, plane'
---	ˣ*ɓɛ?	ɓɛ?	ɓe?	ɓe?^{24}	'clf. long, thin objects'
---	ˣ*ɗa?	---	---	?da?^{24}	'crack open'
---	ˣ*hua?	hua?	---	hua?^{24}	'eat rice'
---	ˣ*ɓɔ:?	ɓɔ:?	ɓo:? mata	ɓo?^{24}	'face' cf. 'nose'
---	ˣ*lɛ?	lɛ?	le?	le?^{24}	'fall into'
ĕmpat	*pa:t	pa:?	pa:?	pa?^{24}	'four'
---	ˣ*rək	rə?	rə?	zə?^{24}	'grass; weeds'
---	*ɓuk -1	ɓu:? -1	ɓu:?	ɓu?^{24}	'head hair'
---	ˣ*?akɔ?	akɔ?	ako?	ko?^{24}	'head'
---	ˣ*paɗia?	pəɗia?	paɗia?	ɗia?^{24}	'hot; sunny'
---	*ŋa?	ŋa?	ŋã?	ŋau?^{24}	'make, do'
---	ˣ*cət	cə?	cə?	tsə?^{24}	'mountain range'
minyak	*miña:k	---	mañã:?	ña?^{24}	'oil'
masak	*tasa?	təsa?	tisa?	sa?^{24}	'ripe; cooked'
sakit	*sakit	-səki:?	saki:?	ki?^{24}	'sick, painful'
langit	*laŋit	ləŋi:?	laŋi:?	ŋi?^{24}	'sky'
asap	*?asap	asa?	asa?	sau?^{24}	'smoke (of a fire)'
---	ˣ*klɛ?	klɛ?	tle?	ke?^{24} -m	'steal'
---	*mat	ma?	mã?	ma?^{24}	'take; fetch, get'
ikat	*?ikat	aka?	ika?	ka?^{24}	'to tie'
urat	*?urat	ara?	ura?	za?^{24}	'vein, tendon'
riak	ˣriya:? -1	ria:?	---	za?^{24}	'wave; ripple; surf'
jahat	*jəha:t	jəha:?	---	sa:?^{24}	'bad; wicked'
jahit	*jahit	si:?	chi:?	si?^{24}	'sew'

From final nasals or vowels

Aside from a handful of final nasals discussed on page 160, the developments with forms ending in final nasals or final vowels parallel the developments with final glottal stop: monosyllables beginning with an originally voiced obstruent have a 11 low-level tone; monosyllables without an originally voiced obstruent initial have a contrasting 33 mid-level tone.

Table 149: Origins of the 11 low-level tone

Malay	PC	Chru	NR	Tsat	
abu	*habɔw	həbəu	habəu	phə¹¹	'ashes'
ada	*ʔada	---	---	tha¹¹	'have, exist'
adik	*ʔadɛy	adəi	adəi	thai¹¹	'younger sibling'
babi	*babuy	pəbui	ba bui	phui¹¹	'wild pig'
dada	*dada	təda	dada	tha¹¹	'chest'
dua	*dua	dua	dua	thua¹¹	'two'
hidung	*ʔiduŋ	aduŋ	idŭk	thuŋ¹¹	'nose'
hudang	*hudaːŋ	hədaːŋ	hudaːk	laŋ¹¹ thaːŋ¹¹	'shrimp; lobster'
hujan	*hujaːn	həjaːn	hujaːt	saːn¹¹	'rain'
těbu	*təbɔw -v	tərbəu	tubəu	phə¹¹	'sugarcane'
ubi	*hubɛy	həbəi	habuəi (m)	phai¹¹	'taro; tuber; yam'
ular	*ʔular	ala	ula	(la¹¹) la³³	'snake'
lipan	*limpaːn	ləpaːn	lupaːt	a¹¹ paːn¹¹	'centipede'
kandung	ˣ*kaduŋ	kəduŋ	---	thuŋ¹¹	'pocket; pouch'
ribu	*ribɔw	rəbəu	rubəu	phə¹¹	'thousand'

The remaining 33 mid-level tone is essentially the residual tone class: it involves no voiced obstruent initials, and, thus, no tone lowering; it involves no Tsat final glottal stop, and, thus, no contour tones; and it involves no final *-h or *-s, and, thus, no high-level tone. In short, the 33 mid-level tone is from the vowel final or nasal final forms lacking a voiced obstruent onset.

To summarize the forms discussed thus far, the forms ending in PC *-h or *-s have modern Tsat 55 high-level tone reflexes. The tones of the remaining forms are conditioned by two factors: whether the onset syllable was a voiced obstruent and whether the PC final was originally a stop. The presence of a voiced obstruent onset resulted in a 42 falling tone, if the form ended in a glottal stop, and in the 11 low-level tone, if it did not. The presence of a final glottal stop resulted in a contour tone: if the form had a voiced obstruent onset, the tone was the 42 falling tone; if the onset was not a voiced obstruent, the tone was a 24 rising tone.

Table 150: Origins of the 33 mid-level tone

Malay	PC	Chru	NR	Tsat	
pinang	*pina:ŋ	pəna:ŋ	pinãŋ	na:ŋ³³	'betel; betel-nut'
satu	*sa	sa	sa	sa³³	'one'
tahun	*thun	thun	thut	thun³³	'year'
tali	*talɛy	tələi	taləi	lai³³	'rope; string'
tangan	*taŋa:n	təŋa:n	taŋãn	ŋa:n³³	'hand; arm'
tuha	*tuha	tha	tuha	ha³³ xau³³	'old (people)'
turun	*trun	trun	trut	tsun³³	'descend'
ular	*ʔular	ala	ula	(la¹¹) la³³	'snake'
lapar	*lapa	ləpa	lapa	pa³³	'hungry'
---	ˣ*ʔasɛh	asɛh	aseh	se³³	'horse'
---	ˣ*pər	pər	pə	pan³³	'to fly'
---	*palɛy	pləi ?-v	paləi	piai³³	'village'
---	ˣ*ruay	ruãi -n	ruai	zuai³³	'fly; bug; insect'
ikan	*ʔika:n	aka:n	ika:t	ka:n³³	'fish'
---	ˣ*ka:ŋ	təlka:ŋ	ka:k	ka:ŋ³³	'chin; jaw'
tulang	*tula:ŋ	təla:ŋ	tula:k	la:ŋ³³	'bone'
mata	*mata	məta	mata	tiŋ³³ ta³³	'eye'

Transparency and phonation spreading

As also occurs in Haroi, Western Cham, and Phan Rang Cham, there was spreading of the breathiness generated by a voiced obstruent in the pretonic syllable to the main syllable, thereby resulting in a lowered tone in the main syllable.

And, as in the other languages in this study, the main-syllable-initial sonorants are transparent to spreading. Notice that the tone class of the examples in Table 151 is predictable not from the initial of the PC main syllable but from the initial of the PC presyllable.

Table 151: Spreading through sonorants

Malay	PC	Chru	NR	Tsat	
dahulu	*dihlɔw	ləhəu	dihləu	lau¹¹	'first (go); formerly'
jarum	*jarum	jrum ?	jurup	sun¹¹	'needle'
bunga	*buŋa	bəŋa	buŋã	ŋa¹¹	'flower'
baharu	*bahrɔw	bərhəu	bahrəu	phiə¹¹	'new; just now'
bulan	*bula:n	ea bla:n	ia bila:t	phian¹¹	'moon; month'
jalan	*jala:n	jəla:n	jala:t	la:n¹¹	'road; path'
---	*bara	bra	bara	phia¹¹	'shoulder'

However, Tsat is unique among the languages examined in also allowing spreading through main-syllable-initial voiceless obstruents. In the examples of Table 152, it is the voiced obstruent of the presyllable, not the voiceless obstruent of the main syllable, that correlates with the Tsat 11 low-level and the 42 falling tone. Thus, in these examples, in which the PC presyllable begins with a voiced obstruent and the main syllable begins with a voiceless obstruent, the second register phonation, undoubtedly, breathiness, has spread from the presyllable to the main syllable.

Table 152: Spreading through voiceless stops

Malay	PC	Chru	NR	Tsat	
dĕpa	*dəpa	təpa	tupa	pa^{11}	'armspan'
dikit	*dikit	təki:ʔ	tiki:ʔ	ki$ʔ^{42}$	'few; little'
---	*batɛy	pətəi	pitəi	u^{11} tai^{11}	'banana'
bĕsi	*bəsɛy	pəsəi	pisəi	sai^{11}	'iron'
buta	*buta	---	---	ta^{11}	'blind'
---	^{x}*batɔ	pətɔ	pato	to^{11}	'teach'
batu	*batɔw	pətəu	patəu	tau^{11}	'stone'
batuk	*batuk	pətuʔ	pituʔ	tu$ʔ^{42}$	'cough'

There seem to be, however, a small set of examples, virtually identical to those in Table 152, in which the PC presyllable also begins with a voiced obstruent and the main syllable also begins with the voiceless obstruent *-h-, but where the tone makes it clear that the breathiness did not spread from the presyllable to the main syllable. That is, it initially appears that, in Tsat, breathiness spread through medial voiceless stops but not through voiceless medial /-h-/.

These patterns were reported as a puzzle in Thurgood (1993), a problem heightened by the contrast with Phan Rang Cham, where just the opposite happened: breathiness spread through medial /-h-/, but did not spread through medial voiceless stops (see Table 153). The essence of the puzzle lay in the fact that in Cham the medial voiceless /-h-/ was apparently more transparent to spreading than the medial voiceless stops (as might be expected), but in Tsat precisely the opposite seemed true.

The resolution to the puzzle, however, turns out to be anticlimactic: as the Northern Roglai column in Table 153 indicates, in forms with medial /-h-/ the voicing of the voiced obstruents was lost before the breakup of Northern Roglai and, more to the point, long before the spreading of breathiness would have taken place in Tsat. As a result, by the time spreading occurred, the presyllables in question no longer had voicing or breathiness.

Table 153: The apparent failure to spread through medial -h-

Malay	PC	NR	Tsat	PR Cham	
jahat	*jəhaːt	---	saːʔ²⁴	çhaʔ	'bad; wicked; badly'
jahit	*jahit	chiːʔ	siʔ²⁴	çhiʔ	'sew'
dahi	*ʔadhɛ̌y	thə̌i	thai³³	ṭhɛ̌y	'forehead'
akar	*ʔughaːr	ukha	kha³³	uḳha	'root'

Despite the obvious typological similarities, the Tsat tonal developments and the spreading patterns are idiosyncratic to Tsat, making it evident that the Tsat tonal and spreading developments are quite independent of those in Haroi, Western Cham, and Phan Rang Cham.

Tones and secondary final constriction

This analysis describes what happens to the vast majority of the voiced syllables. However, two cases remain which involve interesting twists: the first involves the tonal development of PMP *-ay syllables acquiring final glottal stops; the second involves final nasals acquiring glottal constriction. The development of the glottalization of final nasals was discussed on page 160ff.; the development of the final glottal stops from PMP *-ay will be discussed below.

*Secondarily-derived falling tones: PMP *-ay > Tsat -aːiʔ*

Tsat has developed an epenthetic final glottal stop and a 42 falling tone on inherited PMP *-ay forms. Although the original sources show considerable variation in the subphonemic pitch of the tone, as Maddieson and Pang (1993) correctly observe Tsat has only one phonemic falling tone, and thus all the examples in Table 154 are marked as 42.

*Table 154: Tsat reflexes of PMP *-ay finals*

PMP	Malay	PC	Tsat	
*ma-atay	mati	*matay	taːiʔ⁴²	'die'
(*qaqay)	kaki	*kakay	kaːiʔ⁴²	'foot'
---	mari	*məray	zaːiʔ⁴²	'come'
---	padi	*paday	thaːiʔ⁴²	'rice (paddy)'
---	---	*haway	vaːiʔ⁴²	'rattan'
*qatay	hati	*hatay	taːiʔ⁴²	'liver'
---	---	*glay	khiaːiʔ⁴²	'forest; jungle'

The falling tone correlates with two features of the modern Tsat reflexes: the presence of a glottal stop and the presence of a modern Tsat long vowel. These same two features can also be seen in the other source of secondarily-derived falling tones, the glottalized final nasals, which discussed on page 160ff.

The history of Tsat contact

The linguistic evidence reveals the outlines of Tsat contact. More revealing than any other finding is that, as is evident from irrefutable linguistic evidence (page 40), Tsat subgroups with Northern Roglai. Along with various minor pieces of evidence, there are two major shared innovations: Tsat and Northern Roglai share the contextually-restricted loss of final *-s just in the rhyme *-a:s but nowhere else and they share the very, very unusual, and typologically highly-marked innovation of preploded final nasals. Either of these would normally be considered significant subgrouping evidence; the combination is irrefutable.

For those without sufficient linguistic sophistication to appreciate the strength of the linguistic evidence, it is possible to be mislead by the name Tsat /tsa:n?⁴²/, which, as is shown in "Tsat and its fully-developed tonal system" on page 214, is the modern Tsat reflex of the name Cham. However, it is only in con-temporary times that the term Cham picks out, for example, just the Phan Rang Cham and the Western Cham. A thousand years ago, all the Chamic speakers along the coast of Vietnam presumably fell under the designation Cham so the name alone tells us nothing other than what we already know—that the Tsat are Chamic.

The connection of the N. Roglai and northern Cham

The modern N. Roglai are, as the apparent etymology of the name Roglai sug-gests, 'forest people' (*ra < *?ura:ŋ 'people' + *glay 'forest'), but it is unlikely that it was a forest-dwelling group that broke off from the Roglai and fled to Hainan. Instead, they must have been living somewhere else with a different life-style and had not yet come to live in the highlands. Further, both Roglai and Tsat share two marked sound changes—the loss of final PC *-s after *a and stop final reflexes from PC final nasals as the result of the decomposition of final nasals forming preploded nasals. It is also unlikely that the speakers of N. Roglai/Tsat were in the south; rather it is far more likely, particularly in light of the existence of the preploded nasals, that these speakers were at the end of the Chamic dialect chain—presumably, all other things considered, the northern end of the chain. Thus, it is reasonably likely that the forerunners of the modern N. Roglai and modern Utsat were then simply the northern Chams living in and around Indrapura before the fall of the northern capital Indrapura in 982, some of them traders and some from other social groups. And, it was only after the fall of the northern capital Indrapura that these northern Chams split up, with the forerunners of the modern Tsat /tsaːnʔ⁴²/ (< PC *cam) fleeing to Hainan, the forerunners of the modern Roglai fleeing to southern Vietnam, and, speculatively, others fleeing to Cambodia.

It is also reasonable to assume that the composition of the emigrant groups was different depending upon the destination. It is likely that a disproportionate number of the traders went to either the trading colony on Hainan or the new capital in the south, that the majority of the members of the ruling class most likely favored southern Vietnam, and that the rest of southern Vietnam and perhaps Cambodia attracted those with other skills and backgrounds. In any event by around 1000, the northern Chams had abandoned the northern provinces.

This scenario, suggested by the linguistic subgrouping and by the subsequent migration patterns, also gives us an approximate date for the Tsat arrival in Hainan—that is, sometime not too long after 982 when Indrapura fell to the Vietnamese and while the Chams were in the process of abandoning their northern provinces. This date would fit nicely with the Tsat traditions (Schafer, 1967:75) which maintain, in one version, that they came to Hainan from the "Western Regions" in Tang times [618-907], and another version that says that they reached Hainan in the Song period [960-1279]. This would account for the prevalence of stories about the times of the kings among the Roglai and for the stories about the Roglai possessing some of the Cham royal treasures.

The traditional dates match quite nicely with the Chinese dynastic records, which Zheng (1986:37, footnote 4), in a footnote in her article on the genetic relationship of Tsat to the Chamic languages, briefly discusses. The translation has been provided by Hilary Chappell; her comments are in square brackets, while Mark Durie has added two notes in curly brackets.

According to the *Records of Qiong Prefecture* (Qiongzhou Fuzhi), their forebears "came in boats with their families as a result of troubled times in the Song dynasty [960-1279 AD] and the Yuan dynasty" [1279-1368 AD]. ['Qiong' is another name for Hainan Island]. According to extracts from both the *History of the Song Dynasty* (Song Shi) and *True Records of the Emperor Xian Zong of the Ming Dynasty* (Ming Xian Zong Shi), it can now be precisely determined that they came in several migrations from Zhancheng {Champa} to Hainan Island. *The History of the Song dynasty,* v. 489, p. 14 080 (revised edition Zhonghua Publishers) records "(During the third year in the period of Yong Xi (986 AD)) Danzhou [modern Danxian, Hainan Island] reported that a person from

Zhancheng named Pu-Luo-E led one hundred of his clan to the county capital [to give their allegiance], having been harassed by the people of Jiaozhi [northern parts of modern Vietnam and the name given to Vietnam by the Northern Song dynasty]".

Unquestionably, these immigrants are Chamic speakers from Champa. Two years later there is another report of immigrants from Champa, but these immigrants appear to have settled in Guangzhou (Canton City) on mainland China.

In the first year of Duan Gong (988 AD), Guangzhou [Canton City] once again reported that "Huxuan, a person belong to one of the Yi tribes [Yi = non-Chinese 'barbarian'] and others assembled 310 people and came to the country capital from Zhancheng [Champa]".

However, this 988 AD record is difficult to interpret. On the one hand, it is clear that Zheng is citing it in the context of discussing the arrival of the Tsat (Chams) in Hainan. On the other hand, it is quite clear that the report is from Guangzhou (Canton City), not Hainan. The most straightforward reading, however, is that this is a report of Chams arriving presumably in the Guangzhou (Canton) area.

It should be pointed out that Yi is being used here as a general term indicating a non-Chinese barbarian, not as a specific term indicating a member of the Yi people, a Loloish subgroup of Lolo-Burmese branch of Tibeto-Burman.

Then, again, not long after the fall of the southern capital Vijaya, in Binh-dinh, in 1471, there is a another report of the immigration of refugees from Champa. The *True Records of the Emperor Xian Zong of the Ming Dynasty* also records (v.284)

(In the 22nd year of Cheng Hua (1486 AD)), the eleventh month, the Imperial Censor to Guangdong, Xu Tong'ai, and others presented a memorial to the throne, reporting: 'The prince of Zhancheng, Gulai, leading the imperial concubines, the prince's descendants and his clans people--over 1000 people--and carrying local produce [probably as a tribute] came to Yazhou [modern day Yaxian] in Guangdong province, wishing to appeal to the throne'.

Unlike the first two immigrations, since it had been roughly 500 years since the Cham had controlled the northern provinces, these immigrants would not have been from the north, but instead must have been from the south—and, thus, were not the first wave of immigrants, the ones that originally split off from the Northern Roglai. And, again, for the traders the trading post at Hainan would be a likely destination.

Citing these records, Zheng (1986:37) concludes that the Utsat have been in Hainan for over 1000 years, a conclusion that accords very nicely with the subgrouping record and with the consequent conclusion that the first wave of Tsat must have immigrated to Hainan from the northern part of the Champa and thus historically rather early. The Chinese records, however, also suggest that there was a second wave of immigrants roughly five hundred years later.

Correlations with the date of the arrival of Islam

Presumably because the modern Utsat are Muslim, several authors have tried to connect the date for the arrival of the Utsat on Hainan to the date for the arrival of Islam in Champa. Benedict (1941:130), for example, suggests that, although the "date of the introduction of Mohammedanism into Annam remains uncertain", since the earliest Islamic inscriptions are dated 1039 and from 1025 to 1035, "the earliest date potential arrival date was somewhere around the middle of the eleventh century".

Similarly, in her dissertation, Pang begins an appendix entitled "Comment on Utsat's Chamic origins" (1992:431-436) with the statement that she will comment on the dating of the Utsat colony in Hainan and on whether or not the Utsat were already Muslims when they arrived in Hainan. However, much of the argumentation for her dating starts with the assumption that the Utsat were already Muslim when they arrived in Hainan, a position that she provides no evidence for, possibly following Benedict (1941:10) or possibly following Maspero (1928:13-14) who states that the widespread conversion of Cham people to Islam only occurred after the fall of Champa in 1470. Apparently in part as a consequence of this assumption about the Utsat being Muslim upon arrival, Pang argues for a date very roughly 625 years ago. Certainly, if we assume that the Tsat were Muslim when they arrived, the temptation might exist to argue for a later arrival.

It is, however, simply unclear when the Utsat became Muslim. On the one hand, in the literature, it has been argued by some scholars that at least a significant part of the merchant class was Muslim at a very early date. On the other hand, it seems clear that at least the majority of the general population that converted to Islam did so much later. In addition, even if the earlier date of 986 is accepted as the arrival date for the Utsat on Hainan, the arrival of Islam might be correlated, not with this early date, but with one of the later exoduses to Hainan, including those after the fall of Champa in 1470. Given the mixed evidence, it is inappropriate to base any conclusions on putative dates for the conversion of the Utsat to Islam.

For example, a careful reading of Aymonier 1891, Ravaisse 1922, Maspero 1928, Schafer 1967, Manguin 1979 (translation 1985), and Chambert-Loir (1994:96), and Reid (1993, 1995) makes clear there is very early evidence of Islam among the trading community and there is every reason to suspect that it was disproportionately the merchant community who went to Hainan. So if the Tsat were partly Muslim when they left for Hainan, this is not surprising, nor would it call for a date as late as "the middle of the eleventh century". And, if the Tsat were not yet Muslim, it is not surprising that they became so on Hainan, as we know that there was already a Muslim trading community on Hainan.

As for the significance of the Kufic inscriptions dated 1025-1035 and 1039, Ravaisse (1922), who reported them himself, drew limited conclusions. In the words of Manguin (1985:1): "The presence of these two steles indicates nothing more than the existence in the eleventh century of a community of Muslim merchants, strangers to the country." However, it need be added, Cham traders were undoubtedly part of the trading community as well, including quite probably some who were Muslim. Then Manguin adds, providing some perspective, "Nothing could be more normal than this settlement, when it is recalled that Muslim merchants had resided in such great number in South China since the eight century. The trading station in Champa was only one of the links in a long chain, which connected the Middle East with Africa and China."

Thus, while it is true that the bulk of the Muslim influence dates from a later time, the Muslim influence in the trading communities dates from considerably earlier. Various contemporary records indicate that Islam existed among the merchants as early as 958, and probably earlier. Schafer (1967:75), for instance, mentions that the Chinese records show that in 958 the ambassador of the Cham monarch Indravarman III presented to the ruler of Chou "rose water, flasks of Greek firs ("fierve fire oil"), and precious stones, was named (according to the Chinese P'u Ho-San (Pyu Ha-san)—plainly Abu Hasan". Three years later, Abu Hasan was again sent to China by Jaya Indravarman I with "a letter on palmyra leaves in an envelope of fragrant wood, and an offering of ivory, camphor, peacocks, and twenty 'Tajik [Arab] vases' for the new Sung emperor."

Other early accounts also confirm the early existence of Islam, although this may have been largely restricted to the merchant classes. As Schafer (1967:75) writes:

> It seems to me that Aymonier was right when, in 1891, he made the rash statement that there were Muslim Chams as early as the ninth or tenth century. ... This hypothesis, otherwise startling and incredible, would explain the statement in the *History of the Five Dynasties* [907-960] *Wu tai shi,* 74, 448od.] that the customs of the Chams are "the same as those of the Arabs" [lit. Tajik].

Thus, if merchants provided a significant portion of the immigration to Hainan, then an Islam influence may have existed early enough to predate the earliest probable migration.

But, if it was not primarily a merchant class that fled to Hainan, the dates for widespread Islamization of Champa are probably too controversial to be useful for dating the migration. On the one hand, Coedès concluded (1968:239): "We have, however, no real proof that Islam had penetrated into Champa before the Chams were driven out of Vijava in 1471." Henri Chambert-Loir (1994:96) provides an even later date for the Islamicization of the Cham court and part of the population—around the end of 17th century. For instance, the Cham king, as Reid (1993:154) writes, citing Manguin, became Muslim only sometime between 1607 and 1676.

On the other hand, not all scholars agree with this position. Some have concluded that Islam had a much earlier foothold in Champa, and not just among the merchant class. Thus, after citing approvingly Aymonier's claim that Islam was established early in Champa, Schafer (1967:75) writes:

> That the influence of Islam was not restricted to the commercial ports where Arab traders congregated is shown by a statement in the History of Sung. After noting that among the animals used by the Chams, aside from the water buffalo and the yellow ox (both familiar to the Chinese), there was the 'mountain ox' (a banting or a kouprey?) which they did not hitch to the plow but killed as a sacrifice to the ghosts. When about to kill it, their 'shamans' invoked it thus: "A-la-ghwa-gyĕp-băt'"', which can be translated (says our source) as "May it soon live in another body!" Despite the pious Buddhist hope for the reincarnation of even a lowly sacrificial victim, claimed as the meaning of this ritual formula, it can hardly be other than butchered Arabic: "Allāh hu akbar!"—"God is great!"

In short, even if the dates for the arrival of Islam were known, it is not clear that these dates would have any direct bearing on the question of when the Tsat arrived in Hainan. However, the linguistic subgrouping evidence unequivocally places the Tsat and the modern Roglai together as part of what could only have been a northern Cham group, which dissolved into various subgroups with the fall of Indrapura in 982. This scenario accords nicely with the arrival of a Chamic group in 986, one or both of which could have been the Tsat. Thus, the linguistic and the historical evidence substantiate Zheng's conclusion (1986:37) that the Tsat arrived in Hainan roughly a thousand years ago.

Tsat contact on Hainan

After the Utsat arrival in Hainan, Tsat was strongly influenced apparently by Hainanese, the Southern Min dialect that functions as the local lingua franca, but nonetheless, due undoubtedly to a strong communal identity and sense of language loyalty due at least partially to their being set apart by their Islamic beliefs (Keng-Fong Pang, p.c.), the Utsat have retained their language. Nonetheless, not only is the lexicon rampant with Chinese loans, but the Tsat language has converged dramatically with the language structures found in the languages of Hainan.

Since arriving on Hainan, Tsat has gone from atonal to fully tonal, a striking example of phonological convergence with the surrounding languages. Insofar as the contemporary situation is representative of prior history, the obvious mechanism for this change is bilingualism, rather than shift. Not only are many of the Utsat either partially or fully bilingual in the fully-tonal Hainanese, but because the modern Tsat form a rather tight Muslim community, it is difficult for outsiders to marry into it. Thus, the language shift that does occur is from Tsat to Hainanese rather than the other way around.

In earlier times, bilingualism and shift may also have contributed to its restructuring. One Tsat tradition maintains that when the men arrived on Hainan they took wives from among the Li, who are speakers of a tonal language. The women would then have shifted to Tsat, while the children of at least the first generation very well might have grown up bilingual in Tsat and Li. A quite distinct version of the tradition, however, has the men and women arriving together. What does seem apparent from the various stories, however, is that there was some early contact with the Li.

Precisely what sort of tone system did the Tsat come into contact with? Although it is reported that the Tsat are bilingual in Hainanese, it is not clear exactly what this means. As some readers are aware, the term Hainanese is often used as a vague cover term for all the Southern Min dialects found on Hainan island. Probably, the dialect in question is the Tan-chou dialect described by Ting (1980), but it really does not make much difference. All the languages of Hainan that Tsat speakers could have come into contact with have well-developed, typologically very similar tonal systems, any one of which would have provided the typological model needed for the restructuring of the Tsat phonological system.

In Table 155, the tone system of Tsat is compared with the tone system of the Tan-chou dialect (Ting 1980), as it is probably the Tan-chou dialect of Hainanese the Tsat are bilingual in, and with two Lí dialects (that is, the Hlai dialects), as the literature suggests early contact between the Tsat and the Lí (Ouyang and Zheng, 1980; cf. also Thurgood 1991 for a look at the reconstructed Hlai tone system).

The typological approximation of these languages to each other and to Tsat is striking. All the languages have three level tones: Tsat has a high-level 55, a mid-level 33, and a low-level 11; the Tan-chou dialect has a high-level 55, a mid-level 22, and a low-level 11; and, both Li dialects have three level tones. All the languages have a rising tone, and all the languages except Tan-chou have a falling tone.

The differences, such as they are, are minor. Although the Tsat contour tones, the rising and the falling tones, end in glottal stops, only the Tōngshí dialect of Li has final stops (indicated by the final -s) in the contour tones; in neither the Tan-chou nor the Yuánmén dialect of Li are contour tones associated with final stops (although even in Tsat the final glottal stops for the rising and falling were not always transcribed).

Table 155: The tones of Tsat, Tan-chou, and two Lí languages

	Austronesian: Chamic (Hainan)	Chinese: Southern dialect (Hainan)	Tai-Kadai: Hlai (Lí) (Hainan)	
	Tsat	Tan-chou	Tōngshí	Yuánmén
high level	55	55	55	55s
falling tone	42s	---	43s	42
mid level	33	22	33	44
rising tone	24s	35	13s	13
low level	11.	11	11	11

Bear in mind, it is not being argued that the Tsat tonal system is borrowed from one of these languages. Rather, the claim is that the patterns of Tsat bilingualism with these languages influenced the internal paths of change within Tsat itself, ultimately leading to the development of a typologically similar system. Thus, an exact match is not likely, and would, in fact, be rather surprising. Looked at in this way, the interaction between the internal influences and the external factors should typically result in a system distinct from the earlier Tsat system as well as different from the system found in the contact language.

Under extended contact with speakers of the tonal languages of Hainan, Tsat speakers have radically restructured their phonological system, innovating a tonal system through the exploitation of internal paths of change that is extremely similar to the tone systems of the other languages of Hainan.

THE INTERNAL PATHS OF CHANGE

The Phan Rang data and the Tsat data show the chain of developments so clearly that it is valuable to point out that this chain, leading to tonogenesis, may be a model for most if not all tonogenesis—as distinguished from tone splitting. Although it is not all that obvious from the literature, in Southeast Asia true tonogenesis always seems to be mediated through prior or at least coexistent phonation distinctions. There are several arguments for this position. Voicing distinctions alone do not seem to be sufficient for tonogenesis. Further, it is not voicing per se that leads to tonogenesis, as vowels are voiced. Finally, it is frequently not all the voiced consonants that develop the low tones, but rather just the voiced obstruents, which are associated time and time again with breathy voice, while the sonorants are ignored, which if anything are more voiced than the voiced obstruents. Again, it is not the voicing per se that is crucial in the development of low tones, but rather some other quality of the voiced obstruents.

The origins of register complexes and tones

Gaps exist in our knowledge and will continue to do so for some time, but we now know the basic stages in the development of Cham register, and its subsequent development in the Western Cham register system, into the incipient tones of Phan Rang Cham, and into the restructured register system of Haroi. We also know the stages in the essentially independent development of the full-blown tone system of Tsat on Hainan island.

Although Western Cham, Phan Rang Cham, and Haroi appear to have developed a common register system before dividing into separate linguistic entities, the subsequent development were largely independent of one another, aside from some obvious later contact between the groups. As the prior discussion (and Table 156) makes clear, the developmental paths often parallel one another, reflecting the type of convergence common to languages which share an identical starting point, which were probably subject to considerable bilingual contact, and which are guided by what are assumed to be universal phonetic tendencies. Further, with very little exception, the internal paths of change are themselves phonetically plausible.

The initial stage in all cases was to develop a breathy-voiced register complex after the voiced obstruents, with Western Cham, Phan Rang Cham, and Haroi probably evolving the same system before breaking up into dialects and with Tsat doing the same thing but quite independently of the developments elsewhere. Once breathy voice has developed after one set of initials, by default the voice quality after the other consonants constitutes a contrasting register, and, thus, we have register contrasts. Even from this point, although the developments in individual languages may differ in detail, the changes remain similar typologically.

The Western Cham developments involved the fewest adjustments to the already existing register system. The one peculiarly Western Cham modification was the extension of second register to a subset of the sonorant initial forms, an extension not yet fully explicable.

Phan Rang Cham, of course, initially developed along identical lines with Western Cham, with the differences coming after Phan Rang and Western Cham split. The major difference between the two was that in Phan Rang Cham the pitch differences came to the foreground with a corresponding backgrounding of the phonation distinctions. The second register developed into the low tones and the first register the high tones, with both tones being split again into those forms ending in glottal stop.and those not.

The initial developments of the Haroi register also involve modifications of the earlier shared register system. However, unlike Western Cham or Phan Rang Cham, the non-breathy high vowels were further modified apparently by a unique phonation associated with the voiceless stops and affricates, presumably a tense phonation that has left its own special class of vowel reflexes in modern Haroi. Elsewhere, except for some rather odd vowel assimilation, the vowels were essentially unaffected.

This Haroi register system was probably at this point only marginally distinguishable from the system in Western Cham. Aside from differences in details and the possibility it might have had more striking contrasts in vowel quality than Western Cham, the two systems were very much alike typologically. And, most importantly, in both register systems, the vowel quality differences were still fully predictable from the accompanying phonation distinctions. The dramatic Haroi restructuring came with the loss of the phonation differences: when the voice quality differences disappeared, some of the accompanying vowel quality differences were left behind, adding new phonemically distinct vowels to the vowel inventory and making Haroi into a restructured register system.

Although Tsat is closely-related to Northern Roglai and the Tsat changes occurred quite independently of the changes in the other three languages after the Tsat reached Hainan, the Tsat changes also tend to parallel the changes in the other three languages. Tsat initially developed a two-way register contrast distinguishing a breathy register and, by default, a modal (clear) register. Thus, the initial stage was the development of a register system.

Then, in the case of Tsat, the phonation distinctions were backgrounded and the pitch distinctions were foregrounded, leading to the development of tones. In a development unique to Tsat, a special tone class evolved from words ending in PC *-s and *-h. Among the remaining forms, the former breathy register developed into the 11 low tone in forms without a final glottal stop and into the 42 falling tone in those forms with a final glottal stop; similarly, the modal register developed into the mid-level 33 tone in words without a final glottal stop and into the 24 rising tone in those words with a final glottal stop. Thus, aside from some oddities involving glottalized final nasals as well as some epenthetic final stops, the Tsat developments, despite the historical separation from Phan Rang Cham, followed largely parallel lines of change.

Table 156: The paths of development in monosyllables

	Western Cham	Haroi	Phan Rang Cham	Tsat
	register	restructured register	incipiently tonal	fully tonal
voiceless obstruents	first register (default)	vowel reflexes < first register (initial layer)	high tones (default)	33; 24s tones (default)
glottalized obstruents	first register (default)	(default; unaffected)	high tones (default)	33; 24s tones (default)
sonorants	second register also occurs after some sonorants (second layer)	(default; unaffected)	high tones (default)	33; 24s tones (default)
voiced obstruents	second register (initial layer)	vowel reflexes < second register	low tones	11, 42s tones

Despite all the developmental similarities, the resultant modern phonological systems are radically distinct typologically. These striking differences in outcomes have their origins in modest adjustments made to the configurations of features that comprise the register complexes. As Eugénie Henderson noted some thirty years ago, the breathy-voiced second register is composed of a complex cluster of features: a characteristically lax or breathy voice quality, accompanied by relatively lower pitch, but relatively higher vowel quality, while the contrasting first register typically has tense, or modal phonation, accompanied by a relatively higher pitch but relatively lower vowel quality. For reasons related to external contact, not to internal pressures, Western Cham has essentially maintained a modified version of the earlier register system, while the pitch component has risen to prominence in Phan Rang Cham and Tsat, and the vowel quality differences have been focused on in Haroi.

Spreading patterns

The reflexes of main syllables are often not the reflection of the initial of the main syllable but instead are the result of phonation spreading from the presyllable to the main syllable. In this sort of spreading, there are two interacting patterns: one is for certain classes of main-syllable initials to be more transparent than others to the spread of phonation, and the other is for the breathy-voiced second register to be the most likely to spread (Table 157).

Table 157: The paths of breathy voice spreading in disyllables

	through sonorants	through *s, *h	through voiceless stops
Western Cham	yes	yes	no
Phan Rang Cham	yes	yes	no
Haroi	yes	not clear	no
Tsat	yes	yes (*s)	yes

Table 157 summarizes the spreading of the breathy-voiced second register from the presyllable to the main syllable. Note that in all four languages breathy voice has spread through the sonorants, resulting in the main syllable having second register, not first register, reflexes. Notice that medial *s and *h are almost as permeable, with Western Cham and Phan Rang Cham showing clear evidence of spreading, with the Haroi data unclear, and with Tsat showing evidence of spreading through *s. However, spreading of the breathy voice through a medial voiceless stop is limited to Tsat.

The Chamic data tells us little about the spreading of tense voice, primarily because in every language except Haroi the vowel reflexes found after the voiceless obstruents and the vowel reflexes after the sonorants are identical—that is, the same voice quality is found after both the voiceless obstruents and the sonorants. Thus, the Chamic data on the spreading of tense voice is restricted to one instance in Haroi, where tense voice (but only from voiceless stops and affricates but not from *s and *h) spreads through medial sonorants lowering high vowels to mid vowels.

9

PC Morphology:
Some Notes

Even a brief sketch of Chamic morphology lies beyond the scope of this work, let alone any sort of thorough survey. However, it is possible to discuss certain morphological structures found in Chamic, particularly those structures that are reconstructable to PC, with a special emphasis both on the MK influence on Chamic morphology and on the importance of the Acehnese data to the reconstruction of PC morphology.

The existence of a MK element in Chamic has been recognized almost from the beginning of the study of Cham. Crawfurd (1822) recognized the AN core of Chamic early, terming it the "Malay of Champa", but subsequent scholars not only recognized the MK element in Chamic but also were often mislead by it, sometimes going as far as to misclassify it as a MK language. For Étienne Aymonier (1889:5-6), who recognized both its MK and AN elements, Chamic was some kind of intermediary link between Khmer and Malay. Schmidt (1906) also recognized the existence of both a MK element and an AN element when he described the Chamic languages as "Austroasiatische Mischsprache". Thomas Sebeok (1942) was led even further astray by the MK, misclassifying the Chamic as Austroasiatic. None of the investigators seemed to have trouble recognizing a MK element in Chamic. It was only its interpretation that was controversial.

Even the existence of a MK element in Acehnese seems to have been recognized early and with little enduring debate about its existence. Niemann (1891), Cowan (1933, 1948, 1974, 1981, 1982, 1983, 1988, n.d.), Shorto (1975), and Durie (1990a) all have not only recognized the existence of a MK element in Acehnese but also the last three have further recognized that, for the most part, it is essentially the same MK element found in the mainland MK languages. The controversy that exists again revolves around determining the origins of this MK element.

The debates about the genetic affiliations of Chamic have long since been laid to rest, but for those interested in a summary of the positions various scholars have held, see Lafont (1987b; 1994b). However, all modern scholars recognize the AN character of Chamic, with the questions revolving not around the classification of Chamic but around how these AN languages acquired the MK and the typologically MK-like forms and systems which they now have.

Both Cowan and Shorto rejected the possibility that the MK features have been borrowed from MK—the position argued for in this work—and instead argue that in one sense or another the similarities are vestiges of a much, much deeper genetic relationship between MK and AN. In both cases, the crux of their argument is essentially "belief-based"; that is, both scholars are convinced that certain elements are almost in principle unborrowable! In particular, neither the vowel length nor the shared grammatical morphemes are viewed as borrowable.

The assertion that certain elements are *in principle* unborrowable has certainly been rejected by the preponderance of modern scholarship, leaving as the real question to be answered whether the borrowing hypothesis is plausible in this particular case—with the borrowing hypothesis the only position supported by much of the evidence in this work.[1]

Especially interesting is the extent of morphological borrowing. Shorto (1975:82) notes one of the influences of MK when he suggests that the loss of suffixes is an areal feature shared with the neighboring MK languages, a position confirmed by an examination of these languages.

A NOTE ON PC MORPHOLOGY

Much of the borrowing of MK material into AN post-dates the breakup of PC. Though especially notable in the highlands Chamic languages, where the contact with MK has been more intense and for a longer duration, post-PC borrowing is found throughout the mainland Chamic languages. However, a small but significant amount of MK morphology seems to be reconstructable to PC. Both Cowan (1948:432-431) and Shorto (1975:81) recognize verbal and nominal morphology of considerable antiquity found in both Acehnese and the mainland Chamic languages, specifically a causative verbal prefix *pə-, a reflexive/reciprocal verbal prefix *tə-, a verbal prefix *mə-, and a nominalizing instrumental infix *-ən-

---

1. The possibility of a much, much earlier genetic relationship between Austronesian and Austroasiatic, or possibly with just the Mon-Khmer component of Austroasiatic, notwithstanding.

found in both Acehnese and the mainland languages (the reconstructions are those of this work). While the causative verbal prefix *pə- is native apparently to both MK and PAn, the nominalizing infix *-ən- is definitely of MK origin.

In addition to these, there is a negative imperative *bɛʔ, of obvious MK origin, and a nominalizing infix *-əm-, just as obviously of AN origin, as well as a number of nonaffixial grammatical morphemes including pronouns, prepositions, and other connectives, which are sometimes from MK and sometimes from AN.

The borrowing did not all go one way, of course. Bahnar, a MK language, shows the heavy borrowing of AN lexical material as does Katu (Diffloth, p.c.) and various other MK languages of the region.

VERBS AND VERBAL MORPHOLOGY

The two inherited AN prefixes discussed here, the *tə- and the *mə-, are not as semantically transparent. Both are best retained in Acehnese, whose speakers not only left the mainland quite some time ago—thus leaving much of the MK influence behind—and have since been in contact with speakers of other Malayic languages—thus helping preserve these prefixes, which Adelaar reconstructs for proto-Malayic.

A glance at the lexicon makes it clear that not only were verbs borrowed from MK but also so was some of the verbal morphology. The instrumental infix *-ən- is not just MK but may have been at least quasi-productive, if one can judge from the modern languages. Similarly, the negative imperative *bɛʔ is unquestionably from MK. In both cases, the meaning of the borrowed grammatical element is relatively transparent.

The 'inadvertent' prefix

The 'inadvertent' prefix, to use Durie's term, is reconstructed for PC as *tə-, with the possibility that future research might allow the eventual addition of a final -r to the prefix. Aymonier and Cabaton (1906:xxiii-xxiv) describe it as having a range of meanings for Cham including causativity, reciprocity, and stativity. This prefix is reconstructed not just back to the proto-Malayo-Chamic stage but to PAn. Adelaar (1992) reconstructs it as *tAr- for proto-Malayic but with the meaning 'inadvertent' including potentiality, non-controlledness, and excessivity (Adelaar, p.c.). Blust (p.c.) reconstructs it to PMP as *taʀ 'inadvertent; marker of involuntary action' and for PAn as *tar- 'inadvertent'. The match with Adelaar's PMalayic and Blust's PMP and PAn looks perfect, both in terms of form and function.

*Table 158: The PC *tə- 'inadvertent'*

PMalayic	*tAr-	'inadvertent'
PC	*tə-	'inadvertent'
Acehnese	tɯ-	'inadvertent'
Jarai	tə-	'reflexive'
Bahnar	tə-	'passive; reciprocal; causative'
Pacoh	tar-	'reciprocal'
	t-	'resultant state'
	ta-	'involuntary'

However, what look to be variants of *tə- seem to occur not just in the Chamic languages of Vietnam but also in neighboring MK languages. Within the Bahnaric branch of MK, for instance, Bahnar has a form Banker (1964) glosses as 'passive; reciprocal; causative'. Although Banker chosen to treat it as several homophonous prefixes rather than as a single unit, it looks to be the same element historically. The *tə- also seems to be found in Chrau (Thomas 1971:152-153) as *ta-* 'causative, resultative'. And, within the Katuic branch, Pacoh (Watson 1966) lists three prefixes which look as if they might be historically conditioned variants of a single prefix: *tar-* 'reciprocal', *t-* 'resultant state', and *ta-* 'involuntary'.

The apparent relatedness of the MK to the PC forms is of considerable interest. The PC prefix reconstructs to PAn *tar- 'inadvertent' and PMP *taʀ 'inadvertent; marker of involuntary action' (Blust, p.c.). Thus, the form reconstructs back not just to proto-Malayic but to PAn; certainly the Acehnese and, if connected, the Jarai form are also inherited from PAn. How then does one account for the MK forms, that is, the Bahnar (MK: Bahnaric), Chrau (MK: Bahnaric), and Pacoh (MK: Katuic)? The phonetics and the semantics are similar. If not simply lookalikes, which seems doubtful, are these forms the result of borrowing from Chamic? If the forms are borrowed, the borrowings must have been into both Bahnaric and Katuic, two distinct subgroups of MK. If the forms are borrowed, the borrowing would not be too surprising as the evidence of intense contact between Chamic and MK. Of particular interest are the Pacoh forms as they indicate intense contact between ancient Chams and the Katuic. Notice that even this more northerly contact falls within the boundaries of Champa influence, at least before the Vietnamese began pushing southward. Other evidence of a Chamic contact with Katuic include apparently Katuic borrowings into Chamic, particularly into Acehnese, and an apparent Austronesian morphological strata in Katu (Reid 1994), which one would presume were due to Chamic influences.

The obvious way to account for the Katuic strata found in Chamic is to assume that Chamic influence extended up along the coast into Katuic territory. Certainly, an examination of the appendix of forms makes it abundantly clear that there are a considerable number of MK forms, attested in the more northerly Katuic but not in the more southerly Bahnaric. Further, many of these are attested in Acehnese. Thus, the most likely scenario is to assume that the Acehnese are the descendants of the most northerly group of Chamic speakers---the first group forced to leave the mainland. This scenario is consistent with other evidence, specifically, with the fact that Acehnese patterns neither with the remaining mainland coastal Chamic languages nor the remaining highlands Chamic languages. Why not? Because the division of the original dialect chain into coastal and highlands languages only became strongly marked after the Vietnamese push to the south had split up the chain—a division that occurred after the Acehnese had left the mainland.

The other way to account for the Austronesian morphological strata in Katu is to invoke Austric, that is, to conclude that this strata is inherited from a proto-Austric consisting of Austroasiatic and Austronesian (cf. Reid 1994). However, early contact between Chamic and Katuic speakers needs to be recognized anyway to account for the presence of Katuic borrowings in Chamic and Chamic borrowings in various Katuic languages (see Appendix II) so the opportunity for the borrowing to take place has already been established. Further, the parallels between the Cham prefix described by Aymonier and Cabaton (1906:xxiii-xxiv) as expressing causativity, reciprocity, and stativity and the Pacoh prefixal variants described by Watson as expressing 'reciprocal' (tar-), 'resultant state' (t-), and 'involuntary' (ta-) are too close to be accounted for by mutual inheritance from proto-Austric. The notion of mutual inheritance would require that, on the one hand, the Katuic Pacoh inherited the prefix from proto-Austric by way of proto-Austroasiatic with its phonetics and semantics largely unaltered, while on the other hand the PC language Cham inherited the prefix also from proto-Austric but by way of Austronesian, again with the phonetics and semantics largely unaltered. Given that the time depth for PAn exceeds 6,000 years this is implausible.

The *mə- marker

The *mə- marker (< proto-Malayo-Chamic *məŋ-) is a fully productive part of the morphology of the Malayic branch of Malayo-Chamic (cf. its central place in the verbal morphology of modern Malay).

Aymonier and Cabaton (1906:364) describe the prefix mə- in Cham as a causative prefix, indicating a state, possession, reciprocity, or mutuality, further noting that it also occurs in Bahnar as mə-. They specifically equate it with

Malay *mĕ-/mĕng.* An examination of the *mə-* section of their dictionary makes it clear that the prefix is essentially the same prefix as in Malay and that its use, although much diminished in modern Cham, was once far more productive.

Table 159: The PC *mə- 'verb prefix'

Malay	PC	Acehnese	Jarai	Bahnar
mĕng-	*mə-	mɯ-	mə-	---

It clearly reconstructs to PC, as it exists in Acehnese, Jarai, and Written Cham. However, its occurrence in the modern mainland Chamic languages is now far more limited than it once was in PC.

The 'causative' prefix

The PC 'causative' prefix *pə- is found throughout the Chamic languages except for Tsat, where it got lost as part of the loss of almost all initial syllables. The prefix is not just widespread in Chamic languages including Acehnese on northern Sumatra but appears to either be productive or to have been productive in those languages for which we have sufficient evidence and it occurs just as freely with AN as MK roots, except again for Tsat where sound change has led to the dropping of initial syllables. In addition to its appearance as part of the morphology, it also occurs widely in fossilized form as the initial syllable of a number of lexical items in the appendixes.

Table 160: The PC *pə- 'causative'

Malay	PC	Acehnese	Jarai	Bahnar
---	*pə-	pɯ-	pə-	pə-

As early as 1906, Aymonier and Cabaton (1906:xxiii) described the causative *pə- as borrowed from Khmer, a not unreasonable assumption as it occurs not just in MK languages contiguous to the Chamic languages but also in quite distant branches of MK. It certainly occurs in the MK languages of Vietnam. For instance, it occurs as *pə-* in Bahnar, not just with the same form but also the same meaning (Banker 1964:105-106). It also must occur fossilized in Chrau (Thomas 1971:153), cf. the pair *jêng* 'become' and *panhjêng* 'create'. Farther afield, it occurs in Rischel's (1995) Mlabri of northern Indochina, as the only instance of an entirely transparent prefix in Mlabri. Rischel describes this prefix as a causative with two variants *pa-* and *ba-*, with the former occurring before stem-initial voiced consonants, and the latter before voiceless consonants (Rischel 1995:90).

However, the *pa- causative prefix also reconstructs to PAn. It certainly occurs in the Formosan languages, that is, the Austronesian languages of Taiwan; for instance, Ross (1995) includes both the PAn reconstruction *pa- and various instances of pa- occurring as a causative marker in Paiwan (cf. also Wolff 1995:566). Blust, in his dictionary (1990, 1991, 1992, 1993, 1994, 1995) reconstructs it for PAn. He notes the causative *pa- in his reanalysis of Dempwolff's *patay and *matay, which he reanalyses as *pa-aCay 'kill' (with causative *pa-) and *ma-aCay 'dead' (with stative *ma-). It also occurs in the Philippines and in some languages of Borneo. It also seems to occur fossilized in some of the Oceanic languages (reported in Blust's dictionary).

Thus, the causative *pa- is found in both MK and PAn. If its presence in MK had any effect on its presence in Chamic, it is probably nothing more than to reinforce its use, making it less resistant to loss.

The negative imperative

The negative imperative is without doubt borrowed from MK. Although it is found throughout the Chamic languages (Acehnese, Rade, Jarai, N. Roglai, Chru, Jarai, PR Cham), it does not occur elsewhere in Austronesian.

*Table 161: The PC *bɛ?- 'reflexive, reciprocal, inadvertent'*

Malay	PC	Acehnese	Jarai	Bahnar
---	ˣ*bɛ?	bɛ?	be?	be?

Within MK, Smith (1972) reconstructs it for PNB as *beq, noting its appearance in Bahnar and Hrê, among other MK languages.

N. Roglai contains not only the reflex of the older PC ˣ*bɛ? but also a second, far more recent, borrowed negative imperative represented by the form ɗəŋ [di], an obvious borrowing of Vietnamese dùng.

The bipartite negatives

Lee (1996) contains an excellent discussion of Chamic negatives, using N. Roglai as his point of departure, but covering all of Chamic nicely. Lee reconstructs three negation markers: the PC pair ˣ*ɓuh...ˣ*?ɔh 'not, no; negative' and PC *ka, *?aka 'not yet'. The ˣ*ɓuh... and *ka, *?aka 'not yet' typically occur preverbally, often in conjunction with the post-verbal ˣ*?ɔh 'not, no, negative'. Both the simple negation 'not, no' and the 'not yet' usually occur in conjunction with the final *?ɔh, but not always. The bipartite constructions containing these negation markers are limited to the mainland languages, although Acehnese also has a bipartite construction for 'not yet' goh....lom.

The Chamic negatives are difficult to date with any precision. In addition to the apparent absence of cognate negatives in Acehnese, there are other problems for reconstruction. Not only is the very existence of a preglottalized initial a problem (it suggests the form might be a MK borrowing), but the initial and final of ˣ*ɓuh both show irregularities. The origin of the structure is unclear. Cf. Lee 1996 for further discussion.

NOUNS AND NOMINAL MORPHOLOGY

The pieces of the nominal morphology discussed here are the *-əm- nominalizing infix inherited from AN (*-um- 'Actor Focus', cf. Wolff 1973, Dahl 1976, Starosta, Pawley, and Reid, 1982, Ross 1995) and the instrumental infix borrowed from MK. The evidence for the *-əm- nominalizing infix is thus far limited to Acehnese and in fossilized forms in Written Cham; its occurrence in Acehnese is mainly important as it provides evidence that it was once productive in PC. The instrumental *-ən- borrowed from MK is interesting because the presence of a borrowed infix—an apparently productive infix—indicates something about the intensity of the contact.

In addition to these affixes, there were various prepositions, pronouns, and other grammatical words that were borrowed both from MK into AN and from AN into MK.

The -əm- nominalizing infix

The PC *-əm- nominalizing infix is reconstructed for PC on the basis of Written Cham and Acehnese. For Cham, Aymonier and Cabaton (1906:xxiv) do not really define it but instead simply list -mə- (-am-) as an infix and give a set of Written Cham examples: k-am-əraŋ 'deficit' < karaŋ 'less', p-am-əyau 'comparison' < payău 'equal', and b-am-ən-əŋ 'food, provisions' < bəŋ 'to eat' (the morpheme divisions have been added). The last infixed word b-am-ən-əŋ is particularly interesting both because it has a double infix, that is, both the -um- and -ən-instrumental infix and because it suggests that the shape of the -um- nominalizing infix is -am-, not -mə- as suggested by Aymonier and Cabaton.

For Acehnese, Durie (1985:32) discusses it at some length, noting that there is both a prefixal variant and an infix. Cowan (n.d.7) clearly recognized the root as being of AN origin and identified it with marking what Dahl (1976) termed actor focus. Durie gives the forms c-ɯn-arʌŋ 'cleverness'< carʌŋ 'clever' as an example of its use.

Table 162: The PC *-əm- nominalizing infix

Malay	PC	Acehnese	Wr. Cham	Bahnar
-um-	*-əm-	-ɯm-	-mə-	---

Although only occurring in fossilized forms in Malay, the infix is widely attested in AN. Of the fossilized forms of this infix that do occur in Malay, my favorite is *kancil* 'the little one, the pelanduk' < apparently an infixed version of *kěcil* 'little'. Blust (1988:14) offers a similar pair: *gilang* 'luster, glow' and *g-em-ilang* 'very bright, splendid'; the same pair is listed in Coope (1986) as *gilang* 'shining' when in isolation and as *gilang-g-em-ilang* 'radiant, resplendent' in reduplication, with the meanings and forms in Coope making it evident that in Malay the semantics of the infix have been pretty well lost.

The instrumental infix

The instrumental infix PC *-ən- is borrowed from MK. This was recognized long ago by Aymonier and Cabaton 1906:xxiv), who note that the Written Cham infix -n- comes from Khmer [I would say from MK] and serves to form agentive or instrumental nouns e.g., *d-an-ak* 'a pile' < *dak* 'to pile on', *p-an-ṳəč* 'speech' < *pṳəč* 'to speak', and *b-an-ək* 'a dam' < *bək* 'to dam' (the morpheme divisions have been added).

It is found throughout Chamic as Table 162 indicates and as a glance through the glossary of reconstructed forms attests to. Within Jarai, Medcalf (1989:42) discusses the instrumental nominalization which "occurs when the infix *-oN-* is inserted between the initial consonant and the initial vowel of a verb. Thus, *kih*, 'to sweep' becomes *k-ön-ih*, 'broom'." However, while Medcalf equates this with the widespread *-in-* infix in Austronesian, only the form supports the equation; the function seems quite distinct to me, particularly in light of a morpheme with identical shape and function in the neighboring MK languages.

The MK etymology of the form is widely attested. As Aymonier and Cabaton pointed out, a similar infix with a similar range of functions occurs in Khmer. It also occurs in Bahnar, a Bahnar language which has long been in contact with Chamic languages; Banker (1964:100) writes that the instrumental infix -ən- "functions as a nominalizer, converting verbs to nouns." Banker describes the infix as sometimes having the meaning of the result of a verbal action, e.g., *bât* 'to make a dam' becomes *b-ən-ât* 'a dam' and at other times having an instrumental meaning e.g., *păr* 'to fly' becomes *p-ən-âr* 'wing'.

Table 163: The PC *-ən- instrumental infix

PC	Aceh.	Jarai	Chru	PR Cham	Bahnar	
*-ən-	-ɯn-; nɯ-	-ən-	-ən-	-an-	-ən-	'instrumental infix'
*phaːt	phɯət	phǎʔ	phaːʔ	phaʔ	---	'to chisel, plane'
*p-ən-haːt	---	---	pahnaːʔ	---	---	'chisel; plane'
*thow	thɛə; tu-	thəu	thəu	thɔ̆w	---	'know; able'
---	---	---	---	thunɔ̆w	---	'magical knowledge'
ˣ*bət	---	biʔ	bəʔ	---	bât	'to dam; fence'
ˣ*b-ən-ət	---	bəniʔ	bənɯːʔ -f	pinɨʔ	bənât	'a dam; a fence'
ˣ*pɔh	pɔh	---	pɔh	pɔ̆h	--	'strike, pound'
ˣ*p-ən-ɔh	---	---	pənɔh	---	---	'drumsticks'
ˣ*duc	---	duɨʔ	---	ʈŭyʔ	---	'to sting'
ˣ*d-ən-uc	---	---	dənuiʔ	ʈanŭyʔ	---	'stinger'

Although a disproportionate number of forms with this instrumental infix seem to be MK in origin, the infix also shows up in roots inherited from PMP. Thus, in Table 163, the first two roots cited are apparent PMP roots, cf. Malay *pahat* and *tahu*, respectively. According to Blust (p.c.), the PMP root *paqet 'chisel' reconstructs to PMP based on a cognate distribution that includes the Philippines and western Indonesia/Chamic. The infix must have been relatively productive, based on the large number of varied roots in mainland Chamic languages containing it and on the fact that it is still what Durie terms productive in Acehnese.

Prepositions

A number of prepositions can be reconstructed for PC. Table 164 shows three groups of prepositions. The first four show evidence of MK origin: The first has been borrowed in various forms after the breakup of PC, with the variation in initials and finals obvious from the handful of forms given. The second reconstructs to PC as ˣ*jɛʔ. On the one hand, it is reconstructed for PNB as *ajeq 'near' and, on the other, it does not appear to have any AN etymology. The third evolved from a verb meaning 'to follow', which may have a Vietnamese origin, cf. Vietnamese *theo*. The fourth reconstructs to PC but also occurs in Bahnar, making it impossible to evaluate even tentatively without more data.

The next two prepositions (ˣ*məŋ and *hayɔw) both reconstruct to PC, but thus far neither has an obvious AN or MK counterpart, although the vowel in ˣ*məŋ certainly suggests a MK etymology.

Table 164: The Chamic prepositions

PC	Acehnese	Jarai	Bahnar	
---	bak 'at; on'	pə- 'at; to'; ɓəi 'at, on'	bât 'place'	
ˣ*jɛʔ	---	jɛʔ	---	'near'
*tuy	---	tui 'to follow'	---	'to follow; according to'
*gah	---	gah	gah 'side'	'side'
ˣ*məŋ	---	məŋ 'from'	---	'from'
*hayɔw	---	---	---	'like (prep.)'
*dĭ	di	tə-	tə- 'to, in, at'	'to, at'
*dəŋan	ŋʌn	---	---	'with'
*dalam	dalam; lam	dlăm (Lee)	lăm	'in; inside'
*kə-	kɯ-	kə- 'indirect object'; kə- 'in relation to'	kə- occurs both as a prefix and as a preposition	'to; indirect object'

The last four prepositions are not only reconstructed for PC, but they obviously have AN etymologies. All four are found in closely-related Malay, as *di*, *dĕngan*, *dalam*, and *kĕ-*, respectively, and the first two are found in the earliest Cham inscriptions (Marrison 1975:54). What makes this set particularly interesting is that three of the four have also been borrowed into Bahnar, with the forms for 'in; inside' widely enough attested in Bahnaric languages for *lăm to be reconstructed for PNB by Smith!

Pronouns

Among the personal pronouns readily reconstructable for PC, some are inherited from PMP, while others are clearly either secondarily developed or borrowed from MK. The first person singular pronoun PC *kəu 'I' is inherited from PMP, the first person polite form PC *hulun from 'slave' is innovated, but certainly the innovation exists outside of PC; one suspects, however, that while the form *hulun dates back to PC, only the meaning 'slave' existed at the time depth, with the first person meaning a later innovation not just in Chamic but throughout the area. The other polite first person form *dahla? looks to be secondary; it does not seem to be attested outside of Chamic, nor apparently is it widely attested within Chamic. The etymology of one of the second person forms *hã is not firmly established; it is not clear if it reconstructs to a pre-Chamic level or not. The other form in the table, however, ˣih is definitely a post-PC borrowing from MK into Chamic. The third person *ñu is an AN root.

Table 165: The PC singular pronouns

PC	Aceh.	Rade	Jarai	Chru	Haroi	W. Cham	PR Cham	
*kəu	kɛə; ku-	kău	kəu kəmi	kəu;	kău	kau	kŏw	' I (familiar)'
*hulun	ulon	hlŭn	hlun	həlun	həlŭn	hlŭn-; hulĭn	halŭn	'I (polite); slave'
*dahla?	---	---	---	dəlha?	---	-hlă?	ṭahĭa?	'I (polite)'
*hã	---	---	hă (N)	hã	hăi -v	hɨ	hɨ	'you; thou'
ˣih	---	ih	ih	---	---	---	---	'you; thou'
*ñu	---	ñu	ñu -ñəə	ñũ -ñu	ñau	ñu -v	ñu	'he, she; they' in 'we'

Most of the plural pronouns are inherited from AN. The development of the reflexive from a form meaning 'body' is found here and is common throughout Southeast Asia, with the parallel in Tibetan *rang* coming immediately to mind. The plural form meaning 'group; other', which shows up in various plural pronouns, is particularly striking as it is borrowed from MK and, not surprisingly, does not apparently appear elsewhere in PMP. Thus, among the pronouns, the *gəp 'other; group' is borrowed from MK at the PC level.

Table 166: The PC plural pronouns

PC	Aceh.	Rade	Jarai	Haroi	W. Cham	PR Cham	
*kaməi -v	kamɔə; muə-	həmɛi	-găməi (incl.)	kəmei- -v?	---	kami -v	'we (ex.)'
*ta	ta-	---	-ta (excl.)	ata	---	ita	'we (incl.)'
*drəi	drɔə	drɛi in 'we (inclusive)'	-drəi; in 'we (inclusive)'	trəi	ṭray -iv	-ṭrĕy	'we (incl.); reflexive'
ˣɓiŋ	---	---	ɓiŋ	ɓĭŋ	---	---	in 'we'
ˣ*gəp	gɔp; gɯ-; ga- -v	gă?	gă?	---	ḳau?	ḳŏw' (-ḳăn)	'other; group'

Other pronouns of interest are the late post-PC pronominal pieces bor-rowed into various Chamic subgroups from MK sources. Note that ˣɓiŋ and ˣih are found among the Highlands Chamic languages, the languages with the most intense contact with MK.

Other forms

In addition to the demonstratives which can be found in the glossary, there are various other grammatical forms, most of which have AN etymologies.

ya < *yaŋ 'relative clause marker': Marrison (1975:53) notes the exist-ence of this relative clause marker in the older Cham documents.

-kan: Aymonier and Cabaton (1906:xxiv) say about this suffix, widely attested in Malay, "It may have existed in the older language as an analog to the Malay suffixes -an,- i,- -kan. It scarcely exists now except as the suffix -kan (-kanə̄, -kanəy) which, with məljəŋ gave the expression məljəŋ-kan (məljəŋ-kanə̄), comparable to the Malay mĕmulia-kan 'revere, honor'" [The Malay has been respelled here]. Thus, it is likely that the -kan once existed but has long since been lost along with all the other suffixes.

sa-, siy: The older form is clearly PC *si-. Both Aymonier and Cabaton (1906:xxiv) and Marrison (1975:57) note the existence of this honorific-marking prefix. Marrison describes it "as a familiar element in titles, or as the first element in siapa ['who']", while Aymonier and Cabaton simply list it as a prefix and then illustrate it with the following examples: ai 'brother', sa-ai 'elder brother'; nai 'young woman'; sa-nai 'woman'. Cf. also Acehnese si 'title for people's names'. It is also found in Malay.

dom 'all': This quantifier, found in Khmer, is borrowed from MK (Mar-rison 1975:56).

PC ˣˣsɔh 'only; empty, free, leisure': This quantifier is found in a full range of Chamic languages, including Acehnese, but it has an obvious MK source in PNB *sasoh 'only' and in PKatuic *[s/c]ənhɑh 'empty'. It is, thus, reasonable to assume that it is a MK borrowing.

The last three connectives are found in Aymonier and Cabaton's dictio-nary, and all also occur in Malay.

maka:	Aymonier and Cabaton (1906:386) gloss this connective as "well, then, because, and, thus, when".
pun:	Aymonier and Cabaton (1906:288)gloss this connective as "then, if; really; also".
ampun:	Aymonier and Cabaton (1906:1) gloss this word, used in for-mal contexts, as "forgiveness, forgive, ask forgiveness"

Evaluating these forms is problematic. There was obviously a court Malay that existed in numerous courts in the Malay world, a Malay that occurs in the writings of these courts. As a consequence, these specific forms occur in the stories recorded in both the Malay of Pattani and the Malay of Malaka. Since the forms do not occur elsewhere in Chamic, it is not possible to draw conclusions about the antiquity of the forms.

Were this an attempt to provide a full grammatical sketch of PC, numerous other grammatical elements would need to be treated. Additional grammatical forms are found in the glossary, but a large amount of morphological reconstruction remains to be done. The point of this chapter, however, was to provide a preliminary sketch that gave at least a little of evidence of MK influence on Chamic.

10

Contact, Multilingualism, and Change

Although in many ways tentative, unquestionably exploratory in nature, and, of necessity, frequently tedious, this study has nonetheless provided a detailed preliminary examination of the interaction between contact, multilingualism, and change within the history of the Chamic languages. When placed within a broader historical setting, the Chamic linguistic record reveals much not just about the linguistic history of Champa but also about non-linguistic history.

Much of the history of the region is reflected in the patterns of geographical distribution and the deducible patterns of language contact. The early arriving pre-Chamic peoples most likely landed south of Danang and thus probably encountered Bahnarics. Given the major restructuring of the arriving Austronesian language that took place, these pre-Chamic people must have become socially dominant, with this dominance leading many most probably Bahnaric-speaking people to shift to Cham, but bringing with them many MK characteristics. The Vietnamese "push to the south" around 1000 split the northern Cham into a group that moved southward becoming the Roglai and a group that fled to Hainan, becoming the Utsat. Upon reaching Hainan, the Utsat came into close contact with Hainanese and, perhaps, one or more Hlai (Li) languages, leading to the complete restructuring of Tsat.

Probably sometime around the fall of Indrapura in the north, although it may have been as much as several centuries earlier or later, the Chamic speakers who were to become the Acehnese left the mainland on a journey that would ultimately end in northern Sumatra.

The next major restructuring again correlates with a major historical event—the Vietnamese conquest of the south, roughly 500 years ago. With the final conquest of the south by the Vietnamese, the Cham were not only pushed inward from the coast but lost much of their close contact with each other. One major group was pushed into the Central Highlands, becoming the Rade and the Jarai in the process. Somewhat later, the Haroi followed, splitting off from the Coastal Cham and coming under the influence not just of the Rade and Jarai, but more importantly, entering into a close relationship with the MK-speaking Hrê. Under this influence, Haroi was extensively restructured. The Coastal Cham in the south came under increasingly strong Vietnamese influence, particularly in more recent times with the spread of education and so on. The language of these Cham, the Phan Rang Cham, has restructured in the direction of Vietnamese.

NON-LINGUISTIC HISTORY

Much of the interaction between the linguistic developments and non-linguistic history is scattered throughout this work and the outlines of the interaction between linguistic and non-linguistic history are sketched in Chapter 2. However, in addition to the insights the data gives us with regard to earlier contact situations, the linguistic record also clarifies our understanding of two important historical events, one talked about at length in the prior literature and the other scarcely mentioned, that is, the relative positions of the Acehnese of northern Sumatra and the Tsat of Hainan with respect to the rest of the Chamic languages.

With respect to both languages, the careful, detailed establishing and interpretation of correspondence patterns makes the relationships to the rest of the Chamic languages clear. In the case of the relationship between Chamic and Acehnese, long a source of speculation in the literature, the examination of the correspondence patterns between Acehnese and the rest of the Chamic languages provide, at least to a historical linguist, unambiguous and convincing evidence that Acehnese was originally simply another Chamic language, which some time after the breakup of PC, left for northern Sumatra. The evidence for this position is found throughout this work and is summarized in "Acehnese, a Chamic language" on page 47.

In fact, it is also fairly likely that, until they departed for Sumatra, the Acehnese were the more northerly end of the Chamic dialect chain, occupying coastal territory in the regions now occupied by Katuic speaking people. The existence of a clearly Katuic element in Chamic and, significantly, in Acehnese requires this to be so. Being at that point the most northerly group of Chamic speakers, the Acehnese were probably the first to leave as the Vietnamese moved south. In effect, the Acehnese left before any significant breakup of the Chamic dialect continuum into coastal and highlands languages occurred, as the linguistic evidence makes clear.

This departure of the Acehnese left the ancestors of the Northern Roglai and the Utsat as the most northerly group of Chamic speakers and as such these new northern Chamic speakers came under increasingly pressure from the north. The discussion in"The history of Tsat contact" on page 224 makes it clear that, after the fall of the northern capital, some of what were now the new northern Cham fled to Hainan, where their language developed into the modern Tsat, while other northern Cham fled to the south, eventually becoming speakers of Northern Roglai in the southern Vietnamese highlands. The subgrouping evidence unequivocally establishes the connection between Northern Roglai and Tsat from the present locations of the speakers; it has to be inferred that the Northern Roglai and the Tsat must have been in the north when the split occurred, which, in turn, necessitates a date of roughly 1000 AD, a date very much in accord with the Chinese records noting the arrival of groups fleeing from Champa. The rough date may itself be of as much interest to linguists as to historians as it basically marks the point at which Tsat began its transition from a typical post-PC Chamic language to the fully-tonal, monosyllabic language it is today. This date is, of course, of additional interest as the Acehnese must have left the mainland by that date.

CHAMIC AND THE NATURE OF LANGUAGE CHANGE

Despite being rather distinctive and quite varied, the examples discussed in this work nonetheless agree on the respective roles played by external language contact and by internal paths of change: the external contact has provided the impetus and determined the directionality and rate of the changes, while the language internal structures have been largely restricted to providing constraints on the potential paths for the changes.

Certainly, the major changes in these languages have not come about gradually. Rather, the exact opposite is true: the major changes are characterized by short periods of rapid, assimilative restructuring beginning with the onset of intensive contact and are followed by periods of relative stasis characterized only by more minor changes—continuing until the next significant period of contact. The non-contact-induced changes are minimal.

Although the non-linguistic historical findings are significant, the greatest value of the Chamic data may lie in the insights into the nature of historical change that Chamic gives us. At the most general level, the Chamic languages provide insights into the nature of linguistic change itself. In effect, the Chamic data challenges certain assumptions, some implicit and some explicit, about the nature of historical change—not that these assumptions have not been challenged before and not that they will not be made and then challenged again. Specifically, the following assumptions about the nature of linguistic change are called into question: the belief that internal factors are more important than external factors in implementing change, and the belief that rates of change are typically gradual except under catastrophic circumstances.

The influence of internal and external factors

Several linguists have recently commented on the preference given to internal over external explanations of language change. As Grace remarked while talking about subgrouping and the nature of language change (1985:6), "our professional paradigm seems to assume that most linguistic change is caused by conditions internal to the language itself." More recently Thomason and Kaufman in their *Language Contact, Creolization, and Genetic Linguistics* (1988:57-64; 139ff) discussed what they saw as inappropriate prejudice in favor of internal explanations, resulting in what they saw as a tendency to accept contact explanations only in lieu of internal explanations, and then, only if the contact explanations can be completely and fully documented. In fact, in many instances in the literature the suggestion of external causes is rejected outright *simply* because a plausible internal path of development is present.

The preference for internal explanations of change is intimately tied to a related belief that *normally* language change comes about from some sort of disequilibrium in the language undergoing the changes. Since this sort of systemic disequilibrium is assumed to be the typical cause of change within languages, once a plausible internal path of change is found, it is unfortunate but not surprising that this internal development is often automatically taken as the cause of change. Under special circumstances, of course, such as those that lead to the development of pidgins and creoles, it is acknowledged that external pressures can be more influential than internal pressures, but such cases are seen as atypical of normal historical changes. As a corollary, one piece of evidence that supports the atypical nature of such changes is that they cannot be given a plausible internal accounting. Of course, this characterization is in part a straw man, but in part it does characterize many of the implicit if not explicit assumptions about the nature of historical change.

The Chamic changes, which fall well within the range of so-called normal historical change, show an unambiguous relationship between internal and external causation. Despite the existence of not only internally-plausible but often attested paths of internal development for the changes in question, it is the outside, external models provided by bilingual contact—not internal systemic disequilibrium—that has set the changes in motion and determined their directionality. The internal factors do not play a causative role. Rather, the major role played by the internal structures of the languages is the limitations these structures place on the potentially-exploitable paths of change.

Despite the existence of phonetically-plausible paths of change in virtually every case and despite the fact that the preponderance of the evidence is circumstantial, the case for the dominance of the role of external influences in the Chamic changes is compelling. Even a cursory correlation of the Chamic changes with changes in contact patterns makes it obvious that bilingualism with speakers of non-Chamic languages set the Chamic internal changes in motion and gave them their internal direction: in each and every case involving a major restructuring of the phonology of a Chamic language, the timing and direction of the change can be correlated perfectly with a new pattern of bilingual contact. And, in fact, in some cases, such as the development of register complexes, tonality, and restructured register the direction of the change induced by the contact not only matches the language patterns of the contact language but is largely otherwise unattested in the 900 or so other Austronesian languages. The failure to recognize the centrality of external patterns of bilingualism in these changes requires ascribing a considerable role to coincidence to account for countless repeated correlations.

The data leads to the conclusion that for the Chamic changes it is contact, not the existence of a language-internal disequilibrium, that both sets the changes in motion and determines the direction of change. The corollary, of course, is that the major role of language internal patterns is to impose constraints on the possible paths of change in the literature on historical change, these constraints appear to have frequently been mistaken for causes. Certainly, this is particularly obvious with respect to the development of tone, register, and restructured register. The development of phonation distinctions after certain initials left a system with the potential to develop in any one of the these directions—the actual choice was determined by contact.

This conclusion is strikingly reminiscent of the conclusions drawn by Weinreich, Labov, and Herzog's (1968) "Empirical foundations for a theory of language change" in which the authors correlate language change with language variation and ascribe change not to gradual, incremental changes in one register in the dialect of one group of speakers but instead to the spreading of a varying feature. Of course, this is not to say that the variants that spread might not be in and of themselves rather minor with only the accumulation of such variants resulting in dramatic change, but however minuscule the variant, the change itself is abrupt—the change from one variant to another. Looked at in another way, the cause always seems to be adjustment to a new model of language, whether it is a variant within the same language or a model outside the language.

The fact that the significant changes within the Chamic languages correlate with new patterns of contact accounts for the abrupt, non-gradual nature of the changes. For instance, even today the phonologies of Roglai, Jarai, and Chru among the Highlands Chamic languages look very much like the system reconstructed for PC despite the passage of well over a thousand years. In contrast, Tsat and Haroi have undergone intense bilingual contact and have been totally restructured. The pattern that suggests itself is a fairly short period of restructuring followed by a period of relative stasis until new patterns of linguistic contact come into existence (cf. similar conclusions in Grace (1985)).

None of this is to argue that external explanations are automatically to be preferred to internal explanations. That would be nothing more than replacing one prejudice with another. Rather, the suggestion is more balanced. First, the clarity of the Chamic data forces recognition that the role played by multilingualism in areas such as Southeast Asia is far, far more central to language change than previously thought, that the interplay between internal and external factors is just that—an interplay, and that the types of relatively sudden, abrupt changes often found throughout Southeast Asia are more than likely the result of external factors manipulating internal factors—not the result of marked disequilibriums internal to the language itself.

As Thomason and Kaufman have argued external explanations are to be preferred when the balance of the evidence, or else mere simplicity, favors them. As a corollary, such external explanations almost inevitably have language internal correlates.

As an addendum, it must also be recognized that, as Grace (1985) has written, there is another external factor: in times of significant cultural change, there is a tendency for languages to undergo more rapid change than in times of relative stability. Some of this may simply reflect the mixing of various dialects and so on, but some of it may reflect adaptation to a new range of uses that a language is being required to perform—in some cases the change may correlate with the transition from exclusively phatic and social uses to a system in which information transfer plays a much more central role. These considerations, however, lie outside of the scope of this work.

'Inheritance' accounts of the MK substratum

The evidence assembled in this work makes it obvious that the MK substratum in Chamic is due to contact, but there are several older, alternate accounts which attempted to invoke common genetic inheritance as a major determinant of the similarities. These attempts to account for the massive similarities between MK and Chamic run into two related, insurmountable obstacles. Reconstructed PC looks remarkably like proto-Malayic, not like a remnant of Austronesian that remained behind on the mainland, while the rest of Austronesian went out into the Pacific. In fact, the comparative evidence makes it clear that PC and proto-Malayic were either sister languages or something very close to that. Thus, PC is a close-knit, rather shallow subgroup with a time depth of roughly two thousand years. However, the last time the Austronesian languages were on the mainland was at least 6,000 years ago, as the archaeological and linguistic evidence both make clear. Further, it is quite clear that the features shared between Chamic and the MK languages of Vietnam are strikingly similar, almost identical—far, far too close to identical in most cases to reflect common retention from a common relationship some five or six thousand years earlier. At that time depth, even if there were an ancient genetic relationship between Austronesian and Astronautic, it would be too far in the past to account for the striking similarities between PC and MK.

Thus, the 'inheritance' accounts of both Cowan and Shorto are interesting to examine, not for their merits as possible accounts of similarities, but instead to examine why both Cowan and Shorto found it necessary to invoke such accounts in the first place. In both cases, their preference for an inheritance rather than a contact account of the similarities rests on beliefs that certain things are not borrowable in principle and thus must be inherited. Cowan (n.d.:2) simply states that, given that the vowel length agreement is shared by Acehnese and mainland Chamic languages on the one hand and by the neighboring MK languages on the other, and given that the length distinction cannot have been borrowed ready-made from MK into Chamic, the only other possible explanation must be that the agreements point to a common genetic origin of vowel length in MK and PC where vowel length was a distinctive feature. If these principles were to be accepted, it would follow that the length distinction must be the result of a common genetic MK/AN origin, with the vowel length feature having been lost everywhere else in PAn, "except for sporadic remnants reminiscent of it in certain languages" (Cowan 1983:179). In support of his position, Cowan (n.d.:3) argues that Chamic represents a dialect of PAn "which not only remained on the continent but also stayed in the immediate vicinity of the Austro-Asiatic mother tongue", a contention that is demonstrably false.

For similar reasons, Shorto (1975:90) also concludes that the vowel length distinction found in Acehnese and mainland Chamic did not result from borrowing: "...the creation of so fundamental a distinction as that of vowel length by borrowing seems intrinsically unlikely. On the other hand, contact with MK languages, in many of which (as in PMK) a vowel-length distinction operates, would favour the *retention* of an original distinction conceivably lost elsewhere." Like Cowan, Shorto also argues that PAn had an original vowel length distinction which was retained in Chamic but lost elsewhere. However, not only is there no apparent evidence elsewhere for a PAn or PMP vowel length distinction but the Chamic data can be accounted for without positing any length distinctions above the PC level ("PC vowel length" on page 138ff.).

Cowan (n.d.:9) draws a parallel conclusion about the shared morphological elements, declaring that "the agreement which exists between the affixal systems of the Austronesian languages and those of the Mon-Khmer languages is a rather close one" and concludes that the similarities cannot be explained by loans due to contact since grammatical morphemes, unlike vocabulary, are not easily borrowed.

What is interesting about both Cowan's and Shorto's positions is not the ultimate conclusions about the existence of a genetic relationship between MK and AN (a position that ultimately may turn out to be right but which is certainly not relevant to this data) but the fact that their conclusions came out of two false beliefs, one that vowel length could not have developed as the consequence of language contact and a similar belief about the unlikelihood that grammatical morphemes could have been borrowed.

ACCOMMODATION TO A LINGUISTIC AREA

The other value of the Chamic languages is as an example unparalleled in its clarity of the effects of areal influences on language change. As Eric Oey noted earlier, the study of the Chamic languages provide an example *par excellence* of the effects of the three distinct waves of contact—with the Bahnaric and Mnong languages, then Vietnamese and the languages of Hainan.

Intimately interwoven with the various waves of contact are multiple examples of the development of Southeast Asian areal features otherwise largely unattested in Austronesian: the development of rich registral systems, the development of restructured register, the development of full sets of tonal contrasts, the internal development of glottalized obstruents, the drive toward monosyllabicity, and so on. Chamic provides example after example of internal "drifts" given directionality through external contact. (Cf. "Chamic convergence with Southeast Asia" on page 4ff. and "The general tendencies: A broad overview" on page 5ff., for a general discussion, with details and examples found throughout).

Particularly notable among the changes is the complete documentation of the development of register, restructured register, and tonal systems, from a completely atonal, disyllabic origin to monosyllabic, fully-tonal modern language (in the case of Tsat), cf. Chapter 8, in particular. Unless the Chamic developments are somehow inexplicably viewed as an aberration, they provide an intriguing model for the much more inextricably interwoven layers of historical development that characterize the histories of many of the languages that have been intermingling on the mainland for a much longer period of time.

In fact, because so much is known about the insular Austronesian languages and because it is so evident what the pre-Chamic Austronesian languages looked like, the changes found in the Chamic languages of the mainland provide us with invaluable insights into linguistic contact and adaptation to a new linguistic area.

This outline of the history Chamic is a first approximation presented in the hope that it will prove insightful and useful to others interested in these and similar questions.

Appendix I: Language Names
(and transliteration tables)

This appendix contains a list of Chamic language names, information about which names correspond to which, and transliteration tables.

The transliteration tables are just that — transliteration tables. Except by chance, they are not complete phonological sketches of the languages involved. Thus, for example, various diphthongs are not listed separately as their transliteration follows naturally from the transliteration of the individual components.

The transcription systems have been largely standardized. The standardization was necessary for at least three reasons: First, many of these languages have been transcribed in a modified version of the Vietnamese alphabet Quocngu, making the notation readily accessible to those familiar with Vietnamese or with other languages of Vietnam but somewhat opaque to others. Second, in numerous instances, data from the same language has been transcribed sometimes even by the same linguist on different occasions for different purposes. Third, not just intra-language but also cross-language comparability was desired, both for readers and for myself. Sometimes the same symbols are used for different languages with different values, a practice that makes sense on a language-by-language basis but makes cross-linguistic comparison difficult.

Many of the linguists working on Chamic languages are affiliated with the Summer Institute of Linguistics (SIL), an organization motivated in part by its interest in translating the Bible into as many languages as possible. In the early stages of the process this involves a linguistic analysis followed by the development of an orthography. The language data being used in this work comes from all different stages in this process. As a consequence, the earliest work on the language is often in a rather phonetically-transparent transcription system, while later work is sometimes appears in an orthography that differs in certain ways from the earlier phonemic transcription. Even the system of phonemic transcription may be changed somewhat over time. In almost all cases, however, the differences in transcription systems have been purely notational and the systems were standardized by simply substituting one symbol for another.

The varied orthographies used in the transcription of the different Chamic languages have been transliterated with the intention of making the notation maximally transparent to the linguistically sophisticated reader. First, where the same sounds have been transcribed with one symbol in one language and another in another, a single transliteration was chosen in order to make the symbols as comparable as possible across languages. Second, in some cases, where a sound has been transcribed more or less uniformly in the sources, but where the actual phonetic value of the symbol is not obvious to readers not familiar with Vietnamese orthographic conventions, an alternate transliteration was chosen which makes the phonetics more obvious to the non-specialist.

None of these adjustments should be misinterpreted as criticisms of the orthographies originally employed in the works cited. The contrary is true: given the intended purpose and primary audience, these orthographies are admirably well-crafted. However, these orthographies were designed not to provide a maximally transparent transcription system for linguists, but, much more importantly, to provide a maximally readable orthographic system for speakers of the languages in question. And, where the potential users are literate in another language, it is likely in the majority of cases to be in Vietnamese. Thus, in many cases, these orthographic systems often follow the orthographic conventions of Vietnamese. For instance, as in Vietnamese, in Roglai /k/ is represented mainly by < c >, with < k > occurring only before < i >, < e >, and < h >, a system somewhat reminiscent of the distribution of < c > and < k > in English. Similarly, as in Vietnamese, the Roglai < p >, < t >, < ch >, and < c/k > represent unaspirated voiceless stops, while < ph >, < th >, < chh >, and < kh > represent voiceless aspirated stops.

ACEHNESE

Bireuen, a dialect in the North Aceh region

Consonants:

Durie (1985):					Transliteration:				
p	t	c	k-/-k/'		p	t	c	k-/-ʔ /ʔ	
ph	th	ch	kh		ph	th	ch	kh	
b	d	ɟ	g		b	d	j	g	
bh	dh	ɟh	gh		bh	dh	jh	gh	
	s	sy		h		s	ʃ		h
w	1	y			w	1	y		
	r					r			
m	n	ny	ng		m	n	ñ	ŋ	
mb	nd	nj	ngg		'm	'n	'ñ	'ŋg	

Notes:

The last row represents Durie's funny nasals, rather than clusters consisting of nasals followed by homorganic voiced stops.

Vowels:

Durie (1985):			Transliteration:		
i	eu	u	i	ɯ	u
ê, é	ë, ö	ô	e	ə, ʌ	o
e, è	a	o	ɛ	a	ɔ

Nasalization and diphthongs:

Nasalization is marked by ' preceding the vowel, except after nasal consonants, where it is fully predictable.

The shwa at the end of various diphthongs is written in the orthography as -e, but transcribed here as /ə/.

BIH

The Bih may have been originally a Rade group but have diverged due to long contact with the Mnong, although it remains mutually intelligible with Rade. Maitre (1912:400) reported that the Pih (undoubtedly the Bih) spoke a corrupt Rade dialect.

CHRU

Chru, Churu, Chrau Hma, Cadoe Loang, Seyu, Cru, Kru, Rai

Consonants:

Jràng et al. (1977:viii-x):				Transliteration:			
p	t	ch	k	p	t	c	k
ph	th		kh	ph	th		kh
b	d	j	g	b	d	j	g
	jh				jh		
	s		h		s		h
'b	d		-	ɓ	ɗ		ʔ
w	l	y		w	l	y	
	r				r		
m	n	nh	ng	m	n	ñ	ŋ
	n-h				n-h		

Notes:

Intervocalically, the glottal stop is marked in the original as < - >, but finally as part of the marking of length, pitch, and nasalization (see "Length, pitch, and nasalization" below). The peculiar symbol < n-h > represents an aspirated nasal.

Vowels:

Jràng et al. (1977:viii-x):			Transliteration:		
i	ɯ	u	i	ɨ	u
ê	ơ	ô	e	ə	o
e	a	o	ɛ	a	ɔ

Length, pitch, and nasalization:

In the orthography used by Jràng et al. (1977:viii-x) for Chru, a complex system of diacritics has been used to mark three separate features: (a) vowel length co-occurring with the "lowering of voice" (Jràng et al. (1977:viii-x), that is, most likely, the lowering of pitch, although it may actually be some sort of voice quality or phonation change (b) nasalization of the vowel and (c) the presence of a final glottal stop.

In the Jràng et al. system, individual diacritics have different values word-internally than they have word-finally. In addition, these diacritics may mark not a single feature, but a complex of features. Thus, for example, word-internally the diacritic on the vowel < a > in < ả > marks two features: vowel length plus voice lowering and nasalization; word-finally, it marks three features: vowel length plus voice lowering, nasalization, and a final glottal stop.

Despite a reluctance to normalize an orthography, the diacritics in this transcription system have been rewritten to make the phonetics more transparent to those not familiar with Chru orthographic conventions: (a) length plus voice lowering is always marked by a colon, i.e. < a: >, (b) nasalization is always marked by a tilde over the vowel, i.e. < ã > and (c) glottal stops are always marked by a glottal stop, i.e. < ʔ >.

Jràng et al.		Transliteration	
< ã >	ã	a tilde indicating nasalization	
< -à- >	-a:-	medial: a colon indicating voice lowering and length	
< -à >	-a:ʔ	final: a colon indicating both length, and, apparently, lowered pitch, and a final glottal stop	

< -ȧ- >	-ã:-	medial: a tilde for nasalization and a colon indicating voice lowering and length
< -ȧ ·	-ã:ʔ	final: a colon indicating both length, and, apparently, lowered pitch, a tilde indicating nasalization, and a final glottal stop
< -ă >	-aʔ	final: a final glottal stop

HAROI

Haroi, Hrway, Hroi, Hroy, Bahnar Cham

Consonants:

Mundhenk and Goschnick (dictionary):				Other: Mundhenk, Goschnick Lee, Burnham:				Transliteration:			
p	t	ch	k	p	t	c/č	k	p	t	c	k
ph	th		kh	ph	th		kh	ph	th		kh
	s		h		s		h		s		h
b	ɗ		-/q	b;ʔb	d;ʔd		ʔ	ɓ	ɗ		ʔ
	1/r				1/r				1/r		
m	n	nh	ng	m	n	ñ	ng;ŋ	m	n	ñ	ŋ
w		y		w		y		w		y	
w		j-		ʔw-		ʔy-		ʔw-		ʔj-	
-uq		-iq		-ʔw		-ʔy		-uʔ		-iʔ	
-uh				-wh				-uh			

Vowels:

iu̵	u	i		ɨ		u		i	ɨ	u	
ie	uo	ι				ʊ		ι		ʊ	
ê	o̵	ô		ê; e	ə	ô; o		e	ə	o	
e	a	o		e; ε	a	o; ɔ		ε	a	ɔ	

As Mundhenk and Goschnick (1977) note, all the diphthongs begin with one of five onsets: i, ɨ, u, o, or e.

In their dictionary, Mundhenk and Goschnick apparently indicate short and long /ɪ/ by < ie > and < iê >, respectively. However, the marking of length involved in their use of their orthographic representation of /ʊ/ is not as clear. In this work, on the basis of indications found in various articles, the < uô > (with an additional breve over the already marked <o>, < ŭo >, and < uo > are treated as short /ŏ/, and < uô > is treated as long /ʊ/.

Length and nasalization:

In addition, Haroi has both length and nasalization distinctions. Nasalization is marked with a tilde, i.e., < ã >. In the dictionary, long vowels are unmarked, while the short vowels are marked as short, i.e. < ă >. In the other Mundhenk-Goschnick source and in Lee, it is the long vowels that are marked; long vowels are indicated by a grave accent, i.e. < à >, while the short vowels are unmarked. In Burnham, both long and short vowels are marked: the long vowels are indicated by a macron, i.e. < ā >, while the short vowels are indicated by a breve, i.e. < ă >, with the unmarked vowels presumably indicating vowels occurring in contexts where no vowel length contrasts occur (ignoring, of course, the possibilities of errors and forms where the length is unknown).

In this work, Haroi length is unmarked, shortness is indicated by a breve, and nasalization is indicated by a tilde.

JARAI

Two sources have been used for Jarai: Pham Xuân Tin's *Lexique Polygotte* (1955), which is the source of the forms in Lee (1966), who uses a modification of Pham Xuân Tin's orthography and Pierre Lafont's (PL) *Lexique Jarai* (1968), the dialect of Plei Ku. However, it is clear that the two descriptions are of different dialects.

Consonants:

Pham Xuân Tin (1955):

p	t	č	k
ph	th		kh
b	d	j	g
ɓ	ɗ	dj	
m	n	ñ	ng
w	l, r	y	
	s		h

Transliteration:

p	t	c	k
ph	th		kh
b	d	j	g
ɓ	ɗ	ʔj	ʔ
m	n	ñ	ŋ
ʔm	ʔn	ʔñ	ʔŋ
w	l, r	y	
	ʔl, s		h

Lafont (1968):

p	t	ch	k	
ph	th		kh	
b	d	j	g	
ƀ	đ	dj		-
m	n	ñ	ng	
m̶	n̶	n̶h	ŋg	
w	l, r	y		
	ł, s			h

Lee (1966):

p	t	c	k	
ph	th		kh	
b	d	j	g	
ʔb	ʔd	ʔj		ʔ
m	n	ñ	ŋ	
w	l, r	y		
	s			h

Vowels:

Pham Xuân Tin (1955):

i	ư	u
ê	ơ, â	ô
e	a	o

Transliteration:

i	ɨ	u
e	ə	o
ɛ	a	ɔ

Lafont (1968):

i	ư	u
ê	ơ, â	ô
e	a	o

Lee (1966):

i	ɨ	u
e	ə	o
ɛ	a	ɔ

Notes: (1) The *-o*, when it used as an off-glide, is written as *-u*. (2) Final vowels marked with a breve have had final glottal stops added, where this is supported by the evidence.

KRUNG

Krung is the only name reported for this group. They are found along the upper La Liau, Ya Hiau, and Kra Bou north of Ban Me Thuot. Beyond the fact that they are alleged to be Chamic speaking, there is no information on further affiliations.

NOANG

Also called La-Dang. The Noang are located southeast of Dalat in South Vietnam.

PHAN RANG CHAM

Cham has its own literary tradition, one that dates back some 1500 years involving an Indic script. There are two modern descendants of this tradition. One is

Moussay's Phan Rang Cham dictionary, which lists Cham forms in this Indic script and then provides a two transliterations for each item, one representing a variant of the modern pronunciation and the other providing a more historically accurate representation of the writing system. The other is the excellent Cham-Vietnamese dictionary by Bùi Khánh Thế (1995); this dictionary uses the same script as Aymonier and Cabaton (1906), but instead of their transliteration, the author uses one that is useful and quite transparent.

Consonants:

Moussay (1971): (spoken)   Transliteration:

p	t	c	k		p	t	c	k	
ph	th	ch	kh		ph	th	ch	kh	
p̣	ṭ	ç	ḳ		p̣	ṭ	ç	ḳ	
p̣h	ṭh	çh	ḳh		p̣h	ṭh	çh	ḳh	
	s			h		s			h
b	d	'j	'		ɓ	ɗ	ʔj		ʔ
w	l	y			w	l	y		
ẃ	r	ý			ẃ	r	ý		
m	n	ñ	ng		m	n	ñ	ŋ	

Moussay (1971): (written)   Transliteration:

p/p̣	t	c	k		p/p̣	t	c	k	
ph	th	ch	kh		ph	th	ch	kh	
b	d	j	g		b	d	j	g	
bh	dh	jh	gh		bh	dh	jh	gh	
	s	ś		h		s	ś		h
ɓ	ɗ	/ń	'		ɓ	ɗ	ʔj		ʔ
w	l	y			w	l	y		
	r					r			
m	n	ñ	ṅ-/-ñ		m	n	ñ	ŋ	

Note:

In Written Cham, postvocalic k is almost always (but not always) a glottal stop, as indicated by Moussay's transcription of the spoken language, which almost always shows a glottal stop.

The spoken Phan Rang Cham used throughout this work is from Moussay at only one important point does his representation differ significantly from the actual modern pronunciation and that is with the diphthongs written < -ɛy̆ > and < -ɔy̆ >, which are pronounced in modern Phan Rang as /-ăi/ and /-ău/, respectively.

Vowels:

Moussay (1971):			Transliteration:		
i	ư	u	i	ɨ	u
ê, ĕ	ơ	ô, ŏ	e, ĕ	ə	o, ŏ
e	a	o	ɛ	a	ɔ

In addition, for the Moussay and the Aymonier and Cabaton dictionaries two other more specific transliterations are necessary: must be substituted for < -ĕy > and < -ŏy > to bring their transliteration system in line with the other transcriptions and the script.

RADE

Rade, Rhadé, Raday, Rde, Ede

Consonants:

Egerod (1978:49):					Transliteration:				
p	t	c	k		p	t	c	k	
ph	th	ch	kh		ph	th	ch	kh	
b	d	j	g		b	d	j	g	
ˣf	s, ˣz			h	f	s, z			h
ƀ	ʔd	ʔj		ʔ	ɓ	ɗ	ʔj		ʔ
w	1	y			w	1	y		
	r					r			
m	n	ñ	ŋ		m	n	ñ	ŋ	

Tharp (1980:vi):					Y-Chang (1979):				
p	t	č	k		p	t	č	k	
ph	th	ch	kh		ph	th	ch	kh	
b	d	j	g		b	d	j	g	
	s			h		s			h
ƀ	đ	dj	-		ƀ	đ	dj	-	
w	1	y			w	1	y		
	r					r			
m	n	ñ	ng		m	n	ñ	ng	

Notes:

Egerod (1978:49) notes that /f/ and /z/ only occur in loans. He also notes that initial glottal stop is left unwritten, as it is considered automatic before all word-initial vowels.

Vowels:

Egerod (1978:50):			Transliteration:		
i	ï	u	i	ɨ	u
e	ə	o	e	ə	o
ε	a	ɔ	ε	a	ɔ

Tharp (1980:vi):			Y-Chang (1979):		
i	uʼ	u	i	ɨ	u
ê	oʼ	ô	ê	ə	ô
e	a	o	e	a	o

Note:

Egerod marks the long vowels as long, leaving the short vowels unmarked. The remaining authors mark the short vowels as short, leaving the long vowels unmarked. Note that short *a* is written as *â* in Tharp and Y-Chang. In addition, *-ao* has been transliterated as *-au*.

Lee (1974:644) notes that "Rade initial *m, k, h* followed by any consonant except *l, r, h, w, y* is structurally a separate syllable with noncontrastive vowel. Occasionally there is a contrast of consonant cluster and disyllabic word which is handled in the traditional orthography by writing *u* for *w* and *i* for *y* in a cluster (cf. *hwie* 'rattan' which is disyllabic and *huĭ* 'to fear' which is monosyllabic) and by inserting an *a* between *k* and *h* to indicate a disyllabic word (cf. *khǎn* 'cloth' and *kahǎn* 'soldier')." For the sake of making the syllable structure more transparent, the vowels in such words have been re-inserted.

In all the Rade orthographies, the following initial clusters are written with the intervening shwa omitted.

kp-	mp-	---	>	kəp- məp- ---
kt-	mt-	---	>	kət- mət- ---
kk-	mk-	---	>	kək- mək- ---
kb-	mb-	hb-	>	kəb- məb- həb-
kd-	md-	hd-	>	kəd- məd- həd-
kg-	mg-	hg-	>	kəg- məg- həg-

kɓ-	mɓ-	hɓ-	>	kəɓ- məɓ- həɓ-
kɗ-	mɗ-	hɗ-	>	kəɗ- məɗ- həɗ-
km-	mm-	hm-	>	kəm- məm- həm-
kn-	mn-	hn-	>	kən- mən- hən-
kŋ-	mŋ-	hŋ-	>	kəŋ- məŋ- həŋ
ks-	ms-	hs-	>	kəs- məs- həs-
	mh-	hw-	>	məh-həw-
	hj-	h?j-	>	həj- hə?j-

However, in this work, the shwas have been reinserted to make the forms more readily analyzable and more comparable with non-Rade forms.

RAI

The term Rai, according to Grimes (1988), is sometimes used to refer to a dialect of southern Roglai, a usage that coincides with a comment by Lee (1966:3), but also notes that the term is also used to refer to a Chru group. As these two languages are extremely close together genetically, it is still unclear to me whether distinct groups are being referred to or not.

Grimes (1988) lists Rai as related not just to Chru, but specifically to the Seyu dialect.

NORTHERN ROGLAI

Consonants:

Awơi-hathe et al. (1977:vi):   Transliteration:

p	t	ch	c/k		p	t	c	k	
ph	th	chh	kh		ph	th	ch	kh	
v	d	j	g		b	d	j	g	
vh	dh	jh	gh		bh	dh	jh	gh	
	s			h		s			h
ɓ	∂	dj	-/q		ɓ	ɗ	?j	?	
w	l	y			w	l	y		
	r					r			
m	n	nh	ng		m	n	ñ	ŋ	

Notes:

The /r/: About the /r/, Awơi-hathe et al. (1977:vi) write that, in some dialects it is pronounced as trilled, while in other dialects it has, in effect, disappeared, that is, initially, it has disappeared, leaving the onset vowel long medially, it has disappeared, leaving the adjoining vowels as a single long vowel and, finally, it has become a semivowel, somewhat close to the Vietnamese < ư > [ɨ]. (See also the introductory discussion of this section on transliteration.)

The glottal stop < -/q > is marked in the original as < - > between vowels, but as < q > finally.

Vowels:

Awoʻi-hathe et al. (1977:vi):			Transliteration:		
i		u	i		u
e	oʻ	o	e	ə	o
	a			a	

Length and nasalization:

In addition, N. Roglai has both length and nasalization distinctions. Length in isolation is marked with a colon, i.e. < a: >, while nasalization in isolation is marked with a tilde, i.e., < ã >. However, the combination of length and nasalization has been written with < å > borrowed from Vietnamese, which coalesces the marking of length and nasalization into a unitary symbol. In this work, length and nasalization are kept separate and are written as < ã: >, that is, as a nasalized vowel followed by a colon symbolizing length.

CAC GIA ROGLAI

Cac Gia Roglai (Cobbey 1977) or Cat Gia Roglai (Lee 1998) is considerably different from other Roglai dialects (Grimes 1988).

SOUTHERN ROGLAI

Like Chru, Rai is listed by Grimes (1988) as a dialect.

TSAT

As Maddieson and Pang (1993) note, there are two descriptions and two transcriptions of Tsat, one by Ouyang and Zheng (1983), with subsequent work by Zheng (1986) and the other by Ni (1988ab; 1990ab). Both transcriptions essentially agree, with the only apparent differences being in the transcription of tones. However, even with the tones, upon more careful examination it becomes apparent that the two systems essentially agree (Maddieson and Pang, 1993).

Consonants:

Ouyang, Zheng, Ni:					Transliteration:				
p	t	ts	k		p	t	ts	k	
ph	th		kh		ph	th		kh	
	s			h		s			h
ʔb/b	ʔd/d				ɓ	ɗ			
v	l	z			v	l	z		
m	n	ɲ	ŋ		m	n	ñ	ŋ	

Note: The /ph/ is phonetically [ɸ] and /kh/ is phonetically [x].

Vowels:

Except where noted otherwise, the vowels are as in the original sources. Length is not yet completely understood; thus, the tables do not always indicate apparent irregularities in length.

Ouyang, Zheng, Ni:				Transliteration:			
i			u	i			u
e		ə	o	e		ə	o
		a				a	

Tones:

Maddieson and Pang (1993) significantly refines the tonal system of Ouyang, Zheng, and Ni and it is this refined analysis that is used in this work. Certainly the historical data fully supports Maddieson's adjustments. Thus, based on Maddieson and Pang, Tsat is analyzed in this work as having five etymological tones: three level tones in non-checked syllables and two contour tones in checked syllables, one rising and one falling. In addition to these five etymologically-predictable tones, there appear to be a handful of additional tonal configurations occurring only in recent loanwords.

Maddieson and Pang (1993) argue that, despite what might be suggested by the transcriptions used in the various papers on Tsat, the contour tones are always associated with checked syllables. With reference to the various falling tones transcribed in the sources on Tsat, on the basis the absence of instrumental or historical data to support the existence of more than one falling tone, Maddieson and Pang suggest that there is a single falling tone, which only occurs in checked syllables. Similarly, there is only a single rising tone, which again only occurs in checked syllables.

Table 167 shows the correspondences between the Ouyang and Zheng forms, the Ni forms, and the standardized Tsat cited in this paper. Note that the final glottal stop, found in Maddieson's examination of all contour tones has been indicated in the transcription. Further, the pitch values used by Ni are followed, as Maddieson's instrumental work suggests that the pitch range of the contour tones more closely approximates the Ni analysis.

Table 167: Comparison of tone transcriptions

Ouyang and Zheng	Ni	Standardized	
55	55	55	high-level
53	42	42ʔ	high-falling
33	33	33	mid-level
35	24	24ʔ	low-rising
11	11	11	low-level

It is important to emphasize that the Maddieson and Pang (1993) refinements of the Tsat tonal system are completely substantiated by the historical comparisons.

WESTERN CHAM

In the orthography used for Western Cham by Kvoeu-Hor and Friberg (1978), the voiced stops are used for voiceless stops and affricates followed by second register vowels, while voiceless stops are used for, not surprisingly, voiceless stops. However, despite this treatment being etymologically-correct, this work uses voiceless stops for both series, with a following second register vowel being indicated by a subscribed dot under the immediately preceding p, t, k, or c.

Consonants:

Kvoeu-Hor and Friberg (1978):					Transliteration:				
p	t	ch	k		p	t	č	k	
ph	th	chh	kh		ph	th	ch	kh	
b	d	j	g		p̣	ṭ	ç	ḳ	
	s			h		s			h
ɓ	ɗ	dj	-		ɓ	ɗ	ʔj		ʔ
w	l	y			w	l	y		
	r					r			
m	n	nh	ng		m	n	ñ	ŋ	

Vowels:

Kvoeu-Hor and Friberg (1978):   Transliteration:

i	uʼ	u		i	ɨ	u
ê	oʼ	ô		e	ə	o
e	a	o		ɛ	a	ɔ

Note: There is no contrast in Western Cham between -ɛa- and -ea-, nor between -ɔa- and -oa-. Thus, these are written as -ea- and -oa-, respectively. The Kvoeu-Hor and Friberg -*ao* has been transliterated as -*au*.

WRITTEN CHAMIC

Written Chamic data shows up from two sources in this work: in the transcription of Phan Rang Cham used throughout (see Phan Rang Cham section above) and in the citations from Aymonier and Cabaton also scattered throughout this work.

As Eric Oey notes about the 587-page Aymonier and Cabaton Cham dictionary, many of the cognates are incorrect and there are apparent problems with the transliteration. Nonetheless, when used with appropriate caution it constitutes an invaluable source. The older orthography provides numerous insights into earlier stages of the language, almost all of which can be substantiated by other evidence. As Oey further notes (n.d., p. 2), although Aymonier and Cabaton's dictionary contains many variant forms and has inadequacies in the script, "the variants and apparent quirks of the script may provide value clues to the historical development of the language."

The modifications to the transliteration are identical to those employed for Moussay's Phan Rang Cham.

An additional source for Written Chamic forms is the 1995 Bùi Khánh Thế Cham-Vietnamese dictionary Từ Điển Chăm-Việt.

Appendix II: The Chamic Lexicon

The organization of Appendix 2 involves an initial division of the lexicon into those forms that reconstruct to PC and those that do not. Thus, the first major set of forms is those that reconstruct to PC. The forms that reconstruct to PC are further divided into those with Austronesian etymologies, those with MK etymologies, and those without established etymologies. The PC reconstructions with MK etymologies, of course, represent the oldest layer of Chamic and MK contact.

The second major grouping, post-PC borrowings, represent post-PC language contact. Language contact is a major focus of this work so the inclusion of a large section on post-PC loanwords is central to the investigation. In addition, throughout the lexicon, the presence of Chamic loanwords in MK languages is also noted. Loan words both from MK into Chamic and from Chamic into MK help document the extent of language contact while providing evidence about where and when the contact occurred.

The post-PC borrowings have been divided up according to origin, specifically, into words of Indic origin, of Arabic origin, and of MK origin.

Other loans also occur in Chamic, but it is these three groups that represent the dominant cultural contact, at least until more recent times. Now of course the dominance of the Vietnamese would require the analysis of the countless, almost daily loans from Vietnamese. The depth of the historically recent Vietnamese influence is seen in the borrowing of the post-PC borrowing ˣɗəŋ 'IMPERATIVE, negative, don't', cf. Vietnamese dùng. Other loans are common, for instance, ˣvai, 'cotton cloth' is a post-PC borrowing from Vietnamese, which shows up in Chru as baːi, cf. Vietnamese vải.

ˣɗəŋ 'IMPERATIVE, negative, don't', N. Roglai ɗəŋ; ɗəŋ di; Vietnamese dùng. Looks to be borrowed directly from Vietnamese.

ˣvai 'cotton cloth', Chru baːi, Vietnamese vải. Note that the Chru is borrowed from the Vietnamese. However, an etymologically related doublet also exists in Chru in the form kəpaːh 'cotton'; this second form reconstructs to the PC level (cf. 'cotton' below).

277

Over time there have been various Chinese loans, some of considerable time depth like PC ˣ*cawaːn 'cup; bowl, dish', which reconstructs to PC. Others are more recent like the post-PC borrowing ˣɗaw 'sword; knife'.

ˣ*cawaːn 'cup; bowl, dish', Acehnese cawan -v, Chru cuaːn, N. Roglai cawaːt, Haroi cəwan, W. Cham cawan, PR Cham cawan 'petite tasse à alcool', Wr. Cham cawan, Malay cawan; MK: PMnong *ciân 'bowl'. Coope (1976) lists this as a borrowing from Chinese. If so, it looks like the coalescence of a two-syllable construction to one, with the the most likely candidates being 'tea' + 'bowl' [cf. Mandarin chá 'tea' + wǎn 'bowl' = 'tea-bowl; tea-cup' ; Japanese chawan 'bowl' (Baxter, p.c.)] producing Malay cawan 'cup; bowl; dish'.

ˣɗaw 'sword; knife', Rade ɗau, Jarai (PL) ɗau, Jarai (Lee) ɗau, Chru ɗaːu -l, N. Roglai ɗau, Haroi thɨau < *dau; ɗau 'machete'ˢ, like a knife but longer', W. Cham ɗau, PR Cham ɗaw, Wr. Cham ɗaw; MK: Bahnar (AC) dao; MK: PKatuic (DT) *daaw 'knife'. This word is probably a Chinese borrowing, but the intermediate paths are anything but obvious. Cf. Baxter (1992) Old Chinese *taw 'knife', Middle Chinese taw, Mandarin dāo.

However, the handful of Chinese borrowings represent a relatively indirect contact without a significant impact on Chamic languages. Thus, these are left for another study with another focus.

The post-PC borrowings from Indic, Arabic, and MK sources are discussed below in their own sections.

Comments on methodology and the lists

The problem of sorting out which borrowed forms date back to PC and which were borrowed more recently is often present. Thus, comments on the distribution are included with some of the sets. Specifically, the sets are sometimes labelled as either restricted to Highlands Chamic (Rade, Jarai, Chru, N. Roglai, and Tsat (which was a part of N. Rogali until it moved to Hainan)), or as Highlands Chamic plus Haroi and Western Cham, the two originally Coastal Chamic languages that have had an extended period of contact under the influence of highlands MK languages. Thus, words restricted to Highlands Chamic plus Haroi and Western Cham are likely to have been borrowed from MK. Even when the existence of regular correspondence patterns suggests a form reconstructs to PC, the possibility is quite real that some of these regularly corresponding forms are actually later borrowings, particularly in the case of forms that are not only without wider Austronesian attestation but also restricted to Highlands Chamic.

Other potentially valuable distributional information is also evident in the lexicon. Thus, the presence of a Phan Rang Cham form or a Written Cham form is obvious: such a form establishes that a set of words is not just restricted to the languages now found in the highlands, but instead is distributed throughout mainland Chamic and thus reduces the possibility that the form was borrowed from MK only after many of the Chamic languages had moved up into the highlands. More difficult to evaluate is the importance of Acehnese attestation. Certainly the lack of an Acehnese form is particularly difficult to evaluate; it is likely that some forms have simply been lost, while others have been replaced by Malay forms. However, even if there is a related form in Acehnese, it is possible that the word may have entered Acehnese after Acehnese left the mainland. It has, in fact, been suggested that Acehnese has a number of MK words not normally found in Bahnaric and Katuic, but this remains to be established.

Aside from the possibility of inadvertent omissions, the following lists of reconstructions include not only all the reconstructions referred to in the text but also all the reconstructions retained from Lee (1966). However, the list does not begin to include each and every form in each and every language examined. For example, four sources of Rade were examined and analyzed, but only one is included in the list. Similarly, the work on Phan Rang Cham by the David and Doris Blood, by Dorothy Thomas, by Ernest Lee, and by Gerard Moussay were all thoroughly examined and included in the analysis, but only the forms from Moussay are systematically included in this appendix. In each case where multiple sources were examined and used, the source chosen for inclusion in the lexicon is the one that provided the longest list of cognate forms—no other criterion was used. It needs to be emphasized that the analysis itself used all the available forms, and occasionally in the text an alternate source has been used to illustrate a point, usually because that source happened to have fewer gaps than the others. In the list of forms given here, except for Jarai, only one source for each language has been included. As a consequence, a form occasionally appears more marginally attested than it is; in most cases this simply means that the attestation was found, not in the languages given below, but in several of the other languages used for this study. Thus, while in general Appendix 2 includes the data used for the analysis, it does not begin to include the whole data base; that would have led to an appendix extending to hundreds of pages with little corresponding increase in our knowledge.

The decision has also been made to include various problematic sets, clearly labeled as such, in the sets below. Further work and feedback from various readers should clarify much of this sort of indeterminancy; the hope is to see this collection updated at a later time.

If there is a discrepancy between the reconstructions in the body of the text and the reconstructions in the appendix of forms, the appendix of forms is almost inevitably correct. While the various parts of the body of the text were written at different times, the appendix was always updated and represents the final version. One hopes, of course, that no such discrepancies exist, but undoubtedly more than one has slipped by.

1.   CHAMIC VOCABULARY RECONSTRUCTABLE TO PC

As expected, a large number of these forms reconstructed for PC have obvious AN etymologies and these constitute the first set of forms presented. It needs to be noted that many of these Austronesian forms have been borrowed into MK languages of Vietnam and are thus found in both the Bahnaric and in the Katuic branches of MK. As a consequence, it is often only the existence of fairly well-established Austronesian etymologies that allow us to establish their ultimate Austronesian affiliation.

1.1   PC words of Austronesian origin

*-ən- 'INSTRUMENTAL infix', Acehnese -ɯn-, nɯ-, Rade -ən-, Jarai (Banker) -ən-, Chru -ən-, N. Roglai -an-, W. Cham -ən-, PR Cham -ən-.

*ʔabih 'all; finished, done', Jarai (PL) abih, Jarai (Lee) ʔabih, Chru abih 'completely', N. Roglai abih, Tsat phi⁵⁵ phi⁵⁵, Haroi aphĭh; phĭh, W. Cham pih, PR Cham apih, pih, Wr. Cham abih; bih, Malay habis 'done, finished, entirely', PMalayic *habis, PWMP *qabiq, *qabis.

*ʔada 'have, there is, there are', Tsat tha¹¹, W. Cham maṭa iʔ, Malay ada, PMP *adaq; *wada.

*ʔadɛy 'younger sibling; cadet', Acehnese adɔə, Rade adɛi, Jarai (PL) adəi 'soeur ou frère cadet', Jarai (Lee) ʔadəi, Chru adəi, N. Roglai adəi, Tsat thai¹¹, Haroi athĭi, W. Cham ṭay, PR Cham aṭĕy; ṭĕy, Wr. Cham adĕi, Malay adik (Blust (p.c.) notes that the -k is the retention of the PWMP vocative marker *-q), PMP *huaji-q (Blust (p.c.) notes that the *-q is a vocative marker).

*ʔadhĕy 'forehead', Acehnese dhɔə, Rade adhɛi, Jarai (PL) thĕi, Jarai (Lee) thəi, Chru thəi, N. Roglai thĕi, Tsat thai³³, Haroi thəi -v, W. Cham ṭhay, PR Cham ṭhĕy, Wr. Cham dhĕi, Malay dahi, PMP *daqih.

*ʔaduʔ 'room', Rade adŭʔ, Jarai (Lee) ʔadŭʔ, Chru aduʔ, N. Roglai aduʔ (also a clf.), Haroi athŭʔ, PR Cham aṭŭʔ; ṭŭʔ, Wr. Cham aduk, Malay cf. pĕraduan.

*ʔalih 'move residence', Jarai (PL) rĭ ʔ, PR Cham alĭh, Wr. Cham alih, Malay alih, PMP *aliq.

*ʔama 'father', Rade ama, Jarai (PL) ama, Jarai (Lee) ʔama, Chru ama, N. Roglai amă, Tsat ma¹¹, Haroi ama 'father; address term', W. Cham mɨ, PR Cham amɨ, Wr. Cham amɨ, PMP *ama, PAn *ama.

*ʔana:k 'child', Acehnese anɯʔ, Rade anak, Jarai (PL) anăʔ, Jarai (Lee) ʔanăʔ -1, Chru ana:ʔ, N. Roglai ană:ʔ, Tsat naʔ[24], Haroi anaʔ, W. Cham niʔ, PR Cham aniʔ, Wr. Cham anɨk, Malay anak, PMalayic *anak, PMP *anak.

*ʔaŋan 'name', Chru aŋan, W. Cham ŋăn, PR Cham aŋăn; ŋăn, Wr. Cham aŋan; ŋan, PMP *ŋajan; MK: Bahnar (AC) anan ?.

*ʔanan 'name', Acehnese nan, Rade anăn, Jarai (PL) anăn, Jarai (Lee) ʔanăn, N. Roglai anăn, Tsat nan[33], Haroi anŏn -v, PMP *najan.

*ʔanan 'that (third p.)', Acehnese ñan, -nan, Rade năn, Jarai (PL) anŭn, Jarai (Lee) ʔanun < *u, Chru nɨn, Tsat nan[33], Haroi nŏn -v, W. Cham nən 'there', PR Cham năn, Wr. Cham nan, PMalayic *(i)na(n), *(a)na(ʔ), PMalayic *(i)na(n), *(a)na(ʔ), PWMP *-nan (note that this is reconstructed as a PWMP suffix).

*ʔanap 'front (of)', Rade ti anăp, Jarai (PL) anăp, Jarai (Lee) ʔanăp, Chru anauʔ, N. Roglai paʔ anăʔ, Haroi anɨauʔ, W. Cham ḳah nauʔ, PR Cham anăʔ, Wr. Cham anak, Malay hadap, PMP *qa(n)dep.

*ʔaŋin 'the wind', Acehnese aŋɛn, Rade aŋĭn, Jarai (PL) aŋĭn, Jarai (Lee) ʔaŋĭn -1, Chru aŋin, N. Roglai aŋĭn, Tsat ŋin[33], Haroi aŋĭn, W. Cham ŋĭn, PR Cham aŋĭn; ŋĭn, Wr. Cham aŋin; ŋin, Malay angin, PMalayic *aŋin, PMP *haŋin.

*ʔantɔw 'ghost; corpse', Acehnese ɯntɛə, Rade atău 'corpse', Jarai (Lee) ʔatəu, Chru atəu 'corpse', N. Roglai atəu 'underworld', Haroi atău 'ghost, corpse', W. Cham atau -presyllable, PR Cham atŏw, Wr. Cham atuw, Malay hantu, PMP *qanitu, PAn *qaNiCu.

*ʔapuy 'fire', Acehnese apui, Rade pui, Jarai (PL) pui, Jarai (Lee) ʔapui, Chru apui, N. Roglai apui, Tsat pui[33], Haroi apoi, W. Cham pui, PR Cham apuy; puy, Wr. Cham apŭĭ, Malay api, PMalayic *api, PMP *hapuy.

*ʔasah 'sharpen', Acehnese asah in 'whetstone', Rade sah 'whet', Jarai (PL) ăsah, Jarai (Lee) ʔasah, Chru asah, N. Roglai asah, Haroi asăh, W. Cham sah, PR Cham thăh, Wr. Cham thah, Malay asah, PMalayic *asah 'grind; sharpen', PMP *hasaq.

*ʔasap 'smoke (of a fire)', Acehnese asap, Rade săp pui, Jarai (PL) ăsăp, Jarai (Lee) săp, Chru asaʔ, N. Roglai asaʔ, Tsat sauʔ[24], Haroi asău ʔ, W. Cham sauʔ, PR Cham thăʔ; athăʔ, Wr. Cham săk; athak, Malay asap, PMalayic (Adelaar) *asəp, PWMP *qasep.

*ʔasey 'flesh; meat; body; contents', Acehnese asɔə, Rade asɛi 'body', Jarai (PL) ăsar -vf, Jarai (Lee) ʔasəi, Haroi asŏi 'body', PMalayic *isiʔ, PMP *hesi; MK: PKatuic (DT) *sâj 'meat'. Note that this form has been borrowed from Chamic into Katuic, but apparently not into Bahnaric.

*ʔasɔw 'dog', Acehnese asɛə, Rade asău, Jarai (PL) asəu, Jarai (Lee) ʔasəu, Chru asəu, N. Roglai asəu, Tsat a[11] sau[33], Haroi asău, W. Cham sau, PR Cham athŏw; thŏw, Wr. Cham suw; asuŋ, Malay gigi asu 'canine tooth', PMa-

layic *asu?, PMP *asu, Pan asu; MK: PMnong *so. This root obviously reconstructs both in PMK and PAn.

*?ata:s 'far; above; long', Acehnese atɯəh, Rade taih, Jarai (PL) ataih,
Jarai (Lee) ?ataih, Chru ata:h, N. Roglai ata, Tsat ta³³, Haroi atah, W. Cham tah,
PR Cham atăh; tăh, Wr. Cham atah, tah, Malay atas 'above', PMalayic *atas,
PMP *atas.

*?awa 'uncle, aunt', Acehnese abuwa ?, Rade awa 'uncle, aunt', Chru
wa 'paternal', PMP *ua? 'uncle, aunt'; MK: PMnong *wa. This is a variant of
*?awa.

*?ayup 'blow e.g. the wind; whistle, instrument', Acehnese yop 'blow
flute', Rade ayŭ?, Jarai (PL) ayŭp, Jarai (Lee) ayŭp, Chru iu:?, N. Roglai ayu:?,
Haroi ayŭ?, W. Cham yŭ?, PR Cham ayŭ?; yŭ?, Wr. Cham ayuk; yuk, Malay tiup,
PMalayic *iup, PMP *heyup, PAn *Seyup.

*?iar -f 'water (fresh)', Acehnese iə, Rade ea, Jarai (PL) ia, Jarai (Lee)
?ia, Chru ia, N. Roglai ia, Tsat ?ia³³, Haroi ea, W. Cham ea, PR Cham ýa; ier -f,
Wr. Cham ḭā, Malay air; ayer, PMalayic *air, PMP *wahiʀ. There are problems
with the PC correspondences for this form. It is, perhaps, unrelated.

*?iduŋ 'nose', Acehnese idoŋ, Rade adŭŋ, Jarai (PL) aduŋ; ɗuŋ (Ss);
ăduŋ (S), Jarai (Lee) ?adŭŋ, Chru aduŋ, N. Roglai idŭk, Tsat thuŋ¹¹, Haroi athŭŋ,
W. Cham ţuŋ, PR Cham iţŭŋ; aţŭŋ; ţŭŋ, Wr. Cham iduŋ; aduŋ; duŋ, Malay
hiduŋ, PMalayic *hiduŋ, PMP *ijuŋ.

*?ika:n 'fish', Acehnese ikan < Malay, Rade kan, Jarai (PL) akan, Jarai
(Lee) ?akan, Chru aka:n, N. Roglai ika:t, Tsat ka:n³³, Haroi akan, W. Cham kan,
PR Cham ikan; kan, Wr. Cham ikan; kan, Malay ikan, PMP *hikan; MK: PNB
*ka, PMnong *ka, Bahnar (AC) ka, PSB (Efimov) *ka:, PKatuic *?əka:. The
MK and the PC forms both date back to their respective proto-languages.

*?ikat 'to tie', Acehnese ikat, Jarai (PL) aka?, Jarai (Lee) ?akă?; kă?,
Chru aka?, N. Roglai ika?, Tsat ka?²⁴, Haroi akă?, W. Cham kăk, PR Cham ikă?;
kă?, Wr. Cham ikak; kak, Malay ikat, PMalayic *ikət, PMP *hiket; MK: PNB
*kăt, Bahnar (AC) kât, PSB (Efimov) *kət. [The PSB must be borrowed from
PC.]

*?iku 'tail', Acehnese iku < *-r, Rade ku, Jarai (PL) aku, Jarai (Lee)
?aku, Chru aku, N. Roglai iku, Tsat ku³³, Haroi akou, W. Cham hla ku, PR Cham
iku, Wr. Cham ikū, Malay ékor, PMalayic *ikur, PMP *ikuʀ.

*?ina 'mother (animal); big', Acehnese inʌŋ, Rade ana 'female', Jarai
(Lee) ?ana, Haroi aniə, W. Cham nɨ in nɨ taŋin 'thumb', PR Cham inɨ, Wr. Cham
inɨ, Malay betina [be/t/ina] 'female', PMalayic *ina, PMP *(t)-ina.

*?inɨ; *iney 'this', Acehnese ñɔə, -nɔə, Rade tinɛi, Jarai (PL) anai, Jarai
(Lee) ?anai, Chru ni 'here, this', N. Roglai tinɨ, Tsat ni³³, Haroi ni, W. Cham ni,
PR Cham ni, Wr. Cham nɨ, Malay ini; ni, PMalayic *(i)ni(?).

*ʔughaːr 'root', Acehnese ukhɯə < *-r, Rade agha, Jarai (PL) akha, Jarai (Lee) ʔakha, Chru akha, N. Roglai ukha, Tsat (kai³³) kha³³; ha³³; ha³³ eee, Haroi akha, W. Cham k̦ha, PR Cham uk̦ha; ak̦ha; k̦ha, Wr. Cham uk̦hā; aghā, Malay akar, PMalayic *akar, PMP *wakaʀ.

*ʔular 'snake', Acehnese ulɯə < *-r, Rade ala, Jarai (PL) ală, Jarai (Lee) ʔala, Chru ala, N. Roglai ula, Tsat (la¹¹) la³³, Haroi alɨa 'snake (poisonous)', W. Cham la, PR Cham ula; ala; la, Wr. Cham ulā; alā; lā, Malay ular, PMalayic *ular, PMP *hulaʀ, PAn *Sular.

*ʔuraːŋ -1 'person; someone', Acehnese urɯəŋ, Rade arăŋ -1, Jarai (PL) arăŋ, Jarai (Lee) ʔarăŋ -1, Chru araːŋ 'people, clf.', N. Roglai uraːk; raːk, Tsat zaːŋ?³³, Haroi arăŋ -1 'clf.', W. Cham raŋ, PR Cham uraŋ, Wr. Cham uraŋ, Malay orang, PMalayic *uraŋ 'person; someone'. Blust notes that this is restricted to languges in Western Borneo which are either closely related to Malay, or which have been in a borrowing relationship with Malay for many centuries. It is listed under the appendix entitled 'loans' in his comparative dictionary, making the length irregularity in Chamic difficult to evaluate.

*ʔurat 'vein, vessel, tendon' cf. 'root', Acehnese urat; urʌt -v 'vine', Rade aruăt (m), Jarai (PL) arăt, Jarai (Lee) ʔara? -v, Chru ara?, N. Roglai ura?, Tsat za?²⁴, Haroi ară? -v, W. Cham ră? 'thread', PR Cham ră?; ară?; ură?, Wr. Cham arak, rak, Malay urat, PMP *uʀat, PAn *uʀaC; MK: Bahnar (AC) ara, PSB (Efimov) *ʔurat cf. 'root', PKatuic *ʔaraː? 'vein, leaf'. The antiquity of the PAn and PMP forms suggests that the borrowing is into PSB and PKatuic, not the other way around.

*babah; *mabah 'mouth', Acehnese babah, Jarai (PL) băbăh, măbăh, Jarai (Lee) bah; məbah -i, N. Roglai mubah (also a classifier); bah, Tsat pha⁵⁵, Haroi pəphɨah, W. Cham papah, PR Cham papah, Wr. Cham pabah̦, PMP *baqbaq; *beqbaq.

*babuy 'wild pig', Acehnese bui, Jarai (PL) băbui, Jarai (Lee) bəbui, Chru pəbui, N. Roglai ba bui, Tsat phui¹¹, Haroi pəphŭi, W. Cham papui, PR Cham papuy, Wr. Cham pabŭĕi, Malay babi 'pig', PMP *babuy, PAn *babuy.

*bahrɔw 'new; just now', Acehnese baro -f, Rade mrău, Jarai (PL) pəhrəu, phrəu, Jarai (Lee) phrəu -i, Chru bərhəu, N. Roglai bahrəu, Tsat phiə¹¹, Haroi prĭau, W. Cham pahau, PR Cham pirɔ̆w, Wr. Cham biruw, Malay baharu; baru, PMalayic *baharu?, PMP *baqeʀu.

*balɔw 'widowed', Acehnese balɛə, Jarai (PL) bləu, Jarai (Lee) bləu, Chru bləu, N. Roglai baləu, PR Cham pilɔ̆w, Wr. Cham biluw, Malay balu, PMP *balu.

*banut 'banyan, balete', Rade mənŭt, Jarai (PL) mənŭt, bənŭ?, Jarai (Lee) bənŭ?, Chru bənŭː?, N. Roglai binŭ? 'banyan, balete', PR Cham pinu?, Wr. Cham binuk, PWMP *bunut 'Ficus species'.

*bara 'shoulder', Rade mra, Jarai (PL) bra (Pk), Jarai (Lee) bra, Chru bra, N. Roglai bara, Tsat phia[11], Haroi prɨa, W. Cham pra, PR Cham pira, Wr. Cham birā, PMP *qabaʀa.

*barah 'swell; swollen', Acehnese barah, Chru brah, N. Roglai barah, Haroi prɨah, W. Cham parah, Malay barah 'tumor, abscess', PMP *baʀeq; *baʀeq 'abscess'.

*basah 'wet; damp', Acehnese basah, Rade məsah, Jarai (PL) pəsăh, Jarai (Lee) pəsah, Chru pəsah, N. Roglai pasah, Tsat sa[55], Haroi pəsăh, W. Cham pasah, PR Cham pathăh, Wr. Cham pathaḥ, Malay basah, PMalayic *basah, PMP *baseq.

*batɛy 'banana', Rade mətɛi, Jarai (PL) pătəi, Chru pətəi, N. Roglai pitəi, Tsat u[11] tai[11], Haroi pətŏi, W. Cham patay, PR Cham patɛy, Wr. Cham patĕi, PMP *punti; MK: PNB *prɨt, PMnong *prit, PSB (Efimov) *prɨːt, PKatuic *pəriet, *ʔəriet. Despite some similarities, neither the MK nor the PC words for banana are borrowed from the other language.

*batɔw 'stone', Acehnese batɛə, Rade bɔh tău, Jarai (PL) pətəu, Jarai (Lee) pətəu, Chru pətəu, N. Roglai patəu, Tsat tau[11], Haroi pətău, W. Cham patau, PR Cham pitŏw; patŏw; patŏw, Wr. Cham bituw; batuw, Malay batu, PMalayic *batu, PMP *batu.

*batuk 'cough', Acehnese batoʔ, Rade mətŭk, Jarai (PL) pătŭk, mătŭk (Pk), Jarai (Lee) pətŭk, Chru pətuʔ, N. Roglai pituʔ, Tsat tu?[42], Haroi pətoʔ, W. Cham patŭʔ, PR Cham patŭʔ, Wr. Cham patuk, Malay batuk; MK: PMnong *bəsyăk, PSB (Efimov) *bəshiəʔ. Despite the apparent similarity, the MK forms are only lookalikes.

*bilit -i 'twist', Rade blĭt -i, Jarai (Lee) blĭʔ, Chru bli:ʔ 'roll up', N. Roglai bili:ʔ, Haroi pliʔ -first vowel, W. Cham pliʔ 'wrap up, roll, package', PR Cham liʔ -i, Wr. Cham lik, Malay bĕlit 'twining round, coiling round', PMP *belit.

*binay 'virgin', Rade mənie 'daughter', Jarai (PL) bănai, Jarai (Lee) bənai, Chru bənai 'female (animal)', N. Roglai binãi 'of animals', W. Cham panai 'female (animal)', PR Cham pinay 'woman', Wr. Cham binai, Malay bini 'wife', PMP *binay 'virgin', PAn *binay 'female; woman'. The PAn is an infixed form (*b-in-ahi); the infixed variant is not attested anywhere in Taiwan.

*blah 'chop; split', Acehnese plah -i, Rade blah, Jarai (PL) blăh, Jarai (Lee) blah, Chru blah, N. Roglai blah, Tsat phia[55], Haroi plɨah, W. Cham plah, PR Cham plah, Wr. Cham blaḥ, PMP *belaq, Malay bĕlah, PMalayic *bəlah, PMP *belaq 'crack, split open'; MK: PNB *pah, PSB (Efimov) *bɨlah, PMnong *blah 'split'. Note that this root also appears to reconstruct in three branches of Bahnaric.

*blɛy 'buy', Acehnese blɔə, Rade blɛi, Jarai (PL) bləi, Jarai (Lee) bləi, Chru bləi, N. Roglai bləi, Haroi plĭi, W. Cham play, PR Cham plɛ̆y, Wr. Cham blĕi, Malay bĕli, PMalayic *bəli, PMP *beli, PAn *beli.

*bɔh 'fruit; egg; clf. for round objects', Acehnese bɔh, Rade bɔh, Jarai (PL) bɔh, Jarai (Lee) bɔh, Chru bɔh, N. Roglai boh, Tsat pho⁵⁵, Haroi phŭh <phuôh>, W. Cham poh -v, PR Cham pɔh, Wr. Cham buah̥, Malay buah clf., PMalayic *buah, PMP *buaq, PAn *buaq.

(*bɔh) *bətih 'calf of leg', Acehnese bɯteh, Rade bɔh tih, Jarai (PL) pɤtih, Jarai (Lee) pətih, Chru bɔh pətih, N. Roglai boh patih, Haroi pəteh, W. Cham poh patih, PR Cham patĭh, Wr. Cham patih̥, Malay bĕtis, PMP *betis.

*bɔw 'stench', (the initial is a voiced variant of the more frequent *ɓ-, but is also found in Acehnese), Acehnese bɛə, Wr. Cham bau, Malay bau 'smell', PMP *bahu.

*ɓɔw 'stench', Rade ɓɤ̆u, Jarai (PL) ɓɤ̆u, Jarai (Lee) ɓəu, Chru ɓəu, N. Roglai ɓəu, Tsat ɓə³³, Haroi ɓɤ̆u, W. Cham ɓau, PR Cham ɓɤ̆w, Wr. Cham ɓuw, Malay bau 'smell', PMP *bahu.

*braːs 'rice (husked)', Acehnese brɯəh, Rade braih, Jarai (PL) braih, Jarai (Lee) braih, Chru braːh 'pounded rice', N. Roglai bra, Tsat phia¹¹, Haroi priah, W. Cham prah 'pounded rice', PR Cham prah -1, Wr. Cham brah̥, Malay bĕras, PMP *beʀas.

*brɛy 'give', Acehnese bri -f < Malay ?, Rade brɛi, Jarai (PL) brəi, Jarai (Lee) brəi, Chru brəi, N. Roglai brəi, Tsat ?, Haroi prĭi, W. Cham pray, PR Cham prɛ̆y, Wr. Cham brĕi, Malay bĕri, PMalayic *bəri?, PMP *beʀay, PAn *beʀay. [The PC and PMalayic vowels are unexpected; one would expect PMalayo-Chamic *-ay, not the reflexes of what was apparently PMalayo-Chamic *-i]

*brɛy 'to permit' < 'give' cf. *brɛy 'give', Rade brɛi, Chru brəi, N. Roglai brəi, W. Cham pray.

*bru? -n -f 'rotten', Acehnese bro?, Rade brŭ?, Jarai (PL) brŭ?, Jarai (Lee) brŭ?, Chru bru?, N. Roglai brŭk -n -f, Tsat zo?²⁴ ?, Haroi prŭ? -i, W. Cham prŭ?, PR Cham prŭ?, Wr. Cham bruk, Malay buruk 'worn, decayed (of vegetables)', PMP *buʀuk 'rotten meat; addled eggs; bad character'; MK: PKatuic (DT) *qab/ɓ_k.

*bruă? 'do; work', Rade bruă?, Jarai (PL) mă? bruă?, Jarai (Lee) bruă?, Chru brua? -n, N. Roglai bruă?, Haroi prŭ?, W. Cham prŭ?, PR Cham prŭ?, Wr. Cham bruk; MK: PSB (Efimov) *bruə? 'work, industrious'; PKatuic (Dorothy Thomas) *br_q [Pacoh proaq, Katu briaq]. This set of forms plus the set for *buat 'do, work' is inordinately interesting. First, it looks like *buat 'do work', which has an excellent PAn genealogy [PMP *buhat, PAn *buhat]. However, it also occurs in MK in both PSB and in PKatuic. If it is a borrowing from MK, then the PAn forms must be counted as chance look-alikes. If, as is more likely, it

was borrowed into Katuic and PSB from AN, then this is another AN form borrowed into Katuic (or, perhaps, just Katu and Pacoh) from a presumably Chamic
source along the coast, a little north of the northern-most capital of Champa.
Both the PSB and the PKatuic forms contain an infixed -r-, a piece of morphology not expected in Chamic but common in MK. Perhaps it was then reborrowed
into Post-Chamic from one of these sources but with the -r- infix borrowed from
MK; perhaps the -r- was introduced by MK bilinguals speaking Chamic.

*buat 'do; work', Acehnese buət 'action'; buət 'action'; pubuət 'do',
N. Roglai buã?, Tsat phua?[42], Malay buat 'do', PMP *buhat, PAn *buhat.

*bukən 'other; different', Acehnese bukʌn; kʌn 'on the contrary', Rade
məkăn used in the phrase 'the other day', Jarai (PL) păkŏn, Chru pəkən 'different', N. Roglai tukət -i, Haroi pəkŏn 'other', PR Cham (ķŏw')-ķăn -i, Wr.
Cham (gəp)-gən -i, Malay bukan 'not', PMalayic *bukən 'other', PWMP
(Blust) *beken 'other, different'. As Blust has pointed out, the first vowel of the
word *bukən is a Malayo-Chamic lexical innovation.

*bula:n 'moon; month', Acehnese buluɯən, Rade mlan, Jarai (PL) blan,
Jarai (Lee) blan, Chru ea bla:n, N. Roglai ia bila:t, Tsat luŋ[11] phian[11], Haroi
pəlïan, W. Cham ea plan, PR Cham pilan, Wr. Cham bilan, Malay bulan, PMalayic *bulan, PMP *bulan, PAn *bulaN.

*buləw 'hair, body; downy feathers; plant floss', Acehnese buleə,
Rade mlău, Jarai (PL) bləu 'plume', Jarai (Lee) bləu, Chru bləu, N. Roglai biləu,
Tsat phiə[11], Haroi pəlïau, W. Cham plau, PR Cham pilŏw; palŏw, Wr. Cham
buluw, biluw, Malay bulu, PMalayic *bulu, PMP *bulu.

*buŋa 'flower', Acehnese buŋɔŋ, Rade məŋa, Jarai (PL) bəŋă, Jarai
(Lee) bəŋa, Chru bəŋa, N. Roglai buŋã, Tsat ŋa[11], Haroi pəŋïa, W. Cham paŋur -
f, PR Cham piŋu, Wr. Cham biŋū, Malay buŋa, PMalayic *buŋa(?), PMP *buŋa.

*buŋa 'striped' cf. 'flower', Rade məŋa 'checkered, spotted', Chru
bəŋa, N. Roglai buŋã, PR Cham piŋu, Wr. Cham biŋū. The 'striped, checkered'
meaning looks to have evolved from 'flowery' or some such, as the shape of the
etymon is the same as that for 'flower'.

*buŋat 'soul, spirit; shadow, shade', Rade məŋăt, Jarai (PL) bəŋăt,
Jarai (Lee) bəŋă?, bəŋăt, Chru bəŋa?, N. Roglai buŋã?, Haroi pəŋïa?, W. Cham
paŋŭ?, PR Cham piŋŭ?, Wr. Cham biŋuk.

*buta 'blind', Acehnese buta, Tsat ta[11], PR Cham mïta, Wr. Cham mïtā
(same as eye?), Malay buta.

*buya 'crocodile', Acehnese buya, Rade mya, Jarai (PL) bïa, Jarai
(Lee) bia Note: the same as bya, Chru bia Note: the same as bya, N. Roglai
biya, Haroi pəyïa, W. Cham paya, PR Cham piya, Wr. Cham biyā, Malay buaya,
PMP *buqaya, PAn *buqaya.

*bəsɛy 'iron', Acehnese bɯsɔə, Rade məsɛi, Jarai (PL) pə̆səi, Jarai (Lee) pəsəi, Chru pəsəi, N. Roglai pisəi, Tsat sai[11], Haroi pəsŏi, W. Cham pasay, PR Cham pithə̆y; pathə̆y, Wr. Cham bithə̆i; pasə̆i, Malay bə̆si.

ˣ*ɓla:t 'open eyes wide', Acehnese blɯt, Chru ɓla:ʔ, N. Roglai ɓla:ʔ, PR Cham ɓlaʔ, Wr. Cham ɓlak, PMP bulat 'open eyes wide'; MK: Bahnar (AC) blə̆k. If as it appears, the form is descended from PMP *bulat, the initial is quite puzzling. The form has the only example of a PC *ɓl- cluster in the data. Thus, despite the obvious Austronesian etymology, the most plausible account is that the PC was not inherited directly but secondarily borrowed from an Austronesian source.

*ɓɔw see immediately below *bɔw

*ɓuk -1 'head hair', Acehnese oʔ, Rade ɓŭk, Jarai (PL) ɓŭk; ʔmŭk (Pkly), Jarai (Lee) ɓŭk; ɓŭʔ, Chru ɓu:ʔ -1, N. Roglai ɓu:ʔ, Tsat ɓuʔ[24], Haroi ɓuʔ, W. Cham ɓuʔ, PR Cham ɓuʔ, Wr. Cham ɓuk, PMalayic *buʔuk, PMP *buhuk.

*dada 'chest', Acehnese dada, Rade ɗah da 'breast' -i (the first initial is irregular), Jarai (PL) tə̆da (Ouest), Jarai (Lee) təda, Chru har təda 'breast', N. Roglai dada, Tsat tha[11], Haroi cəthia, W. Cham taṭa; çaṭa, PR Cham taṭa, Wr. Cham tadā, Malay dada, PMP dahdah; MK: PKatuic (DT) *tath_. Note that it is only in Katuic apparently that the Chamic form has been borrowed, another small piece of evidence that there was extensive Chamic contact in the Katuic speaking area.

*dalam 'inside; in', Acehnese dalam; lam, Rade hlă̆m lam; elam, Jarai (PL) həlă̆m -i, də̆lă̆m, Jarai (Lee) dlă̆m, Chru dərlam; lam, dəlam, N. Roglai dalap, Tsat la:nʔ[42], Haroi lă̆m; lĭm, cəlĭam, W. Cham ṭală̆m, PR Cham ṭală̆m, Wr. Cham dalə̆m̀, Malay dalam, PMalayic *(d-)aləm, PMP *dalem; MK: PNB *lă̆m, Bahnar (AC) ləm.

*danaw 'lake', Acehnese danɔ, Rade enau, Jarai (PL) dənəu, Jarai (Lee) dənau, Chru dənau, N. Roglai danau -n, Haroi cəniau 'pond', PR Cham ṭanaw, Wr. Cham danaw, Malay danau 'mere, pool, lake', PMalayic *danaw, PMP *danaw.

*dara 'girl (c. teenage)', Acehnese dara, Rade era, Jarai (PL) dra, Jarai (Lee) dra, Chru dra 'teenage girl', N. Roglai dara, Haroi cəria, W. Cham ṭra, PR Cham ṭara, Wr. Cham darā, Malay dara, PMP *daʀa 'girl'.

*darah 'blood', Acehnese darah, Rade erah, Jarai (PL) dră̆h, Jarai (Lee) drah, Chru drah, N. Roglai darah, Tsat sia[55], Haroi cəriah, W. Cham ṭarah, PR Cham ṭară̆h, Wr. Cham daraḥ, Malay darah, PMalayic *darah, PMP *daʀaq.

*dha:n 'branch; bough', Acehnese dhɯən, Rade adhan, Jarai (PL) than; dhan (Ouest), Jarai (Lee) than; dhan, Chru tha:n, N. Roglai tha:t, Haroi than, W. Cham ṭhan, PR Cham ṭhan, Wr. Cham dhan, Malay dahan, PMalayic *dahan, PMP *daqan.

*dĭ 'at', Acehnese di, Rade ti -v (The vowel difference here is probably because as a function word it was subject to a different stress pattern.), Jarai (PL) tə- 'pour - marque le but pour suivi', Chru tə-, N. Roglai ta, W. Cham ṭi sa 'first', PR Cham ṭi, Wr. Cham dĭ, Malay di, PMalayic *di, PMP *di.

*dihlɔw 'formerly'; *hlɔw 'first (go); formerly; before', Acehnese dilɛə, Rade elău, Jarai (PL) hləu, Jarai (Lee) hləu; hlau, Chru ləhəu, N. Roglai dihləu, Tsat lau¹¹, Haroi hlău, W. Cham ṭalau, PR Cham ṭahlŏw, ană?, Wr. Cham dahluw, Malay dahulu; dulu, PMalayic *di hulu(?).

*dikit 'few; little', Acehnese dit -mv, Chru təki:?, N. Roglai tiki:?, Tsat ki?⁴², W. Cham taki?, PR Cham taki?, Wr. Cham takik, Wr. Cham (AC) dikik, Malay dikit, PMP *dikit.

*dilah 'tongue', Acehnese dilah, lidah, Rade elah, Jarai (PL) jəlăh; glăh (Hd.), Jarai (Lee) jəlah -i < *g-, -v, Chru dəlah, N. Roglai gilah < *g-, Tsat la⁵⁵, Haroi cəlḭah, W. Cham ṭalah, PR Cham ṭalah, Wr. Cham dalaḥ, Malay lidah; dilah 'wick, lamp', PMalayic *dilah, PMP *dilaq.

*dɔ:k 'sit; live; stay', Acehnese duə?, Rade dok, Jarai (PL) dŏ?, Jarai (Lee) dŏ?, Chru dɔ:? 'remain, sit', N. Roglai do:?, Tsat tho?⁴² 'sit', Haroi thu?, W. Cham ṭɔ?, PR Cham ṭɔ?, Wr. Cham dauk, Malay duduk, PMalayic *duduk, PMP *dukduk.

*dɔ:k 'still' cf. 'sit', Rade adok, Chru dɔ:?, W. Cham ṭɔ? kuŋ, PR Cham ṭɔ?, Wr. Cham dauk, Malay duduk.

*do:k 'at; in' cf. 'sit', Haroi thu?. This "prepositional" use has developed from the main verb use, apparently through a verb serialization process.

*dras 'fast; short time', Acehnese draih -v, Jarai (Lee) drah cf. ?ɛh drah 'dysentery', Chru drah, N. Roglai drah 'short time', Tsat sia⁵⁵, Haroi cərḭah 'fast (coming back)', W. Cham ṭrah 'short time; early', PR Cham ṭrah, Wr. Cham draḥ, Malay dĕras, PMP *deʀes 'fast, rapid'.

*drɛy 'reflexive (-self); body; living beings', Acehnese drɔə 'self; clf. for people', Rade drei in 'we (inclusive)', Jarai (PL) drəi 'corps'; ha 'même'; ñu 'lui même', Jarai (Lee) drəi, N. Roglai drəi clf. living things, Tsat pi¹¹ se¹¹ -v [(trəi -iv)], W. Cham ṭray 'living beings, animal, clf.', PR Cham ṭrɛy, Wr. Cham drĕi; min ?, Malay diri, PMP *diri.

*drɛy 'we (incl.)' cf. 'body, self', Rade drɛi, N. Roglai labu? drəi; labu? ñũ, W. Cham ṭray, PR Cham khŏl ṭrɛy 'we (excl.), Malay diri, Salako (Adelaar) diri? 'we (inclusive)'.

*dua 'two', Acehnese duwa, Rade dua, Jarai (PL) dua, Jarai (Lee) dua, Chru dua, N. Roglai dua, Tsat thua¹¹, Haroi thua, W. Cham ṭoa, PR Cham ṭwa, Wr. Cham dṵā, Malay dua, PMalayic *dua(?), PMP *duha.

*dua pluh 'twenty', Acehnese duwa plòh, Rade dua pluh, Chru dua pluh, N. Roglai dua pluh, W. Cham doa pluh, PR Cham ţwa plŭh, Malay dua puluh, PMP *duha ŋa puluq.

*dua-lapan 'eight', Acehnese lapan, Jarai (PL) dua rəpan -l (two taken away from ten), Jarai (Lee) cəpan -1, Chru təlpan, Tsat paːnʔ⁴², Tsat (Stübel) /băd/ i.e., /păt/, W. Cham tapăn, PR Cham ţalipăn, Wr. Cham dalipən, Malay dĕlapan.

*durɛy 'thorn', Acehnese durɔə, Rade erue (m), Jarai (PL) drɨi, Jarai (Lee) drəi; trəi, Chru druəi (m), N. Roglai daruəi (m), Haroi cərɨi (m), W. Cham ţaruai (m), PR Cham ţaroy (m), Wr. Cham daruai, Malay duri, PMP *duʀi.

*dəŋan 'with; and', Acehnese ŋʌn, Malay dĕngan, Inscriptional Cham dengan, PWMP *deŋen.

*dəpa 'armspan', Rade pa, Jarai (PL) tŏpa, Jarai (Lee) təpa, Chru təpa, N. Roglai tupa, Tsat pa¹¹, Haroi cəpa, W. Cham tapa, PR Cham tapa, Wr. Cham tapā, Malay dĕpa, PMP *depa.

*gatal 'itchy', Acehnese gatai, Rade kətăl, Jarai (PL) gaɨʔ (Est), Jarai (Lee) kətal, Chru kətal, N. Roglai katan, Haroi kətăl 'to itch', W. Cham kətăl, PR Cham kătăl, Wr. Cham katəl, Malay gatal, PMP *gatel.

*gigɛy 'tooth', Acehnese gigɔə, Rade egɛi, Jarai (PL) tŏgəi, Jarai (Lee) təgəi -i, Chru təgəi, N. Roglai digəi, Tsat (hu¹¹) khai¹¹, Haroi cəkhɨi, W. Cham ţakay, PR Cham tak̆ɛy, Wr. Cham tagɛ̆i, Wr. Cham (AC) tagɛ̆i , Malay gigi, PMalayic *gigi. This root is confined to languages in western Indonesia.

*gila 'foolish', Chru gəla 'foolish', N. Roglai gila pitoːʔ 'foolish', W. Cham ķla 'crazy; mad', PR Cham ķila, Wr. Cham gilā, Malay gila, cf. PMP *ila, *kila 'restless; wild'; MK: PSB (Efimov) *gəlaː.

*guluŋ 'to roll', Acehnese gulòŋ, Jarai (PL) kŏlŭŋ; (Hd.) bŏ-gŏluŋ, Jarai (Lee) gluŋ, Chru pə-rləŋ -v, N. Roglai pa-guluk; ta-guluk, Haroi tə-kəlŭŋ; kəlŭŋ, PR Cham ķalŭŋ, Wr. Cham galuŋ, Malay gulung, PMP *guluŋ. With prefixation: In Jarai, Chru and N. Roglai, the form seems to occur with a causative prefix, not to mention also with a ta- prefixed version in N. Roglai and Haroi.

*gətak 'sap; resin', Rade kətăk, Jarai (Lee) kətăk, Chru kətaʔ, N. Roglai kataʔ, Haroi kətăʔ, W. Cham kătăʔ, PR Cham kătăʔ, Wr. Cham katak, cf. Achnese gɯtah, Malay gĕtah 'sap; latex', PWMP *geteq 'tree sap'. The PWMP (Blust), the Acehnese, and the Malay all reflect an earlier final *-h (< PWMP *-q), while all the Chamic forms (except Acehnese) reflect an unexpected final *-k; the Acehnese is most likely borrowed from the Malay.

*habɔw 'ashes', Acehnese abɛə, Rade həbăŭ, Jarai (PL) həbau, Jarai (Lee) həbau -vl, Chru həbəu, N. Roglai habəu, Tsat phə¹¹, Haroi aphɨau, W. Cham pau, PR Cham hapɔ̆w; pɔ̆w, Wr. Cham habuw, Malay abu, PMalayic *habu, Malay abu, PMP *qabu; MK: PSB (Efimov) *buːh, PKatuic *[s/h]əʔbɑh, *həʔbɑh.

*hadaŋ 'charcoal', Acehnese araŋ -m, Rade hədăŋ, Jarai (PL) hədăŋ, Jarai (Lee) hədăŋ, Chru hədaŋ, N. Roglai hadak, Tsat thaːŋ^{42}, Haroi athĭaŋ, W. Cham ţăŋ, PR Cham haţăŋ; ţaŋ, Wr. Cham hadəŋ; dəŋ, PMP qajeŋ; MK: Bahnar (AC) araŋ.

*halɔw 'pestle', Acehnese alɛə, Rade hlău, Jarai (PL) hləu, Jarai (Lee) hləu, Chru hələu, N. Roglai haləu, Haroi hələu, W. Cham hlau, PR Cham hlŏw, Wr. Cham hluw, Malay alu, PMalayic *halu, PMP *lalu.

*hatay 'liver', Acehnese ate, Rade tie, Jarai (PL) hətai (Ouest), Jarai (Lee) hətai, Chru hətai, N. Roglai hatai, Tsat taːiʔ^{42}, Haroi atăi -i, W. Cham tai, PR Cham hatay, Wr. Cham hatai, Malay hati, PMalayic *hati, PMP *qatay, PAn *qaCay.

*haway 'rattan (generic?)', Acehnese awe, Rade həwie, Jarai (PL) həwei; huai (Hd.), Jarai (Lee) huai 'rod, rush, Chru həwai, N. Roglai hawai, Tsat vaːiʔ^{42}, Haroi həwăi, W. Cham haway -f, PR Cham hawĕy, Wr. Cham hawĕi, Iban uiʔ, PMalayic *(h)ui, PMP *quay, PAn *quay.

*hijaw 'green; blue', Acehnese ijo, W. Cham çau, PR Cham haçaw; çaw, Wr. Cham hajaw; caw, Malay hijau, PMalayic *hijaw.

*hitam 'black', Acehnese itam, Jarai (PL) hətam jŭʔ 'bleu-noir', Tsat taːnʔ^{42}, Tsat (Stübel) /dăn/ i.e., /tăn/, PR Cham hatăm; tăm, Wr. Cham hatəm, Malay hitam, PMalayic *hitəm, PMP *qitem.

*hlɔw see *dihlɔw

*hubɛy 'taro; tuber; yam', Acehnese ubi -f, Rade həbɛi, Jarai (PL) hăbəĭ, Jarai (Lee) həbəi, Chru həbəi, N. Roglai habuəi (m), Tsat phai^{11}, Haroi aphui (m), W. Cham ƀay, PR Cham haƀĕy; ƀĕy, Wr. Cham haƀĕi, Malay ubi, PMP *qubi. Also cf. 'a plant'.

*hudaːŋ 'shrimp; lobster', Acehnese udwəŋ, Rade hədaŋ, Jarai (PL) hădaːŋ, Jarai (Lee) hədaŋ, Chru hədaːŋ, N. Roglai hudaːk, Tsat la^{11} thaːŋ^{11}, Haroi athiaŋ, W. Cham nɨʔ ţaŋ, PR Cham haţăŋ; ţaŋ, Wr. Cham hudaŋ; daŋ, Malay hudang; udang, PMP *qudaŋ.

*hudɛy 'after; behind', Chru hədəi 'after', W. Cham haţay 'then, already', PR Cham haţĕy; ţĕy, Wr. Cham hadĕi, cf. Malay kemudian, PMalayic *hudiʔ, PMP *ma-udehi; MK: Bahnar (AC) hadoi.

*hudip 'live, alive', Acehnese udep, Rade hədĭp, Jarai (PL) hădip, Jarai (Lee) hədip, Chru hədiuʔ, N. Roglai hadiuʔ, Tsat thiuʔ^{42}, Haroi athĭp, W. Cham ţiuʔ, PR Cham haţĭwʔ; ţɨwʔ, Wr. Cham hadjəp, Malay hidup, PMalayic *hidup, PMP *qudip, *quDip, PAn *qudip.

*hujaːn 'rain', Acehnese ujɯən, Rade həjan, Jarai (PL) həjaːn, Jarai (Lee) həjan, Chru həjaːn, N. Roglai hujaːt, Tsat saːn^{11}, Haroi asɨan, W. Cham çan, PR Cham haçan; çan, Wr. Cham hajan; jan, Malay hujan, PMalayic *hujan, PMP *quzan, PAn *quzaN.

*hulat 'worm', Acehnese ulat, Rade hluăt (m) 'caterpillar', Jarai (PL) hlăt, Jarai (Lee) hlăt; hluăt (m), Chru həla?, N. Roglai hula?, W. Cham hlă? 'caterpillar', PR Cham hală?, Wr. Cham halak, Malay ulat, PMalayic *hulət, PMP *qulej, PAn *qulej.

*hulun 'slave; servant; I (polite)', Acehnese ulon, lon, ulŏŋ, ulonŋtuwan, lontuwan (sg./pl.) (polite); ulon, lon-, uloŋ-, ulontuwan-, lontuwan-; -lon, -loŋ, Rade hlŭn, Jarai (PL) hlun, Jarai (Lee) hlŭn, Chru həlun, N. Roglai hulut, Haroi həlŭn, W. Cham hlŭn hlă?; hulĭn ' I', PR Cham halŭn, Wr. Cham halun, Malay ulun, PMP *qulun.

*huma 'cultivated field', Acehnese umʌŋ, Rade həma 'swidden field', Jarai (PL) həmua (m), həma, Jarai (Lee) həma; həmua, Chru həma 'paddy field', N. Roglai humã 'wet field', Tsat ma³³, Haroi həmɨa, W. Cham hamɨ, PR Cham hamu -v, Wr. Cham hamū, Malay huma 'dry field', 'swidden', PMP *quma, PAn *qumah.

*hurɛy 'day; sun', Acehnese urɔə; mata urɔə, Rade hrue (m); yaŋ hrue, Jarai (PL) hrəi, Jarai (Lee) hrəi, Chru hərəi, N. Roglai hurəi; ia hurəi, Tsat zai³³, Haroi hərɨi (m), W. Cham hray; ea hray, PR Cham harɛ̆y, Wr. Cham harɛ̆i, Malay hari, PMalayic *hari, PMP *waʀi.

*hutaːn 'forest; jungle', Acehnese utɯən, PR Cham hatan; tan, Wr. Cham hatan; tan, Malay hutan; utan, PMalayic *hutan, PMP *qutan 'small, wild herbaceous plants; scrub-land, bush'. As Blust (p.c.), points out the meaning 'forest' is secondary, but shared in both Malay and Chamic.

*ɗɔh 'far, distant', Chru ɗɔh 'near', PR Cham haɗŏh 'éloigne'; ɗŏh 'loin, éloigné', Wr. Cham haɗauh; ɗauh, Malay jauh, PMalayic *jauh, PMP *zauq. The PC initial is quite unexpected.

*ita 'we (incl.)', Acehnese gɯ-ta-ñɔə, ta-ñɔə (sg./pl.) (neutral) < *gɯta < *kita plus ñɔə 'this'; ta-; -tɯ(h), Jarai (PL) ɓiŋ ta 'we (excl.)', Tsat ta¹¹-phi⁵⁵; ta³³ 'we (excl.)'; ta³³ za:k³³ 'we (excl.)', Haroi ata 'we (incl.)', PR Cham khŏ̆l ita, Wr. Cham itā, Malay kita, PMalayic *kita?, PMP *kita.

*jaːk 'invite', Rade jak, Jarai (Lee) jak, N. Roglai ja:?, Haroi sɨa?, PR Cham ça?, Wr. Cham jak, Malay ajak; MK: Bahnar (AC) jāk.

*jahit 'sew', Rade jhĭt, Jarai (PL) (cɛt), Jarai (Lee) sĭ?; sit, Chru si:?, N. Roglai chi:?, Tsat si?²⁴, Haroi sei?, W. Cham çhi?, PR Cham çhi?, Wr. Cham jhik, Malay jahit, PMalayic *jahit, PMP *zaqit; MK: Bahnar (AC) çit.

*jalaːn 'road; path', Acehnese -lɯən 'yard; space in front of the house'; jalan -v < Malay, Rade elan, Jarai (PL) jəlan, Jarai (Lee) jəlan, Chru jəla:n, N. Roglai jala:t, Tsat la:n¹¹, Haroi cəlɨan, W. Cham çalan, PR Cham çalan, Wr. Cham jalan, Malay jalan, PMalayic *jalan, PMP *zalan.

*jarum 'needle', Acehnese jarom, Rade erŭm, Jarai (PL) ʔjɜ̆rum; jrŭm (Pk), Jarai (Lee) jrŭm -ə, Chru jrum ?, N. Roglai jurup, Tsat sun[11], Haroi cərŭm, W. Cham çrum -v, PR Cham çarŭm, Wr. Cham jarum̃, Malay jarum, PMalayic *jarum, PMP *zaʀum; MK: PNB *jarŭm, PKatuic (DT) *jar_m.

*judɛy 'after, later; last', Rade edɛi, N. Roglai judəi, Haroi cəthĭi. Restricted to Highlands Chamic plus Haroi. [This form looks to be a variant of *hudɛy 'after; behind', but with an unexplained initial]

*jəhaːt 'bad; wicked', Acehnese jɯhɯɯt; jhɯɯt -v, Rade jhat, Jarai (PL) săt, Jarai (Lee) sat, Chru jəhaː?, Tsat saː?[24], Haroi săt, PR Cham çhaʔ, Wr. Cham jhak, Malay jahat, PMalayic *jah(aə)t, PMP *zaqat; *zaqet.

*kaju 'spear; lance', Rade kəju, Jarai (Lee) təju -i, Haroi kəsu, Malay kujur.

*kakay 'foot', Acehnese gaki -v (< Malay ?), Jarai (PL) təkai, Jarai (Lee) təkai, Chru təkai, N. Roglai takai, Tsat kaːiʔ[42], Haroi cəkăi, W. Cham takai, PR Cham takay, Wr. Cham takai, Wr. Cham (AC) kakai, takai, Malay kaki, PMalayic *kaki, PMP *qaqay. There is a problem with the relationship with the PMP form, already noted by Blust in his dictionary. Note that the *k-reflex of PMP *q- in both PC and PMalayic is unexpected: the expected reflex is /h-/, not /k-/. It could be the case that, despite the similarities, the two forms are simply unrelated, it could be that the PMalayo-Chamic represents an irregular sound, or it could be something else—perhaps the MK velar prefix, which sometimes marks body parts. In any case, the form is valuable for subgrouping; this unexpected form is shared in both branches of PMalayo-Chamic, that is, in both PMalayic and PC.

*kalaːŋ see *ralaːŋ

*kalɛy 'dig', Rade klɛi, Jarai (PL) klɜ̆i, Jarai (Lee) kləi, Chru kləi -i, N. Roglai kaləi, Haroi kəlŏi, PR Cham kalɜ̆y, Wr. Cham kalɜ̆i, Malay kali 'ditch'; gali -i, PMalayic *kali, PMP *kali.

*kamĭ; *kamɛy 'we (ex.)', Acehnese kamɔə; mɯ-; -mɯ(h), Rade həmɛi, Jarai (PL) ɓiŋ gɜ̆məi 'we (incl.)', ɓiŋ məi (Hd.) 'we (incl.)'; ɓiŋ həməi (S) 'we (incl.)', Jarai (Lee) gəməi -iv, N. Roglai labuʔ kamĭn -v?, Tsat mi[33], Haroi kəmei -v hăi -v (grammatical particle); kəmeh (-hăi); kəme hăi -v (grammatical particle), PR Cham kami, Wr. Cham kami, Malay kami, PMalayic *kami, PMP *kami.

*kanam -f 'dark', Jarai (PL) kənam, Jarai (Lee) kənam, Chru kənam 'very dark', N. Roglai kanap -f, Haroi kənăm, W. Cham kanăm 'dark of moon', PR Cham kanăm, Wr. Cham kanam̃, Malay kĕlam, PMP *kelem; MK: PKatuic *kənham 'dark'. [The Katuic form is apparently borrowed].

*kapaːl 'thick', Rade kəpal, Jarai (PL) kə̆pal, Jarai (Lee) kəpal, Chru kəpaːl, N. Roglai kapan, Tsat paːn[11] -t, Haroi kəpal, W. Cham kapal, PR Cham kapal, Wr. Cham kapal, PMP *kapal.

*kapit 'squeeze; pinch, press' maybe the same as *kapit 'close', Jarai (Lee) kəpĭʔ ?, Haroi cəpĕt -vf, PR Cham tapiʔ, Wr. Cham tapik, PMP *ka(m)pit 'hold together, squeeze', *ga(m)pit 'to hold together'.

*karəm 'to hatch', Acehnese karɔm, Rade krăm 'sitting hen', Jarai (PL) krŏm, Chru krəm 'sitting hen', N. Roglai karəp, W. Cham karŏm, PR Cham karăm, Wr. Cham karəm̀, Malay kə̆ram, ram.

*kawat, *kuat 'wire', Rade kəwăt, Jarai (Lee) kuăt, Chru kuat -f, Haroi kəwăt, W. Cham kawĕt -vf, Malay kawat, PWMP *kawad.

*kayɔw 'tree; wood', Acehnese kayɛə, Rade kəyău, Jarai (PL) kəyəu, kəyau, Jarai (Lee) kəyəu, Chru kəyəu, N. Roglai kayəu, Tsat (phun[33]) zau[33], Haroi kəyău -vr, W. Cham kayau, PR Cham kayŏw, Wr. Cham kayuw, Malay kayu 'stick; wood', PMalayic *kayuʔ 'stick, wood', PMP *kahiw.

*klɔw 'three', Acehnese lhɛə, Rade tlău, Jarai (PL) kləu, Jarai (Lee) kləu, Chru kləu, N. Roglai tləu, Tsat kiu[33], Haroi tlău, W. Cham klau, PR Cham klŏw, PMalayic *təlu, PMP *telu.

*klu 'testicles (of animal)', Jarai (PL) tə̆lu, Chru klu 'testicles', PR Cham klu, Malay tə̆lur 'egg', PMalayic *təlur 'egg', PMP *qateluʀ, *qiteluʀ 'egg', PAn *qiCeluʀ 'egg'.

*kɔw 'I (familiar)', Acehnese kɛə; ku-; -ku(h), Rade kău, Jarai (PL) kəu 'de inférieur à son chef direct', Jarai (Lee) kəu, Chru kəu, kəmi, N. Roglai kəu, Tsat kau[33], Haroi kău, W. Cham kau, PR Cham kŏw, Malay aku, PMalayic *aku, PMP *aku.

*kra 'monkey', Rade kra, Jarai (PL) kra, Jarai (Lee) kra, Chru kra, N. Roglai kra, Tsat kia[33], Haroi kra, W. Cham kra, PR Cham kra, Wr. Cham krā, Malay kə̆ra, PWMP (Blust, p.c.) *keraq 'the chattering of monkeys'. The loss of final -q is irregular, but shared with both Malay and Chamic.

*kukɔw 'claw; fingernail', Acehnese gukɛə, Rade kəkău, Jarai (Lee) cəkəu (initial reflects neither *k- nor *t-), Jarai (PL) təkəu < *t-, Chru kərkəu, N. Roglai kukəu, Haroi kəkău, W. Cham kakau, PR Cham kakŏw, PR Cham cəkăw (initial reflects neither *k- nor *t-), Wr. Cham kakuw, Wr. Cham (AC) kukau, Malay kuku, PMP *kuhkuh. Note the sporadic nature of the changes of the presyllable-initial *k-. One contributing factor is interaction with the *k- body part prefix found throughout MK (cf. Smith 1975).

*kulit 'skin', Acehnese kulet, Rade klĭt, Jarai (PL) kə̆lit, Jarai (Lee) klit, Chru kəliːʔ, N. Roglai kuliːʔ, Tsat liʔ[24] -i; loʔ[24] -i, Haroi kəleiʔ, W. Cham kliʔ, PR Cham kaliʔ, Wr. Cham kalik, Malay kulit, PMalayic *kulit, PMP *kulit 'skin; bark'.

*kuñit 'yellow; tumeric', Acehnese kuñɛt 'tumeric', Rade kəñĩʔ, Jarai (PL) kəñĩʔ, Jarai (Lee) kəñiʔ, Chru kəñĩ:ʔ, N. Roglai kuñĩ:ʔ 'yellow-orange', Tsat ñiʔ[24]; ŋi[55], Haroi kəñeiʔ, W. Cham kañiʔ 'orange, safron', PR Cham kañiʔ, Wr. Cham kañik, Malay kunyit 'tumeric', PMalayic *kunit 'yellow, tumeric', PMP *kunij 'tumeric'.

*kura 'tortoise; turtle', Rade krua (m) 'turtle', Jarai (PL) krŏa (Ouest), Jarai (Lee) krua (m), Chru kra, N. Roglai kura, Haroi kroa (m), PR Cham kara, Wr. Cham karā, Malay kura.

*kura:ŋ 'less; insufficient', W. Cham kuraŋ, Acehnese kurɯəŋ, Malay kurang.

*kutɔw 'head louse', Acehnese gutɛə, Rade kətău, Jarai (PL) kŏtəu, Jarai (Lee) kətəu, Chru kətəu, N. Roglai kutəu, Haroi kətău, W. Cham katau, PR Cham katŏw, Wr. Cham katuw, Malay kutu, PMalayic *kutu, PMP *kutu.

*kə- 'to, for (goal), at', Acehnese kɯ-, Rade kə-, Jarai (PL) kə- 'pour - marque le motif', Jarai (Lee) [kə], Chru kə- 'to, concerning', N. Roglai hia ga; ga, Haroi kə-, PR Cham ka, Wr. Cham kā, Malay kĕ-, kepada, PMP *ki- 'to, for (goal)'.

*kəntut 'fart; flatus ventrus', Acehnese toh gɯntət -v, Chru kətu:ʔ, Haroi kətouʔ; tout, Malay kĕntut, PWMP *ka-qetut 'the noise of flatuence', PMP *qe(n)tut. If the Malay and the PC were derived directly from the PMP *qetut, they would have /h-/ as their initial; the actually occurring /k-/ reflects the *ka- prefix, with the nasal an expected secondary development.

*laʔur 'coconut palm', Acehnese bɔh u, Chru ləʔu, N. Roglai laʔu, Haroi ləʔu, W. Cham laʔu, PR Cham liu, Wr. Cham liū, Malay nyor, PMalayic *niur, PMP *niuR, PAn niyuR.

*laba:t 'walk, go', Rade ebat, Jarai (PL) rəbat, N. Roglai luba:ʔ, Tsat pha:ʔ[42], W. Cham k̟apaʔ ʔ-i, PR Cham lipaʔ; lapaʔ, Wr. Cham libak; labak, PMP *lampaqʔ.

*labuh 'fall down; drop anchor', Rade ebuh, Jarai (PL) rŏbŭh, Jarai (Lee) rəbuh, Chru ləbuh, N. Roglai labuh, Tsat phu[55], Haroi ləphŭh, W. Cham lapuh, PR Cham lipuh; lapuh, Wr. Cham libuḥ, Malay labuh 'drop anchor', PMalayic *labuh, PMP *labuq.

*lakɛy 'male; person', Acehnese lakɔə, Rade ekɛi, Jarai (PL) rŏkəi, Jarai (Lee) rəkəi -i; cəkəi -i, Chru ləkəi 'male', N. Roglai lakəi, Tsat kai[33], Haroi ləkŏi, W. Cham lakay, PR Cham likĕy; lakĕy, Wr. Cham lakĕi, Malay lak-ilaki, PMalayic *laki (-laki), PMP *laki.

*laŋa -v 'sesame', Rade eŋu, Jarai (PL) rŏŋa; bŏŋa (Hd.), Jarai (Lee) rəŋa, N. Roglai laŋā, Haroi ləŋa; ləŋău -v, W. Cham laŋɨ, PR Cham liŋɨ; laŋɨ, Wr. Cham liŋɨ; laŋɨ, PMP *leŋa; MK: PSB (Efimov) *ləŋa:.

*lanah 'pus', Jarai (PL) rŏnăh, Jarai (Lee) rənah, N. Roglai lanãh, Tsat lə[11] na[55], Malay nanah, PMP *nanaq.

*laŋit 'sky', Acehnese laŋɛt, Rade eɲit, Jarai (PL) ŋit (Pk), Chru təsi:ʔ ləŋi:ʔ, N. Roglai laŋĭ:ʔ, Tsat ŋiʔ²⁴, Haroi ləŋiʔ, W. Cham laŋiʔ, PR Cham liŋiʔ; laŋiʔ, Wr. Cham liŋik; laŋik, Malay langit, PMalayic *laŋit, PMP *laŋit.

*lapa 'hungry', Rade epa, Jarai (PL) rəpa, Jarai (Lee) rəpa, Chru ləpa, N. Roglai lapa, Tsat pa³³, Haroi ləpa, W. Cham lapa, PR Cham lipa; lapa, Wr. Cham lipa; lapā, Malay lapar, PMP *lapaʀ.

*lasɛy 'rice (cooked)', Rade esɛi, Jarai (PL) asəi -i, Jarai (Lee) ʔasəi -i, Chru ləsəi, Haroi ləsŏi, W. Cham lasăy, PR Cham lithĕy, Wr. Cham lisĕy, Malay nasi.

*layɔw 'withered; faded', Acehnese layɛə 'faded', Chru ləyəu, W. Cham layau, PR Cham liyɔ̆w, layɔ̆w, Wr. Cham layuw; liyuw, Malay layu 'faded; withered', PMalayic *layu, PWMP *laqeyu.

*lima 'five', Acehnese limʌŋ, Rade ema, Jarai (PL) rəma, Jarai (Lee) rəma, Chru ləma, N. Roglai lumă, Tsat ma³³, Haroi ləmĭa, W. Cham lamɨ, PR Cham limɨ; lamɨ, Wr. Cham limɨ; lamɨ, Malay lima, PMalayic *lima, PMP *lima.

*limpa:n 'centipede', Acehnese limpɯən, Rade epan, Jarai (PL) rə̆pan, Jarai (Lee) rəpan, Chru ləpa:n, N. Roglai lupa:t, Tsat a¹¹ pa:n¹¹, Haroi ləpan, W. Cham lapan, PR Cham lipan; lapan, Wr. Cham lipan; lapan, Malay (ha)lipan, PMP *qalu-hipan, PAn *qalu-Sipan.

*lintah -i 'water leech', Acehnese lintah, Rade kətah -i, Jarai (PL) rə̆tăh, Jarai (Lee) rətah, Chru lətah, N. Roglai ritah -i, Haroi lətăh, W. Cham latah, PR Cham lităh; latăh, Wr. Cham lataḥ, Malay lintah 'horse leech', PMP *qali-metaq, PAn *qali-meCaq; MK: Bahnar (AC) lətah, rətah.

*lipih 'thin (material)', Acehnese lipeh, Rade epih, Jarai (Lee) rəpih, Chru ləpih, N. Roglai lupih, Tsat pi⁵⁵, Haroi ləpeh, W. Cham lapih, PR Cham lipĭh; lapĭh, Wr. Cham lipiḥ; lapiḥ, Malay nipis, PMalayic *nipis, *m/ipis, PMP *nipis.

*liya 'ginger', Acehnese haliya, Rade eya, Jarai (PL) rə̆ya, rə̆ia, Jarai (Lee) rəya, Chru lia (note: the same as lya), N. Roglai riya -i, Tsat za³³, Haroi ləyɨa, PR Cham liyā; laya; ḳanroŋ-riya -i, Wr. Cham liyā; layā; ganrauŋ riyā, Malay halia, PMP *laqia; MK: Bahnar (AC) liă.

*luba:ŋ 'hole; pit', Acehnese kubaŋ -i 'wallowing hole', Chru ləba:ŋ, N. Roglai luba:k, W. Cham lapaŋ, PR Cham lipaŋ; lapaŋ, Wr. Cham libaŋ; labaŋ, Malay lubang.

*luka 'wound, scar', Acehnese luka, Rade eka, Jarai (Lee) rəka, Chru ləka 'bite, sore', Haroi ləka, W. Cham laka, PR Cham lika-likĕh, Wr. Cham likā, Malay luka, PMP *luka.

*lumpɛy 'to dream', Acehnese lumpɔə, Rade epɛi, Jarai (PL) rəpəi, Jarai (Lee) rəpəi, Chru ləpəi, N. Roglai lupəi, Tsat pai³³, Haroi ləpŏi, W. Cham lapay, PR Cham lipĕy; lapĕy, Wr. Cham lipĕi; lapĕi, Malay mimpi, PMalayic *m-impi, PMP *h-in-ipi; *hipi; *h-um-ipi.

*ləbɛh 'more; surplus', Acehnese lɯbɛh -v, Rade ebɛh dlai, Jarai (Lee) rəbĕh, N. Roglai lubeh, Haroi ləphɪh, PR Cham lipɛh; lapĕh, Wr. Cham libaih; labaih, Malay lĕbih, PMalayic *lebih, PMP *lebiq.

*ləma? 'fat, grease, oil', Acehnese lɯma?, Rade emă?, Jarai (PL) rĕmă?, Jarai (Lee) rəma? -1, Chru ləma?, N. Roglai lumă?, Tsat ma?[42], Haroi ləmǐa?, W. Cham laməʔ, PR Cham limǐ?; lamǐ?, Wr. Cham lamɨk; limɨk, Malay lĕmak, PMalayic *ləmək, PMP *lemak; MK: PMnong *ramăq, *ramaq, Bahnar (AC) rəmā; ləmā.

*lən 'earth', Acehnese lʌn 'silt, Rade lăn, Jarai (PL) lŏn, Jarai (Lee) lŏn, Chru lən, N. Roglai lət, Haroi lŏn 'ground, floor; country', PR Cham lăn, Wr. Cham lən, PMP *talun 'fallow land, secondary forest', PAn *Calun.

*ləsuŋ -i 'mortar', Acehnese lɯsoŋ, Rade esŭŋ, Jarai (PL) rəsŭŋ, Jarai (Lee) rəsŭŋ, Chru ləsuŋ, N. Roglai risuk -i, Haroi ləsoŋ, W. Cham lasuŋ, PR Cham lithŭŋ; rathŭŋ -i; lathŭŋ, Wr. Cham lisuŋ; rasuŋ; lathuŋ, Malay lĕsung, PMalayic *ləsuŋ, PMP *lesuŋ.

*ma-alas 'lazy', Acehnese malaih, Rade alah, Jarai (Lee) ?alah, Chru alah, N. Roglai alah, Haroi alăh, W. Cham lah, PR Cham alah mɪtăh, Wr. Cham alah mɪtah, Malay malas, PMalayic (Blust) *males.

*ma-bɔh 'to lay egg', Jarai (PL) mĕboh, Jarai (Lee) məbɔh, Chru bɔh, Haroi pəphŭh, PR Cham mɪpɔh, Wr. Cham mɪbuah. Related to 'fruit; egg; small round object' below.

*ma?in 'play', Acehnese mɯ?ɛn, Chru mə?in 'fun', N. Roglai ma?in, Tsat ?in[33], Haroi mə?en, W. Cham ma?ɪn, PR Cham mɪin, Wr. Cham mɨin, Malay main, PMP *ayam.

*mabah see *babah

*mabu? 'drunk, intoxicated', Acehnese mabo?, Chru məbu?, N. Roglai babu?, W. Cham mapŭ?, Malay mabuk, PMP *ma-buhek, PAn *(ma-)buSek.

*mahăw 'thirst; desire', Rade məhau, Jarai (PL) mĕhaŭ -f, Jarai (Lee) məhau, Chru məhău, N. Roglai mahău, Tsat hau?[24] -t, Haroi məhău, W. Cham mahu 'desire; thirst', PR Cham mɪhu, Wr. Cham mɪhū, Malay mahu 'want'.

*mahirah 'red', Acehnese mirah, Rade hrah, Jarai (PL) mriăh (Est), Jarai (Lee) mriah -m, Chru məriah, N. Roglai mariah, Tsat za[55], Haroi məreah, W. Cham mareah, PR Cham mɪryăh, Wr. Cham mɪrɪah, Malay mérah, PMalayic *(ma-)irah, PMP *ma-qiʀaq.

*malam 'night; evening', Acehnese malam 'night', Rade mlam -1, Jarai (PL) mlăm, Jarai (Lee) mlăm, Chru məlam, N. Roglai malap, Haroi məlam -1, W. Cham malăm, PR Cham mɪlăm, Wr. Cham mɪlɑm, Malay malam 'night', PMalayic *ma-ləm, PWMP (Blust) *m-alem 'night', PMP *halem 'night, dark'.

*malɔw 'blush; ashamed; shy', Acehnese malɛə, Jarai (PL) mə̆ləu, Jarai (Lee) mləu, Chru mələu alah, N. Roglai maləu, Haroi mlă̆u, W. Cham malau, PR Cham mɨlɔ̆w, Wr. Cham mɨluw, Malay malu, PMalayic *malu.

*mamah 'chew', Acehnese mamʌh, Rade məmah, Jarai (PL) mă̆h, Jarai (Lee) məmah, Chru bəmah ?*mu-, N. Roglai mumă̆h, Tsat ma⁵⁵, Haroi məmă̆h, W. Cham mamɨh, PR Cham mɨmɨh, Wr. Cham mɨmɨh, Malay mamaḥ, PMalayic *mamah, PMP *mamaq.

*mamih 'sweet', Acehnese mamɛh, Rade məmih, Jarai (PL) mih, Jarai (Lee) məmih, N. Roglai mumĭh, Tsat mi⁵⁵, Haroi məmĭh, PR Cham mɨmĭh 'aigrelet', Wr. Cham mɨmɨḥ 'aigrelet', PMP *mamis.

*mañam -l 'weave; twill', Acehnese mañum, Rade məñam, Jarai (PL) mə̆ñă̆m, Chru məña:m -l 'knit', N. Roglai mañă̆m, Haroi məñɨam, W. Cham mañɨm, PR Cham mɨñim, Wr. Cham mɨñiṁ, PMP *añem, *ma-añam 'plait, weave (mats, baskets)'.

*manɛy 'bathe', Acehnese manəə, Rade mənɛi, Jarai (PL) mə̆nəi, Jarai (Lee) mənəi, Chru mənəi, N. Roglai manî -v, Haroi mnŏi < *-əi, W. Cham manay, PR Cham mɨnə̆y, Wr. Cham mɨnə̆y, Malay mandi.

*manuʔ 'chicken; fowl', Acehnese manɔʔ, Rade mənŭʔ, Jarai (PL) mənŭʔ, Jarai (Lee) mənŭʔ, Chru mənŭʔ, N. Roglai manŭʔ, Tsat nuʔ²⁴, Haroi mənŭʔ, W. Cham manŭʔ, PR Cham mɨnŭʔ, Wr. Cham mɨnuk, Malay manuk 'bird', PMalayic *manuk 'chicken', PMP *manuk.

*maray 'come', Jarai (PL) rai, Chru mərai, N. Roglai mă̆i -r-, Tsat za:iʔ⁴², Haroi ră̆i -m, W. Cham mai -r-, PR Cham mɨray, mai, Wr. Cham mɨrai; mai, Malay mari-lah 'come here', PMP *um-aʀi; *maʀi.

*masam 'sour; vinegar', Acehnese masam, Rade ea məsă̆m, Jarai (PL) məsă̆m, Jarai (Lee) məsă̆m, Chru ia məsam, N. Roglai ia masap, Tsat sa:n²⁴², Haroi məsă̆m, W. Cham masă̆m, PR Cham mɨthă̆m, Wr. Cham mɨthəṁ, Malay masam, PMalayic *asəm, PMP *ma-esem. The word 'vinegar' is simply the word 'sour' plus the word for water.

*masin 'salted; salty', Acehnese masen, Rade məsĭn, Jarai (PL) məsĭn (Hd.), Jarai (Lee) məsin, Chru məsin in 'pickled fish', N. Roglai masit (?), Tsat sen²⁴² -vft, Haroi məsen, W. Cham masĭn in 'fish juice', PR Cham mɨthĭn, Wr. Cham mɨsin, Malay masin, PMP *ma-qasin.

*masuh 'fight (war)', Chru məsuh, N. Roglai masuh, Haroi phia-məsoh -l 'tease each other', W. Cham masruh -r, PR Cham mɨthuh, Wr. Cham mɨsuḥ, Malay musuh 'enemy'.

*mata 'eye', Acehnese mata, Jarai (PL) məta, Jarai (Lee) məta, Chru məta, N. Roglai mata, Tsat tiŋ³³ ta³³, Haroi məta, W. Cham mata, PR Cham mɨta, Wr. Cham mɨtā, Malay mata, PMalayic *mata, PMP *mata; MK: PNB *mă̆t, PMnong *mă̆t, PSB (Efimov) *mat, PKatuic *mat. The PMP and the MK sets of forms date back to their respective proto-languages.

*matay 'die', Acehnese mate, Chru mətai, N. Roglai matai, Tsat taːiʔ[42], Haroi pəthia ?, W. Cham matai, PR Cham mitay, Wr. Cham mitai, Malay mati, PMalayic *mati, PMP *ma-atay.

*matɔw 'son-in-law'; *patɔw 'child-in-law', Rade mətău, Jarai (Lee) pətəu < *p-, Chru mərtəu, N. Roglai matəu, Haroi mətău, W. Cham matau 'son/ daughter-in-law', PR Cham mitŏw, Wr. Cham mituw, Malay měnantu, PMalayic *b-in-antu 'child-in-law'. Confined to languages in western Indonesia (Blust, p.c.).

*miaw 'cat', Acehnese miə, Rade mieo, Chru miau, N. Roglai miău, Tsat miau[33], Haroi meau, W. Cham maŋiau, PR Cham miyaw -v, Wr. Cham miyaw -v; MK: PMnong *miâw, PSB (Efimov) *mɛːw. The imitative nature of this word requires no further comment.

*miñaːk 'oil', Acehnese miñɯ?, N. Roglai mañăː? h?, Tsat ña?[24], W. Cham mañi?, PR Cham miñi?, Wr. Cham miñik, Malay minyak, PMP *meñak 'fat, grease, oil'. The -i- in Malayo-Chamic is another shared irregularity in Malayo-Chamic.

*minum; *minam 'to drink', Acehnese minom, Rade mənăm, Jarai (PL) mənŭm; ñŭm (Hd.), Jarai (Lee) məñum, Chru məñum, Haroi məñɨam, W. Cham mañum, PR Cham miñŭm, Wr. Cham miñuɯm, Malay minum, PMalayic *inum, PMP *um-inum.

*muburɛy 'yesterday', Acehnese barɔə, Rade məbrue (m), Jarai (Lee) brəi, Chru kəbruəi (m), W. Cham maprɔi (m), Malay bahari 'the good old days'.

*muda 'young; unripe; tender', Acehnese muda, Rade məda in 'small intestine', Jarai (PL) məda, Jarai (Lee) məda, Chru məda, N. Roglai mida in 'small intestine', Tsat tha[11], Haroi məthia, W. Cham maṭa, PR Cham miṭa, Wr. Cham midā, Malay muda, PMP *uda, *m-uda.

*mə- 'verb prefix', Acehnese mɯ-/mu-, Jarai mə-, Wr. Cham mə-, Malay měng-, PMalayic *maŋ-, PWMP *maŋ-.

*məntah 'raw; green; unripe', Acehnese mɯntah, Rade mətah, Jarai (PL) mŏtah, Jarai (Lee) mətah, Chru mətăh -n 'unripe', N. Roglai matăh -n; matah, Tsat ta[55], Haroi mətăh, W. Cham maṭa -m, PR Cham mităh, Wr. Cham mitah, Malay měntah, PMP *mataq; *mentaq; *a(n)taq.

*ñamuk 'mosquito', Acehnese jamɔ?; ñamɔ?, Chru jəmũ?, N. Roglai jamõ? -v, W. Cham çamŏ?; çamŭ?, PR Cham çamŏ? -v, Wr. Cham jamauk, Malay nyamuk, PMalayic *ñamuk, PMP *nyamuk; *lamak; *lamuk. In large part the reflexes of initial *ñ- have blended with those of *j-.

*ñawa 'breath, soul, air', Rade ewa < *j-, Jarai (Lee) jəwa, Chru jəwa, N. Roglai lawa, Haroi cəwia 'breath, blow' < *j-; məcəwia, W. Cham (yawa), W. Cham (Headley) /ñawà/ 'soul', PR Cham yawa 'blow out', Wr. Cham yawā,

Malay jiwa, nyawa, PMalayic *ñawa, PMP *jawa 'air, soul, breath', (*ma)-nihawa.

*ñu 'he, she; they', Rade ñu, Jarai (PL) ñu, Jarai (Lee) ñu 'he', Chru ñũ, N. Roglai ñũ, Tsat nau[33] -vi, Haroi ñau -v, W. Cham ñu, PR Cham ñu, Wr. Cham ŋū; MK: Bahnar (AC) ñi. [This form has cognates throughout AN but the vowel correspondences are somewhat irregular]

*ñus 'blow nose; sniffle; nasal mucus', Rade añih, Jarai (PL) ñə̆hŭh ?, Jarai (Lee) ñuih, Chru ñi:h adung, N. Roglai ñũh, Tsat ñau[55] -v, W. Cham ñuh, PR Cham ñuh; hañuh, Wr. Cham ñuḥ; hañuh, Malay inguṣ, PMP *hiŋus 'nasal mucus'.

*nam 'six', Acehnese nam, Rade nă̆m, Jarai (PL) nă̆m, Jarai (Lee) nă̆m, Chru nam, N. Roglai nă̆m, Tsat na:n?[33], Haroi nă̆m, W. Cham nă̆m, PR Cham nă̆m, Wr. Cham nəm̀, Malay ĕnam, PMalayic *ənəm, PMP *enem.

*naw 'go; walk', Rade nau, Jarai (PL) nau, Jarai (Lee) nau, Chru nau, N. Roglai nău, Tsat na:u?[33/42], Haroi nau, W. Cham nau, PR Cham naw, Wr. Cham nau, PMP *panaw 'go; walk'.

*pa:t 'four', Acehnese pɯət, Rade pă̆?, Jarai (PL) pă̆?, Jarai (Lee) pă̆?, Chru pa:?, N. Roglai pa:?, Tsat pa?[24], Haroi pa?, W. Cham pa?, PR Cham pa?, Wr. Cham pak, Malay ĕmpat, PMalayic *əmpat, PMP *epat; MK: PMnong *puân. [The MK forms are not directly related to the PC forms]

*padam 'extinguish', N. Roglai padap, Tsat tha:n?[42], W. Cham paṭă̆m, PR Cham paṭam, Wr. Cham padəm̀, Malay padam, PMP *padem; MK: PNB *pă̆t.

*paday 'rice, paddy', Acehnese pade, Rade mədie, Jarai (PL) pədai, Jarai (Lee) pədai, Chru pədai, N. Roglai padai, Tsat tha:i?[42], Haroi pəthɨai, W. Cham paṭai, PR Cham paṭay, Wr. Cham padai, Malay padi.

*pagar 'fence', Acehnese pagɯə < *-r, Jarai (PL) pə̆ga, Jarai (Lee) pəga, Chru pəga, N. Roglai paga, Tsat kai[33], Haroi pəkhɨa, W. Cham paḳa, PR Cham paḳa, Wr. Cham pagā, Malay pagar, PMP *pager; MK: PMnong *pêr. Note that PMP has a schwa in the second syllable.

*pagi 'tomorrow', Rade məgi -v, Jarai (Lee) pəgi, Chru pəgi, N. Roglai pagi, Haroi pəkhɩ, W. Cham paḳe -v, PR Cham paḳe -v, Wr. Cham pagē, Malay pagi 'tomorrow'. This form does not look to be of any great antiquity.

*pala:t -1 'palm; sole', Acehnese palɯət, Rade plă̆? -1, Jarai (Lee) plă̆? -1, Chru pla:?, N. Roglai pala:?, Tsat pie?[24] -v, Haroi pəla?, W. Cham pla?, PR Cham pala?, Wr. Cham palak, PMP *palaj.

*palɛy 'village', Jarai (PL) plə̆ĭ, Jarai (Lee) pləi, Chru pləi -v, N. Roglai pləi, Tsat piai[33], Haroi pəlŏi, W. Cham play 'region', PR Cham palĕy, Wr. Cham palĕi, Malay balai, PMP *balay 'public building, community house'; MK: PNB *pală̆y, Bahnar (AC) pəley. [If the Malay and PMP are to be connected to the PC, two problems needed to be addressed: the initial is unexpectedly voice-less in PC and the vowel seems to reflect an earlier *-i, not *-ay. Borrowing is most likely involved, probably into Chamic and into MK]

*panah 'shoot (bow); a bow', Acehnese panah 'arrow' (Durie notes variation in nasalization), Rade mənah, Jarai (PL) pănăh, Jarai (Lee) pənah, Chru pənah, N. Roglai panăh, Tsat na⁵⁵, Haroi pənăh, W. Cham panɨh, PR Cham panɨh, Wr. Cham panɨḥ, Malay panah 'bow', PMalayic *panah, PMP *panaq, PAn *panaq 'shoot an arrow; the flight of an arrow' ; MK: PNB *pĕñ, PMnong *păn, PSB (Efimov) *paɲ, PKatuic *ɣəpeɲ. The AN forms reconstruct to PAn. Although the MK forms look related, they are not obviously borrowings as they have good etymologies in the MK languages.

*papaːn 'board; plank', Acehnese papɯən, Chru pəpaːn, Tsat paːn¹¹, W. Cham papan; panah, PR Cham papan 'table', Wr. Cham paban, Malay papan, PMP *papan.

*patah 'vomit', Acehnese muntah -i, Jarai (PL) pătah, Jarai (Lee) pətah, Tsat ta⁵⁵, Haroi mətăh -i, Malay muntah, PMalayic *m/u(n)tah, PMP *pa-utaq (with a causative prefix).

*pha 'thigh', Acehnese pha, Rade pha, Jarai (PL) pha, Jarai (Lee) pha, Chru pha, N. Roglai pha, Tsat pha³³, Haroi pha, W. Cham pha, PR Cham pha, Wr. Cham phā, Malay paha, PMP *paqa.

*phaːt 'chisel, to plane', Acehnese phɯət, Jarai (PL) phă? (Pk), Jarai (Lee) phă?, Chru phaː?, Tsat phaː?²⁴, W. Cham pha?, PR Cham pha?, Wr. Cham phak, Malay pahat, PMP *paqet; MK: PSB (Efimov) *phaːt, *phaː?. The PSB is apparently borrowed. With *-ən- instrumental infix: 'chisel; plane'*p-ən-haːt, Acehnese pɯnɯhɯət, Rade mənhat, Chru pəhnaː? 'a plane', N. Roglai pahnă:?.

*phit 'bitter; bile', Acehnese phet, Rade phĭ?, Jarai (PL) phĭ?, Jarai (Lee) phĭ?, Chru phiː?, N. Roglai phi:?, Tsat phi?²⁴, Haroi phei?, W. Cham phi?, PR Cham phi?, Wr. Cham phik, Malay pahit, PMP *paqit.

*phun 'trunk; log; stem; plant', Acehnese phon, Rade phŭn 'stump, stubble', Jarai (PL) phŭn, Jarai (Lee) phun -1, Chru phun 'stem', N. Roglai phut 'stump', Tsat phun³³, Haroi phon, W. Cham phŭn, PR Cham phŭn, Wr. Cham phun, Malay pohon.

*pinaːŋ 'betel (areca palm); betel-nut', Acehnese pinɯŋ, Rade mənaŋ, Jarai (PL) pănaŋ, Jarai (Lee) pənaŋ, Chru pənaːŋ, N. Roglai pinăŋ, Tsat naːŋ³³, Haroi pənaŋ, W. Cham paniŋ, PR Cham paniŋ, Wr. Cham paniŋ, Malay pinang, late WMP *pinaŋ ?; MK: PSB (Efimov) *pinaːŋ; MK: PKatuic (DT) *panoâng, PKatuic *pɛnhaːn. Ultimately, despite its distribution in WMP, this might be bor-rowed.

*pluh 'ten', Acehnese siploh, Rade pluh, Jarai (PL) pluh, Jarai (Lee) pluh, Chru spluh, N. Roglai sa pluh, Tsat piu⁵⁵, Haroi aploh, W. Cham ha pluh,

PR Cham plŭh, Wr. Cham pluḥ, Malay sĕ-puluh, PMalayic *puluh, PMP *sa-ŋa-puluq; *sa-puluq.

*pɔ 'master; lord', Acehnese pɔ, Rade po wide range of meanings and uses, Jarai (PL) po, Jarai (Lee) po 'self', Chru po -v, N. Roglai po, Haroi po -v, W. Cham pɔ 'title', PR Cham po -v, Wr. Cham pō, Malay empu 'master', PMP *empu 'grandparent'.

*pulaw 'island', Acehnese pulɔ, Rade plau ea, Chru buːt pəlaːu -l, PR Cham palaw, Wr. Cham palau, Malay pulau.

*pusat 'navel; center', Acehnese pusat, Rade məsăt, Jarai (PL) phŭn săt, Chru pəsaʔ, N. Roglai pisaʔ, Haroi pəsăʔ, W. Cham pasăʔ, PR Cham pathă̆ʔ, Wr. Cham bathak, Malay pusat, PMP *pusej.

*putih 'white', Acehnese puteh, Tsat ti⁵⁵, Haroi pəteh 'light, fair', W. Cham patih, PR Cham patĭh, Wr. Cham patiḥ, Malay putih, PMalayic *putih, PMP *putiq.

*pə- 'CAUSATIVE', Rade m-, Jarai (PL) pə-, Jarai (Lee) pə-, Chru pə-; per-, N. Roglai pa-, Haroi pə-, W. Cham pa-, PR Cham pa-, Paiwan pa-, PAn *pa-; MK: Bahnar (AC) bə-. This prefix is reconstructable within AN to PAn and within MK most likely to PMK.

*pə-blɛy (*pə- 'causative') 'sell', Acehnese publɔə, Rade blɛi 'buy', Jarai (Lee) pəbləi; bəbləi, Chru pəbləi, N. Roglai pabləi, Tsat li⁵⁵ -ivt, Haroi pəpli̇̆ -m, W. Cham paplay, PR Cham papli̇̆y, Wr. Cham pabli̇̆y, Malay bĕli 'buy', PMP *beli.

*ra 'person', N. Roglai ra- in ʀadglai, PR Cham ra, Wr. Cham rā. [A shortened form of PC *uraŋ]

*ra-glay (*ra- 'person' + *glay 'forest, jungle') 'Roglai', Rade rəglai -mv, N. Roglai manŭih radlai 'Montagnard', PR Cham ʀaḵlay, Wr. Cham raglai.

*rabuh 'collapse, destroy', Rade ebuh, Malay roboh, PMP *ʀebaq.

*rabuŋ 'bamboo shoot', Rade ebŭŋ, Jarai (PL) rəbiŋ -v, Jarai (Lee) reɓŭŋ -i, Chru rəbuŋ, N. Roglai rubuk, Tsat phuŋ¹¹; phoŋ¹¹, Haroi phŭŋ, PR Cham ripuŋ; rapŭŋ, Wr. Cham ribuŋ, Malay rĕbung, PMP *rebuŋ; MK: PNB *daqbăŋ 'bamboo sprouts', PSB (Efimov) *də'b₁aŋ, PKatuic *ʔəʔbaŋ.

*rakit 'tie together; assemble', Acehnese raket, Jarai (Lee) rəkĭʔ, PR Cham rakiʔ, Wr. Cham rakik, Malay rakit, PMP *ʀakit 'tie together; raft'.

*ralaːŋ; *kalaːŋ 'grass, thatch or congo; roof thatch', Acehnese naluɯəŋ -i, Rade hlaŋ, Jarai (PL) həlăŋ, Jarai (Lee) hlaŋ, Chru rəlaːŋ, N. Roglai ralaːk, Malay lalang 'k. of long grass'.

*ralin 'candle wax', Rade hlin, Jarai (PL) hălin, hlin, Jarai (Lee) hlin, Chru rəlin, N. Roglai ralit (hăli̇̆n 'candle wax'), PR Cham rali̇̆n, Wr. Cham ralin, cf. Malay lilin, PMP *lilin 'beeswax'.

*raŋ 'dry', Rade (Lee, Tharpe) raŋ, Haroi raŋ, PMP *keʀaŋ; (*ma-
)ʀaŋaw; *keʀaŋ; (*kaʀiŋ); MK: PNB *răŋ 'dry wood', PSB (Efimov) *raɲ.
Note that, although it is restricted to Highlands Chamic plus Haroi, it does seem
to reconstruct to PMP.

*ratus -f 'hundred', Acehnese sirɯtoh, Rade etuh -v, Jarai (PL) rɵ̆tŭh,
Jarai (Lee) rɵtuh -v, Chru rɵtu:h, N. Roglai sa ratuh, Tsat ta¹¹ tu³³ -tf, Haroi
lɵtouh -v, W. Cham ratuh, PR Cham ritŭh; ratŭh, Wr. Cham rituh; ratuh, Malay
ratus, PMP *sa-ŋa-ʀatus; *sa-ratus.

*raya ? 'big', Acehnese raya, Haroi lɵyɨa, PR Cham raya, Wr. Cham
rayā, Malay raya, PMalayic *raya, PMP *ʀaya.

*ribɔw 'thousand', Acehnese ribɛə, Rade ebău, Jarai (PL) rɵ̆bəu, Jarai
(Lee) rəbəu, Chru rəbəu, N. Roglai sa ngăn; rubəu, Tsat phə¹¹, Haroi lɵphɨau, W.
Cham rapau, PR Cham ripɵ̆w; rapɵ̆w, Wr. Cham ribuw; rabuw, Malay ribu,
PWMP *ribu, no PMP; MK: PNB *rabăw, PSB (Efimov) *rəbu:.

*rusa 'Sambhur deer', Acehnese rusa, Jarai (PL) rɵ̆sa, Jarai (Lee) rəsa,
Chru rəsa, N. Roglai rusa, Haroi lɵsa, W. Cham rasa, PR Cham ritha; ratha, Wr.
Cham rithā; rasā, Malay rusa, PMP *ʀusa.

*rusuk 'ribs', Acehnese rusoʔ, Jarai (Lee) rəsŭʔ, Chru rəsuʔ, N. Roglai
tula:k risŭk -f, Haroi lɵsoʔ, W. Cham talaŋ lasŭʔ -i, PR Cham rathŭ̆ʔ, Wr. Cham
rasuk, Malay rusuk, PMP *ʀusuk.

*rɵɲa:n -ifl 'ladder, Acehnese rɯnɯn -vm, Rade eñan, Jarai (PL)
rɵ̆ñan, Jarai (Lee) rəñan, Chru lɵya:n -i, N. Roglai riña:t -fl, Haroi lɵñɨan, W.
Cham kañan -i, PR Cham liñan -i; lañan -i, Wr. Cham liñan -i; lañan -i, PMP
*haʀezan 'notched log ladder'. This form, despite being an apparent PMP ety-
mon, is quite irregular in Chamic.

*sa 'one', Acehnese sa, Rade sa, Jarai (PL) sa; ha (article), Jarai (Lee)
sa, hə-, Chru sa, N. Roglai sa, Tsat sa³³, Haroi sa; ha; hɔ, W. Cham sa; ha, PR
Cham tha, Wr. Cham sā, Malay satu, PMalayic *əsaʔ, PMP *esa; *isa.

*sa pluh sa 'eleven', Acehnese siblah, Rade pluh sa, Jarai (PL) pluh sa,
Chru spluh sa, N. Roglai sa pluh sa, W. Cham ha pluh sa, PR Cham tha plŭh
tha, Malay sĕbĕlas.

*sa-lapan 'nine', Chru səlpan, N. Roglai salapat, PR Cham thalipăn,
Wr. Cham salipan.

*sakit 'sick, painful', Acehnese saket, Jarai (Lee) həkit, Chru -səki:ʔ, N.
Roglai saki:ʔ, Tsat kiʔ²⁴, PR Cham hakiʔ, Wr. Cham hakik, Malay sakit, PMalayic *sakit, PMP *sakit.

*samilan 'nine', W. Cham samlăn, Malay sĕmbilan ('one taken from
ten' se ambilan).

*sapuh 'broom; sweep', N. Roglai sapuh, Haroi apoh, W. Cham ḳai puh, Malay sapu -f, PMP *sapu; MK: Bahnar (AC) ço puih. [The Bahnar form is borrowed]

*sarip 'sip; slurp; suck in', Jarai (PL) hrĭp (Pk), Jarai (Lee) hrip, Haroi hərip, Malay irup, PMP *hiʀup. [The Malay and PMP second vowels do not match with the PC]

*saya:p -i 'wing', Acehnese sayɯəp, Rade siap, Chru sia:ŭʔ -n, W. Cham cheauʔ -i, PR Cham thyawʔ, Wr. Cham thiap, Malay sayap, PMalayic *sayap. Blust (p.c.) notes that there are no reflexes of *sayap outside of Malayo-Chamic, but forms reflecting *s-um-ayap 'to fly' are found in the northern Philippines.

*sɛy 'who; question word' cf. also 'honorific prefix' *si-, which might be the unstressed variant of this same morpheme, Acehnese sɔə, W. Cham hay 'who', PR Cham thĕy, Wr. Cham thĕi, PMalayic *sa-apa, *sia, PMP *i-sai.

*si- 'honorific prefix?', cf. also 'who', which might be the stressed variant of this same morpheme, Acehnese si 'title for people's names', Chru sə-in səʔai 'older sibling', Wr. Cham siy (Marrison 1975); sa- (AC), Malay si (No longer has an honorific meaning in Malay). Blust (p.c.) notes that its reconstructed function is as an actor focus marker for personal nominals. In a number of languages, including Thao in Taiwan, and Malay, it has lost all grammatical function and is retained simply as a redundant marker of personal names. That is, the reconstructed function in PAn and PMP was much like the sychronic function of /si/ in Tagalog, marking the actor focus of personal nominals (proper names, plus a few others).

*sidəm 'ant', Acehnese sidɔm, Rade hədăm, Jarai (PL) hədŏm, Jarai (Lee) hədŏm, Chru adəm -i of first syllable, N. Roglai sidəp; sudəp, Tsat a[11] than[11], Haroi athĭam, W. Cham tŏm, PR Cham hatăm; tăm, Wr. Cham hadəm; dəṁ, PMP (Blust; Adelaar) *sejem, *sijem; MK: Bahnar (AC) huduṃ; hadaṃ. [It is the Bahnar forms that are borrowed]

*sira -i 'salt', Acehnese sira, Rade hra, Jarai (PL) hra, Jarai (Lee) hra, Chru sra, N. Roglai sara, Haroi sra -i, W. Cham sra -i, PR Cham sara -i, Wr. Cham śarā, PMalayic *sira, PMP *qasiʀa.

*sukat 'to measure', Acehnese sukat 'of volume', Rade məkă? -i, Malay sukat.

*surat 'write; letter, book', Acehnese surat, Rade hră?, Jarai (PL) hră?, Jarai (Lee) hră?, Chru sra? in the word for paper, N. Roglai sura?, Haroi həră?, W. Cham hră?, PR Cham hară?, Wr. Cham harak, Malay surat; MK: PSB (Efimov) *səra? 'book, written document', PKatuic (DT) *–uraaq 'writing' [Brôu sraq, Pacoh uraq]. The *surat appears to also reconstruct in Efimov's PSB, which, if the reconstruction is correct, suggests the time depth of the borrowing into PSB as well as in Katuic; even should neither the PSB or PKatuic reconstruction hold up, this is evidence of reasonably early borrowing into PSB (or, at least Bahnaric languages) and into PKatuic (or at least Katuic languages). The root itself looks like it reconstructs at least to Malayo-Chamic, but it is unclear what the original Malayo-Chamic gloss was.

    **susɔw > *tasɔw 'breast', Rade kəsău, Jarai (PL) tɞsəu, Jarai (Lee) təsəu, N. Roglai tisəu, Haroi cəsău, W. Cham tasau, PR Cham tathɞw, Wr. Cham tathuw, Written Cham (AC) tasɞu, Malay susu, PMalayic *susu(?), PMP *susu. The reconstruction with the double asterisk is what I assume, on the basis of external evidence and internal reconstruction, the earlier PC form would look like, if it were not for gaps in the data base; the form with the single asterisk is the earliest form reconstructable on the basis of just the evidence now available.

    *taʔ 'chop; cut', Acehnese taʔ, Jarai (PL) tăʔ, Jarai (Lee) tăʔ, Chru taʔ, N. Roglai taʔ, Haroi tăʔ, W. Cham tăʔ, Malay tĕtak, PMalayic *tətək 'chop, hack', PMP *tektek 'chop; cut'; MK: Bahnar (AC) tak.

    *tabaːr 'tasteless; flat', Acehnese tabɯə < *-r, Rade kəba, Jarai (PL) tăba, Chru təba, N. Roglai taba, Haroi cəphɨa, W. Cham tapa, PR Cham tapa, Wr. Cham tabā, Malay tawar, PWMP *tabaʀ.

    *tabus 'ransom; save; rescue', Tsat phu⁵⁵, PR Cham tapŭh, Wr. Cham tabuh, Malay tĕbus, PMP *tebus.

    *talεy 'rope; string', Acehnese talɔə, Rade klεi braŋ, Jarai (PL) tɞləi, Jarai (Lee) tələi, Chru tələi, N. Roglai taləi, Tsat lai³³, Haroi cəlɞi, W. Cham talay, PR Cham talɞy, Wr. Cham talɞi, Malay tali, PMalayic *tali, PMP *talih, PAn *CaliS.

    *tama 'enter', Acehnese tamʌŋ, Chru təma, Haroi cəma, W. Cham tamɨ, PR Cham tamɨ, Wr. Cham tamɨ, PMalayic *tamaʔ 'go inside', PMP *tama.

    *tampεy 'to winnow', Acehnese tampɔə, Rade kəpεi, hədεi, Jarai (PL) tăpəi (Pk), N. Roglai tupəi, Haroi cəpɞi; cəpɞai, W. Cham tapay, PR Cham tapɞy; pɞy, Wr. Cham tapɞi, Malay tampi, PMP *tahepi; MK: Bahnar (AC) təbeh; təpai.

    *tamuh 'grow; sprout', Chru təmŭh, N. Roglai tumŭh, Haroi cəmoh, W. Cham tamuh, PR Cham tamŭh, Wr. Cham tamuh, Malay tumbuh, PMalayic *tumbuh, PMP *tu(m)buq.

    *taŋa 'ask', Acehnese tañʌŋ, Jarai (PL) tɞñă, Jarai (Lee) təña, Chru tənia, N. Roglai tiñă, Haroi cəña, PR Cham tañi < *-ŋ-, Wr. Cham tañi, Malay tanya. [There are minor problems with this root: the medial nasal and subsequent vowels pattern unexpectedly]

    *taŋaːn 'hand; arm', Rade kəŋan, Jarai (PL) təŋan, Jarai (Lee) təŋan, Chru təŋaːn, N. Roglai taŋăn, Tsat ŋaːn³³, Haroi cəŋan 'hand', W. Cham taŋən -

v, PR Cham taŋin, Wr. Cham tangin, Malay tangan, PMalayic *taŋan, PMP *taŋan 'thumb'.

*tanaʔ 'to cook', Rade kənăʔ, Jarai (PL) tənăʔ, Jarai (Lee) tənăʔ, Chru tənaʔ, N. Roglai tanăʔ, Haroi cənăʔ 'cook rice', W. Cham tanəʔ, PR Cham taňĭʔ, Wr. Cham tanɨk, Malay tanak, PMalayic *tanak, *tanək, PMP *tanek.

*tanah 'earth, soil', Acehnese tanɔh, Jarai (PL) tănăh (Pk), Jarai (Lee) tənah, Chru tənah, N. Roglai tanăh, Tsat na⁵⁵, W. Cham tanɨh, PR Cham tanɨh, Wr. Cham tanɨḥ, Malay tanah, PMalayic *tanah, PMP *taneq; MK: PNB *taqneh 'dirt', PMnong *nteh 'earth', PSB (Efimov) *tneːh. The spread of MP forms indicates the word is native to Austronesian; thus, at least the PNB form looks to be borrowed!

*tapay 'rice wine; alcohol', Acehnese tapɛ -v 'fermented rice cake', Rade kəpie, Chru təpai, N. Roglai tapai, Haroi cəpăi, PR Cham tapay, Wr. Cham tapai, Malay tapai, PAn *tapay 'ferment'.

*tapɛy 'yeast', Rade kəpɛi, Jarai (PL) tăpəi, Jarai (Lee) təpəi, Chru təpəi, N. Roglai tupəi. Cf. 'rice wine' [This particular word seems to be related to fermentation, the making of rice wine, and yeast]

*tapuŋ 'flour', Rade kəpŭŋ 'bread', Jarai (PL) tăpŭŋ, Jarai (Lee) təpŭŋ, Chru təpuŋ, N. Roglai tupuk, PR Cham tapŭŋ 'farine', Wr. Cham tapuŋ, Malay tĕpung; MK: Bahnar (AC) təpuŋ.

*tasiʔ 'sea; ocean', Rade kəsĭʔ, Jarai (PL) rəsĭʔ -i, Jarai (Lee) rəsĭʔ -i, Chru təsiːʔ, N. Roglai tasiːʔ, Haroi cəseiʔ, W. Cham tasiʔ, PR Cham tathiʔ, Wr. Cham tathik, Malay tasik 'lake', PMalayic *tasik 'lake', PMP *tasik 'sea, salt-water'. Note that the Malay tasik has undergone a semantic change and now refers only to lakes; the Chamic forms, however, appear to still retain the older meaning 'sea; saltwater'.

*thɔw 'know; can; able', Acehnese thɛə; tu-, Rade thău, Jarai (PL) thəu, Jarai (Lee) thəu, Chru thəu 'understand', N. Roglai thəu, Tsat tiauʔ⁴² -i, Haroi thău, W. Cham thau, PR Cham thŏw, Wr. Cham thŏy̧, Malay tahu, PMalayic *tahu, PMP *taqu.

*thu 'year', Acehnese thon, Rade thŭn, Jarai (PL) thun, Jarai (Lee) thŭn, Chru thun, N. Roglai thut, Tsat thun³³, Haroi thon, W. Cham thŭn, PR Cham thŭn, Wr. Cham thun, Malay tahun, PMalayic *tahun, PMP *taqun.

*tikus 'rat', Acehnese tikoh, Rade kəkuih, Jarai (PL) təkuih, Jarai (Lee) təkuih, Chru təkuːh, N. Roglai tukuh, Tsat (na¹¹) ku⁵⁵, Haroi cəkoh, W. Cham takuh, PR Cham takŭh, Wr. Cham takuḥ, Malay tikus, PMalayic *tikus. [This root is restricted to parts of WMP]

*timun 'melon; cucumber', Acehnese timɔn, Rade kəmŭn, Jarai (PL) təmŭn, Jarai (Lee) təmŭn 'a citrus', Chru təmun, N. Roglai tumŭn, Haroi cəmon,

W. Cham tamŭn 'cucumber'; tamŭn padai 'melon', PR Cham tamŭn, Wr. Cham tamun, Wr. Cham (AC) tamun, Malay timun, PMP *timun.

*tinεy see *tinĭ

*tinĭ; *tinεy 'here', cf. *ti, Acehnese sinɔə, hinɔə, Rade tinεi, Jarai (PL) anai, Chru ni 'here; this', N. Roglai tinĭ, Haroi ni 'here, this', W. Cham ni, PR Cham ni, Wr. Cham nĭ, Malay sini, di sini.

*tiya:n 'stomach; abdomen; belly', Acehnese -tiyɯən in mɯtiyɯən 'pregnant', Rade tian, Jarai (PL) kĭăn, Jarai (Lee) kian < *k- prefix, Chru tia:n, N. Roglai matia:t 'pregnant', Tsat ten?³³, Haroi tean, W. Cham tean, PR Cham tyan, Wr. Cham tian, Malay tian 'uterus of a pregnant woman', PMP *tian.

*ti(?) 'PARTICLE'. Rade ti? -v, Rade (Lee) ti, N. Roglai (Lee) ti, Haroi ti? -v. Cf. 'at'.

*trun 'descend', Acehnese trən, Rade trŭn, Jarai (PL) trŭn, Jarai (Lee) trŭn, Chru trun 'descend; southerly', N. Roglai trut, Tsat tsun³³, Haroi tron, W. Cham trŭn, PR Cham trŭn, Wr. Cham trun, Malay turun, PMP *tuʀun.

*tu?ut 'knee', Acehnese tuot; tɯot, Rade kəŭt, Jarai (PL) kŏtə?ŭt, Jarai (Lee) te?ŭt, Chru tə?ŭ:?, N. Roglai tu?u:?, Haroi cə?u? -v, W. Cham ta?u?, PR Cham tau?, Wr. Cham tauk, Malay lu/tut, PMalayic *tu?(uə)t, PMP *tuhud, PAn *tuSud.

*tuburεy 'yesterday', Acehnese barɔə, Rade məbrue (m), Jarai (Lee) brəi, Chru kəbruəi (m) -i, N. Roglai tubrəi, Haroi məcəprui (m), PR Cham kaproy; paproy, Wr. Cham kabruai.

*tuha 'old (people)', Acehnese tuha, Rade khua (m), Jarai (PL) tha, Jarai (Lee) təha; tha, Chru tha, N. Roglai tuha, Tsat ha³³ xau³³, Haroi cəha, W. Cham taha, PR Cham taha, Wr. Cham tahā, Malay tua; tuha, PMalayic *tuha(?), PMP *tuqah.

*tujuh 'seven', Acehnese tujoh, Rade kjuh, Jarai (PL) təjuh, Jarai (Lee) təjuh, Chru təjuh, N. Roglai tijuh, Tsat su⁵⁵, Haroi cəsŭh, W. Cham taçuh, PR Cham taçŭh, Wr. Cham tajuh, Malay tujuh, but PMP *pitu. [The form *tujuh postdates the breakup of PMP, but precisely at what level it was innovated is not clear yet]

*tula:ŋ 'bone', Acehnese tulɯəŋ, Rade klaŋ, Jarai (PL) təlŏŋ, Jarai (Lee) təlaŋ, Chru təla:ŋ, N. Roglai tula:k, Tsat la:ŋ³³, Haroi cəlaŋ, W. Cham talaŋ, PR Cham talaŋ, Wr. Cham talaŋ, Malay tulang, PMalayic *tulaŋ, PMP *tuqelan; *tuqelaŋ; MK: PMnong *kətiŋ. The similarities between the MK and the PMP words for 'bone' are intriguing.

*tuŋ 'stomach; abdomen', Jarai (PL) tuŋ (Pk), Chru tuŋ, N. Roglai tuk, Haroi toŋ, W. Cham tuŋ 'intestines', PR Cham tŭŋ, Wr. Cham tuŋ, Malay jantung 'heart'. Confined to languages in western Indonesia (Blust, p.c.).

*tə- 'INADVERTENT', Acehnese tɯ- 'inadvertent', Jarai tə- 'reflex-ive', Malay tĕr, PMalayic *tAr- 'inadvertent', PMP *taʀ 'inadvertent; marker of involuntary action', PAn *tar- 'inadvertent'. The PAn, PMP, PMalayic, and PC forms reflect the same etymon; the MK forms (discussed in Chapter 9) look to be more than simply look-alikes. They appear borrowed.

*təbɔw -v 'sugarcane', Acehnese tɯbɛə, Rade kəbău, Jarai (PL) təbəu, Jarai (Lee) təbəu, Chru tərbəu, N. Roglai tubəu, Tsat phə¹¹, Haroi cəphiau, W. Cham tapau, PR Cham tapŏw, Wr. Cham tabuw, Malay tĕbu, PMP *tebuh.

*təliŋa 'ear', Acehnese gɯliñuəŋ -iv; puñuəŋ, Rade kəŋa, Jarai (PL) tŏŋia (m), Jarai (Lee) təŋia (m), Chru tənia (m), N. Roglai liŋiã (m); riŋiã -i (m), Tsat ŋa³³, Haroi cəŋea (m) 'ear, brain (place of thinking and memory)', PR Cham taŋi (m), Wr. Cham taŋĭ, Malay tĕlinga, PMalayic *tɔliŋa(ʔ), PMP *taliŋa.

*təpat 'straight; honest', Acehnese tɯpat, Rade kəpă?, Jarai (PL) təpă?, Jarai (Lee) təpaʔ -l, Chru təpaʔ, N. Roglai tupaʔ, Haroi cəpă?, PR Cham tapă?, Wr. Cham tapak, Malay tĕpat 'exactly', PWMP *tepet 'exact; precise'; MK: Bahnar (AC) təpăt.

*wa 'uncle, aunt', Jarai (PL) wa, Jarai (Lee) wa 'uncle, aunt', Chru wa 'paternal', N. Roglai wa, Haroi wa, W. Cham wa, PR Cham wa, Wr. Cham wā, Malay ua 'old; aunt or uncle older than one's parents', PMP *uaʔ 'uncle, aunt'; MK: PMnong *wa 'uncle, aunt', PSB (Efimov) *wa:. Note the PMnong form, but the antiquity of the PMP form suggests that this was an early borrowing into PMnong and PSB, not the other way around.

*ya:p 'count', Rade yap, Jarai (Lee) yap, Chru ya:uʔ, N. Roglai ya:ʔ, Haroi yiauʔ, W. Cham yauʔ, PR Cham yawʔ, Wr. Cham yap -f, PMP *ihap. The vowel length results from a requirement found not just in Austronesian where it is widespread but in many languages of the world that vowels in monosyllable roots be at least two moras long.

1.2   PC words of MK origin

In addition to the form inherited from Austronesian, there is a second, large set of forms reconstructed for PC. These items are those borrowings from MK sources that were borrowed so early as to be reconstructable to PC. These forms include numerous forms from two distinct MK subgroups, the more southerly Bahnaric and the more northerly Katuic. In many cases, of course, the forms are found both in Bahnaric and Katuic so it is not possible to tell which branch of MK the borrowing came from, but in a significant subset of cases, the form is attested in only one of these branches. It is inevitable of course that there are accidental gaps in the data, but the large number of forms attested in only one of these two branches of MK makes it clear that both branches contributed material to pre-PC

establishing that there was early, intense contact not just with Bahnaric speakers
but also with Katuic speakers.

Establishing that a MK form reconstructs to PC is done almost exclusively on correspondence patterns within PC. In this regard, the existence of an
extra-Chamic Malay form does not mean that a form is necessarily Austronesian
as Malay itself has borrowed a number of MK forms, for example, *ketam* 'crab'
and *semut* 'ant' quite independently of Chamic. Thus the occurrence of a form
both in Malay and Chamic does little to establish either that form must inevitably
be Austronesian nor does it contribute to determining a time depth for a MK borrowing.

It is important to realize that historically there was contact between Austronesian and MK languages before Austronesians speakers reached the coast of
Vietnam. On the Malaysian peninsula, there are still Orang Asli speaking MK
languages, and in Borneo, Adelaar (1995) argues that there is linguistic evidence
of a MK influence on the Land Dayak. Adelaar presents two pieces of evidence
for MK influence on Land Dayak: one is the presence of preploded nasals, found
in MK languages and in Austronesian languages in contact with MK languages,
and the other is the presence of MK vocabulary in Land Dayak. To this evidence
I would add another piece of evidence that suggests the shifting of MK speakers
to the Austronesian languages of Borneo, including proto-Malayic. Specifically,
throughout the proto-Malayic forms found in the lexicon below (from Adelaar
1992) there are a number of forms that, etymologically, should be vowel final but
instead end in a final glottal stop (Blust, p.c., mentioned the difficulty of accounting for these finals etymologically). On the Malay peninsula, much the same
process can be seen with borrowings into Aslian languages from Malay, as is evident in Benjamin's (1976) wordlists in his work the subgrouping of Orang Asli
languages of the Malay peninsula; in those lists, as in Land Dayak, as in proto-
Malayic (cf. the forms in this lexicon), final glottal stops are often present on
Malay words which should end in open syllables. The significance of all this, of
course, is that some MK influence may have already been present in their language when the pre-Chamic speakers arrived in Vietnam.

The evidence that a form is borrowed from a MK source varies from
form to form, but two general types of evidence are widely represented in the following list. One type of evidence is provided by reconstructions of Austronesian
subgroups, on the one hand, and MK subgroups on the other. Certain forms are
found in reconstructed in one or more subgroups of MK but, aside from PC,
apparently nowhere else in Austronesian. Here the unmarked hypothesis is that
such forms have been borrowed from MK. A second type of evidence is found in
the phonology of the reconstruction: a number of specific vowels, certain diphthongs, particular consonants (e.g. the implosives (with a small number of well-

know exceptions), and otherwise unique clusters only occur in MK borrowings (discussed in detail elsewhere in this work). The fact that a word contains one of these elements is by itself evidence that it is a MK borrowing; however, it is almost never necessary to depend upon this evidence alone, as when a word contains one of these elements, it is inevitably the case that the word also lacks an Austronesian etymology. Here again the unmarked hypothesis is that the word is a MK borrowing.

ˣ*ʔaːk 'a crow', Acehnese aʔ-aʔ, Rade ak, Jarai (Lee) ʔaʔ, Chru cim aːʔ, N. Roglai aːʔ, Haroi aʔ 'raven', W. Cham aʔ, PR Cham aʔ, Wr. Cham ak; MK: Bahnar (AC) āk, PKatuic *[k/g]əʔaːʔ, *ʔəʔaːʔ. One has to be careful with such onomatopoetic forms.

ˣ*ʔada 'duck', Chru ada, N. Roglai ada, Tsat tha[11], W. Cham ṭa, PR Cham aṭa; ṭa, Wr. Cham adā; dā; MK: PSB (Efimov) *daː, PKatuic *yədia, *ʔədia.

ˣ*ʔadɔh 'sing', Jarai (PL) ădɔh, Jarai (Lee) ʔadɔh, Chru adɔh, N. Roglai adoh, W. Cham ṭɔh, PR Cham aṭɔh; ṭɔh, Wr. Cham adauh; MK: PSB (Efimov) *ʔədɔḥ. [The vowel also suggests a MK origin]

ˣ*ʔaduan 'old', cf. ˣ*maduan, Rade aduon, Jarai (PL) adɔn, Jarai (Lee) ʔadɔn. This form obviously is obviously related to ˣ*maduan; both forms are restricted to two Highlands Chamic languages. [The vowel also suggests a MK origin]

ˣ*ʔaha; ˣ*ha 'open (mouth to say sthg.)', cf. Vietnamese há, Acehnese hah -i, Rade ha, Jarai (PL) ha, Jarai (Lee) ha, Chru ha 'slightly opened', N. Roglai aha, Tsat ha[33], Haroi ha 'wide open', W. Cham ha, PR Cham ha, Wr. Cham hā; MK: PNB *ha, PMnong *ha, PSB (Efimov) *haːʔ, *haː, PKatuic *təhɑ, *ʔəhɑh.

ˣ*ʔakɔʔ 'head', Rade kŏʔ, Jarai (PL) akŏ, Jarai (Lee) ʔakŏʔ, Chru akɔʔ, N. Roglai akoʔ, Tsat koʔ[24], Haroi akŏʔ, W. Cham kŏʔ, PR Cham akŏʔ; kŏʔ, Wr. Cham akauk; kauk. [The vowel suggests a MK origin]

ˣ*ʔalɛ 'medium bamboo', Rade ale, Jarai (PL) əlɛ -v, ălɛ -v, Jarai (Lee) ʔale, Chru alɛ, N. Roglai ale, Haroi alɛ, W. Cham çŭt lɛ 'small bamboo'; MK: PNB *pale 'bamboo', PMnong *gle, PSB (Efimov) *glɛː, PKatuic *ʔələɛ. Restricted to Highlands Chamic plus Haroi and W. Cham. [The vowel also suggests a MK origin]

ˣ*ʔamuːŋ 'snout; muzzle', Rade amuŋ, Chru mɔːŋ, N. Roglai mũːk -f. Note the restriction to Highlands Chamic. [The vowel length also suggests a MK origin] ˣ*ʔamuːŋ (?) 'bunch; ear of grain; stalk', Rade amuŋ 'stalk (bananas)', Chru amuːŋ -v 'stalk of bananas'; tərmung, N. Roglai amuːk 'stalk', Haroi amuŋ, W. Cham moŋ 'stalk of bananas', PR Cham (Blood) moŋ, Wr. Cham (AC) amuŋ. Cf. MK: PKatuic (DT) *–phoong. [The vowel length suggests a MK origin]

ˣ*ʔatɔːŋ 'hit with implement; beat (gong)', Rade toŋ, Jarai (PL) ătoŋ, Chru atɔːŋ, N. Roglai atoːk 'beat (gong)', Haroi atɔŋ, W. Cham tɔŋ, PR Cham atɔŋ, Wr. Cham atauŋ; MK: PKatuic (DT) *thɨɨŋ. [The vowel also suggests a MK origin]

ˣ*ʔaw 'clothing; shirt', Viet. áo, Rade au, Jarai (PL) au, Jarai (Lee) ʔau, Chru aːu -1 'shirt', N. Roglai au, Tsat ʔaːu¹¹, Haroi au, W. Cham au, PR Cham aw, Wr. Cham aw; MK: PNB *aw, PSB (Efimov) *ʔaːw.

ˣ*ʔawaːk 'spoon; ladle', Acehnese awɯaʔ, Rade awak, Jarai (PL) awăʔ, Chru awaʔ, Haroi awaʔ, PR Cham awaʔ, Wr. Cham awak; MK: Bahnar (AC) uak, PKatuic *həwaʔ 'ladle'.

ˣ*ʔɛh 'excrement; defecate', Acehnese ɛʔ -f, Rade ɛh, Jarai (PL) ɛh, Jarai (Lee) ʔĕh, Chru ɛ̆h, N. Roglai eh, Haroi ɛh, W. Cham ɛh, PR Cham ĕh, Wr. Cham aiḥ; MK: PNB *ĭč, PSB (Efimov) *ʔac, PKatuic *ʔɛh. [The vowel also suggests a MK origin]

ˣ*ʔiaw 'call; cry; yell', Rade ieu -v, Jarai (PL) iau, iəu, Jarai (Lee) ʔiəu, Chru iəu, N. Roglai iəu, Tsat ʔiə³³, Haroi ʔjʊ, W. Cham iau, PR Cham (Lee) ʔăw. [The triphthong suggests a MK origin]

ˣ*ʔjaːʔ 'hold; carry', Rade ʔjăʔ, Jarai (PL) ʔjăʔ, Jarai (Lee) ʔjăʔ, N. Roglai ʔjaːʔ, Haroi jaʔ 'carry in hand'; MK: PMnong *yək 'carry'. Restricted to Highlands Chamic plus Haroi. [The initial also suggests a MK origin]

ˣ*ʔjam 'soup, thin', Rade ʔjam, Chru iăm, N. Roglai ʔjaːp -1. Restricted to Highlands Chamic. [The initial also suggests a MK origin]

ˣ*ʔjuh 'firewood', Rade ʔjuh, Jarai (PL) ʔjŭh, Jarai (Lee) ʔjuh; ʔjŭh, Chru iuh, N. Roglai ʔjuh, Tsat ʔiu⁵⁵, Haroi ʔjŭh, W. Cham ʔjuh, PR Cham ʔjŭh, Wr. Cham ʔjuḥ. [The initial suggests a MK origin]

ˣ*ʔjup 'smoke tobacco', Rade ʔjup hăt, Jarai (PL) ăʔjŭp, Jarai (Lee) ʔjŭp, Chru iuʔ 'smoke', N. Roglai ʔjuːʔ, Haroi ʔjuʔ, W. Cham ʔjuʔ -f, PR Cham ʔjuʔ, Wr. Cham ʔjuk; MK: PKatuic *həʔjeːp, *kəjeːp, *ʔjuːp, *ʔjɔʔ 'suck'. [The initial also suggests a MK origin]

ˣ*ʔjəp 'correct; right', Rade ʔjə̆ʔ, Jarai (PL) ʔjə̆ʔ, Jarai (Lee) ʔjə̆ʔ, Chru iəuʔ, N. Roglai ʔjəʔ; dadi, Haroi jăŭʔ, W. Cham ʔjauʔ, PR Cham ʔjə̆w, Wr. Cham ʔjəp; MK: PNB *joq. [The initial and the vowel also suggest a MK origin] ˣ*ʔñam 'vegetables; food; legumes', Jarai (PL) ăñăm, Jarai (Lee) ʔañam, Chru iăm, Tsat ʔiaʔ³³, PR Cham ʔjăm, Wr. Cham ʔjaṁ. [The initial suggests a MK origin]

ˣ*ʔɔʔ 'vomit', Jarai (Lee) ʔɔʔ; həʔŏʔ; ʔŏʔ, Chru ɔːʔ 'choke', PR Cham (Lee) ʔɔʔ, Wr. Cham (AC) auk; MK: PNB *hăk, PMnong *hok, PSB (Efimov) *hʌʔ, PKatuic (DT) *–hɔɔk 'choke on food'. [The vowel also suggests a MK origin]

ˣ*ʔuːŋ 'husband; male', Rade uŋ, Jarai (PL) ŭŋ (Est), Jarai (Lee) ʔoŋ, PR Cham (Lee) ʔoŋ 'you (to a man), Wr. Cham (AC) oŋ 'grandfather', PNB *ŏŋ 'son-in-law'. [The vowel length also suggests a MK origin]

ˣ*ʔuăʔ -n 'to saw', Rade uăʔ, Jarai (PL) (uă) ănuăʔ, Jarai (Lee) ʔuăʔ, N. Roglai uăʔ, PR Cham (Lee) ʔuaʔ. [The vowel suggests a MK origin]

ˣ*ʔəm 'to roast', Rade ăm, Jarai (Lee) ʔŏm, Chru əm, N. Roglai əp, Haroi ŏm, W. Cham ăm -v, PR Cham (Lee) ăm. [The vowel suggests a MK origin]

ˣ*baːl 'mend; to patch',   Jarai (Lee) bal, Chru baːl, N. Roglai ban, Haroi phĭal, W. Cham pal, PR Cham pal, Wr. Cham bal; MK: PKatuic *–pˍl 'to patch'. With the instrumental infix: ˣ*b-an-aːl 'rag', Rade mənal, Jarai (PL) bənal, Jarai (Lee) bənal, N. Roglai banăn. Note: The connection between the infixed and the non-infixed forms depends upon acceptance of the semantics of the equation of 'rag' with 'mend; path'.

ˣ*bɔh 'wash; launder',   Rade bɔh, Jarai (PL) boh (Ouest), Jarai (Lee) bŏh, Chru bɔh, N. Roglai boh, Haroi phŭh, PR Cham pɔh, Wr. Cham bauh. [The vowel suggests a MK origin]

ˣ*b-an-ət 'a dam; a fence', Rade mənĭʔ, Jarai (PL) bənĭʔ, Jarai (Lee) bənĭʔ, Chru bənũːʔ -f, N. Roglai banăʔ, W. Cham panəʔ 'a dam', PR Cham pinĭʔ, Wr. Cham binĭk; MK: Bahnar (AC) bənot. [The vowel and the infix also suggest a MK origin]

ˣ*baʔar 'paper; book', Rade məar, Jarai (PL) məʔar (Mod.), Chru bəʔaːr, N. Roglai baʔa, Haroi pəʔĭal, W. Cham paʔar -il, PR Cham piʔar, Wr. Cham biar; MK: PNB *baqar 'paper; book', PSB (Efimov) *pəʔaːr.

ˣ*bala 'tusk; ivory', Rade mla, Jarai (PL) bla, Jarai (Lee) bla, Chru bla, N. Roglai bala, Haroi pəlĭa, W. Cham pla, PR Cham pila, Wr. Cham bilā; MK: PMnong *bla, PSB (Efimov) *blaː, PKatuic (DT) palˍk 'tusk' (the final -k is unexpected).

ˣ*batɔ 'teach', Rade məto, Jarai (PL) pʼto, Jarai (Lee) pəto, Chru pətɔ, N. Roglai pato, Tsat to¹¹, Haroi pətɔ, W. Cham patɔ, PR Cham patɔ, Wr. Cham patauw; MK: PSB (Efimov) *pə'd₁aw 'teach, dictate'. [The vowel also suggests a MK origin]

ˣ*bɛʔ 'IMPERATIVE, negative, don't', Acehnese bɛʔ 'don't', Chru bɛʔ, N. Roglai beʔ, PR Cham pɛ̌ʔ, Wr. Cham baik; MK: PNB *beq. [The vowel also suggests a MK origin]

ˣ*biluay 'gourd', N. Roglai biluai, Wr. Cham plyai; MK: PKatuic *ʔəlhuəj. [The vowel also suggests a MK origin]

ˣ*blah 'skirt', cf. 'flat object', Chru blah 'sheet', W. Cham plah 'square of cloth', PR Cham plah 'un habit; sheet', Wr. Cham blaḥ; MK: PNB *blah.

ˣ*blɔ 'split; pierce; earring', Jarai (Lee) blo, Chru blɔ 'earring', Haroi ɓlɔ 'earring'. Restricted to Highlands Chamic plus Haroi. [The vowel also suggests a MK origin]

ˣ*blək 'sound of turbulent water in stream rapids; turn over', Jarai (Lee) blïʔ 'rolled up', Haroi plïʔ -i, W. Cham plïʔ -v 'spin', PR Cham (Lee) plɜ̌ʔ. [The vowel suggests a MK origin]

ˣ*bɔːŋ 'coffin; casket', Rade boŋ, Jarai (PL) ɓoŋ, Jarai (Lee) bɔŋ, Chru bɔːŋ, N. Roglai boːk, Haroi phŏŋ, PR Cham pɔŋ, Wr. Cham bauŋ; MK: PNB *boŋ, Bahnar (AC) boŋ. [The vowel also suggests a MK origin]

ˣ*bok 'to swell', Jarai (PL) təbŭk (Ouest), N. Roglai boʔ, Haroi phŏʔ, W. Cham poʔ -v takuai 'goiter', PR Cham poʔ -v, Wr. Cham bok; MK: Bahnar (AC) bop ʔ. [The vowel also suggests a MK origin]

ˣ*buc 'uproot, pull up; scratch', Rade bŭč, Jarai (PL) bŭc, Jarai (Lee) buc, Chru buiʔ, N. Roglai puiʔ, Haroi phŭiʔ; pŏiʔ -v; pŭiʔ -i, W. Cham puiʔ 'pick, pluck' ?, PR Cham pŭyʔ, Wr. Cham buc; MK: PKatuic *həpɔjʔ, *ɣəpuajʔ 'pull out'. [The final also suggests a MK origin]

ˣ*buhay 'otter', Rade kəmhe, Jarai (PL) pə̆hai, N. Roglai buhai, W. Cham pahas -f, PR Cham phay, Wr. Cham bhai; MK: Bahnar (AC) phây, PKatuic (DT) *pih_, cf. Pacoh pihây.

ˣ*bət 'to dam; to fence', Rade bïʔ ea, Jarai (PL) bïʔ, Jarai (Lee) bïʔ, Chru bəʔ, W. Cham pəʔ 'to dam up'. [The vowel suggests a MK origin]

ˣ*ɓah 'chipped; broken', Rade ɓah 'dented', Jarai (Lee) ɓah, Chru ɓɛh -v, N. Roglai ɓah, Haroi ɓăh. Restricted to Highlands Chamic. [The initial suggests a MK origin]

ˣ*ɓaŋ 'hole; door', Rade ɓăŋ, Jarai (PL) ʔmaŋ, Jarai (Lee) ɓăŋ, Chru ɓaŋ 'door', N. Roglai ɓak, Haroi ɓăŋ, W. Cham paɓăŋ, PR Cham ɓăŋ, Wr. Cham ɓəŋ, Malay pintu; MK: PNB *qmăŋ 'door', Bahnar (AC) maŋ. [The initial also suggests a MK origin]

ˣ*ɓar 'coiled; wrapped around', Rade -ar, N. Roglai ɓa 'coil (snake)',
PR Cham ɓăr, Wr. Cham ɓar. [The initial suggests a MK origin]

ˣ*ɓɛʔ 'clf. long, thin objects', Jarai (Lee) ɓɛ̌ʔ, Chru ɓɛʔ, N. Roglai ɓeʔ
'stick-like objects', Tsat ɓeʔ²⁴, Haroi ɓɛ̌ʔ, W. Cham ɓɛ̌k -f, PR Cham ɓɛ̌ʔ, Wr.
Cham baik. [The initial and the vowel suggest a MK origin]

ˣ*ɓiaʔ 'little', Rade ɓiă̆ʔ, Jarai (PL) ɓiă̆ʔ, Jarai (Lee) ɓiă̆ʔ, Chru lu biaʔ -i,
Haroi ɓĕaʔ 'a moment', PR Cham (Lee) ɓiă̆ʔ. [The initial and the vowel suggest
a MK origin]

ˣ*ɓɔːʔ 'face', cf. 'nose' Rade ɓɔ̌ʔ məta, Jarai (PL) ɓɔ̌ʔ, Jarai (Lee) ɓɔ̌ʔ;
ɓŏʔ, Chru ɓɔːʔ məta 'cheek' and 'eye' ?, N. Roglai ɓoːʔ mata, Tsat ɓoʔ²⁴, Haroi
ɓɔʔ, W. Cham ɓɔʔ, PR Cham ɓɔʔ, Wr. Cham ɓauk; MK: Bahnar (AC) bŏ; buk;
bŏk. [The vowel also suggests a MK origin]

ˣ*ɓrəm 'arrow', Rade ɓră̆m, Jarai (PL) ɓrə̌m, ă̆mrə̌m, Jarai (Lee) ɓrɔ̌m,
Chru ɓrəm, N. Roglai ɓrəp, Haroi ɓră̆m, W. Cham ɓrɔ̌m, PR Cham ɓră̆m, Wr.
Cham ɓram; MK: PMnong *kă̆m, Bahnar (AC) brəm; mrəm. [The initial conso-
nant and the vowel also suggest a MK origin]

ˣ*ɓuːn 'poor, cheap; easy', Rade ɓun, Jarai (PL) ă̆mŏnh, munh (CT),
Chru ɓuən 'easy', Haroi ɓun 'poor, cheap; easy', PR Cham ɓŏn 'cheap; easy',
Wr. Cham ɓyən; MK: Bahnar (AC) bŏñ 'cheap, easy'. [The initial consonant
and the vowel length also suggest a MK origin]

ˣ*ɓuah 'scold', Rade ɓuah, Chru ɓuah, PR Cham ɓwă̆h, Wr. Cham ɓyaḥ.
[The initial and the vowel suggest a MK origin]

ˣ*ɓuh...ˣ*ʔɔh 'not, no; negative', Rade ɓu; ɓu...ŏh; ɓu...ʔjə̌...ŏh; Jarai ɓu
mə̆n 'non plus'; ɓu...oh; Chru ɓuh...əu; N. Roglai ɓuh...oh; Tsat pu³³ -i; Haroi
ʔŏh; W. Cham o; o 'yes/no question marker'; PR Cham ka...o 'pas encore', PSB
(Efimov) *ʔɔːh 'denial particle'. [The initial suggests a MK origin] Note: Not
only do the initial and final of ˣ*ɓuh show irregularities, but the initial itself is
totally unexpected if the form is inherited from PAn. Also, while the negative is
often bipartite, it is not always so. The origin of this structure is still unclear. Cf.
Lee 1996 for further discussion. Acehnese also has a bipartite construction for
'not yet' goh....lom, but the components do not seem related to the constructions
in the mainland Chamic languages. Cf. also 'not yet' immediately below.

ˣ*ɓəŋ 'eat', Rade ɓə̌ŋ, Jarai (PL) ɓɔ̌ŋ, Jarai (Lee) ɓɔ̌ŋ -v, Chru ɓəŋ, N.
Roglai ɓək, Tsat ɓaŋ³³, Haroi ɓɨ̆ŋ, W. Cham ɓəŋ, PR Cham ɓă̆ŋ, Wr. Cham ɓəŋ;
MK: PNB *čŏŋ 'eat rice', PMnong *sôŋ, PSB (Efimov) *soːŋ. The initial of the
MK forms is quite unexpected, so it is unclear if these forms are related to the PC
form. [The initial and the vowel also suggest a MK origin]

ˣ*ɓəŋ 'to burn', Jarai (Lee) ɓɤ̆ŋ, Chru ɓəŋ, W. Cham ɓəŋ, PR Cham ɓă̆ŋ, Wr. Cham ɓəŋ. [The initial and the vowel suggest a MK origin]

ˣ*cacɔh 'chop, strike', Rade kəčɔh, Jarai (PL) tɤ̆cɔh, Chru təcɔh, N. Roglai ticoh, W. Cham tacɔh, PR Cham tacɤ̆h, Wr. Cham tacauḥ; Wr. Cham (AC) čačauḥ, tičauḥ; MK: PSB (Efimov) *cɔh 'chop'. [The vowel also suggests a MK origin]

ˣ*caɗiaŋ 'finger', Rade kəɗieŋ, Jarai (PL) cəɗɛŋ, Jarai (Lee) cəɗɛŋ, Haroi cəɗeaŋ, W. Cham caɗiaŋ -i; MK: PNB *dĕŋ 'little finger', PKatuic *ʔdɑŋ. Restricted to Highlands Chamic plus Haroi and W. Cham. [The vowel also suggests a MK origin]

ˣ*canah 'cross over; crossroads', Jarai (Lee) cənah, Chru cənah 'tributary; crossroads', N. Roglai canah, W. Cham k̆ăn 'crossroad' -i, PR Cham canăh, Wr. Cham canaḥ. If the W. Cham form is related, that would indicate that the rest of these forms have an instrumental infix -an-, an indication of a likely MK origin.

ˣ*caːŋ 'wait; await', Jarai (PL) pɤ̆caŋ, Jarai (Lee) că̆ŋ -1, Chru caːŋ, N. Roglai caːk, Haroi pəcaŋ, W. Cham caŋ, PR Cham coŋ, Wr. Cham coŋ; MK: Bahnar (AC) çaŋ. [The initial at least suggests a MK origin]

ˣ*caramah 'generous', Rade kəmah, Jarai (PL) cəmah, Jarai (Lee) cəmah, N. Roglai caramah -n, PR Cham (Lee) kamah -v; MK: PSB (Efimov) *srəmah.

ˣ*ciaʔ 'peel (with a knife)', Acehnese seʔ -i, Chru ciaʔ, N. Roglai ciaʔ 'split, cleave'. [The vowel suggests a MK origin]

ˣ*cicaʔ 'lizard; gecko; salamander', Acehnese cicaʔ, ticaʔ, Rade tăklelo, Jarai (PL) k̆ăŋ k̆ăʔ (Ouest); că̆ŋ că̆ʔ (Est), W. Cham tacăʔ -i, PR Cham kacă̆ʔ, Wr. Cham kacak, Wr. Cham (AC) čačaʔ, Malay cicak 'garden lizard'.

ˣ*cicɤ̆t 'great grandchild', P-Acehnese (Durie) *(cɛ)cɛt, Acehnese cʌt, Rade čɤ̆ʔ 'great grandchild', Jarai (PL) təcɤ̆ʔ (Ss), Jarai (Lee) təcɛʔ -1, Chru cɛʔ -n, N. Roglai ticɤ̆ʔ, Haroi cəcɤ̆ʔ, PR Cham tacɤ̆ʔ, Wr. Cham tacaik, Wr. Cham (AC) čačaiʔ, tičaiʔ, Malay cicit. [The vowel suggests a MK origin]

ˣ*cih 'write; draw', Rade čih 'to write', Jarai (PL) cih rup, Jarai (Lee) cih, Chru cih, N. Roglai chih 'to draw', Haroi ceh, W. Cham cih, PR Cham cĭh, Wr. Cham ciḥ; MK: PNB *ačhɨ̆h, PMnong *čih, PSB (Efimov) *ciːh 'write, draw'.

ˣ*cim 'bird', Acehnese cicem, Rade čĭm, Jarai (PL) cim, Jarai (Lee) cĭm, Chru cim, N. Roglai cip, Tsat -tsun[33] -v, Haroi cem, W. Cham cĭm, PR Cham cĭm, Wr. Cham cim; MK: PNB *čɤ̆m, PMnong *sĭm, Bahnar (AC) çem, PSB (Efimov) *shim, PKatuic *hacɛːm; *ʔəcɛːm.

ˣ*ciŋ 'small gong', Rade čiŋ 'small gong', Jarai (PL) ciŋ, Chru ci:ŋ 'gong (with hump)', W. Cham ceŋ -v; MK: PNB *čhĩŋ, PSB (Efimov) *ciŋ. Restricted to Highlands Chamic plus W. Cham.

ˣ*cɔh 'dig', Jarai (PL) cŏh, Jarai (Lee) cɔh, Haroi cŏh, PR Cham cŏh, Wr. Cham cauḥ. [The vowel suggests a MK origin]

ˣ*cɔh 'peck (of bird); strike (snake)', Acehnese cɔh, Rade čɔh, Jarai (Lee) cɔh, Chru cɔh, N. Roglai coh, Haroi cŏh 'strike (snake)', W. Cham cɔh; MK: PNB *joh. [The vowel also suggests a MK origin]

ˣ*cɔk 'to cry', Haroi cŏʔ hea 'to wail, cry mourning', W. Cham cɔʔ 'weep, mourn', PR Cham cŏʔ, Wr. Cham cauk; MK: PNB *kro. [The vowel also suggests a MK origin]

ˣ*cuah 'sand', Rade čuah, Jarai (PL) cuah, Jarai (Lee) cuah, Chru cuah, N. Roglai cuah, Tsat tsua[55], Haroi coah, W. Cham coah, PR Cham cwăh, Wr. Cham cụaḥ; MK: Bahnar (AC) čụəḥ; čoâh, PKatuic *səʒuah, *ɣəʒuaḥ. [The vowel also suggests a MK origin]

ˣ*cuan 'grab, seize', N. Roglai cuat, W. Cham cuan. Note the restriction to a Highlands Chamic language plus W. Cham. [The vowel also suggests a MK origin]

ˣ*cuco 'grandchild', Rade čo, Jarai (PL) təcɔ; təco, Jarai (Lee) təcɔ, Chru cɔ, N. Roglai tico, Haroi cəcɔ, W. Cham tacɔ, PR Cham tacɔ, Wr. Cham tacauw, Wr. Cham (AC) čačauv, tičauv, Malay cucu, PMalayic *cucuʔ; MK: PNB *čăw, PMnong *sau, PSB (Efimov) *saw. [Adelaar (p.c.) suggests that this might be a very early Dravidian borrowing; if so, the presence of the form in three branches of Bahnaric suggests either very early borrowing into Bahnaric from Chamic or the possibility it was originally MK, not Dravidian. However, remember that Austroasiatic speakers are found in India. In any case, the vowel suggests a MK origin for the PC variant.]

ˣ*cuh 'burn trns.', Rade čuh 'kindle; barbecue whole animal', Jarai (PL) cŭh, Jarai (Lee) cuh, N. Roglai chuh 'kindle', Haroi coh, W. Cham cuh 'fry', PR Cham cŭh, Wr. Cham cuh; MK: PMnong *čhu 'burn', PSB (Efimov) *jhu: 'burn, set on fire'.

ˣ*cət 'mountain range', Acehnese cʌt 'hill, steep, vertical', Rade čɨʔ -i, Jarai (PL) cɨʔ, Jarai (Lee) cɨʔ, Chru cəʔ, N. Roglai cəʔ, Tsat tsəʔ[24], Haroi cŏʔ, W. Cham cəʔ, PR Cham cəʔ, Wr. Cham cək. [The vowel suggests a MK origin]

ˣ*d-an-uc 'stinger', Chru dənuiʔ, PR Cham ṭanŭʔ, Wr. Cham danuc.

ˣ*dar 'encircle', Rade dar 'go around', Jarai (PL) dar; dar, đar (Ouest) 'circonférence d'un lieu', Jarai (Lee) dar; MK: PNB *tăp dăr.

ˣ*druam 'fell a tree', Rade druom, Jarai (PL) drom; grom (CT), Jarai (Lee) drɔm, Chru drɔːm, N. Roglai droːp, Haroi trŭm dial.; cərŭm, PR Cham (Lee) c̦rɔ̀m, ʈrɔ̀m. [The vowel suggests a MK origin]

ˣ*duc 'to sting', Rade duč, Jarai (PL) duĭʔ, N. Roglai (taʔ), W. Cham ʈuiʔ, PR Cham ʈŭyʔ, Wr. Cham duc. [The final suggests a MK origin]

ˣ*dəŋ 'stand; stop', Acehnese dʌŋ, Rade dĕŋ, Jarai (PL) dɔ̆ʔ dɔ̆ŋ, Jarai (Lee) dɔ̆ŋ, Chru dəŋ, N. Roglai dək, Tsat thaŋ¹¹, Haroi thɨ̆ŋ 'stand', W. Cham ʈəŋ, PR Cham ʈăŋ, Wr. Cham dəŋ; MK: PNB *qyùŋ, PMnong *dɔ̆k, PKatuic *ʔtəjɨŋ, *ʔəʔjɨŋ 'stand'. [The vowel also suggests a MK origin]

ˣ*dər 'bury', Rade dər, Jarai (PL) dɔ̆r, Jarai (Lee) dɔ̆r, Chru dər, N. Roglai də, Haroi thŏl, PR Cham ʈăr, Wr. Cham dər. [The vowel suggests a MK origin]

ˣ*duh 'poor; unlucky' probably connected with 'serve', Tsat thu⁵⁵, W. Cham ʈuh 'sad', PR Cham ʈuh-ʈaʔ 'être de corvée', Wr. Cham duḥ-dak; MK: PNB *d-an-ŭh. Note: The PNB contains an infix.

ˣ*duh 'serve', cf. ˣ*duh 'poor, unlucky', Chru duh, N. Roglai duh hueʔ 'respect, honor', W. Cham ʈuh, PR Cham ʈuh, Wr. Cham duḥ.

ˣ*ɗaːŋ 'lie supine; be on back', Rade ɗaŋ, Jarai (Lee) ɗaŋ, Chru ɗaːŋ, N. Roglai ɗaːk, W. Cham ɗaŋ, PR Cham ɗaŋ, Wr. Cham ɗaŋ, Malay tĕrĕntang; MK: PNB *qdlaŋ 'lie on back', PKatuic *lə-lieŋ 'face-up position'. [If the Malay form is related, it is through borrowing from a MK source] [The initial also suggests a MK origin]

ˣ*ɗaʔ 'crack open', Tsat ʔdaʔ²⁴, PR Cham (Blood) ɗăʔ. [The initial suggests a MK origin]

ˣ*ɗal 'to wedge', Jarai (PL) ɗăl (Pk), Jarai (Lee) ɗăl, PR Cham ɗăl, Wr. Cham ɗəl, Malay sĕndal; MK: Bahnar (AC) stg. dăl. [The initial also suggests a MK origin]

ˣ*ɗay 'very', Chru ɗəi, Haroi ɗăi, PR Cham (Blood) ɗay -y. [The initial suggests a MK origin]

ˣ*ɗɛh 'fry', Rade ɗɛh, PR Cham (Lee) pəɗɛh (with causative prefix). [The vowel suggests a MK origin]

ˣ*ɗiʔ 'climb; ascend', Acehnese eʔ, Rade ɗĭʔ, Jarai (PL) ɗĭʔ, Jarai (Lee) ɗĭʔ, Chru ɗiːʔ 'climb; northerly, easterly', N. Roglai ɗiːʔ, Haroi ɗiʔ, W. Cham ɗiʔ, PR Cham ɗiʔ, Wr. Cham ɗik, Malay naik, PMP *pa-nahik; MK: Bahnar (AC) dɔ̆k. Two distinct possibilities exist with this root: either the root descended from PMP and was borrowed into Bahnar, or the word was borrowed into PC from Bahnar and the PMP forms are simply chance lookalikes. [The initial suggests a MK origin] ˣ*ɗih 'sleep; lie down', Acehnese eh, Rade ɗih, Jarai (Lee) ɗih, Chru ɗih, Tsat ɗi⁵⁵, Haroi ɗïh, W. Cham ɗih, PR Cham ɗïh, Wr. Cham ɗiḥ, Malay tidur u?, PMP *tiduʀ; *tuduʀ. It is not likely that the Malay and PMP are related to the PC. [The initial suggests a MK origin for the PC]

ˣ*ɗɔh 'pull', Rade (Tharpe) ɗɔh, Jarai (PL) ɗɔ̆h (Ouest et S), Jarai (Lee) ɗɔh, Haroi həɗɔ̆h, PR Cham (Lee) ɗoh. [The initial and the vowel suggest a MK origin]

ˣ*ɗua 'carry (wear) on head', Rade ɗua, Jarai (PL) ɗua, Jarai (Lee) ɗua, Chru ɗua, N. Roglai ɗua, Haroi ɗoa, W. Cham ɗoa, PR Cham ɗwa, Wr. Cham ɗụā. [The initial and the diphthong suggest a MK origin]

ˣ*ɗuac 'run; run off; flow', Rade ɗuɛ̆?, Jarai (PL) ɗuaï?, Jarai (Lee) ɗuăi?, Chru ɗuai?, N. Roglai ɗue?; duai?; dlai, Tsat ?doi?⁴², Haroi ɗŏai?, W. Cham ɗuai?, PR Cham ɗoy?, Wr. Cham ɗụəc; MK: PNB *gadăw ?. [The initial and the vowel also suggest a MK origin]

ˣ*ɗuŋ 'wrap up; bundle', Rade ɗŭŋ, Jarai (PL) pə anŭŋ, N. Roglai ɗuk, Haroi ɗŭŋ, W. Cham ɗuŋ, PR Cham ɗŭŋ, Wr. Cham ɗuŋ; MK: Bahnar (AC) duŋ. [The initial also suggests a MK origin]

ˣ*gan 'cross; pass over; go past', Rade găn 'go past', Jarai (PL) găn, Jarai (Lee) găn, N. Roglai gat, PR Cham ḳăn, Wr. Cham gən; MK: PMnong *găn, Bahnar (AC) pəgan, PSB (Efimov) *gan.

ˣ*ganiat 'narrow', Rade kəniă?, Jarai (PL) gĕniă?, Chru gənia? 'narrow; crowded', (N. Roglai cakiă?; pakiă?), Haroi kənĕa?, W. Cham ḳanii? (n), PR Cham ḳanï? (n), Wr. Cham ganik. [The vowel suggests a MK origin]

ˣ*gay 'stick; wood', Rade gie, Jarai (PL) gai, Jarai (Lee) gai, Chru gai 'in various compounds', N. Roglai gai, PR Cham ḳay, Wr. Cham gai; MK: PKatuic *gir.

ˣ*gɛ 'boat', N. Roglai ge, W. Cham ḳɛ, PR Cham ḳɛ, Wr. Cham gaiy. [The vowel suggests a MK origin]

ˣ*glac 'error; sin', Jarai (PL) glaï?, Jarai (Lee) glai?, Chru glaːi?, N. Roglai dlaːi?, Haroi tlïai?, PR Cham ḳlay?, Wr. Cham glac. [The final suggests a MK origin]

ˣ*glɛh 'tired', Jarai (PL) glɛh; dlɛh (S), Jarai (Lee) dlɛh; glɛh, Chru glɛh, N. Roglai dleh, Haroi tlιh, W. Cham ḳlɛh, PR Cham ḳlɛh, Wr. Cham glaiḥ, Malay lĕtih. [The vowel suggests a MK origin]

ˣ*glɔ 'brain; marrow', Rade dlo, Jarai (PL) dlɔ akɔ̆?, Jarai (Lee) dlo, Chru glɔ̄ -n, N. Roglai dlo, W. Cham ḳlɔ, PR Cham ḳlɔ, Wr. Cham glauw. [The vowel suggests a MK origin] ˣ*glɔːŋ 'tall; high; big', Rade dloŋ, Jarai (PL) dloŋ, Jarai (Lee) dloŋ 'long; cf. pəgloŋ 'to lengthen', Chru glɔːŋ, N. Roglai dloːk, Tsat khyoŋ[11], Haroi cətluŋ; tluŋ, W. Cham ḳlɔŋ, PR Cham ḳlɔŋ, Wr. Cham glauŋ. [The vowel suggests a MK origin]

ˣ*gləh 'descend; sink; knock down; collapse, destroy', Acehnese lhʌh, Chru jərləh -i, N. Roglai tadləh 'collapse', Haroi tlɨh, PR Cham ḳləh, Wr. Cham gləḥ. [The vowel suggests a MK origin]

ˣ*gɔʔ 'kettle; pot, glazed clay', Rade gɔ̆ʔ 'cooking pot'; gɔ, Jarai (PL) gɔ̆ʔ, Jarai (Lee) gɔ̆ʔ, Chru gɔʔ, N. Roglai goʔ, Haroi khŏʔ, W. Cham ḳɔ̆ʔ, PR Cham ḳɔ̆ʔ, Wr. Cham gauk; MK: Bahnar (AC) gŏ. [The vowel also suggests a MK origin]

ˣ*guːʔ 'below, lower part', Rade gŭʔ, PR Cham ḳuʔ 'tirer du haut vers le bas', Wr. Cham guk; MK: Bahnar (AC) gut. [The vowel length also suggests a MK origin]

ˣ*gulac 'return; go home; again', Jarai (PL) gəlaïʔ, Jarai (Lee) glăiʔ, Haroi kəlɨaiʔ, PR Cham ḳalayʔ, Wr. Cham galac; MK: PKatuic *gəlhiʌh, *ɣəlhiʌh, *kə[l/lh]aːjh. [The final also suggests a MK origin]

ˣ*guy 'carry on back', Rade gui, Jarai (PL) gui, Jarai (Lee) gui, Chru gui, N. Roglai gui, Tsat khui[11], Haroi khŭi, W. Cham ḳui, PR Cham ḳuy, Wr. Cham gu̯ĕi; MK: PKatuic *gɨj, *kuːj.

ˣ*gəm 'to cover', Acehnese gɔm 'cover with a cuplike object; invert a container', Rade gă̆m, Jarai (PL) gom, Jarai (Lee) gŏm, Chru gəm, N. Roglai gəp, Haroi khŭm; khɨam, W. Cham ḳŏm, PR Cham ḳăm, Wr. Cham gəṁ. [The vowel suggests a MK origin]

ˣ*gəŋ 'pole; post', Jarai (Lee) gə̆ŋ, Chru gəŋ, N. Roglai gək, W. Cham ḳəŋ 'main beam', PR Cham ḳăŋ, Wr. Cham gəŋ; MK: PNB *gă̆ŋ 'pole, spirit', Bahnar (AC) gàŋ; gə̆ŋ. [The vowel also suggests a MK origin]

ˣ*gəp 'other; group', Acehnese gɔp, Rade gə̆ʔ -v, Jarai (PL) gə̆ʔ 'he, she; they', Jarai (Lee) gə-, Chru gəuʔ, N. Roglai -gəʔ, W. Cham ḳauʔ, PR Cham ḳɔ̆w'(-ḳăn), Wr. Cham gəp(-gən); MK: Bahnar (AC) gâp. [The vowel also suggests a MK origin]

ˣ*gər '(knife) handle', Acehnese gʌ, Rade gră̆n -ivf, Jarai (PL) gər, Jarai (Lee) gə̆r, Chru gər, N. Roglai gə, Tsat khan[11], Haroi khŭl, W. Cham ḳăr, PR Cham ḳăr, Wr. Cham gər; MK: Bahnar (AC) gər. [The vowel also suggests a MK origin]

ˣ*ha see ˣ*ʔaha

ˣ*ha:k 'split', Rade hak 'whittle bark off', Jarai (Lee) hak, N. Roglai ha:ʔ 'ripped', Haroi haʔ, Wr. Cham (AC) hak; MK: Bahnar (AC) hak; hek, PSB (Efimov) *[ ]ha:ʔ 'split, tear, divide'.

ˣ*ha:ŋ 'bank (river); shore', Rade haŋ ea, Jarai (PL) hăŋ, Jarai (Lee) haŋ, N. Roglai ha:k, W. Cham haŋ, PR Cham haŋ, Wr. Cham haŋ; MK: PMnong *haŋ, Bahnar (AC) çaŋ. [< MK]

ˣ*haduah 'look for; search', Rade duah, Jarai (Lee) həduah, Chru duah, N. Roglai duah, Haroi athŭh, W. Cham ʈoah, PR Cham ʈwah, Wr. Cham dụah. [The vowel suggests a MK origin]

ˣ*hagɛt -f 'why? what?', Jarai (PL) həgɛt, Jarai (Lee) həgɛt, Chru kəyua gɛ, PR Cham hakĕt -f; k̬ĕt -f, Wr. Cham hagait; gait. [The vowel suggests a MK origin]

ˣ*haluaʔ 'sharp', Chru ləhŭʔ, N. Roglai hluəʔ, PR Cham halwŏʔ -i, Wr. Cham halụak. [The vowel suggests a MK origin]

ˣ*haləʔ 'chaff; rice dust', Chru lɔ:ʔ 'remove husk', W. Cham (Headley) /lŏʔ/. Restricted to Highlands Chamic plus W. Cham. [The vowel suggests a MK origin]

ˣ*haŋ 'hot; spicy', Rade hăŋ, Jarai (PL) hăŋ, Jarai (Lee) hăŋ, Chru haŋ, N. Roglai hak, Tsat ha:ŋ⁴², Haroi hăŋ, W. Cham hăŋ, PR Cham hăŋ, Wr. Cham həŋ; MK: PNB *hăŋ, PMnong *hăŋ 'peppery', PSB (Efimov) *haŋ, PKatuic *ha:ŋ, *hɛ:ŋ 'hot'. Cf. Malay sahang 'black pepper' ?

ˣ*haŋɔ 'pine', Rade həŋo, Chru həŋɔ, N. Roglai haŋŏ; MK: PNB *haŋo, PKatuic *səŋhɔ:. Restricted to Highlands Chamic. [The vowel also suggests a MK origin]

ˣ*hia 'cry; weep', Rade hia, Jarai (PL) hĭa, Chru hia, N. Roglai hia, Tsat hia³³, Haroi hea, W. Cham hea, PR Cham hya, Wr. Cham hịā. [The vowel suggests a MK origin]

ˣ*hɔʔ 'sweat; bleed; leak', Rade kəhŏʔ, Jarai (Lee) hŏʔ 'to bleed', W. Cham hauʔ -v, PR Cham (Lee) hŏʔ, Wr. Cham (AC) huak; MK: PSB (Efimov) *hu:c 'drink; leak'. [The vowel also suggests a MK origin]

ˣ*hɔk 'pour out; spill', Rade hŏk, Jarai (Lee) hɔk 'to abort', Chru hɔʔ 'spill', Haroi hŏʔ 'to spill, pour', PR Cham hŏʔ, Wr. Cham hauk; MK: PNB *ŭk, PKatuic *[t/d]əhɔʔ, *həhɔʔ. [The vowel also suggests a MK origin]

ˣ*hua 'pull', Jarai (PL) hŏa (Ouest), Jarai (Lee) hua, Chru hua 'pull along' hwa -vʀ, W. Cham hoa, PR Cham hwa, Wr. Cham hụā. [The vowel suggests this is of MK origin] ˣ*hua? 'eat rice', Rade huă?, Jarai (PL) huă?, Jarai (Lee) hua? -ă, Chru hua?, Tsat hua?[24], W. Cham hoa?, PR Cham hwă?, Wr. Cham hu̧ak. [The vowel suggests a MK origin.]

ˣ*hual 'cloud, fog, mist', Chru hual, N. Roglai huan, PR Cham hol, Wr. Cham hu̧əl; MK: PKatuic *[h/ɣ]əhuɔl 'smoke'. Cf. ˣdhual/r -f; here the same etymon, but probably with a different prefixal element, has been borrowed more than once into Chamic.

ˣ*hayua? 'harvest (rice)', Chru yua?, N. Roglai riyua?, Haroi yŏ?, W. Cham yoa?. Restricted to Highlands Chamic plus Haroi and W. Cham. [Both the vowel and the restriction suggest this is MK in origin.]

ˣ*hurɛt 'rope; vine', Acehnese urɛt, Rade hruĕ? (m), Jarai (PL) hrĕ? (Hd.), Jarai (Lee) hruĕ? (m), N. Roglai hure?, Haroi hərĕ?, W. Cham hrĕ?. [The vowel suggests a MK origin]

ˣ*hə?a:p'to yawn', Acehnese sɯmɯŋɯp [Note: This Acehnese form looks like it is from *sama + *ŋap], Rade həap, Jarai (Phraya Prachakij-karacak) ?aap, Chru səmaũ:?, N. Roglai sama-?ă:? [Note: Notice the first morpheme], Haroi hə-?au? [Notice that the word is treated as having two morphemes], PMalayic *uap, POc *mawap, PMP (*ma)huab, *huab; PSB (Efimov) ŋga:p, PNB *kaqa⁵⁵p, Vietnamese ngáp, PKatuic *həŋ?ua:p.

ˣ*jaray 'Jorai', Rade jərai -v-i, Chru mənih jərai -i, N. Roglai manũih jərai, W. Cham çarai.

ˣ*jaw 'to deliver', Jarai (PL) jaŭ, Jarai (Lee) jau 'to trust', PR Cham çaw, Wr. Cham jaw. With the *pa- 'causative' prefix: ˣ*pajaw, Jarai (Lee) pəjau, N. Roglai pajau.

ˣ*jɛ? 'near; about to' Rade jĕ?, Jarai (PL) jĕ?, Jarai (Lee) jɛ? -1, Chru jɛ?; məjɛ? 'near', N. Roglai je? si 'about to'; je? 'near', Tsat se?⁴², Haroi sɪ?, W. Cham çĕ?; maçĕ? 'nearly', PR Cham çɛ?, Wr. Cham jaik; MK: PNB *ajeq 'near'. [The vowel also suggests a MK origin]

ˣ*jɔh 'broken; spoilt', Rade jɔh, Jarai (PL) jŏh, Jarai (Lee) jɔh, Chru jɔh, N. Roglai joh, Haroi sŭh, W. Cham jɔh 'snap', PR Cham çɔh, Wr. Cham jauh. [The vowel suggests a MK origin]

ˣ*ju:? 'black', Rade jŭ?, Jarai (PL) jŭ?, Jarai (Lee) jŭ?, Chru ju:?, N. Roglai ju:?, Haroi su?, W. Cham çu?, PR Cham çu?, Wr. Cham juk; MK: Bahnar (AC) jŭ, PSB (Efimov) *ju:? 'black, dark'. [The vowel length also suggests a MK origin]

ˣ*jua? 'step on; tread', Rade juă?, Jarai (PL) juă?, Jarai (Lee) juă?, Chru jəwa?, N. Roglai jua?, Tsat sua?⁴², Haroi sŭ? -i, W. Cham çoa?, PR Cham çwă?, Wr. Cham ju̧ak; MK: PMnong *jot 'trample', PSB (Efimov) *jɔ:t. [The vowel also suggests a MK origin] ˣ*jum 'around' cf. ˣ*pajum 'meet together', Rade jŭm, Jarai (PL) jum, Jarai (Lee) jŭm 'around', N. Roglai pajup 'assemble, gather', PR Cham yɔm; MK: PMnong *jŭm.

ˣ*juəy 'don't', Chru juəi, W. Cham çuai, PR Cham çoy, Wr. Cham juai. [The vowel suggests a MK origin]

ˣ*jəh 'PARTICLE', Rade jih 'completely' PR Cham çəh, Wr. Cham jəḥ 'vraiment'. [The vowel suggests a MK origin]

ˣ*kacua 'firstborn', Jarai (Lee) kəcua, N. Roglai kacua, Haroi kəcoa 'oldest child', W. Cham kacoa, PR Cham kacwa, Wr. Cham kacụā. [The vowel suggests a MK origin]

ˣ*kacua 'to spit', Jarai (Lee) kəcua, PR Cham (Lee) cuwa (the first syllable of the original has dropped).

ˣ*k-am-lɔ ? 'dumb; mute', cf. Mnong, Acehnese klɔ, Rade kəmlo, Jarai (PL) kŭmlo, Chru kəmlɔ̆, N. Roglai kumlo, Haroi kəmlɔ, W. Cham ḳəm lɔ, PR Cham kamlɔ, Wr. Cham kamlauw; MK: PMnong *kəmlo, PSB (Efimov) *kəmlɔ:. Notice particularly the lack of the infix in the Acehnese form, and the treatment of the word as two separate morphemes in W. Cham. [The vowel also suggests a MK origin]

ˣ*ka:ŋ 'chin; jaw', Acehnese kɯəŋ, Rade kaŋ, Jarai (PL) kaŋ, Jarai (Lee) kaŋ, Chru təlka:ŋ; ka:ŋ, N. Roglai ka:k, Tsat ka:ŋ³³, Haroi kaŋ, W. Cham kaŋ, PR Cham kaŋ, Wr. Cham kaŋ, Malay rahang ?; MK: PNB *kaŋ, PMnong *kaŋ 'chin', PSB (Efimov) *ka:ŋ, PKatuic *tə?ba:ŋ 'jaw'.

ˣ*kaduŋ 'pocket; pouch', Jarai (Lee) kəduŋ, Chru kəduŋ 'bag', Tsat thuŋ¹¹, Haroi kəthŭŋ, W. Cham kaṭuŋ 'bag', PR Cham (Blood, Lee) kəṭùŋ, Malay kandung; MK: PNB *gadŭŋ, Bahnar (AC) kəduŋ, PKatuic *kəndo:ŋ, *kəduŋ, *ʒəduŋ 'basket, bowl', Katu AD ʒəduŋ 'men's basket worn around waist' [Note: The form occurs in MK, PC, and Malay, with the core meaning being 'pouch'. Despite its occurrence in Malay, this form looks ultimately to be MK in origin.].

ˣ*ka?u:? 'barkcloth; tree species', Rade (Lee) kə?ŭ?, Jarai (Lee) kə?ŭ?, N. Roglai (Lee) ka?u:?. Note the restriction to Highlands Chamic. [The long vowel also suggests a MK origin]

ˣ*ka?u:? 'worried; sad', Jarai (Lee) kə?ŭ?, Chru kə?ŭ:?, Haroi kə?ou?, PR Cham (Lee) ka?u?. [The vowel length suggests a MK origin]

ˣ*kabac 'scratch (an itch)', Chru kəba:i?, Haroi kəphiai? 'scratch'. Restricted to Highlands Chamic plus Haroi. [The final also suggests a MK origin] ˣ*kabaw 'water buffalo', Rade kəbau, Jarai (PL) kəbəu, Jarai (Lee) kəbau, Chru kəba:u -1, N. Roglai kabau, Haroi kəphɨau, W. Cham kabau, PR Cham kapaw, Wr. Cham kabaw, Malay kĕrbau; MK: Bahnar (AC) kapô; kəpô, PSB (Efimov) *'grəpu:. [Despite its occurrence in various Malayic dialects, this word looks to be a MK borrowing]

ˣ*kacuh 'to spit', Rade kəčuh, Jarai (Lee) kəcuh, Chru kəcuh, Haroi kəcoh -f, W. Cham tacuh -i, Wr. Cham (AC) kačuḥ, PNB *kačuh, PSB (Efimov) *chɔh, *jhɔh, PKatuic *kəcɔh, *kəcɔ:h.

ˣ*kala:ŋ 'hawk; bird of prey', Acehnese klɯəŋ 'kite' -i, Rade tlaŋ -i 'bird of prey; hawk', Jarai (PL) klaŋ, Jarai (Lee) klaŋ 'eagle, kite', Chru kəla:ŋ 'bird of prey', N. Roglai kala:k 'bird of prey', Haroi kəlaŋ, PR Cham kalaŋ, Wr. Cham kalaŋ, Malay hĕlang; MK: Bahnar (AC) klaŋ-an, PSB *tsələŋ, PKatuic *kəlha:ŋ. Headley (1976) also suggested that this was originally a MK etymon, later borrowed into a handful of WMP languages.

ˣ*kapa:s 'cotton', Acehnese gapɯəh, Rade kəpaih, Jarai (PL) kǝpaih, Jarai (Lee) kəpaih, Chru kəpa:h, N. Roglai kapa, Tsat pa³³, Haroi kəpah, W. Cham kapah, Malay kapas, PWMP *kapes 'cotton, Gossypium spp.'; MK: PNB *kapayh, PKatuic *kəpa:jh, PKatuic *kəpa:jh; *həpa:jh. Note that the PC vowel does not match the PWMP, but does match the PNB and the PKatuic. Incidentally, Lee's apparent reconstruction of length in the onset syllable is simply a mistake, probably a typing error. [The origin of this word is a subject of commentary. This word looks like an early loan into WMP, possibly from Indic. Headley (1976:#2.1) notes possible Sanskrit and Hindi sources, cf. Sanskrit karpaasa. Baxter (1989) analyzes it as an Austroasiatic borrowing, that is, from the larger family that includes MK.]

ˣ*kapuat 'to close', Rade (Lee) kəpuat, kəpăt, Jarai (Lee) kəpŏt, N. Roglai (Lee) kapi:ʔ, Haroi kəpŏaʔ. Note the restriction to Highlands Chamic, plus Haroi. [The diphthong suggests a MK origin]

ˣ*kapuat ? 'handful', Rade kəpăt, Jarai (Lee) kəpŏt, W. Cham ha kapoaʔ. Restricted to Highlands Chamic. [The vowel also suggests a MK origin]

ˣ*karah 'ring', Rade krah, Chru krăh -n, N. Roglai karah, Haroi krăh, W. Cham karah, PR Cham karăh, Wr. Cham karaḥ. [The nasalization suggests a MK origin]

ˣ*katər 'corn; grain', Rade kətər, Jarai (Lee) kətər 'corn', N. Roglai (Lee) katɛ, Haroi kətɔl. Note the restriction of the distribution to the Highlands Chamic languages plus Haroi. [The vowel also suggests a MK origin]

ˣ*kɛʔ 'bite; snap at; peck', Rade kĕʔ, Jarai (PL) kĕʔ, Jarai (Lee) kĕʔ, Chru kɛʔ 'bite', N. Roglai keʔ, Haroi kĕʔ, W. Cham kĕʔ, PR Cham kĕʔ, Wr. Cham kaik. [The vowel suggests a MK origin] ˣ*khan 'cloth; blanket', Jarai (PL) khăn, Jarai (Lee) khăn, Chru khan, N. Roglai khat 'cotton cloth', W. Cham khăn, PR Cham khăn, Wr. Cham khən, Malay kain; MK: PNB *khăn 'blanket', Bahnar (AC) khăn.

ˣ*khiaʔ 'burnt smell', Rade khiăʔ 'crust at bottom of pot', Jarai (Lee) khiăʔ, Chru khiaʔ, N. Roglai khiaʔ 'scarred, scorched', Haroi khĕaʔ 'burnt (rice)', PR Cham khyăʔ, Wr. Cham khịak. [The diphthong suggests a MK origin]

ˣ*khɔːŋ 'dry (weather)', Acehnese khuəŋ 'drought' (Durie notes varia-tion in the nasalization), Rade khoŋ 'end of rain', Jarai (Lee) khoŋ, Chru khɔːŋ 'fair', N. Roglai khoːk 'dry, sunny', Haroi khɔŋ 'refers to when it has finished raining', PR Cham khɔŋ, Wr. Cham khauŋ. [The vowel suggests a MK origin]

ˣ*klaːs 'escape', cf. 'lose', Acehnese lhɯəh, Rade tlaih, Jarai (PL) klaih, Jarai (Lee) klaih, Chru klaːh, N. Roglai tla, Haroi tlah, W. Cham klah 'to free', PR Cham klăh, Wr. Cham klaḥ-cǐm ṭi pay; MK: Bahnar (AC) klah, PKa-tuic (DT) *–klah, *–lah. With *pə- causative prefix: 'escape, cause to; save; release' ˣ*pə-klaːs, Acehnesepɯ-lhɯəh 'free', Rade tlaih, Jarai (PL) tăklaih ɗuaï? (Hd.), Jarai (Lee) pəklaih, Chru pəklaːh, N. Roglai tatlah, PR Cham paklăh, Wr. Cham paklah; MK: PMnong *klas 'release'. With *pə- causative prefix: 'take apart, dismantle' *pə-klaːs, Rade mətlaih, N. Roglai patla. Cf. 'escape'.

ˣ*klah 'to lose', cf. 'escape', Jarai (Lee) klah, Haroi tlah 'to slip away or escape, e.g. chicken from being tied', W. Cham lah, PR Cham (Lee) klah; MK: PKatuic (DT) *–klah, *–lah. [Note: This looks to be a doublet of the ety-mon for 'escape'].

ˣ*klan 'boa; python', Acehnese ulɯə lhan, Rade tlăn, Jarai (PL) tlăn, klăn, Jarai (Lee) klăn, Chru klan 'python', N. Roglai tlat, Haroi tlăn 'boa', W. Cham klăn, PR Cham klăn, Wr. Cham klan; MK: Bahnar (AC) klăn, PSB (Efi-mov) *klan.

ˣ*klay 'penis', Chru klai, N. Roglai pitlai 'testicles', Haroi tlai, W. Cham klai, PR Cham klay, Wr. Cham klai, PSB (Efimov) *klʌw 'man, male, penis', PKatuic *[k/g]əlh[ɛ/ə]j.

ˣ*klɛʔ 'steal', Rade tlɛ̆ʔ; kənɛ̆ʔ, Jarai (PL) klɛ̆ʔ, Jarai (Lee) klɛ̆ʔ, Chru klɛʔ, N. Roglai tleʔ, Tsat keʔ²⁴ -m, W. Cham klɛ̆ʔ, PR Cham klɛ̆ʔ, Wr. Cham klaik; MK: Bahnar (AC) klĕ. [The vowel also suggests a MK origin]

ˣ*klɔh 'to break', Jarai (PL) klŏh, Jarai (Lee) klŏh -1, Chru klɔh 'cut (skin)', N. Roglai tloh, Haroi tlŏh, W. Cham klɔh 'cut (skin)', PR Cham klŏh, Wr. Cham klauḥ. [The vowel suggests a MK origin]

ˣ*kluan 'behind; buttocks', Rade tluon, Jarai (PL) klɔn, Jarai (Lee) klɔn, N. Roglai tluat 'buttocks', Haroi tlŏn, PR Cham klŏn, Wr. Cham klauŋ;

MK: PKatuic (DT) *tantuun 'behind'. Note that the MK is spatial, not anatomi-
cal. [The vowel also suggests a MK origin]

ˣ*klun -f 'tadpole', Rade tlŭn, Chru kluːt -f -1; MK: PSB (Efimov)
*klɯn.

ˣ*kləp 'stab; poke', Rade tlŏʔ, Chru kləuʔ, N. Roglai tləʔ, Haroi tlău̯ʔ,
Wr. Cham (AC) kləp; klap; MK: PMnong *tŏp, Bahnar (AC) klak, klâk, klâp,
klǫ̂k. [The vowel also suggests a MK origin]

ˣ*kɔːʔ 'white', Rade koʔ, Jarai (PL) kɔ, Jarai (Lee) koʔ -1, Chru kɔːʔ, N.
Roglai koːʔ, Haroi kɔʔ, W. Cham kɔʔ in patih kɔʔ 'very white', PR Cham kŏʔ;
akŏʔ -1, Wr. Cham kauk; MK: PKatuic (DT) *klook. [The vowel also suggests a
MK origin]

ˣ*kɔːŋ 'bracelet', Rade koŋ, Jarai (PL) koŋ, Jarai (Lee) kɔŋ 'brass',
Chru kɔːŋ, N. Roglai koːk, Haroi kɔŋ, PR Cham kɔŋ, Wr. Cham kauŋ; MK: PNB
*koŋ, PMnong *kôŋ, PSB (Efimov) *kʌːɪŋ 'copper bracelet', PKatuic (DT)
*kóng, PKatuic *həkɑŋ; *həŋkɑŋ. [The vowel also suggests a MK origin]

ˣ*kɔh 'cut off; shorten', Acehnese kɔh, Rade kɔh, Jarai (PL) kɔh, Jarai
(Lee) kɔh, Chru kɔh, N. Roglai koh, Haroi kɔh -1, W. Cham kɔh 'to lop off'.
[The vowel suggests a MK origin]

ˣ*krɔ 'dry', Rade kro, Jarai (PL) krɔ rɔ̆rŏ, Jarai (Lee) kro, N. Roglai kro,
Haroi krɔ; MK: PMnong *kro, PSB (Efimov) *rɔ. Note that this is limited to
Highlands Chamic and Haroi among the Chamic languages, but reconstructs in
two of the Bahnaric branches. [The vowel also suggests a MK origin]

ˣ*krɔːŋ 'river', Acehnese kruəŋ, Rade kroŋ, Jarai (PL) kroŋ, Jarai (Lee)
krɔŋ, Chru ia krɔːŋ 'stream', N. Roglai kroːk, W. Cham karɔŋ, PR Cham krɔŋ,
Wr. Cham krauŋ; MK: PMnong *kroŋ, Bahnar (AC) kroŋ, PKatuic *kərhuaŋ.

ˣ*kruac 'a citrus', Rade kruĕʔ, Jarai (PL) ɓoh krə̆ʔ e, ɓoh krŭə̆ʔ (E)
(Hd.), Jarai (Lee) kruăiʔ, PR Cham kroyʔ, Wr. Cham krụ̯ɑc, Proto-Hrê-Sedang
*kruč; MK: PMnong *kroc, PSB (Efimov) *kruə̆č. [The vowel and the final also
suggest a MK origin]

ˣ*kuac 'gather, amass', Chru kuaiʔ, N. Roglai kuaiʔ, W. Cham kuaiʔ.
Restricted to Highlands Chamic plus W. Cham. [The vowel and the final also
suggest a MK origin]

ˣ*kuah 'shave, scrape', Rade kueh -v, Jarai (Lee) kuah, Chru kuah, N.
Roglai kuah, Haroi koah, W. Cham koah; MK: PNB *akoyh 'shave', PMnong
*kos 'shave off', PSB (Efimov) *kɔːs, PKatuic *kuah, *kuajh 'scrape, shave'.
Restricted to Highlands Chamic plus Haroi and W. Cham. [The vowel also suggests a MK origin]

ˣ*kuan 'gibbon', Rade kueñ -v, Jarai (PL) kra kuăñ, Chru kuan, W. Cham kuan, PR Cham kon, Wr. Cham kɥən; MK: PSB (Efimov) *kuə ₗɲ. [The vowel also suggests a MK origin]

*kulit 'skin' + ˣ*sɔ:ʔ 'lungs; placenta' is 'lungs; placenta', Acehnese sũəp -fn, Rade kəsŏʔ, Jarai (PL) kəsŏʔ, Jarai (Lee) kəsŏʔ, Chru kəlsɔ:ʔ, N. Roglai kuli:ʔ so:ʔ, Haroi kələsɔʔ, W. Cham kasɔʔ, PR Cham thɔʔ 'placenta', Wr. Cham thauk 'placenta; lungs'; MK: PKatuic *sɑh ʔ. [The first morpheme is Austronesian; in the second, the vowels suggest a MK origin]

ˣ*la:ŋ 'spread out (a mat)', Rade laŋ, Jarai (PL) laŋ, Jarai (Lee) laŋ, Chru la:ŋ 'unroll', N. Roglai la:k, W. Cham laŋ, PR Cham laŋ, Wr. Cham laŋ; MK: PMnong *lăk -f 'spread', Bahnar (AC) lāŋ, PSB (Efimov) *laʔ -f 'spread, unroll'.

ˣ*laʔi 'basket, winnowing', Rade ei, Jarai (PL) rəʔi, Jarai (Lee) rəʔi, Chru ləʔi 'basket (shallow)', N. Roglai laʔi, Haroi ləʔi, W. Cham laʔi 'large round', PR Cham lii, Wr. Cham lii; MK: PSB (Efimov) *ləʔi:, PKatuic *ʔərie, *kərie.

ˣ*lac 'say', Rade lač, Jarai (PL) laïʔ, Jarai (Lee) lăiʔ, Chru la:iʔ, N. Roglai la:iʔ, Haroi laiʔ, W. Cham laiʔ cf. 'if', PR Cham layʔ, Wr. Cham lac, PMnong *lah, PSB (Efimov) *lah 'say, scold'. [The final also suggests a MK origin]

ˣ*lahiăʔ 'to lose', Rade luč, Chru ləhĩaʔ, W. Cham lahiɨʔ (n). Restricted to Highlands Chamic plus W. Cham. [The vowel and its nasalization also suggest a MK origin]

ˣ*lamən -v 'tired; weak', Rade emăn, Jarai (PL) rămŭan, W. Cham lamĕn -v 'weak, soft, bloated', PR Cham limăn -v 'feeble', Wr. Cham liman; MK: PKatuic (DT) *qadl_h 'tired'. [The vowel also suggests a MK origin]

ˣ*lɛʔ 'fall into', Rade lɛʔ buh, Jarai (PL) lɛ̆ʔ, Jarai (Lee) lɛ̆ʔ, Chru lɛʔ, N. Roglai leʔ, Tsat leʔ²⁴, Haroi lɛ̆ʔ, W. Cham lɛ̆ʔ, PR Cham lɛ̆ʔ, Wr. Cham laik. [The vowel suggests a MK origin]

ˣ*lɔ:k 'to peel', Acehnese pluəʔ, Rade lok 'take bark off tree', Jarai (Lee) lok -v, Chru lɔ:ʔ; lɔ:h -f, N. Roglai lo:ʔ; calo:ʔ, Haroi lɔʔ, W. Cham lɔʔ, PR Cham lɔʔ, Wr. Cham lauk, PMP *bulut 'coconut husk'; MK: Bahnar (AC) lōk, PSB (Efimov) *plŏ:ʔ 'peel, strip off skin, hull', PKatuic *lɨɛt, *luɔt. [The vowel also suggests a MK origin]

ˣ*lɔ:ŋ 'try, prove, test', Rade loŋ, Chru pərlɔ:ŋ 'try, prove, test', PR Cham (Blood) loŋ, Wr. Cham lauŋ; MK: PNB *loŋ, PMnong *rəloŋ 'try, test'. [The vowel also suggests a MK origin] ˣ*luay 'swim', Rade lue, Jarai (PL) loĭ -v, luaĭ (Hd.), Jarai (Lee) luai, Chru luai ia, N. Roglai luai, Haroi luəi -v, PR Cham loy, Wr. Cham lựai, PMnong *re ?, PSB (Efimov) *rɛ:, PKatuic *[b/ʔb]əluɔ[j]h. [The vowel also suggests a MK origin]

ˣ*luc 'complete; die, end; perished', Rade luč 'lose'; luč lie 'get lost', Haroi lŭi? -v, W. Cham luai -vf 'stop, quit', PR Cham lŭy?, Wr. Cham luc. [The final suggests a MK origin]

ˣ*luəy 'put, place, discard; allow', Rade lui, Chru luəi, N. Roglai luəi, Haroi lui, Wr. Cham buḥ. [The vowel suggests a MK origin]

ˣ*luəy 'reject; quit', Rade lui, Jarai (PL) lui, Jarai (Lee) lui, Chru luəi, W. Cham luai, PR Cham loy, Wr. Cham lựai. [The vowel suggests a MK origin]

ˣ*ləp 'fold', Jarai (PL) lŏp (Ouest); lăp (S), Chru ləu?, PR Cham lŏw?, Wr. Cham ləp; PMP *le(m)pit -f; *lepet -f 'wrap; fold'. Despite the similarities, the PMP forms are not related. [The vowel suggests a MK origin]

ˣ*maduan see ˣ*ʔaduan

ˣ*madəh 'awaken', Rade mədih, Jarai (PL) pɨdih, mədɨh (Hd.), Jarai (Lee) mədɨh, Chru mədəh 'stay awake', N. Roglai madəh, Haroi məthɨh, W. Cham maṭəh, PR Cham mɨṭəh, Wr. Cham mɨdəḥ. [The vowel suggests a MK origin]

ˣ*miaŋ 'cheek; jaw', Acehnese miəŋ, Rade mieŋ, Jarai (PL) mɛŋ, Jarai (Lee) mɛ̆ŋ; mɛŋ, W. Cham miaŋ, PR Cham mieŋ, Wr. Cham mjeŋ. [The diphthong suggests a MK origin]

ˣ*mɔ:? 'wife', Rade mo?, Jarai (PL) mŏ? (Est), N. Roglai mõ:? 'midwife', Haroi mɔ?, W. Cham mă? -v, PR Cham (Lee) mu? -v. [The vowel suggests a MK origin]

ˣ*məŋ 'from', Rade mŏ̆ŋ, Jarai (PL) mŏ̆ŋ, Jarai (Lee) mŏ̆ŋ, Chru mɨ̆ŋ -v -n (prep.), N. Roglai munɨ -vf, Haroi mɨ̆ŋ (grammatical particle), W. Cham məŋ, PR Cham mɨ̆ŋ, Wr. Cham mɨŋ. [The vowel suggests a MK origin]

ˣ*ñu? 'dive; submerge', Rade ñŭ?, Jarai (PL) pəñŭ?; ñŭ?, Jarai (Lee) ñŭ?, Chru ñu? ia, N. Roglai ñŭ?, Haroi ñŭk -f, W. Cham ñŭk -f 'submerge', PR Cham ñŭk -f, Wr. Cham ñuk; MK: PSB (Efimov) *ɲəp 'dive, submerge, set' ? .

ˣ*nɛh 'to elbow', Rade (Tharpe) ñɛh -n, N. Roglai ñeh -n julukiac, PR Cham (Lee) ñɛh. [The vowel suggests a MK origin]

ˣ*ŋɔ? 'upgrade; above; east', Jarai (PL) ŋŏ? 'east', gah yang hrəi ɓlɛ̆?, Jarai (Lee) ŋŏ? 'east', Chru gah ŋɔ? 'east', Tsat ŋoʔ⁴²/²⁴ -t?, Haroi ŋŏ?, PR Cham (Lee) ŋŏ?, Wr. Cham (AC) ŋauk. [The vowel suggests a MK origin] ˣ*padiaŋ -v 'carry; transport', Rade mədiăŋ -v, Jarai (PL) bə̆diaŋ -i, Chru pərdiaŋ, PR Cham paçyə̆ŋ, Wr. Cham pajiəŋ; MK: PMnong *pədiâŋ, PKatuic (DT) *pataeng 'transport'. [The diphthong also suggests a MK origin]

ˣ*pagəm 'dove', Jarai (PL) bə̆rə̆gom ?, Haroi pəkhŭm. Note the restriction to the Highlands Chamic languages, plus Haroi. [The vowel suggests a MK origin]

ˣ*pah 'to slap', Rade pah, Jarai (Lee) pah, Chru pah, N. Roglai pah, Haroi pă̆h, W. Cham pah, PR Cham pă̆h, Wr. Cham pah; MK: PKatuic *[h/s]əm[p/b]ah, *[h/ɣ]əpah, *həbah.

ˣ*paɗar -f 'tell, send; command', Chru pəɗar -1, N. Roglai paɗa 'tell, send', Haroi pəɗal -f 'command, to tell to do sth', W. Cham paɗă̆r 'order, demand, summon'. [The medial consonant suggests a MK origin]

ˣ*paɗaw 'warm, hot', Rade mədau, Jarai (PL) pə̆ɗəu, Chru pəɗau, Tsat ɗa:u?⁴² , Haroi pəɗau 'be warm', W. Cham paɗau, PR Cham paɗaw, Wr. Cham paɗaw; MK: PKatuic *[k/g]əta:w, *[k/g]ətaw 'hot'. [The medial consonant also suggests a MK origin]

ˣ*paɗia? 'hot (weather); sunshine', Jarai (Lee) pə?iă?, Chru pəɗia?, N. Roglai paɗia?, Tsat ɗia?²⁴ , Haroi pəɗĕ̆a?, W. Cham paɗea?, PR Cham paɗyă̆?, Wr. Cham paɗịak. [The medial consonant and the vowel suggest a MK origin]

ˣ*palɛ? 'to drop', Rade kəplĕ̆?, Chru pəlɛ?, N. Roglai palε?, Haroi pəlĕ̆?. Restricted to Highlands Chamic plus Haroi. [The vowel also suggests a MK origin]

ˣ*pɛt 'pick, pluck', Acehnese pʌt, Rade pĕ̆?, Jarai (PL) pĕ̆?, Jarai (Lee) pĕ̆?, Chru pε?, N. Roglai pe?, Tsat pi⁵⁵ -ft, Haroi pĕ̆?, W. Cham pĕ̆?, PR Cham pĕ̆?, Wr. Cham paik. [The vowel suggests a MK origin]

ˣ*pha 'different', Jarai (Lee) pha, N. Roglai pha, Haroi pha; MK: PNB *pha. Restricted to Highlands Chamic.

ˣ*picah 'broken; break', Acehnese picah, Rade mčah, Jarai (PL) pə̆cah, Jarai (Lee) pəcah, Chru pəcah, Tsat tsa⁵⁵ , Haroi pəcă̆h, W. Cham pacah, PR Cham pacă̆h, Wr. Cham pacă̆h, Malay pĕcah; MK: PMnong *bəcah 'break', PSB (Efimov) *'pəcah 'split, smash, break', PKatuic *pəc[ə/a]h, *kəc[ə/a]h 'crack'. Note that this word is found both in Austronesian and MK, but looks to me like it originated in MK.

ˣ*pioh 'put, place', Rade pioh, Chru piɔh, W. Cham mapiah. Restricted to Highlands Chamic plus W. Cham. The vowel suggests that it is either borrowed or the result of the coalescence of two morphemes.

ˣ*pit 'sleep; close eyes', Rade pĭt, Jarai (PL) pit, Jarai (Lee) pit, Chru pi:? 'shut eyes', N. Roglai pi:?, Haroi pei?, PR Cham pi?, Wr. Cham pik 'mourir;

fermer l'oeil'; MK: PNB *qɓĭč 'lie down', PMnong *ɓĭc, PSB (Efimov) *ɓik, PKatuic *ʔɓvjʔ, *ʔɓʌjʔ.

ˣ/*plum -1 'land leech', Rade plum -1, Jarai (PL) plum, Chru ploːm -vl, N. Roglai pluːp, W. Cham plom -v, PR Cham plom, Wr. Cham ploṁ; MK: PNB *plàm, PMnong *plom, PSB (Efimov) *plʌːm, PKatuic *bəlhʌːm, *pəlhʌːm.

ˣˣ*pɔh 'strike; pound', Acehnese pɔh, Chru pɔh, N. Roglai pɔ̆h 'to pound', PR Cham papɔ̆h, Wr. Cham papauḥ. [The vowel suggests a MK origin]. With *-ən- instrumental infix: 'drumstick' ˣˣp-ən-ɔh cf. ˣˣpɔh, Rade hənɔh -i, Chru pənɔh, N. Roglai panɔ̆h, Haroi pənɔ̆h 'to drum'. [The vowel suggests a MK origin]

ˣˣ*pɔk 'to open', Rade pɔ̆k, Jarai (PL) pɔ̆k, Jarai (Lee) pɔ̆k, N. Roglai poʔ; MK: PMnong *pək, PSB (Efimov) *pəːʔ. [The vowel also suggests a MK origin]

ˣˣ*prɔːk 'squirrel', Rade prok, Jarai (PL) pro, Jarai (Lee) prɔ̆ʔ, Chru prɔːʔ, Haroi prɔʔ, W. Cham prɔʔ, PR Cham prɔʔ, Wr. Cham prauk; MK: PMnong *prok, Bahnar (AC) prŏk, PSB (Efimov) *prɔːʔ, PKatuic *[b/ʔɓ]ə(r/rh]oŋ, *tə[r/rh]oŋ. [The vowel also suggests a MK origin]

ˣˣ*prɔŋ 'big', Rade prɔ̆ŋ, Jarai (PL) prɔ̆ŋ, Jarai (Lee) prɔ̆ŋ, Chru prɔŋ, N. Roglai prok, Tsat pioŋʔ³³, Haroi prɔ̆ŋ, W. Cham pruŋ -v, PR Cham prɔ̆ŋ, Wr. Cham prauŋ. [The vowel suggests a MK origin]

ˣˣ*puːʔ 'carry in arms', Rade pŭʔ, Chru poːʔ, N. Roglai puːʔ, Haroi poʔ, W. Cham poʔ, Wr. Cham (AC) puʔ; MK: Bahnar (AC) pók. [The vowel length also suggests a MK origin]

ˣˣ*pə-puh (*pə- 'causative') 'blow away; chase', Jarai (PL) pə̆pŭh, Jarai (Lee) pəpuh 'chase', Chru puh 'blow', N. Roglai papuh; MK: PMnong *pŭh 'blow'. Restricted to Highlands Chamic.

ˣˣ*pulɛy 'gourd; squash', cf. *biluay, Rade plɛi, Jarai (PL) plui (m), Jarai (Lee) pləi, plui, ploi, N. Roglai pluəi (m), W. Cham plɔi (m), PR Cham ploy (m), Wr. Cham plu̦ai -v; MK: PNB *plùy.

ˣˣ*puːŋ 'straw (rice)', Acehnese jɯmpuŋ, Chru apoːŋ, Tsat puŋ³³ 'rice', W. Cham poŋ, PR Cham apyɔ̆ŋ, Wr. Cham apiəŋ. [The vowel length suggests a MK origin]

ˣˣ*puac 'scold; talk', Jarai (PL) pŭaĭʔ, Jarai (Lee) puăĭʔ, Chru puaiʔ, N. Roglai puaiʔ 'strong feelings; impatient', Haroi pɔ̆aiʔ, W. Cham puaiʔ, PR Cham poyʔ, Wr. Cham pu̦ac. [The final suggests a MK origin]

ˣˣ*pə-pət (*pə- 'causative') 'to fan', Jarai (Lee) pəpɨʔ 'to vibrate', N. Roglai pəʔ, Haroi pəpă̆ʔ; MK: PNB *pă̆y, PKatuic *[h/ɣ]əpɨʔ; *ʔəpɨʔ.

Restricted to Highlands Chamic plus Haroi. [The vowel also suggests a MK origin]

ˣ*pəh 'to open', Chru pəh 'open up', Haroi pɔ̆h, W. Cham pəh, PR Cham pɔ̆h, Wr. Cham pəh; MK: Bahnar (AC) pəha, PKatuic (DT) *pəəh. [The vowel also suggests a MK origin]

ˣ*pəŋ 'to nail; to hammer', Rade pɔ̆ŋ, Jarai (Lee) pɔ̆ŋ, Chru pəŋ; pə:ŋ 'to pound', N. Roglai pək, Haroi pɔ̆ŋ, W. Cham pəŋ, PR Cham pəŋ 'frapper sur la téte', Wr. Cham pəŋ, PMP *paku; MK: PMnong *pɔ̆ŋ. [The vowel also suggests a MK origin]

ˣ*pər 'to fly', Acehnese phʌ -i, Rade phiər -iv Note: It is only the Rade that looks to be borrowed after PC, Jarai (Lee) pɔ̆r, Chru pər, N. Roglai pə, Tsat pan[33], Haroi pɔl, W. Cham pɔ̆r, PR Cham pɔ̆r, Wr. Cham pər; MK: PNB *pɔ̆r, PMnong *pɔ̆r, Bahnar (AC) apɔ̆r; pɔ̆r, PSB (Efimov) *par, PKatuic (DT) *pâr, PKatuic *par, *pa:r. [The vowel also suggests a MK origin]

ˣ*radɛ 'Rhade', Rade edʼe, Chru mənih radʼɛ, N. Roglai manŭih radʼe, W. Cham radʼɛ, PR Cham radʼɛ, Wr. Cham radʼē. [The vowel and the meaning suggest a MK origin]

ˣ*ralɔ 'flesh; meat', Rade hlɔ, Jarai (Lee) hlo, Chru rəlɔ, N. Roglai ralo clf., W. Cham ralɔ, PR Cham ralɔ, Wr. Cham ralauw. [The vowel suggests a MK origin]

ˣ*raw 'wash', Acehnese rhah -iv, Rade rau, Jarai (PL) rau, Jarai (Lee) rau, Chru ra:u -1, N. Roglai rau, Tsat za:u[33], Haroi rau, W. Cham rau, PR Cham raw, Wr. Cham rau; MK: PNB *–raw, PMnong *raw, Bahnar (AC) rao, PSB (Efimov) *raw, PKatuic *ʔəriaw.

ˣ*rɛh 'cut', Jarai (Lee) rɛ̆h, Chru rɛh 'clean fish', N. Roglai reh 'operate, dissect', Haroi rɛ̆h, PR Cham (Lee) rɛh, PMnong *sreh, PSB (Efimov) *srɛ:h 'chop', PKatuic *hərɛh, *tərɛh, *[s/c]ərhɛ:ʔ, *tərhɛ:ʔ. [The vowel also suggests a MK origin]

ˣ*ribu:ʔ 'storm', Rade ebŭʔ, Jarai (Lee) rəbuʔ, Chru rəbu:ʔ, N. Roglai rubu:ʔ, Haroi ləphuʔ, W. Cham ŋin rapuʔ, PR Cham ripuʔ; rapuʔ, Wr. Cham ribūk, Malay ribut; MK: Bahnar (AC) həbut, PKatuic (DT) *rapuuq. Within wider Austronesian, this form is restricted to languages in western Indonesia and so is most likely also a loan into these AN languages.

ˣ*rɔ 'cage', Jarai (PL) ro (Pk), Jarai (Lee) ro, Chru rɔ, N. Roglai ro, Haroi rɔ, W. Cham rɔ. [The vowel suggests a MK origin]

ˣ*rɔ:ŋ 'raise; nourish', Rade roŋ 'take care of livestock', Jarai (PL) roŋ, Jarai (Lee) roŋ, Haroi rɔŋ 'raise, feed', PR Cham rɔŋ, Wr. Cham rauŋ; MK: Bahnar (AC) rōŋ. [The vowel also suggests a MK origin] ˣ*ruah 'choose', Rade ruah 'election', Jarai (PL) ruăh, Jarai (Lee) ruah, Chru rəwah, Haroi roah, PR Cham rwăh, Wr. Cham rụaḥ; MK: PNB *ràyh, PKatuic (DT) *r_s (vowel unclear), PKatuic *həriəh. [The diphthong also suggests a MK origin]

ˣ*ruay 'fly; bug; insect', Rade rue, Jarai (PL) ruaĭ, Jarai (Lee) ruai, Chru ruăi -n, N. Roglai ruai, Tsat zuai³³; za:i³³; a¹¹ la?²⁴, Haroi roai, W. Cham ruai, PR Cham roy, Wr. Cham rụai; MK: PNB *roy, PMnong *rəhway, PSB (Efimov) *rəhwəːy, PKatuic (DT) *róóy, PKatuic *[h/ɣ]əruɑj, *rə-ruɑj, *?əruɑj. [The vowel also suggests a MK origin]

ˣ*ruəy 'to crawl', Rade rui, Jarai (PL) rui, Jarai (Lee) rui, Tsat zoi³³, Haroi rui, W. Cham ruai. [The triphthong suggests a MK origin]

ˣ*rək 'grass; weeds', Rade rŏk, Jarai (PL) rək, Chru rə? 'grass; weeds', N. Roglai rə?, Tsat zə?²⁴, Haroi rŏ?, W. Cham rə?, PR Cham rŏ?; harŏ?, Wr. Cham rək; harək. [The vowel suggests a MK origin]

ˣ*sac 'bail (water to catch fish); splash; shake out', Acehnese suɨət 'bail', Rade sač ea 'bail water to catch fish', Jarai (Lee) săi?, Chru saːi?, N. Roglai saːi?, Tsat sai?²⁴, Haroi sŏ? -v, W. Cham sai?, PR Cham thay?, Wr. Cham thac. [The final consonant suggests a MK origin]

ˣ*sadər 'remember', Rade hədər, Jarai (PL) hŏdər, Jarai (Lee) hədər; hədŏr, Chru sədər, N. Roglai sidə, Haroi athŭl 'feel, sense', W. Cham pa-dăr 'remind; cause to remember', PR Cham haṭăr; ṭăr, Wr. Cham hadər; dər. [The vowel suggests a MK origin]

ˣ*sagər 'drum', Rade həgər, Jarai (PL) hŏgŏr, Jarai (Lee) həgŏr, Chru səgər, N. Roglai sagə, Haroi akhŭl, W. Cham ḳăr, PR Cham haḳăr, ḳăr, Wr. Cham hagar, hagər; gər; MK: PNB *hagăr, Bahnar (AC) həgər; çər, PSB (Efimov) *səŋghər, PKatuic *səgɨr; *səŋkəːr. [The vowel also suggests a MK origin]

ˣ*saɗap 'old (things)', Rade həɗăp, Jarai (Lee) hədăp ?ă, N. Roglai saɗa?. The restriction of the distribution to Highlands Chamic suggests that, despite the regular correspondences, this may be a post-PC borrowing. [The medial consonant also suggests a MK origin]

ˣ*saləŋ 'forever; eternally', Rade hlŏŋ lar, Jarai (Lee) hlɔŋ, PR Cham klɔŋ -i, Wr. Cham klauŋ. [The vowel suggests a MK origin]

ˣ*sapal 'arm', Acehnese sapai, Rade păl 'forearm', Jarai (PL) hŏpal, Jarai (Lee) həpal, Chru spal 'forearm', N. Roglai sapan, W. Cham pha pal 'forearm muscle', PR Cham hapăl, Wr. Cham hapəl; MK: PKatuic (DT) *qapaal 'shoulder'.

ˣ*sapuat 'to harvest', Rade puot -v?, Jarai (PL) puă?, Jarai (Lee) həpuă?, Chru spua?, N. Roglai sapuă?; sapua?. Restricted to Highlands Chamic. [The vowel also suggests a MK origin]

ˣ*(si)?jɔh 'drip; a drop', Jarai (PL) cf. tă?jɔh, Jarai (Lee) ?jɔh; cf. tə?jɔh 'to leak', Chru sə?iɔh, N. Roglai si?joh, Tsat ?iu⁵⁵, W. Cham ta?jɔh, PR Cham ta?jŏh, Wr. Cham ta/ñauḥ; MK: PNB *katoh 'drip; drop'. [The initial and the vowel also suggest a MK origin]

ˣ*siyaːm 'good; nice; pretty', Rade siam 'beautiful', Jarai (PL) hiăm, Jarai (Lee) hiam, Chru siaːm, N. Roglai siaːp, Haroi seam, W. Cham seam, PR Cham thyam, Wr. Cham sịaṁ; MK: PKatuic *[l/lh][e?ɛ]ːm, *lə-[l/lh][e/ɛ]ːm.

ˣ*sɔh 'only; empty; free, leisure', Acehnese sɔh, Jarai (PL) sŏh (Hd.), Jarai (Lee) sɔh 'empty', N. Roglai (Lee) soh; W. Cham sɔh, PR Cham thŏh, Wr. Cham thauḥ; MK: PNB *sasoh, PKatuic *[s/c]ənhɑh 'empty'. [The vowel also suggests a MK origin]

ˣ*sua 'pull out; seize', cf. ˣsuac 'pull out', Rade (Tharpe) sua, Jarai (Lee) sua 'seize', Haroi soa 'pull'. Note the distribution is restricted to Highlands Chamic plus Haroi. [The vowel suggests a MK origin]

ˣ*sua 'skin, dead', Jarai (Lee) sua, N. Roglai sua, PR Cham (Lee) sua. [The vowel suggests a MK origin]

ˣ*suay 'fish trap', Rade sue 'long fishtrap, N. Roglai suai. Restricted to Highlands Chamic. [The vowel also suggests a MK origin]

ˣ*sula 'leaf', Rade hla, Jarai (PL) hla, Jarai (Lee) hla, Chru səla, N. Roglai hla:? -h-f, Haroi həla, W. Cham hla, PR Cham hala, Wr. Cham halā; MK: PNB *hla, PSB (Efimov) *ḷhaː, PWB (Thomas) *hlaa, PKatuic *[p/b]əlhah, *həlhah.

ˣ*suəy 'slow; long time', Rade sui, Jarai (Lee) sui, Chru suəi, N. Roglai suəi, Haroi sui, W. Cham suai, PR Cham (Lee) soy; sroy -m. [The vowel suggests a MK origin]

ˣ*səm 'to wrap', Acẹhnese sɔm 'hide, put away' ?, Jarai (Lee) sɔm -1, Chru məsəm 'cover'; MK: PMnong *klăm. [The vowel also suggests a MK origin]

ˣ*səŋ ? 'with; and', Rade məbĭt hŏŋ, Jarai (PL) hăŋ, Chru səŋ; sə- 'negative particle', W. Cham hŏŋ -v 'with; and', PR Cham thŏŋ -v, Wr. Cham sauŋ. [The vowel suggests a MK origin]

ˣ*səna 'crossbow', Rade həna, Jarai (PL) hna (Pk), Chru səna, W. Cham haniŋ -f tapoŋ, PR Cham hani, Wr. Cham hani; MK: PMnong *səna, PSB (Efimov) *sənaː 'bow', PKatuic *sənhaː.

ˣ*tadrua? 'lid', Rade kədruă?, Chru tədrua?, PSB (Efimov) *khʼróːp 'to cover; a lid'. Restricted to Highlands Chamic. [The vowel also suggests this is of MK origin]

ˣ*taguː? 'get up; to stand up', Rade kəgŭ? pit, Jarai (PL) dəgŭ? -i, Jarai (Lee) təgu?, Chru təguː?, N. Roglai taguːk -f, Haroi cəkhʋ?, W. Cham taḳo?, PR Cham taḳo?, Wr. Cham tagok. [The vowel length suggests a MK origin]

ˣ*takuay 'neck', Acehnese takuə, Rade kəkue, Jarai (PL) tŏkuai, Jarai (Lee) təkuai, Chru təkuai, N. Roglai takuai, Tsat kuaːi³³, Haroi cəkŏai, W. Cham takuai, PR Cham takoy, Wr. Cham takṵai. [The vowel suggests a MK origin]

ˣ*taliat f? 'flute (front flute)', Rade ɗɪŋ kliŏ? -v 'side flute', Jarai (PL) tŏliă?, Chru təlia?, N. Roglai talia?. [The vowel suggests a MK origin]

ˣ*taluc 'last, lastborn', cf. ˣ*luc, Rade kluč 'youngest sibling', Jarai (Lee) təlui?, N. Roglai talui?, Haroi cəlŏi?, PR Cham talŭy?, Wr. Cham taluc. [The final suggests a MK origin]

ˣ*taluc plus reflex of *apui 'fire' is 'firebrand', Rade (Tharpe) kluič, Jarai (Lee) təlui?, N. Roglai (Lee) talui?. Limited to Highlands Chamic. [The final also suggests a MK origin]

ˣ*tamɛh 'pillar; post', Acehnese tamɛh, Rade kəmɛh, Jarai (PL) tŏmɛh, Jarai (Lee) təmɛh. [The vowel suggests a MK origin]

ˣ*tanɔ 'male', Rade kəno, Jarai (PL) tŏno, Jarai (Lee) təno, Chru tənɔ, N. Roglai tano -n, Haroi cənɔ; tənɔ dial., W. Cham tanɔ, PR Cham tanɔ 'male; son', Wr. Cham tanauw 'male; son'; MK: PNB *čano 'male; husband'. [The vowel also suggests a MK origin]

ˣ*tarapay 'rabbit', Rade pai, Jarai (PL) pai, Jarai (Lee) pai, Chru tərpaːi, N. Roglai tarapai, Haroi kəpai -i, W. Cham tapai, PR Cham tapay, Wr. Cham tapay, Malay tapai Treng.; MK: PMnong *tərpay, PSB (Efimov) *tsrəpaːy.

ˣ*tatuan 'wobbly', Chru tətuən, W. Cham tatuan. [The vowel suggests a MK origin]

ˣ*taɓak 'hang up', Rade (Tharpe) kəɓak, N. Roglai (Lee) taɓa?, PR Cham (Lee) kaɓă?; MK: PKatuic (DT) *_bak 'hang up'. [The medial consonant also suggests a MK origin]

ˣ*tɛ? 'torn, worn', Rade tĭ? -v, Chru tɛ?, N. Roglai te?. Note the restriction to Highlands Chamic. [The vowel also suggests a MK origin]

ˣ*tɔh 'undress; take off', Jarai (Lee) tŏh -l, Chru tɔh 'dismantle', N. Roglai toh, Haroi tŏh, W. Cham tɔh. Restricted to Highlands Chamic plus Haroi. [The vowel also suggests a MK origin] ˣ*tram 'soak', Rade tram, Jarai (PL) trăm (Pk et N), Jarai (Lee) tram, Chru tram, N. Roglai trap, Haroi trăm; dial. cərăm, PR Cham trăm, Wr. Cham trəm̀, PMP (*r)endem; MK: PNB *trăm, PSB (Efimov) *tram, PKatuic *tərh[ə/a]m.

ˣ*trɔŋ 'eggplant', Acehnese truəŋ, Rade trŏŋ, Jarai (PL) trŏŋ, Jarai (Lee) trɔŋ, Chru trɔŋ, N. Roglai trok, Tsat (hu¹¹) tsioŋʔ³³ -medial, Haroi trŏŋ, W. Cham trŏŋ, PR Cham trŏŋ; crŏŋ, Wr. Cham trauŋ; crauŋ, Malay tĕrung; MK: PNB *trŏŋ, PKatuic *həŋgɨŋ; *səkɨŋ ?. [The vowel also suggests a MK origin]

ˣ*truh 'arrive', Acehnese troh, Rade truh, Jarai (PL) truh, Jarai (Lee) truh, Chru truh, N. Roglai truh, Haroi troh 'escape'; MK: PNB *trŭh.

ˣ*tuːʔ 'to receive', Rade tŭʔ ə 'accept; consent, Jarai (Lee) tŭʔ, Chru [duːʔ maʔ], N. Roglai tuːʔ, W. Cham toʔ, PR Cham toʔ, Wr. Cham tok. [The vowel length suggests a MK origin]

ˣ*tuhɔ 'snare', Rade kəho, N. Roglai tuho, Haroi cəhɔ. Note the restriction to Highlands Chamic, plus Haroi. [The vowel also suggests a MK origin]

ˣ*tulɛh 'untie', Jarai (PL) tŏlɛh, Jarai (Lee) təlɛh, Chru təlɛh, Haroi cəlɛh, W. Cham talɛh, PR Cham talɛh, Wr. Cham talaiḥ. [The vowel suggests a MK origin]

ˣ*tulŏk 'disk shape; spherical shape', Jarai (Lee) təlŏʔ, N. Roglai (Lee) tulŏk -nf, W. Cham (Headley) /talŏk/, PR Cham (Lee) kəlŏʔ. [The vowel suggests a MK origin]

ˣ*tuɓuac 'beak', cf. 'lips', Rade kəɓoč -f, Jarai (PL) tŏɓuk, Jarai (Lee) təɓuăʔ, Chru təɓuaiʔ, N. Roglai tuɓueʔ, Haroi cəɓŏaiʔ, W. Cham caɓuaiʔ 'lips, bill', PR Cham caboyʔ, Wr. Cham cabʉac; MK: PKatuic *caʔɓah, *tərʔɓah ?. [The vowel and the final consonant also suggest a MK origin]

ˣ*təl 'arrive; until', Rade təl kə 'to the point that, so much that', Jarai (PL) tŏl, Jarai (Lee) təl 'sufficient', Tsat tan³³, Haroi tŏl -v 'come' dir. v., W. Cham tăl, PR Cham tăl, Wr. Cham təl; MK: Bahnar (AC) tâl; tol, PSB (Efimov) *tət 'arrive; reach'?. [The vowel also suggests a MK origin]

ˣ*wɨl 'round', Rade wɨl 'circle', Jarai (PL) wɨl, Jarai (Lee) wɨl, Chru wɨl 'circle', N. Roglai win, Haroi wɨl, W. Cham wɨl 'circle', PR Cham wɨl, Wr. Cham wil; MK: PMnong *wɨl, PSB (Efimov) *wil.

ˣ*wir 'turn around; dizzy; churning of rapids', Rade wir, Jarai (PL) wir, Jarai (Lee) wir 'dizzy'; MK: PSB (Efimov) *wiː, *wə: 'dizziness'. Restricted to Highlands Chamic.

ˣ*wər 'forget', Acehnese tuwʌ, Rade wər, Jarai (PL) wər, Jarai (Lee) (rəbit), Chru wər, N. Roglai wəbiʔ, Tsat van³³, Haroi wɔl, W. Cham wăr, PR Cham wăr, Wr. Cham wər. [The vowel suggests a MK origin]

ˣ*yaːŋ 'spirit; god', Jarai (PL) yaŋ hrəi, Rade yaŋ, Jarai (Lee) yaŋ, Chru yaːŋ, N. Roglai yaːk, Haroi yïaŋ, PR Cham yaŋ, Wr. Cham yaŋ, Malay yang; MK: PNB *yaŋ 'spirit', PMnong *yaŋ, Bahnar (AC) iāŋ, PSB (Efimov) *yaːŋ, PKatuic *ʔəjɛːŋ, *ʔəjɛːŋ.

ˣ*yɔŋ 'to lift; take off', Rade yɔ̆ŋ, Jarai (Lee) yɔŋ, N. Roglai yok 'carry by hand', Haroi yɔ̆ŋ; yïŋ ?. Restricted to Highlands Chamic plus Haroi. [The vowel also suggests a MK origin]

ˣ*yuam 'expensive', Rade yuom, Chru yɔːm, Tsat zuan³³, W. Cham yɔm 'price, cost'. Restricted the Highlands Chamic and W. Cham. [The vowel suggests a MK origin]

ˣ*yun 'hammock', Chru ayun, PR Cham ayŭn; MK: Bahnar (AC) ayŭn.

ˣ*yəh 'PARTICLE', Jarai (Lee) yəh 'why', N. Roglai yəh, PR Cham mïyăh, Wr. Cham mïyah; MK: PMnong *yəh 'emphatic'. [The vowel also suggests a MK origin]

ˣ*yər 'lift, raise', Haroi yɔl, PR Cham yer, Wr. Cham yer. [The vowel suggests a MK origin]

1.3   PC words of uncertain (or other) origin

This third list of forms that reconstruct to PC consists of words that, given the current state of knowledge, seem to lack an etymology. Some of these will inevitably turn out to be MK borrowings, but simply have not yet been identified as such. For instance, many of the forms that are listed as restricted to Highlands Chamic are likely to turn out to be borrowings, perhaps even post-PC Chamic borrowings but ones that cannot yet be confidently labelled as such yet.

Note that many of the forms occur both in Chamic and in Bahnaric, but this by itself is not enough to establish that the form is ultimately MK as many demonstrably Austronesian forms are found widespread in Bahnaric languages.

*ʔabaw 'snail', Acehnese ubo, Rade abau, Chru abau, N. Roglai abau 'large ocean snail', W. Cham paw, PR Cham apaw, Wr. Cham abaw.

*ʔagam 'incest; desire, lust', Jarai (PL) ăgăm, Jarai (Lee) ʔagăm, Chru agam, PR Cham akăm, Wr. Cham agaṁ.

*ʔaka see *ka

*ʔala 'below; beneath', Jarai (Lee) ʔala, Chru ala, N. Roglai ala, Haroi alïa, W. Cham la toŋ 'under the house', PR Cham ala, Wr. Cham alā.

*ʔalak 'yolk', Rade ală? 'eye' ?, Jarai (PL) ălăk, Jarai (Lee) ʔală?.

*ʔañu? 'beads', Rade añŭ? 'necklace', Jarai (PL) añŭ?, Jarai (Lee) ʔañu? -vl, N. Roglai añŭ? 'seed bead necklace', Haroi añŭ?, PR Cham ñu?, Wr. Cham ñuk.

*ʔanuŋ 'package', Rade anŭŋ, Jarai (PL) anŭŋ, Jarai (Lee) ʔanuŋ 'to wrap', Haroi anŭŋ -v 'bundle', PR Cham anŭŋ, Wr. Cham anuŋ; MK: Bahnar (AC) anuŋ.

*ʔaŋuy 'to use', Acehnese ŋui, Chru aŋui, W. Cham ŋui 'wear' ?, PR Cham aŋuy; ŋuy, Wr. Cham aŋ*u̯ĕi; ŋ*u̯ĕi.

*ʔapan 'hold; take', Jarai (PL) ăpan, Chru apan, N. Roglai apat, W. Cham păn, PR Cham apăn; păn, Wr. Cham apan.

*ʔariaŋ 'crab', Rade arieŋ, Jarai (PL) arɛŋ, Jarai (Lee) ʔarɛŋ, Chru rə?iaŋ, N. Roglai ayak; ariak, Tsat liaŋ?[33] -i, Haroi areaŋ, W. Cham riaŋ, PR Cham arieŋ; ryăŋ, Wr. Cham arie̯ŋ; rie̯ŋ.

*ʔasuk 'shavings', Jarai (Lee) ʔasŭk, Haroi asok. Note the restriction to Highlands Chamic plus Haroi.

*ʔay 'elder sibling', Rade ie 'older sister's husband, older brother's wife', N. Roglai ai, Haroi ai 'brother-in-law (of elder sibling); sister-in-law', PR Cham ay, Wr. Cham ai.

*ʔura? 'now', Rade ară?, Jarai (PL) ră?, Jarai (Lee) ʔară?, Chru ara? ni, PR Cham ură?; ară?, Wr. Cham urak.

*ʔurah 'bedbug', Rade arɛh -v, Jarai (PL) arah, Jarai (Lee) ʔarăh, Chru arah, N. Roglai ura? -f, Tsat zua[55] (m), W. Cham rah, PR Cham arăh, Wr. Cham araḥ.

*ʔusar 'flesh, meat', Acehnese siə, Jarai (Lee) ʔasar; ʔasăr, Chru asaːr 'soup solids', N. Roglai usa, Haroi asăl, PR Cham athăr, Wr. Cham asar.

*ba 'bring, take, carry', Acehnese ba, Rade ba, Jarai (Lee) ba, Chru ba, N. Roglai ba, Haroi phɨa, PR Cham pa, Wr. Cham bā.

*ba 'to lead', Rade atăt ba, Jarai (Lee) ba, Chru ba in ba jəlaːn 'advise', N. Roglai ba, W. Cham pa, PR Cham pa, Wr. Cham bā.

*babuŋ 'roof; ridge of (house, mountain)', Chru pəbuŋ 'peak of roof', N. Roglai babuk 'tall center pole of house', Haroi pəphŭŋ 'roof', W. Cham papuŋ, PR Cham papuŋ, Wr. Cham pabuŋ, Malay bumbung; bubung, PMP *bubuŋ; MK: PKatuic (DT) *–phuung 'roof'.

*bantal 'pillow', Acehnese bantai, Jarai (PL) hănal akö?, Chru pətal, W. Cham patăl, PR Cham patăr -f, Wr. Cham patər -f, Malay bantal.

*bap 'fill; full', Jarai (PL) buă?; bö?, Jarai (Lee) bă?, N. Roglai paba?, Haroi phɨau?, W. Cham pau?, PR Cham pă?, Wr. Cham bak.

*bapha see *mabha

*bhaːn 'sneeze', Jarai (PL) phăn (Pk), Jarai (Lee) phan, Chru phãːn -n laːiʔ, N. Roglai phaːt, Haroi aphan, W. Cham pahan -v, PR Cham phan, Wr. Cham bhān.

*bhu 'dry' cf 'dry in the sun', Rade (Lee) bhu, Jarai (Lee) bhu, PR Cham (Lee) phu.

*biaʔ 'true, right; good', Chru biaʔ, Haroi phiaʔ, W. Cham peaʔ 'indeed; true; very', PR Cham pyăʔ, Wr. Cham bjak, Malay baik 'good'.

*bijɔw 'shaman', Rade mjău 'diviner', Chru pəjəu, N. Roglai bijəu, Haroi pəsĭau, PR Cham paçŏw, Wr. Cham pajuw; MK: PNB *pajăw 'sorcerer'.

*binuh 'to butt', Rade mənuh, Jarai (PL) băbănuh, Jarai (Lee) bənuh, N. Roglai binũh, W. Cham panuh, PR Cham pinuh, Wr. Cham binuḥ.

*bit 'forget', Rade wər bĭt, Jarai (PL) rəbĭt, Jarai (Lee) rəbit, N. Roglai wəbiʔ -1, Haroi phĭʔ, PR Cham piwăl.

*bituʔ 'star', Rade mətŭʔ, Jarai (PL) pătŭʔ, Jarai (Lee) pətuʔ, Chru pətuʔ -f, N. Roglai pituʔ, Haroi pətoʔ, W. Cham patŭʔ, PR Cham pitŭʔ; patŭʔ; patŭʔ, Wr. Cham bituk; batuk.

*blah flat object', Jarai (Lee) blah, Chru blah clf., PR Cham plah, Wr. Cham blaḥ.

*blus -f 'to blow', Jarai (Lee) bluh -v, Chru bluːh, N. Roglai bluh, Haroi plŭh, W. Cham pluh 'breathe, puff', PR Cham pluh, Wr. Cham bluḥ.

*bɔh maw 'mushroom', Rade məmau, Jarai (PL) bɔh mău, Jarai (Lee) bəmau, Chru bəmau, N. Roglai bumãu, Haroi pəmĭau, W. Cham poh mau, PR Cham pimaw, Wr. Cham bimaw. [The first element is the widespread AN round object classifier PC *bɔh; it is the second element that has the unknown origin]

*bruːŋ 'streaked; colorful, striped', Rade bruŋ 'striped', Jarai (Lee) broŋ, Haroi pruŋ. Restricted to Highlands Chamic plus Haroi.

*buh 'wear ornaments', Jarai (PL) buh, Jarai (Lee) buh, Chru buh, N. Roglai buh, Haroi phŭh. Restricted to Highlands Chamic plus Haroi.

*buŋ 'large basket', Rade bŭŋ 'back basket', Jarai (PL) bŭŋ -i, Jarai (Lee) buŋ, Chru buŋ 'storage', Haroi phŭŋ, PR Cham puŋ, Wr. Cham buŋ, Malay rombong.

*cam 'Cham', Rade čam, Jarai (PL) cam, Chru mənih cam, N. Roglai manũih cap, Tsat tsaːnʔ[42], Haroi căm 'Montagnards, highlanders', W. Cham căm, PR Cham căm, Wr. Cham cāṁ.

ˣˣcaɓaːŋ 'branch; fork of tree', Acehnese cabɯəŋ, Rade kəɓaŋ, Jarai (PL) təɓaŋ iʔ, Chru cəɓaːŋ, W. Cham caɓaŋ, PR Cham caɓaŋ, Wr. Cham caɓaŋ, PMP *cabaŋ 'bifurcation', Malay cabang; MK: PKatuic (DT) *–beeng. The glottalized ɓ- is quite unexpected, as is the medial /b/ in Malay, which probably should be /w/. Although this forms seems to be attested in Austronesian, within PC it certainly patterns as a borrowing.

*campa < *cam + pa 'Champa', Acehnese jɯɯmpa, PR Cham campa, Wr. Cham campā, Wr. Cham (AC) campā.

*cata 'parrot', N. Roglai cata, W. Cham cata, W. Cham (Headley) cata. Restricted to Highlands Chamic.

*cut 'pierce, prick', Rade čŭt 'wear (ring)', Chru cuːʔ. Restricted to Highlands Chamic.

*cut 'to dress; wear', Rade čŭt, Jarai (Lee) cut, W. Cham cuʔ, PR Cham cuʔ, Wr. Cham cuk.

*dadit 'a fan', N. Roglai dadiːʔ, Haroi cəthiʔ 'to fan', PR Cham taṭiʔ, Wr. Cham tadik.

*dahlaʔ 'I (polite)', Jarai (PL) dăm 'de supérieur à inférieur', Chru dəlhaʔ, W. Cham hlŭn hlăʔ 'I', PR Cham ṭahɩ̆aʔ, Wr. Cham dahlak.

*dap 'line up; straighten', Jarai (PL) dăp, Chru daʔ 'put in, place', N. Roglai daʔ, PR Cham ṭăʔ, Wr. Cham dak.

*dih 'that; there', Acehnese hideh, sideh 'there (far)', Rade adih, Jarai (PL) ădih, Jarai (Lee) dih, Chru dih 'there (far)', N. Roglai udih, Haroi thɩ̆h, PR Cham ṭeh -v, Wr. Cham deḥ -v.

*draːŋ 'hornbill rhinoceros', Chru draːŋ, N. Roglai draːk, cf. Malay ĕnggang. Restricted to Highlands Chamic.

*draʔ -n 'hands on hips', Jarai (Lee) drăʔ, N. Roglai drăʔ -n. Restricted to Highlands Chamic.

*duy 'to guide', Jarai (PL) dui, Jarai (Lee) dui, Chru dui, duːi, N. Roglai dui, Haroi thui, PR Cham ṭuy, Wr. Cham dy̆ĕi.

*gah 'side, direction; bank', Jarai (PL) gah, Jarai (Lee) gah, Chru gah, N. Roglai gah, Haroi khɩ̆ah, W. Cham ḳah, PR Cham ḳah, Wr. Cham gaḥ; MK: Bahnar (AC) gaḥ.

*gahnap 'wealth(y)', Jarai (Lee) gənam -f, Chru gəñəp -vʔ, N. Roglai gahnăp, PR Cham ḳanŭp-miṭa, Wr. Cham ganup.

*gaw 'rim', Rade gau 'back of knife', Jarai (Lee) gau 'helix', Chru gau, PR Cham ḳaw 'dos'; haḳaw, Wr. Cham gaw; hagaw.

*giŋ 'stove', Chru giːŋ apui 'cooking fire', W. Cham ḳiŋ 'cooking fire', PR Cham ḳiŋ 'cusine', Wr. Cham giŋ.

*glaŋ 'look at; watch' Rade dlăŋ, Jarai (PL) lăŋ -i; dlăŋ (Est), Haroi tlɩ̆aŋ, PR Cham ḳlăŋ, Wr. Cham glaŋ; MK: Bahnar (AC) lăŋ.

*glay 'forest, jungle; wild, savage', Rade dlie lui, Jarai (PL) glai, dlai (N et S), Jarai (Lee) glai, Chru glai 'jungle; forest; wild'; kaih, N. Roglai dlai; kaih, Tsat khiaːiʔ⁴² , Haroi tlɩ̆ai [cf. tlua], W. Cham ḳlai, PR Cham răm-ḳlay, Wr. Cham rəṁ-glai.

*gulam 'carry on shoulder', Acehnese gulam, Rade klam, Jarai (PL) gɐ̆lăm, Jarai (Lee) glăm, Chru gəlam, N. Roglai gulap, Tsat khiaŋʔ⁴² -ft, Haroi kəlɩ̆am, W. Cham ḳlăm, PR Cham ḳilăm; ḳalăm, Wr. Cham gilăṁ; galəṁ.

*gunam 'cloud', Rade kənam, Jarai (PL) gənăm, Jarai (Lee) gənăm, Chru gənam 'rain cloud', Haroi kənĭam, PR Cham ķanăm, Wr. Cham ganəṁ.

*gut 'cave', Jarai (Lee) gŭʔ, Chru gu:ʔ 'lair', N. Roglai gu:ʔ 'cave', PR Cham ķoʔ, Wr. Cham gok.

*hă 'you; thou', Acehnese gata (sg./pl.) (neutral); ta-; -tɯ(h), Jarai (PL) hă (N), Jarai (Lee) ha, Chru hă, N. Roglai hă, Tsat ha³³, Haroi hăi -v, W. Cham hɨ, PR Cham hɨ, Wr. Cham hɨ̇.

*hadum -l 'how much, many?', Rade dŭm, Jarai (PL) hədŏm, Jarai (Lee) hədom; dom -v, Chru hədu:m -vl, N. Roglai hadu:p -l, Haroi athŭm, W. Cham haṭom -v; haṭòm -v, PR Cham haṭom -v; ṭom -v, Wr. Cham hadoṁ.

*halɛy 'who; question word', Rade hlɛi, Chru hələi, N. Roglai aləi, Tsat ʔa³³ za:ŋ³³ -i vʔ, Haroi hələ̆i -v (grammatical particle), W. Cham hlay 'whatever', PR Cham halɛ̆y; lɛ̆y, Wr. Cham halɛ̆i.

*halim 'rainy season', Rade hlĭm 'rain for two or three days'; lip 'flood', Jarai (Lee) hlim, Chru həlim 'wet weather', N. Roglai halip 'continual rain; flood', Haroi həlĭm 'flood', PR Cham halĭm 'rainy season', Wr. Cham haliṁ.

*haluh 'perforated; pierce', Rade hluh, Jarai (Lee) hluh, Chru həluh, N. Roglai haluh, Haroi hələ̆h 'to have a hole', PR Cham halŭh, Wr. Cham haluḥ.

*hayɔw 'like (prep.)', Chru yəu, W. Cham yau, PR Cham yŏw, Wr. Cham yuŋ ?.

*hunaʔ 'asthma', Chru hənaʔ, N. Roglai hunãʔ, W. Cham hanɨc -f, PR Cham hanɨ̆ʔ, PR Cham hanɨ̆ʔ, Wr. Cham hanɨk.

*jah 'weed, clear brush', Rade jah, Jarai (PL) jah, Jarai (Lee) jah, Chru jah 'chop small wood', N. Roglai jah, W. Cham çah 'cut with a knife', PR Cham çah, Wr. Cham jaḥ.

*jaluʔ 'bowl', Rade elŭʔ, Chru jəluʔ, N. Roglai jaluʔ (also a clf.), PR Cham (Lee) paŋɨn-çalŭʔ; MK: Bahnar (AC) jəlu.

*ka, *ʔaka 'not yet', Rade ka...oh; Jarai (Lee) ka; ʔaka; Chru ka...əu; N. Roglai ka; ka ɓuh; Haroi kaʔ; W. Cham ka...o; PR Cham ka...o 'pas encore'.

*ka:l 'to lock; bolt', Rade kal, Jarai (Lee) kal, Chru kal -l; k-ən-al 'a lock', PR Cham (Lee) kiən -vf.

*kaʔiaŋ 'loins; waist', Rade kəieŋ 'rib (back)', Jarai (Lee) kəʔiaŋ, Chru kəʔiăŋ 'waist', N. Roglai kaʔiak 'lower back', Haroi kəʔeaŋ, W. Cham kaʔɨŋ, PR Cham kaʔɨŋ, Wr. Cham kaiŋ.

*kacaw 'scratch, scrape', Rade kəčau, Chru kəcau, N. Roglai kacau. Restricted to Highlands Chamic.

*kadɔw 'jump', Rade kədău, Jarai (Lee) kədəu, N. Roglai kadəu, Haroi kəɗău -ɗ, PR Cham katŏw, Wr. Cham kaduw.

*kaka:s 'fish scales', Rade kaih, Jarai (PL) rǎkǎh -i, Chru kǝrkǎːh -n; kǝrkaːh, N. Roglai kaka, Tsat ka[33], Haroi kǝkǎh 'fin of fish, shell of anteater', W. Cham kakah, PR Cham kakǎh, Wr. Cham kakaḥ, Wr. Cham (AC) kakaḥ.

*kala 'bald; bare', Rade kǒʔ kla, Jarai (PL) kla, Chru kǝla akǒ, N. Roglai kahlo, Tsat kiu[33] -fʔ, Haroi kǝla; kǝlɔ, W. Cham kla, PR Cham kala, Wr. Cham kalā.

*kalih 'miserly', Jarai (PL) kǎlih, Jarai (Lee) klih, Chru kǝrlih, Haroi kǝleh, PR Cham kali̇h, Wr. Cham kaliḥ.

*kapit 'to close', Rade (Lee) kǝpi̇ʔ, Jarai (Lee) kǝpit, PR Cham (Lee) kapiʔ. Restricted to Highlands Chamic.

*karam 'sink; sunk', Jarai (PL) krǎm, Jarai (Lee) krǎm, Chru kram, N. Roglai karap, Haroi krǎm, PR Cham karǎm, Wr. Cham karǝmi̇, Malay karam; MK: PNB *krǎm.

*kata:l 'thunder (-bolt); lightning', Jarai (PL) kǎtal, Chru kǝtaːl, N. Roglai katan, PR Cham katal, Wr. Cham katal.

*kata:ŋ 'strong; well', Rade kǝtaŋ, Jarai (Lee) kǝtaŋ, Chru kǝdaŋ -1, Haroi kǝtaŋ, PR Cham (Lee, Blood) katǎŋ -1.

*katit 'to crush', Rade kǝtit -1 'wring, twist', Jarai (Lee) kǝtit, N. Roglai katiːʔ, Haroi kǝtět -f 'fall on something', W. Cham katě? 'pinch'. Restricted to Highlands Chamic, Haroi, and W. Cham.

*katrɔw 'pigeon', Rade kǝtrǎu, Jarai (Lee) kǝtrau, Chru kǝtrɔu, N. Roglai katrɔu, Haroi kǝtrǎu, W. Cham katrau play, PR Cham katrǒw-catoy; MK: PNB *čatrǎw, PMnong *kǝtǝp.

*katuŋ 'pull', Rade kǝtǔŋ, Jarai (Lee) kǝtuŋ, Chru kǝtuŋ, N. Roglai katuk, Haroi kǝtoŋ 'tear (thread)', PR Cham (Lee) kǝtuŋ.

*kayua 'because', Rade kǝyua dah, Jarai (PL) yua (kǝ), Jarai (Lee) yua kǝ, Chru kǝyua, N. Roglai kayua, Haroi kǝyua kǝ-, W. Cham kayoa, PR Cham kaywa, Wr. Cham kayu̇ā.

*khaŋ 'hard; stiff; strong', Acehnese kʌŋ 'strong' -v, Rade khǎŋ, Jarai (PL) khǎŋ, Jarai (Lee) khǎŋ, Chru khaŋ, N. Roglai khak 'solid, dense', Tsat kha:ŋʔ[42], Haroi khǎŋ, W. Cham khǎŋ, PR Cham khǎŋ, Wr. Cham khǝŋ.

*klam 'afternoon; night', Rade tlam, Jarai (PL) klǎm (Hd.), Jarai (Lee) klǎm, Chru klam, N. Roglai tlap, Tsat kianʔ[33], Haroi tlǎm 'night', W. Cham maklǎm, PR Cham klǎm; mǝklǎm, Wr. Cham klǝmi̇; mǝklǝmi̇; MK: Bahnar (AC) klam.

*klap 'old', Chru klaʔ, W. Cham klauʔ, PR Cham klǎʔ, Wr. Cham klak; MK: PNB *krǎq.

*klaw 'laugh', Rade tlau, Jarai (PL) klǎu, Jarai (Lee) klau, Chru klau, N. Roglai tlau, Tsat kiau[33], Haroi tlau, W. Cham klau, PR Cham klaw, Wr. Cham klaw. [The forms in Malay tawa, PMalayic *tawaʔ, and PMP *tawa do not appear related to the PC]

*klum 'to cover', Jarai (Lee) klŭm, Chru klum 'cover up', N. Roglai tlup, Haroi tlŏm; kəlom.

*krăh 'middle; half', Rade ti krah, Jarai (Lee) krah, Chru krăh, N. Roglai khrăh -i, Tsat kia⁵⁵, Haroi krăh, W. Cham krih; kih, PR Cham krih, Wr. Cham krih.

*kraːŋ 'clam; shellfish', Acehnese krɯəŋ, Chru kəraːŋ -v, N. Roglai kraːk 'clam', Malay kĕrang.

*krih 'whittle', Rade krĭʔ -f 'whittle, sharpen', Jarai (PL) krĭh, Jarai (Lee) krih, Chru kriːh -l, N. Roglai krih, Haroi kreh 'sharpen'; cərăh -v, PR Cham krĭh, Wr. Cham krih.

*kumɛy 'female, woman', Jarai (PL) kămăï, Jarai (Lee) kəməi, Chru kəməi, N. Roglai kuməi -n, Tsat mai³³, Haroi kəmŏi, W. Cham kamay, PR Cham kamĕy, Wr. Cham kamĕi.

*la 'spleen; pancreas', Jarai (PL) la, Jarai (Lee) la, N. Roglai diːʔla, PR Cham la, Wr. Cham lā.

*labua 'a plant; taro', Chru ləbua 'spinach', Haroi ləphua 'taro root', PR Cham (Lee) kəpùa -i.

*lagah 'tired', Rade egah, Jarai (Lee) rəgah, Chru ləgah, N. Roglai lagah, Tsat khe⁵⁵ -v, Haroi ləkhĭah, W. Cham lakah 'ache', PR Cham likah; likoy; likah, Wr. Cham ligah; liguai; lagah; MK: Bahnar (AC) rəgah.

*lajaw or *rajaw 'hammock', Jarai (PL) răjau, Jarai (Lee) rəjau. Restricted to Highlands Chamic.

*lakɔw 'ask for', Rade akău, Jarai (PL) rəkəu, Jarai (Lee) rəkəu, N. Roglai lakəu, W. Cham lakaw, PR Cham likŏw; lakŏw, Wr. Cham lakaw.

*lamaːn 'elephant', Rade eman, Jarai (PL) răman, Jarai (Lee) rəman, Chru ləmaːn, N. Roglai lumăn, Haroi ləmian, W. Cham lamin, PR Cham limin, Wr. Cham limin.

*lanaŋ 'earthworm', Rade enăŋ, Jarai (PL) rănăŋ, Jarai (Lee) rənăŋ, Chru lənaŋ, N. Roglai lanak -f, Haroi lənăŋ, W. Cham lanəŋ, PR Cham lanĭŋ, Wr. Cham laniŋ.

*lasun 'onion', Rade esŭn, Jarai (PL) rəsŭn, Jarai (Lee) rəsŭn, W. Cham lasŭn, PR Cham lithŭn; lathŭn, Wr. Cham lisun; lithŭn; lathun.

*lawaːŋ 'thin; lean; emaciated', Rade ewaŋ, Jarai (PL) răwaŋ, Jarai (Lee) rəwaŋ, Chru ləwaːŋ, N. Roglai luwaːk 'lean; thin', Tsat vaːn³³ -f, Haroi ləwaŋ, W. Cham lawaŋ, PR Cham liwaŋ; lawaŋ, Wr. Cham liwaŋ; lawaŋ, PMP *niwaŋ.

ˣ*ləmɔ 'cow; ox; cattle', Acehnese lɯmɔ, Rade emo, Jarai (PL) rəmo, Jarai (Lee) rəmo, Chru ləmɔ, N. Roglai lamo -n, Tsat mo³³, Haroi ləmɔ, W.

Cham lamɔ, PR Cham limɔ; lamɔ, Wr. Cham limauw; lamauw, Malay lĕmbu; MK: Bahnar (AC) rəmō; ləmō. [This word has a limited distribution in AN.]

*liyah 'lick; taste', Acehnese liəh, Jarai (PL) liah, Jarai (Lee) liăh-i, Chru ləyah 'taste', N. Roglai liah, Tsat lia⁵⁵, Haroi leah, PR Cham lyăh, Wr. Cham liah; MK: cf. PEastern MK *liət 'lick'.

*lu 'much, many', Acehnese lə, Rade lu, Jarai (PL) lu, Jarai (Lee) lu 'very', Chru lu la; lu biă, Tsat lu³³, Haroi lu; lo -v, W. Cham lo ṭay, PR Cham lo -v, Wr. Cham lo; MK: Bahnar (AC) lə.

*lukut 'absent', Rade ekŭt, Jarai (PL) rəkut, Chru ləkuː?, N. Roglai likuː? -v, Haroi ləkou? 'avoid; escape'?, PR Cham (Lee) liku?.

*ma?iăk 'urinate', Acehnese ?iə?, Rade mə?iek, Jarai (PL) mə̆ñă? · ñă?, Chru mə?ia?, N. Roglai ma?iă?, Haroi mə?ĕă?, W. Cham ma?ii? (n), PR Cham miiʔ -v (n), Wr. Cham miik; MK: Bahnar (AC) ik.

*(ma)(sa)lun 'naked', Acehnese lon, Rade mlŭn, Jarai (PL) hlun, məhlun, Jarai (Lee) məhlŭn, Chru sərlun, N. Roglai salut, Haroi məhəlŭn, PR Cham milŭn, Wr. Cham milun.

*ma?ih 'soured', Jarai (Lee) mə?ih, W. Cham ma?ih 'spoiled', PR Cham mimĭh, Wr. Cham mimih.

*mabha, *bapha 'divide; share', Rade məbha, Jarai (Lee) pəpha < *p-, Chru pərpha, N. Roglai mupha, Tsat pha³³, W. Cham papha, PR Cham pha; parapha; rapha, Wr. Cham bhā; pārabhā; rabhā; MK: PMnong *pa?.

*magɛy 'move, agitate; wobbly, shaky, loose', Rade məgɛi, Chru məgəi, N. Roglai magəi, W. Cham maḳay.

*maja 'fox', Rade mja 'weasel', Jarai (PL) mə̆ja, Chru məja 'weasel', N. Roglai maja, PR Cham miça 'civette', Wr. Cham mijā.

*makrah 'middle; half', cf. *khrah, Rade ti krah; məkrah, Jarai (PL) mə̆krăh, Jarai (Lee) məkrah, Haroi məkrăh, W. Cham krih.

*mal 'beam', Jarai (Lee) mal, Chru mal, N. Roglai măn, Haroi măl, PR Cham măl, Wr. Cham məl.

*mam -v 'suck; suckle', Rade mam, Jarai (PL) pə̆mĕm, Jarai (Lee) mĕm -v, Chru mɛm -v; mum -v, N. Roglai măm, Haroi mem -v, W. Cham mŏm -v, PR Cham mŭm -v; măm, Wr. Cham mum; məm̄.

*marus 'itch', Rade ruih lak, N. Roglai maruh 'itchy, sores'. Restricted to Highlands Chamic.

*mat 'take; fetch, get', Acehnese mat, Rade mă?, Jarai (PL) mă?, Jarai (Lee) mă?, Chru ma?, N. Roglai mă?, Tsat ma?²⁴, Haroi mă? 'to take, get, catch, seize', W. Cham mə?, PR Cham mĭ?, Wr. Cham mik.

*mit 'always', Chru mit, W. Cham /mĭt/ (Headley). Restricted to one Highlands Chamic language plus W. Cham.

*ŋaʔ 'make, do', Rade ŋăʔ, Jarai (PL) ŋăʔ, Jarai (Lee) ŋăʔ, Chru ŋaʔ, N. Roglai ŋăʔ, Tsat ŋauʔ[24], Haroi ŋăʔ, W. Cham ŋăʔ, PR Cham aŋăʔ cf. ŋăʔ, Wr. Cham aŋap; ŋap.

*paʔ -i 'to, towards', Chru paʔ 'at', N. Roglai paʔ, Haroi pə- 'at, in (far distance)', PR Cham (Lee) paʔ, Wr. Cham (AC) phak -i; MK: Bahnar (AC) phŏ (?).

*paʔaːk 'armpit', Rade păl-ak, Jarai (PL) pŏʔăʔ, Jarai (Lee) pəʔăʔ, Chru pəʔaːʔ, N. Roglai ala paʔaːʔ, Haroi pəʔaʔ, W. Cham paʔaʔ, PR Cham paaʔ, Wr. Cham paak.

*pabah 'spittle, slaver, drool', Rade bah, Chru ia pəbah, Tsat pha[55]. Restricted to Highlands Chamic.

*padar 'spin; turn', Jarai (PL) pădar; pŏɗar (Ouest), Jarai (Lee) pədăr; pədər, Chru pədar -1, N. Roglai pada 'turn upside down', W. Cham ʈăr, Wr. Cham (AC) padar.

*padɛy 'rest', Rade mədɛi, Jarai (Lee) pedəi, Chru pədəi, N. Roglai padəi, Haroi pəthɨi, PR Cham paʈĕy, Wr. Cham padĕy; MK: PNB *badăy.

*pagaːŋ 'protect', Rade məgaŋ used in a phrase meaning 'to get a shot', Jarai (PL) pŏgaŋ, pŏgiŋ -v, Jarai (Lee) pəgaŋ, Chru pəgan -fl 'to barricade'. Restricted to Highlands Chamic.

*paɗiʔ 'pain; ache', Jarai (Lee) pəʔiaʔ -m, Chru pəɗiːʔ, N. Roglai paɗiːʔ, Haroi pəɗiʔ, W. Cham paɗiʔ, PR Cham paɗiʔ, Wr. Cham paɗik. Note: Acehnese puɪdeh, Malay pĕdih represent a distinct etymon; the Acehnese may, in fact, be borrowed from Malay.

*pajum 'meet together', cf *jum, Jarai (Lee) bəjənŭm, N. Roglai pajup, Haroi pəsŭm, PR Cham paçŭm, Wr. Cham pajum.

*pak-ke 'lizard; gecko', Acehnese paʔɛ, Rade păk ke, Jarai (PL) pŏk-kɛ, Jarai (Lee) pakəke, Chru pak kɛ, N. Roglai pakĕ, PR Cham pakɛ, Wr. Cham pakaiy.

*paŋ 'to make a wall', Jarai (Lee) păŋ cf. khăn păŋ 'curtain', W. Cham (AC) paŋ; MK: Bahnar (AC) pŏŋ; pŏŋ. Restricted to Highlands Chamic and W. Cham.

*pataw 'master; lord', Rade mətəu, Jarai (PL) pətəu, Jarai (Lee) pətau, Chru pətau, N. Roglai pitau, Haroi pətau, W. Cham patau, PR Cham pataw, Wr. Cham patau; MK: PNB *patăw, PSB (Efimov) *ʼpataw 'king, state'. Marrison (1975:53) follows Aymonier and Cabaton (1906) in suggesting that this word might be composed of *pɔ plus *tau 'person' as in Tagalog tao 'man'.

ˣˣ*piŋan 'bowl; dish', Acehnese piŋan, Rade məŋan 'plate'; bɨŋ 'bowl or plate made from squash or gourd', W. Cham pañin , PR Cham paŋĭn-çaluʔ, Malay pinggan, PMP *piŋgan; MK: PMnong *tiŋgan 'bowl'; *bəŋ 'bowl', PSB (Efimov) *[bə]ŋgan, PKatuic (DT) *p/tingan, PKatuic *pəŋhaːn 'bowl'. This word, according to Coope, is a Persian borrowing by way of Hindi; certainly, the vowel length of all the Chamic forms suggests a short vowel, rather than the long vowel that would be expected from the proposed PMP reconstruction. Note not only that the form also occurs in PMnong, PSB, and PKatuic but that it shows considerable variation in these MK languages, strongly suggesting it was borrowed into MK. This form is a borrowing into all the languages of the area.

*pioh 'keep, store; conserve', Rade piɔh 'to put, to place', Jarai (PL) pioh wai, Jarai (Lee) piɔh, PR Cham pyɔ̆h, Wr. Cham piəh.

*plaŋ 'citronella grass', Rade plă̆ŋ, Chru pla:ŋ -1, N. Roglai plak, Haroi aplă̆ŋ, W. Cham plă̆ŋ, Wr. Cham (AC) plaŋ.

*pras 'scratch (of chicken)', Rade (Tharpe) praih, Chru pra:h, N. Roglai pipra. Restricted to Highlands Chamic.

*pula 'to plant', Acehnese pula, Rade pla, Jarai (PL) plă̆, Jarai (Lee) pla, Chru pəla, N. Roglai pila, Tsat pia[33], Haroi pəla, W. Cham pla, PR Cham pala, Wr. Cham palā.

*pusa:ŋ < (? *pɔ + *sa:ŋ 'master' + 'house' (AC)) 'husband', Chru pəsa:ŋ, N. Roglai pisa:k, W. Cham pasaŋ, PR Cham pathaŋ, Wr. Cham pathaŋ. [The word for 'house' looks borrowed but the word *pɔ 'master' may be inherited]

*pə-gha:ŋ (causative prefix *pə-) 'dry over fire', Rade bhaŋ -i (appears to have coalesced), Jarai (PL) khă̆ŋ, Jarai (Lee) pəkhaŋ, N. Roglai pakha:k 'roast, broil', Haroi pəkhaŋ, PR Cham pakhaŋ. The Malay form pang-gang 'to roast' makes a tempting comparison, but the *g- to > gh- change that it would require would be unique.

*pə-ghaʔ (*pə- 'causative') 'forbid', Jarai (Lee) pəkhă̆ʔ, Chru khaʔ, Haroi khă̆ʔ, PR Cham k̟hă̆ʔ trı̆h, Wr. Cham ghak drı̆h.

*pə-klah 'divide; separate', cf. *klah 'to lose', Rade kah, Jarai (PL) pă̆klah; pă̆că̆lah (Pk), Jarai (Lee) peklah, Chru klah, N. Roglai patla; pak, PR Cham klă̆h-nı̆h, Wr. Cham klah-nih.

*pə-pah (*pə- 'causative') 'clap, slap; rub', Rade pah, N. Roglai papah 'clap hands', W. Cham pah. Restricted to Highlands Chamic plus W. Cham.

*rah/s -f 'separate a fire', Rade raih pui, N. Roglai raih -f pui, PR Cham ră̆h, Wr. Cham rah.

*ram 'dead fire', Rade pui ram, W. Cham pui ră̆m.

*ranam 'love', Chru rənam, Haroi W. Cham rană̆m, PR Cham rană̆m, Wr. Cham ranəṁ.

*rawaŋ 'visit', Chru rəwaŋ, N. Roglai lawak -i, PR Cham rawă̆ŋ, Wr. Cham rawəŋ.

*riya 'land, interior; earth', N. Roglai riya, PR Cham (Lee) riya, Wr. Cham (AC) riyā.

*rəta:k 'bean; pea', Acehnese rɯtɯəʔ, Rade etak, Jarai (PL) rɜ̆tă̆ʔ, Jarai (Lee) rətaʔ, Chru rəta:ʔ, N. Roglai rata:ʔ, Haroi lətaʔ -1, W. Cham rataʔ, PR Cham riṭaʔ; rataʔ, Wr. Cham ritāk; ratāk.

*sa:ŋ 'house', Acehnese sɯəŋ 'hut, tent', Rade saŋ, Jarai (PL) saŋ, Jarai (Lee) saŋ also 'family', Chru sa:ŋ, N. Roglai sa:k, Tsat sa:ŋ³³, Haroi saŋ, W. Cham saŋ, PR Cham thaŋ, Wr. Cham saŋ.

*saʔay 'elder sibling', Chru səʔai, N. Roglai saʔai, Haroi cəʔăi -i (Note: looks like a compound, not a disyllabic root), PR Cham ay, Wr. Cham ai; MK: PKatuic *sa:j; *sə-sa:j 'older sibling'. The existence of this root in both PC and PKatuic needs some explanation.

*salih 'trade', Rade məlih < *pə-, Chru səlih, W. Cham halih. Restricted to Highlands Chamic (Chru) and W. Cham.

*samaw 'prompt; on time', Jarai (Lee) həmau, Chru səmŭ -f, Haroi həmĭau. Restricted to Highlands Chamic plus Haroi.

*samu 'compare; comparable', Rade (Tharpe) həmo, Rade (Lee) həmo, N. Roglai (Lee) samŭ, PR Cham (Lee) hmu.

*sana 'roast; parch', Jarai (PL) hɜ̆nă, Jarai (Lee) həna, Chru səna 'fry', N. Roglai sana -n, Haroi həna, W. Cham hana (first syllable atypically retained), PR Cham hana, Wr. Cham hanā.

*sanal 'pillow', Rade anal kɜ̆ʔ -i, Jarai (PL) hɜ̆nal akɜ̆ʔ, Jarai (Lee) hənal, N. Roglai sanăn. Restricted to Highlands Chamic.

*saniŋ 'think', Rade hənĭŋ; mĭn, Chru sənəŋ, N. Roglai sinĭŋ, Haroi hənĭŋ, W. Cham sanəŋ -i, PR Cham sanĭŋ -i, Wr. Cham śanĭŋ.

*sarăw 'sting, hurt', Chru srău, N. Roglai sarau, W. Cham hrau. Restricted to Highlands Chamic and W. Cham.

*sarum 'sheath-like', Jarai (Lee) hrum 'scabbard', Chru srum ?, Haroi hərŭm, PR Cham harŭm, Wr. Cham harum; MK: Bahnar (AC) co rum. Although the final nasal is a complete mismatch, Malay *sarung* comes to mind.

*satuk 'boil; cook', Rade tŭk, Jarai (PL) hɜ̆tuk, Jarai (Lee) hətŭk, Chru stuʔ 'boil', N. Roglai satuʔ 'boil', Tsat tuʔ²⁴, Haroi atoʔ, W. Cham tŭʔ, PR Cham hatŭ̆ʔ; tŭʔ, Wr. Cham tuk; hatuk; MK: Bahnar (AC) hətŭk.

*sijaw 'hammock', N. Roglai sijau, Haroi asiau. Restricted to Highlands Chamic plus Haroi.

*sukat 'cork; stopper', Rade kăt, Jarai (PL) həkăt, Jarai (Lee) həkɜ̆t -v, Chru skaʔ, N. Roglai sukaʔ -v 'poke in; insert' . Restricted to Highlands Chamic.

*tagak -f 'cleaver', Rade kəgă̆ʔ 'small bush knife', Jarai (Lee) təgă̆ʔ, Chru təgak -f 'bushknife (long curved handle)', N. Roglai tagak -f 'bush knife', Wr. Cham (AC) tagaʔ; MK: Bahnar (AC) təgă̆k.

*tamaha 'parent in-law', Acehnese tuwan -mf, Rade kəmha, Jarai (Lee) təhma; təhmua, N. Roglai tamaha, Haroi cəhma 'also an address term', W. Cham tamaha, PR Cham (Lee) hma.

*tamut 'hammer', Rade kəmŭt, Jarai (PL) mut, t̆əmut, Jarai (Lee) təmŭt, Chru mŭ:ʔ, N. Roglai mŭ:ʔ, W. Cham muʔ. Restricted to Highlands Chamic plus W. Cham.

*tana:ʔ 'fagot; bamboo strip', Jarai (PL) cɛ̆năʔ, Jarai (Lee) tənăʔ 'fagot', PR Cham tană; cană ?, Wr. Cham tanak.

*taŋal 'deaf', Rade kəŋăl, Jarai (PL) t̆əŋĭl; tɛ̆ŋəl (N), N. Roglai (dən), Tsat (ŋa³³) ŋin³³ vʔ, W. Cham taŋɔh -f, PR Cham taŋɔ̆h -fv, Wr. Cham taŋauḥ.

*tapaʔ 'lie full length', Rade kəpăʔ, Chru təpaʔ 'standing upright', W. Cham tapăʔ also 'sit up'. Restricted to Highlands Chamic plus W. Cham.

*tarah 'trim; cut up; to sculpture', Jarai (Lee) trah 'to sculpture', N. Roglai tarah, PR Cham tarăh, Wr. Cham taraḥ.

*tasaʔ 'ripe; cooked', Rade kəsăʔ, Jarai (PL) təsăʔ, Jarai (Lee) təsăʔ, Chru təsaʔ, N. Roglai tisaʔ, Tsat saʔ²⁴, Haroi cəsăʔ, W. Cham tasăʔ, PR Cham tathăʔ, Wr. Cham tathak.

*thu 'dry', Acehnese tho, Rade thu, Jarai (PL) thu, Jarai (Lee) thu, Chru thu, N. Roglai thu; pathu 'to dry', Tsat thu³³, Haroi thou, W. Cham thu, PR Cham thu, Wr. Cham thū.

*timiya 'dance', Chru təmia, N. Roglai timiya -v, W. Cham tamanea, PR Cham tamya; mya, Wr. Cham tamĭā; mĭā.

*tiya:p 'chase, run after', Acehnese tiyɯəp, Rade tiɔ̆ʔ -fv, Chru tia:uʔ, N. Roglai tia:ʔ, Haroi teauʔ, PR Cham tyawʔ, Wr. Cham tĭap.

*trɛy 'full, satiated', Rade trɛi, Chru trəi, N. Roglai trəi, Tsat tsiə³³ vʔ, Haroi troi -1, W. Cham tray, PR Cham trɛ̆y, Wr. Cham trɛ̆y.

*tuh 'change; metamorphose', Jarai (PL) tuh, Jarai (Lee) tuh, N. Roglai tuh, Haroi toh 'give birth (animals)'. Restricted to Highlands Chamic and, possibly, Haroi.

*tuh 'pour', Rade tuh, Jarai (PL) tuh, Jarai (Lee) tuh, Chru tuh, N. Roglai tuh, Haroi cətoh; toh, W. Cham tuh, PR Cham tŭh, Wr. Cham tuḥ.

*tuy 'follow' > 'according to', Rade tui hluɛ 'imitate, copy, follow', hluɛ 'according to', Chru tui 'according to', N. Roglai theu -v 'follow' < Vietnamese, W. Cham tui 'according to, with', PR Cham tuy 'suivre', Wr. Cham tŭɛ̆i.

*tuy 'to follow', Rade tui hluɛ, Jarai (PL) tui, Chru tui, N. Roglai theu; dõm, Haroi toi dir. v. only occurs as an auxiliary verb, W. Cham tui, PR Cham tuy, Wr. Cham tŭɛ̆i.

*tuy 'to mate', Chru tui; tu:ʔ, W. Cham tui. Restricted to Highlands Chamic plus W. Cham.

*təglak 'choke; cough', Acehnese tɯrhoʔ -m, Rade kədlăk, Jarai (Lee) təglăk, Chru tərglaʔ, Haroi cətlĭaʔ.

*wah 'to fish', Rade wah, Jarai (PL) wah, Jarai (Lee) wah, Chru wah 'fish with pole', N. Roglai wah, Tsat va⁵⁵, Haroi wăʔ -f 'hang on a hook', W. Cham wah, PR Cham wăh, Wr. Cham waḥ.

*wah 'weave; twist', Rade (Lee) wah, Jarai (Lee) wah, N. Roglai (Lee) wah, PR Cham (Lee) wah.

*waŋ 'sickle', Rade wăŋ kuok 'hoe', Chru waŋ, N. Roglai wak 'blade for weeding', Haroi wăŋ, W. Cham wăŋ, PR Cham wăŋ, Wr. Cham wəŋ; MK: Bahnar (AC) uāŋ.

*yah 'destroy; take apart', Haroi yĭah, W. Cham yah, PR Cham yăh, Wr. Cham yaḥ.

*yɔw 'yoke', Chru yəu, W. Cham yau, PR Cham yɔ̆w, Wr. Cham yuw.

*yua 'to use', Rade (Tharpe, Egerod) yua, Haroi yua. Restricted to Highlands Chamic.

2.   WORDS BORROWED AFTER THE BREAKUP OF PC

This section contains lists of forms borrowed into Chamic languages after the breakup of PC. In addition to the continued borrowing of MK forms throughout the history of the Chamic languages, there were also contributions of loanwords from two main sources of cultural influence: India and Arabia.

2.1   Of Indic origin

The oldest layer of Indic borrowings in insular Southeast Asia seems to date back a little over two thousand years. As discussed earlier in this work, Indic loanwords are found in the earliest Indic inscriptions and six forms that reconstruct to the PC level have proposed Indic etymologies.

ˣˣʔasar 'seed', Rade asăr -1, Jarai (PL) ăsar, Tsat saʔ⁴² -f, Haroi asăl 'grain', W. Cham săr, PR Cham athăr, Wr. Cham asar; MK: PMnong *ŋgăr ?, PSB (Efimov) *'ŋgar. [? < Indic, cf. Sanskrit saara. It is unclear if the MK forms listed are related.]

ˣˣʔasɛh 'horse', Rade asɛh, Jarai (PL) asɛh, Jarai (Lee) ʔasɛh, Chru asɛh, N. Roglai aseh, Tsat se³³, Haroi asɛ̆h, W. Cham sɛh, PR Cham athɛ̆h, Wr. Cham asaiḥ; MK: PNB *aseh; MK: PMnong *ʔaseh, PSB (Efimov) *ʔasɛːh, PKatuic *ʔəsɛh. [< ? Indic; Headley, #2.2; cf. Sanskrit ashva] ˣ*bih 'poison; venom', Jarai (Lee) bih, Chru bih, Haroi phĭh, PR Cham pih, Wr. Cham biḥ. [< Indic; Headley, #2.9; cf. PIE *visa]; MK: PKatuic (DT) *piih.

ˣ*bijɛh 'seed', P-Acehnese (Durie) *bijeh, Acehnese bijɛh, Rade mjɛh, Jarai (PL) pɔjɛh; bɔ̆jɛh (S), Jarai (Lee) pɔjɛ̆h -ɛ̆ -i, Chru pɔjɛh, N. Roglai bijeh, Tsat se⁵⁵, Haroi pɔsɨh, W. Cham pacɛh 'seed for planting', PR Cham pacɛh, Wr. Cham pajaih -i, Malay biji. [? < Indic cf. Sanskrit; according to Coope, this form is from Sanskrit]

ˣ*kapa:s 'cotton'. MK < Indic ?; Headley, #2.1; Hindi; Sanskrit kar-paasa; Note: There is, so far, no PC internal grounds for designating this as a borrowing. Incidentally, Lee's apparent reconstruction of length in the onset syllable is simply a mistake, more than likely simply a typing mistake. Much ink has been spilled discussing this form and its origins.

ˣ*radɛh 'vehicle', Rade edɛh, Jarai (PL) rɔ̆dɛh, Jarai (Lee) rɔdɛh, Chru rɔdɛh, N. Roglai radeh, Tsat the¹¹, Haroi lɔthɨh, W. Cham raṭɛh, PR Cham riṭeh -v; raṭeh -v, Wr. Cham rideh, radeh; MK: PMnong *rɔndeh, PSB (Efimov) *rɔndɛ:h. [? < Indic; Headley, #2.8; Sanskrit ratha]

For these six, it is likely that they were already in the Austronesian language that developed into Chamic.

The remaining Indic loans clearly postdate that period, as may one or two of the forms above now reconstructed to PC. For some of the words listed below, Indic languages are suggested as the source. In most cases, it is clear that the words are borrowings and in some but not all cases it appears that the ultimate source was an Indic language. However, it is not likely that the Indic language itself was always the immediate donor. Instead, it is likely that some of these forms were borrowed from other Austronesian languages of the area, such as Malay.

ˣʔama(:)s 'gold' , Acehnese mɯh, mɯih (long), Rade mah (short), Jarai (PL) mah, Jarai (Lee) mah, Chru mî:h (long), N. Roglai mãh, Tsat ma³³ (long), Haroi mah, W. Cham mɨh, PR Cham mĭh (short), Wr. Cham mɨh (short), Malay ĕmas, mas; MK: PNB *mah, PMnong *mah, Bahnar (AC) maḥ. [< ?]. In addition to its apparent resemblance to Sanskrit hema-; heman (Headley, #4.5), it looks remarkably like Chinese, cf. Baxter (1992:768) Old Chinese *krjɨn, Middle Chinese kim, Mandarin jɨn.

ˣʔamrɛc 'pepper; hot', Rade amreč -v, Chru amrɛʔ -f, N. Roglai amreʔ 'red pepper', Haroi amrɛ̆k 'red pepper shaker (bamboo tube)', W. Cham mrɛ̆ʔ -f, PR Cham amrɛ̆ʔ -f; mrɛ̆ʔ -f, Wr. Cham amraik; mraik; MK: Bahnar (AC) amre, PSB (Efimov) *mrɛʔ, PKatuic *pə[r/rh]iʔ, *pə[r/rh]iʔ. [? < Indic; Headley, #2.7; Sanskrit marica]

ˣjaːl 'casting net', Acehnese jɯə, Rade jal, Jarai (Lee) jal, Chru jaːl 'conical net', N. Roglai jan, W. Cham çal, PR Cham çăl -1, Wr. Cham jal, Malay jala; MK: Bahnar (AC) jâl; jol. [< ? Indic; Headley, #2.6; Sanskrit jaala]

ˣjaːŋ 'to guard; gate(way)', Acehnese jaga < Malay, Rade gak -i, Chru jaːŋ, N. Roglai jaːk, Malay jaga. [? < Indic, cf. Sanskrit (according to Coope)]

ˣmanaːs -f 'pineapple', Acehnese bɔh anɯh -f, Chru mənaih -f, W. Cham manas -f, PR Cham mɨnăh, Wr. Cham mɨnaḥ, Malay nanas. [< Portuguese, apparently by way of Hindi]

ˣmanus -f 'man; person', Rade mənuih, Jarai (PL) mənuih, Jarai (Lee) mənuih, Chru mənih 'person', N. Roglai manŭih -f, Haroi mənĭh -v < *-s, W. Cham manus -f, PR Cham mɨnuyh -f, Wr. Cham mɨnṵiś -f, Malay manusia. [? < Indic; Headley, #2.4; Sanskrit manus, manushya, manusha]

ˣ‾naːn 'pineapple', Rade tɛinan -i, Jarai (Lee) pənan, N. Roglai inaːt -f; rinaːt -f, Malay nanas. [< Portuguese apparently by way of Hindi. Pineapples were introduced from South America]

ˣnagar > ˣlagar 'country; city; area', Acehnese naŋgrɔə < *-i 'country' (independently borrowed into Acehnese), Chru ia ləgar, N. Roglai laga, W. Cham naḳăr -i, Malay nĕgeri. [< Indic cf. Sanskrit nagara]. The irregular correspondences make it clear that this form was a post-PC borrowing.

ˣrupa 'form; image; body', Acehnese rupa, Rade rup, Jarai (PL) rup, Jarai (Lee) rup, Chru ruːp -f, N. Roglai ruːp -f 'body', Haroi rup -fl 'picture', W. Cham rup -f, PR Cham rup -f, Wr. Cham rūp, Malay rupa; MK: PSB (Efimov) *ruːp. Note that this is an Indic loanword; the PSB is borrowed from Chamic. [< Indic; Headley, #2.3; cf. Sanskrit rūpa]

ˣsap 'sound; voice; language', Rade săp 'hear; obey; tape-recorder', Jarai (PL) săp; hiăp, Jarai (Lee) săp, Chru sap -f 'voice, sound', N. Roglai (s-an-ăp -f), Tsat seʔ[24], Haroi săp -f, W. Cham săp -vf, PR Cham săp -f, cf. chăp -f, Wr. Cham śap. [? < Indic; Headley, #2.11; Sanskrit shabda]

ˣtara 'sky', PR Cham tara, Wr. Cham tarā. This form may (or may not) be related to PSB *truːʔ and PMnong *trôk. If so, the phonetics of the Chamic forms may eventually provide clues as to which language was the donor. [? < Sanskrit tārā; a Sanskrit source has also been proposed, a suggestion not necessarily mutually exclusive with the MK suggestion. In all this, the one thing that is clear is that it is a borrowing.]

ˣˣyuan -v 'Vietnamese', Rade yuăn -v, Chru mənih ʀuən, N. Roglai manŭih yuat, Haroi yŏn, W. Cham ʀuan, PR Cham yon, Wr. Cham yṵən; MK:

PNB *yun, PSB (Efimov) *'yyuən. [? < Indic; Headley, #2.10; Sanskrit yavana 'barbarian, Greek']. This last proposed Indic etymology is, at the very least, speculative.

In the literature Indic etymologies have been proposed for two forms that can now be shown to have Austronesian origins.

*phit 'bitter; bile', cf. Sanskrit pitta., see Acehnese phet, Rade phĭʔ, Jarai (PL) phĭʔ, Jarai (Lee) phĭʔ, Chru phiːʔ, N. Roglai phiːʔ, Tsat phiʔ[24], Haroi pheiʔ, W. Cham phiʔ, PR Cham phiʔ, Wr. Cham phik, Malay pahit, PMP *paqit. Although it has been suggested that this form is Indic in origin, the suggestion lacks any merit as the form is reconstructable back to PAn.

*sira -i 'salt', Acehnese sira, Rade hra, Jarai (PL) hra, Jarai (Lee) hra, Chru sra, N. Roglai sara, Haroi sra -i, W. Cham sra -i, PR Cham sara -i, Wr. Cham śarā, PMalayic *sira, PMP *qasiʀa. Aymonier and Cabaton suggested a Sanskrit source for this form but it now can be established as Austronesian.

2.2   Of Arabic origin

Even the earliest Arabic contributions are much later than the earlier Indic contributions. None of them reconstruct to PC, nor are the relatively few post-Chamic borrowings as widely distributed as the Indic forms.

ˣʔalak 'rice wine; liquor; alcohol', Acehnese araʔ -i, Jarai (PL) ălak, Chru alak -f, N. Roglai alak, W. Cham lăc patih -f, PR Cham alăk; lăk, Wr. Cham alak, lak, Malay arak 'rice wine; liquor'; MK: PSB (Efimov) *ʔəlak. As Coope correctly notes, the form is a borrowing from Arabic, so the Efimov reconstruction bears closer examination. Either the PKatuic time depth is rather shallow, or the reconstruction has some problems. [< Arabic]

ˣtalabat 'worship', Chru təlbat -f, N. Roglai talabat -f, PR Cham talapăt -f, Wr. Cham talabat -f. [< Arabic]

ˣumur 'age, e.g. the modern age', Acehnese umu, Malay umur. [< Very late borrowing from Arabic umuru].

This handful of forms underplays the Arabic contribution. Even a cursory examination of Aymonier and Cabaton's dictionary of Chamwould show a large number of Arabic loanwords, but a survey of the rest of the Chamic languages would indicate that the Arabic loans were not widely disseminated.

2.3   Of MK (and other) origin

The overwhelming majority of the words in this section are of MK origin. Many have been provided with partial MK etymologies and many more are found restricted to the Highlands Chamic area, where the only neighbors are MK speaking. Only a handful of these words have been borrowed from another source, such as Malay or French.

ˣʔabual -v 'blunt; dull', Rade băl -v, Chru buəl, N. Roglai abən -v, PR Cham bul; MK: PKatuic (DT) *p̱1 'dull'.

ˣʔamiat 'uncle, aunt', Rade amiet -v 'uncle, aunt', Jarai (PL) mɛt 'frère cadet du père', Chru miaʔ 'maternal', N. Roglai miăʔ, Haroi met -v, W. Cham miïʔ (n)'uncle, aunt', PR Cham mïʔ (n) 'paternal', Wr. Cham mik.

ˣʔamuan see ˣkəmuan

ˣʔanrɔːŋ 'carry (two objects suspended from a stick)', Rade enoŋ -v, Jarai (PL) anɔŋ; ʔnɔŋ (N), Jarai (Lee) ʔanɔŋ, Chru anɔːŋ, N. Roglai anroːk, Tsat noŋ³³, Haroi anɔŋ, W. Cham nɔŋ 'carry with pole (shoulders)', PR Cham anɔŋ, Wr. Cham anauŋ; MK: PNB *tùŋ 'carry on pole', Bahnar (AC) anoŋ, PSB (Efimov) *tuːŋ 'carry on pole'.

ˣʔanrɔŋ -f 'toad', Jarai (PL) ajĭ-ărɤ̆ʔ, N. Roglai anroʔ -f, Haroi arɤ̆ʔ -f, PR Cham arɤ̆ʔ, Wr. Cham arauk.

ˣʔiăw 'left (side)', Rade ɗiău -iv, Jarai (PL) ïaŭ, Jarai (Lee) ʔiɛau -v, Chru iău, N. Roglai iău, Tsat taːïʔ⁴² -iv, Haroi eau, W. Cham iu, PR Cham iw, Wr. Cham iw; MK: PNB *haqɛw, PMnong *kiâw, PSB (Efimov) *'giəw.

ˣʔjraw 'bamboo sp.', Rade ɗrau 'thornless long-sectioned bamboo', Chru iraːu -1 'thornless, long-sectioned', N. Roglai ʔjrau, Haroi ʔjrau, W. Cham çrau < *jr- 'thornless, long-sectioned', PR Cham (Lee) ʔjaw, ɗraw, PKatuic *kə[l/lh]aːw, *ʒə[l/lh]aːw.

ˣʔjruah 'barking deer', Achenese glɯh; jlɯh, Jarai (PL) ʔjruăh, Jarai (Lee) ʔjruah, Chru iruah 'barking deer', N. Roglai ʔjuah, Haroi ʔjroah 'barking deer', W. Cham ʔjoah 'mousedeer', PR Cham ʔjrwăh, Wr. Cham ʔjrụah.

ˣʔəm-ˣaguăh 'morning; dawn', Rade ïm 'early', aguah 'morning'; məŋač 'light, morning', Jarai (PL) măguah, guah, Jarai (Lee) məguah, Chru əːm -1, guăh, N. Roglai muguăh; guăh, Haroi əm. Both forms are restricted in their distribution to Highlands Chamic plus Haroi; both forms contain loan phonemes.

ˣʔəmraːk 'peacock', Acehnese mɯraʔ -v, Rade amrak, Jarai (PL) amrăʔ, Chru amrăːʔ, N. Roglai amraːʔ, Haroi amraʔ, W. Cham mraʔ, PR Cham mraʔ; amraʔ, Wr. Cham amrak; mrak, Malay mĕrak; MK: PMnong *brak, Bahnar (AC) amra, PSB (Efimov) *braːʔ, PKatuic *riaʔ.

ˣaguat -vf 'jew's harp', Rade aguat -v 'one string instrument', Chru aguat -f 'jew's harp'. Restricted to Highlands Chamic.

ˣbamɔːŋ -f 'banana blossom', Rade moŋ 'stalk of bananas', Rade (Tharpe) məmoŋ, N. Roglai bumoːk -f, Haroi pəmuŋ, PR Cham (Lee) mŏʔ -f.

ˣbarəm -i 'light (fire)', Rade răm, Chru pərəm -i, Tsat zan[11]. Only found in the highlands languages.

ˣbay 'basket, kind of', Rade bai, Jarai (PL) bai, Jarai (Lee) bai, Chru baːi (large, round), N. Roglai bai, Haroi bai; phɨai, W. Cham ɓai (ķep), PR Cham ɓay; haɓay, Wr. Cham bai; MK: Bahnar (AC) bai.

ˣbiam -lv 'crop (of bird)', Rade biăm 'goiter', Jarai (PL) bɛm (Ouest); MK: PKatuic (DT) *phl_m 'crop, craw', PKatuic *biam 'craw of fowl'. Restricted to Highlands Chamic.

ˣbɔ 'empty', Rade (Tharpe) bŏ, Jarai (Lee) bo. Restricted to Highlands Chamic. [The vowel indicates a MK origin]

ˣbuːr -f 'soup', Acehnese bu 'rice, Rade bur -f, Jarai (Lee) bur, Chru bu 'porridge', N. Roglai bu, Haroi phu -f 'cooked rice', W. Cham ɓu, PR Cham ɓu -f, Wr. Cham bū, Malay bubur 'broth', PMP *buʀbuʀ; MK: PSB (Efimov) *pɔːr 'gruel, soup'. Although this form is also found in PMP, within Chamic it has quite irregular reflexes.

ˣbubɛ 'goat; sheep', Rade be, Jarai (PL) be, băbe (S), Jarai (Lee) bəbe, Chru pəbɛ, N. Roglai mube, Tsat phe[11], Haroi phɪ, W. Cham ɓaɓɛ, PR Cham ɓaɓɛ 'goat'; ɓaɓo 'sheep', Wr. Cham ɓaɓaiy 'goat'; ɓaɓauḩ; MK: PNB *babe, PMnong *be, PSB (Efimov) *bəbɛː, PKatuic *ʔb[e/ɛ]ː, *ʔb[e/ɛ]ːʔ.

ˣbum -vl 'blind', Rade bum -1, Jarai (PL) bɔm; bum, Jarai (Lee) bum; bom -v, Chru boːm məta -vl, N. Roglai buːp -1, Haroi phum -1, PR Cham (Lee, Blood) bom 'night blind'.

ˣɓaʔ -i 'carry on back', Rade ɓăʔ, Jarai (PL) ɓăʔ, Jarai (Lee) băʔ -i, Chru baʔ -i, N. Roglai baʔ -i, Haroi ɓăʔ 'carry in carrying cloth', W. Cham pă̆ʔ -i, PR Cham pă̆ʔ, Wr. Cham bak -i; MK: PNB *pòq ʔ, PMnong *baʔ, PMalayic *baʔ 'carry'. The irregularities in the Chamic forms plus existence of the two Bahnaric forms mark the word as MK; thus, the PMalayic form looks to be borrowed.

ˣɓaŋ 'table', Chru ɓaːŋ, N. Roglai ɓaŋ -f, Haroi baːŋ -i-vʀ; MK: PSB (Efimov) *'bá(o)ːŋ. Restricted to Highlands Chamic plus Haroi.

ˣɓiŋ 'we', Jarai (PL) ɓiŋ-, Haroi bĭŋ sɨa 'other'; MK: PNB *(q)bèn '(incl.)', PMnong *băn, PSB (Efimov) *bəːₙn 'we (incl.)'. Restricted to Highlands Chamic.

ˣɓlaŋ 'plains, delta; yard', Acehnese blaŋ 'rice field, rice growing plain, cultivated flood plain', Chru ɓlaːŋ 'yard', N. Roglai ɓlaːk, W. Cham ɓlaŋ 'plains, delta', PR Cham ɓlaŋ, Wr. Cham ɓlaŋ; MK: Bahnar (AC) blaŋ; bəlaŋ, PKatuic *trəəɲ 'field, plain'.

ˣɓlit see ˣ(ma)klit

ˣɓluar -f 'to tell a lie', Rade luar -v, Jarai (PL) ɓlər, Jarai (Lee) ɓlɔr -v; blɔr -v, Chru lər -i, N. Roglai lə -i, PR Cham (Blood) ɓăr -f 'slander'.

ˣɓuan -ivf 'island', Jarai (PL) ɓul (Ss), Chru buːt -ivf pəlaːu, N. Roglai ɓuat, PR Cham ɓon 'island; small hill', Wr. Cham ɓųən.

ˣɓuh 'see', Rade ɓuh, Jarai (PL) ɓûh, Jarai (Lee) ɓuh, Chru ɓuh, N. Roglai ɓuh, Tsat ɓu⁵⁵, Haroi ɓŏh -vʀ, W. Cham ɓoh -v, PR Cham ɓɔh; ɓoh -v, Wr. Cham ɓôh; MK: Bahnar (AC) bôh.

ˣcaːi -f 'sap; resin', Jarai (PL) cai, Chru caːi -f, N. Roglai traiʔ -f, PR Cham cay, Wr. Cham cai.

ˣcabiʔ 'sack', Jarai (PL) cǎbïʔ (Ouest), Jarai (Lee) cəbiʔ, Chru səbiːʔ, PR Cham capiʔ; kapiʔ, Wr. Cham cabik; kabik.

ˣcagam 'handspan', Rade kəgam, Jarai (PL) cǎgam, Jarai (Lee) cəgam -1, Chru səgam, N. Roglai cagap 'thumb to middle finger', Tsat khaːŋ¹¹ ?-1, Haroi cəkhiam 'measure from thumb to middle finger', W. Cham caḳam -1, PR Cham caḳam -1, Wr. Cham cagaṁ.

ˣcagɔw 'Malaysian bear', Acehnese cagɛə, Rade kəgău, Jarai (PL) jəgəu, Chru səgəu 'black bear', N. Roglai cagəu, Haroi cəkhiau, W. Cham caḳau duʔ 'black bear', PR Cham caḳŏw, Wr. Cham caguw; MK: PMnong *čəkăw, Bahnar (AC) çagâu, PSB (Efimov) *ʼjrəkaw. This word for 'bear' is found throughout Southeast Asia. Probably originally a MK word.

ˣcaɗaːŋ; ˣraɗaːŋ 'crack open', Rade kəɗaŋ 'split, divide', Jarai (Lee) cəɗaŋ, Chru cədaːŋ; səɗaːŋ, N. Roglai caɗaːk, Haroi cəɗaŋ, PR Cham raɗăŋ -mi, Wr. Cham raɗəŋ.

ˣcaɗɔŋ -f 'flat basket', Chru cəɗɔŋ 'large, round winnowing basket', N. Roglai caɗok -f 'large, round basket', Haroi cəɗŏŋ, PR Cham caɗɔŋ -1, Wr. Cham caɗauŋ; MK: PMnong *dôŋ 'winnowing basket', PKatuic *kəduŋ, *kəndoːŋ, *ʒəduŋ.

ˣcakuːŋ 'carry (several)', Rade kəkuŋ, Jarai (PL) cǎkuŋ (Pk), Jarai (Lee) cəkuŋ, Chru səkoːŋ, N. Roglai cakuːk, Haroi cəkoŋ 'two carry something heavy on a stick over the shoulders', W. Cham cakoŋ, PR Cham cakoŋ; takoŋ, Wr. Cham cakoŋ; MK: Bahnar (AC) çəkuŋ; čokəŋ ?, PKatuic *cəkaːŋ 'carry on pole'.

ˣcana:ŋ 'furniture; bed', Jarai (PL) cənaŋ, Jarai (Lee) cənaŋ, Chru cəna:ŋ, N. Roglai canăŋ, W. Cham caniŋ 'wooden bed', PR Cham taniŋ -i, Wr. Cham taniŋ 'bed'; MK: PSB (Efimov) *ˈcʌ:ŋ 'bed'.

ˣcantik 'beautiful', Acehnese cantɛʔ, Wr. Cham (AC) čantik, Malay cantik. This is a late borrowing from Malay into both Cham and Acehnese.

ˣcaŋuar -f 'flat basket', Rade kəŋuor, Jarai (PL) cə̆ŋua -f, Jarai (Lee) cəŋua -f, Chru cənua -ŋf 'winnowing basket (pointed)', N. Roglai caŋuã 'winnowing basket', Haroi cəŋoa, W. Cham caŋoa -vf 'winnowing'.

ˣcap 'bundle, tie', Rade čắp, Jarai (Lee) cắp, cắʔ -f caʔ -f 'of chignon', Chru ciauʔ ʔi, Haroi cău? 'to tie', W. Cham cauʔ, PR Cham (Lee) că?, Wr. Cham (AC) čap.

ˣcataʔ see ˣtatuh

ˣch-an-ər, 'dibble stick', cf. ˣchər 'plant with stick', Chru cənər, N. Roglai chanə cf. chə; chanəʔ kaləi 'posthole digger'.   Note the restriction of these terms to Highlands Chamic.

ˣchar -f 'gong', Rade čhar, Jarai (PL) car, Chru sa:r, N. Roglai cha, Haroi sal, PR Cham char, Wr. Cham char; MK: Bahnar (AC) čar.

ˣcho? 'scoop up; ladle out', Jarai (PL) sŏ? ia, Jarai (Lee) sŏʔ, Chru so? ia 'dip water', N. Roglai cho? (ia), W. Cham chŏʔ, PR Cham çhŏʔ, Wr. Cham jhauk; MK: Bahnar (AC) kh. čhak.

ˣchum -1 'pants; clothes', Rade čhum -1 cf. čhiăm 'cloth', Jarai (PL) sŭm gloŋ (Mod.), Jarai (Lee) som -v, Chru sum pha -1, N. Roglai cupha -1, W. Cham capa -v 'trousers'. Restricted to Highlands Chamic plus W. Cham.

ˣchəp 'dirty', Rade čhŏʔ, Chru səuʔ, N. Roglai ticəʔ; magap -f, W. Cham soc -fv groc, PR Cham tasŏwʔ, Wr. Cham taśəp.

ˣchər 'plant with stick', Chru cər, N. Roglai chə cf. chanə. Note the restriction of these items to the Highlands Chamic languages.

ˣciam 'feed; nourish', Rade čiem -v; mčiem, Jarai (Lee) [pə] cɛm -v, Chru ciam -1, N. Roglai ciap, Haroi ceam, W. Cham kiam -iv, PR Cham ciem -v, Wr. Cham ci̯em, PSB (Efimov) *siəm, PKatuic *həcɛ:m, *ʔəcɛ:m.

ˣciaŋ 'carry on side', Rade čieŋ, Jarai (PL) cieŋ -v, Chru cɛ:ŋ -v, Haroi ceŋ -v, Wr. Cham (AC) či̯əŋ.

ˣcrɛh 'mark; draw line', cf. 'write; draw', Rade trɛh 'make lines', Jarai (Lee) crɛh 'to strike', PR Cham crɛh, Wr. Cham craih.

ˣcrih 'strange; unusual', Chru crih craŋ, N. Roglai crĭh -n, PR Cham crĭh, Wr. Cham crih.

ˣcrɔh 'stream, creek', Rade crɔ̆k -f, Jarai (PL) crŏh, Jarai (Lee) crɔh, Chru crɔh, N. Roglai croh, Haroi cərŏh, W. Cham crɔh, PR Cham crŏh, Wr. Cham crauh̞.

ˣcuːr 'lime (for betel)', Rade čŭr -f, Jarai (PL) cŭr, Jarai (Lee) cur, Chru cuːr, N. Roglai cu, Haroi col, W. Cham cu -f, PR Cham cur, Wr. Cham cur; MK: PSB (Efimov) *cuːr.

ˣcum 'kiss; smell', Acehnese com, Rade (bi) čŭm, Jarai (PL) cum, bəcum, Jarai (Lee) cum, Chru cum 'nose kiss', N. Roglai cum -f, Haroi com, W. Cham cum, PR Cham cŭm, Wr. Cham cuṁ, Malay cium 'kiss, smell'; MK: PNB *tačhŭm, PMnong *cŭm, PSB (Efimov) *cum 'nuzzle'.

ˣcupa/et -vf 'squeeze; grasp', Acehnese jupat -i, Rade kəpăt, Jarai (PL) kăpit, căpit (Pk), Jarai (Lee) cəpă? 'to knead', Chru cəpa?, N. Roglai capa?, Haroi cəpă?, W. Cham capĕt -f.

ˣcuɓuay; ˣtuɓuay 'lips; gums', cf. 'beak', Rade kəɓue, Jarai (Lee) cəɓuai; təɓuai; təbuai; səɓuai, Chru səɓuai, N. Roglai cu ɓuai; cuɓuai, Haroi cəɓŏai, W. Cham caɓuai, PR Cham caboy, Wr. Cham caɓy̆ai; MK: PKatuic *hə?bər, *təm?bər 'lips' ? [cf. Malay bibir].

ˣdhual/r -f 'dust; fog, mist', Acehnese dhoi < *-1, Rade dhul 'fog, mist, vapor', Chru thul -v, N. Roglai thun -v, W. Cham ṭhŭl -v, PR Cham ṭhŭr -vf, Wr. Cham dhur -v. [The vowel indicates a MK origin]

ˣdian 'candle', Rade pui diăn, Chru diən -v, N. Roglai diăn -f, Tsat then?⁴², W. Cham ṭian, PR Cham ṭien, Wr. Cham djen, Malay dian; MK: PKatuic (DT) *taen.

ˣdriaw 'exclaim; acclaim', Jarai (PL) dreu, Haroi trɨau, PR Cham ṭriew, Wr. Cham drjew. [The vowel indicates a MK origin]

ˣdrən -if 'numb', cf. ˣnrən -if, Chru drɨn -v, N. Roglai drɨn -vf, Haroi trŭn 'benumbed; asleep (foot)', PR Cham ṭrăn, Wr. Cham dran.

ˣdəp -ifv 'hide', Rade ɗuɛ̆? dăp -fv, Jarai (PL) kădŏp, pădŏp; bădăp 'quelque chose', Jarai (Lee) (pə)dŏp -fv, Chru pədəu?, N. Roglai də?; paɗə? -i; kada:? -v, W. Cham paṭau?; ṭau?, PR Cham thŏw?; pakaɗŏw? cacher dans un endroit secret; paṭŏw?; kaɗŏw?; kawă?, Wr. Cham thəp; pāgaɗəp; gaɗəp etre cacher; kawək, Malay ĕndap.

ˣɗaw 'all', Chru ɗau 'at all', Tsat ?dau³³. Only found in Chru and Tsat so far, both Highlands Chamic languages. [< MK]

ˣɗɛl 'shallow', Acehnese dɯə -i, Rade eɗal -v, Chru ɗɛl, N. Roglai ɗen; MK: PMnong *thəl, PKatuic *[h/s]əndial, *[p/b]ə?di:l.

ˣɗiŋ -f 'tube; pipe (for smoking)', Rade ɗïŋ, Jarai (PL) ɗiŋ, Jarai (Lee) ɗïŋ; ɗïŋ, Chru ɗiŋ -1, N. Roglai ɗit -f, Haroi ɗiŋ, W. Cham ɗïŋ v? ?ju? 'pipe'; ɗïŋ tju?, PR Cham ɗiŋ, Wr. Cham ɗiŋ; MK: PNB *qɗĩŋ 'bamboo pipe', PMnong *ɗíŋ, Bahnar (AC) diŋ, PSB (Efimov) *diŋ.

ˣɗiəp 'glutinous rice', Rade ɗiɔ̆?, Jarai (PL) ɗiəŭ? ?, Haroi ɗiu?, W. Cham (Headley) /diau?/. Restricted to Highlands Chamic plus Haroi and W. Cham.

ˣɗɔh 'flow; run off', Rade ɗɔh, N. Roglai ɗoh 'subside'. Note the restriction to two Highlands languages. Cf. 'run; run off; flow' ˣ*ɗuac.

ˣɗuːŋ 'float', Rade ɗuŋ, Jarai (PL) pɔ̆ɗuŋ; ɗuŋ hleŋ hlɔ̆ŋ, Chru ɗoːŋ, N. Roglai ɗuːk, Haroi ɗoŋ -vʀ, W. Cham ɗoŋ, Wr. Cham (AC) ɗoːŋ; MK: Bahnar (AC) dôŋ.

ˣɗuan 'bamboo hat', Rade ɗuon, Jarai (PL) həɗoăn, Jarai (Lee) ɗuăn -v, N. Roglai ɗuat, Tsat ɗuat³³ -f, PR Cham ɗon, Wr. Cham ɗon; MK: PMnong *?duân, Bahnar (AC) duən, PSB (Efimov) *'duən, PKatuic *?duan.

ˣɗvt -v 'small', Rade ɗiet, Haroi ɗăt. Restricted to Highlands Chamic plus Haroi.

ˣgalɛk -lv 'tickle', P-Acehnese (Durie) *gle?, Acehnese gli?-gli? -vi, Jarai (PL) glɛk, Jarai (Lee) glɛ̆k ?ɛ̆, Chru gəlɛk -f; glɛk -if, N. Roglai gilet -f, Haroi kəlɛ̆k -vf, PR Cham k̟alɛ̆k, Wr. Cham galaik, Malay gĕletek; gĕli; gĕlak 'laugh'; MK: PKatuic (DT) *–lek.

ˣgiam/p -ivf 'carry under arm', Jarai (PL) gɛ̆p, Chru kiap -1, N. Roglai kiap 'clutch, carry under arm', W. Cham k̟iam -v. Restricted to Highlands Chamic, Haroi, and W. Cham.

ˣgɔh 'clean', Chru gɔh, N. Roglai goh; MK: PNB *ragoh. Note the restriction to closely-related Chru and N. Roglai.

ˣgriaŋ 'fang; tusk', Rade griăŋ -v, Chru griaŋ, N. Roglai giaŋ -f 'incisor', W. Cham k̟rɛ̆ŋ -v, PR Cham k̟rɛ̆ŋ, Wr. Cham grɛ̆in, PSB (Efimov) *gənɪːŋ 'fang; eyetooth'.

ˣgrit 'dirty', Jarai (PL) grĭ?, Jarai (Lee) grĭ?, Haroi khri?; kri?, W. Cham k̟roc -vf, PR Cham (Lee) krĭ?.

ˣgrɔh 'to bark', P-Acehnese (Durie) *grɔ̆h, Acehnese dloh; kloh -i, Rade grɔh, Jarai (PL) grɔ̆h, Jarai (Lee) grɔh, Chru grɔh, N. Roglai groh, Tsat khiə⁵⁵, Haroi krŭh -v; krouh -v, PR Cham k̟rɔ̆h, Wr. Cham grauh; MK: PMnong *groh, PKatuic *gəruah.

ˣgruă? 'lie prone'.

ˣgrək 'vulture; garuda', Jarai (PL) grĭ?, Jarai (Lee) gri?, N. Roglai grə?, Haroi kri?, W. Cham k̟rə?, PR Cham k̟rɔ̆?, Wr. Cham grək, Malay ɢaruda 'eagle of Vishnu'.

ˣgrəm -vf 'thunder', Rade grăm, Jarai (PL) grŏm, Jarai (Lee) grŏm, Chru grəm, N. Roglai grəm -f, Tsat khi:n¹¹ or khien¹¹, Haroi kriam, W. Cham ḳrəm -v, PR Cham ḳrŭm -v, Wr. Cham gruṁ; MK: Bahnar (AC) grâm, PKatuic *gərim.

ˣguaʔ 'lie prone'.

ˣhadruam 'book', Rade hədruom hrăʔ, Haroi cətrŭm; hətrŭm -i. Thus far, this seems restricted to two languages, one a Highlands language and the other now found in the highlands.

ˣham -1 'greed', Jarai (Lee) ham, Chru ha:m -1 la:m, N. Roglai ham -f; MK: Vietnamese thám lam, PKatuic *ha:m 'greedy'.

ˣhanuăʔ -v 'right (side)', Rade hənuăʔ, Jarai (PL) hənuăʔ, Jarai (Lee) hənuăʔ, Chru hənuaʔ, N. Roglai ha nuaʔ (this form either indicates the original form was bimorphemic, or that it was reanalyzed in Northern Roglai), Haroi hənŭʔ, W. Cham hanuïʔ, PR Cham hanŭʔ; nŭʔ, Wr. Cham hanuk; nuk, PMP *kawanan, *qaqay; *taqu 'right hand', Malay kanan. Note that it is possible that this form may ultimately turn out to be related to the Austronesian forms given here, and the irregularities may simply reflect the reduction of a multi-syllabic, multi-morphemic entity to a single disyllabic form.

ˣhɔ:ŋ -f 'wasp', Acehnese hŭəŋ, Rade hoŋ, Jarai (PL) hoŋ, Jarai (Lee) hoŋ, Chru hɔ:ŋ, N. Roglai hoŋ -f, Haroi hɔŋ, W. Cham hɔŋ; MK: PNB *oŋ, PSB (Efimov) *ʔɔ:ŋ, PKatuic *ha:ŋ.

ˣhuac 'fear', Rade huïʔ -f, Jarai (PL) huïʔ -f, Jarai (Lee) huïʔ -f, Chru huəiʔ -f, N. Roglai hueʔ, Haroi hwăiʔ -vʀ, W. Cham huaiʔ, PR Cham (Blood) hoc; MK: PSB (Efimov) *rəhyu:.

ˣhuc 'whistle', Rade hoč, Jarai (PL) hoac, Chru srui:t -if, N. Roglai huaiʔ -v, W. Cham huiʔ, PR Cham huyt -f, Wr. Cham huit -f; MK: PKatuic *gəhɔ:jʔ *həhɔ:jʔ.

ˣhuni 'bee; honey', Acehnese unɔə, Rade ea hənue (m), Jarai (PL) həni, Jarai (Lee) həni, Chru həni; həni:ŋ 'honey', N. Roglai huṅi, Tsat ni³³, Haroi həni, W. Cham ea hani; hɔŋ, PR Cham hani, Wr. Cham haṅi. It is the unexpected final /i/ that primarily marks this as a borrowing; it may, however, have some related forms in Malayic (Adelaar).

ˣhəməʔ -ivf 'hear', Rade həmïʔ, Jarai (PL) həmïʔ, Jarai (Lee) hmïʔ, Chru məhŭʔ, N. Roglai hmỗʔ -v, Haroi hmăk -f, W. Cham hamït -f meţialʔ, PR Cham hamït -f, Wr. Cham hamit -f.

ˣih 'you; thou', Rade ih 'you (sg.)', Jarai (PL) ih 'to a single person (polite)'; MK: PNB *ĩh.

ˣjam 'plate; dish', Rade jam 'dish', Jarai (PL) jam, N. Roglai (jiə), W. Cham çam -1, PR Cham çam -1, Wr. Cham jaṁ; MK: PMnong *jam, Bahnar (AC) jâm.

ˣjaɓu 'dry in sun', Rade ɓhu mədie, Jarai (PL) cǎɓǔʔ -f, Chru səɓu -i 'dry rice', N. Roglai jaɓu padai, Haroi cəɓu, W. Cham caɓu -i 'spread rice to dry', PR Cham paɓu -i, Wr. Cham ɓaɓu. The first syllable varies inexplicably.

ˣjhuəŋ -n (?) 'long-legged', Jarai (Lee) sɨŋ 'stilts', PR Cham (Lee) chɨ̀ŋ; MK: PSB (Efimov) *jɔːŋ 'long', PKatuic *(hə)ʔjoŋ, *gəʔjoŋ 'long'.

ˣjiǎ 'taxes', Rade jia, Jarai (Lee) jia, Chru jiǎ, N. Roglai jiǎ, Haroi sia -v, PR Cham (Lee) cɨ̀.

ˣjɔːŋ 'axe', Rade joŋ, Jarai (PL) jɔŋ, Jarai (Lee) jɔŋ, Chru jɔːŋ, N. Roglai joːk, Tsat suoŋ[11]; soŋ[11], Haroi suŋ; suŋ, PR Cham çɔŋ; açɔŋ, Wr. Cham jauŋ; ajauŋ; MK: PNB *čùŋ, PMnong *suŋ, PSB (Efimov) *suːŋ, PKatuic *cu[ə/ɑ]ŋ.

ˣjrǎw 'medicine', Rade drau, Jarai (PL) jrau, Jarai (Lee) jrau, Chru jrǎːu, N. Roglai jrǎu, Tsat sia(ː)u[11], Haroi cərɨǎu, W. Cham çru, PR Cham çru, Wr. Cham jrū; MK: Bahnar (AC) jərâu, PSB (Efimov) *'jrʌːwʔ, PKatuic *hərhaw, *təhaːw.

ˣjrɔ 'large jar', Chru jrɔ, N. Roglai jrɔ 'water crock' (also a clf.). Restricted to Highlands Chamic.

ˣjrɔ 'rainbow', Rade keñ ero; keñ kro, Jarai (PL) cro (Sɛ), Jarai (Lee) cro ?, N. Roglai tagalo jro, Haroi cərɔ -vʀ, W. Cham crɔ -i. Restricted to Highlands Chamic plus Haroi and W. Cham.

ˣjut -fl 'small bamboo', Rade jǔt, Chru jut -fl, W. Cham çǔt -f. Restricted to Highlands Chamic plus W. Cham.

ˣjəŋ -vf 'become', cf. *pajəŋ, Rade jiŋ -v, Jarai (PL) pǎgiŏŋ, Jarai (Lee) jiŋ -v, Chru jiəŋ -v, N. Roglai jək, Haroi sɨ̆ŋ, W. Cham çiaŋ -v, PR Cham çyəŋ -v, Wr. Cham jiəŋ; MK: PMnong *jêŋ, PSB (Efimov) *jɛŋ 'be born; become'.

ˣkaɗual 'heel', Rade kəɗul, Jarai (PL) kǎɗul, Jarai (Lee) kəɗul, Chru kəduəl 'elbow', N. Roglai kaɗuən, Haroi kəɗul, W. Cham kaɗual, PR Cham kaɗol, Wr. Cham kaɗʉəl; MK: PNB *kaqnèl, PMnong *kəndəl, PSB (Efimov) *'gəndʌːl, PKatuic *gənʔdʌːl, *səndual.

ˣkasuǎr -f 'porcupine', Rade kəsua -f, Jarai (PL) kətsǔa, Jarai (Lee) kəsua -f, Chru kəsuǎ -f, N. Roglai kasuǎ -f, Haroi kəsoa, W. Cham kasur, PR Cham kathǔr, Wr. Cham kathur; MK: Bahnar (AC) gəçor, PKatuic *[h/ʔ]əŋkʌjh, *ɣəŋkʌːjh.

ˣkatri 'scissors', Rade kətrɛi, Chru kətrəi -f, N. Roglai katri, Haroi kətrɔ̆i, W. Cham katray, Malay kĕlĕkati 'areca-nut scissors' from Tamil?; MK: PKatuic *-dərh[ɛ/ə/a]j, Bru kəntraj.L.

ˣkhiːn 'dare; brave', Jarai (PL) khɨn, Jarai (Lee) khin, Chru khin, N. Roglai khin -f, Haroi khɛ̆n, W. Cham khɨ̆n 'covet; desire', PR Cham khɨ̆n, Wr. Cham khin, Proto-Hrê-Sedang *khɨ̆n.

ˣkhiaŋ -fi 'want; desire; marry', Rade čiăŋ -v, Jarai (PL) kiăŋ, Jarai (Lee) kiăŋ -iv, Chru khiaŋ -v, N. Roglai khiaŋ -f also verbal auxiliary, Haroi ceaŋ -i, W. Cham khĭn -f, PR Cham khĭŋ, Wr. Cham khiṅ-khĭŋ; MK: PSB (Efimov) *kʌːŋ 'want, desire'.

ˣkrăm -lvn 'bamboo', Rade kram, Jarai (PL) kram, Jarai (Lee) kram, Chru kraːm -l 'large, thornless', N. Roglai kram -f, Haroi kram -l, W. Cham krɨm -v, PR Cham krɨm -v, Wr. Cham krɨṁ.

ˣkriăw 'castrate', Jarai (PL) krɛŭ, Jarai (Lee) krɛu, N. Roglai kiău -i, Haroi pə-kreau 'to cut off dead branches' -v.

ˣkúit 'tangerine', Rade kuĭt, Chru kuit, N. Roglai cit.

ˣkuac 'scratch, claw', Rade kuač -f 'scrape, Jarai (Lee) kuac -f, Haroi koai? -l 'pick up (handful)'; MK: PNB *kuč. Again, restricted to Highlands Chamic plus Haroi.

ˣkuhɔ -iv 'Koho', Rade kəhɔ -iv, Chru mənih kəhɔ -v, N. Roglai manũih kuho; manũih crău 'Tring, Koho', W. Cham kahɔ.

ˣkun -f 'fold; bundle; curled', Rade kŭn, Jarai (Lee) kun 'curled', N. Roglai kun -f 'lie in a heap'. Restricted to Highlands Chamic.

ˣkutɔːk/p 'grasshopper', Rade kətuop -vf, Chru kətɔːk -f, N. Roglai kutoːk -f, Tsat tɔ?[42] ?, Haroi kətɔk -f, W. Cham katɔk -f; MK: PKatuic *gu[ə/o]?.

ˣkəjap 'firm; solid', Rade kajăp, Chru kəjap -f, W. Cham kaçăp -vf; MK: PMnong *kəljăp. Restricted to Highlands Chamic.

ˣkəmuan, ˣ?amuan 'nephew; sister's son', Acehnese kɯmuən, Rade amuon 'nephew, niece', Jarai (PL) amŏn, Jarai (Lee) ?amɔn, Chru kəmuan 'nephew, niece', N. Roglai kamuăn, Haroi amɔn, W. Cham kamuan, PR Cham kamon -v, Wr. Cham kamɥən; MK: PNB *mon 'nephew', PMnong *kəmon, PSB (Efimov) *kəmɔːn 'nephew, niece', PKatuic *[s/?]əmhaːn, *kərmhaːn 'nephew, niece'.

ˣlaːt 'flat', Rade lat, Jarai (PL) lat, Jarai (Lee) lat; la?, N. Roglai laː?, Haroi la?, PR Cham klɛt -ivf, PMnong *rəlat. Headley (1976) identified the PC form as borrowed from MK, an analysis supported both by the internal irregularities and by the presence of the form in various MK languages. Two lookalikes, Acehnese rata and Malay rata 'smooth; level' are unrelated to the PC. As Adelaar (p.c.) noted, the ultimate source of the Malay and the Acehnese is PMP *datar. From PMP *datar, Malay has, not unexpectedly, datar, but in addition Malay has rata, borrowed from Javanese (also descended from PMP *datar). The Malay form rata was then borrowed into Acehnese.

ˣla?ən 'cold', Rade eăt -f, Jarai (PL) rə?ŏt -fv, Jarai (Lee) rə?ŏt -fv, N. Roglai la?ət, Tsat ?an[33], Haroi lə?ə? -vf, W. Cham la?ăn -v, PR Cham liăn; laăn, Wr. Cham lian; laan; MK: PMnong *?lik, PSB (Efimov) *lə?iː? 'cool, chill'.

*lən 'earth' + ˣkliat -v '?' > 'clay', Rade lăn tliet, Jarai (PL) lŏn, Chru lən klia?, N. Roglai lət matli:?. The ˣkliat -v '?' is restricted to Highlands Chamic.

ˣ(li)huŋ 'papaya', Rade tɛi huŋ -1, Jarai (PL) hoŋ (Pk), Jarai (Lee) huŋ, Chru ləhɔŋ -v, N. Roglai 1ahoŋ -f, W. Cham 1ahŏŋ -v, PR Cham (Lee) lihɔŋ; MK: PNB *rahŭŋ.

ˣliŋiaw 'outside', Rade eŋau -v, Jarai (PL) rɜ̆ŋɨaŭ, Jarai (Lee) rəŋiau, Haroi ləŋɨau -v, W. Cham 1aŋiu, PR Cham liŋiw; 1aŋiw; ŋiw, Wr. Cham liŋiw; 1aŋiw; ŋiw. [The vowel suggests a MK origin.]

ˣluən -v 'to swallow', Rade 1un, Jarai (PL) lŭn, Chru luən, N. Roglai luət -v, Tsat 1uan³³ -vf, Haroi 1un, W. Cham 1uan -v, Malay tĕlan, PMP *telen; *tilen; MK: PKatuic *həli:n, *həlʌ:n.

ˣləyuh 'shake', Rade eyuh, Jarai (PL) rəyŭh, Jarai (Lee) rəyuh, Chru ləyuh, N. Roglai yuh 'wiggle', Haroi ləyŭh, W. Cham yuh 'chill, shivering', PR Cham yŭh; rŭh -i, Wr. Cham yuḥ; ruḥ; MK: PMnong *rəgu 'shake', Bahnar (AC) ruḥ.

ˣ(ma)klit; ˣɓlit 'sticky; pasty', Acehnese kliət -iv, Rade ɓlĭt 'stuck; caught', Jarai (PL) ɓlit, Jarai (Lee) tli? -i, N. Roglai tli:? 'in sticky rice', Haroi ɓli?; MK: Bahnar (AC) klep.

ˣmadar -f 'rich', Jarai (Lee) mədăr 'to cheat', Chru məda -f, N. Roglai mada, PR Cham miṭa -f, Wr. Cham mɨdā.

ˣmɛ? -vf 'mother', Acehnese mak, ma, umi, mi, Rade amĭ?, Jarai (PL) amĭ?, Chru amɛ -f, N. Roglai (awəi), Haroi amĭ? 'mother; address term', W. Cham mɛ?; mă?, PR Cham amɛ?; mɛ?, Wr. Cham maik, Malay (ĕ)ma(?); MK: PMnong *me; *me?, PSB (Efimov) *mɛ: 'mother, female', PKatuic *həmbɛ:?, *?əmh[e/ɛ]?.

ˣmray 'thread', Rade mrai, Jarai (PL) mraĭ, Jarai (Lee) mrai, Chru məra:i, N. Roglai mrai; murai, Tsat za:i³³, Haroi mərai; cəmroi 'string', W. Cham mrai, PR Cham mray, Wr. Cham mrai; MK: PNB *bray, PMnong *bray, PSB (Efimov) *bra:y 'web, thread', PKatuic *[h/s]əmriaj, *pəriaj, *pɛj.

ˣmuăr -f 'termite', Rade muor -v, Jarai (PL) mua, Jarai (Lee) mua, Chru mua, N. Roglai muă, Tsat mua³³ 'termite'?, Haroi moa, W. Cham mur, PR Cham mu -f, Wr. Cham mū; MK: PKatuic *kəmhuar.

ˣnrən -if 'numb', cf. ˣdrən -if, Jarai (PL) krŏn, Jarai (Lee) nrən -v?, Chru prən -i; MK: PKatuic *səbɨ:n.

ˣˣŋan 'money' from 'silver', Rade ŋăn, Jarai (Lee) ŋăn, cf. Tibetan dŋul 'silver'. [This form is from the Tibeto-Burman word for 'silver'.]

ˣpajəŋ -vf 'create', cf. ˣjəŋ, Jarai (PL) pə̆jiŋ -v, Jarai (Lee) pəjiŋ -v, Chru pəjiəŋ -v, N. Roglai pajək, Haroi pəsɨ̆ŋ, W. Cham paçiaŋ -v.

ˣpatuh 'to explode', Acehnese bɯrɯtoh -i, Rade mətuh, Jarai (Lee) pətuh, Chru pərtuh -r, N. Roglai patuh, Haroi pətouh -v, PR Cham patŭh, Wr. Cham patuḥ; MK: PSB *brətɔh, PMnong *bərtoh, PSB (Efimov) *brətɔh.

ˣpayər -f 'to offer', Rade myər, Jarai (Lee) pəyər, Chru pəyəʔ -f, N. Roglai payə ga, Haroi pəyɔl, PR Cham (Lee) payal, Wr. Cham (AC) payər, cf. Malay bayar 'to pay'.

ˣpetruŋ -v 'rich', Rade mədrŏ̆ŋ, Haroi petrŏ̆ŋ -vʀ; MK: PMnong *pədrŏ̆ŋ. Restricted to Highlands Chamic plus Haroi.

ˣphaw 'gun', Rade phau, Jarai (PL) phau (modern), Jarai (Lee) phau, Chru pha:u -l 'rifle', N. Roglai phau, Haroi phau, W. Cham phau, PR Cham phaw, Wr. Cham phaw.

ˣphuŋ 'leper; leprosy', Rade phŭ̆ŋ, Jarai (PL) phŭ̆ŋ, Jarai (Lee) phuŋ, N. Roglai phuŋ -f, Haroi pŭ̆ŋ -i.

ˣpirak -lf 'silver; money', Acehnese piraʔ, Rade prăk, Jarai (PL) prak, Jarai (Lee) prăk, Chru priaʔ jèn -l (m), N. Roglai pariaʔ (m), W. Cham pareaʔ (m), PR Cham paryă̆ʔ (m); pirak 'white', Wr. Cham pariak; birak 'white', Malay pérak; MK: PKatuic *[p/b]ərhaʔ, Khmer prak 'silver; money'. Blust (p.c.) notes that this form is a loan in many AN languages and is found in some MK languages as well.

ˣpliar -f 'hail', Rade plier 'snow, Chru plia -f, Haroi pəleal, W. Cham (Headley) /plia/; MK: PNB *prĕl, PMnong *pliâr, PSB (Efimov) *pḷiər, PWB (Thomas) *priaw, PKatuic *pərhiɛl. Restricted to Highlands Chamic plus Haroi.

ˣpra:l -vf 'strong; well', Rade pral 'well, healthy', Jarai (PL) pran, Jarai (Lee) prăn -f, Chru pra:n -f 'strength', N. Roglai pran -f, Haroi pral; pran -f, W. Cham prin -f, PR Cham prin -f, Wr. Cham prin.

ˣpruac (?) 'stomach; intestine, large', Acehnese pruət, Rade proč -v, Jarai (PL) proaĭʔ, pruaĭʔ, Jarai (Lee) prŭăiʔ; prĕ̆ʔ -f, Chru pruaiʔ, N. Roglai parəʔ -f; puaiʔ, Haroi prŏ̆aiʔ, W. Cham proiʔ -f, PR Cham proyʔ, Wr. Cham prựac; MK: PKatuic *ruajʔ 'instestine'.

ˣprus/h -vf 'to squirt', Rade pruih, Chru kəpru:h, N. Roglai kapru -vf, Haroi prouh -v 'spit out', W. Cham pruh. Restricted to Highlands Chamic plus Haroi and W. Cham.

ˣpək -fvl 'granary', Rade (Lee) pɨ̆ʔ -v, Jarai (PL) pɨk -f, Jarai (Lee) pɨk -f, N. Roglai pə:ʔ -l. Restricted to Highlands Chamic.

ˣraba:ŋ -if 'bridge, suspension', Rade kəban -if, Chru rəba:ŋ, N. Roglai raba:k, W. Cham rapɔŋ 'canal' -v, PR Cham ripaŋ; rapaŋ, Wr. Cham ribaŋ; rabaŋ.

ˣraɗaːŋ see ˣcaɗaːŋ

ˣramah 'rhinoceros', Rade emɛh -v 'rhinoceros horn', Jarai (Lee) rəmah, Chru rəmah, N. Roglai rumãh, Haroi ləmɨah, W. Cham ramɨh, PR Cham ramɨh, Wr. Cham ramɨḥ; MK: Bahnar (AC) rəmai, PKatuic (DT) *ramaas.

ˣramiat 'prepare; put away', Rade emiet -v, Jarai (PL) rə̆mɛt pioh, Chru rəmiaʔ, N. Roglai lumiã̆ʔ -i, Haroi ləmɨaʔ, W. Cham ramiiʔ (n), PR Cham ramɨ̆ʔ (n), Wr. Cham ramik; MK: Bahnar (AC) rəmĕt, PKatuic *miən 'prepare'.

ˣraŋuat 'sad', Rade eŋuot -v, Jarai (PL) rə̆ŋɔt, rəŋuă̆ʔ, Jarai (Lee) rəŋuă̆ʔ -v, Chru rəŋet-f. Restricted to Highlands Chamic.

ˣrimɔːŋ 'tiger', Acehnese rimuəŋ, Rade emoŋ, Jarai (PL) rə̆moŋ, Jarai (Lee) rəmoŋ, Chru rəmɔːŋ, N. Roglai lumõ̆ŋ -i, Haroi ləmuŋ -vʀ, W. Cham ramɔŋ, PR Cham rimɔŋ; ramɔŋ, Wr. Cham rimauŋ; ramauŋ, Malay rimau; hari-mau. This history of this word is quite unclear; Hudson reports the same word in the West Barito branch of his Barito languages (1967:14) of southeast Borneo, but with the meaning 'leopard': Kapuas harimau, Ba'mang harimau, Ketingan haramauŋ, Dohoi haramauŋ, Murung (II) hɔrɔmauŋ, and Siang hɔrɔmauŋ. Note the final velar nasal in several of these.

ˣriyaːʔ -1 'wave; ripple; surf', Acehnese riɯəʔ, Chru riaːʔ 'wave', Tsat (phoˡˡ) zaʔ²⁴, W. Cham rayaʔ, PR Cham rayaʔ, Wr. Cham rayāk, Malay riak. Blust (p.c.) notes that ˣriak is confined to a few languages in Borneo, plus Malay and Malagasy (which, of course, is a Southeast Barito subgroup of Malayic languages of Borneo); the Malagasy form riaka is a borrowing from Malay as evidenced by it /r/ to /r/ correspondence with Malay (Adelaar).

ˣrɔŋ 'back (anat.)', Acehnese ruəŋ, Rade rõ̆ŋ 'upper back', Jarai (PL) rõ̆ŋ, Jarai (Lee) rɔŋ, Chru grɔŋ < *k- 'upper back', N. Roglai tulaːk turok 'back bone', Haroi rõ̆ŋ -vʀ, W. Cham rõ̆ŋ, PR Cham rɔŋ -1, Wr. Cham rauŋ; MK: PNB *(ka)rõ̆ŋ, PKatuic *[k/g]rhaŋ; *[k/g]əlhɔŋ; *[k/g]əlhɔːŋ.

ˣruaʔ -v 'painful', Rade ruă̆ʔ, Jarai (PL) ruă̆ʔ, Jarai (Lee) ruă̆ʔ, Chru rəwaʔ -v səkiːʔ, N. Roglai ruạʔ 'ache', Haroi rŭ̈ʔ; ruă̆ʔ -v -vʀ, W. Cham roaʔ 'sick', PR Cham rwă̆ʔ, Wr. Cham rụak.

ˣruc 'pull', Jarai (PL) rɔ̆t; rŭh, Jarai (Lee) ruc, Chru gruiʔ; pruiʔ, N. Roglai ruiʔ 'set trap or bow', Haroi ruiʔ -v, PR Cham rŭy, Wr. Cham ruc; MK: PKatuic (DT) *r̩q 'pull up'.

ˣrəga 'shake', Rade ega; MK: PMnong *rəgu 'shake', PSB (Efimov) *rə'ŋguː. Restricted to Rade.

*sa ˣsit 'little; a few', Chru sit -1f, Haroi aset -vf 'a little', W. Cham hasɨ̆t -f; sit -f, PR Cham asit -i, sit; sɨ̆t 'petit, peu', Wr. Cham asit, śit; śɨ̆t 'peu petit'; MK: Bahnar (AC) toçiet, PKatuic *[h/s]əŋʔiːt.

ˣsaŋ 'gasoline', Rade ea săŋ, Chru saŋ, N. Roglai ia saŋ -f, W. Cham mañĩʔ săŋ.

ˣsaŋat 'asthma; rhinitis', Jarai (PL) bəŋɤ̆t -i, Jarai (Lee) həŋɤ̆t -vi 'asthma', N. Roglai saŋăʔ 'stuffed-up nose'. Restricted to Highlands Chamic. [Probably MK]

ˣsiʔjual -v 'light (not heavy)', Rade həʔjul, Jarai (PL) ʔjul; ʔjhul, Jarai (Lee) ʔjhul -v, Chru səʔuəl, N. Roglai siʔjuən, Haroi həʔjul, W. Cham ʔjual, PR Cham haʔjol; ʔjol, Wr. Cham ʔjʉəl; haʔjaul; MK: Bahnar (AC) hajəč.

ˣsimaŋ -iv 'cement', Rade simăŋ -i, Chru səmaŋ, N. Roglai simăŋ, W. Cham samɤ̆ŋ -v [< French].

ˣˣsisi(r) > ˣtasi 'a comb; hand of bananas', Rade kəsi; kəsir mətɛi, Jarai (PL) tɤ̆si; tɤ̆si, Jarai (Lee) təsi; sir; si -if, Chru təsi; təsi, N. Roglai kasi; tasi, Tsat si³³, Haroi cəsei; casei, W. Cham tasi; tasi, PR Cham tathi; tathi, Wr. Cham tathĩ, Malay sisir; MK: PKatuic *kəci:ʔ; *[h/s]ənci:ʔ. The post-PC borrowing ˣˣsisi(r) form is what I assume the earliest Chamic form looked like (cf. Malay sisir) before it underwent dissimilation).

ˣsrăp 'crossbow', Jarai (PL) harəu, Jarai (Lee) hraʔ -f, Chru srã:uʔ -l, N. Roglai srăʔ, Haroi srăuʔ, PR Cham thruʔ, Wr. Cham thruk.

ˣsra:p -f 'tired of', Jarai (Lee) hrăp, Chru srăp -f 'fed up with', Haroi srăp -fv 'tired of'. Restricted to Highlands Chamic plus Haroi.

ˣsrɛ̃ 'debt, owe', Chru srɛ̃, N. Roglai srɛ̃, W. Cham srɛ. Restricted to Highlands Chamic plus W. Cham.

ˣsrɔh -nʔ 'polish rice', Acehnese srɔh; rhɔh, Chru srɔh 'pound rice', W. Cham srɔh; MK: PKatuic *səruah 'pound'.

ˣsrɔ:k 'fishtrap', Rade hrok, Chru srɔ:ʔ, N. Roglai srɔ:ʔ. Restricted to Highlands Chamic.

ˣsrɔ̃ʔ -n 'subside', Rade hrɔ̃ʔ, Chru srɔ̃ʔ -n. Restricted to Highlands Chamic.

ˣsrŭh 'nest; swarm', Rade hruh, Jarai (PL) hrŭh, Jarai (Lee) hrŭh, Chru srŭh, N. Roglai srŭh, Haroi srouh -v; cəhrouh -v, W. Cham sruh, PR Cham thrŭh, Wr. Cham thruh; MK: PKatuic (DT) *sr̥h, PKatuic *soh, *so:ḥ. Note that this form borrowed into PC is only attested in Katuic thus far.

ˣsuac 'pull out', Rade kəsuɛ̆ʔ, Jarai (PL) soăʔ, Chru suaʔ -f 'pull, extract', N. Roglai suaiʔ -f, Haroi sŏaiʔ, W. Cham soaʔ -f 'extract'. Restricted to Highlands Chamic plus Haroi and W. Cham.

ˣtali -if 'flat (of large rocks)', Jarai (Lee) kli -i (borrowed), Haroi cəlei, PR Cham tali, Wr. Cham tali.

ˣtaŋəy -v 'corn; grain', Chru təŋəi,W. Cham taŋəi, PSB (Efimov) *təŋʌːy.

ˣtatuh; ˣcatəʔ 'shake (blanket); tremble', Chru tərtuh, N. Roglai tatəh, W. Cham catəʔ, tatəʔ. The first variant seems restricted to Highlands Chamic; the second occurs in coastal Chamic dialects.

ˣthaum 'visit', Rade ɓi tuom 'visit', Chru tɔːm 'meet', Haroi thăm, W. Cham tɔm; tɔm ḳauʔ. Restricted to Highlands Chamic plus Haroi and W. Cham.

ˣthuŋ 'barrel', Rade thŭŋ, Chru thuŋ, N. Roglai thuŋ -f, W. Cham thuŋ. Restricted to Highlands Chamic plus W. Cham.

ˣťien 'money', Chru priaʔ jen, N. Roglai jin pariaʔ, Haroi sɯn, W. Cham çen. < Vietnamese tiền 'money'. The other root is 'silver'.

ˣtioŋ -fvl 'mynah bird', Chru tiɔːŋ iraːu, N. Roglai tioŋ -f, Malay tiung. This word has been independently borrowed into Malay and Highlands Chamic.

ˣtraːp 'heavy', Rade kətrɜ̆ʔ -vf, Jarai (PL) trəu, kə̆trɜ̆ʔ, Chru traʔ, N. Roglai traːʔ, Haroi trăuʔ, W. Cham trauʔ, PR Cham tră̆ʔ -1, Wr. Cham trak.

ˣtuăy 'guest; visitor; stranger', Rade tuɛ -v, Jarai (PL) toai -v, Jarai (Lee) tuai, Chru tuãi, N. Roglai thuãi -i, Haroi tõai, W. Cham țuai, PR Cham toy, Wr. Cham țuai; MK: PNB *tamoy.

ˣtruam -f 'trunk (of animal)', Jarai (PL) trom, Chru trɔːm, N. Roglai trom -f, Haroi trom, W. Cham trɔm, PR Cham trɔm, Wr. Cham trauɱ; MK: PMnong *təm 'trunk' not clear from gloss what sort of trunk . [The vowel also suggests a MK origin]

ˣtuki -v 'horn; antler', Rade ki -v 'antler (deer)', Jarai (PL) tə̆ki, Jarai (Lee) təki, Chru təki, N. Roglai tuki, Haroi cəke -v, W. Cham take -v, PR Cham take, Wr. Cham takē; MK: PNB *ake, PMnong *ŋke, PSB (Efimov) *ŋkɛː, PKa-tuic *ɣəkɛː, *ɣəkiː.

ˣtuɓuay see ˣcuɓuay

ˣtəbiat 'go out; appear', Acehnese tɯblet, Rade kəbiăʔ 'go out', Jarai (PL) təbiăʔ, Jarai (Lee) təbiă̆ʔ, Chru təɓiaʔ, N. Roglai tubiaʔ, Tsat phiaʔ⁴², Haroi cəphɨaʔ, W. Cham tapeaʔ, PR Cham tapyă̆ʔ, Wr. Cham tabɨak.

ˣwaːr -fl 'stable; pen', Acehnese wɯɯə, Rade war -f, Jarai (PL) war, Jarai (Lee) war, Chru waːr 'pen', N. Roglai wa, Haroi wal, W. Cham war -1, PR Cham wal -f, Wr. Cham wal -f; MK: PSB (Efimov) *waːr, *waːŋ 'shed, cattle pen'.

ˣwaːs -f 'wipe away', Rade waih 'clean up, Chru waːih -f 'clear away'. Restricted to Highlands Chamic.

ˣway -f -vʀ 'spider', Rade wăk wai, Jarai (PL) wăŋ wai, Haroi wɨai
-vʀ; MK: PNB *way 'spider web'; *wey 'spider web'. Restricted to Highlands
Chamic plus Haroi.

ˣwɛh -vf 'turn aside; visit along the way', Rade wɛh 'turn (right or
left)', Jarai (Lee) we -f, N. Roglai weh, Haroi wĕh; wĭh -v, W. Cham wɛh
'dodge', PR Cham wĕh, Wr. Cham waiḥ; MK: PNB *weh 'turn aside', PKatuic
*wih, *wiːh 'turn'.

ˣyuː? 'descend', Jarai (PL) yŭ? 'ouest', yŭ? gah yang hrəi lĕ? (Ouest),
Jarai (Lee) yŭ? 'west', Haroi yo? -vʀ, PR Cham (Lee) yo?, PNB *jŭr, PMnong
*jŭr. If the MK forms are related, the final -r is unexpected.

3. ENGLISH-CHAMIC INDEX

References

Abdul Hamid Mahmood. 1994. *Sintaksis dialek Kelantan.* Kuala Lumpur: Dewan Bahasa dan Pustaka. Kementarian Pendidikan Malaysia.

Abdul Rahman al-Amadi. 1994 [1987]. Champa in Malay literature. *Actes du Seminaire sur le Campā organise a l'Universite de Copenhague,* Le 23 Mai 1987. English translation in *Proceedings of the Seminar on Champa* (1994), Huynh Dinh Te, trans., Rancho Cordova, CA. Pp. 100-109.

Adelaar, K.A. 1988. More on Proto-Malayic. *Rekonstruksi dan Cabang-Cabang Bahasa* Melayu Induk. Edited by Mohd. Thani Ahmad and Zaini Mohamed Zain. Kuala Lumpur: Dewan Bahasa dan Pustaka, Kementerian Pendidikan Malaysia. Pp. 59-77.

———. 1992. *Proto-Malayic, the reconstruction of its phonology and parts of its lexicon and morphology.* Pacific Linguistics, Series C-119. Canberra: The Australian National University.

———. 1993. The relevance of Salako for proto-Malayic and for Old Malay epigraphy. *Bijdragen tot de taal-, land-, en volkenkunde* 148:382-408.

———. 1995. Borneo as a cross-roads for comparative Austronesian Linguistics. In Peter Bellwood, James A. Fox, and Darrell Tyron (eds.), *The Austronesians: Historical and comparative perspectives.* Pp. 75-95. Canberra: The Australian National University.

Anttila, Raimo. 1972. *An introduction to historical and comparative linguistics.* New York: Macmillan.

Asmah Haji Omar. 1983. *The Malay Peoples of Malaysia and Their Languages.* Kuala Lumpur: Dewan Bahasa dan Pustaka. Kementerian Pelajaran Malaysia.

Awoi-hathe, Aviong, A-Ty, A-Ly, Maxwell Cobbey, and Vurnell Cobbey. 1977. *Suraq vunga sanap Radlai: Ngu-vung Roglai: Northern Roglai vocabulary* [Roglai-Vietnamese-English vocabulary], Manila, SIL.

Aymonier, Étienne François. 1889. Grammaire de la langue chame. In *Excusions et reconnaissances.* Saigon. XIV.31:1-92.

———. 1891. Les Tchames et leurs religions. *Revue de l'histoire des religions* 24:187-237 & 261-315.

——— and Antoine Cabaton. 1906. *Dictionnaire cham-français.* PEFEO 7. Paris, Leroux.

Banker, Elizabeth M. 1964. Bahnar affixation. *Mon-Khmer Studies I.* The Linguistic Circle of Saigon & The Summer Institute of Linguistics. Pp. 99-118.

Baxter, William H. 1989. An Austroasiatic word for cotton in Chinese. ms.
———. 1992. *A handbook of Old Chinese Phonology.* Berlin: Mouton de Gruyter.
Bellwood, Peter. 1978. *Man's conquest of the Pacific.* Auckland, Collins.
———. 1985. *Prehistory of the Indo-Malaysian Archipelago.* Orlando: Academic Press.
———. 1991. The Austronesian dispersal and the origin of languages. *Scientific American* 265.1:88-93.
———. 1992. Southeast Asia before history. *The Cambridge History of Southeast Asia. Volume 1. From Early Times to c. 1800.* Nicholas Tarling (ed.). Cambridge University Press. Pp. 55-136.
———, James J. Fox, and Darrell Tryon (eds.). 1995. *The Austronesians: Historical and Comparative Perspectives.* Canberra: The Australian National University.
Benedict, Paul K. 1941. A Cham colony on the island of Hainan. *Harvard Journal of Asiatic Studies* 4:129-34.
———. 1984. Austro-Tai parallel: A tonal Cham colony on Hainan. *Computational Analyses of Asian & African Languages* 22:83-86.
Benjamin, Geoffrey. 1976. Austroasiatic subgroupings and prehistory in the Malay peninsula. In Philip N. Jenner, Laurence C. Thompson, and Stanley Starosta (eds.), *Austroasiatic Studies* Part I:37-1128. Honolulu: University of Hawaii Press.
Blagden, C. O. 1929. Achinese and Mon-Khmer. In *Feestsbundel, uitgegeven door het Koninklijk Bataviaasch Genootschap van Kunsten en Wetenschappen bij gelegenheid van zijn 150 Jarig Bestaan 1778-1928.* Vol. 1. Weltevreden: G. Kolff, 35-38.
Blood, David L. 1967. Phonological units in Cham. *Anthropological Linguistics* 9.8:15-32,
———. 1977. A three-dimensional analysis of Cham sentences. *Papers in South East Asian Linguistics No. 4: Chamic Studies.* Edited by David Thomas, Ernest W. Lee, and Nguyen Dang Liem. Pacific Linguistics Series A, No. 48:53-76.
——— and Doris W. 1977. East Cham working dictionary. SIL. mf.
Blood, Doris Walker. 1962. Reflexes of Proto-Malayo-Polynesian in Cham. *Anthropological Linguistics* 4.9:11-20.
———. 1977. Clause and sentence final particles in Cham. *Papers in South East Asian Linguistics No. 4: Chamic Studies.* Edited by David Thomas, Ernest W. Lee, and Nguyen Dang Liem. Pacific Linguistics Series A, No. 48:39-51.
———. 1980. Aspects of Cham Culture. *Notes from Indochina on ethnic minority cultures.* Dallas, Texas: SIL Museum of Anthropology. Pp. 11-33.
——— and David Blood. 1977. Eastern Cham working dictionary. SIL. microfiche.
———, David Blood, and Thien Sanh Canh. 1976. Eastern Cham vocabulary. SIL. microfiche.

Blood, Henry F. 1967, 1968, 1974. *A reconstruction of Proto-Mnong.* MA thesis, U. of Indiana; publ. 1968, SIL/University of North Dakota, 115p.; republished 1974, 122p.

Blust, Robert A. 1969. Some new proto-Austronesian trisyllables. *Oceanic Linguistics* 8:85-104.

———. 1972. Proto-Oceanic addenda with cognates in non-Oceanic Austronesian languages --- a preliminary list. *Working Papers in Linguistics* 4.1:1-43. Honolulu: Department of Linguistics, University of Hawaii.

———. 1974. Eastern Austronesian: a note. *Working Papers in Linguistics* 6.4:101-107. Dept. of Linguistics, University of Hawaii.

———. 1976. Austronesian culture history: some linguistic inferences and their relations to the archaeological record. *World Archaeology* 8:19-43.

———. 1977. The proto-Austronesian pronouns and Austronesian subgrouping: a preliminary report. *University of Hawaii working papers in linguistics* 9.2:1-15.

———. 1980a. Austronesian etymologies. *Oceanic Linguistics* 19:1-2:1-181.

———. 1980b. More on the origins of glottalic consonants. *Lingua* 52:125-156.

———. 1981. The reconstruction of Proto-Malayo-Javanic: an appreciation. *Bijdragen tot de taal-, land-, en volkenkunde* 137.4:456-469.

———. 1983-4. Austronesian etymologies—II. *Oceanic Linguistics* 22-23.1 & 2: 29-150.

———. 1986. Austronesian etymologies III. *Oceanic Linguistics* 25.1-2:1-123.

———. 1987. The linguistic study of Indonesia. *Archipel* 34:27-47.

———. 1988. Malay historical linguistics: a progress report. *Rekonstruksi dan Cabang-Cabang Bahasa Melayu Induk.* Edited by Mohd. Thani Ahad and Zaini Mohamed Zain. Kuala Lumpur: Dewan Bahasa dan Pustaka.

———. 1989. Austronesian etymologies-IV. *Oceanic Linguistics* 28.2: 111-180.

———. 1991. Patterns of sound change in the Austronesian languages. In *Patterns of change, change of patterns: linguistic change and reconstruction methodology.* Edited by Philip Baldi. Berlin: Mouton de Gruyter. Pp. 129-165.

———. 1992a. The Austronesian settlement of mainland Southeast Asia. *Papers from the Second Annual Meeting of the Southeast Asian Linguistics Society,* Edited by Karen L. Adams and Thomas John Hudak, pp. 25-83.

———. 1992b. *Tumbaga* in Southeast Asia and South America. *Anthropos* 87:443-457.

———. 1995a. The prehistory of the Austronesian-speaking peoples: A view from language. *Journal of World Prehistory* 9.4:453-509.

———. 1995b. The position of the Formosan languages: Method and theory in Austronesian comparative linguistics. *Austronesian Studies Relating to Taiwan,* edited by Paul Jen-kuei Li, Cheng-hwa Tsang, Ying-kuei Huang, Dahan Ho, and Chiu-yu Tseng. Symposium Series of the Institute of History and Philology, Academica Sinica, No. 3. Pp. 585-650.

————. 1990, 1991, 1992, 1993, 1994, 1995. Austronesian Comparative Dictionary. [Work in progress].

Brennan, Hugh. 1992. Peminjaman leksikal dalam Bahasa Melayu. *Jurnal Dewan Bahasa* 36.6:552-565.

Briggs, Lawrence P. 1951. *The Ancient Khmer Empire.* Philadelphia: American Philosophical Society.

Bùi Khánh Thế. 1995. Từ Điển Chăm-Việt. Nhà Xuất Bản Khoa Học Xã hội.

Burnham, E. C. 1976. The place of Haroi in the Chamic languages. MA thesis, University of Texas at Arlington.

Cabaton, Antoine. 1901. *Nouvelles recherches sur les Chams.* Publications de L'École Français D'Extrême-Orient. Volume II.

Capell, A. 1949. Two tonal languages in New Guinea. *Bulletin of the School of Oriental and African Studies (London)* 13:184-99.

Chambert-Loir, H. 1988. Notes sur les relations historiques et littéraires entre Campā et monde malais. *Actes du Seminaire sur le Campā organise a l'Universite de Copenhague,* Le 23 Mai 1987. Pp. 95-106. English translation in *Proceedings of the Seminar on Champa,* Huynh Dinh Te, trans., Rancho Cordova, CA, 1994. Pp. 87-99.

Chao, Yuan Ren. 1930. A system of tone letters. *Le Maître Phonétique.*

Ciochon, Russell L. and Jamie James. 1992. Land of the Chams. *Archaeology* (May/June) 52-55.

Cobbey, Maxwell. 1977. Word lists from ten villages and Du Long word list. MSEA: VD 57/58/59-71. [Note: the Du Long list was completely unreadable and thus not analyzed].

————. 1979. A statistical comparison of verbs and nouns in Roglai. *South-East Asian Linguistic Studies.* Edited by Nguyen Dang Liem. Volume 4:207-212.

————. 1980. A first case of historiography among the Roglai. In *Notes from Indochina on ethnic minority cultures,* edited by Marilyn Gregerson and Dorothy Thomas. SIL Summer of Anthropology, Dallas, Texas. Pp. 61-83.

————, and Vurnell Cobbey. 1980. *English — Northern Roglai Dictionary.* Dallas: SILMP. 5mf.

Coedès, Georges. 1939. La plus anienne inscription en langue cham. *New Indian Antiquary.* Extra Series I. Bombay. No. 48. Pp. 39-52.

————. 1968. *The Indianized states of Southeast Asia.* Ed. Walter F. Vella. Trans. Susan Brown Cowing. Kuala Lumpur: U. of Malaya Press.

Collins, I. Vaughn. 1975. The Austro-Asiatic substratum in Acehnese. Ph.D. dissertation, University of California, Berkeley.

————. 1969. The position of Atjehnese among Southeast Asian languages. *Mon-Khmer Studies III,* Saigon. Pp. 48-60.

Collins, James T. 1991. Chamic, Malay and Acehnese: the Malay world and the Malayic languages. *In Le Campā et Le Monde Malais.* Actes de la Conférence Internationale sur le Campā et le Monde Malais. Kuala Lumpur: Nur Niaga Sdn. Bhd.

Coope, A. E. 1986. *Macmillan's Malay—English English—Malay dictionary.* Singapore: Macmillan.

Costello, Nancy and Judy Wallace. 1963. Katu-English-Vietnamese Dictionary. 87pp.

———— and Judy Wallace. 1976. Katu linguistic articles. 10pp., 24pp., and 8pp.

———— and Kitrunh. 1976. Katu ethnographic texts. 40pp.

———— et al. 1976. Katu notes and word lists. 72pp.

Court, Christopher. 1967. Some areal features of Mĕntu Land Dayak. *Oceanic Linguistics* 4.1:46-50.

————. 1970. Nasal harmony and some Indonesian sound laws. *Pacific Linguistics,* Vol. 13: *Pacific linguistic studies in honour of Arthur Capell.* Linguistic Circle of Canberra, 203-217.

Cowan, H. K. J. 1933. Het Atjèhsch metrum 'sandja'' in verband met een Tjamsch gedicht. *Bijdragen tot de Taal-, Land- en Volkenkunde van Nederlandsch-Indië* 90:149-55.

————. 1948. Aanteekeningen betreffende de verhouding van het Atjesch tot de Mon-Khmer-talen. *Bijdragen tot de Taal-, Land- en Volkenkunde van Nederlandsch-Indië* 104: 429-514.

————. 1974. Evidence of long vowels in early Achehnese. *Oceanic Linguistics* XIII. 187-211.

————. 1981. An outline of Achehnese phonology and morphology. *Bulletin of the School of Oriental and African Studies,* LXIV 3:552-49.

————. 1982. The Achehnese metre *sanja'* and the Thai klɔːn pɛːt'. *Journal of the Royal Asiatic Society of Great Britain and Ireland* 2: 156-60.

————. 1983. The Achehnese diphthong ɯə and its possible implications for proto-Austronesian. *Acta Orientalia* 44:153-85.

————. 1988. Achehnese dialects in connection with Chamic migrations. Paper presented at the fifth International Conference on Austronesian Linguistics. ms.

————. 1991. Acehnese dialects in connection with Chamic migrations. *VICAL 2: Western Austronesian and contact languages: papers the fifth congress on Austronesian linguistics.* Part I: Edited by Ray Harlow. Auckland, New Zealand. Linguistics Society of New Zealand. vi, 478 p.

————. n.d. The Mon-Khmer-related element in Chamo-Achehic: Mon-Khmer adstratum or direct Austro-Asiatic heritage. ms.

Crawfurd, John. 1822 [1967]. *Journal of an embassy to the courts of Siam and Cochin China* [reprinted]; with an introduction by David K. Wyatt. Kuala Lumpur, London, New York: Oxford University Press.

————. 1852. *Grammar and dictionary of the Malay language; with a preliminary dissertation.* Volume I: Dissertation and Grammar. London: Smith, Elder, and Co., 65, Cornhill.

Dahl, Otto Christian. 1976. *Proto-Austronesian.* Scandinavian Institute of of Asian Studies Monograph 15. Sweden: Studentlitteratur.

Daud, Bukhari and Mark Durie. n.d. Thesaurus of Acehnese. computer disk.

Denning, Keith. 1989. The diachronic development of phonological voice quality, with special reference to Dinka and the other Nilotic languages. Ph. D. dissertation, Stanford University.

Diffloth, Gérard. 1977. Mon-Khmer initial palatals and "substratumized" Austro-Thai. *Mon-Khmer Studies* VI. Edited by Philip N. Jenner. Pp. 39-58.

―――. 1990. Vietnamese tonogenesis and new data on the registers of Thauvang. Sino-Tibetan Conference.

Djajadingrat, Hoesein. 1934. *Atjèsch-Nederlansch Woordenboek.* 's Gravenhage: Martinus Nijhoff.

Donegan, Patricia J. 1985. *On the natural phonology of vowels.* Garland Publishing, Inc. New York & London.

―――. 1993. Rhythm and vocalic drift in Munda and Mon-Khmer. *Linguistics of the Tibeto-Burman Area* 16.1:1-43.

Drewes, G. W. J. 1979. *Hikajat Potjut Muhamat. An Achehnese epic.* Edited and translated by G. W. J. Drewes. The Hague: Martinus Nijhoff.

Durie, Mark. 1985. *A grammar of Achehnese on the basis of a dialect of North Aceh.* Dordrecht: Foris.

―――. 1990a. Proto-Chamic and Acehnese mid vowels: towards proto-Aceh-Chamic. *Bulletin of the School of Oriental and African Studies (London)* 53.1:100-114.

―――. 1990b. A proto-Aceh-Chamic database. Hypercard program.

―――. 1996. Framing the Acehnese text: Language choice and discourse structures in Aceh. *Oceanic Linguistics* 35.1:113-137.

Dyen, Isidore. 1953. *The Proto-Malayo-Polynesian laryngeals.* Linguistic Society of America.

―――. 1965. *A lexicostatistical classification of the Austronesian languages.* Bloomington: Indiana University Publications in Anthropology and Linguistics, Memoir 19; supplement to the *International Joural of American Linguistics.*

―――. 1971a. The Chamic languages. In Thomas A. Sebeok (ed.), *Current Trends in Linguistics.* Mouton: The Hague: Volume 8.1:200-210.

―――. 1971b. The Austronesian languages of Formosa. In Thomas A. Sebeok (ed.), *Current Trends in Linguistics.* Mouton: The Hague: Volume 8.1:171-199.

―――. 1995. Borrowing and inheritance in Austronesianistics. *Austronesian Studies Relating to Taiwan,* edited by Paul Jen-kuei Li, Cheng-hwa Tsang, Ying-kuei Huang, Dah-an Ho, and Chiu-yu Tseng. Symposium Series of the Institute of History and Philology, Academica Sinica, No. 3. Pp. 455-519.

Edmondson, Jerold A. and Kenneth J. Gregerson. 1993. Western Cham as a register language. *Tonality in Austronesian Languages.* Edited by Jerry Edmondson and Ken Gregerson. Oceanic Linguistics Special Publication No. 24. Honolulu, Hawaii: University of Hawaii Press. Pp. 61-74.

Efimov, Aleksandr Yu. 1987. *Historical phonology of South Bahnaric languages.* Ph. D. thesis. Moscow: Academy of Sciences of USSR, Oriental Institute. 240 pp. [Wordlist translated by William Gage].

Egerod, Søren. 1978. *An English-Rade vocabulary.* The Museum of Far Eastern Antiquities, Stockholm. Bulletin 50:49-104.

Ferrell, Raleigh. 1969. Languages of aboriginal Taiwan. *Taiwan aboriginal groups: problems in cultural and linguistic classification.* Institute of Ethnology, Academia Sinica. Monograph No. 17. Pp. 63-75.

Friberg, Timothy and Kvoeu-Hor. 1977. Register in Western Cham phonology. *Papers in South East Asian Linguistics No. 4: Chamic Studies.* Edited by David Thomas, Ernest W. Lee, and Nguyen Dang Liem. Pacific Linguistics Series A, No. 48:17-38.

Fuller, Eugene. 1977. Chru phonemes. *Papers in South East Asian Linguistics No. 4: Chamic Studies.* Edited by David Thomas, Ernest W. Lee, and Nguyen Dang Liem. Pacific Linguistics Series A, No. 48:77-86.

Goschnick, Hella. 1977. Haroi clauses. *Papers in South East Asian Linguistics No. 4: Chamic Studies.* Edited by David Thomas, Ernest W. Lee, and Nguyen Dang Liem. Pacific Linguistics Series A, No. 48:105-124.

———— and Alice Tegenfeldt-Mundhenk. 1976. Haroi dictionary. SIL. Huntington Beach, Calif. 325pp. ms.

Grace, George W. 1964. Movements of the Malayo-Polynesian 1500 BC - 500 AD; the linguistic evidence. *Current Anthropology* 5:361-368, 403-404.

————. 1985. Oceanic subgrouping: retrospect and prospect. In *Austronesian Linguistics at the 15th Pacific Science Congress,* edited by Andrew Pawley and Lois Carrington. *Pacific Linguistics* C-88:1-18.

Greenberg, Joseph H. 1970. Some generalizations concerning glottalic consonants, especially implosives. *IJAL* 36:25-45.

Grimes, Barbara F. (ed.). 1988. *Ethnologue: Languages of the world.* Dallas, Texas: Summer Institute of Linguistics, Inc.

Gregerson, Kenneth J. 1976. Tongue root and register in Mon-Khmer. *Austroasiatic Studies* I, edited by Philip N. Jenner, Laurence C. Thompson, and Stanley Starosta. Oceanic Linguistics special publication no. 13. Honolulu, Hawaii. Pp. 323-70.

Gregerson, Marilyn and Dorothy Thomas. 1980. *Notes from Indochina On Ethnic Minority Cultures.* Dallas, Texas: SIL Museum of Anthropology.

Hall, Daniel George Edward. 1955. *A history of South-East Asia.* First edition. New York: St. Martin's Press.

————. 1981. *A history of South-East Asia.* Fourth edition. New York: St. Martin's Press.

Hall, Kenneth R. 1985. *Maritime trade and state development in early Southeast Asia.* Honolu: University of Hawaii Press.

Hån, Phú Vån, Jerold Edmondson, and Kenneth Gregerson. 1992. Eastern Cham as a tone language. *Mon-Khmer Studies* 20:31-43.

Haudricourt, André-G. 1950. Les consonnes préglottalisées en Indochine. *Bulletin de la Société Linguistique de Partis* 46:172-182.

―――. 1954. De l'origine des tons viêtnamien. *Journal Asiatique* 242:69-82.

―――. 1956. De la restitution des initiales dans les langues monosyllabiques: le problème du thai commun. Originally published in *Bulletin de la Soiété de Linguistiqe de Paris* 52:307-322. Reprinted in *Problèmes de phonologie diachronique.* Paris, 1972: 235-51.

―――. 1965. Problems of Austronesian comparative philology. *Lingua* 14:315-329.

―――. 1966. The limits and connections of Austroasiatic in the northeast. *Studies in Comparative Austroasiatic Linguistics.* The Hague: Mouton & Co. Pp. 44-56.

―――. 1968. Deux langues mélanésiennes à tons. *Maitre Phonetique* 129:7-9.

―――. 1971. New Caledonia and the Loyalty Islands. In Thomas A. Sebeok, editor, Current Trends in Linguistics, volume 8: *Linguistics in Oceania.* Pp. 359-396.

―――. 1984. Tones of some languages in Hainan. *Minzu Yuwen* 4:17-25. Also published in *Bulletin de la Société de Linguistique de Paris* as "La tonologie des langues de Hai-nan." 79.1:385-394.

Headley, Robert K. 1976. Some sources of Chamic vocabulary. *Austroasiatic Studies, Part I.* Oceanic Linguistics Special Publication No. 13:453-476.

―――. 1991. The phonology of Kompong Thom Cham. *Austroasiatic Languages: Essays in honour of H. L. Shorto.* Edited by Jeremy H. C. S. Davidson. University of London, School of Oriental and African Studies: 105-121.

Henderson, Eugénie J. A. 1952. The main features of Cambodian pronunciation. *Bulletin of the School of Oriental and African Studies (London)* 14.1:149-74.

―――. 1965. The topography of certain phonetic and morphological characteristics of South East Asian languages. *Lingua* 15:400-434.

―――. 1967. Grammar and tone in South-East Asian languages. *Wissenschaftliche Zeitschrift der Karl-Marx-Universität-Leipzig.* Gesellschafts- und Sprachwissen-schaftliche Reihe. Part 1/2:171-178.

Hickey, Gerald Cannon. 1982. *Sons of the mountains: ethnohistory of the Vietnamese Central Highlands to 1954.* New Haven: Yale University Press.

Hoang, Thi Chau. 1987. He thong thanh dieu tieng Cham va cach ki hieu [The system of tones in Cham and their symbolization]. In *Ngon-Ngu* [Language] 1-2:31-35. Institute of Linguistics, the Social Sciences Committee of Vietnam.

Hudson, Alfred B. 1967. *The Barito dialects of Borneo; a classification based on comparative reconstruction and lexicostatistics.* Ithaca, N.Y., Department of Asian Studies, Cornell University.

Huffman, Franklin E. 1976. The register problem in fifteen Mon-Khmer languages. In *Austroasiatic Studies*, edited by Philip N. Jenner, Laurence C.

Thompson, and Stanley Starosta. Special publication of Oceanic Linguistics no. 13. 2 volumes. Honolulu, Hawaii: University of Hawaii Press, I:575-90.

————. 1986. *Bibliography and index of mainland Southeast Asian Languages and Linguistics.* 1986. Yale University Press.

Joseph, Brian. 1983. *The synchrony and diachrony of the Balkan infinitive; A study in areal, general, and historical linguistics.* Cambridge University Press.

Jrang, Ja Kuang, Ja Wi, Ja Dai, Ja Ngai, and Eugene Fuller. 1977. *Chru Vocabulary.* Summer Institute of Linguistics. Manila.

Keyes, Charles F. 1995 [1977]. *The golden peninsula: Culture and adaptation in mainland Southeast Asia.* Honolulu: University of Hawai'i Press.

Kvoeu-Hor and Timothy Friberg. 1978. Western Cham Vocabulary. SIL.

Ladefoged, Peter. 1971. *Preliminaries to linguistic analysis.* Chicago and London: University of Chicago Press.

———— and Ian Maddieson. 1996. *The Sounds of the World's languages.* Cambridge Massachusetts: Blackwell Publishers.

Lafont, Pierre-Bernard. 1968. *Lexique Jarai: parler de la province de plei ku.* Publications de L'École Française D'Extrême-Orient. Volume LXIII. Paris.

————. 1987a. Aperçu sur les relations entre le Campā et l'Asie du Sud-Est. Pp. 71-82. *Actes du Seminaire sur le Campā organise a l'Universite de Copenhague, Le 23 Mai 1987.* English translation in *Proceedings of the Seminar on Champa* (1994), Huynh Dinh Te, trans., Rancho Cordova, CA. Pp. 65-75.

————. 1987b. Research on Champa and its evolution. *Proceedings of the Seminar on Champa,* Huynh Dinh Te, trans., Rancho Cordova, CA. Pp. 1-20.

————. 1994a. *Proceedings of the seminar on Champa: held at the University of Copenhagen on May 23, 1987.* Huynh Dinh Te, trans., Rancho Cordova, CA.

————. 1994b. Research on Champa and its evolution. *Proceedings of the Seminar on Champa,* Huynh Dinh Te, trans., Rancho Cordova, CA. Pp. 1-20.

Laver, John. 1994. *Principles of Phonetics.* Cambridge: Cambridge University Press.

LeBar, Frank M., Gerald C. Hickey, John K. Musgrave. 1964. *Ethnic Groups of Mainland Southeast Asia.* New Haven: Human Relations Area Files Press.

Lee, Ernest Wilson. 1966. Proto-Chamic phonologic word and vocabulary. Ph.D. dissertation. Indiana University. 67-3690.

————. 1974. Southeast Asian areal features in Austronesian strata of the Chamic languages. *Oceanic Linguistics* 13.1-2:643-668.

————. 1977a. Introduction. *Papers in South East Asian Linguistics No. 4: Chamic Studies.* Edited by David Thomas, Ernest W. Lee, and Nguyen Dang Liem. Pacific Linguistics Series A, No. 48:vi-vii.

————. 1977b. Devoicing, aspiration, and vowel split in Haroi: evidence for register (contrastive tongue-root position). *Papers in South East Asian Lin-*

guistics No. 4: Chamic Studies. Edited by David Thomas, Ernest W. Lee, and Nguyen Dang Liem. Pacific Linguistics Series A, No. 48:87-104.

———. 1996. Bipartite negatives in Chamic. *Mon-Khmer Studies* 26:291-317.

———. 1998. The contribution of Cat Gia Roglai to Chamic. *Papers in Southeast Asian Linguistics No. 15: Further Chamic Studies.* Edited by David Thomas. Pacific Linguistics. Series A-89. Canberra: The Australian National University. Pp. 31-54.

Lewis, Martha Blanche. 1960. Moken texts and word-list, a provisional interpretation. *Federation Museums Journal 4 N.S.* (102 pages).

Li, Ce Jin and Tian Guang. 1986. Hainan Dao Yanglan Huizu De Li Shi Ji Xian Zhuang Diao Zha [The history and current investigation of the Hui nationality in Yanglan Hui nationality on Hainan Island]. *Minzu Yan Jiu Dong Tai* [Current Nationality Research] 4:26-31.

Li, Fangkuei. 1977. *A handbook of comparative Tai.* Honolulu: The University Press of Hawaii.

Li, Paul Jen-kuei. 1995. Formosan vs. non-Formosan features in some Austronesian languages in Taiwan. *Austronesian Studies Relating to Taiwan,* edited by Paul Jen-kuei Li, Cheng-hwa Tsang, Ying-kuei Huang, Dah-an Ho, and Chiu-yu Tseng. Symposium Series of the Institute of History and Philology, Academica Sinica, No. 3. Pp. 651-681.

Maddieson, Ian and Keng-Fong Pang. 1993. Tone in Utsat. *Tonality in Austronesian Languages.* Edited by Jerry Edmondson and Ken Gregerson. Oceanic Linguistics Special Publication No. 24. Honolulu, Hawaii: University of Hawaii Press. Pp. 75-89.

Maitre, H. 1912. *Les jungles Möi.* Paris: Larose.

Majumdar, R. C. 1927. *Ancient Indian Colonies in the Far East, I: Champa.* Lahore.

Mak, Phoeun. 1987. La communauté cam au Cambodge du XV° au XIX° siècle. *Actes du Seminaire sur le Campā organise a l'Universite de Copenhague,* Le 23 Mai 1987. p. 78: English translation in *Proceedings of the Seminar on Champa,* Huynh Dinh Te, trans., Rancho Cordova, CA, 1994. Pp. 76-86.

Mandelbaum, D. G. (ed.). 1949. *Selected writings of Edward Sapir.* Berkeley: University of California Press.

Manguin, Pierre-Yves. 1979. Etudes cam. II. L'introduction de l'Islam au Champa, *Bulletin de l'Ecole Francaise d'Extreme-Orient* 66:255-87.

———. 1985. The Introduction of Islam to Champa. *Journal of the Malaysian Branch of the Royal Asiatic Society* 58.1:1-28. Translation of Manguin (1979) by Robert Nicholl.

Manley, Timothy M. 1972. *Outline of Sre structure.* Oceanic Linguistics Special Publication No. 12. Honolulu: University of Hawaii Press.

Marrison, Geoffrey E. 1975. The early Cham language and its relationship to Malay. *Journal of the Malaysian branch of the Royal Asiatic Society* 48.2:52-59.

————. 1985. The Chams and their Literature. *Journal of the Malaysian Branch of the Royal Asiatic Society* 58.2:45-70.

Maspero, Georges. 1928. *Le Royaume de Champa.* Paris and Brussels.

————. 1949. The kingdom of Champa: a translation of chapter I of *Le Royaume de Champa.* New Haven, Conn.: Yale University. Southeast Asian Studies.

Matisoff, James A. 1973. Tonogenesis in Southeast Asia. In *Consonant Types & Tone.* Edited by Larry M. Hyman. Southern California Occasional Papers in Linguistics No. 1. Los Angeles: USC. Pp. 71-96.

————. 1985. Rhinoglottophilia: the mysterious connection between nasality and glottality. In *Nasalfest,* edited by C. A. Ferguson, L. M. Hyman, and J. J. Ohala. Stanford University Press. Pp. 265-287.

McNair, J. F. 1972 [1878]. *Perak and the Malays.* Kuala Lumpur: Oxford University Press.

Medcalf, Anne-Marie. 1989. Jörai sentence and phrase structure. B.A. Honours thesis. Murdoch University.

Moussay, Fr. Gérard. 1971. *Dictionnaire Cam-Vietnamien-Français.* Phan Rang: Centre Culturel Cam.

Ni, Dabai. 1988a. The genealogical affiliation of the language of the Hui people in Sanya Hainan. *Minzu Yuwen* 2:18-25.

————. 1988b. The Kam-Tai of China and the Hui of Hainan. *Bulletin of the Central Institute of Minorities* 3:54-65.

————. 1990a. The origins of the tones of the Kam-Tai languages. ms.

————. 1990b. The Sanya (= Utsat) language of Hainan island: a living specimen of a linguistic typological shift. ms.

Niemann, G. K. 1891. Bijdrage tot de Kennis der Verhouding van het Tjam tot de Talen van Indonesië. *Bijdragen tot de Taal-, Land- en Volkenkunde van Nederlandsch-Indië* 40:27-44.

Nothofer, Bernd. 1975. *The Reconstruction of Proto-Malayo-Javanic.* Verhandelingen van Het Koninklijk Instituut Voor Taal-, Land-, en Volkenkunde. 73. The Hague: Martinus Nijhoff.

————. 1985. The subgrouping of the languages of the Javo-Sumatra hesion: a reconsideration. *Bijdragen tot de Taal-, Land- en Volkenkunde van Nederlandsch-Indië* 141.2-3:288-302.

Oey, Eric M. n.d. The linguistic position of the Chamic languages. [preliminary draft]. ms.

Ouyang, Jueya and Zheng Yiqing. 1983. The Huihui speech (Tsat) of the Hui nationality in Yaxian, Hainan. *Minzu Yuwen* 1:30-40.

————. 1980. *A brief description of Li (Hainan).* Chinese Minority People's Language, Basic Description Series. Beijing.

Pang, Keng-Fong. 1992. The dynamics of gender, ethnicity and state among the Austronesian-speaking Muslims (Hui/Utsat) of Hainan island, People's Republic of China. UCLA. Ph.D. dissertation.

————. 1998. On the ethnonym 'Utsat'. *Papers in Southeast Asian Linguistics No. 15: Further Chamic Studies*. Edited by David Thomas. Pacific Linguistics. Series A-89. Canberra: The Australian National University. Pp. 55-60.

Parkin, Robert. 1991. *A Guide to Austroasiatic Speakers and Their Languages*. Oceanic Linguistics Special Publication No. 23. Honolulu: University of Hawai'i Press.

Pawley, Andrew and Malcolm Ross. 1995. Prehistory of Oceanic languages: A current view. In *The Austronesians: Historical and Comparative Perspectives*. Edited by Peter Bellwood, James J. Fox and Darrell Tryon. Canberra: The Australian National University. Pp. 39-74.

Peiros, Ilia. 1996. *Katuic Comparative Dictionary*. Canberra: Pacific Linguistics, Series C-132.

Pham Xuân Tin. 1955. *Lexique Polyglotte*. Dran, Vietnam.

Pittman, Richard S. 1959. Jarai as a member of the Malayo-Polynesian family of languages. *Asian Culture* 1.4:59-67.

Prachacakij-karacak, Phraya. 1995. *Some Languages of Siam*. Translated and annotated by David Thomas and Sophana Srichampa. Institute of Language and Culture for Rural Development. Mahidol University.

Priebsch, R., and W. E. Collinson. 1966. *The German language*. Revised. London: Faber and Faber.

Ravaisse, P. 1922. Deux inscriptions coufiques du Campa. *Journal Asiatique* 11 serie, no. 20, (1922) pp. 247-59.

Reid, Anthony. 1993. Islamization and Christianization in Southeast Asia: The critical phase, 1550-1650. In Anthony Reid (ed.), *Southeast Asia in the early modern era*. Ithaca: Cornell University Press. Pp. 151-179.

————. 1995. Continuity and change in the Austronesian transition to Islam and Christianity. In Peter Bellwood, James J. Fox, and Darrell Tryon (eds.), *The Austronesians: Historical and Comparative Perspectives*. Canberra: The Australian National University. Pp. 314-322.

Reid, Laurence A. 1994. Morphological evidence for Austric. *Oceanic Linguistics* 33-2:323-344.

Richards, Anthony. 1988. *An Iban-English dictionary*. Petaling Jaya: Oxford University Press, Penerbit Fajar Bakti Sdn. Bhd.

Rischel, Jørgen. 1995. *Minor Mlabri: A hunter-gatherer language of northern Indochina*. University of Copenhagen: Museum Tusculanum Press.

Ross, Malcolm D. 1992. The sound of Proto-Austronesian: An outsider's view of the Formosan evidence. *Oceanic Linguistics* 31.1:23-64.

————. 1995. Reconstructing Proto-Austronesian verbal morphology: the evidence from Taiwan. *Austronesian Studies Relating to Taiwan*, edited by Paul Jen-kuei Li, Cheng-hwa Tsang, Ying-kuei Huang, Dah-an Ho, and Chiu-yu Tseng. Symposium Series of the Institute of History and Philology, Academica Sinica, No. 3. Pp. 727-791.

————. 1995b. Proto-Oceanic terms for meteorological phenomena. *Oceanic Linguistics* 34.2:261-304.

Sapir, Edward. 1915. Notes on Judeo-German phonology. *The Jewish quarterly review,* n.s. 6:231-266. Reprinted in Mandelbaum 1949:252-272.

Schafer, Edward H. 1967. *The vermilion bird; T'ang images of the south.* Berkeley: University of California Press.

Schmidt, Pater Wilhelm. 1906. Die Mon-Khmer-Völker, ein Bindeglied zwischen. Völkern Zentralasiens und Austronesiens. Archiv Anthropologie (Braunschw) n.s., 5:59-109.

Schrock, Joann L., William Stockton, Jr., Elaine M. Murphy, and Marilou Fromme. 1966. *Minority Groups in the Republic of Vietnam.* Ethnographic Study Series. Department of the Army.

Scott, N. C. 1956. *A dictionary of Sea Dayak.* London: University of London, School of Oriental and African Studies.

————. 1964. Nasal consonants in Land Dayak (Bukar-Sadong). In David Abercrombie et al. (eds.), *In honour of Daniel Jones.* London: Longmans, Green and Co. Pp. 432-436.

Sebeok, Thomas A. 1942. An examination of the Austroasiatic language family. *Language* 18:206-17.

Shorto, Harry L. 1975. Achinese and Mainland Austronesian. *Bulletin of the School of Oriental and African Studies* 38:81-102. University of London.

————. 1977. Proto-Austronesian *taqǝn: An anomaly removed. *Bulletin of the School of Oriental and African Studies* 40:128-129. University of London.

Smith, Kenneth D. 1972. *A phonological reconstruction of Proto-North-Bahnaric.* (Language Data, Asian-Pacific series, no. 2). Santa Ana, CA, SIL. 109p.

————. 1975. The velar animal prefix relic in Vietnam languages. *Linguistics of the Tibeto-Burman Area* 2.1:1-18.

Solnit, David. 1982. Linguistic contact in Ancient South China: the case of Hainan Chinese, Be, and Vietnamese. *Berkeley Linguistics Society* 8:219-230.

————. 1993. Glottalized consonants as a genetic feature in Southeast Asia. *Acta Linguistica Hafniensa* 25:95-123.

Stampe, David. 1972. On the natural history of diphthongs. *Papers from the Eighth Regional meeting of the Chicago Linguistic Society,* pp. 443-454.

Starosta, Stanley. 1995. A grammatical subgrouping of Formosan languages. *Austronesian Studies Relating to Taiwan,* edited by Paul Jen-kuei Li, Chenghwa Tsang, Ying-kuei Huang, Dah-an Ho, and Chiu-yu Tseng. Symposium Series of the Institute of History and Philology, Academica Sinica, No. 3. Pp. 683-726.

————, Andrew K. Pawley, and Lawrence A. Reid. 1982. The evolution of focus in Austronesian. In Amran Halim, Lois Carrington, and S. A. Wurm, eds., *Papers from the Third Interational Conference on Austronesian Linguistics.* vol. 2. *Tracking the travellers,* 145-170. Pacific Linguistics C-75. Canberra: Australian National University.

Strecker, David Shalom. 1984. Proto-Tai person pronouns. University of Michigan Ph.D. dissertation.

Tadmor, Uri. 1995. Language contact and systematic restructuring: The Malay dialect of Nonthaburi, Central Thailand. Ph.D. dissertation, University of Hawaii.

Tarling, Nicholas (ed.). 1992. *The Cambridge History of Southeast Asia. Volume 1. From Early Times to c. 1800.* Cambridge University Press.

Taylor, Keith W. 1922. The early kingdoms: Champa. Nicholas Tarling (ed.). *The Cambridge History of Southeast Asia. Volume 1. From Early Times to c. 1800.* Cambridge University Press. Pp. 153-157.

Tegenfeldt-Mundhenk, Alice and Hella Goschnick. 1977. Haroi phonemes. *Papers in South East Asian Linguistics No. 4: Chamic Studies.* Edited by David Thomas, Ernest W. Lee, and Nguyen Dang Liem. Pacific Linguistics Series A, No. 48:.1-15.

Tharp, J. A. and Y-Bham Buoy-Ya. 1980. *A Rhade-English dictionary with English-Rhade finderlist.* Pacific Linguistics. Series C - No. 58.

Thomas, David D. 1964. Comment appended to Grace (1964).

————. 1971. *Chrau grammar.* Oceanic Linguistics Special Publication No. 7. Honolulu: University of Hawaii Press.

————. 1979. The place of Alak, Tempuan, and West Bahnaric. *Mon-Khmer Studies* VIII:171-186.

———— (ed.). *Papers in Southeast Asian Linguistics No. 15: Further Chamic Studies.* Pacific Linguistics. Series A-89. Canberra: The Australian National University.

————, Ernest Wilson Lee, and Dang Liem Nguyen. 1977. *Papers in South East Asian Linguistics. No. 4. Chamic Studies.* Canberra: Pacific Linguistics. Series A, No. 48.

Thomas, Dorothy M. 1963. Proto-Malayo-Polynesian reflexes in Rade, Jarai, and Chru. *Studies in Linguistics* 17:59-75.

————. 1967. A phonological reconstruction of Proto-East-Katuic. MA thesis, University of North Dakota. Dallas: Summer Institute of Linguistics. microfiche.

Thomason, Sarah Grey and Terrence Kaufman. 1988. *Language contact, creolization, and genetic linguistics.* The University of California Press: Berkeley.

Thompson, Laurence C. 1984-1985. *A Vietnamese reference grammar.* Edited by Stephan O'Harrow. *Mon-Khmer Studies* XIII-XIV.

Thurgood, Graham. 1980. Consonants, phonation types, and pitch height. *Computational Analyses of African and Asian Languages* 13:207-19.

————. 1982. A comparative note on the Indian linguistic area. *South Asian Review* 6.3:23-9.

————. 1988a. Notes on the reconstruction of Kam-Sui. *Comparative Kadai: Linguistic studies beyond Tai.* Edited by Jerold A. Edmondson and David B.

Solnit. Summer Institute of Linguistics and The University of Texas at Arlington Publications in Linguistics No. 86:179-218.

———. 1988b. k̲- prefixes in Kam-Sui and Kadai: some notes. *Languages and History in East Asia: Festschrift for Tatsuo Nishida on the Occasion of his 60th Birthday.* Edited by Paul K. Eguchi, Yukio Fujimoto, Nobuyoshi Fukuhara, Masura Hashimoto, Koichi Miyamoto, Atsuchi Iwamoto, Tatsuo Kondo, Masaoki Miyamoto, Osamu Sakiyama, Akihiro Sato, David Sell, Norio Shibata, Ken-ichiro Shirai, Mashiro Shogaito, Shiro Yabu and Kazuhiko Yoshida. Kyoto: Shokado. Pp. 229-235.

———. 1991. Proto-Hlai (Li): A look at the initials, tones, and finals. *Kadai: Discussions in Kadai and SE Asian Linguistics* 3:1-49.

———. 1992a. The aberrancy of the Jiamao dialect of Hlai: speculation on its origins and history. *Southeast Asian Linguistics Society I,* Edited by Martha Ratliff and Eric Schiller. Tempe: Arizona State University Southeast Asian Studies Publications. Pp. 417-433.

———. 1992b. *From atonal to tonal in Utsat (a Chamic language of Hainan). Proceedings of the Eighteenth Annual Meeting of the Berkeley Linguistics Society. February 14-17, 1992.* Special Session on the Typology of Tone Languages. Edited by Laura A. Buszard-Welcher, Jonathan Evans, David Peterson, Lionel Wee, and William Weigel. Pp. 145-156.

———. 1993. Phan Rang Cham and Utsat: tonogenetic themes and variants. *Tonality in Austronesian Languages.* Edited by Jerry Edmondson and Ken Gregerson. Oceanic Linguistics Special Publication No. 24. Honolulu, Hawaii: University of Hawaii Press. Pp. 91-106.

———. 1994. Tai-Kadai and Austronesian: The nature of the historical relationship. *Oceanic Linguistics* 33.2:345-368.

———. 1995. Southeast Asian languages--prehistory of. *The Asian American Encyclopedia,* vol. 5. New York: Marshall Cavendish. Pp. 1418-1421.

———. 1996. Language contact and the directionality of internal 'drift': the development of tones and registers in Chamic. *Language* 71.1:1-31.

———. 1998. The Austronesian and Mon-Khmer components in the proto-Chamic vowel system. *Papers in Southeast Asian Linguistics No. 15: Further Chamic Studies.* Edited by David Thomas. Pacific Linguistics. Series A-89. Canberra: The Australian National University. Pp. 61-90.

——— and Hector Javkin. 1975. An acoustic explanation of a sound change: *-ap to -o, *-at to -e, and *-ak to -ae. *Journal of Phonetics* 3.3:161-5.

Ting, Pang-hsin. 1980. The Tan-chou dialect of Hainan. *Cahier de linguistique Asie Orientale* 8:5-27.

Tran, Ky Phuong. 1987. *Museum of Cham sculpture in Da Nang.* Hanoi: Foreign Languages Publishing House.

Tryon, Darrell. 1995. Proto-Austronesian and the major Austronesian subgroups. In Peter Bellwood, James J. Fox, and Darrell Tryon (eds.), *The Austronesians: Historical and Comparative Perspectives.* Canberra: The Australian National University. Pp. 17-38.

Tsuchida, Shigeru. 1982. *A comparative vocabulary of Austronesian languages of Sinicized ethnic groups in Taiwan, Part I: West Taiwan.* Tokyo, Memoirs of the Faculty of Letters, University of Tokyo, No. 7.

―――. 1995. Alienable and unalienable distinction in Puyuma? *Austronesian Studies Relating to Taiwan,* edited by Paul Jen-kuei Li, Cheng-hwa Tsang, Ying-kuei Huang, Dah-an Ho, and Chiu-yu Tseng. Symposium Series of the Institute of History and Philology, Academica Sinica, No. 3. Pp. 793-804.

Watson, Sandra K. 1966. Verbal affixation in Pacoh. *Mon-Khmer Studies* II:15-30.

Weinreich, Uriel, William Labov, and Marvin I. Herzog. 1968. Empirical foundations for a theory of language change. In Winfred P. Lehman and Yakov Malkiel (eds.), *Directions for Historical Linguistics.* Austin: University of Texas Press. Pp. 95-195.

Wolff, John U. 1973. Verbal inflection in Proto-Austronesian. In Andrew Gonzalea, ed. *Parangal kay Cecilio Lopez,* 71-91. Quezon City: Linguistic Society of the Philippines.

―――. 1991. The Proto-Austronesian phoneme *t and the grouping of the Austronesian languages. In *Currents in Pacific linguistics: Papers on Austronesian languages and ethnolinguistics in honour of George W. Grace,* edited by Robert Blust, pp. 535-549. Pacific Linguistics C-117.

―――. 1995. The position of the Austronesian languages of Taiwan within the Austronesian group. *Austronesian Studies Relating to Taiwan,* edited by Paul Jen-kuei Li, Cheng-hwa Tsang, Ying-kuei Huang, Dah-an Ho, and Chiu-yu Tseng. Symposium Series of the Institute of History and Philology, Academica Sinica, No. 3. Pp. 521-583.

Wyatt, David K. 1967. Introduction. *Journal of an embassy to the courts of Siam and Cochin China* [reprinted], by John Crawfurd. Kuala Lumpur, London, New York: Oxford University Press. 4pp.

Y-Chang, Niê Siêng. 1979. *Rade vocabulary.* Summer Institute of Linguistics. Huntington Beach, California.

Zheng, Yiqing. 1986. A further discussion of the position of Huihui speech and its genetic relationship. *Minzu Yuwen* 6:37-43.

Zorc, R. David. 1978. Proto-Philippine word accent: Innovation or Proto-Hesperonesian retention? In *Second International Conference on Austronesian Linguistics: Proceedings,* edited by S. A. Wurm and Lois Carrington, pp. 67-119. Pacific Linguistics C-61.

―――. 1983. Proto-Austronesian accent revisited. *Philippine Journal of Linguistics* 14.1:1-24.

Author Index

Topic Index

OCEANIC LINGUISTICS SPECIAL PUBLICATIONS

Byron W. Bender
General Editor

Editorial Board

Joel Bradshaw, George W. Grace, Howard P. McKaughan,
Kenneth L. Rehg, Albert J. Schütz, Donald M. Topping

Oceanic Linguistics Special Publications are occasional publications issued under the editorial sponsorship of the Department of Linguistics of the University of Hawai'i. The series consists of independently subsidized studies bearing on the languages of the Oceanic area. The "Oceanic area" is defined for this purpose as the combined Austronesian, Papuan, and Australian language areas. The Special Publications are published and distributed for the Department by the University of Hawai'i Press.

Manuscripts may be submitted to:
Oceanic Linguistics Special Publications
Department of Linguistics
1890 East-West Road
Moore Hall 569
University of Hawai'i
Honolulu, Hawai'i 96822

Publications may be ordered from:
University of Hawai'i Press
2840 Kolowalu Street
Honolulu, Hawai'i 96822